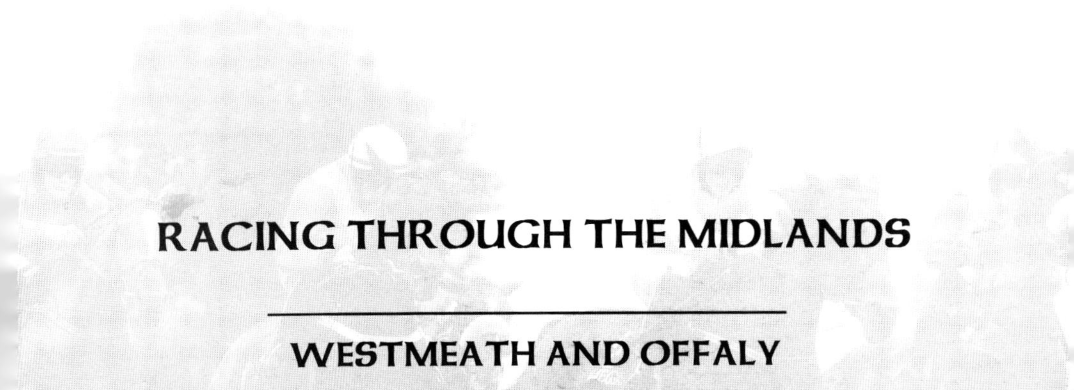

RACING THROUGH THE MIDLANDS

WESTMEATH AND OFFALY

by

Stan McCormack

First Edition: August 2015

ISBN NO:

Hardback No 978-0-9933243-0-7

Paperback No 978-0-9933243-1-4

Published by Stan McCormack

Tullamore Road, Kilbeggan, Co Westmeath, Ireland

Email: racingthroughthemidlands@gmail.com

Phone No: 057 9332683 / 087 7499857

Printed by Print Plus, Tullamore, Co Offaly.

SPONSORS

I wish to thank the following sponsors for their generous support:

Kilbeggan Preservation & Development Association (KPDA);

Kilbeggan Race Committee; Kilbeggan Distillery, Lower Main Street,

Kilbeggan; Joe Scally, Killarney Royal Hotel, Kilarney, Co Kerry;

Next Bet, Lucan Racing, Kilbeggan, Ronan McCarthy, Centra, Kilbeggan

and Peter Downes, Russelstown Stud.

ACKNOWLEDGEMENTS

I wish to acknowledge many people for their support and help over the past few years. I received great assistance from Margaret, Ray, and the staff in Kilbeggan Library; Gretta & staff in the Mullingar headquarters and Gearoid O'Brien in Athlone. I also wish to thank all the people I interviewed, for their help and who also provided photos, including Cecil Ross, Paddy O'Roarke, Michael Geraghty, Connie Cleary, Cecil Ronaldson, Jim Tormey RIP, Cecil Ronaldson RIP, Martin Dibbs, Dot Love, Ciaran Murphy, Tony O'Callaghan, Jim McCartan, Martin Lynch, Eddie O'Leary, Tom Cleary, Frank Fagan, Christy Maye, Frank Kiernan, Shane Shortall, Pat Smullen, George Webb, Paul Daly, Pat McCormack, Arthur Boyd Rochfort, Sir Michael Oswald, Tommy Kinane, Francis Shortt, Jim Dreaper, Paddy Woods, John Oxx, Ted Walsh, Robbie Irwin, Ann Fallon, Tony Costello, Ted Bourke, Tom Lacy, Frank Daly, Michael Scott, John Dolan, P.J.Murphy, Mary Kilduff, Sir Nicholas Nugent , Gerry McCormack, Edwina Maloney, Michael Byrne & John Kearney, Offaly Historical Society, Therese Kinahan, Pat McCormack,Teresa Dunne, Kitty Flynn, Kieran Sheedy, Anthony Glennon and anyone else who helped. I especially wish to thank Guy St John Williams for his help and advice along the way. I also want to thank the sponsors listed in the book for their generous financial support. It was great to have the support of Paddy Dunican, Manager, Paul Daly, Chairman and the Kilbeggan Race Committee in addition to Healy Photos, Caroline Norris and any others who provided photos. The horses head on the back page is from a painting by Joanne Dunne, Cleaboy Stud and I am very grateful to her for providing it. I would also like to thank Tony, Lorraine, and Print Plus for printing the book.

Finally, I wish to thank my wife Flor and son Simon (not forgetting Dexter our dog!), who have had to put up with me writing five books in the last 20 years, although thankfully they raised funds for the Westmeath Hospice, Caring for Kids and the local schools. It is difficult to self- publish without back up and without the support of your family, it's almost impossible. The good news for everyone is that I will not be writing anymore, so I want to thank all those who generously supported me in the past.

DEDICATION

JIM TORMEY RIP,
CECIL RONALDSON RIP,
SEAN DALY & TOM LYNAM

I wish to dedicate this book to four people, who represent a generation of people who have contributed so many positive things to their communitie and to Irish racing over many years. I interviewed both Cecil Ronaldson, RIP and Jim Tormey, RIP once for the book. I could not claim to know them and they were clearly different in many ways, but I was impressed with both of them in their own way. I have included part of their life story in the book, as a representation of their achievements and that of many others from that era.

The book is also dedicated to two Kilbeggan people, who were part of the reason Kilbeggan was the only racecourse to survive. Sean Daly is the last member of the new committee set up in 1956 to save Kilbeggan races. He was also there in 1963 and 1969, when it was under threat. He has been on the gate at the cross over into the stand for many years, where you can still have the pleasure of meeting him at the races. Tom Lynam is the heart and soul of Kilbeggan races for many years and also a major contributor to the Kilbeggan area from being Santa Claus to running the local bingo. He almost literally knows every blade of grass on the course, as he has cut it, watered it, and rolled it for many years. He also has the task of being Treasurer and controller of finance for the Kilbeggan Race Committee over 8 meetings each year. Four unique people who should be acknowledged for what they achieved in sporting terms and in the real world. It is a great honour to dedicate the book to their successful lives.

CONTENTS

INTRODUCTION

Whether it is the rich texture of the soil or the strong imposing character of the midland racing fraternity, the midlands has a tradition of breeding great horses and great racing men from champion trainers like Sir Cecil Boyd Rochfort, to champion jockey Pat Smullen.

Horse Racing in Ireland probably began in pre-Christian times and many traditions are handed down about the Fianna warriors racing their horses at aristocratic assemblies. The most famous of the assemblies was held at The Curragh, Co Kildare now the headquarters of Irish Racing. Racing had developed to the extent that John Cheney's Racing Calendar, which mainly covered British racing ncluded prizes & plates run in Ireland from 1741. Eventually, the Irish Turf Club was formed in 1790 and this led to the publication of the Irish Racing Calendar. Steeplechasing was considered the poor relation to flat racing at this time but this gradually changed in the 19th century. Generally, meetings were organised by the gentry for the gentry, as part of a social lifestyle. In 19th century Ireland, agrarian agitation and faction fighting meant that policing was a big issue at any public event, which included large numbers of the lower classes.

The very successful Kilbeggan meeting is the only racecourse still operating in Westmeath and Offaly, under the rules of racing and it has taken place there since 1840. This year it is celebrating its 175th anniversary. Major historic towns like Mullingar, Athlone, Tullamore and Birr had racecourses up to the 20th century. However horse racing on the flat and over fences has taken place in many areas in Westmeath since the 18th century. Dr Tony Sweeney in his book ***"The Sweeney Guide to the Turf 1501-2001"*** includes many of the Westmeath meeting's which were recorded in the Irish Racing Calendar as follows: **Athlone** (including courses **Garrycastle, Bushfield** etc) 1761/62, 1775/78, 1790/92, 1807, 1811, 1843, 1858/68, 1893/96, 1898/1904, 1906, 1913/16, 1919/20 and 1922/23; **Ballymore, Castlepollard** (Associated Hunt Beggars Benison) 1801,1803, 1845; **Castletown Delvin** 1842, 1844; **Coole** 1874; **Finea, Killucan** 1881/84; **Kinnegad** 1765, 1767, 1802, 1878; **Ledestown** (confined to polo ponies) 1884, 1895/1902, 1904; **Loughegar** (Associated Westmeath Hunt) 1861/62, 1867/68, 1870/71,& 1873/79; **Moate** (Aughafin-Associated Hunt South Westmeath) 1891/96; **Mullingar** (Newbrook, Associated Hunts - Westmeath, Multyfarnhan Harriers, Newbrook Harriers etc) 1754/56, 1768/70, 1776/78, 1783, 1785, 1787/93, 1803, 1820/21, 1843/46, 1848/50, 1852/57, 1859/60, 1863/66, 1869, 1872/74, 1877/84, 1886, 1890/1942, & 1946/67; **Multyfarnham** 1765, **Slanemore** 1872, and **Ballinacaragy** 1846.

The Offaly meetings were recorded in the Irish Racing Calendar as follows: **Banagher** 1763,1770,1841 and 1844; **Birr** (named courses Parsonstown, Coherhoerigh Associated Hunt, Ormond & King's County) - 1761/62, 1764/66, 1769, 1773, 1789/97, N, 1854/55, 1860/61, 1864, 1870, 1887/94, 1896, and 1901/07; **Ferbane** 1858; **Frankford** 1809 & 1867; **Geashill** Associated Hunt Ballymooney 1846; **Munny plains of Offaly** 1795/96 and **Tullamore - Ballykilmurray** 1766, 1851/64, 1866, 1885/90, and 1893/1903.

These are only recorded meetings, but in reality there were many other local meetings or point to points during this time. Racing in Westmeath & Offaly is linked to some of the greatest horses in history from Brown Jack the most popular horse in Britain in the 1930's, who was bred by the Webb family in Corolanty, Birr Co Offaly to Arkle, who famously was beaten in his first ever race at Mullingar. The first owner to win over £5,000 was Lord Rossmore, Offaly who won £6,440 in 1813 and more recently Michael O'Leary's powerful Gigginstown Stud became the leading owner's for the third time ahead of J.P. McManus. They continue to dominate National Hunt racing in modern times, as Gigginstown House hope to add to their success with War of Attrition in the Gold Cup in 2006 with powerful candidates next year like Don Cossack and Don Poli.

Many famous Aintree Grand National winners like Why Not, Drumcree, Ally Sloper, Shaun Spadah, Sergeant Murphy, Quare Times, Mr What, Kilmore, L'Escargot (a dual Gold Cup winner also) and Comply or Die are linked to the counties. Aubrey Hastings from Offaly trained four winners and Lady Margaret Nelson who was the first woman to own a winner was from Westmeath. Irish Grand National winners trace from The Admiral in 1894 to Dot Loves recent winner Liberty Counsel. Some of the most famous studs in Irish racing history are in Westmeath like Tally Ho Stud, Cleaboy Stud, Middletown Park and Gigginstown House Stud. Famous flat horses like Vaguely Noble (one of the few horses to defeat Sir Ivor), Airborne, Hethersett, up to more recent top class horses like Ivawood and Tiggy Wiggy are associated with the area. Racing is about people, and many racing families down the years in the area have been associated with everything Champion Hurdler's to classic success on the flat.

No other sport in the midlands can compete with this kind of international success, which solidifies a great tradition going back hundreds of years. The intention in the book is to capture some of the stories, as a representation of a great generation of people in different eras. It is not possible to cover everything or all the people from jockey's to studs. I tried to cover a representative group from the small to the large including some examples of women in racing, an international connection, the lighter side of racing, and touching on point to points.

chapter 1
RACING IN THE 18th CENTURY

Racing and Hunting were the main outdoor pursuits of the gentry in the 18th century and many had stables of hunters & foxhounds. Both activities, could only be afforded by the rich landed owners, but the poorer classes enjoyed it, as a sport or break from the drudgery of their existence. Gambling huge amounts was common amongst the young landlords, as fortunes were won or lost with bets from £100 to £1,000. In those terms Horse Racing meant very little to the ordinary people. One of the great figures of Irish racing was Sir Edward O'Brien, 2nd Baronet of Dromoland who up to his death in 1765 was a patron of Irish & English Racing. In Clare he named a village *"Newmarket on Fergus"* and laid a track around a Turret hill on his demesne, where he could observe the races. It was also in the O'Brien Papers that the first steeplechase from Buttevant to Doneraile in 1752 was recorded.

A COFFIN FOR 1,000 GUINEAS

One of the more striking figures of the 18th century was Sir Ralph Gore who brought a horse called Othello from England and renamed him Black & All Black. He matched him against the great mare Irish Lass owned by Mr Archibold. The mare won and because she wore a rosary around her neck she became known as the *"Paddereen"* (Gaelic for Rosary) Mare. Gore's horse ran in a great Match at The Curragh against the Earl of March's Bajazet. The Earl led a life of debauchery and later became the Duke of Queensberry and gave his name to the rules of boxing. The match according to Pues Occurances was for a 1,000 guineas. To avoid bribery Gore had a number of jockey's stand by for the race and he only nominated one at the last minute. He won the race and apparently bonfires were lit all around Dublin. Gore observed that the Earl cheated by trying to lose his weights this and challenged him to a duel at 5am the following morning. Gore turned up with a coffin which was put on the ground in front of Lord March with the latter's name and title on the coffin, with the date and year of March's death. Gore said *"Why my dear fellow you are of course aware that I never miss my man".* March quickly apologised and left the country.

The main Stewards of the Turf Club in the 18th century were Francis Savage, Hillsborough, John Dennis, John Taylor, Charles O'Hara, Annaghmore, Sligo, John Kirwan, Denis Bowes Daly, Robert Hamilton and John Whaley. Many of these raced their horses at meetings in Westmeath & Offaly over the years. John Swift Dennis was a Steward of the Turf Club from 1792-1810 and with his brother Rev. Meade Swift Dennis, Mullingar (1753-1837) he inherited a fortune from his maternal uncle John. Their horses raced mainly in the name of Rev. Mead Dennis, which was unusual. He lived at Lynnbury ANS Union Hill in Westmeath and later moved to Cork. John Dennis was admitted as Freeman of the Downroyal Corporation of Horsebreeder's in 1789 and had useful horses like Morgan, Boxer & Kitty. Denis Bowes Daly had a long association with horses in the Galway and Offaly area where he was elected an MP and was a friend of the Prince of Wales, the future King George IV. Towards the end of the 18th century he lived at Banagher's Cuba Court. He won the Gold Cup on The Curragh on numerous occasions and died in 1821.

John Kirwan and his son John were two of the leading figures in racing in this era and they lived at Castlehackett House, Knockma, Galway for 200 years in the 18th and 19th century. They converted to Protestanism and owned around 8,000 acres. They owned the famous Friar & many other good horses. Friar's head was preserved when he died and kept in the house until 1923, when the house was burned down during the troubles and the head destroyed. In 1817, he won the first Irish Derby called the O'Darby Stakes with Souvenir. Lord Clanwilliam was very successful in the 1770's winning races in Westmeath and around the country, but like a number of gentry at that time his lifestyle led to mounting debts.

WESTMEATH

Race meetings were gradually advertised in the 18th century, usually with plates valued at £10 or more plus additional prizes. At Monksland, Athlone in 1731 the meeting took place over 4 days and one of the novelty events was a 10 mile race for "running footmen" with a silver watch for the winner. Almost all of the meetings in Westmeath were sporadic, as prizes were not sufficient, and running a meeting was not viable financially, as there was no entry fee. Aside from finance, organising meetings and travel were major issues. Many of the meetings were organised through Inns in the locality with horses given up to 8 days to register, otherwise they would have to pay double at the post to run the horse. The Inns were used for entries, breeding horses, providing facilities and entertainment at night. The additional entertainment usually involved balls to attract the ladies, cock fighting, and hunting. Steeplechasing was considered the poor relation to flat racing at this time but it would gradually change in the 19th entury. Generally, races were held over three heats over 2 or 3 miles (for Cups and Whips) but there were variations across the country. Whoever, won two of the heats was the winner, bearing in mind that fields were small. If the same horse won the first two heats then the race was over. Horses that were distanced in the first heat were eliminated. In races from two miles up, a distance post was placed 240 yards from the winning post and any horse which had not passed this post before the winner had reached the winning post was said to be *"distanced"* and was eliminated.

Reports on race meetings gradually increased in newspapers and became quite extensive in local papers in the 19th century. Racing was held in Mullingar, Athlone, and Parsonstown (Birr) in the final decade of the 18th century but the 1798 Rebellion was to alter the landscape for many years in the midlands, as the rebellion affected places in Westmeath from Kilbeggan to Mullingar. It lead to very little racing in the midlands through most of the first half of the 19th century, as there was a sense of insecurity with the Napoleonic Wars, development of agrarian agitation and secret societies in Westmeath.

THE "INNS" AND OUTS OF MULLINGAR RACES

Inns, Hotels and public houses have a long association with the history of horse racing. In both Ireland & Britain in the 18th century, horses were often accommodated in the stables of innkeepers prior to a race meeting and many advertisements specified that horses had to be stabled at local inns. This was to allow local innkeepers recoup their investment in prize money and as the groom, owner and anyone associated with a horse often stayed at the inn he could make a profit. Some inns and pubs with a racing connotation like the Horse & Jockey, Co Tipperary have names dating back to the 18th century or earlier. At the Killucan Races of 1719 entries were made to Thomas O'Reilly's Inn, in 1735 to John Heney's Inn, Kinnegad, and in 1765 to Richard Dallton's inn. Two of the most important Westmeath breeders in the 18th century were John Heney (later his son Francis) and Richard Dalton. The Heney's stood stallions at the White Hart Inn, Mullingar and also their Killucan Inn, while Richard Dalton owned the George Inn, Mullingar and the White Lyon Inn, Kinnegad where stallions stood. The other main figures in the breeding industry in Westmeath were Edward Sims, Thomas Nugent, Donore, Robert Dillon, Clonbrock, and Mr Smyth Thompson, Ballinamona, Mullingar.

ACTRESS PEG WOFFINGTON AT MULLINGAR RACES

Edmund Dease in his book *"A History of the Westmeath Hunt"* mentions that a meeting took place in 1742. In a book *"Hallmarks on Gold & Silver Plate"* by William Chaffers there is an entry *"Plate won by Cheshire Tom, Mullingar Races 1737-Sir C. Domville"*. Faulkner's Journal of June 1737 also refers to a play called *"The Conscious Lives"* intended as a benefit for gentlemen in distress was not being put on in Dublin *"as the actors are at Mullingar Races"* including the famous Peg Woffington and they were also performing there that night. John Heney had an inn at Killucan, which was destroyed by fire in 1736 and he moved to Mullingar where he established The White Hart Inn. He had been the prime mover in the Killucan races and in 1737 he took the entries for Mullingar as Clerk of the course. The 1735 races at Killucan were organised by the Subscriber's Club and by Heney, who took the entries 6 days beforehand, and the horses were at his inn until the day of the races. The meeting was held over

5 days (30th May Monday-3rd June Friday) with a brace of bucks hunted, and with plays and balls at night. On the first day a plate of £15 was held, given by the Manor and Town of Mullingar by any horse at 9 stone, with 4 mile heats and on the other days there was a £10 plate given by inhabitants for Galloways at 9 stone, with £20 for hunters that never started in Curragh Plates. In 1737 we have no results other than Cheshire Tom winning.

COCK FIGHTING IN THE AFTERNOON - OVER DINNER!

In 1740, racing took place over a new course with articles for two races published but many races were cancelled that year. Mullingar was held again in September 1741 with £20 purses for horses at 10-14st. John Heney announced *"As the fox hunting season will be at the same time . . . there will be fine fox hunting each day between days of running. Balls and Plays each night and very good Ordinaries each day".* In 1742 the races were postponed because they clashed with Castlebar but were held over 5 days in July. There was a match between Thomas Nugent and Arthur Mervyn from Meath for 40gns aside, over 3 heats, and horses were carrying 14 stone (the old neighbour rivalry!). Mervyn was President of the Jockey Club in 1758.

In the 1740's there was an improved network of roads and coaches & cars provided services between towns like Mullingar and other towns. John Heney's White Hart Inn and the George Inn which was owned by Richard Dalton up to 1746, provided a good service e.g. a coach from Dalton's George Inn went to Dublin every Monday-Friday, with a return service on Wednesday & Saturday. In 1744, John Heney had a purse of £20 over 3 days racing run for by "cattle" bred in Ireland that have not won a race value £50 plus (Please note that **"cattle" in the 18th century referred to horses**). The winners in 1746 were Coe Lyons and John Dillon's top class horse Ground Ivy who beat Dr Medlicot's Poor Robin. He went on to be a successful stallion. In 1748 a 20 guinea purse was won by Maurice Keating's Kettlebender and a four horse race for £15 was won by George Lowther's horse. The latter was much better known for his interest in cock fighting. In July 1751 the flying chaises began a service to Mullingar from Dublin. It was a 7 hour journey for 13/= and passengers were allowed 14 lbs of luggage and holsters were provided for *"gentlemen's pistols to render them safe and ready".*

In 1754, the Sportsman's Subscription Purse for 5y/o's was of 150 guineas and it was won by John Browne's gelding Piper (he was a brother of Lord Altamont) from John Hill Forster's mare Amelia. There was a great deal of money laid down between the two famous 5 y/o' but the colt won both heats, as the mare drifted from 6/4 to 2/1. In 1755, John Dillon won with Duchess in the Sportman's Subscription Plate from John Browne's Smoker and Ralph Jones's Crab and Mr Brown won the race for Irish Breds with Bolton.

From newspaper accounts at this time a lot of horses were stolen from stables but with 2 guinea awards and the possibility of being hanged for the offence it was a dangerous enterprise. In Mullingar in April 1757, two men James Hughes & James Geraghty were convicted of murder and the judgement was that *"they be taken to the gallows and hanged for some time and then taken down & quartered, their bowels taken & thrown on their faces and their bodies brought back to gaol to be gibbeted at Knockdine Hill".* Crime was taken very seriously and usually to the disadvantage of the poor. In 1759-62, races were held at Empor and entries were to Richard Nugent, Churchtown. The rules included *"No horse to be entered to qualify as a runner. Any combinations between owners, as to winners will require owners to verify affidavit that such does not exist".* It seems that races may not have been fair at all times in 18th century! The Clondalever Races were held on 24th September 1764 on the course near Robert Hood's house. The winners were Thomas Tennison's Juliet and Francis Heney's Creeping Gate.

When John Heney died, his son Francis took over The White Hart Inn and he ran the Mullingar Races. He requested that subscribers pay their subscriptions before the first day of the races, as he would have to pay the respective winner's at the post. Edward McDermott's Old Bawn won the £50 purse and was immediately put up for sale. Charles O'Hara won 2 races with Wichnor and Charlotte in 1768. In 1769, a meeting was held from 14-17th August with £50 purses. One interesting conditions race for horses was *"that it never ran for a prize or had a sweat or a galloping horse before 20th July".* In that year Mr Armstrong sold his horse Aimwell to Mr T. Lambert and he won in Mullingar in July, before further success at The Curragh. In 1775, the meeting took place at Walshestown with wins for Lord Clanwilliam's Sweetbriar; Josiah Shadwell's Olympia; and Dennis B. Daly's Jenny Diver. In 1777, Thomas Nugent one of the major figures in Westmeath won with Dangler and Francis Heney won a race with a filly by Fribble, confined to Westmeath bred horses.

BUMBRUSHER OUT OF BANKER

In July 1778, it was announced that the proprietor of the Race Ground had refused to allow the races to go ahead and that no racing would take place and at the end of the month *"there being now a certainty of obtaining the race ground with a new agreement being made with the proprietors".* The races were held from 3rd to 8th August 1778, with disputes decided by Lord Granard and Belvedere. The most successful owner was the most famous in the land, the Rt Hon Thomas Connolly with the interestingly named *"Bumbrusher"*, especially as he was by *"Banker".* There was an interesting notice stating *"It is hoped that the Gentlemen of the neighbourhood, so remarkable for their hospitality will not invite company during the races, which are calculated for the benefit of the*

Town". In October 1784 Francis Heney died but his son John Heney announced he would carry on his father's business at the Inn. Robert Hamilton's horse Lazarus rose from the dead to win two stakes on Thursday and Friday.

In 1787 John Kirwan's Ormond won at Mullingar by 50l's and apparently didn't race again and in 1789 Kirwan won again with Cherokee, Kitty, and Chance. In 1791, Colonel Lumm also had a treble with Boxer, Mendoza and Lady Emily. The Birr meeting required competitors to *'cross over a sporting ditch and 4 foot double stone wall'*. At Athlone that year the Social Hunt for Real Hunters gave £60 for a weight for age race. In Mullingar a Sweepstake of 10gns, play or pay, over 1 3/4 miles was held. John Dennis had first and second with Quiz and Penultima. The meeting was held in November perhaps because there was some dispute in the summer. No other race meetings were held for the rest of the 18th century.

KINGS OF RACING IN WESTMEATH - JOHN AND FRANCIS HENEY

John Heney (1700-65) was Clerk of Mullingar course in 1737. His Inn at Kinnegad was burnt down in 1736 and he moved to Mullingar. He was enterprising, and in August 1747 he advertised a stage coach in Mullingar to run from Dublin to Lanesborough and to Roscommon once per week. In 1734, he stood the stallion Trumpeter at a location between Carrig Drumrisk, Co Leitrim and Sligo. He was by Lord Gowran's Arabian out of his mare Old Blossom and an own brother to Careless *"that beat all England & Ireland"*. In 1736 Trumpeter still owned by John Heney, was with Bryan Fallon, in Roscommon and then at Killucan. He stood Jolly Foxhunter at Killucan at 3 crowns. This horse was *"fit to breed hunters"* and challenged all *'cattle'"* to run 12 miles carrying 12st for 100gns and *"was not answered by any"*. By 1738, a third stallion Smuggler was at the White Hart Inn, Mullingar for £1-5s. He had been brought over from England by Henry Stanly Monk where he raced under the name Sprat. In 1741, John Heney bought James Lennox Napers great stallion Lamporee. Mr Naper said *"he will run four of the said horses against any four cattle of the best stallions in this kingdom for 50 guineas aside"*.

John also owned stallions jointly with Edward Sims, and they advertised Marlborough bought from the Duke of Marlborough and stood Champion at Castlelost (1745-47) and at Mullingar; Louse also stood at Castlelost and Birr between 1745/47. Bolton Starling came from Mr Croft's Barforth Stud and was bought by Edward Sims on 1st October 1739 and he spent up to 1744 at Castlelost. Fox Childers was with John Heney from 1745 to breed *"hunters, officer horses, and running horses"*. He was brought to Ireland by Captain James Baillie in Northern Ireland & sold to Heney. Someone questioned the breeding of the horse and when Captain Baillie returned to Ireland he stated *"that he will punish every evil minded person that maliciously inversed such a falsehood, if they can be discovered".* Their best known stallions included Bustard (full brother to Black and Black), Hurlothrumbo, and Bajazet. The latter won at Epsom, Newmarket etc and was sent to Westmeath for several seasons, before being brought back around 1758. John Heney died in 1765 and his son Francis took over. In 1780, Francis became embroiled in a long standing dispute with Henry Browne, Rathmore, Galway (brother to Lord Altamont) concerning the sale of famous stallion Gamahoe, which he lost.

In the 1780's Francis Heney's name appears regularly, as a subscriber to the Racing Calendar until his death in October 1784 and he was Secretary of the Westmeath Hunt in 1778. He took the entries for Mullingar Races at the White Hart Inn during 1770-80's. Constant Betty won some races for him including Kinnegad and at Banagher, by 50 lengths in August 1763 and Lady Georgina won at Mullingar in August 1778. Charles O'Hara's horse Wichnor won at Mullingar in 1768 and was later sold to Heney but without winning.

RICHARD DALTON - PROVIDES WARM BEDS AND NICKED TAILS

Richard Dalton owned the George Inn, Mullingar and he repaired it in June 1742 including the house and stabling and had the best wines, malt, liquors, eating and other entertainment and *"as he is a new beginner will take care to be well sorted and will do a reasonable rate. He had stabling for 50 horses and food & bedding".* In September 1746, he sold the George Inn and it was reported that he had removed to the New Inn, Kinnegad next door to the Market House at the Sign of the Running Horse, with a good stock of wine, hay and 20 rooms with *"good bedding"* and *"as warm & snug as any beds in the country".* He had stables for 50 horses. He claimed that he *"nicks horses tails after the best manner done in Yorkshire and will engage any horses he takes in hand at a shilling to the pound insurance".* In 1747, he built The White Inn, Kinnegad and it is not clear if he moved to Kinnegad, as his stallion Privateer stood at The George Inn in 1752 and two others Windsor Shades and Snake stood at Kinnegad. Thomas Tyrrell, Postmaster at Mullingar opened The George Inn in Jan 17, 1747 and the stage coach, which formerly ran from John Heney's, now ran from Tyrrells.

EDWARD SIMS, CASTLELOST, TYRRELLSPASS, WESTMEATH (1700-1763)

In the 1730's, Edward Sims was a well-known Westmeath breeder and importer of horses and cattle. In 1735 he stood the stallion Dimple at Tuam and in 1736 at the Pass of Kilbride near Kinnegad. In the 1740's he stood the stallions Terror, Louse, and Young Starling. In October 1739 he imported the stallion 10 y/o Starling (Bay Bolton) bred by Charles Paulet (1685-1754), 3rd Duke of Bolton and had four successful years. He got other good horses like Skim, Ancaster and Teazer.

Stallions were purchased in the joint ownership of Edward Sims and John Heney and advertised for the first time in 1748, when they bought Marlborough from the Duke of Marlborough (bred by Lord Godolphin), which stood initially at the White Hart Inn for 2 guineas. They quietly used the established contacts in various parts of the country to stand as stallions and switched stallions between them. Interestingly, Edward Sims daughter married John Brooker, a nephew of Sir William Glendower Newcomen, who was connected to Sims through horses like Hands. In FDJ 1st November 1748, it stated that Edward Sims, Castlelost & John Heney, Mullingar had 9 draught mares and a 4 y/o black stallion brought over by John Smith, Violetstown, one of the best judges in England. Sims was still in England waiting to bring over mares required for premiums offered by the Dublin Society. In February 1749 they received from the Trustees of the Navigation Society premiums of £380, £90, and £50 for importing the best 3 sets of mares kept by Heney in Mullingar.

OTHER BREEDERS IN THE 18th CENTURY

Robert Dillon, Cloonbrock who had Son of Dimple, who was bought by Xaverus Blake, Dunmanway, in April 1745 and the dam was Marygold, brought from England by Robert Dillon. He won two plates including at Mullingar and at Assolus, Clare. In 1747, he brought Webster from England. He won 2 plates at 5 y/o but at 6y/o but had a bad fall in Mullingar and retired. George Galbraith had the horse Bay Dick in April 1745 standing at Aneskenon, Kinnegad not far from Killucan at *"a guinea a leap".* Between 1745 and 1747, Mr Smyth Thompson advertised Hobglobin at Ballinamona near Mullingar and Thomas Nugent, Donore, sold the stallion Star (Othello-Smallhopes) to Henry Dougherty and it stood at Multyfarnham in 1745. He bred Fearnought (by Godolphin) and this animal was sold by Peter Lesac, Richardstown in 1762. In 1758 the stud of the late Thomas Nugent was sold at Multyfarnham in October. Walter Nugent, Moretown, Castlepollard, was a breeder early in the 18th century but on his death the stud was sold in 1731.

In 1734 Dominic Fullam, Fullwort stood an Arabian stallion at John Morron's, The Sign of the Swan Inn and in 1736 the same Arabian stood with William Dardis, Multyfarnham. In 1750 the stallion Godolphin (by the Godolphin Arabian) stood at Gigginstown (we only know that Michael O'Leary was not the owner!), but the same animal was later with Patrick Dardis, Bellenalack in 1755. Kilbeggan had a few breeders at this time when Sultan stood with John Read in 1759 and an unnamed stallion by Old Bashaw stood with John Higgins the same year. In 1782, John Forster, Killion, Kinnegad stood Young Sampson and in 1785 Cardinal a full brother to Friar stood at Rathcolum. In April 1755, the stallion Young Marlborough was kept by Hugh Killeen, Robinstown, Mullingar. He was got by the great Marlborough and bred by John Neville, Gaulstown. On 24th June, on the fair green in Ballymore, part of the stock of Owen Coffey consisting of horses, mares, colts, fillies, and some choice jumpers & brood mares were present. Young Childers 1747, who was to be let at Frankford, Offaly between Birr & Tullamore, was a son of the Duke of Devonshires famous Childers. He was brought from England by Captain Dickson of Mount Pleasant, Kings County and sold to Mr Thomas Exham, Frankford.

ATHLONE HORSE RACING IN 18th CENTURY AND "THE PINT AND PINT" PUB

Horse Racing in Athlone took place from 1731 to 1923, but it was very periodic with many breaks over the years. The most extensive periods were from 1858-1868 and 1893-1904. In 1731 a meeting took place in the first week of August at Monksland near the town with 4 races taking place over 6 days. It was ideal for viewing, as the Monkslands hills formed part of the Esker Riada across the midlands and acted as the grandstand. The races were won by Mr Edgeworth's Poleboy, Colonel Trench's mare, Colonel Stafford's Budroe (winner of the King's Plate at The Curragh) and Mr Ian's horse. The most interesting race was on the Friday when there was a 10 mile races contested by footmen for the prize of *"a good strong watch"*, which was won by Loughlin Prassagh, a servant of Lord Netterville. The evenings were spent with music *"on the delightful River Shannon, which was made infinitely more so by the company of ladies".* An additional £20 plate was presented on behalf of the Athlone Corporation by Councillor William Harwood, with a subscription for a £100 plate.

In 1733, the meeting was changed to the Leinster side of Athlone for 2 days and the last 2 days were held on the Connaught side. It was held in the last week of August with the strong support of the local Corporation. Entries were to be lodged 6 days before at Francis Johnson's Inn in Athlone for the Leinster side, and at Christopher Dillon's Inn for the Connaught side. Dillon advertised that *"the Subscriptions for the Long Room not being full, it is hoped that the Ladies will breakfast in public at the Town House, so that they may set out together for the entertainment of the day; the music to play till the Ladies set out".* The gentlemen of Athlone presented a £20 Plate for Wednesday; John Browne, The Neale, Mayo, gave a £10 Plate for Thursday (Connaught side) for Galloways; and on Saturday (Connaught side) the Barony Plate of £25 was held. Francis Johnson was an Innkeeper in Athlone in 1719 and in 1748 he had an inn called '*The Pint & Pint*' (Maybe it sould have been called The Two Pints!) In 1734 racing took place over 3 days in the first week in September, with the same races as 1733, but it is not clear if two courses were used. It stated that David Potts, Vice Sovereign of the Borough had the Articles of Racing on display at the houses of Mark Begg, John Plummer, James Galvin, and at Thomas Robinson's Union Flag Inn. Unfortunately, no results were given for these meetings and as it turned out no race meeting was held again until 1761, even though the publication of racing calendars commenced in 1741.

A PUBLIC HORSE WHIPPING AND 'THREE BLACKMOORS HEADS'

It is interesting to look at the people who were involved at that time in organising the races. David Potts was a son of William Potts from Cheshire who settled in Tinamuck, Offaly around 1688. In 1729, David Potts is described as a 'yeoman' who married Jane Trumperant, daughter of an Athlone merchant. James Potts, another member of the family was a proprietor of the newspaper *Saunders Newsletter* and he died in 1795 after a public horsewhipping by Francis Giffard owner of the *Faulkner's Dublin Journal* (A variation on the rivalry between newspapers?). Mark Begg was an innkeeper and in 1736 he set up a stage coach route to Capel Street from Athlone from the interestingly, named *Three Blackmoors Heads* at a cost of 10d, which was probably on the Main Street. He died in 1739 and is buried in the Abbey Graveyard. The inn was later leased by Michael Byrne, who also leased a mill on the bridge of Athlone in 1754. In 1742, he was owner of The Raven Inn and could furnish '*a new chaise and a good horse or saddle horses to any part of the kingdom at a reasonable rate*'.

John Plummer was a vintner and innkeeper who lived in the '*Mansion House*' and he was town bailiff in 1723. In 1737 he claimed he was the only Protestant innkeeper in Athlone. He had stabling for 50 horses and two carriage houses were available. In 1729 James Galvin was also an innkeeper and Thomas Robinson, Union Flag Inn was an innkeeper from at least 1721. He had stables at Hatter's Lane (close to the current AIB). Most of them were connected with inns or local businesses rather than being landed gentry, as was the case later in the 19th century.

It was not until 1761, that Athlone races re-commenced with the articles published in October that year, The Clerk of the Course was Thomas Cooke, who was described as an 'ale draper' in 1753 and as an innkeeper in 1760. In 1754 he was lessee of 'The New inn' later called '*The New Black Horse Inn*' which was on Church Street. He was Churchwarden at St Mary's and died in 1798. The meeting started on 19th October and lasted for 6 days. It was very wet and the races were put back for a week to avoid a clash with Kilkenny. The winners included Andrew Armstrong's Whimsey who beat Mr Lamberts White Nose and Charles O'Haras Sejanus. Sir Edward O'Briens Brutus also won and went on to further success at The Curragh. In 1762, racing was brought forward to 19-24th July and it took place on a new course near Athlone with entries taken by local innkeeper Barclay Corr, whose premises were in the vicinity of Costume Place, near the market house. The main owners participating at a modified programme included Charles Newcomen, Georges Lowther, Charles Donnellan, John Knox (he was MP in Donegal & Mayo), Thomas Smyth, Thomas Walpole, Lord Mounteagle, Andrew Armstrong, Xaverius Blake, Colonel Archdale, and Darcy French. Gorges Lowther won the main race with Granby, who had been beaten the previous year by Andrew Armstrong but this time he beat the latter's Cheshire Tom.

M.P.'S IN RACING DUEL AND SEVERAL MISHAPS ON THE COURSE

The meeting failed and it was another 13 years in 1775 before a determined effort was made to revive it at the old course in Monksland. The races were held between the 7th and 12th August. Entries were taken at the house of Lackey Dunne near the Navigation Bridge. Mr Higgins was running his Fly Coach three times in the Race Week from Dublin to Athlone and ensured that people will arrive before the races. It was claimed that *"This was the largest meeting ever seen at a horse race in Ireland and the Company seemed, unanimously, to be pleased"*. The conditions for the opening race for a £50 purse was for real hunters *"that had been fairly rode last season to the death of, or the earthing of 2 braces of foxes or the death of 4 brace of hares"*. It was won by John Fallon's Governor from Thomas Moland's Orlando. The highlight on Saturday was a £100 purse given by the Town of Athlone and it was won by John Kirwan's famous horse Friar from Lord Clanwilliam's Irish Hero and the Earl of Altamont's Bald Jack. Friar won 8 Royal Plates, 3 Lord Lieutenant Plates, 3 Jockey Club plates and 3 Sweepstakes and 19 other races.

In 1777, James Browne's appropriately named Mother Browne won a £50 purse. She went on to win in 1780, beating Adonis & Droleen and at the same meeting beat the famous mare Lalage. She was then sold to John Kirwan and won another £50 purse for her new owner in 1781 from Titania & Spectator. She was certainly a course specialist at Athlone in this period. Lord Clanwilliam had a double with Hippolitus his star beating Jolly Bacchus by 50l's (he was only beaten by a few horses like Friar and Olympus). The Clerk of the Course for 1778 was Luke Conniff and racing took place over 6 days from 10-15th August. The Duke of Leinster's Cromaboo won twice at the August 1778 meeting and went on to be a successful stallion. In 1782, racing took place over 2 weeks from Thursday 10th October to Wednesday 16th October with entries taken by John Mecham, Clerk of the Course with Darcy French and John Burke as Stewards.

DEATH KNELL - INCAPACITATED HORSES AND INJURED JOCKEY'S

After another break, racing resumed in 1790 when it was the first year in which the Irish Turf Club was mentioned, with all its rules & ordinances printed in the Irish Racing Calendar. The full results were given for the first time and even the betting, although there were few reports on betting trends at the tracks. In that year of the 22 meetings on the Calendar five were from around the midland's - Mullingar, Athlone, Birr, Roscommon, and Longwood. The Freeman's Journal was not impressed with Athlone Races in August 1790 *"The shortness of the turns in a small & ill laid out course occasioned..... accident's to horses & jockey's during the running. Three of the jockey's lie dangerously ill and three of the running horses are incapacitated from ever appearing on the turf in future. Many accidents happened to the spectators, amongst whom was a man who on Tuesday was killed by a horseman, who overturned him with such violence that his ribs were all broken and killed him on the spot".* In 1790, the first day had a race for £60 for any horse that had not won a race valued at £50. It was won by Thomas Conolly's Engineer from Anthony Daly's and Giles Eyre's horse Jane Harold. In 1792, a race for hunters carrying 12 stone led to a contest between the two local M.P.'s Richard St George on Friar and William Handcock on Bennison Jack. Victory went to St George even though Handcock's horse was 1/2 in the betting.

The debacle of 1790 and small fields the next few years was the death knell for the meeting. It was strongly supported by most of the main owners of that era but without strong support from the locals it was not going to last and the relationship between the two local MP's could not have helped in the organisation of racing. Racing in Athlone was to become very sporadic in the 19th century, with only 3 meetings in the first half of the century in 1807, 1811, and 1843. It was only when they commenced at Garrycastle in 1853 (sometimes at nearby Bushfield) that there was any continuity & even then it was spasmodic with meetings on in 1853-68, 1893-6, and also breaks in the period between 1899/1923 when it ended.

BIRR RACES AND OTHER MEETINGS

It was an important meeting with initiatives to include 3 y/o and 2 y/o races, the inclusion of jumps in Hunter races and with good prize money on offer in the latter part of the century. The meetings were sponsored by the Parson's family. In 1731, a 3 day meeting took place in May with entries taken by Anthony Fennell, The Parson's Arms and with a fee of one Pistole *(*A pistole was a Spanish gold coin sometimes called a doubloon. By `the mid-C18, it was almost worth a pound (0.83) or a little over 18 shillings)* for the £10 plate. Results started appearing from June 1761 when Thomas Lambert, John Foster with Promise and Darcy French's Humbug all won. In August 1762, John Julian's Sprightly (121 heat results) won a 4 y/o race, James Daly's Chaffinch walked over in the 5 y/o, and Georges Lowther's Granby won the hunter race. In 1765 the two £100 races were won by Lord Mounteagle and Charles Lambert with unnamed horses (it was common in the 18th century). The race won by Mounteagle, was one of the first 3 y/o races in the country and there was two weight for age races and in one race there was a prize for second place which was unusual. The three year old race was run in three 1 1/2 mile heats.

In 1768 William Jones, Clerk of the Course, took the entries for the races on 27 June-2 July. Any disputes were to be determined by Sir Laurence Parson's. In 1769 the races were similar and John Drought won with Farewell and Sportsman and in 1770 the racing was postponed from September to mid-October. John

Kirwan, Castlehackett, Galway had a runner plus Denis Daly, Josiah Shadwell and the people of Loughrea must have been disappointed when their purse of £50 ended up as a walk over, with the prize going to Thomas Lambert's Aimwell. Lord Clanwilliam, a major figure in racing before being almost bankrupted through his extravagant lifestyle won two £50 purses in 1775 at a 6 day October meeting with a newly purchases gelding by Hippolitus and Carlos.

It was another 14 years before the next meeting from 28 September-3rd October 1789 which featured some of the top horses of the era. Anthony Daly had a few wins with Young Hero and Young Friar, Colonel Eyre with Atalanta and Sir Oliver, John Fallon's hunter Batchelor etc. In 1790 it was another 6 day meeting with entries from many of the leading owners and the wall on the course caused a lot of problems. Colonel Lumm's rider was disqualified on Mendoza for jostling John Fallon's Fair Eliza.

The Stewards at the 1793 meeting were Sir Laurence Parsons, T.R. Pepper, and Denis B. Daly and John Kirwan won the main race with Drone. The entries in 1795 were taken by Robert Poynings, Clerk of the Course, the winning owners to pay one guinea to sworn judge. One race of £50 was sponsored by the people of Parsonstown. There was interesting information regarding the betting for the first time John Whaley's Scratch and Mr Phelan's Viceroy were coupled at 1/1 to beat the field. The individual odds were Scratch 2/1, Viceroy 3/1, Breslaw 3/1, Deceiver 4/1 etc. After winning the first heat Scratch went on to win the second race to take the prize. They had to cross a sporting ditch and a 4 foot double stone wall. It was won by Mr Bell's Boldface, who later turned out again in a race with a 5 foot stone wall. He beat Captain Marlay's Young Friar but the latter disputed the win and issued a statement to the Turf Club for a decision. In 1797, there was victories for John Edwards Viceroy, Thomas Kelly's Cornet, (the prize given by the people of Birr), and John Kirwan's Tom Tit.

Racing also took place on other sites in the 18th century. In 1718 a meeting was held in Clonohill (near Birr) in July for a Plate of £14. The race was organised by Matthew Hobard who provided the Plate but owners had to pay an unspecified sum to him. At Tullamore in 1730 a three day meeting took place in mid-September with entries to Thomas Atkinson, Moore Arms Inn, Tullamore on Tuesday 8th September and be kept there until time of the race. Judges were appointed on the course to decide on any disputes and a ball was held that night for the ladies. Interestingly, it was stated that "*No horse was to jostle or cross for any of the Plates except for the first and that only for the last mile*" A similar meeting was held in 1735 over 2 days including a £20 plate, with one Moydore entrance *(*a moidore was a Portuguese gold coin, minted from 1640-1732. It was the principal coin, current in Ireland at the beginning of the C18 and spread to the west of England. They became 30s in Ireland)*. In 1766 a five day meeting took place starting 29th September when Mr Boarman's horse won both heats beating the horses of Thomas Tennison, Robert Gore and Edward Armstrong and collecting £50.

Race meetings also took place in Banagher in 1763 and from 1768/1770. It was a four day meeting from 29th Aug-1st September, probably associated with the famous fair. The races in 1763 were -£50 for any horse; 30 guineas for maiden hunters; £50 for 5 y/o's; and £50 for 4 y/o's. They were won by Mr Donnelly's Modesty, Mr Ramsay's Roger, John Heney's good horse Constant Betty, and Mr Lambert's Prim. In 1769, the winners were John Drought's Farewell and also his good horse Sportsman, Andrew Armstrong's Slug and Mr Smith's Nimrod, who beat Mr Leslie's Munster Lass and William Parson's Champion. Thomas Thompson Junior took the entries in October 1770 and advertised good ordinaries for ladies and balls at night. Another feature at this meeting was *"a great cock fight between the gentlemen of King's County and County of Galway."*

chapter 2

THE RISE AND FALL OF MULLINGAR RACECOURSE

It was the century of O'Connell and the Catholic Emancipation and Repeal Movement; the Young Irelanders; the Fenian Rising; the formation of the Land League by Davitt & Parnell with the Home Rule movement. It was also a century where poverty was the normal way of life for the majority of people leading to the Great Famine in the 1840's. Race meetings were affected by economic circumstances, faction fighting, politics including hunting and issues of drunkenness and gambling.

It was mainly in the second half of the 19th century that racing spread across the county, but very rarely was their long term consistent meetings. Kilbeggan had three phases 1840-55, 1879-85; and 1901 to the present. Mullingar had racing every decade from the 1840's to the 1960's but with gaps occurring about 10 times. Athlone had a 25 year gap from 1868 to 1895. Tullamore re-commenced in 1851 after nearly a century and was gone after 1903. There was a close connection beween hunting and racing, as it was often members of the hunt who organised the racing like the South Westmeath Hunt Club and individuals like John Malone, Ballymore (12,554 acres in 1875), and Cecil Fetherstonhaugh, Bracklyn. Later in the 19th century, a division occurred between the official Irish National Hunt Steeplechase Committee (INHSC), who ran races with a minimum prize of £5. Local gentry, business people who were getting more involved in racing, better off farmers etc started running meetings where the prize was £4-19s, therefore they did not come under INHSC rules. Generally, races were held over one day unlike the 18th century or early 19th century when they were held for up to five days. In spite of more involvement by non-farming business people, it was still through landlords like John Longworth, Glynwood, (3,264 acres in 1854) that racing took place in Athlone. J.M. Naghten, Athlone, (4,829 acres), was one of the most successful owners in this era and Lord De Freyne (34,000 acres), Frenchpark Roscommon was a breeder, owner and contributor to the development of meetings.

LEADING OWNERS AND BREEDERS IN WESTMEATH

The most successful people in Westmeath from the late 19th century were the Boyd- Rochforts, Middleton Park as outlined elsewhere, A.J. Pilkington, Cornelius Hannan, Frank Mitchell, James Cole, Christopher Taaffe, James Yourell, T.M. Reddy, Cleary's, Purcells, Hams, etc and some of their stories are told elsewhere under the Aintree Grand National, Irish Grand National, family racing histories and international connections. Powerful figures like Captain Cecil Fetherstonhaugh (4,711 acres), was a director of the Mullingar Race

Company and a breeder in the late 19th century. He ran the company in 1890 and had runners at the local meetings. In 1890, he organised a two day event in Bracklyn to entertain friends & farmers.The winner of each race was presented with *"Whippy's Best Hunting Saddles".* A few of the personalities of that that time are briefly outlined below:

Christopher Taaffe, Rathaspic, Rathowen (118 acres) was an owner breeder and he had a private trainer Frank Byrne at his small stable in the 1890's. In 1891 he was fined by the National Hunt Committee for putting up an English jockey G.Morris on Lovely Annie one of his most successful horses. He also had champion mare Darling Nancy, Derravaragh, and St Dermot. He was a large farmer, horse owner, and his son J.P.Taaffe was his jockey. He won the Royal Whip in 1877 with Piersfield, who won 10 races between 1876/77 and was still a stallion in 1895 as a 21 y/o. He sired a number of winners including Baldoyle Derby winner Charming Nancy. He had Connaught Ranger as a sire in 1900, when he was around 70 y/o. His son J.P was well known in Irish Racing circles having had a career as a jockey & breeder (he died in 1948).

James Cole, Pass of Kilbride, Killucane was on the 1911 Census, described as a 70 y/o farmer, wife Mary 65, son Christopher 31 y/o, and daughter Millie 24 y/o. His most successful season was in 1896 when he won £385 with 5 wins. He bred Abbot (1887), who was out of the half-bred Little Agnes (1876, by Delight). He won a National Hunt flat race and eleven steeplechases, including the 1893 Conyngham Cup over four miles, beating Wild Man from Borneo (who won the 1895 Grand National Steeplechase at Aintree). Little Agnes also produced Novice (1884), a winner of a National Hunt race on the flat and a hurdle race and later dam of seven steeplechase winners, including Kilbride (1891) winner of seven steeple chases); Hercules II (1896) who had 7 wins in chases; Spotted Lady (1903), winner of 5 chases and Prioress (Ascetic-Little Agnes), won 7 chases and in her last, at Kempton Park, beat Grand National winner Grudon.

His horse Millie (possibly called after his daughter) with T. Dowdall up won at Navan in May 1897 and in 1896 St Michael was described as a horse rapidly making a name for himself bred M.J. Saurins good horse Anchony. Other successful horses were Heretic, No Sir a prolific winner around the country, Johnny Mac, Hermit etc. In February 1914, a 7 y/o horse called The General (Serviton-Novice) won the Grand Prize at Karlshorst in Germany worth £2,200. He was bred by James Cole and won over fences and hurdles in Ireland and his first win was at the Mullingar Spring meeting in 1910. The horse was sold to Germany and won a number of races there.

J.H. Locke, Ardnaglue, Kilbeggan was the son of John Locke, who arrived in

Kilbeggan in the 1840's and took over the oldest Pot Still Distillery in the world (established 1757). He died in 1868, and by 1887 it was a much larger plant run by his sons John E. and James Harvey. John was a Steward at Kilbeggan in the 1840's and when racing resumed at Kilbeggan in 1879 they provided the course at Ballard. It was his son James Harvey who was interested in hunting, polo, and horse racing, especially flat racing. He was born in 1860 and his horses were trained by professionals on The Curragh including Prudence who won the Irish Cesarewich in 1899 and 1900 worth 200 sovereigns and Jurisprudence won the National Produce Stakes before competing in the first ever meeting at the Phoenix Park in the Phoenix Plate of 1,500 sovereigns (later to be famed as the *"Park 1,500"*). He was fifth to Bushey Park giving 12lbs. The family were involved in supporting Kilbeggan Races from 1840 and the revival in 1901. He was famous for riding his horse *"Black Skin"* on the course to control the crowds. In 1898 he won £1,084 in prize money and was in the top three owners. He had a few other horses like Bivouac, Black Mint and Cowslip who won in this era.

MULLINGAR RACES IN THE 19TH CENTURY WAS OPEN TO "VERY FAST WALKERS"

The earliest accounts of a meeting in the Westmeath papers was in 1823 when a 2 day meeting was held at Hopestown and it remained the venue up to 1826, when it was moved to Gainstown in December. Slanemore was in use in 1829 and in 1831 it was held at Walshestown before returning to Gainstown for a 3 day meeting in 1832 and racing continued there up to 1835, when it changed to Culleen. In 1836, at Culleen there were 6 runners for the Westmeath Urn a 4 mile steeplechase and there was also a selling race over 4 miles. In 1838 the famous Lynn course came into the picture with the Stand *"near Swift's back gate"* and the race was around the *"borders of Boorstown"*. In 1839, Culleen was used again with the featured Urn valued at 100 guineas with 20 guineas added and also the Mullingar Salver of 50 guineas with 15 sovereigns added. The Clerk of the Course was James Quirke. The Lynn course described as *"behind Kieran Ward's"* was the main venue in the 1840's with occasional meetings in the area at Gainstown, Ballymore, and Ballynacarrigy during the Famine period, until 1848 when Newtown came into use. The railway is said to have changed horse racing from a comparatively local event to a more commercial & professional recreation. The number of meetings in Westmeath and surrounding counties increased and were held more often.

Newtown was the predecessor of Newbrook and its use coincided with the opening of the railway line between Dublin and Mullingar. It was situated on the Russelstown Road convenient to the railway line and the lands are long associated with the Downes family, who contributed so much to racing in Westmeath. It was 2 miles round and 17 jumps had to be negotiated. Aside from a donkey race there were two stake races. The railway was available from 1848 and trains from Dublin stopped at Saunders Bridge. Passengers were informed in the press that *"it was a three minute walk"* to the course but they would have needed to be *"very fast walkers"* to cover that distance. A stand was erected for the meeting and it held 500 people and a refreshment bar was underneath.

NEWBROOK OPENS, AS THE RAILWAY CHANGES RACING

Racing at Newbrook opened on 2/3rd November 1852. Originally it was a one man business owned & Conducted by Pat Costello who came from Howth to Mullingar, as the proprietor of the first MGW Railway Saloon at the Mullingar Station. He built a stand and ladies enclosure and stated that *"a new road has been made from the railway terminus to the course at Newbrook".* The stand could hold 2,000 people and the interior was divided into two saloons, and Midlands and Great Western Railway (MDGWR) offered cheap return fares. The balcony was erected at the front of the stand and many of the gentry dined in Costello's each evening and H. Murray presided over food of good quality. The railway changed the whole perspective of racing making it more accessible and commercial and Mullingar was in a good position to benefit. Costello was attempting to bring more professionalism into the business. In 1850/51 he was involved in promoting Lynn with train specials from Dublin with 200 passengers, but it was not a great success. He leased lands at Newbrook closer to the train and passengers could disembark on a special platform built by the railway company. The new course was considered much better with a 2 mile circuit of 14 fences and 6 water jumps. He maintained his involvement until the 1870's (Costello was Secretary 1852, Treasurer, Clerk of Course 1853 etc). Subscriptions were a major part of racing at this time e.g. Sir Richard Levinge gave £25 in 1851 and local inhabitants gave £30 in 1853 as it would benefit business.

The numbers on the trains increased in the 1860's with 28 carriages from Broadstone 1,200 people, from Killucan 500, from Boyle 500, Cavan 400 and Ballinasloe 400, even though the description in 1866 of Mullingar *"being only second to Punchestown"* was somewhat exaggerated. In that year, there was a new *"commodious"* Stand House erected by Mr Costello, the course was described as excellent, and the jumps had improved. The priests had directed people to desist from alcohol and intoxication. By 1870, the Railway Company increased its contribution to the races and business traders in the town doubled their contribution.

Even though Costello was still Secretary, there was a Committee working with him at this time. In 1871, the numbers by train was reduced because of excessive charges by the MGWR Company. The prize money stopped Mullingar being one of the leading courses. In 1874 Costello was Clerk of the Course but he left shortly afterwards, as there was no racing in 1875/76. In 1877, it was revived but there was clearly an issue between the owner and the people with several letters appearing in local papers. In one case the *"want of energy"* in the people was mentioned. The writer hoped *"that that it was not too late to bestir themselve's and show that it was not just trade but the love of sport that induced them to take an interest in the races"*. P.N. Fitzgerald, Soho House, Multyfarnham the owner (who ran it from 1877-89), even wrote that he would be glad to give the Newbrook course and accept the small sum of £70 from townspeople & trader, as their subscription. Eventually, it was resolved and racing took place. In 1878 correspondence on Westmeath Guardian, Fitzgerald stated in response to an allegation that 7s 6d was too expensive for the Stand House that it was the same as some other larger meetings and that others were charging 10/-. He said the writer did not understand the cost of running a meeting including stakes, fences, damage to land etc.

In 1880, the price of admission to the stand was reduced to 5/-. Fitzgerald's own horse New Meadow won at this meeting. He went on to be 2nd in Irish Grand National in 1884 to The Gift. The "river jump" was cut out and part of the ladies stand carpeted. The races were not held in 1884/85. A letter appeared in Westmeath Examiner in June 1886 referring to the great loss of the races but it did not return until 1890.

MULLINGAR RACE COMPANY 1890 - 1935

A limited company took over the races in 1890 with share capital of £2,500 to be raised by £1 share. The aim was to re-establish the famous old races and promote steeplechasing and flat racing in addition to sports, cricket, and other amusements plus the agriculture and horse show. It very much involved landed gentry. Lord Greville was Chairman and owner of Mullingar other big landowners included Captain Ralph Smyth, Gaybrook, 6,287 acres, Captain Cecil Fetherstonhaugh, Bracklyn, Killucan, Colonel J.R. Malone, Ballynacaragy, etc. The commercial and trading people involved included Christopher Downes lawyer, Joe Dowdall, leather dealer, John Gordon draper, and Owen Sullivan publican and all of them were involved in hunting & steeplechasing.

In 1891, the addition of the fields in Clown helped to improve the track plus better conditions for vehicles. The company bought the land on which the old racecourse stood and made improvements to the stands and general buildings. P.J.Carroll became the Secretary and he drove on the races for many years. In 1893 an issue arose, which was to be a constant for the lifetime of Mullingar races. The Town Commissioners met in May to arrange for a collection for the Town Plate. They pushed the point that merchants & the town should come forward *"with a heart & a half"*, while making the point that *"shopkeepers have ill requited the exertions of the company"*. Lord Greville raised the issue of enclosing Newbrook to institute *"gate meetings"*, as they do in Britain and places like Tramore and a 1/- charge would double the income. Meanwhile, the Race Committee were planning to build a wall around the course (about 400 perches). The wall meant that it could be used by other sporting bodies. The Directors agreed to ask Hibernian Bank to advance £1,800 and it would run around company farm. They hoped to make around £200 with about 10,000 attending. The wall was expected to cost £50 which would leave something for shareholders with additional revenue from other organisations (coursing, football and athletics).

ONE OF THE BEST COURSES IN IRELAND

Within a few years Newbrook became one of the best courses in Ireland. In 1895 the company built the Horse Show and Sports Ground around the Newbrook course and raised the status of the meeting. They encouraged the best owners to run their horses with increased prize money. P.J. Carroll was also Secretary of the Horse Show. The Stand enclosure was enlarged and in 1899 it was decided to have 2 meetings in June and September, mainly due to E.A. Shaw, Solicitor, who guaranteed £50 and it was a great success. The other big issue was the siding at the racecourse plus the cost of 2/6d from Mullingar Station to the racecourse, which should only be 1/-. Many meetings were lost because of extortion by jarveys and hotels and it needed to stop.

The course ceased to be free and admission charges were introduced for spectators and vehicles, when the wall was built. The driving forces at this time were C. Downes, J. Dowdall, P. Cleary, P.J. Carroll, Secretary, and John Cahill, Assistant Secretary. In later years it was taken over by J.J. Parkinson & Fred Myerscough who ran it for some years. By 1902 the MWGR had at last erected a siding platform at the Stand House, which meant that you walked off platform and into the track. As the course progressed a new improved weigh room, dressing room, jockey's room, press room, trainers and owners stand, and new telegraph board were put in place by 1905/1906. Pressure brought the combination of a single price for the rail ticket and the ticket for the races. When Richard "Boss" Croker visited in May 1906 for the first time he said *"it was the nicest racecourse in Ireland".* A new 7 furlong 150 yards flat track was used in the Lough Ennel Plate in 1905 for the first time, and the new buildings were erected by the committee and were well constructed.

In 1907, it was noted that there was a major emphasis on motor vehicles with the sporting fraternity as *"mechanism seems to have superceded horseflesh"* and anyone with train tickets got in free. Special platforms were erected for the bookies for the first time, but they were not allowed to use boxes, the telegraph arrangements were praised by the press. The Stewards in 1908 were Lord Greville, Sir Walter Nugent MP, J.R. Malone, Captain Fetherstonhaugh, Frank

Barbour MFH, Phillip O'Reilly, Harry Whitworth, J.H. Locke, Colonel G.C. Hall, T.J.Shaw, and Pat Cleary.

By June 1910, a beautiful new stand was completed and it was twice the size of the old one and completely covered (Contractor Charles Doyle). Each side of the new stand was enclosed with glass and the upper stand was over 100ft in length and 16ft in breath, surrounded by concrete walls and iron ornamental rails. It could hold 2,000 people. It was also proposed to have a feature race worth 200 sovereigns at each of the three meetings. In 1912, the regretted death of C.Downes took place and he was one of the big organisers of the Company full of enthusiastic energy. He acted as Chairman and was missed for his work & energy. The vacancy was filled by N.J. Downes. In 1913 a new motor enclosure was added near the main enclosure. At each of the 3 meetings they hoped to have a 200 sovereign race - in the 2 mile chase in April, the 2 1/2 mile chase in June and the 1 1/2 hurdle in September. A report for 1914 showed profits dropped considerably due to the weather and the war, but in 1918 they showed profits of £519-19s-4d and the Directors gave a donation of £125 to the Bloomfield & Tudenham Red Cross Hospitals.

In March 1922, the 32nd Annual General Meeting (AGM) was held in Mary Street with R.J. Downes presiding. Owing to an increase in general expenses, value of stakes, and loss on farm profit the profits were only £470-10s-1d. In 1923 R.J. Downes said *"There is great dissatisfaction across the country as to these excessive costs, which are destroying racing in some districts. It is time that the Stewards of the National Hunt & Turf Club reconsider the amount and also the amalgamation of some of their offices to reduce the number of officials."* They paid £700-900 per year in Government Entertainment Tax (7-10%). The IPREA (Irish Provincial Race Executive Association) of which Downes and R. Dowdall were senior officials got generous concession from the railways after negotiation with them with regard to the carriage of horses and grooms, but charges for passengers were still too high. In 1927 The IPREA had at last, after negotiation, got a reduction in Turf Club Officials fees, but it was still very high. In 1928 they only held 3 meetings with a loss of £548-17s-10d and after the September Meeting they had to dismiss all the staff. In 1929 only one race meeting was held and by 1935 the company losses totalled £968.

MULLINGAR RACES 1823 - 1967
"NUMEROUS AMUSING FALLS"

In 1823, the Westmeath Journal advertised the Silver cup value 60 guineas given by W. H. Magan to be run on Easter Monday 31st March 1823 and on Easter Tuesday 1st April a Silver Cup value 30 guineas was given by Ralph Smyth, Gaybrook, for hunters bred in Westmeath and entries were made to Henry Wilton, Mullingar, 3 days before the race. The horses had to qualify the day before running, by leaping a 4 foot wall, a 10 foot drain, and a sporting ditch (it was tough in those days!). The races were held at Hopestown and the Stewards were Hon. J.C.Browne, S.Vignoles, Alexander Murray, William Robinson, and Francis P. Smyth. The race was won by William Kelly's Sir Edward (Mr Clarendon) from Mr McEvoy's mare Granuaile (Mr Ferguson). A dispute arose when Mr McEvoy objected stating that the winner went the wrong side of a post near the end of the race. The Journal said it was well contested and *"was rode in the astonishing short space of 18 minutes".* Mr Kelly held the race, as he won the cup after three consecutive wins, when his bay Off-She- Goes defeated his own horse Sir Edward in 1825. Meetings about the races in this era were held in Murray's Inn, Mullingar.

By 1825 it was a 3 day meeting from Thursday to Saturday. It was dangerous in many ways as Captain Sheil fell off Governor and injured his collar bone. Sporadic meetings were held and in April 1830 a Salver was put up by the Westmeath Fox Hounds and it was won by Mr C. Fetherston, Ballintubber with Forget Me. Apparently, there were *"numerous and amusing falls",* which might not have been so funny for those involved. The races at Hopestown in March 1835 were described as *"not calculated to do justice to either men or horses".* Mr Murray's Nettle distanced all the other horses even though he had to turn back after going the wrong side of a post. In 1836 the Westmeath Urn was advertised with William Casey, Mullingar taking entries before 10 am on the day (5/- to enter). Entries were made by Messrs Dennis, Briscoe, Nagle, Nugent, Murray and Knaresboro (owner of the great Brunette). In 1837 the racing was at Cullion and by 1pm the roads were thronged with people, carriages & other vehicles. The course formed a circle around Keene's Hill from which you had a great view. It seemed as if they didn't have the hedges trimmed and the Stewards had to do it just before the race. Mr Nagle's Sportsman dominated the race in both heats.

THE FRIGHTENING FENCE AND THE DRUNK DUBLIN JOCKEY

In 1838, the races were held in Lynn where there was a good course commencing near Mr Richard Swift's back gate. In the race Sportsman was back to win against Mr Fox's Now or Never (McDonagh). In 1839, the Lynn committee were J. Callanan, Treasurer and Secretary, Hugh Tuite, Henry Murray, Sir Percy Nugent, W.Reilly, Richard Coffey, Thomas F. Uniake, Cuthbert Clibborn, R.W.Reynell, Samuel Hendy, John Vignoles, Owen Daly, Robert Holmes, and Edward Briscoe. It was the usual three 2 mile heats over 17 fences some of which could compete with the Liverpool Swampers, especially the double ditch which was described as *"the last barrier to the beaten nag".* Bells Life, London reporter described the fence as *"a double ditch of immense height, narrow on the top with a ditch full of water, fourteen feet wide on the other side. I trust for the sake of humanity, I may never see such another leap in the latter end of a race".* The favourites were old Sportsman, Mr Reilly's Sir James and Sir

Percy Nugents Honesty (Vitch). After many fearful crashes it was won by Sportsman from J. Nugent's Prendergast (T. Nugent). On the second day old Sportsman was "fagged" with Harkaway winning the first heat. In the second heat the rider of Harkaway *"slipped softly off and let the horse go".* It turned out the jockey, who was from Dublin, was quite drunk but at least he had a soft landing and he could explain his sore head.

In 1840, Richard Swift gave his lands again and provided accommodation. In the race for the Urn, Hotspur upset Don Cataract at a fence and Mr Callanan had a bad fall but was uninjured with just a black eye and the *"loss of a beaver"?* There was an objection to the winner Mr Reynell's Priam (Johnston) that he went the wrong side of a post but the Stewards allowed him to start again and Mr Leving's withdrew Hotspur in protest. Priam went on to win the race by a few lengths.

THE FIGHTING GENTRY AND A BEAUTIFUL BRUNETTE

In 1841, the seven runners represented the racing gentry of this era with the names of Crofton, Dennis, Connolly, Reynell, Sir P.Nugent, Knaresboro, and H.Tuite. However, the race turned out to be a battle between Mr Crofton's Mavourneen who just caught Mr Dennis's Victoria on the line. Mr Crofton went the wrong side of the post and there was an objection, but he blamed Mr Knaresboro for pushing him of the course causing him to go the wrong side. A Mr Power, Longford backed up Mr Crofton's version and said he saw Knaresboro push him and would swear to it. A row broke out between Power & Knaresboro leading to Power riding over and striking him 2/3 times with a whip and Knaresboro did the same. The Stewards intervened and both were arrested and bound to the peace. The end results, was that Victoria was given the race.

In 1842, one of the greatest steeplechasers in Ireland during this era called Brunette and owned by Mr Knaresboro won the Westmeath Urn defeating Mr Drought's The Cob This was to be the start of a sequence of wins for the great horse in Westmeath. On the second day Mr Connolly's Tidings was going for three in a row in the Salver and when The Cob who had been 2nd to Brunette lost his rider Tidings went on to beat Mr Preston's Riding Sun and win the Salver outright. In 1843, one of the main organisers of the races was Henry Murray, Mountmurray, who had bred a horse called Tinder Box, which ran in the Aintree Grand National in March 1843 won by Vanguard. He fell at the stone wall fence and threw his rider Mr Moore who fractured his collar bone. The horse was sold at a hunt in Ballinasloe for £120. He was going well when he fell. After the races Murray was offered £450 for him but refused.

John Preston, Ballinter owned Brunatte who won the Kilrue Cup in 1843 (she went on to finish 3rd in the Aintree Grand National in 1847 when well past her best) and was back to retain the Urn. The opposition included Richard Connolly,

Drogheda who owned Tidings winner of the Mullingar Salver three years in a row. In the first race Wild Irish Girl took the lead but came down in a ploughed field but got up to save her distance. Brunette beat Sam Slick by 1/2 lengths in a great finish and then beat Tidings in the second heat to win. There were 13 fences and two double ditches. Mr Thompson the jockey on Brunette dined at an ordinary with Richard Connolly owner of Tidings and Thomas Abbot the jockey at about 10.30pm. They went off in a coach but ended on the Killucan Road, when it overturned and Thompson fell under the wheel and died.

In 1844, racing was held at Gainstown (3 miles from Rochfortbridge) with 17 jumps. James Quirke was Clerk of the Course. John Preston's favourite Brunette (Alan McDonagh) was back against Sam Slick his old rival again making it tough for him in the first heat, but then he fell and Brunette went on to win it for the third time. Preston did not win it outright because Mr Knaresboro owned him the first time. The races were normally the 3rd week of March but in 1845 they clashed with the Catholic Easter ceremonies and it was postponed to 8 September to give Mr Preston's Brunette a chance to win the Urn. There was praise for the track, a good view with three hills and a vast crowd. Brunette was back against the old enemy Sam Slick (Kelly). Brunette fell at the second and unhorsed the jockey but amazingly got back up and went in pursuit of Sam Slick, and was just beaten with the others all distanced. Brunette won the 2nd heat and then Sam Slick was withdrawn leaving Brunette to win four in a row and keep the Urn, which would grace Preston's board at Bellinter after 11 years. The course did not impress some, who described it as crooked, with very deep ground and the run home was through the crowds. The next races were in April 1848 with 17 jumps over 2 miles and a splendid view. Captain Thompson's horse Abdel Kader dominated the race winning the first two heats beating two "insects" in Mr Magan's Spider and Mr Malones Insect.

PRIEST SAVAGED IN MEDIA OVER EVIL HORSE RACING

The above might be a heading in some tabloid but there is some truth in what happened in 1848, as a letter appeared in a local paper, following a comment that the races were on because of the exertions of a Catholic priest Fr Savage. The writer disapproved stating that the conduct of the priest was *"a fearful departure from the high and holy obligations, which belong to a Christian Ministry"*. He felt it was an unsuitable time for horse racing with people suffering from disease & famine. The writer asks *"have the hungry been fed, have the naked been clothed and the destitute relieved"*. Racing and the problems of gambling, drinking, and fighting had always been issues and many attempts were made to stop it as it was deemed to be evil. The writer in this case wanted Fr Savage to make a public acknowledgement of a breach of duty towards God and his neighbour. In 1849 there was a very interesting horse when Farnham owned by Mr Abbot failed to Mr Doyle's Rory- be-aisy, as this horse went on to be 5th in Aintree Grand National in 1850.

Sir Percy Nugent did agree to give £20 towards a new trophy now that the Urn & Salver were both won by Meath owners. He was now a major player in the development of Mullingar races into the future & was one of the Stewards in 1850 with Edward Tyrell, Secretary, and Henry Murray, Treasurer plus Richard Connolly, William Magan, John Malone, John D'Blaquiere. In 1851, there were 26 fences over 3 miles and in 1852 a good field of 14 runners participated in the Westmeath Handicap won by Mr Murphy's Lamienne and the selling stakes was won by Mr De Blaquieres Farmer (Savage). A lot of accidents occurred at this meeting with Legacy falling and his jockey Hughes injured, and another horse ran through the crowd injuring several people and one young woman had a broken collar bone. The real issue that arose was that 3 horses were killed during the races - Mr Osbornes Poll, Mr Jenkin's Don Juan and Mr O'Reilly's Vesper.

ANATIS AND "MASSACRED AS IN A SPANISH BULLFIGHT"

After the races, a letter appeared in the Westmeath Guardian dated 21/4/1853 from J. Middleton Berry, who stated that in future he would not support steeplechasing as the noble horse, *"was not given to be massacred as in a Spanish bullfight"*. Edward Tyrrell, Secretary, replied that Sir Percy Nugent & Henry Murray had looked at the ground and the fence that caused the deaths was a small one and everyone was astonished at what occurred. He said he consented to be Secretary to bring people to the town. Middleton Berry responded that in withdrawing his support *"I blamed no ONE"*. Amazingly, in 1854 three more horses were destroyed at Lynn - Mr Dunnes Tipton Slasher with a broken back, Mr Martin's Fury broken back, and Mr Smart's horse with a leg broken.

In 1856, it was a much improved racecourse and the 3 mile steeplechase provided a significant moment in Newbrook's history, when Sir E.Hutchinson's 5 y/o Anatis was 2nd to E.J.Irwins Eugenia (F.Martin). In 1860 this horse ridden by Mr Thomas won the Aintree Grand National at 7/2 favourite. This great horse bred by Mr Langan ran in Aintree Grand National four times from 1859-62 (5th in 1859, fell in 1861 and pulled up in 1862).

In June 1861 Mr McCormacks Yaller Gal (J.Wynne) won the Westmeath Handicap Stakes from Mr Dennis's Glendalough in a canter. Wynne and his brother Danny were two of the leading jockey's in this era, Thomas Naughton renowned for being the owner of Thomastown, won with Nanny O'Leary and her sale afterwards brought £36 to the committee and presumably the horse was bought by Captain Ormsby, because the next day she won the seller and was sold again for £71, which brought another £41 to the committee. Martha was a horse who completed in Newbrook regularly in this era and she was unplaced in the 1864 Grand National.

In 1865, two local hopes P. Nugents Maligned and Mr Pilkington's Chasseur fought out Westmeath Handicap Stakes with O'Connell third. The papers said *"the struggle was not excelled by any of the head to head struggles, which have given such a sensational interest to Liverpool & Punchestown".* One of the big problems was people encroaching on the track near the finish. In the great finish Chasseur won by *"1/2 a neck"*. An objection was lodged on the grounds of crossing but the Stewards did not change the result. As confidence grew in the meeting it was described in advertisements in 1866 *"as only second to Punchestown in importance".* In the late 1860's another issue was raised that it was almost *"inhumane"* to have a horse run 6 miles in 3 heats to win just £20. It was the beginning of modernising some of the extreme races. One of the classier horses in this era, which brought the first Irish Grand National in 1870 was Mr A Purcell's Jolly Girl, who was unplaced in the Irish Grand National in 1871 but won a race in 1870 at the revived Corkaree races, and then won the two chief races at Newbrook - the Westmeath Handicap of 80 sovereigns and the Mullingar Handicap of 40 sovereigns added. In the Westmeath Handicap Jolly Girl (W. Craven) beat Smoker (who was 3rd in the Irish Grand National in 1872) and in 3rd place was Mr Taaffe's Little Annie who was 5th in the same race in 1873 and 6th in 1874. It was a clear sign that the quality of the horses was improving. In 1874 the Irish Grand National winner P.J. Reynold's Torrent was hot favourite but could only finish 3rd to Mr Swan's Revenge.

REVIVAL AND ROWDYISM AT THE RACES OR WHO CURSED THE QUEEN?

In April 1877, a meeting was held in the Market House with Dr Dillon Kelly JP, Chairman, for promoting the races as people showed great enthusiasm for reviving the races. The issue of the relationship of the people with the owner P.N.Fitzgerald was apparently raised but it was hoped that a two day Whit meeting could be organised. Fitzgerald offered to accept a small sum of £70 from the townspeople & traders and in return he would undertake to carry out the entire days racing expense. Fitzgerald won two races with his horse Sweet Meadow (Haymaker-Souvenir) ridden by W.Hope-Johnstone. She was described *"as the best little mare in Ireland".* Mr Lindes New Purchase won the featured Westmeath Open Handicap of 100 sovereigns with T. Beasley riding. He had been 3rd that year in the Aintree Grand National won by Liberator (G.Moore). Fitzgerald had luck at Newbrook in 1880 when his good horse New Meadow (Mr D.Russell) won the Traders Plate and went on to be 2nd in the Irish National in 1884 to dual winner The Gift.

In 1882, an epidemic at The Curragh & other places led to small fields & poor racing. Aside from the poor racing the main issue was the number of assaults & violence on the courser as shown by the long list at the Petty Sessions. Michael

Shaughnessy, Newdown assaulted 2 men at the races; James Keena, Irishtown, was pursued and arrested for *"cursing the Queen"* in front of witnesses; Robert Grave & Pat Lynch had a row about a roulette table; and Captain Barney said that *"He never saw such ill-disposed men as parties that were going around that day"*. One man Michael Kelly, Curraghmore was confined to a house outside the course and he tried to escape. In court he told the judge *"How Could I, I was handcuffed"*. It was a strange day at Mullingar races! Captain Meysey Thompson was a major figure in racing in Ireland and Britain and his horse Belmont (Cambuslang-Geraldine) ridden by E.R.Owen won. The horse ran twice unplaced at Aintree in 1885 and 1886.

From 1883 to 1890, a number of meetings were lost and it seemed that Newbrook races was coming to an end. A public meeting was held in the Lecture Hall on 7th June 1886 to try to save the races but it was not revived until 1890.

THE MYSTERY OF THE PECULIAR COSTUME

The revival of 1890, included a Traders Plate of £70, Westmeath Cup £120, Clonhugh Plate £50 and Newbrook Plate £35 Cabs, cars, carriages & every other vehicle were on the roads, streets packed with cheery pedestrians, shops from hotel to humble eating places were packed until 12.30PM when everywhere closed. Christopher Corcoran, Austin Friar Street was the caterer in the Stand and a Temperance Bar was run by Rev Robert Barry CC and the National Workman's Club Bar had people like Hubert Rogers, Daniel Moran, Michael Murtagh, John Connolly, Peter Hope, and Thomas Mahon working with them. The races included runners like Mr L'Estrange's Bass (L.Yourell) 3rd in the Irish National and he beat C.Hope's Witching Hour, who was the dam of Drumcree (Ascetic-Witching Hour) winner of Aintree National in 1903.

In 1891, the local winners included J.Brabazon's Prussia and A.J. Pilkington's Aristocracy. In October the final Stewards's Plate was almost declared void, as all the horses fell or persistently refused, before T.Burns on Daisy got home and after discussion the Stewards allowed it. Westmeath trainers were doing very well nationally at this time and A.J.Pilkington won 5 races at Phillipstown (Daingean) in 1891. In 1892 Frank Mitchell had a double with The Admiral & Albert. One paper made a strange comment that one jockey went out in a *"peculiar costume"* and '*seemed to be out of place at a gathering with pretensions or indeed any other meeting*'. The mystery of the costume was never resolved?

Other interesting contenders in 1894 were The Soarer who won at Aintree in 1896 and two time Aintree runner-up Cathal (1895 and 1898). The Soarer was unplaced in the Westmeath Plate to Larry Hope's Lady Raimont and was then owned by David Campbell of the 9th Lancers, who bought him cheaply and rode him before selling him in 1896 for £500. It was also agreed that he would ride him, if he was in the Grand National. He was sold to William Hall Walker MP and won the race at 40/1. In 1895 Jockey C.Hogan had a double with Jim Locke's horse Cowslip 1/1 trained on The Curragh. T. Dowdall in 1897 had 4 wins in 5 rides with Clanricharde, who beat Percy Maynard's Royston Crow winner of the 1896 Irish National. The winner was owned by Gustavus Briscoe, Ballinter, Co Meath father-in-law of Cecil Brabazon and Aubrey Brabazon's grandfather. He also won with Harmony II who beat the 5 y/o Boreenchreogue (J.Kelly) who went on to win the Galway Plate in 1898 for James Cheshire.

ALICE ROCHFORT INVOLVED IN TWO OBJECTIONS IN A FAMILY QUARREL

In 1898, Frank Mitchell's Attraction won his 6th consecutive race and B Gill's Springfield (St Michael) with Eddie Dempsey on board won the Mullingar Town Plate and went on to be 2nd in the Galway Plate in 1900 to Ivanoff. In April A.J. Pilkington, Woodlands, was injured at P. McCormack's corner when he was thrown and his instep was broken. James Cheshire the local based jockey was also seriously injured when his horse fell and he was rushed to hospital with a broken thigh. This injury was to end his career but he had success as a trainer. In a match between P.P. O'Reilly's Baronet and G.R. Reid on Mrs Boyd-Rochfort's Satisfaction there was a grudge history involved, because Mrs Boyd-Rochfort objected to her daughter Alice's marriage to O'Reilly (who was a Catholic) and a court case ensued between Alice & her mother about ownership of a horse. The whole area turned out for the race, which ended in a thriller with O'Reilly winning narrowly and he received a massive cheer. Given the family history it was no surprise when there was an objection, but it was overruled after the Stewards Enquiry and the deposit of £50 was forfeited. An amazing tale with an amazing finish!

"THE DOMAIN OF THE DRESS"

An interesting winner was Honeymoon II (Monsieur-Moonrise) in the Clonhugh Plate, as this horse was 2nd in the Irish National in 1902 to Tipperary Boy and was 3rd in 1903 to a Westmeath horse M.J. Cleary's Patlander ridden by A.J.Pilkington. In 1901, Dan Kiernan's two related horses Gay & Sweet and Sweet & Gay won plus other local winners like T.Dibbs Rathgowan, who also won in September at 5/2, and Frank Mitchell's Lady Hermit. Harold Boyd Rochfort won the Light Weight Cup with The Unknown (Hackler) in April 1902 before joining the army.

Mr C. Cole, son of James Cole, Kilbride was thrown from his horse Drummeel in April 1903, and apparently, was seriously injured in a race won by Lady Fortune. The horse rolled over him when he fell and he was taken away by ambulance and went to the infirmary under Dr Middleton & Miss Elliott. He had a fracture and concussion but it was not serious. In June 1903, the ladies dresses were described as *"The variety of thought, of idea, of shade of material, and of style displayed- no two costumes alike, bore testimony to the great fund of endless variety, which exists in the domain of the dress"*. Larry Hope, Clongiffen, Meath, but with strong Westmeath connections, had a treble with Cumber in the Newbrook Hurdle, Propose in the maiden plate, and the Greville Cup winner Ethna- all ridden by Johney Lynn.

In 1905, rows were a thing of the past, and the flat track was in great condition and it had an air of *"comfort and cleanliness".* A figure that was to play a major part in Irish racing in the coming years, Matthew Dawson won with localman M.J.Clearys Sleep (Enthusiast), who also bred the winner. At this time, Lord Greville who had contributed to the rise of Mullingar Races was seriously ill in London. In September 1905 the new buildings with weigh room, jockeys room, dressing room and press room were all ready for use plus the new 7 furlong 150 yards flat track. Sir Walter Nugent grand mare Sincerity (St Hilaire-Purity) beat the Lord Lieutenant's The Hawk. The new owners and trainers stand and the new telegram board were on display in April 1906. Harold Boyd-Rochfort fell on H.Whitworth's Boothman in the Hunt Cup and was concussed. Willie Dillon another jockey fractured a leg & dislocated his shoulder when he fell on The Harlequin III. E.A Shaw's Happy Result (Gay Reveller-Diversion) beat G.A. Boyd Rochfort's Australia.

'BOSS CROKER' IN MULLINGAR AND THE BOOKIE WHO USED "EMPHATIC LANGUAGE"

Richard 'Boss' Croker visited Mullingar for the first time in 1906 and he was very impressed. He had a local connection with M.J.Cleary the vet who bred Hayden, one of Croker's best horses. Cleary had a winner with Lediston (Sir Patrick Mary Kathleen). John Thompson, champion jockey and soon to be tragically killed, was third in two races. Bergomask bred two winners in Tom Killian's Rustic Queen 10/1 in the Newbrook Hurdle and also with Fantime 10/1 in a day of shocks. Another local stallion General Symons bred Merry May to win for A.J. Pilkington. In June, an interesting innovation was platforms for bookies which meant that boxes were no longer allowed in the enclosure. This led to some trouble as two bookies. A. O'Kelly, Belfast and Kearney, Dublin refused to comply with the regulations but changed their mind when they were about to be removed. O'Kelly wrote a letter to the Midland Reporter newspaper on the issue stating there was *"no violation of the rules".* He said there was no room when he arrived and they refused him accomodation and admitted that he used *"emphatic language"*, but that it was different than not complying with the rules. He stated that the paper gave a false impression.

The free special train from The Curragh ensured plenty of runners from the big stables. Some good horses ran including M. Farrells Schwarmer who won

Galway Plate in 1909 and ironically P. McLoughlin's Rosy Symons who won at Mullingar went on to be 2nd to Schmarmer in the Galway Plate and was also 2nd in 1908 to Shady Girl. In 1908, there were 48 runners for 6 races. T.M. Reddy's Rose of Culleen (General Symons-Rhodine) named after his home area of Culleen won in September, after losing a Stewards Enquiry in April when beaten by Prince John. The real drama at the April meeting was when Hon R. Bruce got caught in the reins of his horse Benbrack, when he fell at the last fence, and was dragged along the track, until Mr W. Langan dismounted from his horse Golden Mask and assisted him, but he was not seriously injured.

ENGLISH RUNNERS FROM CHELTENHAM AT MULLINGAR

In 1909, one reporter commented that a new parade was going to be erected and another issue was that a glass of sherry cost 1/- but generally it was very positive. Three short priced favourites won but the highlight was when E.A. Shaw won the Westmeath Plate with Ilovit (Bergomask-Diversion) and after his third success he was able to keep the trophy. We are used to horses travelling to the Cheltenham Festival but in June 1909 Mr Lucy from Cheltenham sent a few horses to race at Mullingar. His horse Pressman won twice in Britain and was 2/1 favourite to win the Belvedere Hurdle over 2 miles with O. Anthony on board. He duly obliged as he won by 4 lengths. Another Cheltenham trainer Mr Cuthbertson ran his horse Shoeblack in the Director's Plate but he was only 1/1. He was not good enough to beat Schwarmer trained by Matt Dawson. The English horse Pressman was made favourite for the race in September 1909 after travelling from Cheltenham again, but Frank Barbour's Good Lord recorded his first win for the MFH.

E.A. Shaw had a double in April 1910 with Helena (Avidity-Florida) and Ilovit in the Hunt Cup and anther local double winners was J.Cole including The General bred by A.T.F.Briscoe, Killucan, and trained by C.Cole, Milltownpass. Rose of Culleen had won well at the Phoenix Park was all the rage in the Lough Ennel Plate of 7 furlongs, but T.M. Reddy's other horse Culleen won the race for local trainer Captain E.A. Gargan. In April 1911 the charge for ladies was reduced to 5/- and it was hoped that they would induce their male friends to attend. The Newbrook Plate was worth 200 sovereigns and it was won by L.Hope's Thimblerigger 4/1 with runner up T.Killian's Shaun na Scuab (T. Dowdall), who won the Conyngham Cup. Unplaced in this race was J.J. Maher's 5 y/o Covertcoat who won the Aintree National in 1913, when owned by Sir C.Assheton Smith. In June 1912 the Directors Plate of 150 sovereigns was won by Piccaninny (Sir Patrick-Kentucky Octoroon) beating Small Polly, who won the Irish National in 1912 and was trained by C.Hope, Mabestown. Algy Anthony was one of the top jockey's of his era and he trained his first winner at Mullingar when Ballyscadden (J.Cahalan) won the Newbrook Hurdle.

A MINER VICTORY AND W.J. PARKINSON'S FIRST WIN

In 1913 J.P. Dowdall was Chairman & P.J.Carroll was still Secretary. Christy Dunne one of the great characters died before the races and was noted for his kindness and obliging manner. Bob Fetherstonhaugh trained Sensible Symons (General Symons) to win the Newbrook Plate. The Miner ridden by Leslie Brabazon won the Westmeath Plate of 50 sovereign's with Lady Symons II another General Symons horse unplaced. The Miner was 2nd in the Galway Plate, 6th in Irish National in 1911 and in 1913 ran in one of the strangest Aintree Nationals ever (the story is recounted elsewhere). Privit was unplaced but went on later to win the Galway Plate. A sensational event occurred on the train platform when a horse took flight causing damage to some people before escaping towards Castletown. A Mr Dowling was knocked down, kicked on the forehead, and had his ribs cracked before been taken to the infirmary but it was not too serious. The featured Newbrook Chase of 200 sovereigns was won by Sir J.D.Tickbornes General Athel (Wynn) as 6/4 favourite, challenged by Red Damsel (Red Prince II- Gay Lass) with the latter winning, before going on to win the first ever Galway Hurdle in 1913. The stand was extended by 1/3 for the September meeting and was now one of the largest in Ireland.

In April 1914, there were drastic restrictions in runners & attendance due to the Foot & Mouth Disease. The current MFH E.Hope Johnstone won the Westmeath Hunt Cup with Rattles (C.Brabazon). Harry Whitworth had the pleasure of seeing his horse Break Out (Outbreak-Connie II) winning the Mullingar Chase, with brilliant jumping to add to his Baldoyle win. W.J. Parkinson son of JJ had made his first mount a winning one on Feudalism in the Belvedere Plate. He was warmly congratulated for a great start to what was a great career. The rumours at the June meeting were that Captain D.M. McCalmont's (who won with future Galway Plate winner Privit) champion The Tetrarch was to come to Tally Ho Stud in Westmeath for stud purposes, and it was also rumoured that Atty Persse would start a stud in Ireland. Well known English jockey George Duller was at the meeting but was beaten on the favourite Suffragette Sally by E.J. Hope's Don't Worry (T.Dowdall). Joe Canty rode M. Dawsons Tickler to win 7 furlong handicap and he also won the handicap chase with Fast Brendan, who went on to be 2nd in the Galway Plate to Alice Rockthorn.

THE GREAT ERA - GOLDEN FLEECE, ALL SORTS, & SHAUN SPADAH

As 1915 moved on, the impact of World War 1 was to bring many changes with an influx of English owners, trainers, jockeys, bookmakers and pickpockets because of the impact on English horse racing. It was also to be a great era for top class horses like Shaun Spadah, Sergeant Murphy, All Sorts, Ballyboggan, Privit, Golden Fleece, Alice Rockthorn, Silver Dart etc all running in Mullingar. Local trainer Dick Cleary had a treble in April with J.Kiernan's Rathna, Royal Spinner in the Greville Cup and H.Keanes good chaser My Royal (Avidity-Bit of

Thought). Rathna won easily but the horse that finished fourth was Golden Fleece, who proved to be one the great horses of this era. He won the Galway Plate in 1918 and was 2nd in 1917 and 3rd in 1916. He had the speed to win from 6 furlongs to 2 miles on the flat and with stamina to win the Galway Plate. He was known as the *"punter's friend"* because he was a winning favourite 26 times in his career. Silver Dart (who was 3rd in 1914 Galway Plate only beaten 2 lengths) carried 12st 6lbs to success in the featured Director's Plate of 150 sovereigns. He had a light preparation for the race, as there was coughing in Larry Hope's stable. He was considered one of the best 2 mile chasers of this era. H.Ussher had returned from England to his Galway base and had a double with Frank Barbour's Newsham, who beat Dick Cleary's 5y/o All Sorts, who went on to win the Irish National on Easter Monday 1916.

In September 1915, Shaun Spadah, bred by Paddy McKenna (won the Aintree National in 1921 and was 3rd in 1923 in 6 attempts) as a 4y/o was 4th to Stone Chase (C.Hawkins) and Bachelors Gift. Lord Saville's Raventhorpe (W. J. Parkinson) 5/2F beat a useful field, which extended Parkinson's lead in the Jockey Championship. He had now beaten the record figure of 53 wins set by John Thompson. Harry Ussher was leading trainer in Mullingar in 1915 with 5 winners. In the Westmeath Chase future Galway Plate winner Privit (1917) beat future Aintree National winner Sergeant Murphy (1923) in the Westmeath Chase by 15 lengths. In September 1916, Privit won again in the Stand Chase over 2 miles carrying 12st 6lbs with All Sorts (1916 Irish National winner) and Golden Fleece (1918 Galway Plate winner) was unplaced. In April 1917, the Bob Fetherstonhaugh, Carriick, Mullingar trained Ballyboggan (Frustrum-Gentle Annie) who won the Hunt Cup over 3½ miles and in December won the Ring Plate over 3 miles at a meeting.

The most successful trainers were M.Arnott, Clonsilla who had a treble in July including Privit again and R.H.Walker, Athboy. A couple of popular local winners were committee member Robert Downes success with Ardanage (Ardoon-Turkish Delight II) at 100/8 and J.H.Taylor's Worthy Earl won a 1 ½ hurdle race in December 1917. A list of the horses who failed to win in 1918 gives a good indicator of the quality of the racing. They included Irish Grand National winners Punch (1915), All Sorts (1916), Ballyboggan (1918), and Fly Rose (favourite for the race in 1921) in addition to Galway Plate winners Hill of Camas (1915), Privit (1917), and Semper Idem (2nd 1918). At the December meeting in 1918, H. Usshers Picture Saint won the handicap chase and J.McKeevers Jenny Jones won the Newbrook Hurdle and both went on to win the Galway Plate & Hurdle respectively in 1919.

CLONSHEEVER, INCREASE IN PRIZE MONEY AND MAJOR LIONEL HOLLIDAY

In 1919, one of the great legends of Galway Races was defeated at Mullingar when Paddy Cullinanes Flying Lady beat Clonsheever, who went on to win the Galway Plate in 1923 and 1924 and was 3rd in 1925. He was sold to J.E.Tyrell and trained by F.F. McDonagh and then Harry Ussher. He won 12 chases and when going for the record third win he carried 13st 1lb and was beaten by another Westmeath connected horse in the Barbour owned Blancona. In addition, there was great sadness on the death of Bob Eivers who was strongly associated with the races for many years. In June 1920, there was great praise for the committee when the prize fund for the Director's Plate went up to 300 sovereigns, with all other prizes at least 100 sovereigns. Frank Barbour's 6y/o Sir Huon (Huon II-Lady Daffodil) ridden by Canty won with 12st 7lbs in the Westmeath Plate (2nd Galway Plate 1921 and fell at Aintree) and in third place was Tainted Goods (2nd in IGN 1920 giving 13lbs to the great Halston). The September races were postponed with work on the buildings and the new stand.

In 1921 all the work on the stands with a new refreshment bar brought great praise from one journalist that the *"turf reputation of Westmeath was brought into the front ranks of Irish racing"*, especially as the value of the Director's Plate was raised to 500 sovereigns from a pre-war figure of 150 sovereigns. Martin Quirke had first win over hurdles riding J.J. Parkinson's Fane Lady 5/2F and his brother Danny recorded his first ever win in the Lough Ennel Plate with Rathforan. Harry Ussher's, Eastwell stable won 4 of the 6 races with three ridden by English jockey Frank Wootton. One of them was Max 4/7 and he won the Galway Plate that year. He *"jumped the others silly"* beating that year's Irish National winner Bohermore giving him a stone. One race had 30 runners in 1921 and in 1922 a field of 27 runners competed. The 1920's brought whole new issues to Irish Racing and to provincial tracks like Mullingar. In 1922 crowds were down nationally as rail fares went up affecting patrons. Perhaps a record was set in April 1923 in the 7 furlong Lough Ennel Plate when First Consul ridden by Martin Quirke and Pacifier ridden by his brother Danny Quirke dead heated. Was this the first time it happened in Ireland?

GOLD CUP WINNERS KOKO AND EASTER HERO

In April 1924, the most interesting runners were Royal Dennis (6th Irish National) and Don Sancho then owned by Tom O'Roarke, who went on to win the Irish National in 1928 when owned by V.H.Smith (who later became successful owner Lord Bicester). In 1925, the highlight of the year was the success of East Galway bred by J.A. Trench, Galway who won the Galway Plate in 1928 and 1930 and was 2nd to Guiding Light in 1929. He won a 2 mile flat race by 10 lengths and won again in 1926. Another winner at the December meeting was Frank Barbour's Koko 1/1 winner of the Winter Handicap Chase, and he went on to win the Cheltenham Gold Cup in 1926. At two consecutive meetings there were walkovers leaving only 5 races, as it was a difficult time for racing in Ireland which was to last many years. The great Joe Canty had a treble at the October meeting, which brought him over 100 winners for the year.

Probably, the greatest horse to compete in Mullingar aside from Arkle was Easter Hero in September 1926. Easter Hero (My Prince-Easter Week) was described as a light framed, athletic, and spectacular jumper, who was sold to Frank Barbour MFH for £500, changed owners several times and won two Cheltenham Gold Cups in 1929/30 and ran in three Aintree Grand Nationals (1928-F, 1929 2nd of 66, and 1931 fell but turned out to win the Champion Chase the next day). He beat Don Sancho by 6 lengths in the Stand Chase and the latter went on to win Irish National in 1928.

The economic depression of the late 1920's and 1930's had a major impact on Irish Provincial Racing in particular, and racecourses found it very difficult in lean times. In June 1927 hard ground led to a poor meeting and even in September due to the betting tax, entertainment tax, good weather for harvesting, and a full week of national racing - all added to the problems. Reduced admissions charges were having some positive effect with 500 more people at this meeting. There was also a need for a more equitable distribution of meetings by the racing authorities. In 1928 the reduced charge of 1/- to the stand and enclosure had improved the crowds. The number of local people involved in racing was diminishing, but in 1928 James Yourell won with Spring Dennis ridden by his son and Dick Cleary brought some joy to the crowd when Tangmalangaloo who won for owner Fred Pope.

THE TOTE AND CONTEMPLATING CLOSURE OF THE TRACK

Trying to run three meetings was a burden during an economic depression and Mullingar like many other tracks had to cut back or go out of business. The shareholders and committee were very cautious during the 1920s/30's about improvements or extensions. They hoped to have three meetings in 1930 and a major change was the installation of the Pari Mutuel system of betting as set up in France and it became known as *"The Tote"* in Britain & Ireland. In April, two local's won with Tom O'Roarkes Arizona Knight (Arizona-Victrice) and E.J. Hopes Prudent Ross (Captain Ross-Prudent Miss) in the 7 furlong Lough Ennell Plate.

In the Stewards Handicap Chase, J. Wallace's Geoginatown (Kronstad-Georgina Mac) ridden by J.Maxwell (brother of Freddie Maxwell) from near Birr won and went on to win a number of races and ran well in the 1931 Aintree National. J.E.Ryan who was long associated with the Cleaboy Stud before moving to the USA, where he had further success with steeplechasers, also had a winner with

Sagushen. In 1931, many ladies had success with Lady Helen McCalmont's Kilcash Hill, Mrs M.Websters Essex Hill, who won with Copper Court, Irish Grand National winner and Miss E.Laidlow's Hy Spy, all winning. In June 1933, Lady Nugent's Lacatoi won the Clonhugh Plate and later went on to win the Welsh Grand National having moved to J.V. Rank's stable in England.

Captain Edward Gargan's useful chaser Southernmore (won Galway Plate 1935) won the Westmeath Plate in 1934, over 3 miles at 6/4 following a recent win at Gowran Park. In 1935, Mullingar was down to one meeting, as support had fallen away. Rathfriland 5/4 for T.R. McKeever supplemented his Irish National success with a win in the Director's Plate by 6 lengths. Flying Rose (Aeroplane-Red Rose) with 12st 3lbs, ridden by Willie O'Grady and trained by Harry Ussher won impressively. Sir James Nelson, with strong local connections through the Hope family, won the bumper with Kandako. In 1936 a reserved stand was added to the grand stand. The management had been contemplating a close down of the track, buildings, and land due to lack of support. A local reporter wrote *"it would be a shame to lose it, as people look back on the halcyon days, rich in tradition with good attendances".*

A totally new management took over in 1937 and very few were locals. The races started at 3pm instead of 2pm and the enterprise of the Tote Board carrying all the horses free to the track had its reward, with takings of £1,293-8s-6d compared to £734 the previous year. Sir James Nelson won again with Owen More in the Belvedere Hurdle (later 3rd to Clare County in Irish National 1938). Jimmy Cleary was removed to Mullingar with concussion after a fall. The highlight of the meeting was the clash of two of the top chasers in Ireland in the Director's Plate. Southernmore (W.T. O'Grady) with 11st 12lbs met Royal Danielli (F. McKeever) with 12st 7lbs. The 9lbs made a difference with the former succeeding by a length. The top weight was 2nd in the Aintree National in 1938 with 36 runners, and fell in 1939/40 (when favourite at 4/1 & still in contention at the 2nd last).

Not too many Irish classic winners ran at Mullingar but Lindley, who won the Irish 2,000gns as a 3 y/o, won a handicap hurdle for Dan Moore at this meeting. In 1939, the most significant winner was H.L. (Larry) Egan's chaser Jack Chaucer (Jackdaw of Rheims-Miss Chaucer), who won at 1/1 in the Mullingar Chase with Westmeath's Cecil Brabazon his trainer. This horse went on to win the most valuable chase ever run up to this point in 1940 when he won the Irish Red Cross & Hospital's Trust Chase worth an unbelievable £2,610 to the winner during WWII. He also won the Irish Grand National that year worth £740 beating Cabin Fire. Larry Egan had a double with Two Irish Eyes (Irish Battle-White Eyes) ridden by Paddy Powell and trained by Jimmy Cleary. Fred Myerscough, (who was to play a major part in the future of Mullingar

Racecourse) won with Prince Sublime beating T.P. Downes horse Graceful Anne in the Greville Challenge Cup of £100. In September, that year the Stand Plate was the main feature and it was subsidised by the Government of Ireland. A young Tom Dreaper trained My Branch to record third successive win in the Westmeath Plate (2nd in Irish National 1938 at 4/1 to Clare County).

JIMMY CLEARY - A CRACK AMATUER WITH A NIL DESPERANDUM EFFORT

The Mullingar Chase was won by Lt Col Hill Dillon's Luxury Tax ridden by Dan Moore. Since coming to Ireland he owned useful horses like Yellow Furze, Symaethis (won Galway Plate 1938) and Le Cygne. The most interesting horse was Golden View II bred locally by T.P. Downes, a member of the committee and the son of a half bred local stallion Johnny Roebuck. In 1946, when owned by Margaret Lillington and P.A. O'Reilly the horse won the Irish Grand National at 11 y/o beating Klaxton and favourite St Martin (carrying 12st 7lbs). The horse was killed in November 1946 at Aintree in a three horse race for the Champion Chase. The January meeting of 1941, was postponed until 22nd March due to ground conditions. This meeting just barely beat the ban on racing but it brought two of the best chasers of this era in Dorothy Paget's Golden Jack and Golden View II both 6 y/o's. In the Mullingar Chase, Golden Jack (Goldcourt-Jackagu) 1/1F, and future Irish National winner, won easily ridden by Dan Moore and beating J. Kennedy's Offaly Chieftain (Leo McMorrow).

Jimmy Cleary won on Amorite and one paper said *"Jim Cleary showed clearly he can ride as well as any of the crack amateurs by a nil desperandum effort".* He died in December 1966 and in February 1967, C.J. Corcoran, Secretary of the Westmeath Harriers presented a memorial cup to P.J.Collins, Chairman of South Westmeath Harriers for Kilkenny West Point to Point, in memory of Jimmy Cleary. He was a well known trainer and rider in Westmeath & at Kilkenny West, Slanemore, and Ardivahan. Phone Castletown was one of his popular horses and he won at Leopardstown one Christmas with Pat Taaffe riding. He was a gelded son of Consequential and 1/2 brother to Galway Plate winner Relax. Jimmy introduced Larry Egan to racing through Two Irish Eyes who won at Longford in May 1938. The following year Two Irish Eyes won at Mullingar (three times) and Longford, by which time 'Lucky Larry' had moved on to greater heights with Jack Chaucer, trained by Cecil Brabazon. In June 1937, he was severely injured when schooling a horse at Newbrook. The horse rolled over him and sent him to Mullingasr Hospital. In 1938 Jimmy Cleary rode 3 winners and trained 2 to win at Hazelwood Course near Sligo, which was soon to close. He was tough jockey on the track and difficult to pass. In later years at the hunt it was said *"he was a bad man to follow"* as he was fearless.

MULLINGAR RACECOURSE TO BE AUCTIONED? AND ODDS OF 845/1

On 27th March 1941, the Minister for Agriculture made orders prohibiting home racing including Westmeath & Offaly as 8 fresh cases of Foot & Mouth in Donegal and Kildare and 3 in the Birr District. The Government hadn't taken it seriously at the beginning and now drastic steps were needed. The Irish Times announced on 24th April 1941 that racing would resume on 1st May after the Minister met delegates from the racing authority. The prohibition would remain, but by means of a licencing system would ensure adequate safeguards against the speed of infection. Mullingar races were arranged for 10th May, but the Kilbeggan meeting of 19th May was abandoned. Racecourses were disinfected with Jayes Fluid. Charlie Rogers had a double with Lord Queensborough Sir Sen and Dorothy Paget's Bannerman. In September, a local jockey Mr C. Daly rode Bennies Battle owned by Matt Farrell, Streamstown, to win on his first appearance on a track. One lady put 2/- on the horse and won £84-10s (odds of 845/1). This was a tote record beating Naas in 1936 (£50 4s).

It was also reported that Mullingar Racecourse, one of the best in Ireland, would shortly be put up for auction as land for farming, as the company which maintained it was going into voluntary liquidation. An article in the *Westmeath Examiner* in February 1942, spoke about the great history of Mullingar races before it struck difficult economic times & perhaps a lack of enthusiasm by management and the people. The company wound up in 1941 and a new one was formed mainly based in Dublin. The company maintained staff at Newbrook and everyone in the area was urged to support them. In April 1942, it was announced that Mullingar was on the list of forbidden meetings, as World War II was now about to intrude on horse racing in Ireland and end it until 1946.

POST WAR MULLINGAR AND RACE BOXES 1946 - 1967

Tommy Fleming was the new Secretary/Manager when racing resumed in 1946 and on 18th January he stated that *"unless there is an extraordinary change in conditions the meeting will be held"*. The track, fences, and facilities were all in good order. The featured Mullingar Chase was won by Tim Malony on Sentoi beating Klaxton 5/2 F (he won 3 Military Cups at Sandown) with Golden View II, and Lough Conn (2nd in the Aintree National) and Swindon Glory (Dual Galway Plate winner in 1943/44) all behind. The local winners were Captain E.A.Gargan's Southern Lass and E.J.Kings Zarna. During this era the Sligo meeting was transferred to Mullingar in June on a number of occasions, as they were working on the track. The highlight in November was the visit of Prince Aly Khan to see his horse Nussarat run and in 1947 he rode his horse River Trout to win on the track. In 1947, there was a coughing epidemic, which reduced the number of runners. Barney Nugents Charles Edward was a lucky winner in a novice chase; as two fell, but he went on to win the Galway Plate in 1948. Cloncarrig was targeted by Joe Osborne for the Mullingar Gold Cup and won by

15l's and he had a unique record in that he never got around Aintree in 6 attempts. In December, an unknown horse called Knock Hard was 4th in a maiden hurdle and went on to legendary success for Vincent O'Brien. He won the Cheltenham Gold Cup in 1953, in spite of his questionable jumping. In November 1947, Dreaper & Newman had a treble with J.V. Rank's Greenogue, Lord Bicester's Clover Mor and S.H. Martin's Ardnacrassa.

HATTON'S GRACE AND THE HORSE WHO WON BY A "STRONG HEAD"

In February 1948 an interesting innovation occurred when Count Gabrial won in tight finish and Judge Tuthill's verdict was that he won by a *"strong head"*. The meant, that it was more than a *"head"* and less than a *"neck"*. Some interesting chasers ran during the year like Derrinstown (Galway Plate winner 1950 and 3rd in Aintree Grand National in 1951) and E. Shortiss's Coupe carrying 12s tone beat Rockcorry and Highland Lad with his brilliant jumping and he won the Leopardstown Chase in 1950 beating Shagree, Cottage Rake etc. A handicap hurdle of £300 was won by Jimmy Mangan's Amritsir but the most notable participant was Mrs M.Keogh's Hatton's Grace who fell on the flat carrying 12st 7lb. He was one of the great champion hurdlers and winner of 3 Champion Hurdle from 1949-51 (aged 9-11). In February, P. Bell's Royal Tan was beaten a head by Raloo and he was later trained by Vincent O'Brien to win the Aintree Grand National in 1954. He carried 11st 7lbs in 1954 when ridden by Bryan Marshall and held off Tudor Line by a neck. Argus Mount won 5 races at Mullingar and 2 at Kilbeggan and obviously loved the Westmeath air. Miss Mabel Wallace, Birr owner of the famous Barbour Cup winner Baykora won a 2 mile handicap hurdle with Baygina (Baydrop-Georginatown). Con Collins son of M.C.Collins now in India rode his first winner when Consuella Rose won the bumper at 10/1 in January. Captain E.A.Gargan had a rare local winner with Southern Coup (Coup de Lyon-Southernmore). In August easily the most interesting horse was the unplaced Dreaper horse Bright Cherry who became the dam of the greatest ever chaser Arkle.

W.E Kelly was appointed Secretary/Manager of Mullingar Racecourse in 1949 and made sure everything was in order for 1950. Annual badges could be purchased for £2 and £1-5s for ladies. First Battle (Irish Battle) won at Naas for Jimmy Cleary. Another winner was Edward Charles who was a 1/2 brother to the Galway Plate winner Charles Edward and traced through Prudent Toi to Insurance the dual Champion Hurdler bred in Westmeath. In 1950, John J.Dolan's, Farnagh Stud, Moate won a bumper in February with Right Drop (Baydrop-Right of Way) and the same horse won the Keith Donaldson Cup in December. He later bred Fair Astronomer, who in 1962 was the first 2 y/o to win in Ireland, France, and Britain. Royal Tan 4/6 won the Belvedere Novice chase. Harold Boyd Rochfort's Wild Delight gave a home winner and Offaly man P.J.Guiney, Edenderry won with Swindon Robin.

RONALDSON'S FIRST WIN

Cecil Ronaldson has contributed much to the development of racing in his long career and he will always be remembered as the man who rode Lady Flame to defeat Arkle in his first ever race at Mullingar. He had his first ever winner at Mullingar with Royal Stuart and his second winner in 1951 on C.McCartan's Highland Chief 5/1 in the bumper. In November he owned, trained, and rode Another Madcap (Sir Walter Raleigh-Lady Madcap) in the Railway Plate beating Con Collins on Robinstown. T.P.Downe's Doctor Dandy won the Newbrook Chase beating decent horses like Game Toi, Pint of Law and Colin Bell, who all competed successfully at a higher level. The most interesting runner that year was In View (J'Arcure-Rathview) only bought a few days earlier by Major Victor McCalmont and won the bumper with Bunny Cox on board at 6/4. He went on to be the favourite in the Irish Grand National in 1953 but was only 8th. He was Westmeath bred and a full brother to Golden View II and was 2nd in the National Hunt Chase at Cheltenham and most famously ran in the international chase in the USA. In February 1953 Tom Dreaper had a treble with Lord Bicesters Black Prince 4/5, Silver Toe 6/1, and J.V.Ranks Greencore (the first two went on to be successful in Britain) Mrs M.Willington, Birr won with Solwink (Soldado-Drop A Wink) at 11/10 in the Keith Donaldson Cup.

At the end of the year Mullingar & Kilbeggan did well, as the Racing Board was putting money back into racing with a percentage of the takings for the benefit of race-goers. Entrance prices were at pre-war levels, car parks free, stake money increased and some new semi classic races like the Desmond & Athasi Stakes were added. The average stakes per race was £299 and in 1938 it was £100. The average number of runners was 12. With regard to the racecourse the road from the town was widened and re-surfaced, new tote facilities were put in and since 1946 the Racecourse Executive stated that over £650,000 was spent by them on the track & buildings. In June, the track was considered unfit for racing being too rough and slippery at bends. An Enquiry was held and Mullingar was fined £50 and they also lost the December meeting due to flooding and Leopardstown cancelled for the same reason. In 1954 the featured £500 An Tostal was won by course specialist Ballyscadden (unbeaten on his third win on track) at 9/2 beating Nibot (2nd Leopardstown Chase 1956). In December that year Jimmy Cleary, W.D. Kelly, and Major R. Scott were appointed inspectors of courses. Local man Cleary was noted for flying around to racecourses to do his inspections. The first Aer Lingus plane the DH84 Dragon EL-ABI was named the "Iolar" (meaning "eagle"). Jimmy Cleary had a pilot fly him around to the various racecourses, when he was an inspector. It seems that this plane was a "sister plane" of the "Iolar" from Darby Kennedy's aerodrome at Weston, Leixlip, (founded by him in 1931). They used to land in the green park at the back of Cleary's. It was the only plane that Jimmy Cleary ever went in.

Only 5 of the 18 runners completed the course in the Belvedere Novice Chase but it was a local win with T.P.Downes 6y/o Soir winning at 6/1. In July the tote aggregate was £6,797 (£4,007 the previous year), which was an improvement. E.J.Fagan's Mighty Inquisitive (Grand Inquisition- Mighty Prudent) won a maiden plate at 100/8 and former Champion Hurdle contender Cloncaw, showed his class by winning a chase carrying 12st 7lbs. Offaly's E.F. Lacy trained Limeona (T.F.Lacy) to follow up a Phoenix Park success when winning by 8 lengths. It was Tom's Lacy's second riding success.

In December 1953, Meath trainer Matt Geraghty had a double with Duffle Coat & Aesculus but in reality the trainer was Peggy St John Nolan but women were not allowed a training licence at this time. In April 1954, Captain Denis Baggaly had a last success with Good Berth, who won the opening race in July before he took- up an appointment with the Turf Club. Local horses ran well in 1955 with Tom Groarke's Gallant Gale winning the Newbrook Chase (after success at Baldoyle); B.B. Scott, Moate trained Knight Willow to win the Athlone Handicap Hurdle; Mrs M.Willington's Solflame was second and then with Toss Taaffe on board beat Sentina (dual Cheltenham winner) in May; and Captain Gargan won with Southerntown. At the first meeting in 1956 Flashaway with Cecil Ronaldson on board beat B.B. Scott's Knight Willow in a handicap hurdle and in the Newbrook Chase it was an Offaly success for owner J.F. Reid who won with Artistic. In March 1956, Paddy Sleator's Knight Errant owned by R.More O'Farrell won the Greville Cup with Francis Flood on board carrying 12st 3lbs. He was a brother of Galway Plate winner Amber Point and went on to win the Galway Plate in 1957, as 4/1F and the Galway Hurdle in 1958 as 5/2F. The star of the day was Lord Fingall's Roddy Owen who was 9/4JF in the Midland Handicap Hurdle trained by Danny Morgan and he won after surviving an objection. He went on to win the Leopardstown Chase in 1958, and Cheltenham Gold Cup 1959.

KILMORE, PEADAR MATTHEWS AND HARD RIDDEN'S EPSOM DERBY WIN

Major R.Bermingham had a stable just a short distance from the track and won with Diamond Page (Diamond Link-Gold Page) which beat Pontiac & East End (C.Ronaldson). He was ridden by Frankie *"Singing Star"* Carroll. Pat Taaffe had just returned to riding after fracturing his skull at Kilbeggan the previous year. Local successes included Captain Gargan's Culleenroi, E.F. Lacy's Nethy Bridge, B.B.Scott's Knight Willow and Mullingar born jockey Peadar Matthews won the Newbrook Handicap with Son of the Morning for Mick Hurley. It was his first ever success on his home track in Mullingar. He went on to ride for P.J. Prendergast for many years. The most interesting horse for future reference was J.J. Ryan's Kilmore (Zalophus-Brown Image) ridden by C. Kinane and bred in Offaly by G.C.Webb. Kilmore ran 4 times in the Aintree Grand National winning in 1962 (5th in 1961, 6th of 47 in 1963 and fell in 1964). One of the highlights of the year was the commentary over the PA system of Ballymoss's battle with Crepello in the Epsom Derby. It brought the excitement of the famous Epsom Derby straight on to the track. In 1958, the March meeting was abandoned due to snow. The President of Ireland, Sean T. Kelly in July had his 2nd winner in 4 days when Tulagorm won a maiden for John Oxx. There was great excitement at the June meeting with a commentary on Hard Ridden's win in the Epsom Derby from Paddy's Point and the cheers for the Irish win drowned the commentary. This was the first Irish winner of the Epsom Derby since Orby in 1907. The owner Oliver Lambert had a strong association with Kilbeggan, as the family owned the town.

Some very useful horses ran during the year including J.F.K.Farrell's Take Time (Grand Inquisition-McKeogh's Girl), who won the Greville Cup, as a 6y/o trained by J.A.Wilson and ridden by Eddie Harty. He was 2nd to Olympia in the 1969 Irish Grand National and won the Conyngham Cup in 1959. The Mullingar Cup in June was won by Mrs M. Willingtons Baby Bunting beating Kilballyown winner of the Irish National in 1957, and Quita Que twice 2nd in the Champion Hurdle. In November, the highlight was Nat Galway Greer's Another Flash (Roi D'Egypte-Cissie Gay) bred in Westmeath by A.Duncan and a future Champion Hurdler. He cantered home by 8 lengths with Francis Flood riding. Other local winners were E.F.Lacy's Count Tony and Cecil Ronaldson won on his own Magic King 3/1F in the Newbrook Chase and also on Toby Downes horse Rare Record in a bumper. In 1959, the name of the first winner was No Joke and with heavy rain, bitter cold, and conditions like *"a ploughed garden"* there was a certain irony. The final nail in the coffin was when the last race was won by Fork Lightning II but at least it was a double for J.Bryce Smyth.The February meeting had to be transferred to Navan as the track was unraceable. In March, Another Flash returned to win his maiden hurdle and an unplaced horse was Nicklaus Silver who went on to win the Aintree Grand National in 1961. Highfield Lad won the Gold Cup over 2 miles 3 furlongs from Knockacunna and Knight Errant and went on to win the Galway Plate a few months later beating Mazzibell another Mullingar winner and was 2nd in 1964 to Ross Sea.

Dorothy Paget died on 9th February 1960 just one day before the Mullingar races, where she had many winners over the years. Mullingar jockey Paddy Broderick rode Balnagar to victory before he went to Britain to ride Night Nurse & other great horses. At the May meeting the field included Storming who was 2nd to Epsom Derby winner Die Hard at the Phoenix Park but the winner was Peggy St John Nolan's Dear Sma' ridden by Mullingar jockey Peadar Matthews from Buckaroo ridden by Brendan Mooney also from Mullingar. Kevin Prendergast rode the winner of the bumper in Ballydavid and the Parish Priest in Kilbeggan Fr Nicholas Casey had an interest in Rory O'Moore 2/1F but he was beaten by Sir Vodka. A case of drink triumphing over religion! In the Bunbrosna Chase F.D.Farmer's Owen's Sedge (C.Kinane), which was soon to be purchased by Hollywood Legend Gregory Peck and challenging him was Kilmore (T.Kinane) who went on to win the 1962 Grand National for trainer Ryan Price and Fred Winter. Owen's Sedge met Kilmore again in 1963 Grand National having won the Leopardstown Chase. The first one mile 2 y/o race of the year was held each year at Mullingar in September and this year there was a dead heat between Jimbo owned by Mrs Read wife of New York sportsman Colonel Read and John Oxx's Buckaroo.

Young apprentice Timmy Hyde won with a late run on Whispering Breeze in the Newbrook Handicap Chase of £300 over 3 miles at the first meeting of 1961. It was his 15th winner and he quipped *"Getting down to 9st 2lbs was a bit of a problem"*. The Tote aggregate was £9,147 (£7,883 in 1960). In July, the largest crowd since 1952 attended and Cecil Ronaldson won the opening race with Another Flame.

TIME TRAVEL WITH DOUG PAGE AND MULLINGAR OUT OF DATE

One man who appreciated the advantages of the *"Jet Age"* in 1962 was jockey Doug Page. The previous week he rode Albergo to win at Windsor, on the Saturday he rode at the Phoenix Park, on Monday he rode Albergo into 3rd place at Paris, and the next day the 1st June he was in Mullingar to ride Jungle Trix a horse going for a four timer (he was unplaced) and he was flying back at the weekend to ride Albergo in Paris. Little Champ added to his victory in the Usher Cup at Kilbeggan by winning the Mullingar Gold Cup for H.R.Catherwood and trained by George Dunwoody (Richards father). George said *"It's the biggest trophy, I have ever won"*. In February the ground was atrocious but a very interesting 3rd in the Athlone Handicap Hurdle was was Winning Fair, which went on to win the Champion Hurdle in 1963 trained by George Spencer.

There was heavy criticism of Mullingar races during the summer where the horses were kicking up dust, as were the spectators unlike other courses like Sligo, Roscommon etc. The complaint was that the executive had done little to improve *"its grossly out of date facilities"*. In July, there was some improvements including a new surface in the enclosure, which added to the comfort of patrons Charlie Weld had a double with prolific winner Arctic Kanda and Galway Plate winner Highfield Lad. Paddy O'Roarke's Mr Nelson won a maiden hurdle; Mullingar jockey Peadar Matthews won on Jungle Trix; and Mrs E.J.King's Migoli Slipper won a 3 y/o handicap for Sir Hugh Nugent. Ferry Boat who was placed to Arkle on several occasions, including the 1964 Irish National, won at the July meeting.

FRANK PRENDERGAST PLASTERED BUT STILL WINS!

In 1963, Highfield Lad was favourite for the Gold Cup carrying 12st 7lbs but was beaten by George Verling's Knockanacunna by 2 1/2 lengths. Johnny Roe had just returned from Rhodesia to ride for Vincent O'Brien and he had a double at the May meeting. In July Tony Redmond just rode the 4th winner of his career as first jockey to Paddy Norris on Persian Signal in the Bunbrosna Handicap beating Mrs A. Biddles Island (L.Ward), which was 1/1 as he had been 6th in the Queen's Vase to Hereford at Royal Ascot. In July, Frank Prendergast who had broken a bone in his arm 5 weeks before, rode a winner for his brother J.J., even though his arm was still in plaster! In 1964, Pat Taaffe and Willie Robinson had a great rivalry riding Arkle and Mill House. At Mullingar that year they rode the two favourites for the local Gold Cup with Willie on Devenish Artist who had won at Punchestown & Dundalk and Pat was on Dashed Lad who had won by 8 lengths at Limerick. Liam McLoughlin spoiled the plan by winning on Trial Game for J.Bredin owner/trainer. Paddy O'Roarke had another hurdle win with Mr Nelson and unusually an English trained horse Callow Rock won twice at Mullingar over hurdles and on the flat for owner Michael O'Connell, who was based in Manchester.

STORY OF FRANK ROE AND ME OUL SEGOTIA

Ted Walsh recalls riding in Mullingar in 1964 at Mullingar. He said that *"Frank Roe owned a horse called Me Oul Segotia that ran in Mullingar & he put himself down as the rider. At that time there could be a change of jockey up to 10 minutes before a race, if the declared jockey was overweight for some good reason. Frank was not a great jockey & many punters were aware of it, so he was able to back the horse at a good price. He went to the stewards then and explained that he was overweight because he had been injured after a fall in a Donkey Derby and he had put on some weight. They accepted his explanation and professional jockey Tony Redmond was waiting outside and he took the mount and won easily. The horse later won an Ulster Cesarewitch".* His explanation was confirmed in a newspaper report, where Frank explained that he had an injury that caused him to put on a few pounds, therefore he could not ride the horse. In 1966, Ted rode Straight Devon in a race at Mullingar and he caused Dermot Weld to fall and he broke a collar bone. Evilo was in that race and later won the Amateur Handicap in Galway. Ted said that Mullingar was a good track but always had heavy ground. He never had a winner there. Dermot Weld who rode his first winner at Galway had his second success when he made all the running on Wise Knight for his father Charlie in the Streamstown Plate.

In December, former Champion Hurdler 1963 Winning Fair won the Keith Donaldson Cup, which had been postponed from the previous Saturday. He had been 3rd to Fort Leney and Greek Vulgan in the Power Gold Cup at Fairyhouse only beaten 8 lengths. This was his first success since 1963 and George Spencer said afterwards that he was in the Cotswold Chase at Cheltenham *"and he will take a deal of beating".* Knocknacunna added to his good Mullingar record with his 6th win but it was the third horse that was to go down in racing history, as it was Foinavon (P.Woods) who won the the most famous Grand National of 1967.

In May 1965, Height O'Fashion (T.F.Lacy) trained by Frank Lacy carried 12st in the Phoenix Beer Chase over 2 miles 3 furlongs, giving 5lbs to Irish National Splash and nearly 2 stone to Moonsun. In the race at Mullingar Height O'Fashion was virtually tailed off with Tom Lacy pushing for all his worth (common in many of her big races). When Splash & Moonsun went clear she was still 7 lengths behind and 2 lengths down at the last but still got up to beat Moonsun by a nose. The horse had made a specialty of winning races sponsored by the brewing industry having won the Guinness Chase at Punchestown 2 years running. Lacy said later *"I was exhausted pushing and kicking for the first mile but once she began to pick up, I knew she had a chance. However, Splash & Moonsun put in a spurt going to the last and my heart sank but she put in a great jump and got up in the last yard".*

In June, Bobby Coonan had a double with Mrs Biddles Indian Chief who was a full sister to Amber Point and Retinue Jungle. Coonan had 6 winners that week and Retinue Jungle had three runs with 2 wins. Cecil Ronaldson won the bumper with Mountcashel Prince 2/1F. The track seemed to have on-going problems and in December, Sir Peter Nugent, Manager, said on 8th December that *"The Track had been passed for racing and provided the weather does not worsen we will be able to hold the meeting".* It went ahead and two jockey's had their first ever successes when John Enright an 18 y/o rode Bryce Smyth's Pitroddie to win the Kinnegad Maiden Hurdle and Declan Winter, Termonfeckin, was only having his 4th ride when he won on Vulgan's Girl in the Keith Donaldson Cup.

THOU SHALT NOT PASS PADDY WOODS, WHO TAKES HOME THE BEER

Paddy Woods started out riding with Dan Moore before he moved to Tom Dreaper, where all the lads were expected to go to mass. He rode out Arkle every morning and won on him at Gowran Park. He also won the Irish Grand National on Last Link in 1963 and Splash in 1965; two Troystown Chases and on Fort Leney at Leopardstown. He trained for a while and won 11 races with one horse for Jimmy Robinson. He rode the 1967 Aintree National winner Fonavon to be third in Mullingar in a chase in 1964. He recalls his biggest success at Mullingar was with Mrs A.Craigies Splash in the Phoenix Beer Chase in 1966 carrying 12 stone against good horses like Interosian, Ross Sea (dual Galway Plate winner), Flying Wild (one of the few horses to beat Arkle) and Greek Vulgan. He had been just beaten by Height O'Fashion in the race in 1965. He remembers that it was a very rough race just like the Guinness Chase at Punchestown the same year when he was nearly put through the railings. He was determined that it would not happen again and when the chance came he cut across some of the others to grab the lead and he could hear a lot of cursing behind him. After the race some of the jockey's spoke to him (probably using *"emphatic language"*), but he mentioned Punchestown & said *"what goes around, comes around"*. He said *"it was an enjoyable & fair track, with good racing, and should not have closed down. It was one of his favourites"*. He said there were *"rumours about financial difficulties"*. Jim Dreaper said he was there with his father, as a young fella & remembers that the horses used to get frightened with the noise from the railway station which was close by. He rode Black Secret to win a point to point there in 1969 two years after it closed and it was a good track. He mentioned that Jim Tormey's great mare Leney Princess provided many winners for Sir John Thompson and his father from Fort Leney to Tuscan Prince. Paddy Murray from Moate was the Head Lad in the Arkle era and Eddie Newman was the stable jockey before Pat Taaffe -both from Westmeath.

The maiden hurdle was won by Jim Tormey's Evilo beating Jim Cleary's Proud Mardi. The winner went on to win the Player's Navy Cut Handicap at Galway and a few days later was only beaten a 1/2 length in the Galway Hurdle by Tom Dreaper's Muir (winner of the Champion 2 mile chase in 1969. In August the first 2 y/o race the Harp Lager Plate was won by Henry the Fifth trained by Brud Fetherstonhaugh & ridden by Peter Boothman. The horse was to be aimed at the Beresford or Larkspur Stakes. The bumper was like a war of attrition, as a number of horses fell including Killkillrio who took off and jumped a 6 foot stone wall, then Ted Walsh was brought down on Straight Devon and Dermot Weld on Irish Memories was also brought down. The race was won by George Dunwoody's Zel.

1967 THE END

Paddy Dunne Cullinanes great chaser Royal Day won the the Rathowen Handicap Chase in Mullingar carrying 12st 3lbs by 4 lengths. In May the Phoenix Beer Chase of £2,300 had a high quality field with Paddy Sleator's San Jacinto 7/2F even though he had fallen in his last three races- the Leopardstown Chase, Irish Grand National and Guinness Chase at Punchestown. The reason he was favourite was that he fell at the last fence each time when looking a winner. Against him were Tom Dreapers Muir winner of the Galway Hurdle 1967, Champion Chase and Cathcart Cup at Cheltenham; Royal Day one of the few horses to win the Galway Plate 1967 and the Galway Hurdle in 1968 & even more uniquely he won the Plate before the hurdle; the great Height of Fashion and many more. Muir made a few mistakes over the last few fences and San Jacinto got his just reward winning by 6 lengths and appropriately for the last big race at Mullingar the runner up was Anne Duchess of Westminster's horse

Corrie Vacoul.

In June the very versatile Terossian winner of the Galway Hurdle and more recently a winner over fences at Punchestown was favourite for the Mullingar Gold Cup. Trained by GeorgeWells he loved to hear his hooves rattle and he was up against Clusium a very decent horse trained by Dan Moore for W.L. Pilkington. All the money went on Willie O'Grady's Vicon at 9/4F with Dick McIlhagga's Terossian 11/4. John Crowley travelled from Middleton, Cork to ride him and it was his only ride. Clusium made all the running and cantered home by 5 lengths. However, Terossian went on to win the Galway Plate in 1968 as 7/2F. Royal Day had fallen in the Phoenix Beer Chase but he was 1/2F when he won the Tullamore Novice Chase. It was ironic that Mullingar closed in 1967 and two horses that ran there won the Galway Plate in 1967 and 1968 plus the Galway Hurdle in 1969.

When people attended the Mullingar races in July 1967 they did not know that it would be for the last time. The days aggregate for the last meeting was £11,463-2s-6d (In 1966 it was £16,534). One lucky punter won the jackpot of £1,188-0s-6d. The last hurdle race was won by Pat Rooney's Arctic Find (P.Ennis). The last 2 y/o race was won by Stitch (Lambo-Silken Princess) ridden by George McGrath at 7/1. A 16y/o apprentice James Cosgrove had the 2nd win of his career on Hopeful Sunshine in the Lough Owel Handicap for trainer Paddy Mullins. The last flat race ever was won by Clem Magnier with Meddling Polly (J.Roe) and the final race was the bumper won by Longford with Mrs E.Finn's Moigh Star (Mr E.J.Cash). The runner up was the favourite After Eight ridden by Cecil Ronaldson. It would have been appropriate if he had ridden the last winner as he was the man who rode the first horse Lady Flame to beat Arkle. R.M.Willington's Shakledrop was 3rd and this Offaly family had great success over the years. Local men Jim Tormey, Peter Downes and D.J.Moorehead all rode in the final race.

JOCKEYS REMEMBER MULLINGAR

I spoke to Francis Shortt about riding in Mullingar before it closed in 1967. He broke his leg at Tralee in September 1964 and on 13th February 1965 he returned to ride at Mullingar on Chelsea Set. At the 2nd fence he went through it and fell to break the same leg in the same place. It was turned in and set crooked. He was on crutches for 5 years, he got it operated on and pins put in. After that he lost his nerve & he said it was not fair on owners & trainers. He tried training but the recession's ended it. He rode a horse for Richard (Dick) Murray, Mullingar won on him. Murray was under 4 feet and his horse was 18 hands. He said *"Between us we could hardly reach him to pat him on the head"*. He rode Miss Hunter in the Grand National twice and got around finishing third on one occasion. He said *"Mullingar was a lovely track"*. They got £3.50 per ride (now

£180 per ride) and the entry was £3. Unspoken rules were *"do not come up the inside and do not cross anyone"*, but still there was rough riding. He trained for Frank Roe and Ted Walsh rode for him. He said it was true that they could change jockeys up to 10 minutes before a race and when there was a novice chase he said jockeys would jump out windows to avoid being picked for a novice chase with poor jumpers.

He remembers P.F. Conlon's death at Kilbeggan in 1952. He said older jockeys went wide at the bend but he came in tight and was forced out by the bend and then cannoned into the other horses leading to so many coming down & the unfortunate accident. He said that Mullingar had very good horses because the prize money was good, including the big race (Phoenix Beer Chase). He rode in 8 Grand Nationals and three Irish Nationals, 3 Munster Grand Nationals, 1 Kerry National, and 3 Thyestes Chase. He was placed in Aintree and the Irish National and he won the Galway Plate on Lisnaree in 1970, won the Grand Annual Chase at Cheltenham on Top Twenty etc. He was twice joint champion jockey. He dead heated with Pat Taaffe for the jockey's title in 1962 and four shared the title in 1963.

Tommy Kinane in a phone call remembered *"riding three horses at Mullingar for M. Browne. Out & About, which later went to Josh Gifford ran in the first & his brother Christy wouldn't ride, as he would runaway with you. He took the mount and was told to settle him but he took off and was never caught & won by 10 lengths. His second winner was Vulcanian and then he was to ride Gregory Peck horse Owen's Sedge, trained by F.D. Farmer and Christy was riding Kilmore winner of the 1962 Aintree Grand National for Fred Winter. Christy said before the race that he wouldn't let Tommy get a treble. During the race Christy hit Owens Sedge over the head as he challenged to slow him down and eventually won the race".* Tommy just had to put up with it. He mentioned *"one day at Mullingar they were told that they would have to ride in a race even though the sun was shining in their eyes in the straight."* He went out on the track with Bobby Coonan, and Cathal Finnegan to check it but they knew they wouldn't see the fences. Bobby turned round and said *"I hope the f..cking horses can see more than we can".* He said that he broke a finger in Kilbeggan on Height O'Fashion's brother Fashions Future, when the horse fell at the third last and stood on his finger.

He said *"that I lost my best horse Smoke Charger, when he fell in Roscommon in a chase".* He rode Kilmore 7 times for his brother Dan before Christy started riding him (he rode him 9 times and won Munster Grand National 1960). Francis Flood said on the phone *"that Champion Hurdler Another Flash, won a bumper there and that the Galway Plate & Hurdle winner Knight Errant also won there. It was a good track & heavy in the winter. Many came from Dublin by train to the races as the station was beside the track. He had ridden Another Flash when he started with Sleator He said he never wanted to be a pro but sometimes an owner put on a bet for him".* He trained great horses like Glencarrig Lady, Garoupe, and Bobsline in addition to training Nancy Myles for Foster & Allen. Clem Magnier recalled *"His first winner was Cavaliero and ridden by Paddy Lenehan at Rathkeel, Co Limerick. I think it may have been its last meeting. My brother Tom was the owner and I won 3/4 races with Cavaliero, who was then sold to Dorothy Paget. My first double was the same year at Mullingar with Cavaliero and Overshadow".*

MULLINGAR RACECOURSE - CLOSURE AND SALE

An article in the Irish Field in January in 1968 announced that Mullingar Racecourse was to be offered for sale by public auction at the end of February or March. Sir Peter Nugent, Manager since 1953 and one of the four Directors added *"The board decided at their annual meeting that the racecourse should be publicly auctioned in the near future probably in late February or March".* He continued *"we spent a lot of money in recent seasons on improvements at Mullingar and in the purchase of 9 acres to provide extra car parking facilities but there has not been any boom in revenue so the directors feel that they cannot carry on. This of course doesn't mean that Mullingar will be lost to racing. That decision depends on the purchaser".* It was one of the earliest courses to stage evening meetings, which proved extremely popular with race goers. In 1967 the Racing Board stopped a takeover bid for Leopardstown by purchasing a large block of Leopardstown shares to prevent the course being lost to racing but this was not an option for Mullingar.

Early in March 1968, the racecourse was put up for auction at the Greville Arms Hotel but it was withdrawn at £25,000. The 126 acre site, which was more than 100 years old was offered to private bidders. The auction opened with Denis Johnstone, Solicitor, Mullingar reading the conditions of sale after a local auctioneer Anthony Cleary asked bidding to start at £25,000, there was no response from the large gathering, which included many racing personalities. Bidding started at £20,000 and then to £25,000, with two bidders but there was no sale. Early in June, the Racing Board were asked to receive a deputation of Mullingar racing enthusiasts to discuss the future of the racecourse and the possibility of getting dates for meetings. Since March an acceptable bid had been made, but it was withdrawn after it was learned that the racecourse was not allocated any racing for 1968/69. Through the efforts of Matthew Burke Jnr, who farmed near the course a committee of people formed to raise sufficient money locally to ensure the continuance of racing in the area. A meeting was held in the County Buildings on Monday 19th June to try to save the races. A Committee was set up following a public meeting to send a deputation to the Racing Board and money was offered towards the purchase of the course. Matthew Burke Jnr,

Clonmore who was made Chairman, with his brother Peter of the *"Save the Racecourse"* meeting explained to those present that the main purpose was to see if enough money could be raised locally to save racing at Newbrook. P.J. Shaw, Solicitor said the meeting should be the nucleus of a much bigger and more widely representative meeting, as it affected the bloodstock industry in every way.

The Committee elected were M. Burke, Chairman, W. Curran, M.J. McDonagh Junior, Secretaries, S.K. Brabazon, R. Duncan, M. Murphy MRCVS, M. Cox MRCVS, Primrose Downes, J. O'Brien CC, J.Weir, Comm. M.J. O'Donnell,Tom Lynch, Joe Nangle, Gerry L'Estrange TD, and J. Bennett MCC, TC. M Burke said he understood that £14,000 was needed to buy out three shareholders and Mr Weir said it would be better to buy the Race Company than the racecourse. Mr A.C. Hanna, Cleaboy Stud, said he did not think people would be prepared to put money into the racecourse, unless they feel it could be turned into a profit making company. He said it could be turned into a sports centre for Mullingar and that a racecourse was a difficult thing to maintain, as a paying proposition. The issue of getting a licence and meetings was raised by Comm. M.J.O'Donnell & Paul Dunican, Kilbeggan, as the meetings were already allocated for the next year. Several executives from other courses claimed the Mullingar dates and it would be difficult to get them as no application was made by Mullingar for 1968 and 1969. Mr Burke said he was reliably informed that it would be possible to hold the August meeting, if everything was in order and Reggie Bermingham said he was told the same thing by Mr Dunican. Unfortunately, nothing happened for a few years even though point to point's were held there for a few years.

In 1972, Mullingar came under the hammer again in the Greville Arms and a bid of £38,500 was made. A number of parties were interested, some with the intention of resuming racing others like the Rugby Club and Show Committee were interested in what way the sale would go, as they had been using the show grounds at Newbrook. A special meeting was called by the Agriculture Show Committee to consider the position but when Pat Fletcher, Mullingar applied to the Turf Club for racing dates for the next 3 years, it was turned down. It was felt that the racecourse would be sold for around £40-50,000 and that it would take about £90,000 to get it ready for racing. People filled up slips of paper at the end of the meeting indicating what they would give towards the purchase of the course. It came to £13,455 and was not considered enough even though it was generous for a relatively small crowd. They said they would back a bona fida bid that would support racing plus the rugby club and Show Committee. It was said by some that the course had been bought in 1968 by a group called Mullingar Estates including trainer Charlie Rogers and T. McCairns and they were closely connected with the Racing Board.

In June 1972, the racecourse was eventually sold for £45,000. Apart from the annual point to point it had not been used for 5 years. It was purchased by Robert Downes, the young Mullingar Solicitor, and two others were involved. He said *"Every effort will be made to have the racecourse re-opened for racing and a considerable sum of money will be spent on improvements".* The earliest date for racing would be in 1974, as all dates were allocated to the end of 1973. The Auctioneers were Shrewsbury Estates Ltd, Dublin and Patrick Cleary & Son, Mullingar. The sale was conducted by Sir Peter Nugent, Moyvore. Bidding started at £30,000 and went quickly to £40,000 with about five people bidding. Eventually, it was sold to Mr Downes for £45,000.

In June 1973, it was announced that Mullingar Racecourse was again sold for a figure of around £150,000 and it was clear that Mullingar people & racing followers would never see racing again at this venue. The land was purchased by the IDA, who had no particular project in mind but hoped that Mullingar could have a large industry of its own employing 300/400 people said Paddy Murphy, Development Officer. Tom Moloney, Midland Regional Manager told reporter that they reached the final stages of purchasing the racecourse with the present owners Robert Downes and John Connaughton, Ballingall. They made an offer & it was accepted by them. No immediate plans were made for the site. On 30th June 1976 the official dedication ceremony for the £15 million factory site of GAF at Newbrook took place. John Bruton, Parliamentary Secretary to the Minister for Industry & Commerce was present. The General Manager P.J. McLoughlin was Master of Ceremonies of the 40,000sq foot factory. They were apprehensive that the site was of former community facility (racecourse) but mentioned that the new facility would be of far greater benefit to the district by providing jobs.

JOE DOLAN AND MULLINGAR "THE DREAM" RACECOURSE

In Ronan Casey's biography of Joe Dolan it seems that the great Westmeath singer was interested in saving Newbrook in 1968. The last meeting was held in July 1967 but Joe was apparently interested in buying the course and developing it. With support from the band and others he wanted to have 12 meetings per year, have the railway station re-opened, new bars, restaurants, etc that would attract non-regular race goers. He proposed a multi-purpose ballroom, which could be used for concerts & conferences plus other sporting bodies could also use it. They even planned to write songs about the race track. The proposal was put forward and they met with the Racing Board but could not convince them or the company who owned the course that their investment of £28,000 would make it viable. Some months later, it was sold to the Industrial Development Authority. Joe always felt that it would have brought a lot of business to the town. The full story of the loss of Mullingar racecourse is still to be told, as there is so much that is not known.

Guy Williams in his book ***"Winner All Right"*** said *"The closure of the attractive midland course was a tragedy of mis-management, though no fault of the manager per se. Capable of racing in virtually any weather conditions, equally adapted to the needs of the Flat and National Hunt and enthusiastically supported by sponsors, Mullingar should have been a prosperous concern. Unfortunately, there existed amongst the country set a conviction dating back from olden times that it was their God given right to race for free. This they did to such effect and in such numbers, as to render turnstile revenue virtually non-existent. With the increasing value of land on the outskirts of this bustling midland's town the outcome was inevitable".* Sir Hugh Nugent in his book *'The Sir'* said Mullingar was *"my dream racecourse"*. It had the rail line, water from the canal, centrally situated with access from the west and south. He said it was not a great track when it closed but it had great potential in the right hands.

RATHMOYLE STUD, RHODE

RIVER PRINCE

Chesnut (1935)

By ROSE PRINCE, out of VIESTE by PHAROS

Sire of SANGRO and MARFLOW respectively placed second in good class T.Y.O. Races at Ascot and Stockton from his first crop of five runners in 1944.

RIVER PRINCE was one of the best horses of his time. He was not entered in the Classics, but when winning the Chippenham Stakes he beat by four lengths Scottish Union, who had won the St. Leger, and been second in the Derby and Two Thousand Guineas. He won five other races and stakes value £5,090, including Ribblesdale Stakes, Ascot; Boscawen Stakes, Newmarket; Rous Plate, Doncaster; Breeders' St. Leger, Derby and Midland Breeders' Foal Plate. He was allotted 8st. 11lb. in the Free Handicap.

Rose Prince is the sire of Prince Rose, one of the best racehorses and sires on the Continent in recent years, and sire in England of Pappageno II, winner of the Manchester November Handicap in 1938 under the heaviest weight ever carried by a three-year-old.

Fee £24 - 19 - 0 (inclusive).

Apply: F. B. O'TOOLE, as above

'The Irish Horse 1944'

Famous stallion River Prince stood at Rathmoyle Stud in the 1940's

MULLINGAR RACES

(OVER THE NEWBROOK COURSE)

SUMMER MEETING

MONDAY, 5th JUNE, 1939.

SIX RACES. RECORD ENTRIES.

2 Flat Races. 2 Hurdle Races. 2 Steeplechases.

FIRST RACE, 2.30 P.M.

FIRST-CLASS CATERING AT POPULAR PRICES.

ADMISSION

COURSE AND PUBLIC STAND 2/-

GRAND STAND .... 10/- LADIES 5/-

MOTORS

RESERVED ENCLOSURES 5/-

SHOW GROUND 2/-

See Special Posters for Train Service. 2-27-5

Advertisement for Mullingar Races, 1939

chapter 3
RACING IN ATHLONE, BIRR, TULLAMORE AND MOATE

ATHLONE RACES 1858 - 1923

Thomas Naghten hosted a meeting at Thomastown Park in March 1857, but in 1858 it was transferred east of the Shannon to Garrycastle. In 1858 some of the Stewards included John Longworth, John J.Nugent, Thomas Naghten, Pat Grehan, Robert Mooney, plus military like Colonel Gooderough, Captain Chadwick and a Captain Byam. Mr Longworth, Master of Hounds in the neighbourhood held it at Glynwood? (1$^{1}/_{2}$ ml from town). It was a 3 mile course with 18 jumps, consisting of walls and an artificial brook. Hope with J.Kelly up got home from Mr Coghlan's horse and Mr Cusack won on Mr O'Ryan's Little Tiney. Athlone was described as a *"city of the dead"* as the streets were deserted because everyone was at the races. One reporter commented on *"the place of tents and awnings from orthodox marquee to ingenious combinations of old blankets, patchworks quilts, and sack clothes, cars and carriages for four in hand to donkey car, thimble riggers, trick o'the loops, rouge & noir tables, shooting galleries".*

The races were at Garrycastle in 1859, with the stand having a jockey & refreshment room. John Longworth presented the Glynwood Hunt Cup, value 100 sovereigns. In the race Mr Usher's Pedlar beat Mr Naghten's Peter Simple and Mr O'Ryan's Little Tiney won 2 races in 2 days. Mr Naghten won with Peter Simple & Blind Hooky. In 1860 one major difference was the arrival of the trains; the Midland Great Northern & Southern brought a huge influx of visitors, never equalled in the town. Mr Usher's Pedlar repeated his previous success in the Glynwood Cup ridden by the owner. The Garrycastle Handicap was won by the Marquis of Drogheda's Oberon. Mr Naghtens won with his two regular runners Nannie O'Leary & Kate. Pedlar was favourite to win the Glynwood Cup in 1861, but unfortunately broke down on the first round and the race was won by Musician (Thompson) owned by Mr Masters. The Garrycastle Handicap was won by Lord de Freynes O'Connell (D.Broderick) who completed in the Aintree Grand National in 1862 when he finished 10th. In 1862 there was a sense of gloom and lack of confidence in the favourites and the results did throw up shocks, with a stakes sponsored by Sir Charles Domville won by Kathleen the outsider of three.

YOUNG OFFICER KILLED AND CLASH WITH DERBY DAY

Significant work was done on the course in 1863, when the wall of loose stones was removed and sunk and raised fences were substituted. This prevented some of the accidents that occurred in previous years. Thomastown (Broderick) 5/1 won the Garrycastle Handicap beating a couple of celebrated horses of this era in Lightheart 2/1F & O'Connell (Ryan) by 6 lengths. Captain Machells Leonidas and J.H. Moore's Outsider were unplaced in this good quality race but the former won the Glywood Cup on the second day with Molly Ashore (Whelan), formerly owned by Mr Coffey. In the Hunt Cup, Mr Malone's The Orphan receiving 3 stone from The Youth 1/1 won easily. The latter had his turn in 1864 winning the Glynwood Cup carrying 13st 8lbs from T.Coles horse Jones. The Garrycastle Handicap was won by National Petition (D.Meany) 5/2, who had failed to finish in the 1864 Aintree National beating Goldfinder 1/1 (Monahan) by a length. The runner-up in the famous Conyngham Cup was B.Persse's Tophorne, which won the Glynwood Cup from The Youth. In 1866 entries were down as the meeting clashed with Ardee. The meeting had the tragic death of a young officer Mr Saunders of 5th Regiment who fell at a jump and broke his leg, which had to be amputated. After the operation he gradually deteriorated and died.

The Secretary in this era was J.W.Fair with Stewards like John Malone, John Longworth, Thomas Naghten, John Nugent, Robert Mooney ever present. Athlone continued its unfortunate habit of clashing with major events and this time it was Derby Day in England and many of the professional layers were in Surrey. Mr Malones Red Tape (White) 4/1 won the Glynwood Cup for the second consecutive year beating Mr Knox's Hard Times. In 1868 the Prince of Wales came to Ireland but was not in Athlone. The rain fell heavily badly affecting the attendance at what was to be the last races at Thomastown. The highlight was when John Malone's Red Tape won the Glynwood Cup for the third consecutive year beating Souvenir by a length and thus retained the trophy. When the Prince and Princess of Wales attended Punchestown for the inaugural Prince of Wales Plate, they saw Olympia ridden by Mr W. Trocke 35th Sussex Regiment win the Conyngham Cup. The Thomastown track had the good fortune to see the same horse Olympia 6/4F win the Glynwood Cup at this meeting with Mr Trocke aboard. This was to be the last meeting in Athlone for 25 years.

PROPOSALS TO REVIVE ATHLONE RACES - "LETHARGY" THE ENEMY

In December 1873, a writer on the Westmeath Independent calling himself *"Julius"* sent in a letter mentioning *"that it's a surprise that a large enterprising town like Athlone could get along without an annual steeplechase- the cities of Galway, Ballinasloe, Roscommon etc deserve great praise for the way they have kept up their splendid meeting. We have a great racing track, furnished with a stand house where the best horses in the kingdom contended for the prize".* He suggested if the wealthy & influential people of the district used their influence then *"Athlone would regain her ancient sporting renown and Garrycastle would shine with all her glory"*. In January 1874 a very important figure in the area John J. Ennis, Ballinahown Court, wrote in support of the idea *"I always deeply regretted that these races had been given up and I shall most willingly do anything in my power to have them restored, with the hope of getting horses from all over Ireland for valuable stakes"*. *"Julius"* responded by suggesting *"that Mr Ennis could provide a portion of property nearer to the town than the old racecourse at Coosan with a temporary wooden stand and 4 races supported by the farmers, gentry, hunt, and business people of the town".* Other letters supported the project but all attempts at this time failed whether from *"lethargy"*, or lack of financial support from gentry and businesses.

In consequence of a large and influentially signed requisition of all classes of the town Mr L.Kelly JP convened a meeting about Athlone races in March 1886. Present were L. Kelly JP, presiding A. Moore TC, PLG, B. Macken TC, M. Geoghegan, J.C. Kelly, J. Coen, J. Lyster, T. Mullins, L. Watson, P. Neary, H. Murray etc. Mr J.C. Kelly was appointed Secretary. In mid- April 1886, a meeting was held in the Town Hall regarding a revival of the races and it was attended by Messrs B.Macken, Chairman and a decision was made to approach Mr Dames Longworth regarding the old course and a group of five were appointed. He declined to meet them alleging that *"a personal interview would lead to no satisfactory result"* in other words he refused to give the use of his course. It was noted that around £200 was already received in subscriptions and Mr Kilduff had offered the use of the old racecourse.

The committee were Messrs Moore, Mullins, Macken, Milligan, and M. Geoghegan and in St Peter's Ward were Messrs Coen, Phillips, Neary & Geraghty With J.C.Kelly, Secretary and A.Moore, Treasurer. They thanked Mr Kilduff and his son for offering the course. Whether they did not receive enough in subscriptions or the course was not suitable the races again did not proceed. In February 1892, a meeting was held in the Town Hall at 8.30pm called by H.B. Adderly proprietor of Westmeath Hounds, John Murtagh, Ballykeeran House, M. Kilkenny TC, M. Geoghegan TC, PLG, J.Duffy, J.G.Ryan, Solicitor, Major Banbridge, Lt Price, J.C.Kelly, Town Clerk, T.Mullins, and J.Coen TC. Mr Adderly said he intended having a race meeting in Athlone, under Steeplechase Rules. The course proposed was Bushfield owned by Mr Kilduff. The problem was that a portion of the course was divided by a public road. Mr Brindly was to inspect the course & give his opinion. John Murtagh was made Secretary and he was to write to Mr Brindley about a date near Easter week.

REVIVAL OF ATHLONE RACES AT BUSHFIELD IN 1893

It was revived after 25 years at Bushfield about a mile from Athlone. They came by train (Midland Great Western & Great Southern Lines), it seemed every brake and carriage in the area was present, and also the *"fair sex were in gayest bunting, like ships at sea".* Racing officials from The Curragh were met by the committee and *"the most respectable of metropolitan bookmakers were present".* The key people were Joint Secretaries P & John Murtagh, W.Kearney, M.Geoghegan, Andrew Moore, John Hunt, Humphrey Milligan, and Pat Kilduff. Mr Prendergast supplied the plan for the erection of the grandstand & enclosure, which dealt with a crowd of around 12,000. The Tally Ho Plate brought a great local win for H.Adderly and Frank Mitchell, who trained that remarkable Irish Grand National winner The Admiral, won with one of his many horses starting with the letter "A" when Albert won the Farewell Plate ridden by his son Stewart. In 1894, a Public Meeting was held in the Town Hall with John J.Coen, Chairman, presiding and he apologised that racing people were not present and admitted maybe there was not enough publicity in circulars. The Murtagh's resigned as Secretaries and Mr Coen took the job with M.Geoghegan, Treasurer. The meeting the previous year was a success but they were surprised that local people did not take an interest in the races. He stated that the Steeplechase Committee might not approve Bushfield and that they should approach Dames Longworth about Garrycastle, for the 16th April a week before Punchestown. The stand would have to be enlarged by at least 1/3 with a barrier in the lower part and they would ask the Railway Company for more subscriptions.

It rained all day for the races and it was turned into a mud bath but the attendance was around 6,000. Many mishaps occurred on the course and the most notable winner was J.Yourell's Bass (L.Yourell), who had been 2nd to The Admiral in the Irish Grand National and easily won the Bushfield Plate and local trainer Larry Hope won the Farewell Plate with Traynor defeating Lognavadogue (who was 5th in Irish Grand National in 1896). One paper said it was a bad day for favourites but oddly three favourites and three second favourites won. The usual roulette tables, Aunt Sally, thimble rigger, shooting range, fortune tellers, ventriloquist, & conjurors were present. Local owner R.K.Price won the maiden plate with Battlemount (Baily) trained by D.Broderick, Mountjoy Lodge, Kildare and he also won the Tally Ho Plate with Starlight V trained by himself and he won by 50 lengths, but oddly had to survive an objection for crossing! In 1896, the committee carried forward £10-4s-6d from 1894 and their total balance for 1895 was now £22 and the races were on 18th May. A huge crowd turned up for the races with the Stand House full and some horses even came on Saturday even though the races were not on until Monday. Leading trainers like Fred Cullen had runners at the meeting and he won with Gay Girl in a four horse race where all the horses either fell or refused at some point and he had a double with Golden Hair. Captain Dewhurst's useful Wild Flower (Florian-Cora) won the Athlone Plate and young Alice Boyd- Rochfort won with Vexation 1/1.

In 1897, they had some difficulty securing a suitable date and on 10th July 1897 held a meeting in the Town Hall. They had a balance of £21 in the account with some bills still outstanding. A dispute arose as to why the books were not balanced and why vouchers for bills were not paid yet. It was pointed out that there would be no subscribers without proper accounts. The previous Secretary refused point blank to attend the meeting, so it was left to present Secretary John Murtagh & Mr Millican to answer questions. It was pointed out that proposed date of 16th September clashed with Banagher fair, Moate Market & other markets. The main issue was that the cost of Mr Kilduff's field at Bushfield was £20 and the three tenants were paid over £30. Due to all these difficulties & the lateness in the year no race meeting was held.

1899 - GARRYCASTLE RACES REVIVED, AS SOME "FACED DEATH IN THE DUST"

Very few regretted the demise of Bushfield and when the Longworth family and in particular E.Dames Longworth gave Garrycastle, there was renewed interest in the races. Numerous tales of fun, frolic and fighting, coloured with a tinge of exaggeration, were the order of the day after 31 years. The Committee responsible were W.Kelly CC, Chairman, John Murtagh, Ballykeenan, John Gaynor, Solicitor, A. Moore, J.Coen, P.J.Prendergast, H. Millican, J. Bolton VS, Dr F. Moorehead, Moate, and P.B.Tracey. They visited the racecourse to see arrangements and had £210 in prize money for the meeting in April. As one paper stated *"The recollection of the old course was as the memory of an old friend to many, who are now kindly laid to the rest".* The stand was on the side of the course near the Moate Road, and could hold 800, even with a ladies room.

Tropical style heat meant firm ground & a number of withdrawals. There was also a delay of 45 minutes, due to a hitch regarding the hurdles and also an objection delayed proceedings. Around £200 was taken at the gate. With regard to the racing, Baldoyle winner Hawker was a hot favourite but Westmeath trainer Dick Cleary won with Stephens 10/1 in the first race. Major trainers like J.J.Parkinson & W.Meredith were present and the latter won the Garrycastle Plate with Bait. E. Malone jockey had a double with Borjulie & Sweet Star but an objection to the latter for running at an illegal meeting led to an enquiry which lasted 5 months, as Captain Bob Dewhurst and Mrs Stacpoole proceeded with a case, which they eventually lost. It was noted that that the Father Matthew Club had a *"perceptible air of respectability and more attractions than the others, where Guinness & Jamison were detailed at more than their ordinary price".*

In 1899, John J. Coen was now Secretary and many improvements were made for the meeting on 17th September with all rocks removed, the run home had a railing, and it will avoid the crowding by supporters the previous year. A huge problem was the cloud of dust due to the hot weather. One man mentioned *"facing death in the dust on the way to the course through the reckless conduct of money grabbing car drivers".* It was suggested that the stand be moved back to the original site with Mr Longworth's approval. Amongst the entertainment was a machine that purported to show you your future husband or wife or even your mother-in-law! Local jockey T. Dowdall had a double with Goodshot in the Athlone Plate and The Don in the Town Plate.

A CRUEL BOOKIE AND A 3 MILE RACE OVER 2 $^{1}/_{2}$ MILES?

The meeting on 30 April 1901 was again held in good weather and watering carts had to dampen down the dust. The locals cleverly walked through the fields to avoid this problem. The first race commenced at 1.45pm & was won by the appropriately named Roman Child (Roman Emperor- Lady Childers) trained by Matt Dawson, The Curragh beating previous local winners like Stephens & Gay & Sweet. Dr J.A. Coen, Frenchpark, won the Athlone Plate with course specialist and favourite Killastar (Duncombe-Bagenalstown). Champion jockey John Thompson & R.Greville Nugent rode at the meeting without success. J.Cole had a local success with Johnny Mac 4/6F, following up a recent Baldoyle win. The gate receipts were £50 higher than previous years. A reporter from the Westmeath Independent put 5 shillings on a 4/1 winner *"but imagine my disgust when all that remained of the refinedly cruel bookie was a green baize and a mineral water case"*. A horse ran loose in the town belonging to Mr Patrick VS and overturned a trap on Mardyke Street. J.J. Coen hosted a function for the Press & officials after the races. J.Meleady, Leixlip, trained two winners in Mary Anne in Shannon Plate and Benvenir won Glynwood Plate. In the plate Benvinir won but the horses started at the $2^{1}/2$ mile post and not the 3 mile post. The owner of Little Star objected and as the starter had left the course to catch a train, the Stewards decided they would have to race again. Only three of the horses remained and once again Benvinir won to great cheers from the crowds, as he was the favourite on both occasions.

BUSHFIRE 1, BUSHFIRE 2 AND BECKY SHARP

In 1903, it was noticeable that Mullingar, Kilbeggan, and Athlone Races were held within a few weeks of each other from 18th April to 4th May, which seemed a strange decision. The Athlone Races was on 4th May and as the Westmeath Independent stated *"Hedgegrows smiled and birds sang blithely, as the throngs of people moved out towards the race ground".* The recent rains kept down the dust and many felt that Athlone was becoming a very successful meeting. The opening race was won by Christopher Hopes horse The Chief (Marmiton- Baby Girl) by making all the running beating Favonius, which had won at Strokestown and Kilbeggan (won two races in a row at Kilbeggan). Local owners had entries like Colonel Hall, Dr H.Moorehead, Moate, J.Malone, Mullingar, J.Murtagh, Athlone, E.Wakefield, Moate, Mrs Adamson, Mullingar and Colonel Hall's Needful won the Ballinahown Plate beating Dr Moorehead's Light 'Un. One big issue was the placing of the last fence at an angle, which caused some falls and many wanted the stand to be moved back where the old stand was in mid 19th century.

When the people arrived at the racecourse for the May meeting in 1904 they were greeted with the sight of the bush fence of fire. It was not unknown for jockeys to burn down a fence (see the Lighter Side of Racing), but it was not clear whether it was by accident or design. The blaze lasted for over two hours and nothing but the side rails were left. The burning bush was a sign in biblical terms for the punters in the last race. Amazingly, a horse appropriately called Bushfire II (Bushey Park- Greek Fire) won the final race beating a good horse Thiggin Thu. As the local Westmeath Examiner stated *"the meeting opened & closed with a bush fire, the first which gave owners some anxiety, as to regulations and the second which caused numerous "dollors" to vanish from the pockets of even the most successful sportsmen of the day".* The Field Artillery Brigade Cup turned into *"laughable burlesque"*, as it involved a number of horses that couldn't even crawl over a stone fence never mind jump it, and they had to be pulled off the fence by spectators. Only one horse appropriately named Banker got round but the comedy was not over, when Captain Hill on Becky Sharp appeared for the last lap and passed the judges first before being declared the winner. She was objected to for not completing the course and the jockey reported to the Turf Club. At least A. Anthony rode a double with Dutch Roll & Mount Hillery. The newspapers found great fault with the track, the facilities, and the accommodation in general. On the stand the timber was rotting and because it needed a major overhaul no races were held in 1905. In 1906 J.J.Coen was no longer Secretary due to illness and J.Conway was now Secretary with assistance from John Murtagh & Robert English. In 1906 it was difficult to get entries for provincial meetings e.g. Nenagh only had 17 entries, Athlone only had 27 runners for 7 races. It did not make for good betting with 4 favourites beaten and two odds on winners. Some local winners included C.Cole, Milltownpass, with Dominicam a recent Birr winner and J.Cole's No Sir both ridden by T. Dowdall. J. Smith, Kilpatrick, Mullingar won with Sweet Cecil (Sweetheart-Cistus).

ATHLONE RACES 1913 - 1923

The races were revived in 1913 after a break of 7 years due to the many difficulties that arose at that time. A meeting in the Imperial Hotel included Robert Elder, Chairman, Henry Connell, E.J.Bolton VS, H. W. Percy VS, Frank Cox, James Fleming, J.J.Coen, C.Bigley, James Sweeney, Frank Daly, V.D. C. Doyle, and M.J.Cassidy, Secretary. They approached T.H. Montgomery agent for Dames Longworth, and after some weekly meetings the races went ahead. People came on Saturday before the races to stay and accommodation was provided by the committee. They also provided conveyances at a reasonable rate to stop people being victimised- donkeys and jennets could be got for 6d. Athlone was one of the few left handed courses and it was suggested that some trees be cut down on the hill to give a better view. W.A.Ussher, Eastwell, Galway, had a treble winning the Moydrum plate with Abregate (Red Prince II) from Frank Barbour's Bachelors Gift, the Ballinahown Chase with H.F. Malcolmson's Ripe Cherry and H.J. Ussher rode Double Mac to win Glynwood Chase.

MAJOR IMPROVEMENTS IN 1914 - JOCKEY'S WILL NOT HAVE WET FEET!
A number of changes were made, with the clump of trees, which hid the view of the course from the Grand Stand being cut down. The grandstand & offices were overhauled and the floor of the weigh-room concreted, meaning the jockey's and anyone else were no longer standing in wet feet all day. The Press, Ambulance & Jockey's Room were remodelled. This year the committee had turnstiles erected for the day to avoid a crush or delay. The meeting was now to be self-supporting for the first time. The course was railed for a distance to avoid the problems of 1913 when people encroached on the track. Dick Cleary had a treble having had one the previous Monday at Kilbeggan. The most popular was Royal Spinner (Royal Hackle) a 4 y/o brother of Spinning Queen owned by J.Groarke and ridden by Tom O'Roarke. M.J. Cleary's Feakle carrying 12st 11lbs was made favourite 4/7 for Ballinahown Plate with W.Lynn on board and won easily by 1½ lengths The treble was completed by Tom Killian's Happy Go Lucky II (by Cleary's dam Easter Prize).

In 1915, the races were in aid of the Red Cross Funds in view of developments in WW1 and the course was in good condition with a good view. It was a meeting which had better quality runners than previous years, including a number who ran in the Irish Grand National like Ballyneety, Tirhugh (2nd in the Irish National in 1915), General Blane, Dundesert and J.Kiernan's All Sorts, who won the Irish Grand National on Easter Monday 1916. On this day he beat Ballyneety in the Ballinahown Plate but was disqualified by the Acting Steward Robert Elder for bumping and boring. The Red Cross Plate of 45 sovereigns was won by Malcolm Arnotts Gris de Lin ridden by champion amateur W.J.Parkinson. In 1916 there were two meetings and the Stewards were Lord Castlemaine, John Murtagh, R.S.English, J.J.Coen, T.H.Montgomery, E.J.Bolton, plus the committee of R.Elder, J.Fleming & M.J.Cassidy, Secretary. W.A.Ussher's very useful horse Crovederg owned by Mrs Croft won at both the August & September meetings in Athlone at odds of 10/1 and 4/1 respectively and he managed to also win in Galway. The old proverb of backing the outsider of three came true in September 1916, when Ussher's hotpot The Cardinal was beaten by Tom O'Roarkes Poor Willie at 4/1.

Athlone didn't race again until 1919/20, as continuing troubles over the track and a lack of support for the races in the middle of a difficult time for provincial racing. Only a total of 14 runners appeared for 6 races with two walkovers in August 1919 and a maximum field of 4 runners. The purpose of the meeting was to raise funds for the Four Masters Memorial Church. Two local horses R.G.Adamson's Red Spider and J.Kiernan's Rathdrisheogue walked over. Prolific winner Sigram won the Garrycastle Plate for owner, trainer and jockey Mr J.Coghlan. In September warm autumn sunshine brought the *"peasantry and gentry"* to the races according to a local paper. It is interesting that the word *"peasantry"* was still being used in reports. The meeting was for funds for the Franciscan Order and the commemoration of the Four Masters and it brought large crowds on trains, cars, ass and carts, bicycles. Many businesses gave a 1/2 day to the staff and factories gave a full day. Aside from the dust it was a nice walk. At the course some elevations blocked the view but all the usual entertainments were there. J.J.Ham's Kingfisher (Fly Fisher-First Cherry) was 6/1 outsider of three but still won, and another local winner was Dick Cleary's Ratcore (Avidity) owned by J.Kiernan. Arbor who was a lucky winner at a previous meeting had his race won but a late challenge from Coldeen trained by jockey G.N.Bennett got up by a neck. The Champion trainer J.J. Parkinson won with Dark Cider in the Garrycastle Handicap.

RUMOURS SPREADING ABOUT THE RACES

In May 1920, a lot of rumours were spreading that, because of agrarian agitation and the land driving campaign, there would be no races. The course had changed ownership and it was again rumoured that there would be a *"cattle drive"* at the races in protest against the imprisonment of the Ballinahown Drivers, which was a big issue in the Athlone area. There was uneasiness in the area but the rumours were not correct and Ballinahown people said they were strongly in favour of the races and they even offered volunteers to help with security. The weather was bad, but the races proceeded with 32 runners. Two interesting winners were H.V. Kenny's Silvo who won the flat race over 2 miles by 2 lengths at 5/1. The horse went on to be 3rd in the Aintree Grand National in 1924 and unplaced in the same Grand National was Fly Rose and this horse won the Athlone Handicap Chase at 20/1. Fly Rose was then owned by T.J.Weir but when 7/4F for the 1921 Irish Grand National he was owned by Frank Barbour & trained by Dick Cleary. Interestingly, Greeneogue was unplaced in the Ballinahown Plate to Silvo but was 2nd favourite for the Irish Grand National to Fly Rose in 1921. Little did people at Athlone know this day that two rank outsiders would be 1st and 2nd favourites in the Irish Grand National in 1921. The Crofts had a double with Marlien & Leddiston, both trained by Harry Ussher, Eastwell.

Aside from a strong wind, which taxed the wearers of slouch hats it was a good day at the September meeting. The race meeting was to raise funds for the Four

Masters Memorial Committee and while this was a very worthy cause it was also an indicator that the Athlone race committee were not developing into a commercial enterprise looking into the future and planning on further development. Like many other racecourses the signs were there that it would not last much longer. The fine weather meant farmers were missing and rail restrictions from the west prevented people attending. Local volunteers did the police work. Four favourites from 4/5 to 2/1 won, so it was a good day for punters Fly Fisher (Fly Fisher- Royal Rose III) repeated her May win in the Shannon Plate. Silvo failed to win again with the legendary Harry Beasley on board the winner Podarces trained by J.Trench, Tipperary,who was strongly associated with Offaly. Mrs Croft had yet another win at Athlone with her useful horse Max (Zria-Bauble).

The races were not held again in 1921 probably due to the political situation that year. The Anglo Irish Treaty brought a pleasant change, with horses now accommodated & stabled at Costume Barracks. The local IRA Police Force were reinforced and on duty in the town & at the races, under the command of J.J.Elliott, Brigade Chief of Police. The races in May 1922 were packed with cars and refreshments provided by P.J.Lennon, Bastion Street. The Athlone Brass and Reed Band provided pleasant music under the direction of Bernard Burke & E.Farrell. After the successful meeting £200-300 was handed over for the building of the church. Two local people J.J.Coen and J. McDonnell provided plates for the meeting, and local subscriptions from the people saved expenses for the committee. The money was spent on fencing and preparation of the course and plans for more meetings. Harry Ussher continued his love affair with Athlone races with three winners, including Saxham (H.Beasley) beating two Westmeath horses in E.J.Hopes Floral Way & M.Ballesty's Rathmore; Mrs Shaw-Taylor's Gristle (H.Beasley) beat Peter Fitzgeralds Ballyna; and Mr A.Comyn's Mr Vigorous. The Athlone Handicap of 40 sovereigns was fought out by two local horses with J.Kiernan's Rathdrisheogue (Avidity) ridden by J. Doyle beating Tom Killian's Coola II (J. McCarthy). Great work was done by the Joint Secretaries J. Fleming & R.S.English.

The final meeting was, very oddly, held on 31st July 1923 the day before the revived Galway Races, based on the theory that people would stop off on the way to the races.The crowds was not too bad, but only 32 runners turned up for six races in spite of the best efforts of M.J.Cassidy, Secretary. It was ironic that at the last meeting a horse called Doldrums was beaten in the Stewards Plate by local horse Rathcreevagh (repeating the 1922 win). Mrs Croft's Yours Only won over 20 races and beat the favourite Start Again. Frank Barbour had his last win with Soot at 1/4F. The final race was the Shamrock Lodge Chase of £40, over 2 1/2 miles. It was won by Mr T. Whites's Tullylost, ridden by J.Moloney, who beat Little Mick in a 4 runner race at 1/1F. Truly, Athlone was in the doldrums, with no where to go and like many other racecourses they lost the uphill fight to survive.

MOATE RACES 1889 -1897

JACK THE RIPPER WINS AS GRANDSTAND COLLAPSES

On 1st April 1889 a meeting was held on George Gaynor's land about $^1/_2$ mile from town on the Athlone Road. The Stewards were Luke J. Egan, Pat Duff, Dr Moorehead, J.J. Hurley, E. Kelly, John Lowe, George Woodburne, John Murtagh, James Gaynor, Secretary, L.D. Byrne, P. Fallon, S. Boland, John Egan, Peter Marshe. Hurley & Woodburne were joint Treasurers. It was only a month since they decided to race at Aughafin and the course was supplied by Messrs Gaynor. It was a beautiful day & the trains came from Athlone at 8.45am and 12.45pm with extra carriages and great arrangements by Mr Jennings at the Railway Station. Interestingly, placards were put up everywhere on the road into the track with an extract from an Act of Parliament referring to the prosecution of parties engaged in gaming in any public highway or place. It lessoned the number of speculators attending. The sale of drink, including non-alcoholic, was prohibited and with police there in force it was a dry meeting with just some fruit to quench the thirst. Rev Canon Kearney who was probably very influential regarding the drink ban was an expert huntsman and helped to control the crowds on his horse. All the races were of the £4- 19s class.

Jack the Ripper fell at the first but he couldn't be kept down, as the jockey remounted and he fell again on the second round, but somehow he recovered to win the race for Mr S. Gaynor. He turned out again to win a second race and Mr Gaynor won the private sweepstake with his horse Barricade. Well known Westmeath breeder James Yourell won the Pony Race with Wild Deer beating the equally renowned Frank Mitchell on Gamester. During the Pony Race a greater portion of the grand stand collapsed and gave way with a crash and the occupants & timber ended up on the ground. There were hundreds of people on the stand including children, but the only injuries were to a gentleman, a lady and 2 children. People in the enclosure rushed in to assist and afterwards it was discovered that Mrs Haveley, Miss Lissie Potter, Mr Jenston, and a son of Columb Kelly were all checked for bruises.

"MOATE TOWN IN MOURNING ABOUT THE RACES"

It was not an auspicious start, but the Committee held a meeting in March 1890 to organise the races with John Lowe as Chairman and Mr Daly as Secretary. It was held on 8th April and Canon Kearnry had the strictest instructions regarding drink (not even mineral water was allowed), which reduced the crowd, as he patrolled the whole area. As one report said *"Moate town in mourning about the races, as there was no rejoicing with shutters up in the pubs"*. It was also noted that *"punctuality was remarkable by its absence"* with the 2.30pm race starting at 3.45pm. One race was not run due to the lateness of the time. The stand was more substantial on this occasion and mainly occupied by the gentry. The problem with the "£4-19s" races was that there were no rules except what the Stewards laid down and no penalties could be imposed for infringing the rules of justice.

One race had the future Irish Grand National winner The Admiral (1894) as a participant. He won the Consolation Stakes but was also 2nd in the Ladies Plate. The Admiral was fancied for the latter race but M.J.B rabazon's Moonrise was made favourite after the off and apparently lead all the way. The problem was that Mr Costello's mount There She Goes, supposedly was brought out early and taken out of the course until the second round when she joined in and cantered home in front of Moonrise. She was disqualified, the jockey was severely censored, but the bookies paid for the first horse over the course and this annoyed backers of Moonrise, as racing at Moate had provided plenty of controversy.

A meeting was held in Mrs Harford's Hotel early in 1891. Columb Kelly, Treasurer y said he was in touch with Mr Adderley about having a meeting under Hunt Rules and about giving 2 cups for 2 hunt races, which he gave. The main controversy was the last race, which was won by A.J. Pilkington's Aristocrat but there was an objection on the grounds that he was incorrectly weighted, as he had won a previous race. Backers of the 2nd Sunbeam wanted the winner disqualified but Aristocrat supporters gathered around the bookies for payment. After a 15 minute delay the bookies paid first past the post. Mr Brindley gave instructions to hoist the winning number and then immediately left the course in his trap (something he did before!). One of the big changes was that the races were now under the auspices of the South Westmeath Hunt. Proceedings took place under INHS rules with cups, plates, and prizes from £11 to £25 were awarded instead of "£4-19s". On top of all the problems Mr Brindley, Clerk of the Course on his arrival at the track changed the order of the races therefore times on the race cards was wrong. The other problem that arose was due to Canon Kearney's strict instruction on drink, which meant people kept coming and going from the pub to the racecourse all day.

NO ALCOHOL - BUT BASS WAS A BIG FAVOURITE

By February 1893, Mr Adderley wanted to change the races from Moate to Athlone, but the businessmen & traders at a meeting in Harford's Hotel were determined to keep the races in Moate. At this point it seemed that two groups were in dispute, as one group wanted the races under the auspices of Mr Adderley's committee and the other wanted it under the South Westmeath Hunt. Mr Gaynor was again providing the course at Aughafin, but he was resigning as

Treasurer due to work commitments. The races were down for late in May. John Gaynor won the Welter Hunt Cup with Sunfield (by Piersfield) the horse who won the recent private sweepstake & Secretary John Lowe won with Gunshot (Buckshot). It was said that the course from the point of view of both spectators and jockey's was *"not delectable"* and the *"double"* just past the stand caused widespread grief amongst the already small fields with only a few finishing each race. In addition on this occasion there were no refreshments either liquid or solid.

In 1895, the old committee resigned, as there was an on-going issue of the Hunt Committee taking over and local people not being involved. At a meeting in Harford's Hotel the Trustees P.Fallon & J.J.Hurley raised the issue of being empowered to keep possession of the Grandstand and the balance of the money to be used for the athletic club. It was eventually decided after discussion to hand them over to a new committee of John Gaynor, F.Russell, James Gaynor, J. McCormack, J. Lowe, T. Murphy, J. Mahon, J. Wyer, & Stafford Halpin, Manager, National Bank. The Grand Stand could hold 700 and was completed by Pat Heffernan with a substantial enclosure and the enclosure for the Buff's Regiment, Athlone was at the East End. The subscription list was £200 with trains from Mullingar & Dublin & it started at 2pm. Mr Gaynor's horse Sunfield won the opening Hunt Race again at 2/5 and obviously loved the track. The star of the show was the prolific winner J.Yourell's Bass and he won both the Farmer's Race of 20 sovereigns and the Subscriber Stakes of 20 sovereigns.

In 1895, there was another change as they were no longer under the rules of the Hunt Club but under the National Hunt Rules. It was an *"oppressively sunny day"* on Friday 3rd May. In the Stand House there was a long line of vehicles, tents were not allowed on the course, and the refreshment ban in the stand was conducted by John W. Murphy, Athlone. For the first time five races were held instead of four races. Horses that had run in Athlone a few days before did well with R. K. Price's Battlemount winning a maiden plate; Athlone winner W.Coghlan's Tell Tale (M.Powell) won the Moate Plate of 40 sovereigns at 1/1; and Mr Price had a double with his Athlone winner Star Light V in the South Westmeath Hunt Cup.

The committee met in the courthouse in January 1896, including S. Halpin, Secretary John Gaynor (Solicitor/Coroner), and Peter Mahon, Treasurer. They agreed on a Pony Race for the meeting on 12th May and that *"Any pony whose height is disputed will be thrown out"*. The Westmeath Independent stated on 9th April that *"the progress of the meeting is remarkable"*. It was held at James Gaynor's land at Campfield which was I mile in length and level, the bushes blocking the view are cut down, and the old wooden stand gone and a new commodious one. The jockey's room was spacious, the stand cost £70, but was now a permanent fixture, and the enclosure was 50 yards x 30 yards which could hold 800 people. A.J.Pilkington dominated proceedings having a double with Lord Greville's Bonnie Rath 4/5 and James Coles Rattan (Marmiton-Sweet Anchoress). They only had 19 runners for 4 races and two for the Pony Race.

GRAND FINALE FOR MOATE RACES IN 1897

A meeting was held in March after a circular issued by Columb Kelly whereby the Directors of Moate Fair were considering a proposal for a race meeting on the Fair Green and Samuel Belton was presiding. A discussion developed as to how the Race Committee were proposing to move the stand to the Fair Green without having asked the Fair Green Committee who decided not to give permission. The races were to be held over the Moyally Course. They were now being held under the rules of the Irish Racing Association for the first time. The Stewards for the final meeting were Samuel Belton, J.R. North, J. McCormack, T. Murphy, John Daly, Secretary, J.H. Blackburn, Treasurer, John Weir, Eddie Kelly, T. Belton, C. Ross, and T. Lowe. The races included the Drapers Plate of £10, the Granoge Plate of £15 a hurdle race; Westmeath Plate of £20 was an open handicap over hurdles; the Farmer's Plate of £10 confined to farmers and traders in Kings County & Westmeath; and the Consolation Stakes for all beaten horses of £10.

The first time a meeting was held outside the Westmeath Hunt proved to be a success in April, with great credit to the Working Committee. Valentine Dunbar, Clerk of the Scales was described as *"meeting was in charge of genial Valentine Dunbar, who like our famous poet touches nothing that he does not adorn"*. The course was about 15 minutes driving time from the town and was given by Mr J.Raferty, Athlone for the day and it was one mile round & a little hilly. O'Brien the jockey had a few winners including Hazelhatch in the Greeneogue Plate. J.Daly's Little Annie won the last race ever run in Moate and was famous amongst the locals for many years. The Moate races failed for a number of reasons. It is clear that finance and in particular the subscription system never really raised enough money for to develop the races, especially after they lost Aughafin. Then there were the disputes with the South Westmeath Hunt and in particular Mr Adderley and the business people and traders in the town, as to who was in charge. Raising finance was a problem for all courses at this time and when people were not operating on a united front it was always going to be difficult. The quality of horses did not compare to Mullingar or Athlone. In addition, the numbers running were small with only around 18 runners for 4 races. Moyally was described as a hilly course, so it may not have been ideal and given the financial difficulties of the committee Mr Rafferty may not have given it for the following year.

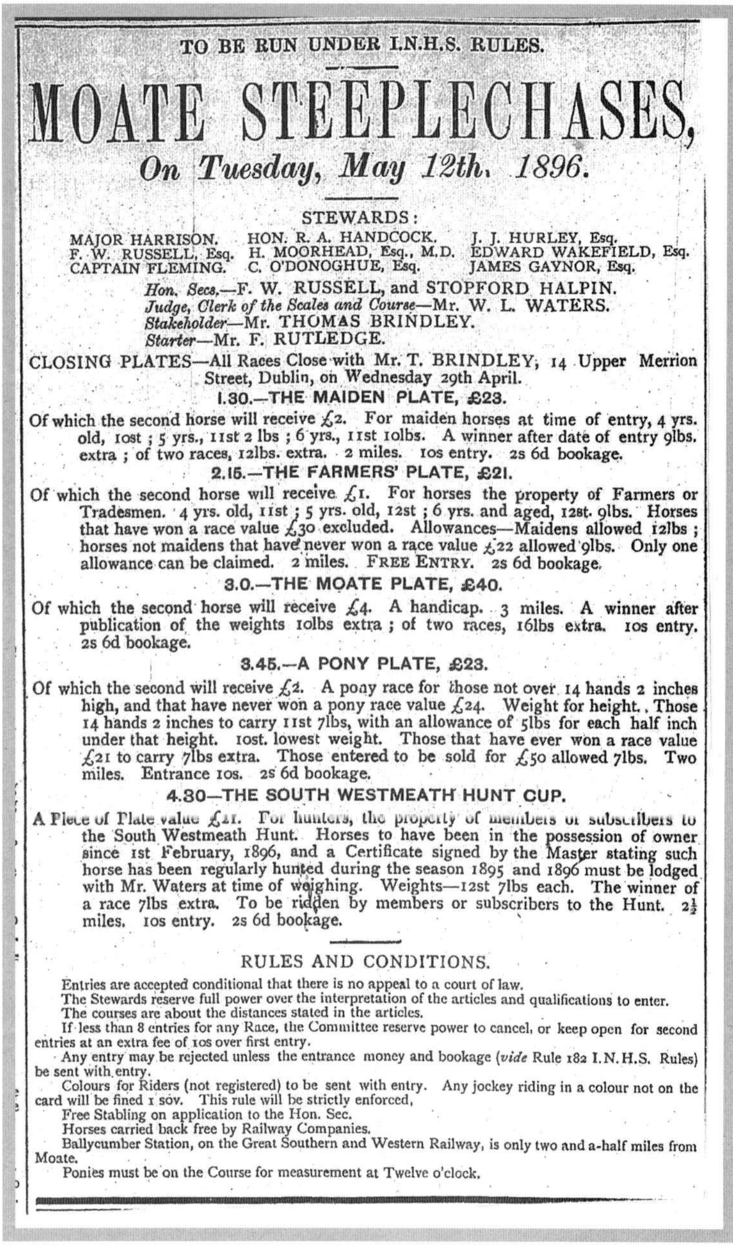

TO BE RUN UNDER I.N.H.S. RULES.

MOATE STEEPLECHASES,

On Tuesday, May 12th, 1896.

STEWARDS:

MAJOR HARRISON. HON. R. A. HANDCOCK. J. J. HURLEY, Esq.
F. W. RUSSELL, Esq. H. MOORHEAD, Esq., M.D. EDWARD WAKEFIELD, Esq.
CAPTAIN FLEMING. C. O'DONOGHUE, Esq. JAMES GAYNOR, Esq.

Hon. Secs.—F. W. RUSSELL, and STOPFORD HALPIN.
Judge, Clerk of the Scales and Course—Mr. W. L. WATERS.
Stakeholder—Mr. THOMAS BRINDLEY.
Starter—Mr. F. RUTLEDGE.

CLOSING PLATES—All Races Close with Mr. T. BRINDLEY, 14 Upper Merrion Street, Dublin, on Wednesday 29th April.

1.30.—THE MAIDEN PLATE, £23.

Of which the second horse will receive £2. For maiden horses at time of entry, 4 yrs. old, 10st; 5 yrs., 11st 2 lbs; 6 yrs., 11st 10lbs. A winner after date of entry 9lbs. extra; of two races, 12lbs. extra. 2 miles. 10s entry. 2s 6d bookage.

2.15.—THE FARMERS' PLATE, £21.

Of which the second horse will receive £1. For horses the property of Farmers or Tradesmen. 4 yrs. old, 11st; 5 yrs. old, 12st; 6 yrs. and aged, 12st. 9lbs. Horses that have won a race value £30 excluded. Allowances—Maidens allowed 12lbs; horses not maidens that have never won a race value £22 allowed 9lbs. Only one allowance can be claimed. 2 miles. FREE ENTRY. 2s 6d bookage.

3.0.—THE MOATE PLATE, £40.

Of which the second horse will receive £4. A handicap. 3 miles. A winner after publication of the weights 10lbs extra; of two races, 16lbs extra. 10s entry. 2s 6d bookage.

3.45.—A PONY PLATE, £23.

Of which the second will receive £2. A pony race for those not over 14 hands 2 inches high, and that have never won a pony race value £24. Weight for height. Those 14 hands 2 inches to carry 11st 7lbs, with an allowance of 5lbs for each half inch under that height. 10st. lowest weight. Those that have ever won a race value £21 to carry 7lbs extra. Those entered to be sold for £50 allowed 7lbs. Two miles. Entrance 10s. 2s 6d bookage.

4.30—THE SOUTH WESTMEATH HUNT CUP.

A Piece of Plate value £21. For hunters, the property of members or subscribers to the South Westmeath Hunt. Horses to have been in the possession of owner since 1st February, 1896, and a Certificate signed by the Master stating such horse has been regularly hunted during the season 1895 and 1896 must be lodged with Mr. Waters at time of weighing. Weights—12st 7lbs each. The winner of a race 7lbs extra. To be ridden by members or subscribers to the Hunt. 2½ miles. 10s entry. 2s 6d bookage.

RULES AND CONDITIONS.

Entries are accepted conditional that there is no appeal to a court of law.

The Stewards reserve full power over the interpretation of the articles and qualifications to enter.

The courses are about the distances stated in the articles.

If less than 8 entries for any Race, the Committee reserve power to cancel, or keep open for second entries at an extra fee of 10s over first entry.

Any entry may be rejected unless the entrance money and bookage (*vide* Rule 182 I.N.H.S. Rules) be sent with entry.

Colours for Riders (not registered) to be sent with entry. Any jockey riding in a colour not on the card will be fined 1 sov. This rule will be strictly enforced.

Free Stabling on application to the Hon. Sec.

Horses carried back free by Railway Companies.

Ballycumber Station, on the Great Southern and Western Railway, is only two and a-half miles from Moate.

Ponies must be on the Course for measurement at Twelve o'clock.

Advertisement for Moate Races in 1896

BALLYMORE RACES 1843 - 1857

Like many other places racing at Ballymore was sporadic. In 1843 it was held in February but the prize money was low and it was a bit out of the way in the view of some people. Around 10,000 people still attended the meeting. The course had to be covered twice to run a 2 mile steeplechase with 15 fences. Most were fair except for the stone wall and a high narrow-backed fence, both artificial & anything but sporting. Mr Browne's horse Fencer won the first heat easily but his jockey Kenny was overconfident and gave Miss Stapely too much of a lead to win the second heat. Only three were left for the third heat and when Fencer fell at the 5th fence, Miss Stapely went on to finish on her own. In 1844, they decided to have a two day meeting (10th-11th February) with The Megan Cup with 20 sovereigns added the feature, plus the Garrison Stakes confined to the military. Amazingly, Mr Browne's Mayboy beat Miss Stapely in two pulsating heats winning by a head and a neck, getting sweet revenge. The Ballymore Challenge Cup was won by Mr Fitzgerald's Allspice beating Mr Wyer's Betsy.

FACTION FIGHT IN A PITILESS STORM AND ARRESTS MADE BY "BOOKEY"

In February 1845, the meeting was hit by a *"pitiless storm"* according to the Westmeath Guardian.The carriage stand was quite full and some horsemen braved the pelting rain. Mr Malone's Insect (Maloney) won two of the three heats in the Megan Cup ahead of Mr Bond's Blue Maid (Abbot) and Mr Fitzgerald's All Spice. The Farmer's Race was won by Mr Casey's Guarantee, who had been ploughing all season and he turned down £60 for the horse after the race.

On the first day a faction fight broke out between two parties on the course. The police interfered and took some prisoners even though assaulted by stones. One man McCaffrey was knocked off his horse by a stone and others received injuries. Three were arrested and Mr Bookey (appropriate name!) Sub Inspector, received an order to proceed to Ballymore with 20 policemen, accompanied by Head Constable Horne and 10 men from other stations also came to assist Mr Bookey in the operation. One horse fell carrying Darby Casey and he was injured when the mare rolled on him. In 1846, Captain Gamble of Washford agreed to become a Steward and he put up a Silver Cup and 5 sovereigns. The meeting was held in February on the Milltown course and the Clerk of the Course was John Hoare. Mr Malone's Insect (by Verulam) repeated his win of the previous year with Maloney on board beating Mr Naghten's Prince Albert & Allspice and turned out the next day to win the Gamble Cup.

The meeting in 1847 was postponed until 13th December. The Megan Cup had

9 runners but 6 were distanced after the first race. It came down to a match between Insect (Maloney) and Mr Moorehead's Cruikshanks, who just failed by a length to stop Mr Malone keeping the trophy after three consecutive wins. Unfortunately, as the tents were being taken down a row broke out and not even the police or clergy could stop it, as *"many skulls were laid bare".* The loss of the Megan Cup and the on-going fighting led to the end of this meeting but by 1857 a local meeting was held again and E. Irwin won again with Dunmurray D. Meaney) in a sweepstakes of 60 sovs.

OTHER MEETINGS - TWO JOCKEY'S TOOK REFUGE IN THE DITCH FROM THE RAIN

The old Rathowen Races were revived in September 1901 on the Joanstown Course given by R.H.Bond with Tim O'Dea, Secretary and John Tynan, Clerk of the Course. They went on for a few years and even in 1909 a point to point it was held on Carrigy's land at Rathganny and again in 1911. After a lapse of 52 years the Milltown Races were revived in 1909 thanks to William Lennon, Chairman. The Hunters Chase was won by H.Russell's Spotless (M.Browne), The Hunters Flat Race went to J. Byrnes Dairy Meadow (M.Cunningham) and T.Lennon won the Hack Race with Harrigan & the Pony race with Little Annie. Other meetings were held in 1910 and 1912 ('£4-19s races'). Delvin races were held at Mooretown Course with the featured Delvin Challenge Cup of 50 sovereigns. Mr Connolly's Tidings won two of the three heats. The race was left between two old 13 yo mares with Lord Howth's Betsy Bedlam beating Tidings in the first heat. They battled it out again in the second heat with Tidings winning by a length and in the final heat they ploughed through the fields as Tidings won by a 1/2 length. The course was 2 miles long with 14 jumps but no *"raspers"*, except a high ditch & grip plus a stone wall 4 feet high. Corkaree races are first mentioned in 1838 and took place over the Multyfarnhan (Fearbranagh) course and five horses competed in the Farmer's Challenge Cup of £20. Percy Nugent donated a plough for another race and the following year it was in Grange when Mr Gaynors Quakerness won the cup. It was held in various places like Ballindurrow 1840, Bunbrosna 1841, and Soho 1842 where the weather was terrible. Mr Gaynor's Smallhopes won the Cup beating Mr De Blaquieres Penelope and Mr Jessops Paganini. After being unseated, two jockeys took refuge in the ditch from the rain. The races ended until 1869, when they were revived at Bunbrosna. A great attendance brought back fond memories and in 1870 it was in Ballinafid on a course provided by Mr Nally. The weight for age race was interesting as the winner was Mr Purcell's Jolly Girl who ran in the Irish Grand National in 1871. Within a few years the races lapsed again although revived in 1881, when held near Multyfarnham Railway Station. Short term races were also held at Leney, Bunbrosna and Multyfarnhan at the *"old Ballinderra course".*

BIRR RACES

Race meetings were held in Birr sporadically in the first half of the 19th century with Mr Kirwan's Drone winning a prize of £50 in October 1802 beating Mr Kelly & Captain Caldwell. Meetings were held in 1802, 1810/14, 1817/18, 1828, 1837, 1839/44, and 1846/50 at Birr. In 1817 the Marquis of Sligo won a stake of 20 guineas with Tenpenny from Mr Kirwans Platoff. In 1855 races were held at Clonkelly, Crinkle on the lands of Thomas Hackett and they were also held there during the 1860's. The Secretary was George Dooley, Royal Arms Hotel, Birr The races were not great with walk overs and easy win's as Mr Walshe's Noisy Boy and Mr Thompson's Grizette outdistanced their rivals in the first heat. This was probably why the races were not held again until 1860 at Ballyatty near Sharavogue, where there was a great view of the course *"as you could see the cars, gigs, carts, nondescript vehicles, and others on foot".* Mr Fitzpatrick's Post Horn (Chiffney) won the first race after much controversy, when Twilight pulled up after two laps thinking it was over and Pass Horn went on to win. The judge decided there was *"misdirection"* to Twilight's jockey M. Broderick and decided to race again. The other two owners refused and Captain Shaw's Twilight was given the race.

In the 1880's racing became more developed in the Birr area and the revival took place in 1886, after 18 years, under the auspices of Secretary/Treasurer J.P. Fagan. It was held at Clonbeg on 6th April and races included the Kings County Hunt Race of £4 for Kings County & Ormonde Hunt, Cob Plate £4-19s, Farmers Race £4-19s, Pony Race £4, Military Chase for Officers based in Birr and a Consolation Stakes for £3. Races run by the Irish National Hunt Committee had prize money from £5 up and this is why the *"£4-19s"* races arose as they were not within the rules of racing. There were portable shops with tempting cakes, all kinds of games & tricks and even a group singing a mournful song about the Land League & Boycotting. The first race at 2PM was a Cob Plate and was started by Gerald Ryall. Rev Frost a Catholic priest accompanied many of the riders on his horse part of the way and jumped some of the fences. The first race was won by Mr Lewis's Little Ned (M.Horan) and he was carried shoulder high by the *"peasants"* after the race. Lord Huntington rode J.P.Fagan's horse Ravensdale in the hunt race. As the came to the last jump a stone wall the young Lord raced into the lead and to great cheers galloped home to success.

1887 "MARK ANTHONY" AND THE "YOUNG DEMOISELLE"

All classes were present from the Earl to the Beggar at Clonbeg, but this time the reporters both local and from Dublin were not happy. The stand house was a problem as people could not see the main fence or final fence from the stand and it was suggested that it be moved back for a better view. It was painful to see the crowds pouring on to the track during races and especially near the finish, where several were knocked down. It was also mentioned that there was no need for the security forces to be going around with guns, when batons would suffice if there was trouble. All in all the committee were left with plenty to think about. J.P. Fagan won again on his good hunter Ravensdale in the Welter Race, but when he turned out again in the Hunt Race it was a comedy of errors. Lovely Weather won the race but was disqualified then Ravensdale was also disqualified for carrying the wrong weight, as he should have carried 7lbs extra for winning the first. The winner eventually was Roelight owned by Mr A. Nolan.

In 1888 (17th May), the committee changed the course from Clonbeg to Thomas Wallaces land at Castletown, which was a wise move. The going was much better for the horses, even though the number of runners didn't improve. One strapping young man carrying a stone to break on his chest *"with a head and a chest like Mark Anthony"* passed some remark with a wink to a *"young demoiselle"* who blushed and ran away. Mr J Meredith had a double with Mocking Bird and Pinkeen.

In 1889, the races were held again at Castletown for a meeting on 9th September. The prize money varied from the five races from £21-£25 with the Birr Plate the feature at 50 sovereigns. On the road to the course the *"noble donkey"* competed with the more aristocratic neighbours. Five jumps were set up by Messrs Waters of Monastrevan. John Galbraith and Mr Rochfort, Secretary were busy on the track and Captain W.E. Head, Lord Huntington, and Assheton Biddulph MFH did their best to keep the track clear but in spite of their efforts a few were injured near the winning post. A man from Aghancon called Simms and a pensioner Connolly, Birr had stomache and hip injuries. Connolly had lost his leg in the Crimea War and therefore the hip injury was very serious for him. In racing terms Frank Mitchell's future Irish Grand National winner The Admiral was ridden to success by him in the Stewards Plate A.J. Pilkington a leading trainer in this era in Westmeath won with Country Dance (P. Fiely) 2/1.

In May 1890, the Secretary was Dr J.W.Goldon and the Treasurer William O'Meara. Improvements were made to the fence in the hollow and the last fence. The races were not always supported on a national level with a few exceptions like Mr M. Dennehy, French House, The Curragh, who won with Miss Lurgan and F.F. Cullen, Rossmore Lodge, who won with Mr Coghlan's Crescent. John Hubert Moore at 80y/o attended the meeting and W. Ronaldson gave the ride of the meeting when only third on Tanner Girl to Galway mare Widgeon (Mr M.Harty), as he went two rounds with broken traces and could have been thrown at any fence.

In April 1891, a meeting was held in Dooly's Hotel to arrange for the races. The erection of the stand cost £40 in 1890 and it was necessary to reduce it. Estimates were £28 for timber and £5 for erection. A permanent stand would need three walls and £40 but by June they had secured sufficient funds to run the races. The races on 11th June 1891, which was a beautiful day, were very successful. In this era Thomas Brindley was Clerk of the Course and J.Dibbs the Starter at most meetings. Unfortunately, only 20 runners turned out for the five races. The popular Thomas Lewis won the hunter chase with Starlight but was disqualified, as Major Craddock's horse was not a proper hunter and the race went to the favourite Merry Heart.

1892 - A FIASCO AND "AS DEAD AS JULIUS CAESAR'S TOM CAT"

It was a nice spring day for racing in May 1892. The course was passed by Parnell Gilpin, and the run home was well kept by Assheton Biddulph MFH, Ormonde Hunt and E.F. Saunders, who were dressed in their brilliant hunting costumes. A few reports referred to problems like poor facilities for the press and the small fields of only 17 runners in five races. However, the Kings County Chronicle had a different view describing it as a *"fiasco"* and a *"failure".* The reporter stated that *"under the present management the Birr meeting is fast degenerating to very little better than an ass race".* He stated that it was necessary to reconstitute the race committee or *"the Birr race meeting is as dead as Julius Caesar's tom cat".* He claimed that they had never published a balance sheet showing expenditure and their idea of success was *"the gathering of thousands of people together to bite their finger nails on the course, drink whiskey on the stand, or fight for spite".*

The races were held on 2nd May 1893, at Castletown and Mr Wallace had the land in great condition for the meeting. In March the committee were trying to raise subscriptions to run the meeting and and some complaints were made that business people who benefitted were not *"liberal"* in subscribing. They had a new Treasurer in J.F.Dooly and J.W.Nolan was a new Secretary. It was described as better than Clonbeg and Clonkelly, as a course but it suffered from small fields, firm ground, and it came after many other meetings including Fairyhouse & Punchestown. Young Aubrey Hastings who was to train four Grand National winners some years later was unplaced in the Stewards Plate riding Laurence Taylor's Lady Rose in a race won by the legendary champion Irish trainer/jockey J.J.Parkinson (his first winner in Birr) with Noiseless 2/1F.

In 1894, some small improvements were made to the stand and some stewards were placed at the bend to ensure proper riding. A big marquee was set up that night and it brought some itinerant musician's but the number staying in hotels was down. The Stewards Plate of 25 sovereigns was the most interesting race as M.J. Harty's Apollo's dead heated with T.J. Maher's Norissa ridden by Mr

J.Taaffe over 2 miles. After passing the post, Apollo collided with one of the mounted stewards leading to him being knocked down and Mr Harty shaken. Then Mr Harty objected to Mr Taaffe for foul riding which was over ruled. They went out for a second heat and although Apollo was apparently hindered, he managed to win the race. In May 1896, the last Birr races of the 19th century was held at Crinkle. A large crowd attended at the new course and £120 was taken at the grand stand. The weather was balmy and the course within walking distance of the town. The problem was again only 18 runners participated in five races, with Frank Mitchell supplying three of them. Amy 4/7F & Ambrose 2/1 had been beaten in Nenagh on Wednesday but both won at Crinkle John H.Locke from Kilbeggan Distillery won with his Tullamore specialist Cowslip 4/5F.

BIRR RACES 1901 - 1907

The Birr races were revived on Monday 29th April 1901, with £150 in prize money and significantly the advertisements were headed *"Birr Steeplechases and Flat Races"*. The latter had played very little part in the history of racing in Birr and it seems likely that it was to try to improve the number of runners. This time they had Joint Secretaries in J.W.Nolan and G.Browne. The Treasurer was G.Etherton, Hibernian Bank, Birr. The Committee was R.F.Barry, H.V.Goldon, H.Gairdner, Wm and M.J. O'Meara, Richard Wallace, James Dooley, John Dooley, P.J. White, D.P. Clavin, P. L'Estrange, H.S. Henny, J. Wright, J.F. Dooley, J. Powell, H.S. Davidge, R. Jackson, D.J. O'Regan MD, and D. Doorly JP. Subscriptions and investment were the two keys for initial success. The races were held at a former old racecourse on Mr Marshall's land in Caherhoerigh about 1 1/2 miles from the town.

The town, including all three banks, were closed for the day, as contingents from all parts of the compass in cars, brakes, and bikes began to arrive and by 10.30am the town was packed with people arriving by train. The Young Mens Society Band played a selection of tunes from marches to Irish songs like *"Garryowen"*. A 1/2 hour delay occurred when the favourite Old Beau in the first race was killed at the regulation fence and it took a long time to get him out. E.P.Ryan contributed on the double by winning the last two races with The Nore 3/1 and Clear Note 5/4, both ridden by E.Sullivan. The Foxhunters Plate had 15 runners, and the favourite D.Craigs Kylemore 2/1F won.

In 1902, the stand was rebuilt and extended but the crowd was somewhat smaller. The best race was the Stewards Plate won by Mr T.L. Smith's Fortune Hunter and he held off Metal Man and G.W.Robinson's, interestingly named Here She is Punchestown.The Committee Plate flat race had an even money favourite, E. Richies Matagon ridden by E Sullivan and he won impressively by 4 lengths. Sullivan had another double with E.P.Ryan's Clear Note1/1F. In 1903 the reporter claimed that even the card sellers blamed the committee. It was a difficult time with land issues related to the hunt and rights of tenants and farmers all coming to the forefront. It seemed that local people were not supporting the races, as much as expected. In 1904 John Dooley JP and Chairman proposed that they have three hurdle races and three flat races with no chases to get larger fields. The National Hunt Committee turned it down, as the programme remained 4 chases and a flat race for the 2nd May 1904. In fairness to the Committee the flat race had 12 runners and always had the most runners. H.V. Jackson dominated the day with 2 winners in the Committee Flat Race of 25 sovs with Bould Derry 5/1 (R. Sherwin) carrying 10st 9lbs and the Birr Plate with Little David 3/1 (P. Sherwin).

On 28th April 1905 it was held again in Caherhoerigh and it was advertised that the Great Southern & Western Railway would bring horses free and ample stable accommodation was available.There was also the issue of collecting subscriptions from local businesses but then getting outsiders to print the cards and do other tasks, which would not help the cause. H.V.Jackson had another double with Black Friar and Clear Artist both ridden by J.Smyth. The Kenny's took each other on in the Ormond Hunt Cup and H.B.Kenny won with Adopted Boy who was an own brother to Standard Bearer, who won the previous year.

MERRY MAY FINALE

It seemed that this was to be the last Birr Races, but in spite of great negativity the Committee persisted and put on the races on 25th April 1907, even with only 22 runners. It was ironic that J.J.Parkinson decided to send a runner, after a number of years, for a 2 miles chase. Golden Morn was 5/4 JF for a 2 mile chase but was a poor jumper and ended up last of three. Mr Ferzen's Annie Symon's had won some races around the country and she added to her successes by winning the Corinthian Welter Plate at even money. The final race at Birr was won by Mr T.J.Daly's Merry May 6/4 (J.Rafferty), who appropriately finished alone not knowing that it was truly the end for Birr. Some years the crowds were excellent but it never attracted many runners, didn't have local financial support, clashed with other meetings, and probably had a wrong programme to attract horses.

TULLAMORE RACES 1850 - 1904

On 24th April 1850 the Tullamore Challenge Cup was raced for at Ballykilmurray within a few miles of the town. The cup had £10 added and it was won by Mr Patrick Boylan's Paddy Carey from William Kelly's Peg Waters over 2 heats. The other races were a Lady's Purse of 3 sovereigns won by John Green's Mavourneen, who was a regular horse around the midland courses. In 1851 the

Stewards included S.Drought, Paul Fawcett, R. Scally, N.M.Delamere, J.Belton, Joseph Fuller, Alexander McMullen, Treasurer, and John Guilfoyle, Secretary. The races were held over 2 heats. Around 120 members of the RIC from Tullamore to Kinnity were present under the control of DI Gamble & Inspector Garrett. As one paper reported they marched to the course *"in clouds of dust in perfect formation"* and were led by Constable Phillips. Their presence prevented rows & thieves, in addition to crushing at certain points. Mr Connolly's Dove won the Challenge Cup by a neck from Mr Green's Brown Bess. Mr Colgan's Hoggerwolf won the Tullamore Stakers beating Mr O'Sheas horse. In 1852 there was a two day meeting with the Ballymooney Steeplechase Cup value 50 sovereigns and it was confined to horses within 12 miles of Ballymooney. The Challenge Cup for those residing in the King's County or within 20 miles of Tullamore was won by Mr Smith's Napier (Cowell) in both heats. In May 1854 the ground was so hard that the only race was the Ballymooney Cup of two runners, with Mr Meredith's Verulam (Jones) beating Mr McMullen's Nanny over 3 heats.

A JOCKEY KILLED AND A "STEEPLECHASE AT MIDNIGHT"

In 1856, in the Ballymooney Cup there was a tragedy on the second lap of the first heat when St Canice attempted to jump a fence at the winning post field but hit it and rolled over on top of the jockey Darby Jennings, who was killed almost instantly. Another horse fell over him but the Jockey F. Martin was uninjured and remounted to finish second in the heat. He went on to win the next two heats on H. Thompson's Grizette and win the trophy. It was a tragic day for everyone involved but the risks were very high for jockey's riding on temporary tracks. The Stewards had changed considerably by March 1858 with Loftus H. Bland MP, P. O'Brien MP, J. Yourell, Bernard Daly, T.M. Biddupph, J.W. Tarleton and N. Delamere, Secretary. It is not clear if some internal difficulties occurred or that it related to the death of the jockey. In 1859 a new branch of the Great Southern Railway from Tullamore to Athlone arrived and this affected the programme, as part of the bend on the course was taken. The Ballymooney Cup was won by Mr H. Thompson's Fairy Anne (jockey Dan Henry) beating Mr Sterling's Mary Anne (Tobin). In 1860, Col J.C. Westenra and J. Pope Hennessy were additional Stewards, but heavy showers and hail delayed proceedings. Mr Connolly's Tenant Right won the Ballymooney Cup, but he was lucky in that Gladiator went the wrong side of a pole. Mr Scott's Little Bob repeated his previous win on the track in the Tullamore Handicap beating local landlord Lord de Freyne's Little Charlie. Many bets were struck as the two horses battled it out for the last 1/2 mile - a bit like Betfair in the 21st century.

A fine April day was a good sign in 1861 but delays at the start meant a late evening. Mr Cusack's horse Canary (D.Meany) won the Cup beating Mr Cassidy's Trunculo, but the latter later won with Ben Brace (Hanlon) who beat the Marquis of Drogheda horse The Twin. The races gradually seemed to be running into difficulties, as there were only two races in 1862 and even then they caused problems. In the Free Handicap, Mr Bigg's Mont Blanc won beating Mr Dunnes Phoenix, but there was an objection for going the wrong side of a post & it was referred to The Curragh for a decision. In 1864 Captain Beresford's Signal (J.Murphy) won the Free Handicap and Lord Conyngham's Paris also won. Racing ended around this time probably for economic reasons or lack of support in difficult times. We live in an era of *"selfies"* and *"self-promotion"*, where people try anything for attention, perhaps a novel *"Steeplechase at Midnight"* might appeal to them. In 1864, at the Dowdallshill Course in Louth, a Lieutenant Farquhar of the 4th Dragoons, decided to ride a 3 mile steeplechase course on his mare Annie at midnight. He did it unscathed, winning £100 in bets. Hopefully, Annie got her oats too.

MICHAEL GORRY TOWN CRIER WAS "GLISTENING IN THE SUNSHINE"

The revival meeting in 1885 had inauspicious weather but a thronging crowd. The Committee were P. Egan TC, W.Adam's TC, A. Connolly JP, F. Biddulph, W. Hoey, P. Lenihan, A. O'Carroll, C. Kenny, J. Sheil, C. Quirke, Dr Carr and B. Smith. The Ballymooney Cup of £50 was back with the Tullamore Plate £60, and the Ballykilmurray Plate of £40. After nearly 20 years the races were back and one local paper reported *"it does not seem to have lost any of its pristine attractiveness"*. The streets were crowded, as they went into the Charleville Arms Hotel and then a *"surging mass"* headed for the races from the Dublin, Athlone, Cork, Portarlington trains. The only real crib was the tall trees that interspersed the track & blocked the view from the stand. J.L. Sterling was the Secretary and the driving force. Major Trocke the well-known jockey rode his own horse Brown Betty, one of the few favourites to win. Other major figures in racing in this era were all at the Tullamore races like W.P.Cullen from Galway(who won three Galway Plates between 1885-96), Willie & Harry Beasley from the great family of jockey's, Rice Meredith (who trained four Irish Derby winners), Richard Brabazon of the famous Westmeath racing family, and Frank Mitchell who trained The Admiral.

Gorry's news agency was legendary in Tullamore long after Tullamore Races was gone but Mickey Gorry was on the track, as a sort of town crier announcing the *"correct card"*. Mr Gorry was spotted on one occasion at the races *"wearing a hunting frock coat of flaming red with brass buttons, glistening in the sunshine"*. He was also ringing his bell as he announced the sale of the race cards (sold about 900). In May 1886, the rain poured down for 2 days before the races, as people went the 2 1/2 mile journey to the track on everything from a four wheeled dray to Tom Carpenter's family car in ankle deep muck. Rice Meredith won the Farmers Plate on his horse Sorrow 6/4F and Mr Latham won on Sunlight in the Challenge Cup.

THACKERAY SAID AN IRISHMAN WOULD GO 160 MILES TO A RACES

William Makepeace Thackeray in his Irish Sketch Book mentioned that an Irishman would travel 160 miles for a race meeting. The entertainers, the three card trick men, thimble riggers, Aunt Sallys etc often had to travel long distances by hitching lifts on trains to get from one race meeting to another. The Kings County Chronicle reporter in March 1887 had little sympathy. He said that they degraded racing with their *"shabby genteel clothes, dirty hands, absence of linen and dingy faces did not we are happy to say attract attention"*. The big problem at the track was people racing out through the ropes to see the finish. In a race won by Waxy Timmy a young man rushed out and did not see two late finishers, who knocked him over but he was not seriously injured. James Cheshire who won the Irish Grand National on Patlander in 1902 and the Galway Plate on Boreenchreogue added to those successes by winning on Mr McManus's horse Beatrice in the Ballymooney Cup. Before the 1888 meeting, the Committee decided to cut down the tall trees in the centre and also some fences that did not leave enough room for a few horses to jump together. The big stable of C.J. Blake, The Heath, Portlaoise, won the Tullamore Plate with Dismantine (Harris) and W. Coghlan's Lochinvar (who was 2nd in the Irish Grand National in 1890) won the Farmer's Race ridden by W.P. Cullen. The Ballymooney Cup was won by Count G.Erdody's Eccentric a son of Aintree Grand National winner Empress. In 1890 there was a local success in the Ballymooney Cup won by W.Meredith with Geashill (E. Malone), who was trained privately in Tullamore. It is interesting that some of the top families in racing were supporting Tullamore races including Linde, Cullen, Blakes, Moore, Brabazon, Meredith etc, so it is not clear why the races was not held again until 1893. A lack of local subscriptions and financial support, causing disputes was often a big factor as shown at other courses.

A NEW COMMITTEE AND CRUSHED ALMOST TO JELLY!

The new committee announced in March 1893 that a meeting would be held in June. The races were held on Mr Gonoude's land at Ballykilmurray. The place and the stand was overhauled completely and made more suitable for a larger attendance. A section was set aside for the ladies for the first time and it was a half crown extra for the men to stay with them. Captain Bernard Daly was the force behind it and he was noted for his open hospitality in Tullamore at race time and on the course. William Hoey was Secretary at this time. The races were won by J.H. Moore with Captain Lloyd's Cranagh in the Tally Ho Plate and Mr Bull's Toss Up won the Ballymooney Cup. V.J. Blakes prolific winner Lognavadogue also won by making all the running.

The Grand Stand had around 150 vehicles with Captain Daly & Mr Locke dispersing hospitality. The cycling fraternity were supplied by Messrs Walsh, Crinkle, Molloy & Guinan, even against the blinding dust and crowded traffic.

Brakes were supplied by Dooley's & Mathews Hotels, Birr. Larry Hope, won with Traynor in the Provincial Plate and Frank Mitchell rode V.J.Blakes Loughnavadoge to win the Ballykilmurray Plate. The real drama occurred when a man called Davey, Ballinagar was seriously injured (described as *"crushed almost to jelly"*), when C.Taaffes Bloomfield (jockey Mr J.P.Taaffe) crossed another horse Kohima at the last fence, forcing him & jockey Barnes on to the rails. They crashed through it and Davey was struck & had to be rushed to Tullamore Hospital. Kohima had a stake driven through him & Barnes was also injured. Taaffe was suspended by the Stewards, but he appealed without success. The fact that Kohima was the favourite caused some tension in the crowd. In 1895 it was said that a 1,000 stood on the stand. James Coles Millie was a lucky winner when Larry Hopes Bit of Lightning was disqualified for crossing.

WATER CART DAMPENS DOWN THE DUST AND BARBOUR CRASHES INTO A TREE

In May 1896, the beautiful weather meant that the water cart was brought in to dampen down the dust created by the traffic. The fences were better designed with *"no ugly swerves on the fences"*, as one paper reported. The enclosure was enlarged and the *"pretty paling"* moved to a new site. The Secretary, T.Freyne was busy ensuring that everything was in order. Alice Boyd-Rochfort was a young 19 y/o woman & sister of Cecil. On this day she won the Ballymooney Cup with Vexation (W.Costello) and also won in 1898 with Cavan Lass II. Lord Greville had a rare win with Bonnie Rath. Frank Barbour rode in the Tally Ho Plate and nearly got killed when he was thrown from his horse, as it crashed into a tree. Springfield won in 1898 in the Provincial Plate beating big race winners Boreenchreogue & The Admiral and J.H.Locke's Cowslip also repeated his previous success with Cowslip. The most amazing winner was C.Gaynor's Springfield, as he fell at the first and then remounted to win. In 1899 Alice Boyd Rochfort continued her success rate with Cherry Hampton winning the Ballymooney Cup.

PENNY WISE AND POUND FOOLISH AT LAST RACES

The new century started with Westmeath horses again dominating. P. Casey's Bullfinch won the opening race but he went the wrong side of a post and the runner-up James Yourell's Lady Angelos took the prize when he was disqualified. This was followed by Captain Dewhurst's Wildflower trained by A.J. Pilkington; J.J. Hams Springfield won the Ballymooney Cup; and H.B. Blacks Glencoe completed the quartet of successes. In 1901 J.J.Ham repeated his success with Springfield in the Ballymooney Cup beating Bernica by 2 lengths. The committee received great praise for their layout and control of the large crowds. In 1902 visitors were taken care of by Captain Daly, Dr Moorehead, and J.H. Locke. The fields continued to be small with only 23 runners for 5 races. All the businesses closed for the races and assistants were allowed go to the races. Harold Boyd Rochfort had a winner with The Unknown ridden by M. Lowe. James Cheshire the well-known jockey and the trainer was injured when his horse had a crashing fall in the Ballymooney Cup and he broke his leg. Mrs F.L. Rochforts horse Well Done won the race.

One reporter wrote *"there is nothing half so magnetic for drawing such a large crowd of all classes as the Sport of Kings".* It was either too firm or too heavy but the reality was that horses were not being entered in Tullamore in sufficient numbers. The maiden plate had no runners and only 17 runners in total turned up for 4 races and the majority came from Westmeath stables. The meeting was not supported by subscriptions like others (Kilbeggan was revived in 1901). Another problem was that the course did not give a full view of each race and the other big issue with Tullamore was that it was not advertised properly. As stated in one paper *"a policy of pennywise and pound foolish has been adopted".* A few pounds were saved by not advertising but hundreds were lost from lack of support, which affected the prestige of the meeting. The papers even commented that business people like Captain Daly, R.Bull, J.H.Locke, B.S.Mara, W.R.Power, J & M.C. Quirke and T.Frayne, Secretary *"seemed to be asleep".* The reality was that 56 horses were entered and only 17 ran, which was a disaster. Course specialist Merville was 5/2F in the Tullamore Plate, especially after being 2nd at Leopardstown but Mrs Fetherstonhaugh's horse Friendship (E.Graham) proved too strong. The Ballymooney Cup was won for the last time by Hilary1/1F, who won in a canter beating Harry Whitworth's Little Peg. The final winner at Ballykilmurray races was The Hawk 1/2F (Anthony) owned and trained by D.Shanahan, The Curragh. It was a disappointing end to 18 years of endeavour at Ballykilmurray and it seemed that the committee felt it was going nowhere.

John Preston's Brunette who won the Westmeath Urn four years in a row (1842-45) and also the famous Kilrue Cup four times (1843-46)

The Westmeath Challenge Cup Urn

Colonel J.C.Westenra, Offaly was the leading owner in Irish racing and won the most prize money four times between 1843/1848

Captain Reginald Greville Nugent was a great jockey in this era, and tragically was killed in 1878

The hoof of Drumcree, winner of the Aintree Grand National 1903

Why Not won the Aintree Grand National in 1894 and was bred by Sir Percy Nugent's aunt Miss Fitzgerald Nugent

Drumcree won the 1903 Aintree Grand National for the Nugent family

Ascetic Silver winner of the Aintree Grand National in 1906 and was trained by Aubrey Hastings from Offaly

Leslie Brabazon and Harry Ussher on The Miner after both fell in the Aintree Grand National in 1913 (from Racing Through My Mind by Aubrey Brabazon)

Ally Sloper was the first Aintree Grand National winner to be owned by a woman Lady Nelson from Gartlandstown, Westmeath

Shaun Spadah, the winner of the Aintree Grand National in 1921. He won in Kilbeggan in 1917

Sergeant Murphy the winner of the Aintree Grand National in 1923

Dick Cleary's House and Stables at Bishopstown, where Michael Jackson almost came to stay?

Richard G. and Catherine Cleary

"Atty" Persse, Frank Barbour, Reggie Walker and G.A.Boyd Rochfort at Barbour Cup day in Slanemore in the early C20

The Athlone Race Committee preparing for the races in 1914

From Left to Right - Pat, Michael and Dick Cleary who contributed so much to racing in Westmeath

Mrs Muriel McCall the founder of Tally Ho Stud and she ran it for 50 years

Culleen House was owned by T.M.Reddy who made his fortune in Argentina before returning to Ireland and having success with his horses

chapter 4

THE LIGHTER SIDE OF RACING OR THE CORONER WHO PUT THE BODY ON ICE

A series of articles by Leslie Brabazon in the Irish Press in the 1930's and Aubrey Brabazon's memoir *Racing Through My Mind,* give a good idea of a different world of racing in the early part of 20th century. A time with less emphasis on political correctness, patrol cameras, whip controversies, and more on humour or pulling the odd stroke. The Brabazon family are long associated with Westmeath and racing, from the time of William T. Brabazon, Johnstown House near Mullingar who later moved to Woodlands, Multyfarnham. (Cecil & his brother Leslie later trained at Rossmore Lodge, The Curragh). His son Cecil was a successful jockey & trainer and his grandson Aubrey is remembered as one of the great jockey's associated with many racing champions on the flat & over the jumps. He won 3 Gold Cups, 2 Champion Hurdles, Irish 2,000gns, Irish Oaks, Champion Jockey 1949 etc.

Cecil's brother Leslie in many ways was the most interesting of the family. He rode his first winner on Wrong Age at Skerries Strand in 1907. The horse was owned by Christopher Hope, Mabestown, Delvin, Co Westmeath. He was champion amateur jockey on six occasions and overall Irish Champion in 1913 (37 winners) and 1914 (39 winners). He rode in the Aintree Grand National on two occasions on The Miner in 1913 and the favourite Irish Mail (pu) in 1915 before his career was cut short after a serious injury at Tramore in September 1915 (which left him in a coma for 98 days). He rode again subsequently and trained horses for a time but was never quite the same. He once rode 11 winners in a week -2 at Kells, 4 at Longfield and 5 at Mullingar.

Aubrey recounts the story of Leslie arriving in Ballyhaunis one evening for a ride on a well- fancied mare in a chase the following day. The problem was that the mare hated open ditches and was likely to refuse at the jump. To overcome this problem Leslie and Harry Ussher went out in the middle of the night with a can of petrol and burned the fence to the ground thus resolving the problem (Warning - punter's or jockey's nowadays should not attempt this tactic or they could be prosecuted!). Leslie Brabazon recounts a fascinating story of a race that ended in a court case involving a famous old character called Coroner Friery who always wore a top hat & attended race meetings all over Ireland. A story was told of him being at Galway Races when he got a wire summoning him to Dublin to hold an important inquest. Coroner's as they say were not *"two a penny".* However this did not influence Coroner Friery who without qualms wired back and told them to put the corpse on ice! He must have had some good tips for Galway.

A BRISK BETTING MARKET IN COURT!

The race that caused all the controversy was held in Kells. Leslie rode Lisngarvey for Larry Hope and his brother Cecil rode Another Delight for Christopher Hope and only three ran. It was a mile flat race and all the money was on Lisnagarvey. Before the race, Leslie had to take some lead out of the saddle cloth before his weight was right. He won the race easily but when he got on the scales he was a stone too light, as the Clerk made a mistake & he had to be disqualified, leaving Cecil as winner of the race at 6/1. One bookie Jack Casey lost £600 on the race & a week later in Ballinasloe in a hotel he accused Leslie of cheating. He refused to withdraw it & Leslie took him to court.

Casey's Solicitor was the same Coroner Friery (!) and Eddie Shaw, Mullingar acted for Leslie. Shaw was also a great sportsman & Leslie won the Westmeath Hunt Cup for him on Ilovit. When the case started there was strong betting in the courtroom with Casey at 4/6 to win. As the case proceeded voices could be heard shouting *"I'll take £60 to £40 Casey".* Casey started to drift in the betting, as bets were put on Leslie to win, when the jury went to consider the verdict. Nearly £1,000 changed hands in the ante post betting market during the case. When the jury returned with the verdict there was dead silence in the court, but Leslie won the case and the jury awarded him £10 damages (he was only an amateur). Leslie and Casey were the best of friends afterwards. He recalled that the Marquis of Headford used to throw a big luncheon party for all at Kell's races and you never left thirsty or hungry - but particularly you never left thirsty!

A RACE WITH NO WINNER AND A RACE WON TWICE ON THE SAME DAY

Leslie Brabazon rode a horse called Marble Hall one day at The Curragh in a 1 1/2 mile race against St Dunstan ridden by John Doyle and Bell H ridden by J. Thompson. He thought he had no chance and his money went on St Dunstan. The other two were fighting out the finish and Thompson tried to snatch a length or two at the bend but the horse swerved and ran into a pillar and was killed instantly. St Dunstan romped home and Leslie was second. Shortly afterwards the objection flag was raised and it was discovered that St Dunstan was not eligible to run in the race, leaving Marble Hall with Leslie up as the winner. That evening a trainer checked the rules of the race and discovered that it was for riders with 5lbs extra and under rules as an amateur Leslie was not eligible to ride in the race. This meant that the race was declared void as the only eligible horse was killed during the race.

Leslie also rode in a three horse race at Baldoyle, which he had to win twice! He rode Rayon de Sol for Maxwell Arnott in a 1mile 7 furlong hurdle race. One horse tore loose at the start with bared teeth and made a dash for the starter Major

Blennerhassett who lashed out with his flag, which he dropped and shouted at the animal. The Major shouted *"away"* and dropped the flag. The jockeys thought he shouted *"go"* and took off. Leslie and the other jockey, jumped off thinking it was the start. His horse was in the lead all the way and finished alone, but the 2nd horse stopped and went back to the start. Then he heard it was a false start and they had to go again. Punters joked that he had run the horse off its feet and backed against him but he had the last laugh and won the race again.

CHAMPAGNE CORKS POPPING IN THE JOCKEY'S ROOM - BEFORE THE GRAND NATIONAL 1915?

Many extraordinary races have taken place since the first official Aintree Grand National race in 1839. When Leslie Brabazon rode W.A.Wallis's The Miner in the 1915 race it had its own moments. To quote him *"The morning of April 4, 1913 broke fine and clear-and yet the Grand National run that afternoon, in which I made my first acquaintance with the Liverpool fences, deserves to go down in history as one of the wettest on record".* The public never knew that cases of champagne arrived in the jockey's room shortly before the race started and all were empty before they went down to the start. As Leslie said *"Champagne corks were popping like machine guns and the contents were vanishing like snow in June".* Some of the jockey's could see two fences and jumped the wrong one! Covertcoat easily won the race and Leslie's mount The Miner landed on top of a fence. He pulled him up but on the way back he picked up Harry Ussher and carried him on the back of the horse. Mr Wallis didn't mind his horse losing but objected to him being turned into an ambulance.

CUP GOES TO BLAZES!

T.C. Foster (Died 31st May 1939-aged 87), Bunbrosna was headmaster of Farra School. At one time he was prominent figure in sporting and social life. He was associated with the Westmeath Polo Club, Cricket Club, and founder of Belvedere Rugby Club where he played as full back. In 1880/81 he was amateur lightweight Irish boxing champion, and a member of Westmeath Hunt. Before the war he owned famous chaser Sunburst II, which won a score of chases including the Cochrane Cup outright in Cavan.

Leslie had met T.C.Foster at school. Foster owned Sunburst II, which he bought after he retired from teaching. He was trained by Larry Hope at Enfield and then went to Cecil Brabazon at Multyfarnham. Leslie rode him 4/5 times to win and at Cavan he won the Cochrane Cup presented by Sir Stanley Cochrane. He was determined to win it again the following year and keep the cup but in the meantime he sold Sunburst II to Germany. He then bought a mare called You to Blazes to try to win it but the horse was so bad he wouldn't beat a clothes horse. The entry that year was the best on record, as all the best Irish horses including

Harry Ussher's Galway Plate winner Ashbrook were in the race. It seemed that all the owners & trainers thought that it would be an easy race to pick up and entered their best horse. When they saw the entries and realized how tough the race would be they all decided to take out their horses leaving just one entry - You to Blazes. Harry Ussher was a very disappointed man and if he could *"have got the horse to Cavan by telegraph he'd have done it"*. The articles for most Cup events stipulated three runners were necessary to race but a walk over was acceptable in the Cochrane Cup. A walk over was You to Blazes only chance and if he had to jump he wouldn't have got round. He strolled past the judge's box and Mr Foster won his Cup.

The 37 $^1/_2$ MINUTE RACE AT DUNMORE!

Dunmore was one of the many racecourses in existence in the early 20th century and it was about 9 miles from Tuam. Harry Ussher rode the favourite Stone Wall in a three horse race. It was the first runner for the owner T.G.Fletcher, Navan and all parties were anxious for a win. Leslie was riding Wrong Age who had a habit of refusing to jump, as did the third horse. Wrong Age ran out at the first fence and was followed by the third horse. He turned round Wrong Age & jumped the fence, only for the horse to run out at the 2nd and again he turned and jumped the fence and went in pursuit of Stone Wall. The third horse copied everything that Wrong Age did and they ran out at the 3rd and 4th fence until he eventually jumped the fifth, where the third horse fell. He galloped on hoping to get 2nd place and then found Harry & Stone Wall stuck in the regulation fence. Leslie continued on with Wrong Age refusing at different fences and when he came back to the regulation Harry had got his horse out of the ditch and joined up with Wrong Age although a full lap behind!

Gradually, the favourite pulled away from Leslie's horse, as his brute continued to refuse but when he came back to the ditch Harry was stuck in it again with the favourite. Things got worse when his horse fell over the fence, dumped him, and bolted. At this stage the crowds were laughing and cheering their heads off but they caught his horse and brought him back to Leslie, who was lying dazed on the ground. They lifted him up and put him back in the saddle and eventually he got past the post. To quote Leslie *"the race took about 37$^1/_2$ minutes to run and I imagine it must have been near a world record".* The judge Waring Willis had been seriously thinking of leaving his box with Reggie Walker and getting a side car back to Tuam to catch the train. Luckily, he stayed and he won the prize. Wrong Age had provided him with his first ever winner at Skerries Strand and the horse also went on to win races for Harry Ussher.

THE CARD GAME, THE FOAL, AND JACK McCALL

The McCall family were long associated successfully with Tally Ho stud, which is now one of the most successful studs in the world for the O'Callaghans. Jack

McCall came up to Leslie Brabazon when he was training at Bellinter near Navan to look at The Boss a stallion at a stud farm called Garlow Cross belonging to John Reid. The latter had won a Galway Plate with Royal Tara. They called to Reid's to look at a filly foal by The Boss out of Golden Hen. McCall was anxious to buy her but Reid wouldn't sell for less than £300 and he didn't want to pay that amount. McCall passed uncomplimentary remarks about the stalls and found fault with all the horses. They spotted a lovely blue-grey bullock that looked good for any prize at a show and John Reid said he would sell him for £50 but there were no takers. They adjourned to the house for a drink and John suggested a game of cards.

They played for the bullock and for some ewes and a horse (won by Leslie) with two other visitors until Reid suggested the foal *"I want to sell it but I'll tell you what I'll do. If McCall & Brabazon put up £100 each against the foal the three of us will have another game"*. At the end of a tricky game Reid won his own horse plus their £200. Even worse for McCall he decided to buy the horse and had to pay the full £300. When he sent the filly to the sales the following year he only got £75, as it proved a white elephant. Harry Ussher bought it and it turned out to be very successful. All round a bad day for Jack McCall. He used to run horses under the name of "Mr Fersen", which was a common thing at that time. The best he had were two mares called Golden Egg a good 2 y/o and Annie Symons. One day at Laytown they met two magpies and that day Jack McCall had four winners at the races. Racing is strange but as a friend of Leslies who finished 2nd said once said *"I am not beaten yet - I'm going to object"*. Perhaps racing is now better organised, more international in outlook, safer, with more quality and better courses, but is it as much fun as 50 or 100 years ago? I doubt it very much.

AUNT SALLY, THE THIMBLE-RIGGER, AND THE THREE- CARD -TRICK

Albert Einstein once said *"You can't beat a roulette table unless you steal money from it"*. Over a century ago in Ireland we had more than 50 racecourses and roulette tables were part of a whole world of entertainment on what was called the "outside" of the track. One famous autotype called *"The Outside"* by J.O'Hea was taken on the occasion of the Prince of Wales trip to Punchestown in 1868. In the background in the Stand is Prince of Wales and the gentry, but at the front on *"the outside"* are a motley crew a ballad singer, three card trick man, the thimblerigger, a bookie, a pipe smoking woman selling oranges, a pick pocket, hurdy gurdy man, a fiddler and his dog, a Punch and Judy show etc. All these were part of life at the races well into 20th century.

Authorities in 19th century Ireland viewed gatherings at sports events like horse racing as occasions for *"spirit drinking and mischief"*, such as faction fights, drunken violence, thieves, and pick pockets. For most ordinary people they were wonderful occasions that enlivened the hum drum daily existence. William Makepeace Thackeray on a visit to Killarney races in 1842 wrote *"the sight of so much happy laziness did one good to look on".* He also mentioned *"There was a brightness and intelligence about this immense Irish crowd, which I don't remember to have seen in an English one"*. The many entertainment's at race meetings included Aunt Sally, which was a game in which the head of an old woman was set up with a clay pipe in her mouth and for a penny, player's threw sticks at it to break the pipe. The trick-of-the-loop is still familiar to our present generation, where a leather belt using the figure eight was set up and for a charge you had to guess the centre of one of the loops. The Thimble-Rigger asked people to identify which of three thimbles contained a hidden pea. The thimble-rigger could hide the pea under a thumbnail and ensure that it was never under the selected thimble. The same principle applied to sleight of hand in the three-card trick game in which the victim was asked to pick out the Queen. Bets were laid, but the operator had associates who "won" to encourage patrons to bet on a game they could never win.

At Athlone races in 1901 when a writer went to collect his winnings he discovered *"that all that remained of the refinedly cruel bookie was a tattered account book, a square yard of green baize and a mineral water case"* His joy on the day was meeting a crickity croupier who wanted him to back red, white, black or blue, anchor star or feather and then he met *"the sunburnt man who manipulates three playing cards on the end of a porter barrel and his ability to make you doubt your eyes is amazing".* At Birr in 1904 there was another popular feature of the American machine, which would show you a picture of your future husband or wife. All meetings had fruit stallholders with oranges and apples and in Roscrea one man was tempted by the forbidden fruit, but *"they were too green to be allowed into any self- respecting stomache".*

At the Heath Races in 1859 the local gentry were playing Aunt Sally. The basis for playing the game went back to an incident at Brighton races in 1858 when the Duke of Beaufort struck a vet for crossing his path during the game leading to a trial reported on the Times and Punch magazine. The game was popular with the nobility for a number of years. The French version of the game was appropriately called jeu de massacre (wholesale slaughter). At The Heath there was also a Diorama with a view of the Indian Rebellion and this was the pre-cursor to a startling announcement in Mullingar Races in 1907 of showing the *"Destruction of San Francisco by Earthquake and Fire".* It was just a Penny Peepshaw. At The Curragh in 1884 a row broke out between English travellers with a game called *"Shake the Monkey"*, where 7 tables were drawn with a monkey attached to them to pull out a winning ticket. Business was brisk but local players attacked them and even beat the monkeys. Reporters at meetings were often nostalgic about the entertainment. In 1906 at Kilbeggan one wrote that *"the little lady who told your fortune was there too and also the lady with the strident voice, who sold large penny oranges with thick skins and little juice. And my old friend the acrobat was there twisting his poor little body into queer shapes for his living; in fact all my childhood friends were, I was perfectly happy".* At Tullamore in 1895 there was a tipster *"who gave the winner of the New York Plate to the President of the United States and he proclaimed that he had all the winners on his card for 1/-".*

It was wonderful for the crowds but there was a harsh reality and unrelenting existence for those people travelling from Punchestown to Araglen in Derry or from Clifden in the west to Tramore in the south, travelling was a real issue and paying train fares was not realistic. The Kilbeggan meeting held on a Monday in 1913,was followed by Rathkeale, Limerick, on a Tuesday, and many were overheard discussing how to sneak on to a goods train. It was not a glamorous existence, which was why some like street musicians stayed 3 or 4 days in a town playing a tin whistle, melodian or barrel organ until they were debarred. A huge influx of beggars came into towns, as described by one reporter *"those submerged units of human society on whom we occasionally practice a little charity".* Times changed and as many racecourses closed the marquees and entertainers disappeared on *"the outside".* Of course you can still meet *"the hawkers"*, swinging boats etc at some courses but as the world changes it is more likely bouncing castles and face painting for children. Having said that the next time you go to the races remember a quote from W.C. Fields *"Horse sense is a good judgement, which keeps horses from betting on people"*

CAPTAIN BOYCOTT, THE MOVIE, AND THE MULLINGAR RACING CONNECTION

Captain Charles Cunningham Boycott has gone down in Irish history, as the man who created a new word in the dictionary as a lasting memorial to an unfortunate life. He leased land and lived at Lough Mask House in Co Mayo in the 1870's. It was a time when Charles Stewart Parnell and Michael Davitt were Irish leaders and they encouraged tenants to fight for their rights and legally refuse to work, socialise or deal with certain land agents. Captain Boycott was the land agent for Lord Erne and he was picked for the exercise which over a period of time led to Captain Boycott losing and being left in isolation in spite of protection from the military. The word *"boycott"* was to symbolise the fight by tenant's to win their rights. Captain Boycott loved steeplechasing and he rode a winner at Newbrook Racecourse in Mullingar in 1877 when Martinet (Voltigeur-Parade) beat J.R.Gubbin's horse New Purchase ridden by Harry Beasley. He also rode Butte Des Mortes to win twice at the Galway Festival in 1883.

Little was he to know that 70 years later a British film called *"Captain Boycott"* (1947) starring Stewart Granger & Kathleen Ryan would cover the story of his life with Cecil Parker acting his part. In addition the film would return to Newbrook Racecourse to re-enact a horse race for the film. Phillip Rooney (who worked in a bank in Mullingar at one stage) wrote a novel about Captain Boycott and part of it was filmed in Westmeath at the racecourse and Ledeston House. Advertisements in the newspapers sought a crowd of 1,500 people for film work in Mullingar Racecourse. A daily rate of 15/- per adult was given with an additional 5/- to anyone wearing costumes or dress from the year 1880. Because of his association with Captain Boycott, 92 y/o Mr Uniake, Millmount House, Mullingar, retired District Inspector of the R.I.C. in Mayo was invited to see the film in the making. Interestingly, the sequences at the start of the race and the finish are from Mullingar, but for some reason the middle section was a problem and some scenes were re-shot on Naas Racecourse. As one wit said *"The race started in Mullingar, did several laps at Naas, and finished back in Mullingar".* Major Tom Crean a former rugby player was doing the riding for Captain Boycott, with other ex-sevicemen also participating. Two other local stars were in the film. Young Pat Layde, Patrick Street, Mullingar went on to be a great actor with the Abbey Company and movies like Ryan's Daughter. Bernadette Farrell from Birr starred in other films like the St Trinian's series in the 1950's and 1960's. She is also remembered for playing the part of Maid Marian in 1955-57 in the Robin Hood series on television.

FILM PEOPLE ARE "CURIOUS MORTALS"

The Mullingar Racecourse was chosen because of the original ornate stands. The weigh- room was used as dressing rooms, film equipment was stored in the Stand House and cameras were concealed in the stands. The racing scene involves the crowds surging forward to stop Boycott's horse winning at Corran Races. It is worth checking out the film to see this scene. Ledeston House near Mullingar was used to represent Lough Mask House in Mayo. J.C.Lyons author of the History of the Grand Juries of Westmeath resided at Ledeston in the late 18th century and early 19th century. He was High Sheriff & later Chief Magistrate from 1817 to 1837 being the last person to hold the office. Mrs Gladys Macarthney (a member of the Lyon's Family) owned the house when Captain Boycott was being filmed and described filmmakers as '*curious mortals*'. The house appears in a number of scenes in the film, which was a big hit in Ireland. Mrs Macarthney was visited by a reporter during the filming in September 1946. She was described as a *"short, jolly little person who wears a sort of jockey cap and pearls and smokes incessant cigarettes".* The house was altered to represent a 19th century look and the reporter who oddly arrived at 4am to meet the crew slept for a few hours, and when he came down at 8am for breakfast he walked into a strange film world. Frank Launder and others were playing poker in the dining room at 9.30am as it was raining outside. Thelma Myers the editor was sleeping on the floor and the actor Mervyn John's who played Boycott's bailiff *"sat stiffly in another chair dressed in leggings, heavy tweeds, and crepe sideboards"*. At 5pm the rain stopped and people appeared from everywhere for a scene in a *"two sided roofless room with seven people, an outsize camera, and trolley on rubber-tyred wheels concentrated in a space the size of a cupboard."*

Apparently, 'film rushes' were shown at Healy's Coliseum Cinema in Mullingar to great acclaim. The producer Frank Launder kept race horses in Ireland with J.T. Doyle in Shankhill, Co Dublin. He had a nice mare Windsor Cottage (Long Walk-Coigne), which was beaten a head by Zircon III in the Hillside Handicap Chase at Leopardstown. The horse had a joint engagement across the sea in the USA in racing & acting in a film. To quote one paper *"She was expected to acquit herself adequately in this dual role"*. Exactly 20 years after the film came out and 90 years after Captain Boycott had a winner in Mullingar the racecourse was closed (1967).

chapter 5
FAMOUS STUDS - GIGGINSTOWN TO TALLY HO

CAPTAIN CECIL BOYD-ROCHFORT

Cecil Boyd Rochfort once said *"he was born in a place that no Englishman can pronounce correctly"*. The place was Castletown-Geoghegan, Co. Westmeath and the house he was born in was Middleton Park. At the end of a great career as a trainer of horses, he had won 13 English classics, 7 Irish classics and the major cup races 15 times. He trained 772 winners of 1,169 races value £1,651,432. He was 5 times leading trainer in 1937/38, 1954/55, and 1958. It was said that he was the first trainer to win over 1 million in England and the first trainer to win the Epsom Derby, with a double barrelled name! His father was Hamilton Boyd Rochfort a large land owner in Westmeath and High Sheriff of Westmeath. He died in 1887 at the age of 43, when Cecil was around 6 months old. His grandfather, George Augustus built Middleton Park around 1842 and in his will he laid down that his eldest son should take the name Boyd Rochfort, as the estate was originally Rochfort property. Hunting was a major part of Cecil's boyhood.

His brother Arthur had an early interest in horse racing and won at Baldoyle with Pride of Middleton. He married Ellie Ussher, Eastwell, Loughrea, sister of Harry Ussher one of the great jockey's and trainer's in this era. Arthur was awarded a Victoria Cross during World War 1, when a bomb landed in a trench and he picked it up and threw it back saving many soldiers. When Arthur (1880-1940) took over Middleton Park Stud he had stallions like The Solicitor and Simony II. His brother Harold (1882-60) bred Airborne who won the Epsom Derby & St Leger in 1946. He also bred Flying Wild owned by Raymond Guest and one of the few horses to beat Arkle.

Cecil was educated at Eton, but with many of his family like Arthur, Alice and his mother, he was involved with horses. At the age of 10, he paid his first visit to Punchestown races and ironically, he saw Atty Persse ride Sweet Lavender to victory beating favourite Breemount Oak, ridden by his owner Bob Dewhurst in the famous Conyngham Cup. The irony is that he started work with Persse in 1906 and became Assistant Trainer to Dewhurst in 1908. He was 19 y/o when he started with Persse, the trainer of The Tetrarch. He specialised in 2 y/o's and was very disciplined in his approach as a trainer. He nearly won the Grand National in 1906 with Aunty May. At the age of 21, he became assistant trainer to Captain Bob Dewhurst at Bedford Lodge, Newmarket. He had been with the army in Ireland and trained horses at Clonsilla, Dublin before going to Newmarket. In 1911, Cecil, because of his ability and contacts, became Racing

Manager to Sir Ernest Cassel business millionaire and financial advisor to King Edward VII. During WWI he was wounded fighting with the Scots Guards on the Somme in 1915 but received the Croix de Guerre. After the war he returned to Cassel, but in 1919 he met American Marshall Field III, who had been educated in England, and he was appointed to take over his racing interests. They became friends for life and Field and Cecil's mother helped him financially to set up as a full time trainer, which he paid back by 1936.

He set up at Freemason Lodge, Newmarket and from there he had his first classic success with Amethysline in the Irish Oaks. It was the first runner he brought over to his native country and it was a great occasion with all his family there to support him. In the late 1920's he was introduced to American owners like John H.Whitney & William Woodward. The former had great success with Royal Minstrel winning the St James Place Stakes in 1928, Eclipse Stakes in 1929 etc. His 1927 Cambridgeshire winner Double Life became the foundation mare for Sir Harold & Lady Zia Wernher and was kept by Arthur at Middleton Park. The other great mare was Black Ray for Marshall Field who provided many good horses like Jacopo, Foray, Infra Red etc. William Woodward bought a good filly called Brown Betty (named after Cecil's favourite sister Betty McCall) and she became his first classic winner in the English 1,000gns. Precipitation (out of Double Life) won the Ascot Gold Cup in 1937 and Cecil became leading trainer without a classic success. He won the title again in 1938 with another success in the Ascot Gold Cup with Woodward's Flares, as part of a Royal Ascot treble. His nephew Peter McCall was his Assistant Trainer from 1934. Cecil's success was helping both Muriel at Tally Ho Stud and Harold at Middleton Park to build up their own studs. By the end of the 1930's, he was one of the most successful trainers in Britain, with international owners and held in great respect.

World War II brought many problems, as he lost many American owners and Marshall Field sold all his horses in 1943, as he became more involved in American politics. During this time he met Rohays Cecil a young widow (her husband was killed in late 1942 and after his death the twins David & Henry Cecil were born in January 1943). A relationship developed with the apparent confirmed 57 year old bachelor Cecil, but with petrol rationing he used to have to go by bicycle to meet her. On 24th July 1944 they were married. Their son Arthur was born in July 1945 with Atty Persse as godfather. In 1943 Cecil was appointed the royal trainer after an interview with Captain Charles Moore (another Irishman). Moore was determined to restore the Royal Family's fortune in racing after some lean years. In 9 years Cecil won 57 races for the King.

In 1944, he won his first English Oaks with Hycilla. Peter McCall was a prisoner of war in WWII but after the war he returned as Cecil's assistant. Cecil was delighted in 1946 when the grey Airborne won the Epsom Derby, as he was bred by his brother Harold at Middleton Park. It was this year that Harry Carr took over as first jockey for the stable. In 1947 his horse Black Tarquin was unplaced in the Derby, but went on to win the St Leger and was 2nd in the Ascot Gold Cup in 1949. One of his most unfortunate horses was Prince Simon who was beaten in photo finishes in a whole series of races from the English 2,000gns, Epsom Derby, and Royal Ascot. Harry Carr was blamed by some for the Epsom Derby defeat because he hit the front too soon and was caught on the line by Galcador. Cecil did not blame him and his owner William Woodward, as always, took the defeat very well. In his lifetime, he won three Kentucky Derbies and four classics in Britain. Woodward died in September 1952, after being a wonderful and generous owner to all the staff.

King George VI died in 1952 and Princess Elizabeth took over and she had six horses with Cecil. One of the Queen's horses was Aureole, who was 5th in the English 2,000gns and 2nd in the famous Epsom Derby in 1952 won by Pinza, and ridden by Gordon Richard, the most famous jockey of his era. It was his only success in the big race and it was acclaimed by all lovers of horse racing in Britain. Aureole won the King George & Queen Elizabeth Stakes in 1954. Cecil was leading trainer for the third time in 1954 and the Queen was the leading owner. Meld his great filly was the star of 1955, winning the 1,000gns and then the Oaks by 6 lengths. The 1,000gns was 39 y/o Carr's first classic win and also the first classic win for Lady Zia Wernher. Cecil was the first trainer to win over £1 million in a year, as he won his 4th trainer's title.

In June 1956, the horse that he always deemed his best was born. Alcide (Alycidon-Lightning) was sent to Muriel McCall at Tally Ho Stud because he was in such poor condition, but a dose of cow's milk & glucose contributed to great improvement in his condition when he went into training. He won the Lingfield Derby Trial & Chester Vase and he was favourite for the Derby, but could not run. People had different views on the reason why, but Cecil & Bruce Hobbs always believed that he was got at in the box, while Harry Carr thought he injured himself. He won the Great Voltigeur on his return and then the St Leger by 8 lengths (his 6th St Leger success) at 4/9. In 1958 Cecil, became leading trainer for the 5th and last time. In 1958 he won the English 2,000 guineas for the first time with Pall Mall for The Queen even though Harry Carr was on the better fancied stable companion Bald Eagle (who went on to be a very successful horse in the USA, winning two Washington DC Internationals). Alcide was Sir Humphrey de Trafford's first classic success after 30 years of ownership, but in 1959 he had his greatest and last classic success when Parthia (Persian Gulf-Lightning), who was related to Alcide, won the Epsom Derby. He won the Lingfield Derby Trial & Dee Stakes at Chester before going on to win the Derby at 10/1 beating Fidalgo. He was the favourite for the St Leger but was only fourth to Cantelo after recovering from the cough. He ran as a 4 y/o winning the Jockey

Club Cup and was 2nd to Petite Etoile in the Coronation Cup.

Things were changing in 1960, with Harold's death after selling Middleton Park in 1959 and Bruce Hobbs his Assistant Trainer left, to start training for himself. He had some success in the 1960's with horses like Canisbay winning the Eclipse Stakes in 1965 and he had some interesting owners like Harry Guggenheim and Elizabeth Arden. He had no success with the former but two of the horses, who were unsuccessful in Britain, were Bald Eagle and Iron Peg (who even beat the great Kelso in a race) and both had great success in the USA. His biggest mistake in his career was to advise Guggenheim not to buy Ragusa (Ribot-Fantan), who was 3rd in the Epsom Derby to Relko, and winner of the Irish Sweeps Derby, King George & Queen Elizabeth Stakes, St Leger etc. Guggenheim sent a mare Fantan to be mated with Ribot and Iris Boyd Rochfort (widow of Harold) described him as *"a great colt that never leaves an oat".* The problem was that Cecil didn't like Ribot horses and advised Guggenheim to sell. The horse was bought by Jim Mullion for 3,800 guineas and went to trainer P.J.Prendergast. In April 1967 on his 80th birthday, he got a beautiful cigarette box as a present from The Queen and in the New Years Honours list he was made Knight Commander of the Royal Victorian Order (KCRVO). His last big winner for the Queen was Castle Yard in the Zetland Gold Cup in June 1968.

In his career he had 57 wins for the King, 126 for the Queen, and 3 for the Queen Mother. In 1968, Cecil decided to retire and live in Kilnahard Castle in Co Cavan and in 1977 he celebrated his 90th birthday with his sister Muriel (two years younger), who was still living at Lynnbury, Mullingar. He continued his interest in horse racing. His good horse Croghan Hill won races including the Rank Cup at Phoenix Park in 1981 and a two year old filly Valentia also won at the Park. In March 1983 he died in Cavan and was buried at Moylisker Cemetery near Mullingar. The mourners included former jockey Harry Carr, his wife Lady Rohays Boyd Rochfort, his son Arthur, sister Muriel McCall, and nieces and nephews the McCalls, Cecils etc. Looking back he had trained great horses like Meld, Alcide, and Parthia. He was one of the greatest trainers of the 20th century, who loved his work, treated staff well, and delivered success for his owners.

His nephew Henry Cecil had been his Assistant Trainer and after Cecil retired in 1968 he started a career that would even outdo the great maestro. Throughout his life he continued his strong association with his native county Westmeath through his sister Muriel McCall, Tally Ho Stud and both Harold & Arthur at Middelton Park Stud to leave a great family legacy in racing terms.

SOME OF THE McCALL FAMILY

The McCall's all became involved in horse racing and breeding in some form, with David McCall as Racing Manager to Charles Engelhard and he also owned Ile De Bourbon, winner of the 1979 St Leger Peter McCall (Died 26/11/86) was born in Westmeath and in 1934 became Assistant Trainer to Cecil Boyd Rochfort. He was captured during WWII and was a prisoner for the duration of the war from 1940. He later Managed Sir Harold Warner's Someries Stud, until retiring to Ireland where he ran Calverstown House Stud, Kildare. Betty McCall was Cecil's favourite niece and William Woodward's Brown Bess who won the English 1,000gns in 1933 was named after Betty. She married Robert Hoare in October 1939 and he was Master of the West Norfolk Hunt. Major Angus McCall (died October 2009) fought in WWII from Normandy to 1945 and he was awarded a Military Cross after fighting in Palestine in 1947. He went to work with Elizabeth Arden, who had horses with Cecil and mares with Muriel at the time. Rather than working for the cosmetic firm he was an advisor on horses. He stayed with the firm for 30 years and while the firm wanted him working in London, she wanted him to escort her round the race tracks, which he did in considerable luxury. When he retired he lived in Cork with his daughter Susan Gornall where he died and is buried.

THE TALLY HO STUD STORY FROM GOLDEN MYTH TO IVAWOOD & TIGGY WIGGY

As you looked at the statistics on *'The Irish Field'* each week, with particular reference to leading sires of two year olds in 2014, two stallions were on top of the table most of the time in July and August. Kodiac (Danehill-Rafha) had over a 40% win to runners success rate at the end of July with the brilliant Tiggy Wiggy leading the way, as winner of the National Stakes and Weatherby's Super Sprint by 6 lengths carrying 9st 1lbs. Tiggy Wiggy's brilliant win over Cursory Glance and Anthem Alexander in one of the best ever Lowther Stakes cemented her reputation. Zebedee (Invincible Spirit- Cozy Maria) was in second place mainly due to the exploits of Richard Hannon's Ivawood who became the favourite for the 2015 English 2,000gns. What both of these horses have in common is that they were bred at the Tally Ho Stud near Lough Ennel in Westmeath, which is run by Tony and Anne O'Callaghan with their two sons Roger & Henry. They have described themselves as one of the leading consignors of thoroughbreds in Ireland & Great Britain and no one could dispute it. Recent Group1 winners produced include Sky Lantern (three Group1's 1000 Guineas, Sun Chariot Stakes, Moyclare Stud Stakes), Dream Ahead (5 Group 1's and Champion Sprinter), Bushranger (Champion 2-Y-O), Myboycharlie (Group 1 Prix Morny), Kingsgate Native (Group 2 Temple Stakes twice), Lahaleeb (Group 1 E.P.Taylor Stakes), and Dubawi Heights (two Group 1's in the USA). Sky Lantern becomes the 8th Classic winner to have been bred and raised at Tally Ho Stud in 2013.

The story of Tally Ho Stud began with the Boyd-Rochfort family, long associated with the nearby Middleton Park Stud, as outlined above. Cecil, Muriel & to some extent Arthur all played a part in the development of Tally Ho Stud. Muriel became interested in racing as her mother and sister Alice had horses in training and Arthur had some success with Pride of Middleton and went on to set up a stud at Middleton Park. Muriel married Jack McCall who bought a long lease of a farm near Lough Ennel and the Ennel Lodge (where The Tetrarch was due to stand at one stage) and he called it Tally Ho in 1918. They sold horses for the first time in July 1919, and 3 of the 4 sold were winners with a top price of 1,400gns for a colt by Tredennis. The horse who was bought by Jack Jarvis was Golden Myth, who won the Gold Vase and Gold Cup in 3 days at Ascot and later dropped down in trip to win the Eclipse Stakes at Sandown. The McCall's did not do as well as they hoped and were in financial difficulty by 1923 when they only got 1,440gns for 8 horses. The irony of the situation was that one of the yearlings sold was by their mare Himalaya and she produced Capture Him, bought for only 120gns. This horse went on to win eight out of nine races as a 2 y/o and was the top rated 2y/o of the year. Marshall Field one of the American owners who helped to set up Cecil Boys Rochfort as a trainer at Freemason Lodge in 1922, decided to buy Tally Ho Stud, which was now run by Muriel McCall and continued to be for the next 50 years. Black Ray was to be one of the foundation mares of Tally Ho Stud and helped to repay Field's financial input as she produced Jacopo & Foray, who were top class 2 y/o's plus fillies like Éclair, Infra Red and Dawn Ray.

In 1924, Cecil brought over Amethystine to win the Irish Oaks (the first horse he brought over to race Ireland) and later she won the Kempton Park Great Jubilee Handicap before being sent to Tally Ho Stud. By 1931, Marshall Field had 14 mares at Tally Ho stud but by 1943 Field was now very involved in politics in the USA and decided to go out of racing. At this time Muriel's mother was living with her at Tally Ho Stud. In 1951, Bill Woodward sold a granddaughter of his broodmare Priscilla Carter called Niobe II to Muriel McCall, and she brought great success to Tally Ho when breeding Aurelius who won the English St Leger in 1961. One of Cecil's most interesting owners was Elizabeth Arden Graham, who had 3 mares standing with Muriel at Tally Ho in the 1950's and she took on her son Angus McCall when he left the army to work for her company. Sagacity was bred at Tally Ho and bought as a yearling for 2,220gns in 1959 and went on to win the Goodwood Cup in 1962 amongst other successes.He was 2nd to Balto in the Ascot Gold Cup.

Other quality horses bred at Tally Ho over the years included Hard to Beat (Hardicanute- Virtuous) who won the Prix de Jockey Club, the French Derby at Chantilly, 3rd Prix de L'Arc etc,Wollow (English 2,000gns, Eclipse Stakes, Sussex

Stakes etc), and Exar won the Gran Premo d'Italia, Goodwood Cup etc. A number of high class horses not bred in Tally Ho came to be reared there and a good example was Alcide, who won the St Leger in 1958 and the King George & Queen Elizabeth Stakes in 1959. He was trained by Cecil and when he came to Tally Ho Stud at 3 months he was *"a tiny miserable creature"*, but they gave him plenty of cow's milk, glucose, and the limestone in Westmeath's soil to help him turn into a strong high class horse. Parthia (Persian Gulf-Lightning) winner of the Epsom Derby was also weaned at Tally Ho Stud and her mother Lightning was there.

Cecil's son Arthur Boyd Rochfort took over the Tally Ho stud when Muriel retired in 1968 and she moved to nearby Lynnbury. In 1967, Rohays Cecil his mother went over to Tally to help Arthur set it up. Arthur bred Wollow winner of the English 2,000gns and Cloonagh winner of 1,000gns in 1973. In 1976, Wollow (Wolver Hollow-Wichuriana who was a 1/2 sister to Exar) won the English 2,000 guineas. Many thought he was a certainty for the Epsom Derby, but three months earlier Arthur said *"just as long as we win the guineas, that is the main thing."* He only finished fifth to Empery (Vaguely Noble-Pamplona) in the Derby, a horse that had Westmeath connections through Vaguely Noble, never looking a winner. Sir Winston Churchill's Vienna was the grandsire. Some complaints were made of Giafranco's Dettori's ride, but the stud did not blame him. The horse won 9 of his 11 races including the Eclipse Stakes, Sussex Stakes, and the Benson & Hedges Gold Cup. He had been the top rated two year old winning the Dewhurst Stakes. He was descended from Black Ray and related to Mill Reef and Blushing Groom. Cecil had advised the purchase of Wollow's fourth dam and trained his sire Wolver Hollow, before his stepson Henry Cecil took over. Arthur bought Cloonagh (High Hat-Zoom) and the dam had produced the winners of 30 races.

At this stage Muriel's son David was Racing Manager to Charles Engelhard, Peter was managing Calvestown House Stud, Kildare and Angus was working for Elizabeth Arden. His step son Henry started his career as Assistant Trainer to Cecil and took over Freemason Lodge when Cecil retired to Cavan in Ireland after seeing Henry's first major success with Wolver Hollow in the Eclipse Stakes in 1969. Henry used to stay at Tally Ho stud with his Aunt Muriel and remembered fishing evenings in Lough Ennel.

A NEW ERA AT TALLY HO

Tony O'Callaghan and his wife bought Tally Ho Stud from Arthur Boyd Rochfort in the late 1970's when Arthur moved to England. It has become one of the most successful studs in modern times due to their hard work with the assistance of their sons Roger and Tony. The one thing that didn't change over the years was the quality of the horses and the commitment of the owners to quality. In 1932,

Harold Cayzer's bought a filly for 800gns called Dalmary out of Simons Shoes by Blandford & Cecil trained the filly to win the Yorkshire Oaks after which she went to Tally Ho Stud. Leading sires like Sadler's Wells and Nureyev trace back to her as do Sky Lantern and Sir Prancelot, who is a recent addition as a stallion to Tally Ho. Many useful stallions like Beckett, Danetime, Indian Rocket, Redback, Tillerman, Chevalier, Chineur, Mr Dinos etc have passed through Tally Ho over the years under the care of the O'Callaghan's.

Speed is the common denominator with many of the Tally Ho stallions and a strong connection with some of the faster Richard Hannon young horses. Baltic King was a winner of the Hong Kong Jockey Club Sprint and Wokingham Handicap plus winning every year from 2 to 6 year old. Bushranger won the Prix Morny and Middle Park Stakes breaking the track record as a two year old. He was 2nd to Mastercraftsman as the best two year old in 2008. Sir Prancelot won the National Stakes and Gr2 Flying Childers Stakes; and Society Rock was the winner of Gr1 Golden Jubilee and Newbury Sprint Cup beating amongst others Group 1 winners like Gordon Lord Byron, Lethal Force etc. Undoubtedly, the success of Kodiac and Zebedee with 2 y/o's this season, highlights the international importance of Tally Ho Stud. Richard Hannon compared Ivawood (Zebedee-Keenes Royale) to his sire Zebedee when he romped home in the Richmond Stakes at Goodwood at odds of 2/5 but also added he had more scope for the future. Tiggy Wiggy (Kodiac-Kheleyf's Silver) was so impressive in the Weatherby's Super Sprint that she got the highest Racing Post Rating by a 2 y/o over 5 furlongs since 1992 and she was entered for the Prix L'Abbaye at Longchamp in October, (which was last won by a 2 y/o Sigy in 1978) but she didn't run.

The hard work of Tony and Anne O'Callaghan has made Tally Ho stud a modern racing success story. In 2009, they received a Special Recognition award. Tony's advice then was *"I'v seen about three recessions and I'd say just be patient and it will come"*. Very appropriate for the era we now live in when there is nothing certain about our future.

Ivawood went on to be third to Gleneagle and Territories in the English 2,000 guineas and he was also 3rd to Gleneagles in the Irish 2,000 guineas. Tiggy Wiggy was 3rd to Legatissimo in the 1,000 guineas.

FRANKEL AND THE UNIQUE WESTMEATH CONNECTION

Even those who only have a slight interest in horse racing have heard of Frankel the wonder horse, who retired unbeaten after 14 races and captured news headlines around the world. He was trained by the great Henry Cecil and ridden by Irishman Tom Queally and is now rated one of the greatest horses in history after winning nine Group 1 races in succession. It is not necessary to go into the full exploits of the great horse, as his wins from the English 2,000gns to the Champion Stakes are well recorded.The first Irish connection is that Frankel is a son of Aidan O'Brien's champion Galileo and a grandson of the most successful stallion of modern times in Saddler's Wells in addition his regular jockey is a Waterford man Tom Queally. Henry Cecil has a strong Irish connection, as his stepfather was Captain Cecil Boyd Rochfort who was born in Middleton Park, Castletown Geoghegan, Co Westmeath and learned his early trade with him.

HENRY CECIL FISHING ON LOUGH ENNEL AND EATING APPLE TART

Henry and his twin brother David were born in Aberdeen in January 1943, around 6 weeks after their father Henry was killed by a mortar bomb. Their mother Rohays later met Cecil Boyd Rochfort and they were married in July 1944. When the Westmeath bred Wolver Hollow owned by Mrs Iselin (aged 100) finished 2nd in the English Cambridgeshire in 1968, it was his last runner in a major race at 81 years old. At the end of the year he passed on Freemason Lodge to his stepson Henry. In 1969, Wolver Hollow continued to improve and ran in the Eclipse Stakes to provide Henry Cecil with his first Group 1 winner, even though most of the credit went to Cecil Boyd-Rochfort. Even Henry Cecil admitted that it was more luck than ability that gave him the prize.

The Burke family, who lived near Newbrook Racecourse in Mullingar, befriended Henry Cecil on his visits to his Step Aunt Muriel McCall at Tally Ho stud. Ted Burke said that he used to go coarse fishing along the banks of Lough Ennel and then he would call to Burkes because *"he loved my mother's apple tarts"*. Ted described as him *"the greatest trainer in history"*. He was invited to The Curragh some years ago when Henry Cecil had a runner. A few years before he died there was an article in the local Westmeath Examiner paper about famous Westmeath people and it referred to Cecil Boyd Rochfort and Ted sent it to Henry and received a reply and Henry wrote *"Thank you very much for sending the article on my stepfather in the Westmeath Examiner. I enjoyed reading it and it brought back memories. I have very happy memories of Mullingar, as well. We used to stay at my stepfather's sisters Muriel and I remember evening's fishing at the lake"*.

However, in many ways the third person associated with Frankel's success his work-rider Shane Fetherstonhaugh is the most interesting historically. Shane 35 was first assigned to Frankel in January 2011, and he is the work rider who has ridden the great horse almost every day. He was born in Skerries and is a son of Brian Fetherstonhaugh, an Irish Press Journalist for many years. His brother Neil is a journalist and joint author with Tony McCullagh of the story of the Stardust fire called *"The Never Came Home"*. His grandfather Francis was a racing correspondent with the Irish Field and the Horse & Hound, until his death in 1981. Shane started out with Dublin trainer Peter Casey (original trainer of champion novice chaser Flemenstar) and his father brought him around to race meetings, which developed his interest in the sport. Henry Cecil summed up Shane's contribution to the success of Frankel in a quote *"This season, Shane has ridden Frankel entirely at home. I've managed his training schedule and preparation, but Shane has carried out the orders to perfection. So, perhaps, it could be said that we - Shane and I - have trained Frankel together".* Shane has won awards as a groom, and praise from other sources, but the above comment from one of the legends of racing is the ultimate comment.

The story does not end there, as the Fetherstonhaugh family have contributed greatly to the history of horse racing in Ireland and around the world. The family came to Ireland after the Civil War in England. Early in the 19th century Thomas Fetherstonhaugh, Grouse Lodge, Moate, a Solicitor & JP kept a number of horses. Captain Cecil Fetherstonhaugh owned 4,700 acres in late 19th century and was a director of the Mullingar Racing Co in 1890. However the most notable contributor was Bob Fetherstonhaugh (1873-1950) from Carrick, Mullingar, He trained 3 winners of the Irish Grand National in Ballyboggan (1918 also 2nd in Aintree Grand National), Dog Fox (1925), and Copper Court (1932). He trained for 10 years in Mullingar, before the Land Commission took over the lands and he then moved to Loughbrown Cottage, The Curragh, where he had great success with horses owned by Dermot McCalmont, Mount Juliet Stud, Kilkenny. He trained 9 Irish Classic winners on the flat including 2 Irish Derbies with Slide On (1944) and Piccadilly (1945). His son "Brud" who was successful in 2 Irish classics, succeeded him in 1950, and in 1961 had 3 winners with 3 runners at Royal Ascot with Bun Penny, Silver Tor, and Prince Tor. The greatest horse he trained was Busted, which had some success for him in Ireland, but when he was sent to Noel Murless he became a champion, winning the Eclipse Stakes, King George VI & Queen Elizabeth Stakes etc in 1967. "Brud" had a brother called "Aintree" named after the course, but it could have been worse, the family were initially going to call him "Ballyboggan" after the Irish Grand National winner!

Other notable members of the family were Major Francis Fetherstonhaugh (1858-1931), who won an Irish Oaks in 1897 and trained at The Curragh, but more importantly he became Racing Manager to King George VI in 1923. It was said that he got the job through the influence of his wife Beatrice, who was related to Lord Woverton and the family lived in The Royal Lodge, Windsor Park. Beatrice was affectionately known to the king as 'Mrs Fethers', because she placed bets for him. Under his management the royal horses won 19 races and prize money of £12,095, in the first season. The influence of the Irish Fatherstonhaugh's on racing even stretched to Australia. Cuthbert Fetherstonhaugh (1837-1925) originally from Dardistown, Westmeath was a natural horseman and wrote about his time in Australia in his autobiography

'After Many Days'. Thomas Strettel Clibborn (1837-1910), Moate Castle who went to Australia in 1859, was a nephew of the Fetherstonhaughs, and went on to become one of the great developers of horse racing in Sydney and New South Wales, when he became Secretary of the Australian Jockey Club.

Shane Fetherstonhaugh is part of a great family tradition stretching back a few hundred years and maybe it is no surprise that he has made such a contribution to the success of one of the greatest horses in racing history as declared by Henry Cecil.

MIDDLETON PARK STUD

The Barony of Moycashel represents much of the territory of the ancient country of Cineal Fiachra or Kinaleagh which varied at times but the McGeoghegan Clan were the main landowners in the Castletown Geoghegan area in the Middle Ages. In the 19th century, it was bought by George Augustus Rochfort Boyd (1817-1888). His father was Abraham Boyd, but he also adopted his mother's name which was Jane, Countess of Belvedere widow of George Augustus Rochfort. He had the reputation for evicting tenants but he did set up two soup kitchens during the famine. The house was destroyed by fire in 1838 and he built a new mansion overlooking Lough Ennel. When he died in 1888, Hamilton his son took over and he died in 1891. It was left to his wife Florence Louise to run the estate with eight children.

Arthur Boyd Rochfort (1880-1940) was third in the family and even as a 21 y/o in 1901 he helped set up the Middleton Kennels, with him as master & the famous Will Matthews as huntsman. A presentation was made to him of a Silver Tray with a Coat of Arms for his 21st birthday. On New Years Day he won on Pride of Middleton at Baldoyle to great rejoicing. Arthur won the Victoria Cross during WW1, when he picked up a mortar bomb in the trench and he threw it out saving many lives. After the war, he started building up Middleton Park with Cecil's help. The horse that helped launch the Stud was the foundation mare Double Life, bought by Lady Zia Wernher in 1927 and great horses like Precipitation, Doubleton, Persian Gulf, Meld etc descended from her. In 1929 William Woodward, sent Priscilla Carter to Arthur and in 1940, as the war began he gave Arthur & his wife Ellie (a sister of the great Harry Ussher) two mares. He was a generous man and when Boswell won the St Leger in 1936 he sent £250 to Arthur. He died in 1940 at the age of 60. He was a kind landowner and no staff member was ever fired, but it was expensive to run. Earlier in life, he had horses like Old Times, Lady Boreen, The Unknown, and Vera. He served as a Steward on the Turf Club and National Hunt Committee. Two horses bred by him before he died were very successful in the USA - Ended (Felicitation-Last Act), who won 33 races and $107,315 and Haile (Rameses the Second-Banditry) with 21 wins and $98,000. It is recalled by locals that many celebrities like Rita

Hayworth visited the house in the 1930/40's.

Harold Boyd Rochfort (1882-1960) was educated at Eton and was an officer in the 4th Scottish Rifles 1900-01 and fought in the Boer war and later in WW1, and was decorated with a Military Cross in 1916. In 1899, he sold The Masher for 280 guineas to Sandringham, as a mount for Princess Victoria of Wales and in August that year he won 15 prizes at Moate Show. Arthur took over Middleton Park in 1940 after working as a stockbroker for a time. His wife Iris ran the estate for a number of years and one mare that Harold had, called Bouquet (Buchan-Hellesport), was to play a big part in its history. Arthur bought the mare for 400gns. She never ran due to an injury but when mated with Precipitation, she produced an Epsom Derby winner in Airborne. Lord Portal bought Bouquet in 1943 at Cecil's suggestion, as Harold needed the money. Harold sold the colt by Precipatation for 3,300gns to John Ferguson.The misfortune was that Airborne won the Derby & St Leger for trainer Dick Perryman and Lord Portal had great success with Bouquet. The good news was that because of Airborne's success, Harold became Breeder of the Year in 1946, beating Lord Derby and was apparently the first Irish person to win it. The loss of Bouquet put the Stud under pressure, although Judy bought by Cecil bred a number of winners and Lone Pat a mare of Iris's also had some success.

Harold had to sell the stud in 1959, due to financial pressure, upkeep, and inability to pay and he was able to buy back 400 acres in the north-west of the estate. A year later he died and Iris continued to run it up to the 1970's. Airborne was not a great success at stud, but one famous horse was a steeple chaser Flying Wild (Airborne-Wild Delight) owned by American Ambassador Raymond Guest (owner of Sir Ivor and remembered for his ante-post bet on Sir Ivor to win the Epsom Derby at 100/1). Flying Wild, was one of the few horses to beat the great Arkle over fences and the only mare to win the Massey Ferguson Gold Cup. She also won the Stone Ginger Wine Chase, Cathcart Cup, and was 2nd to Flyingbolt in the Two Mile Champion Chase. The mare Wild Delight won ten races for Iris before she went to stud. The Stud was retained by the Boyd-Rochfort's, but the Land Commission took some lands and a German group set up a pig and sheep farm, before it was sold to the O'Callaghan's. Iris (who died in 1973) carried on with the stud, until she left it to her niece Suzanne Cramphorn.

Middleton Park has been used for many purposes not related to horse racing. In the 1970's it was owned by Mr J.G.and Mrs Rosalie O'Callaghan and a 3 day international event was held with riders from Holland, Italy, England etc. It was to prepare the Irish team for the Olympics. British Movitone News filmed highlights of the event in 1976 including a 4 minute film of the Westmeath Hunt, which was shown in Dublin Cinemas. The course cost £5,000 to build and it was designed by Juliet Jobling Purser former Irish Olympic rider, with locals doing voluntary work. The Irish Olympic team used it as their final pre-Olympic outing, including Ronnie McMahon, Ned Cash, Gerry Mullins, Eric Morgan, and John Watson. They only stayed for a few years probably because of the maintenance costs.

BARNEY CURLEY

For over 40 years Barney Curley, the legendary and controversial Northern Ireland-born gambler and racehorse trainer, has lived on his wits winning and losing sums of money unimaginable to most of us. The seminary and the sanitorium, he claims, taught him never to worry about anything again. He was born in Irvinestown, Co Fermanagh, in 1939 in a strong Catholic family. His father loved drink and gambling, which left the family poor. His father was only interested in the dogs but he was interested in the horses from an early age. He was educated by the Jesuits, which influenced him to some extent for the rest of his life. In his show biz career Frankie McBride & Polka Dots were the first band to get into British top ten with *"Five Little Fingers"* and by the time he quit showbiz, Barney had a stable of bands, which included Brian Coll and the Buckaroos and Hugo Duncan and the Tall Men. His wife Maureen was a bookies daughter of Irish extraction from Cheshire.

The famous coup at Bellewstown in June 1975 is well known through a series of books. Yellow Sam was an average but well handicapped horse in a bad race. He spent a long time planning the coup with a large number of 'layers' spread around the country, all ready to place bets from £50 to £300 on off course bookies at 15 minutes before the start (3pm). Around £15,000 was bet. The horse was a 20/1 shot, but the key was the off track bookies would not hear about the gamble. Bellewstown had only one telephone and a friend Benny O'Hanlon went in to make a call at 2.30pm and stayed on the phone until after the off. Barney said he watched the race concealed in a bush, as Yellow Sam won easily by 2½ lengths and he collected £300,000 from the bookies. It was precise and he would argue not illegal. The alternative view is that he outwitted the bookies in a very unique way.

His interest in Middleton Park arose directly out of the famous Yellow Sam coup. When he saw Middleton Park he fell in love with it. He used it primarily for 'store horses'. He had three children at this time. They spent nine years at Middleton before leaving in 1984. He always said it was impossible to maintain and heat, and the farming side was not successful.

He bought Silver Buck from Paul Doyle for 8,000gns and vet Pat McCann, Tullamore looked after him. He won a bumper at Clonmel by 8 lengths and after a short holiday in Mullingar with him, he sold the horse to the Dickinson's in

1977. He said it was on condition he would be tipped off when he was fancied! First time out he was 8th of 12 and the plan was to win at Catterick. Michael Dickinson, apparently, rang him at Mullingar the night before the race to tell him the horse would win. He opened next day at 10/1 and finished at 9/2. He had around £10,000 on him, but the price should have been much bigger as Yellow Fire was hot favourite. He was annoyed & suspected that it was the operators on the phone in the area, who passed on information to the locals in the Mullingar area. He claims he devised a plan with Michael and arranged conversations about horses that would not win, to catch out the operators. The problem was that, in an era without mobiles, he had to go to a public telephone to make his calls and he used to go to place inside the Fermanagh-Cavan border, as it was the nearest place to dial direct and he needed around £5 worth of coins. Silver Buck went on to win two King George VI Chases, 29 races and nearly £160,000 in prize money.

In 1981, he bought a 4 y/o by Precipice Wood for £4,000. He had taken away his horses from Liam Brennan the trainer because of a dispute, but met him at the sales and asked him if he would train the horse. It was therefore appropriate that he called the horse Forgive N'Forget. He ran in bumpers under Liam's wife's name. He was beaten first time out but was backed heavily to 5/2 F next time and won by 8l's. This led to enquiries, which ended with Liam and Anthony Powell being warned off for 4 months. He later sold him for £45,000 to Tom Kilroe, Manchester who had horses with Jimmy Fitzgerald. He won the Cheltenham Gold Cup in 1985, but before that he had some gambles. His biggest win was the Coral Golden Hurdle Final in 1982/83 where he had very good form for it.

RAFFLE AT MIDDLETON PARK AT "THE BIGGEST CLUB IN THE WORLD"

He thought of having a raffle for the house, which was worth around 1 million, and if he sold enough tickets to cover that, he would be even. It was said by Gardai that any draw or raffle over £300 was illegal and if the prize was more than that, it had to be charitable or philanthropic. It was called the Private Limited Subscribers Draw and they intended to sell 9,000 tickets at €200, $275 or £175. It was decided that all subscribers would have to become members of the Ballinagore GAA Club, answer 3 simple questions and make a donation to the Irish Wheelchair Association. The club were going to get a new pitch, changing rooms, and a social club. He had a video made with a Michael O'Hehir commentary. The Trustees were Tommy Stack, Michael O'Brien trainer, and Mick O'Toole. The raffle was organised with the help of the club. Once you bought a ticket you were a member of the club.

The Irish Times said one day *"The biggest club in the world, bigger even than the New York Yacht Club or Lords"*. He was on the Late Late Show and on BBC.

Celebrity entrants included Eric Clapton, Harry Carr, and Robert Sangster. When he went to the USA that year around 6,000 tickets were already sold. It was on TV across the USA and the New York Post had a headed article *"Irish betting legend comes to America"*. He could not sell tickets in the USA but he was over 4 months there to publicise the draw. Just a few weeks before the draw there was a Garda raid. It was based on the Gaming & Lotteries Act and they took possession of items related to the draw. Having commentator Michael O'Hehir was a big plus, as he was so well respected in the GAA and racing. He tried to persuade him not to draw the ticket in case it would affect his reputation but he insisted. He said *"My Word is My Bond"* and Barney called a horse that name, as he was so impressed.

In 1984, on Thursday 9th February 19, the draw was held and he allowed the BBC to cover it exclusively. The Guards were around the house and they had received 4 visits that week. He sold all the tickets with receipts of £1.8 million. Around 3pm the draw took place at the staircase. Three detectives from Mullingar were there at the door. Michael drew the winning ticket 41877 and it was a British Syndicate from Gloucester headed by Tony Ray with 5 others. They celebrated later in the Bloomfield Hotel, Mullingar. The end result was that he had made nearly a million after expenses. It seemed that was the end until he was charged with an illegal lottery and also Michael O'Hehir.

Five in total were charged and it was held in the court in Ballynacaragy in July. Three local people were fined £100 for selling tickets. Judge Tormey convicted him with the maximum sentence of 4 months and Michael O'Hehir's case was dismissed. He got a jail sentence but appealed it, as he intended to train in Britain. At this point he had horses like Silver Buck, I'm A Driver, and The Haciendos. The family stayed in the Lodge House at Middleton. In November he returned for the Court Case in Mullingar. Judge O'Malley said he was Guilty, but he got probation and a fine of £5,000 to be paid to St Vicent de Paul. Curley said I would double it and this was the end of the story.

He was then able to get a trainers licence in Britain. The British Syndicate sold it and there have s been a number of owners since then. Barney Curley stayed eight years at Middleton Park and it became famous worldwide for a short time.

MARTIN LYNCH AND THE PRIEST AT AINTREE

Martin was born in 1949 and he married Suzanne Finn (Lady Champion 1986 and 1990). He rode many good horses over the years like Nick the Brief, Cool Ground, Auntie Dot, Mr Frisk etc and a number for trainer John Webber. He jokes that he rode a Cheltenham Gold Cup winner, but the problem is that it was in the Aintree Grand National 1992, where he finished 10th on Cool Ground after Adrian Maguire got injured. He rode 5 winners between the flags and as an amateur rode Royal Dipper to win the Morgiana Hurdle, as a professional won the Thyestes Chase in 1985 on Sheskin Bridge owned by The President and was also 2nd on him in the Irish Grand National, to dual Grand National winner Rhyme N'Reason. He rode in England for 6 years and won the Mildmay of Flete on Elfast (1992) and the Vincent O'Brien Gold Cup in 1990 on Nick the Brief beating Carvill's Hill.

With regard to the Aintree Grand National he rode Barney Maclevie in 1981. He had ridden the horse for Jim Dreaper just a few weeks before in his first professional ride and was offered the ride in the big race. He was excited, as he crossed the Melling Road to the first fence, but the horses landed too steep and he was thrown from the saddle and got a kick in the leg. As he stood, stooped over and cursing with the pain at the side of the first fence, he looked up and there was a priest standing blessing him. The priest uttered the immortal words *"I don't blame you my son".* To this day he doesn't know why the priest was at the first fence!

He began training by renting a yard from Bill Durkan in Dublin in 1993. They bought a cottage, stable yard and 20 acres and put up an all-weather gallop & moved into it in 1997. He bought a horse for Cathal Ryan a Ryan air pilot for 15,000gns, as an unbroken 3 y/o. He was named Colonel Yeager, after Colonel Chuck Yeager the American air force test pilot, the first to break the sound barrier in the desert. He was only beaten by Joe Mac in 1998 and big offers were made for him (Ryan also bought a 1/2 sister and called it Amelia Earhart). Colonel Yeager won the Punchestown Champion Bumper. The following year he was 4th in the Supreme Novices Hurdle, but then he got a leg injury and was out for 2 years but by that time Martin had given up his licence (he beat Moscow Flyer at Gowran Park on his return). Martin had to give up training because *"I had two young children and it was a combination of factors. Trying to get the right horses and the right staff was never easy and it was too much hardship".*

He filled various consultant & bloodstock roles in the industry, before he decided to have a go again at his new base in Middleton Park, where he has an old stone coach yard with around 30 stables. His son Mark was also starting out and he hoped to get him some rides.

OSCAR TIME AND SAM WALEY COHEN

From his birth in 2001 to May 2014, Oscar Time (Iscar-Baywatch Star) ran 37 times, won 6 races, 2nd on 11 occasions and 6 thirds. It was a very consistant record which more importantly included a win in the Paddy Power Chase at Leopardstown, 2nd to Ballabriggs in the Aintree Grand National in 2011 and 4th to Auroras Encore in the same race in 2013. He was the horse that brought Martin Lynch into the public eye and in many ways the Waley Cohen family.

He realised that riding and training were two different businesses. The horse that was to bring him to the forefront was Oscar Time, whom he purchased for £37,000 in 2004. He resold him for a profit of £3,000. Robbie Power rode Oscar time to win the 190,000 Paddy Power Chase at Leopardstown in December 2009, when he was backed from 20/1 to 10/1. Martin said afterwards *"Luckily, my jockey wasn't listening, when I told him not to hit the front until after the last".* He gave much of the credit to his wife Suzanne, who is a herbalist & acupuncturist and helped out the horse, who was not a great eater. In 2010, Oscar Time 22/1 was second to Bluesea Cracker 25/1 in the Irish Grand National. In 2011, the objective was to win the Aintree Grand National and at that stage the owner Robert Waley-Cohen had his son Sam riding the horse. Sam rode the family's horse Long Run to success in the Cheltenham Gold Cup 2011 and the King George VI Chase in January 2011. In 2007, he was 5th on his father's horse Liberthine in the Aintree Grand National and Oscar Time was purchased, as the horse who might deliver the Aintree Grand National. Eamonn Keane only wanted to sell him to an owner that would leave him with Martin, who rang Robert Waley Cohan and the rest is history.

Martin had known the family going back to the 1980's and it was natural that he should continue to train the horse. Sam rode the horse for the first time at Thurles in November 2010. At Aintree in 2011, he was up against Ballabriggs trained by Donald McCain, who had to live up to the family tradition set down by his father Ginger McCain with Red Rum. Both horses were 14/1 and fought out a great finish with Ballabrigs succeeding by 2 1/4 lengths. In 2012 Oscar Time was withdrawn from the race due to a tendon strain. He had two runs before the 2013 Grand National without making much impact and was 66/1 to win the race. Amazingly, the 12 y/o ran another great race and led with three fences to go but weakened near the final stages and finished 20 lengths 4th to Sue Smith's Aurora Encore who was also 66/1. He returned to Robert Waley Cohen after receiving a knock and did not return to the racecourse until May 2014, when he won two hunter chases at Wetherby & Uttoxeter at odds of 1/2 and 8/13. There was still life in the old dog! Martin hopes that some day soon another horse like Oscar Time will appear on his horizon.

CLEABOY STUD

The beginning of Cleaboy Stud is all about Major Lionel Holliday (1881-1965). Lionel Brook Holliday was born in 1881 and died in 1965, he was educated at Oatlands School Harrogate, and later went to Bonn University. He served as a Major in France in World War 1, but in 1915 he was recalled from the front line, as he had a working knowledge vital for the production of explosives for the war. In the same year, Read Holliday was nationalised and became British Dyes. He received £10,000 for his share of the business, which was used to purchase a site at Deighton, where he founded in 1916 a new dye manufacturing business called L.B.Holliday and Co Ltd. The business prospered under Holliday and eventually, after World War II, he employed over 800 people.

Tom Cleary lived at Kilpatrick in the 19th century, and after his death it passed to M.J.Cleary the vet. Then it was owned by Owen Ryan (1872-1942), Kilpatrick, Mullingar, and in 1911 (aged 38) he lived at Cleaboy, Ballintobber, Roscommon (where possibly he got the name for the stud, although it is also said that the *"Cle"* refers to the Cleary's?) and he married Anne Doherty. When WW1 broke out he was technically out of business, as there was no trade with England and he sold it to Major Holliday in 1915 and remained on as Manager contributing to its great success. He was succeeded by his daughter Sheila as Manager, and his son James Edward was a successful trainer in the USA, often with horses provided by his father. He worked in Holliday's dye factory in England, while riding steeplechasers at the weekend. Holliday bought Cleaboy Stud in Co.Westmeath in 1915, and had his first winner in 1918, although it was years later that he was most successful. He was married twice, and it was his son Brook, who was most involved in his breeding operation. He was a very difficult and tough character. He rented Copgrove Hall in Yorkshire and eventually bought it in 1936. Holliday also owned Sandwich Stud in Newmarket, which was bought in 1958. It was largely used, as a base for mares visiting Newmarket stallions and as a stud for some of Holliday's stallions including Hethersett and Narrator.

The most important horse and foundation of future success in the development of Cleaboy Stud was Lost Soul (1931 f by Solario - Orlass). She was purchased as a yearling for 1,800gns at the Doncaster St Leger yearling sales of 1932, but in 1936 Major Holliday purchased her for 4,000gns when in foal to Blenheim. Solario was one of the leading sires at that time, and Orlass had already bred six winners including the Derby third Shian Mor. Lost Soul won two races at three, and at four was placed in the City and Suburban Handicap and the Victoria Cup. At stud she bred seven winners, including four really good horses in Nearly, Goldsborough, Saved, and Dumbarnie. Mick Easterby's good horse Lochnager (King's Stand Stakes, Nunthorpe Stakes) traces back to the family, who in turn was dam sire of the popular sprinter Lochsong.

Phase (1939 f by Windsor Lad) was to be the most successful of Lost Souls offspring. In 1940, he decided to sell all his yearlings and they were bought together by leading Irish owner Joe McGrath except for the filly Phase. Holliday liked naming most of his horses starting with the letter "N" after his favourite sire Nearco. He was unbeaten in 14 races including the Grand Prix De Paris and in 1962, 33 of his 53 mares had Nearco in their pedigree. Lost Soul won three times in the war years at Newmarket, but it was at stud that she showed her true merit where she produced nine winners from fourteen foals including horses by Nearco like Neasham Belle, who won the Epsom Oaks; Netherton Maid, who won the Princess Elizabeth Stakes, and was second in the Epsom Oaks; Narrator, who won the Champion Stakes (as a maiden at 20-1) and Coronation Cup; and None Nicer who won the Yorkshire Oaks, and the Ribblesdale Stakes. Other horses bred there were No Argument (Narrator), High Flown, up to Hard Fought (Habitat-Ambrosia) winner of Prince of Wales Stakes (Group2), Jersey Stakes (G2), Earl of Sefton (G3), and disqualified in the Eclipse Stakes in 1977.

Most of these horses were bred or reared on the rich limestone soil at Cleaboy Stud. By the end of 1965, he claimed the winners of 937 races worth £721,050, at a time of low prize money. He was leading owner in Britain in 1956, 1961, and 1962 and leading breeder 1954, 1956, and 1962. In 1956, he won 43 races with 21 horses worth £37,333. He sacked Geofrey Brooke (1952) and Humphrey Cottrill (1957) as trainers. He was difficult and ungenerous, when he said about trainers that *"they arrived on bicycles and left in Bentley's"* and was notorious for his toast *"Well here's damnation to the working man"*. The great Dick Hern was there from 1957 but left in 1962 in his last year as Holliday's trainer. The stud Manager in Hern's time was Desmond McKeever, who loved horses and was very dedicated. His wife Maureen and her sister Maeve worked there also rearing the animals under Hern's instructions. The two most notable horses who came out of Cleaboy Stud were Hethersett and the great Vaguely Noble.

HETHERSETT

Hethersett (Hugh Lupus) was the best of the Lost Soul family to race in the Holliday colours. First time out in 1961, he won the Duke of Edinburgh Stakes at Ascot by five lengths for Dick Hern, with Harry Carr up and in his only other race at two, he was only fifth in the Timeform Gold Cup G1. At three he won the Brighton Derby Trial impressively and was made favourite for the Derby. This was the famous Larkspur Derby, where on the descent to Tattenham Corner a number of horses, including Hethersett, were brought down, and thus Holliday's best chance of winning the Derby failed. He was badly injured, and on his return could only finish seventh on firm ground at Goodwood in the Gordon Stakes. He won the Great Voltigeur at York and then the St Leger by an easy four lengths, with Larkspur back in sixth place. On his final run, Hethersett was second to Arctic Storm in the Champion Stakes at Newmarket. His exploits enabled Holliday to claim the 1962 Champion Owner and Breeder crowns (the latter championship for the second season in a row). Hethersett failed to win in his four outings the next year. His best horse as a stallion was Blakeney who won the Epsom Derby in 1969.

After a very successful career, he died on 17th December 1965 (aged 85), when he had around 50 horses in training. His son Brook took over and he retained

Cleaboy Stud until 1978. Even after selling it, horses were officially bred by "Cleaboy Farms Ltd". The useful filly Pugnacity was inherited by Brook Holliday and she produced seven winners including one of his best horses in the shape of Relkino (1973 by Relko), whom he sold as a yearling from Cleaboy for 58,000gns, the top price for a yearling in England or Ireland in 1974, to Lady Beaverbrook. He went to Dick Hern where he won the Benson & Hedges Gold Cup G1, Lockinge Stakes G2, and was second in the Epsom Derby G1) to Empery, who's sire was of course Vaguely Noble.

THE GREAT VAGUELY NOBLE

However not only was the best horse he ever bred, Vaguely Noble, not a classic winner, but Holliday died the year the horse was foaled at Cleaboy Stud. At the time of his death, aged 85, Holliday's horses were trained by Walter Wharton. The winding-up of the estate took some time, so the final group of horses to be sold by the executors did not reach the sales ring until 1967. The best horse to come out of Cleaboy Stud in his era was undoubtedly, Vaguely Noble. He was a beautiful bay colt by Vienna out of Noble Lassie. Vienna was Sir Winston Churchill's horse and the filly, as always, was by Nearco. Trained as a two-year-old by Wharton for Brook Holliday, who leased him from the Executors, he was beaten into 2nd place in his first two races. The softer ground in the autumn, allowed Vaguely Noble to show his full potential, and he inflicted a twelve length victory on the opposition in his next race and, two weeks later, he won the Observer Gold Cup at Doncaster by a very impressive seven lengths.

Due to the death of his owner there were no classic entries for the colt and Brook Holliday pressed ahead with plans to sell him at Tattersalls, mainly to help settle the massive death duties he had incurred. He was one of 16 horses sold for 180,740 guineas. The opening offer quickly rose to 80,000gns, events were quickly wrapped up with the winning bid of 136,000gns being a then world record price for a racehorse. Vincent O'Brien bid up to 110,000gns for him before dropping out. The purchaser was a plastic surgeon to all the stars, and a notable dog breeder, Dr. Robert Franklyn (who swiftly sold a half share to fellow American Nelson Bunker Hunt) and the horse was transferred first to Paddy Prendergast in Ireland, but he was quickly moved to France to be trained by Sea Bird's trainer, Etienne Pollet.

He won the first two races of his three-year-old career, the Prix de Guiche and the Prix du Lys, but was then only third in the Grand Prix de Saint-Cloud. However, he quickly bounced back for an easy win in the Prix de Chantilly, before the final racecourse appearance of his short career, where he won the greatest race in the racing world, the Prix de L'Arc de Triomphe by three lengths from Sir Ivor, with one of the best fields ever seen, trailing in behind him. Sir Ivor has often been mentioned as the best horse trained by Vincent O'Brien, even ahead of Nijinsky. In their only meeting in the best race in the world, Vaguely Noble proved he was the best horse and undoubtedly the greatest flat horse to come through Westmeath. Dr Franklyn, later praised Major Holliday for prodicing the best horse in the world.

He was voted the 17th best horse of the 20th Century by *'The Racing Post'*, Vaguely Noble became a great sire of turf horses including Dahlia, Estrapade, Nobiliary, Lehmi Gold, Exceller, Gay Mecene, Empery and Noble Decree, and an equally renowned sire of broodmares (the dams of Golden Fleece, Indian Skimmer, Dahar, Tamarisk, River Memories, Touching Wood and L'Emigrant), which will ensure his legacy lives on for many years to come. The last good horse that Brook Holliday had with Dick Hern before they ended their relationship was the filly Highest Hopes (Hethersett-Miranda) who was 2nd to Sweet Mimosa in the French Oaks in 1967, but won the Prix Vermeille and Fred Darling Stakes.

THE McKEEVER'S SELL RED SETTERS TO PRESIDENT RICHARD NIXON

Des McKeever managed Cleaboy Stud for many years for Major Holliday. He was a member of the Irish Guards and a tank regiment in WWII and was injured in an explosion, leading to hearing problems, but he learned to lip-read. His wife Maureen was daughter of James A.Kiernan from Derrycarne House, Annaduff, Co Leitrim. In 1924, it was bought by Colonel Kirkwood from the great racing family and in 1937 her father bought it. Her father died in 1944 and it was put up for sale and bought by Lady Dorothy Mack, married to a British officer, and when she banned hunting and fishing it created a bad relationship with locals, at a time when the IRA was active in Leitrim. One night, shots were fired at the house and they put it up for sale. They couldn't sell it and decided to demolish the house. After her marriage to Desmond, she and her sister Maeve went to work at Holliday's Cleaboy Stud. She reared and nursed horses like Brown Sabre, Valetta, Foxtrot, and Silver Fox. The sisters reared foals up to yearlings for selling at Newmarket mainly in October.

She said people were keen to buy *"the Holliday lot"*, as they used to say because of their great success at the time. She was specifically a night nurse, with a lot of stress and hard work, but was very much helped by local vet Michael Murphy. The great limestone grazing land meant that foals who arrived often from England with thin legs, returned with powerful muscles. She remembered Vaguely Noble, as being the outstanding horse at the stud. She also bred champion setters from 1939 and some of her setters were of such quality that they were purchased by the White House, during the time of Richard Nixon. In 1966, the King of Belgium once chartered a plan and sent Francis Leo Goffart, Belgium Ambassador to purchase a dog. It brought her into contact with people like comedienne Rosaleen Linehan, and she almost got in a film role when the author Richard Hayward came there, as he was a friend of Maurice Walshe, whose book Castle Gillian was adapted and made as *'The Quiet Man'.* Because of this, plans were made for another book *'The Road to Nowhere,'* as a screen play, and Maureen was offered a part. Unfortunately, it did not happen due to WWII.

SALE OF CLEABOY STUD IN 1978

The clearance sale of Cleaboy Stud on 422 acres was advertised in 1978 and was held on 6th February 1978 in the Shelbourne Hotel. Brook Holliday auctioned everything from cattle down to racing books. Over 60 years, Major Holliday acquired the stud that covered 300 acres and it grew to 422 acres. He had a lifelong interest in hunting and by the time he died in 1965, there was scarcely a country that did not feel impact of Cleaboy Stud. He had great managers like Owen Ryan, Des McKeever and Sheila Ryan up to this time. The latter later set up the Littlewell Stud, Hopestown, Mullingar, in Westmeath in 1954 and she managed Cleaboy Stud for 13 year after. Her father died in 1941. In July 1996 after her death, the executors put it up for auction at the Greville Arms. Interestingly, the auctioneer was Paddy Cleary & Son because Mr Cleary's great grandfather, also an auctioneer, lived there and his grandfather was born in Cleaboy. Sheila Ryan had horses with Kevin Prendergast and her best horses included Anxious Moment in the USA, Magic Boy (Wokingham Stakes, Royal Ascot), Gustave Dorc (Errol Stakes, at Ascot), Ludgam (won 13 races in the USA and Britain worth $195,000 and £3,542). Her best buy was Sol Anza (grand-dam of Ludham) at 250gns. Her brood mares included Sol Anza, Gayness, Tasmania, Fair Renown, Short but Sweet, Even Me, and Itoldyouso (kept at Littlewell Stud).

Paddy Clarke took over Cleaboy Stud in April 1978 from Brook Holliday, after the death of Major Holliday in 1965. Paddy Clarke was in his 20's and his family bred horses going back to 1847 at Balreask near Navan. He paid £¾ ml for Cleaboy and sold 140 acres of his Navan land. They steadily switched to chasers and then more to the flat. He studied at Warrenstown Agriculture College and spent 12 months in New Zealand working at the famous Ra Ora Stud, and later worked in South Africa and in America. He had sprint sires Golden Cloud & Proud Chieftain at Balreask. After he bought Cleaboy Stud, he had Runnett (owned by Vee Evans, Rathconrath, Co. Wesmeath), Hays, Sandhurst Prince etc. In 1979 he purchased Orchestra by Tudor Music, as a stallion (winner of John Porter Stakes) and he took up duties at the stud in 1981. Runnett was trained by John Dunlop for Miss Evans and won the Matt Gallagher Sprint at the Phoenix Park in July 1981. He later won the Vernon Sprint at Haydock. In April 1981, the Board of the National Stud intended to buy multiple the winner Runnett, but due to many delays they missed their chance and he was sold.

In January 1995, Patrick J.Clarke his son died suddenly, while on holiday in

Kenya aged 44. He had taken over Cleaboy Stud from his father. This led to the sale of the stud in 1996 to John McKay, when he paid £630,000 for 220 acres. He had played hurling for Clonkill & Westmeath and football with The Downs. He was nominated for the Irish Race Horse Owners Ltd Awards in the *"New Owner"* category, after the exploits of his horse Magical Lady in 1995. In December 1996, one of the top fillies sold at Newmarket for £82,000 was bred by Cleaboy Stud. The dam of the foal was one of the leading mares in Ireland and had winners like Verglas who won Coventry Stakes and Persian Secret a listed winner in England. McKay gave a lot of credit to John Kirby, Castletown-Geo who prepared the foals for sales.

He had a winner at Irish Derby Festival with Generous Lady trained by Dermot Kelly, The Curragh, won by 4 1/2 lengths. She won two of her three races and was the daughter of Generous-Northern Blossom, who was a top champion filly in Canada. John was assisted later by his son David and daughter Suzanne. The stud had top class horses including Magical Lady, 9 mares and foals including Rahaam dam of Verglas, and 5 top bred national hunt 2y/o colts among them Comanche Court and Supreme Leader. He had a successful year with mares and 100% success rate. At the end of 1998, it was another successful year with sales at Newmarket realising excellent returns on a number of their horses with one of the top mares Rahaam and a foal making £380,000. She was originally bought for £24,000. Her first foal was sold for £24,000, 2nd for £82,000, and third for £160,000. They also sold Generous Lady who won 4 races for £100,000 and Noble Dane £85,000. He bought 6 top class American brood mares to replace them. For a time, he had fantastic success with Magical Lady (2nd in Triumph Hurdle), Generous Lady, Strategic Ploy and other horses with his trainer David Kelly and jockey Wayne Smith.

He had been a successful business man and developed one of the largest Equestrian Centre in Southern England. In October 1997, plans were made to develop a luxurious Equestrian Village at Cleaboy Stud the first of its kind in the world. He proposed to have 8 houses, paddocks, stables and plenty of open spaces on 7 acres, with walks around the village and bounded by road & forestry. It was to be beside Kilpatrick Railway Bridge and a 1/2 ml from Fagan's Equestrian Centre and Charlestown jumping and equestrian enterprise. Unfortunately, the successful years did not last and the Stud was sold yet again to Sean O'Gorman.

SEAN O'GORMAN

In 1990, he bought 36 acres of land in Enfield and built a new house and had a few old mares. When things started to go wrong for John McKay he decided to sell it and Sean bought it in the Greville Arms over a handshake and eventually moved into Cleaboy in 2005. He has 43/44 mares and takes mares to foal, where they are held until they foal. It is mostly Nationl Hunt horses, although they had some flat mares but they weren't a success. He had seven who were not a success and he sold a few of them. Oh Cecilia went to Pat Flynn who won at Downroyal and Galway in a nursery during the festival, as a 2 y/o and was 2nd to Ridgewood Pearl in the Charlie Weld Stakes in 1994 and also won in the USA, as 4 y/o. She bred Newgate Lodge who won twice in Ireland (€18,600). There is a steady flow out and big sums keep you going to pay off the bills. He used to sell them all, but now retains some mares to spread it out. He trys to get €30,000, but it gets tighter all the time and also sells some to France and the USA. You need to produce quality horses and it takes around 4 years to bring them to fruition. Sean reduced numbers in time in order to increase the quality. He said you need knowledge and a lot of luck. He said *"a few nice winners always help's you sell other horses".*

Sean O'Gorman buys and sells under Cleaboy & Coppice Farm and some of the horses involved over a number of years were six time winner Heltornic, purchased for £65,000. The nine-year-old, who was offered with both a filly foal by Kayf Tara and a covering by the Overbury Stud stallion, won the Towton Novice Chase at Wetherby and Red Square Vodka Gold Cup in February, 2007, and joined an older sibling Glenmoss Tara. At the time Sean said "*We're always interested in any good mares who come up for sale and I think her price reflects the market. Hopefully she's a really nice young mare with her future in front of her.*"

The New One was sold at the 2011 Derby Sale by Cleaboy Stud and Coppice Farm for €25,000 to Highflyer Bloodstock. In recent years Cleaboy & Coppice Farm sold a 1/2 sister to Willie Mullins' high-class chaser J'y Vole, who won at Grade 1 and 2 level, for €45,000 to Richard Cotter and they also sold a sister of chaser Heltornic for €44,000. Ben Case paid €30,00 for a son of of Robin Des Champs from Cleaboy Stud and Bobby O'Ryan paid €40,000 for a Sakhee colt. In the past, they sold the first foal of French Hurdler La Zingarella for €62,000 and a son of Milan. The family goes back to Francois Doumen's Triumph Hurdle winner Snow Drop. In June 2010, O'Ryan paid €125,000 for a son of Westerner from Cleaboy Stud & Coppice Farm. The gelding was out of Grade 3-winning handicap hurdler Monte Solaro. John Fallon originally from Athlone, was a friend of the O'Gorman's and he owned the successful African Moon associated with the Scott family in Moate. He left four mares with Sean & Katherine - two flat & two National Hunt horses. He bought a mare with Sean at Keeneland and called Hidden Heart and hopefully she will be a success.

GIGGINSTOWN HOUSE STUD

In 1750 the stallion Godolphin (by the Godolphin Arabian) stood at Gigginstown (we only know that Michael O'Leary was not the owner!), but the same animal was with Patrick Dardis, Bellenalack in 1755. In 1909, there is a reference to Frank McCrath, Gigginstown, who sold a Bergomask mare to Mr Quinn, Mount Pellier, Dublin. All this tell's you, is that in the past 265 years horses were bred at Gigginstown, Co Westmeath. In more recent times, the name of Gigginstown House Stud has become a major player in National Hunt racing in Ireland and Great Britain. His father Ted always had an interest in a few National Hunt horses and his brother Eddie was part of the bloodstock industry, at a very young age and was a successful pin-hooker. Michael attended local point to points at Castletown Geoghegan (an area associated with Middleton Park Stud & Sir Cecil Boyd-Rochfort) and enjoyed the day out. From the very start he had no interest in flat racing. The horses run under the banner of his Gigginstown House Stud in Mullingar, because as he once said ,*"I'm running a low-fare airline, so I don't really want my name bandied about as a rich, lazy bastard with lots of horses in training"*. The other point he makes is that he pays for the horses, but his brother Eddie of Lynn Lodge runs the stud and racing operation, *"therefore the credit for any success should go to him"*.

He has stated that he loves Mullingar and living in Gigginstown House, Collinstown, where he is a pedigree Angus farmer. The story of one of the richest men in Ireland and his association with Ryanair, which has benefitted people so much in Ireland, has been well documented, but we are only interested in his involvement with horse racing. He has used the media very effectively on the one hand, but he is also clearly a loving family man. It could be argued that he is mellowing, as he gets older and that he would get more pleasure out of winning another Cheltenham Gold Cup than anything to do with Ryanair?

O'LEARY'S WAR OF ATTRITION

The first horse he ever bought was Tuco trained by David Wachman and he won the Goffs Land Rover bumper in 2001(Beef or Salmon was 3rd) and a novice hurdle at Naas in 2002, before being put down after falling in a Grade 2 novice. It was a good and bad experience but he was determined to buy more horses, which grew to 50 and more over the years. Mouse Morris the trainer has been associated with great horses like Buck House, Trapper John, Cahervillahow, Boss Doyle and many more, but the one that delivered his most important victory was War of Attrition on 17th March 2006. He bought the horse after he fell in the lead at a point to point in Horse & Jockey in 2003. The horse was sold by Ger Hourigan to the O'Leary's and it was the first horse they sent to Mouse Morris. After a few runs he won at Punchestown & Navan beating Mac's Joy when ridden by Conor O'Dwyer for the first time. It was only then that they began to believe that they had a good horse. After running down the field when sick, he was 33/1 for the Supreme Novice Hurdle, but ran a great race to be only beaten a neck by Brave Inca. It was one of the few occasions that Michael O'Leary backed one of his own horses and he won a few bob at various prices. It was after this, that Conor O'Dwyer became the first jockey to be contracted with Gigginstown House Stud mainly through Eddie O'Leary. Although fancied for the Arkle at Cheltenham, he was run off his feet and it was a bitter disappointment, but the he went on to be second at Aintree and won a Grade 1 novice chase over two miles at Punchestown. In October 2005, he beat the Gold Cup winner Kicking King in the Daily Star Chase and in his last run before Cheltenham he was second in the Lexus Chase to Beef or Salmon in unsuitable soft ground.

The plan at Cheltenham was to go for the Ryanair Chase, but the ground was good, so they decided to go for the Gold Cup. With 22 runners it was an open race with Beef or Salmon 4/1F and War of Attrition 15/2. They decided to run on the outside which allowed the horse to jump well. Conor O'Dwyer was one of the greatest jockey's ever and he brilliantly got the horse into a rhythm on the outside. He fought off Forget the Past (B. Geraghty) and then Ruby challenged with Hedgehunter, but he was always confident and put in a great jump at the last to guarantee the win. Conor said that the horse gave him a great feel at the last fence and he knew he would win the cup and add to his success on Imperial Call. As Michael O'Leary said *"War of Attrition - he was named after his owner"*.

The dream had come true for the O'Leary's and they flew back home to Mullingar and many celebrations took place in the town that night, as the locals backed the horse each way. The Gold Cup was paraded by the Camogie Club through Delvin on that Sunday, which was St Patrick's Day. At the subsequent Kilbeggan races, around 6,000 people turned up to see War of Attrition in the parade ring. In March 2007, Mouse Morris's War of Attrition developed a leg problem in his tendon, so he was out for the season. The horse retired in 2010 after the World Hurdle and a final race at Punchestown and went to retire at Gigginstown. He said about War of Attrition *"I want to make sure we get War home in one piece, so that he and I can look at each other for years"*. They later had the experience of Hear The Echo the Irish Grand National winner (outlined under the Irish Grand National) who collapsed and died on the run-in of the Grand National in 2009.

AN EMOTIONAL DAY AT CHELTENHAM

In the following few years they produced horses like Sir Des Champs, First Lieutenant, Carlito Brigante, Toner D'Oudaries, Trifolium and Weapon's Amnesty to win at Cheltenham. In 2011, Michael O'Leary almost broke down before the cameras, as his father Ted was seriously ill. His great servant First Lieutenant (winner of 7 races and over €620,000) won at Cheltenham, as his father was home watching it. He said it's an *"emotional day"*, as his father was undergoing chemotherapy. He had three winners at the meeting and Carlito Brigante gave him a double on the Wednesday. Gordon Elliott said about the 5 y/o Carlito Brigante after his success that *"It's great to get a winner for Gigginstown. They are one of our biggest supporters in the yard".* He had sourced the horse for Gigginstown Stud and paid €40,000 for him. Willie Mullins's Sir Des Champs completed a treble on Friday in the Conditional Jockeys Hurdle. The latter went on to be second to Bobsworth in the Cheltenham Gold and in 2013 got up to beat Sam Waley Cohen on Long Run and First Lieutenant at Punchestown by 3/4 length and 1/2 length. He had to be ruled out for the 2014 Gold Cup after an injury. First Lieutenant has been a great servant with two Grade 1 wins, but just fell short at the very highest level in major races. Weapons Amnesty trained by Charles Byrne won the RSA Chase at Cheltenham in 2010 by 7 lengths beating Punchestown, Long Run & Burton Port from Nick Henderson's stable after winning the Albert Bartlett Novice Hurdle in 2009 (Byrnes first winner at the Festival). He then received a serious tendon injury and had to be retired in January 2013. Eddie O'Leary considered him to be the best chaser they ever had.

The end of the 2009/10 National Hunt season marked something of a changing of the guard in Irish jump racing, as Gigginstown beat JP McManus at the top of the owners prize money list, it was the first time since 1995 that JP hadn't been champion owner.

DAVY RUSSELL AND THE COMPLEXITIES OF A SPORTING LIFE

The year 2014 was a difficult one for Gigginstown House, with blanks at Cheltenham and Leopardstown at Christmas, but stable jockey Davy Russell rode his 1,000th winner. He was a tough, reliable jockey and at 34 was still a major figure in races having spent seven years with Gigginstown Stud. It was therefore a surprise to him that he was sacked on New Year's Eve to be replaced by Bryan Cooper 21 y/o. He said he was disappointed for himself, but not blaming Michael O'Leary. When Gigginstown House & Russell look back on the previous 7 years they will appreciate it was a golden spell. In his time he had ridden good horses like Sir Des Champs and First Lieutenant, but they hadn't won the major races.

The complexities of sporting life, and the part that chance plays in events, is always fascinating and inexplicable. Bryan Cooper who was on a high with his new appointment was injured in a fall on the first day. The irony for Davy Russell was that he got the mount of Lord Windermere in the Cheltenham Gold Cup for Jim Culloty and he was offered and accepted rides on Gigginstown House horses. As Lord Windermere trailed behind the field for most of the trip it looked like the best Davy Russell would do was collect his fee as a jockey. However, in the latter stages he started picking up the whole field, and with as many twists as a Hitchcock movie on the run-in, he got up to beat Ruby Walsh and On His Own in a driving finish. At that moment Davy thought that it couldn't get better than this and Michael O'Leary, as he watched, probably thought it couldn't get any worse with no winners after three days. However, on a freaky Friday afternoon at Cheltenham, Gigginstown House and the O'Leary brothers were to have an astonishing four winners. It started with Tiger Roll 10/1 (ridden by Davy Russell) winning the JCB 4 y/o Hurdle; then Noel Meade's good horse Very Wood 33/1 (P.Carberry) winning the Albert Bartlett Novice Hurdle; Willie Mullins won with Don Poli (M.P.Fogarty); and in the last Davy Russell completed his hat-trick of wins on Savello trained by Tony Martin. It was joy all round for the O'Leary's and Russell in your ultimate happy ending, if it was a movie. It was all achieved with four different trainers.

THE MYSTERY AND POTENTIAL FOR CHELTENHAM 2015

It has been noticeable that Gigginstown House Stud gradually has more horses with Willie Mullins, Gordon Elliott and Noel Meade the three top trainers in Ireland with an increased number of French imports, but having said that Charles Byrnes, Tony Martin, Mouse Morris and Eoin Griffin also had had winners. It seems that Gigginstown's influence (and others) in purchasing horses is raising the profile of the sport and also bringing in buyers for other participants, thus enabling them to get a better deal. The quality of horses running at point to points is sometimes better than the racecourse with future Grade 1 winners often found there. The horses are usually bought by Eddie O'Leary and Mags O'Toole.

Going into Cheltenham 2015 many of the horses had great potential. Noel Meade's Road to Riches has gone on a path similar to J.P.McManus's horse Carlingford Lough via success in the Galway Plate. In spite of that success it was still a surprise to many when he won the Group 1 Lexus Chase 150,000 at Leopardstown ridden by Bryan Cooper to beat On His Own and Sam Winner. The horse had won Down Royal's JNwine.com Champion Chase in November beating Rocky Creek by 11 lengths, but this time he beat the last two Gold Cup winners (Lord Windemere & Bobs Worth). Noel Meade said *"Since we changed his diet at Punchestown last season he hasn't stopped improving"*. The horse's only defeat in his previoust four races was against Sizing Europe and he had won 8 out of 15 by Christmas 2014.

Don Cossock had won 10 of 19 runs including the Grade 1 Drinmore Chase in December 2013 beating Carlingford Lough and Road to Riches, which in hindsight was brilliant form but Gordon Elliot's relationship with this horse, that he once described as an *"aeroplane"* was mixed. He was not progressive and it seemed he might disappear, as a Grade 1 horse. However, from his return in October until January 2015 he rolled off 4 consecutive wins on ground from Good/Firm to soft (three in a row over 2 $^1/_2$ miles).When he won the €80,000 John Durkan Chase at Punchestown more people began to notice, as it was his second Grade 1. Gordon Elliott was quick to say that if he had his way the horse would go for the Ryanair Cup and not the Gold Cup.

Other good horses going into Cheltenham included Lieutenant Colonel, who won the Hatton's Grace Hurdle at Fairyhouse, where he gave Sandra Hughes her first major win since Dessie passed away the previous month. Don Poli a 5 y/o won the Topaz Novice Chase Grade 1 over 3 miles beating Apache Stronghold and Lots of Memories and was now one of favourites for RSA or JLT at festival. He had been bought privately by Willie Mullins & Eddie O'Leary. Clarcam won the Racing Post Novice Chase (Grade 1) beating hotpot Vautour by 17 lengths. It seemed a slightly strange result and Cheltenham was to prove that it was false. Valseur Lido won the Drinmore Chase in Nov 2014 easily for his second win over fences and his main challenger was Noel Meade's Apache Stranglehold, but he went on to win by 8 lengths. He was to have his day in the sun after Cheltenham. Petite Parissiene won the Gala Retail Spring Juvenile Hurdle Grade 1 4 y/o hurdle over 2 miles in February 2015 at 6/1. It all looked good for Cheltenham.

At Cheltenham, there were some disappointments including Don Cossack's only defeat of the season in a strange race. Don Poli delivered a brilliant win in the RSA Chase to become a favourite for the Gold Cup in 2016 (7/1 from 12/1). Willie Mullins said *"He has Gold Cup written all over him. If he can do that to the best novices in England & Ireland at Cheltenham, there is only one road on which to go".* Rivage D'Or 16/1 travelled well, and in a career best he won the cross country race. Michael O'Leary said Tony Martin gave him confidence and was the right man for the job. He was having lunch, when the race was on, and only saw the last few furlong. He threatened to sell him a few months before, but he failed his vet test and he took him back. The Punchestown Festival brought a brilliant performance in the Punchestown Gold Cup by Don Cossack beating Djakadam with Road to Riches third. Valseur Lido came back to his best at Punchestown beating the disappointing Don Poli. Petit Parissienne was also very impressive in victory. The potential for next year with all this depth of talent will mean that Gigginstown House Stud have plenty to look forward to in 2016.

A variety of other good horses have shown up from chasers to bumper horses including Tony Martin's Dedigout, to Wounded Warrior, Very Wood, Bright New Dawn, Rule the World, General Principal, Whistling Dixie, McKinley, Stone Hard, Tycoon Prince etc. Two promising young novice hurdlers with Westmeath connections are the Cathal Ennis, Castletown-Geoghegan bred Identity Thief trained by Henry de Bromhead, and the Peter Downes, Russelstown, bred No More Heroes (related to Fiveforthree and Celestial Gold). Gigginstown House Stud were crowned the Irish National Hunt Champion Owner's for the third time in 2015, getting the better of J.P. McManus.

GOOD DEED'S AND STRONG VIEWS

John Thomas McNamara, famed Irish Amateur jockey, was riding Galaxy Rock for Jonjo O'Neill, when they fell at the first fence in the Kim Muir Chase at Cheltenham in March 2013. He was seriously injured. In addition around that period Jonjo Bright, an 18-year-old point-to-point rider, also suffered a serious neck injury in a fall at a meeting at Tyrella. Both riders benefited from a €200,000 gift that Michael O'Leary, one of jump racing's biggest patrons, donated to the Injured Jockeys Emergency Fund that week. He had pledged to pay €200,000 for the winner of the bumper. He won the race himself with Akorakor (a recent Kilbeggan winner) and then he phoned from Portugal and instructed that the money go to the Injured Jockey's Fund. It was a generous gesture for a great cause. It was the same day that Dot Love, Mullingar won the Irish Grand National with Liberty Counsel. There was a great connection with Gigginstown House Stud, as their horses are sent to her to learn how to race & jump before they go to a racecourse. He has also been a great supporter of his local racecourse in Kilbeggan, when Gigginstown House Stud sponsored its featured race the Midland's National each July for four years and he had success in the race as outlined elsewhere.

It was reported in January 2014, that Michael O'Leary had purchased Newmarket's 210 acre Plantation Stud in a private deal (it had come up for sale in May 2012). The intention as reported by Eddie O'Leary was to send the National Hunt horses over there for rehab.

VIEWS ON RACING

At times, Michael O'Leary has given his views on racing. With regard to owners like himself and J.P. McManus he said on occasions it seems to some people that the taxpayer is subsidising rich people like them, but the reality is that they lose millions each year. This has become very clear with the cost of purchasing top National Hunt horses in Ireland or France, all reaching six figure sums. Many are injured and most don't make the grade, therefore there is a massive loss (in one year alone they lost 15 horses through injuries). It does seem as if more of his better horses are going to the top three trainers Willie Mullins, Gordon Elliott and Noel Meade in more recent times. It is likely that the overall number of trainers will stabilise and that more French bred's will be bought, as they are racing as mature horses at a younger age. In spite of all the money going into racing he feel's there is still a need to generate money at the turnstiles, as it competes with other sports.

Pat Doyle prepares the Gigginstown youngsters in their point to point year and he works closely with Eddie O'Leary on how horses should be prepared, so that they can have the best chance of enjoying success under rules. It is usually O'Leary that sources the horses and they are then handed to Dot Love and Ciaran Murphy, who are based near Gigginstown headquarters in Mullingar to be broken and pre trained. The three and four year olds then move onto Doyle, who has been in the business for over 30 years. Most of their horses are given a run in a point to point for experience purposes. The horses are then dispersed amongst a select number of trainers including Gordon Elliot, Charles Byrnes, Mouse Morris, Dessie Hughes, Paul Nolan and MichaelHourigan. This policy of using a number of trainers negates the risk of the whole string being struck with a virus.

EDDIE O'LEARY AND LYNN LODGE

The recession in recent years with the loss of many owners (and trainers like Charlie Swan, Joanna Morgan most recently), who had made fortunes in the building industry had badly affected horse racing, which is just recovering now. Breeders were also badly affected, especially on the National Hunt side. Eddie O'Leary has a 200 acre farm at Lynn Lodge, Killucan, which he started in the 1980's. He was born in 1962 and he admits that the recession did not affect flat racing, as much as National Hunt, as most of his sales were to Britain, France and other international countries (he is around 95% export).

Lynn Lodge breeds foals from around 30 mares and then sells them at the Autumn yearling sales and they also purchases yearlings to be sold as 2 y/o's at the "breeze ups" sales in the spring. This keeps them busy all the year round with mares, foals, and yearlings needing constant care. More than half of Lynn Lodge's stock, which runs to around 50 animals each calendar year are bred at the stud, with the rest bought as foals or yearlings. They bring in some yearlings, break them and train them and then they are sold at breeze ups in Newmarket, Kempton, and St Cloud, France, but the main job is selling yearlings at Goffs, Doncaster, & Deauville. Eddie says there is an art in spotting a foal that will improve as a yearling. It's an inexact science but he gets it right more times than wrong. He knows bloodlines are important but physical attributes are also just as relevant. He has had success with a number of horses in recent years. As he has said in the past *"The way I think of it, is it gives you a good kick when you get it right, and a good kick in the ass when you get it wrong".*

Lynn Lodge has had international success both sides of the Atlantic. Passinetti won the Group 1 San Juan Capistrano at Santa Anita in 2003; Castledale won two Group 1's, the Santa Anita Derby and Shoemaker Breeders Mile at Hollywood Park. Benbaun won the Group1 Prix de I'Abbaye at Longchamp and six Group 3 races trained by Mark Wallace. Other winners were Killybegs, Red Jazz, and Hellvelyn. He breeds horses for 2 y/o speed to try to get a horse of championship class over a mile as a 3 y/o. He would love to breed a winner of the Guineas, because he think's it is the real big race not the Derby. Eddie O'Leary has carved out his own position in racing and the operation at Gigginstown House Stud is very different to Lynn Lodge and he is a familiar figure at National Hunt fixtures. The older O'Leary summed up the Gigginstown operation a little more colourfully when he said *"Eddie runs the stud, buys all the horses, does all that"* he said last year. *"I just write the cheques. We have an appropriate division of labour!"'*

Some examples of successful sales in recent years include in October 2013 a colt by Mastercraftsman-Splash Mountain sold to David Elsworth for 200,000 guineas to be trained by James Fanshawe on behalf of Ben Wong, Hong Kong. This horse was pinhooked by Eddie O'Leary, who purchased him as a foal for 44,000 guineas. In April 2013, there was a European Record broken at Tattersalls Craven Breeze Up Sale, when an Elusive Quality colt by Gender Dancer consigned by him was sold for 760,000 guineas to Jamie McCalmont. It was in January 2013 that Canford Cliffs' first foal was born, when Gigginstown House Stud's Smartest (Exceed and Excel) produced a bay colt at Lynn Lodge Stud. Eddie O'Leary described the foal as: *"a really good, strong colt with plenty of quality and a great colour".* Outside racing he likes rugby and played for Mullingar and goes to see Leinster & Ireland. He is also involved in the GAA, as his daughter's Megan & Jodie plus sons Jack and Ted play for Raharney hurling and The Downs football. Jack his son is a very good athlete having represented Ireland at under age level.

To sum up the operation in Gigginstown House Stud it is not the number of wins, the prize money or leading owner that matters. The objective is to win the Group 1 races and in particular the Cheltenham Gold Cup

chapter 6
JOCKEYS - PAT SMULLEN AND "THE MAN WHO BEAT ARKLE"

PAT SMULLEN - INTERNATIONAL JOCKEY AND ONE OF OFFALY'S GREATEST SPORTSTAR'S

Pat Smullen was not born into a racing family and when he was young, his father Paddy was much more involved with greyhounds than horses. He was one of four sons and the connection with racing developed due to his older brother Sean, who was working with Joanna Morgan former successful jockey & then trainer. When he was 11 y/o, Sean brought him to the yard. Sean loved horses and had started with Joanna Morgan, where he prepared horses for breeze up sales. It was here that he learned about riding a pony not just on the flat but jumping a pole. When I interviewed Pat in December 2014, he said it was tough working at Joanna's but *"within a year he was riding thoroughbred's including two year old's".* Sean later went to Canada and is in charge of one of the leading bloodstock farms in North America, owned by the powerful Frank Stronach. He also trains some horses in Toronto. Pat could no longer work in Meath without a means of transport.

He left school at fifteen and his father got him a job with Tom & Peg Lacy near home in Rhode, Co Offaly. The *"Rhode to success"* was possible, as Tom Lacy himself was famed because of his connection with the great mare Height O'Fashion, who gave both Arkle and Flyingbolt two of the toughest races of their great careers. Barry Lacy son of Tom worked with Pat on his riding and he found a very willing and determined young man at the age of 15. Even as a young man Pat was not really interested in other hobbies, but he had a great love of all farm animals and to this day when he is not riding his hobby is *"spending time with all the animals on his stud farm"*. He worked on the farm as a youngster, but his great success as a rider gave him the opportunity to purchase the land, many years later. The Lacy Family were almost like second parents and even though it was a small yard, they ensured that he got every opportunity to succeed at riding. He has always stated that he put him up on almost every horse he ran. His father had brought him to all the pony tracks and he rode for the Fahey's and others, before winning the Pony Rider's Title in 1992. His first ever ride on a horse was on Lacy's Power Source at Listowel, where he finished 9th of 11 runners, but it was not until June 1993 that he recorded his first ever win on Vicosa at Dundalk for his mentor. In 1993 he had 5 wins, 1994-11 wins and he was deemed the Most Improved Jockey. He went on to win the Apprentice Title in 1994 with 26 winners and in 1995 with 29 winners. This gave him the opportunity to ride in the Tokyo World Apprentice Series in Japan, which was a great experience. In 1995/96, he rode 6 winners from 20 rides for his future brother-in-law Aidan O'Brien, and one way or another his life has crossed with his brother-in-law throughout his career.

It was during this period that he had issues with his weight, as he was over 8 stone and he rode over hurdles for a short period including a couple of placed mounts, and then he went to Australia to work at Randwick but returned home weighing over 9 stone. It was then the will power and determination that he shows on the track focused him on the issue and gradually he got his weight under control. He started to get outside rides with other trainers and then he was offered the opportunity to ride as second jockey to Johnny Murtagh at John Oxx's stable.

His first major success was on Tommy Stack's Tarascon in the Moyclare Stakes in 1997, but in the long term his most significant success was in the CL Weld Park Stakes in October 1996 when Mick Kinane, the No 1 jockey for Dermot Weld, chose to ride Absolute Glee leaving young Pat Smullen to ride stable companion Token Gesture. In a driving three way finish with Kinane & Christy Roche he succeeded by a head and a neck with Absolute Glee in third place. He has described it as *"the turning point of my career"*, as events that day stayed in the mind of Dermot Weld when Mick Kinane decided to move to Aidan O'Brien's powerful Coolmore Stud stable in 1999. I asked Pat did he have to do an interview for the job? The reality is that racing is not run like a company and he received a call to meet with Dermot and after discussions he was offered the job. As it was one of the most prestigious jobs in Irish Racing there was no doubt that the 22 y/o would accept it but it was a major responsibility for a young man.

He has been described as everything from calm, courteous, intelligent, capable, determined, and he is all of these and more recently Dermot Weld called him *"the professional's professional"*. As you look back on 2014, you see a jockey who did not quite get the credit he deserved in Britain until his two dramatic successes at Royal Ascot on Mustajeeb in the Jersey Stakes and the horse that Eddie Lynam called *"the real deal"* Anthem Alexander in the Queen Mary Stakes, which somehow focused attention on his abilities. His ability was recognised in Ireland and he rode around Galway in a style similar to his idol Mick Kinane. Whether it was right or wrong, there is no doubt that Royal Ascot in June 2014 changed the international view of Pat Smullen and there was much written about where he might be riding in the future. He has just ignored the media speculation and carried on become champion jockey for the seventh time.

It was very different when he started with Dermot Weld, as in the early days analysis of races on video was a common feature. He was still very young and needed advice from Dermot Weld and Mick Kinane, as it was a learning process. He listened, he learned, and then he applied it on the track like a professional jockey should. Even at an early age he ensured that he was always on time, didn't miss work and controlled his weight. He has mentioned that there was great respect between them. In numerous interviews he has always stated that he has received other offers but he is happy and enjoys working for the owners that support the stable. Dermot Weld has broken records all over the world from the USA to Australia. Go and Go was the first European horse to win an American Classic, Vintage Crop was the first European horse to win the famous Melbourne Cup, which he then repeated with Media Puzzle. In addition he has broken all records at Galway races over a number of years and he has a high percentage strike rate when he sends runners to Britain, as they only run if they have a chance. Most of Pat's main winners were trained by Dermot Weld.

In 2014, he won his 7th Irish Jockey's Championship and in addition he had over 100 winners for the first time. In September 2014, Brooch gave Pat Smullen his 100th winner of the season when she maintained her unbeaten record in the Denny Cordell Lavarack & Lanwades Stud Fillies Stakes, the feature race at Gowran on Sunday. The horse had won at Galway & Killarney and was 11/8 favourite for the Group 3 race. It was a typical powerful ride as he caught and beat English raider Regardez.

VINNIE ROE WAS A TWO YEAR OLD BRAT!

The above may sound like a criticism of one of the most popular flat horses in recent times, but it was in reality an affectionate reference to Vinnie Roe by Pat Smullen when he said *"He was a brat as a two year old"* and they had to put blinkers on him, as a three year old. It was all worthwhile, because he went on to win four Irish St Leger's between 2001-2004, Prix Royal Oak, 2nd and 4th in the Melbourne Cup, 5th in the Prix De L'Arc, and 2nd in the Ascot Gold Cup to Royal Rebel in 2002. He was the horse that put Smullen in the international map. In 2002, the very useful filly Dress To Thrill, won the Matron Stakes and then the Sun Chariot Stakes in England before going on to win the Group 1 Matriarch Stakes at Hollywood Park in December. I asked Pat about how he approached riding in the USA and Australia for the first time, as the local media can often be critical of foreign jockey's. He said that he doesn't change his approach, as it is all about the feeling of the horse through your hands and natural instinct. He had his first Royal Ascot winner with Irresistible Jewel in the Ribblesdale Stakes in 2002, his first and only English classic success with Refuse to Bend in the English 2,000guineas in 2003. It was then that Dermot Weld said to him *"Ride him like the top class international jockey you are"*. He went on to beat Zafeen, but this was as good as is got with the horse, that finished 13th in the Epsom Derby. In 2004, he rode Vinnie Roe to be an excellent second to Australian favourite Makybe Diva, who was receiving weight and as usual with the Australian press, the *"foreign"* jockey did not escape criticism for going wide on the top weight. Pat had no regrets about his ride, even if the style of racing and riding is different in most countries, you can only ride your normal professional race.

One of his most important wins was on Grey Swallow in the Irish Derby in 2004. The horse was the top rated two year old in Ireland, but had not quite delivered before the big race at The Curragh, where he ran against Epsom Derby winner North Light. He came sweeping through to catch the latter and amid emotional scenes was very pleased to win the most important classic in Ireland. The horse went on to win the Group 1 Tattersalls Cup the following year and prove his class. One of his most liked horses was Famous Name multiple Group winner of 21 races, out of 31 races (placed in 8 others). Perhaps his unluckiest reversal of all at Group 1 level that season came in the French Derby in 2008 where Famous Name was beaten by just a head. He also rode good horses like the Ralph Beckett trained Muhannak who won the Group 1 Breeders Cup Marathon at Santa Anita; Emulous added to her earlier victories with a stunning success in the Group 1 Coolmore Fusaichi Pegasus Matron Stakes at Leopardstown in 2010, and Rite of Passage when he won the Ascot Gold Cup.

FREE EAGLE - THE PRINCE OF WALES

In 2014, the quality and quantity of top class horses increased at Dermot Weld's stable and with a number of Group and high class winners like Mustajeeb, Forgotten Rules, Pale Mimosa, Vote Often, Fascinating Rock, Afternoon Sunlight, Tarfasha and Edelmira plus outside rides like Eddie Lynam's Anthem Alexander. Pat has ridden many fine horses but none of them were career defining like Sea the Stars or Frankel, but undoubtedly the horse that he is looking forward to is the four time raced (2 wins) Free Eagle, who was third in the Quipco Champion Stakes and was once rated higher than Australia, until defeated by him as a two year old. He said the race he wants to win the most is the Prix De I'Arc de Triomphe and he thinks this is the horse that might give him that win in 2015. Another race he has in his sights on is the Champion Bumper at Cheltenham, as he loves National Hunt racing and rode over hurdles. What about the double in the next few years?

On Wednesday 17th June 2015, Free Eagle had his first run of the year in the Group1 Prince of Wales Stakes. Dermot Weld was worried about his race fitness, even though he was in great form. It was only his 5th race ever but Pat Smullen had great faith in him, which he showed by making a vital move about 2 1/2 furlong's out and getting first run on The Great Gatsby who was legally kept in by Frankie Dettori and his late run came up a fraction short as Free Eagle got his deserved Group 1 win. The objective is still the Prix de L'Arc in October a race that Pat & Dermot Weld would love to win. If this horse stays healthy and fit he could deliver that important win. Pat also rode a brilliant race on Sir Michael Stoute's horse Snow Sky to make all the running in the Hardwicke Stakes and win easily.

Exciting times seem to be on the horizon for the Dermot Weld stable and it seems unlikely that he will move anywhere. He is now 37, and will ride for as long as possible because training is an unlikely career move. Some day he will retire to his farm near Rhode with his love of animals, but hopefully not for some years. Martin Davey from Kilbeggan was a jockey some years ago with Tom Lacys and Mouse Morris and he mentioned that the jockey' there scratched their names around an old fireplace at the yard. Pat Smullen confirmed that he also scratched his name while there and it is a name that will be embedded in the mind of racing supporters for many years to come.

Frances Crowley who is married to Smullen, with three children, retired in 2008 after 10 years. She won the Irish 1,000gns with Saoire (M.Kinane) in 2005, after training about 350 winners. She was a daughter of Joe Crowley and sister of Anne Marie (Aidan O'Brien's wife). They met in 1998 at Dubai and she later started training in Piltown, Carlow. They were married in 2001. Her best horses were Saoire and Cheyanne Star on the flat plus Moscow Express (who won £326,866 in prize money for Frances Crowley), who won 26 races with 17 over fences, including the Galway Plate 2001. Sackville was the winner of 18 races and won eight consecutive novice chases including the Drinmore Chase and the Power Cup during the 2000/01 season, before adding the Charlie Hall Chase and the Tommy Whittle Chase the following season. In her first year she trained 42 winners and was third in the Jumps Championship. She won seven races with Nil Desperandum, most notably the Drinmore Chase at Fairyhouse in 2003. She was twice Irish Champion Amateur rider.

CECIL RONALDSON (1928 - 2014) - THE MAN WHO BEAT ARKLE

Cecil Ronaldson died on 4th November 2014 at the Midland Regional Hospital, Mullingar and following the Funeral Service at All Saints Church his burial took place on Friday 7th November in Enniscoffey Cemetery. He is one of the people the book is dedicated to, because of his personal contribution, but also as a representation of the many families in Offaly and Westmeath who contributed so much to racing over several generations.

Cecil was involved in all aspects of racing from riding, training and breeding and was a leading amateur jockey in the 1950's and 1960's. He even rode against a young Ted Walshe and Dermot Weld. He was Champion Amateur Rider in 1959 and he won our 'Amateurs' Derby at the Galway Festival on Charlie Weld's Ballyflame in 1960 and Many Mansions in 1966 for Mick Connolly. However, he is best remembered as the man who on 9th December 1961 rode his wife's mare Lady Flame to beat Kilspindie and Arkle the greatest horse in racing history. The story has been recorded so many times that most racing people know it well. I interviewed Cecil last year in connection with the book and there was more to the story, that is not often mentioned. On the Monday before Mullingar races, Tom Dreaper rang Cecil (which was not unusual as he rode for him in bumpers) and said he had two entries in the bumper at Mullingar and would Cecil ride one of them. He said they were not likely to win, which interested Cecil, as his good mare Lady's Flame was in the race. He said he would let Tom know after his horses morning gallop. After a good workout, he rang back to say he would ride his own horse and Lady's Flame will be remembered forever in racing history. She had been second in Clonmel when she was in season, and he said *"I really fancied her that day in Mullingar and she didn't let me down. She developed a shoulder problem later on that meant she didn't thrive when she went jumping"*. Dreaper only ran Arkle in the race and Cecil did wonder if he said yes would he have been riding Arkle? He would then have gone down in history as the first jockey to ride Arkle rather than the first jockey to beat Arkle ! Interestingly, Lady Flame was later always lame, which limited her career but she was the dam of Tomboy II, who was a good winner for him and as outlined below, one ride on the horse led to great acclaim for him in the media.

Mark Hely Hutchinson has gone down in history as the only man to ride Arkle and not win on him and as he has always said *"nobody told me I was riding a famous horse"*. The runner up was John Bryce Smyth's Kilspindie, who was a likeable horse in his future career over hurdles and fences. Lady Flame was only 8th in a maiden hurdle at Mullingar in February 1962. The Arkle connection with Mullingar could have been extended, as he was entered for a handicap hurdle in Mullingar in March 1962 but the meeting was transferred to Naas due to the condition of the ground in Mullingar. He was 2/1F and he won in his first handicap, the first time he started favourite and the first time he was ridden by Pat Taaffe. He beat the Offaly horse Mrs M.Willington's Soltest by 4 lengths giving 2 stone and T.P.Downes fron Mullingar, owned the 4th horse Mariner's View. Another horse of Mrs Willington's Soldropina was 2nd last in Mullingar on Arkle's debut and finished 3rd at Naas in the bumper. Paddy O'Roarke rode his own horse Prudent Gertie in Arkle's race and Frank Lacy rode Painters Cottage.

Another Westmeath connection with Arkle was the Head Lad Paddy Murray, who was originally from Moate and worked with John Dolan at Farnagh Stud, until he went to Dreaper's in 1942. He was born very close to Farnagh Stud. He looked after Prince Regent the 1946 Gold Cup winner and also Shagreen, who won the Irish National in 1949. He was made Head Lad in 1951 until he retired in 1982 and all the great horses went through his hands. He was up at 7.20am and gave the last feed at 8pm. He didn't take off time except a 1/2 day on Friday for a few pints. He'd take out a drop of Guinness himself when feeding the horses. He went to Leopardstown one year at Christmas and they had a few winners. He used to ride out horses in the morning like Prince Regent, as he rode hunters at an early age in Moater. He was very fond of Prince Regent & Arkle, but Flyingbolt was a horse of a different colour and not as kind as Arkle. The horses were given plenty of time to develop by Tom Dreaper & the owners. Jim was more a farmer than a racing man so he never had the same success. Paddy very seldom backed a horse. He was the unsung hero of the Arkle era at Tom Dreaper's Greenogue yard and his funeral in 2005 brought back golden memories for many.

RIDING IN AN "IMPOSSIBLE FASHION"

Cecil was a brave and determined jockey and this was proven in January 1971, when his horse Tomboy II ran in the Slaney Hurdle at Naas. One of the leathers broke on the way down. Undeterred he tied it up and carried on but at the 5th last hurdle it broke again leaving him without the stirrup and only his balance to keep him on. He was challenged and overtaken by favourite Eternal Hope, but riding in an *"impossible fashion"* (as one paper said) he got up to somehow win by 3/4 length. Just a few yards after the line, he finally slipped off the horse to tremendous applause. Louis Gunning, a reporter gave his top award for riding to the amateur on that Saturday and added *"indeed for that matter for a hundred Saturdays".*

He was the son of a successful owner /trainer in W. Ronaldson and one of the most resourceful amateurs to emerge in the post WWII era. His first ever winner in Mullingar was on Royal Stuart, but he added many more over the years from Another Madcap to Highland Chef. In 1957 he entered Magic King in the Aintree Grand National where he fell half way round. He trained multiple winners like Foxbat and Another Flame. In 1981, Foxbat won at Aintree in April in the Skol Chase from Irian, but was disqualified as he hung left. He was later killed in a novice chase in Ayr when falling at the last. A feature at the Ballinrobe meeting in June 1959 was the third Corinthian Plate Bumper success in a row for Cecil .On Tuesday he won with Another Flame at Leopardstown; on Wednesday he won at Mallow with Solbaygina and on Thursday won at Ballinrobe with Scotch Koffee for Willie O'Grady. He rode for Charlie Weld, the Downes family, Mrs Rochfort Hyde and others like John McQuaid, Irishtown owner of Glasslough Monica a Punchestown winner.

STEWARDS "TWILIGHT SEARCH FOR HOOF MARKS"

Dan O'Neill was better known for his involvement with greyhounds but he leased a horse called *Owen's Image* from Barney Noughton and the horse ran in a bumper at Mallow on 23rd November 1955 ridden and trained by Cecil Ronaldson. He was backed from 6/1 to 1/1 and Ronaldson was one of the best amateur jockeys of this era. The horse made rapid progress from the back to overtake everything and win easily by 1 $^{1}/_{2}$ lengths from Kumala. Eddie Harty riding the runner-up, objected to the winner on the grounds that he had gone inside a post on the far side of the course. After some deliberation the Stewards decided to go with Mr Harty and have a look at the spot even though it was now twilight. After a while they returned to the Stewards Room. The enquiry carried on for another hour before, amazingly, it was announced that the winner was disqualified for going the wrong side of the post and Kumala was declared the winner. The horse later left Cecil, and went to the Willie O'Grady stable and eventually to Fulke Walwyn in England, where he continued to compete successfully.

Cecil Ronaldson bred a useful horse more recently in Weird Al (Accordion-Bucks Gift), who was trained in Britan and won over £133,000 in prize money, including the Charlie Hall Chase at Wetherby and also ran in the Cheltenham Gold Cup in 2011. He was purchased at the 2006 Tattersalls Ireland Sale for 60,000. He started with Venetia Williams and then went to Ian Williams, but only ran a few times before showing his ability over fences at the end of 2009 by winning novice chases twice at Cheltenham. In February 2010, he won the Grade 2 Towton Novice Chase at Wetherby and was aimed for the RSA Chase at Cheltenham, until he fractured a cannon bone just a few days before the race. In 2010, he won at Carlisle in an intermediate chase, before finishing 8th to Diamond Harry in the Hennessy Gold Cup. He ran in the Gold Cup at Cheltenham in 2011 but was pulled up with a broken blood vessel. He then went to Donald McCain and ridden by Timmy Murphy. He won the Charlie Hall Chase at Wetherby in October and was only beaten 10 lengths by Kauto Star on the Betfair Chase at Haydock. He ran in the Gold Cup again, but had another broken blood vessel & was pulled up again. He never had the opportunity to show his full potential because of all his problems but won 6 of his 11 starts and over £133,000.

I would not claim to know Cecil after an interview but he was reserved and I had to persuade him to give me a few photos to copy. I promised that they would be returned by 10am the following Wednesday morning. I made sure to be there by 9.45am and then he invited me in for tea and a chat. He was a great representative of a generation of people in racing and point to points, who have left many great memories. He lived a sporting life to the full but as it said on the front of the Funeral Service leaflet he is now *"Peacefully at Rest".*

THE CLEARY FAMILY, ATHLONE

On Saturday 1st November 2003, Sean Cleary an apprentice and 5lbs claimer (aged 22) died. He had suffered severe head injuries in a fall at Galway races the previous Sunday, 26th October 2003. He rode All Heart for Paddy Mullin's in the 7 furlong Corrib Oil Auction Race, when his mount clipped the heels of another horse about a 1/2 mile from finish. He was taken to Galway University hospital and transferred to the neuro-surgical department of the intensive care unit at Beaumont Hospital. He had been in a coma on a life support machine. Sean rode 14 winners and spent 3 years with Jim Bolger, before joining Pat Flynn in Waterford for the previous two 2 seasons. His biggest success was in 2001 in the Leopardstown November Handicap s on Bubble N'Squeak. He was the third in 15 months to have suffered such injuries following Jimmy Mansell at Ballinrobe and Kieran Kelly at Kilbeggan (3 months earlier). A total of 11 riders died since 1981 in Ireland & Britain. In a tragic twist his girlfriend Maggie Farrell gave birth to a baby boy on Wednesday in the Rotunda Hospital, while he was in a coma.

The Cleary's are a Racing family with 40 acres outside Athlone. His father Tom, got ponies for the 4 boys-Paul, Sean, and twins Rory & Thomas. At three their father would leg them up and lead them round. By the age of nine they were ready for the pony circuit. Rory Cleary was born on 25 June 1987 and he went on to do an apprentices course over 2 years, but he was still going to RACE & was called "grandpa" by the others apprentices. His first ride was in July 2003 on Tom Hogan's No Frontier and his first winner was on Ger Keane's Keen Look at Fairyhouse on 15th August 2003. His second winner came on Mango Catcher at Gowran just 4 days, after his brother Sean died. Rory Cleary won his first Dubai Carnival race when steering the Dhruba Selvaratnam-trained Almaram to victory in the Dubai Handicap at Nad Al Sheba in 2003.

One of his most emotional wins at Galway in 2004 was on Peter Casey's Palace Star in the McDonagh Handicap, the horse who won the race in which Sean was tragically killed. His parents Tom & Kathleen and all the family were present to see this emotional victory. Rory won the leading rider award with further wins on Michael O'Brien's High Priestess and Tom Hogan's Rooftop Protest. RTE Commentator Robert Hall said *"You don't have to say anything over those pictures"* and Rory said afterwards that *"Sean was definitely smiling down on me"*. He was runner-up to Cathy Gannon in the Champion Apprentice title in 2004. He won the the Irish Cesarewitch with Essex and had 4 wins on Joanna Morgan's Lough Gem. In 2005, he rode 20 winners for Michael Halford and at the end of season he had 32 wins and was runner up to Chris Hayes for the Apprentice Title. He had 20 wins in 2006; 30 in 2007 and 34 in 2008. He won three Group 3 races in 2007 and in 2008 he won twice at Galway on his father's Miranda Girl including the race in which Sean was killed in 5 years previously.

He had relatively bad years between 2009/2011, as the wins were sporadic and it was a difficult time. In 2011 his career slumped and he was wondering about his future. He said *"It was going all right before I broke my jaw a couple of years ago. When I came back it was hard to get going again. Michael Halford didn't have a job for me anymore, so I tried freelancing."* He felt his riding career might be ending, but in May 2011 he got a job with Jim Bolger after a vacancy came up. In his first ride for Bolger at Navan he won on File & Paint. It was over a year since his last win. He said *"Mr Bolger is a great man to work for, as long as you are on time and do your work".* The jockey drives from his Curragh home and rides out some of the top horses. He won his first group race in the Group 3 Flying Five with My Girl Anna at The Curragh trained by Muredach Kelly, who had also helped with rides.

At Dundalk in March 2013, he rode his first treble with General Bunching 16/1 for his father Tom Cleary, Cash or Casualty (5/1) and Saga Eider (3/1). In Dec 2013, had a double with Ballyadan Brook at 25/1 and Ned's Indian. On 4th April 2015 he had a double with Damien English's Cash or Casualty 14/1and John J.Walsh's Never Again 28/1 to show he could still deliver. Queen of Alba was 4th in the Irish Lincoln for his father Tom and was 3rd in listed race in May 2015. He has ridden winners of Group 3 races like Miss Sally in the Concorde Stakes (2005); Eastern Appeal in Athasi Stakes in 2007; Nicks Nikita in the Noblesse Stakes (2007) and Snaefell in Phoenix Sprint Stakes in 2008.

Tom Cleary father of Rory and trainer is based at Carrick O'Brien, Athlone. His most successful horses in recent times are Queen of Alba, who has won three races but was 4th of 23 in the Irish Lincoln beaten 7 1/4 lengths. In 2014, she was 3rd in the EBF fillie's handicap at Galway and won the first Connacht Derby in August in Sligo. Other successful horses include General Bunching (5 wins), Truly Delightful (4 wins), Sweet Annathea (2 wins), Sophies Echo (3 wins), etc. At Ballinrobe on 26 July 2014, Tom & Rory won with Truly Delightful over 9 furlongs and beat the favourite Fav Que Sera Sera by 3/4 length. Tom said *"That's my first winner here and this is my home town. It's good for the syndicate (Galway, Mayo, Offaly Syndicate), as they are relatively new to racing and she has won three for them. She'll be going to Galway next week".*

J.P. McNAMARA, SHINRONE

John Patrick McNamara from Shinrone, Birr, Co Offaly got his interest in horses from his father, who had show horses and ponies at home. It was only when he went to Victor Bowen's, as a 16 y/o that he seriously thought of becoming a jockey. He then ended up with Sean Treacey and rode 20 winners under Rules in Ireland and another seven or eight winner's in point-to-points. He went to Britain and linked up with the successful Ferdy Murphy yard. In December 1998, he rode a four timer at Musselborough for Ferdy Murphy. He also had a winner at that time on Kates Charm at Ascot after having a double at Wincanton. He was always full of praise for Murphy and his operation at Middleham (Ferdy Murphy eventually went to France in 2013). J.P. lost his claim on a horse of Val Wards called Profiler at Folkstone, though at that time he was still entitled to ride in conditional races and restricted bumpers. He was the riding for other stables like Val Ward, John Mackie, James Given, and Les Eyre. His agent at that time was Dave Roberts and he knew it would be difficult once he was a full professional. In that respect his whole world changed in 2006.

On Saturday 22nd April 2006 J.P.McNamara rode a horse called Three Lions in the 2.45 race at Bangor. At the 4th last the horse fell crashing to the ground. The serious injuries started him on the road to Wrexham Hospital then to the Robert Jones & Agnes Hunt Orthopaedic Unit in Oswestry, and the International Spinal Injuries and Rehabilitation Centre at Royal Buckinghamshire Hospital. *"I remember hitting the ground and looking at the horse and thinking that if I had any brains I'd get up quick. He was lying beside me and I knew he could roll over at any second. I couldn't move anything though, I knew something wasn't right".* He told the racecourse Doctor he couldn't move and that evening he could feel nothing in his legs. He said someone took off his *"bloody boots"* he might feel something until Josh Byrne said he was actually naked. (Aged 27 then). The Doctors were not saying much and he didn't know how serious it was for 5/6 weeks. The prognosis was that he wouldn't stand or walk again. He asked the doctor if 100 people were in same position how many might walk. He replied *"two".* J.P. said that meant it was a 50/1 chance, which in racing terms made it possible. He needed help for a long time but improved gradually.

He saw a future with a few horses around the place but not as a trainer. He wanted to be involved in racing maybe on the racecourse side like clerk of the course. He made progress over two years. He recovered the ability to walk and is swimming. He also took up a Stewards Secretary role with the Turf Club at point to points.With regard to work he was a young man in his twenties who needed a career. Through help from various people he received training and the result was that he started work for Liam Quinn of Baltinglass, as an Equine Sales Representative for the Irish Horsefeed Distributor. As part of support for all the various charities & groups that help people he went on a walk with Richard Dunwoody (his 1,000 Miles in 1,000 Hours' charity challenge) starting on Monday, June 29 in 2009. He started with a walk around his home town, Shinrone, County Offaly, with his four dogs: a St Bernard, a boxer and two terriers. He called to see Liam Quinn on the way and met Mick Naughton from Middleham and stayed with them during the walk. He and his wife Nicola saw him through some bad days when he was in hospital in Oswestry. Sometimes he seizes up if he doesn't exercise and needs to walk and swim a lot. He has great admiration for Richard Dunwoody as a jockey and a man. He found the experience an endorsement of the good things in life.

PADDY BRODERICK

Paddy Broderick was born on 1st September 1939 in Rathowen, Mullingar. As a boy he always said he would be a jockey and he had his first ride on a pony at age 5. He rode his first winner in an apprentice race at Navan on Pipe Band in 1953 at the age of 13 1/2, while in his early teens and he went to Kells to join Cyril Bryce-Smith. As he became heavier, he turned towards jumping and moved to Arthur Stephenson in Britain in 1961 and spent eight years with him. They had some good horses like Cock Concert & Easby Abbey, who won four in a row at Market Rasen. He won the Welsh Grand National on Rainbow Battle and won on Pawnbroker in the Mackeson Cup. He had a crashing fall on a horse called Dashing White Sergeant and was unconscious for 2 weeks in Derby Hospital. The trainer put him up on Dashing White Sergeant on his first ride back test his nerve. He was northern champion three times and his best score was 50 winners. When he got into his thirties the rides began to decrease and only when Night Nurse came along was he looked at as a top class jockey. He won the Irish Sweeps Hurdle in him in 1975 and it was his first ride in Ireland for 14 years (Bernard Ryan a shopkeeper in Kilbeggan got some sweeps luck when he shared £954 with a Mayo man). Paddy Broderick was described as having wonderful hands and an uncomplaining nature, but he was defined by Night Nurse the horse that brought him to the forefront with back to back Champion Hurdle wins in 1976/77 (the horse died in 1998 at the age of 27). He summed it up *"Night Nurse was the best by a long way. His biggest asset was that he was a brilliant jumper and he'd pick up from outside the wings sometimes. He was a great horse at a time when Bird's Nest, Dramatist and Monksfield were around, yet he beat them all".*

Night Nurse was described as a *"bully"* and Broderick called him *"the machine of my career".* It was a great era for high class hurdlers with Comedy of Errors, Lanzarote, Monksfield, Sea Pigeon and Birds Nest. In reality he only beat Monksfield once in 5 races and Sea Pigeon once in 6 races, Paddy's only mount in the Champion Hurdle had been Pawnbroker in 1964. In 1976 he made all the running, as Night Nurse was a brilliant jumper and kicked on to beat Bird's Nest by 2 lengths. Night Nurse had won 10 races in a row before a few defeats and Birds Nest was the favourite for the 1977 Champion Hurdle, as he beat Night Nurse by 15 lengths in the Fighting Fifth Hurdle, but on the day he battled on to beat Monksfield by 2 lengths at odds of 15/2. Monksfield went on to win the race in 1978/79. In 1977 he dead heated with Monksfield in the Templegate Hurdle at Aintree giving 6lbs. It was ironic that after that the 1977 hurdle he decided not to ride over fences again (as he did not want to lose out on riding Night Nurse), but fell on Night Nurse in the Christmas Hurdle at the last hurdle. The injury ended his career of over 500 winners and his association with Night

Nurse (won 18 of his 26 races). He went on to be third to Monksfield in 1978. He was the best horse he rode in 25 years of riding.

It should be noted that he was also associated with Red Rum in his earlier career. In 1969 he rode him over hurdles five times between March 27th and May 20th winning three times in April in the Bilton Hurdle (Wetherby), Bradmore Handicap Hurdle (Nottingham), and Teeside Celebration Handicap Hurdle at Teeside plus being 2nd in the Lancashire Hurdle at Liverpool in March. His last ride on him was in a handicap hurdle later in November 1969, when he was unplaced.

WILLIAM GLYNN, DECD MULLINGAR JOCKEY

He was born on 28 July 1961, the son of Anne & Owen Glynn, Empor, Ballynacaragy. He was educated in the National School, Empor and the Vocational School, Ballymahon. He started as apprentice on 1976, where he attended the Racing Apprentice Centre at The Curragh. He got 1st place there and joined Buster Harty and then Michael J. O'Brien, Rathbride after 2 years. His first winner in November 1981 was at Limerick Junction with O'Brien's horse Dr Livingstone in a 2 1/2 mile hurdle race. Other useful winners were Ballygriffin, Grangeview Lad, Spanish Train (Chris de Burgh owner), Sean Ogue (Aidan Comerford), Surprise Slipper, Run for Gold, and Miss Curraghmore. In March 1984 he travelled to Pennsylvania to join the stable of Russell Carrier, who had raced many horses in Ireland and won there in South Carolina. Tragically, just days before he was due home, he was killed on 14th November at the age of 23 and he is buried at Milltown Cemetery. The family had a sponsored race in his name for many years at Kilbeggan.

OWEN BRENNAN, BALLINAGORE / KEIHAM, NEWARK-ON-TRENT

Owen Brennan was born on New Year's 1935 just a few fields from Loughnagore (at Toarlisnamore) near Kilbeggan Races and he attended national school in Ballinagore with his brothers Paddy & Oliver. He worked in the evenings for local farmer's and earned half a crown (2/6) a week. At 14, he went to work with Dick Sweeney stables and did well at show jumping including at the RDS. After 3 years he went to Quigley Stables, Rathnure, Wexford to ride their point- to-point horses. He spent 5 years there and had plenty of winners, especially on Good Leather. Then he went to Paddy Sleator stables for a short time, and rode for Paddy Prendergast. He eventually went to Sligo man Martin Cowley in Morton near Chesterfield. His first winner in England was on Sea Tiger at Uttoxeter in October 1957. He rode a winner on his third mount for Cowley on Skegby. He also rode for Walter Wharton and George Beeby.

On June 16, 1962, he married Maureen Keegan and had 3 daughters Helen, Cindy, and Bonnie and all of them worked with horses. Owen took out a trainer's licence in 1965, and moved to Park Leys, Newark. He travelled, frequently, to Ireland to race meetings & to buy bloodstock. Owen's father also Owen had an interest in horses and his uncle Jim was a blacksmith, & bred hunters in Clondra, Longford. Two other uncles Owen & Ned both emigrated to America, where they became famous as jockeys. Sadly, Owen was killed in a race riding accident in the USA. In 1993, Owen trained 25 horses (he owned around 1/2 of them) at Sloswicks Farm, Worksop, Notts. His best horses over 40 years, included two of his best known chasers the multiple winning Speaker Weatherall winner of the Great Yorkshire Chase at Doncaster and Strath Royal (both owned by his biggest benefactor, Lady Anne Bentinck). The latter won the Rowland Meyrick Chase at Wetherby in 1997, the Charlie Hall Chase at Wetherby in 1998, and was 9th in the Cheltenham Gold Cup in 1998. He ran in 57 races, winning 20 of them and won nearly £150,000, in win and place prize-money. He won eight times over hurdles, but it was over fences that he made his biggest impact winning twelve races. Speaker Weatherill was foaled in 1989, and made his racecourse debut in 1994 in a bumper at Doncaster (He won 8 of his 28 races). In January 1998 he won the Great Yorkshire Chase at Doncaster, his biggest win, but then suffered injury before retiring after breaking down in 2000.

Other favourites were Vulrory's Clown, Arctic Wings (9 wins), and Threeoutoffour. The vast majority of Brennan's horses were owned by Lady Anne Cavendish-Bentinck who had supported the yard since 1991. She died at the age of 92 on 12th January 2009 and was one of the richest landowners in Britain and worth £158 million. Owen Brennan, who trained for her for many years based at her 17,000-acre estate in Nottinghamshire or in Scotland, said after her death: *"She was the best owner anybody could have had. She never bothered you and always understood."*

One horse not mentioned so far is Aintree Grand National winner Minnehona. Owen's contribution is often under estimated.It was on Owen's recommendation that, comedian Freddie Starr bought the future National winner Minnehoma, named after the place in Texas where Paul Getty had first struck oil. This horse was to replace Kouros, which Owen had trained for Starr. Owen bought the horse for 35,000 guineas and turned him out for the summer. Minnehoma proved to be a very difficult to break in, to ride and constantly unshipped any jockey who tried to ride him. He caught salmonella poisoning and became very ill. Owen's son Martin had put a lot of work into getting the horses confidence, but he broke his collarbone in a fall at Nottingham and it was left to Owen to continue his development. He brought the horse to Uttoxeter on 28th March 1989 for his first bumper. Before the race the horse got rid of jockey Jamie Railton twice and he went out to 33/1 in the betting and Owen put a £5 on him. The horse won by 5 lengths before going to Martin Pipe on the road to Aintree success in 1994. The horse lived until the age of 29 and died in 2012. He made a return to the training ranks in February 2013 at the age of 77, saddling three winners from his new stable at Bretby near Derby. He suffered a stroke in September 2012 that left some memory loss. On December 17th 2012 he suddenly disappeared. On that day Owen and his wife Pat dropped off presents to a friend. His daughter Cindy Beadling-Brennan said her father's disappearance was out of character. She said: *"He is such a family man. It's so odd. To us he's just vanished off the face of the Earth".* It was a terrible Christmas and New Year for the family (his 78th birthday was on January 1st). On Wednesday, 9th January, 2013, his body was dragged from the River Derwent. He had been missing for more than three weeks and that included what would have been his 78th birthday. His son, ex-jockey Martin Brennan, said at the time: *"It is just nice that the uncertainty is over and we know where he is. We can now move on and get things planned."*

Martin Brennan, who rode more than 350 winners, began his career with Jimmy Fitzgerald before having spells with John Blundell and Walter Wharton and then his father at Worksop. His first winner was Arctic Menelek at Kelso on March 3 1981 and biggest successes came in 1998 on Strath Royal His last winner came on Common Man for his father at Cheltenham. He retired to go to Dubai after 19 years in the saddle and was presented with a picture of his victory on Strath Royal in Wetherby`s Charlie Hall Chase at Leicester. Brennan went to be a work rider for leading trainer Kieran McLaughlin. Three years later Martin (39) he was enjoying life in Dubai, where he spent winter's looking after two-year-olds for Sheikh Hamdan Al Maktoum and had about 150 through his hands. They are broken and then sent to the various trainers. Martin then became Flight Transport Manager for the Dubai World Cup Quarantine as the horses arrive. The hardest part was at the airport & getting in and out with all the documentation at one of the biggest events of the year.

REGINALD NUGENT

Hon Reginald Greville Nugent called *"Mr St James"*, when he was riding, died in a tragic fall in 1878. His popularity was widespread over Britainand Ireland and he was familiar on Irish racecourses. He was the 4th son of Foulke Southwell Greville-Nugent, Colonel in the Westmeath Militia and was born in 1848. He was educated in England and on the Continent and he joined the Coldstream Guards Regiment. Since leaving the army, he has been steeplechasing. In 1870 he was elected MP in Longford beating *"honest John Martin".* Within two months he was unseated after a petition. He eventually opened his own training quarters at Rossmore Lodge and had horses like Mrs Star & Melitta. Within two years he ceased training but kept a few chasers under his white and crimson hooped banner.

In the previous 5 years he was a busy amateur. He was called *"The Limb"* by friends. One of his best horses was Revoke and he won the Galway Plate with Tom Miller riding. He also rode for C.J. Blake at The Curragh on the flat and over hurdles. Just a few days, before, he won on Rocksavage in the Birmingham Grand Annual.He fell on Longford in a Selling Chase and died from injuries. In the race before, Pride of Kildare and Martha two Irish mares (G.Moore & T.Beasley) fought it out and he was on Mabel, who also fell but there was no injury. When racing in front on Longford, a lady walked across his path and knocked him down. He fell on his head and had severe concussion of the brain. Medical aid was given but he died. He had suffered fractured legs twice, and broken bones. When he fell in Paris on Pilgrimage people people shouted *"He's dead"* as he didn't move face downwards and when he was turned over he said *"What won".* For a few years he was MFH in Westmeath. He was small and under 8 stone. He was genial, jovial, and kindly and was married to Hon Louisa Yarde Buller daughter of Lord Churston in 1871. He won races like the 1875 Conyngham Cup with Milltown and the 1874 Galway Plate with Revoke (he was owner). In 1874 he was champion jockey, even though an amateur with 21 wins.

STEPHEN DONOHOE APPRENTICE CHAMPION 2006

He was born on 28 February 1984 and began his career in Athlone with Gerry Moran, before joining RACE in Kildare and training under Christy Roche, David Evans and William Musson Newmarket. He learned to ride at the Racing Academy at the Curragh. He had great time for Christy Roche who was the first man he worked for and he was a total professional in everything he did. But after a bright start, he ended up quiting in the summer of 2004. He ran into a problem with his weight and fell out with David Evans the trainer and went to live with his sister in Brighton. He gradually got sorted out and his weight down to 8st 5lbs. He restored his relationship with David Evan's and he won on his horse The Kiddykd in a listed race at Chester. His first winner back was also on Evan's horse Risk Free. The highlight of his earlier career was in 2006 when he became British Champion apprentice The Athlone man rode 44 winners in 2006 and finished four ahead of his main challengers Adam Kirby and James Doyle, when he claimed the title in late October. The trophy was presented by Pat Eddery. He sealed the prestigious award with victory on a 14/1 shot, Show Trial, at Musselborough Racecourse in Scotland. Stephen has now established himself as one of Irelands's most promising jockeys and by winning the Lester Award for *Apprentice Jockey of the Year.* Now attached to the Newmarket stable of Willie Musson, Donohoe was rewarded for his decision to return to the saddle having quit race riding last year because of weight issues. He now has just 17 winners to go before losing his claim and may pick some of these up quickly on the all-weather over the coming weeks before heading off to California in USA America for the off-season.

He also made a bit of history when riding Ed Dunlop's Temple of Thebes to victory in the first race ever at the new race track in Great Leighs in a 6 furlong maiden. He had ridden at the trials earlier in the weekend had got familiar with the track. In 2008 he was riding for owners like Dr Marwan Koukash and he had 57 winners that year. The 24 y/o who was based at Newmarket injured himself after a freak accident that year and broke his hand when slipping on a door step. He was out for 6 weeks in his first year as a professional, and it was a set back to his progress in a competitive industry. In 2014 he had 21 wins out of 329 rides and his minimum weight at that stage was 8st 6lbs. He had around 290 winners in the last five years and was riding for Brendan Powell and Lee Carter. He has had 21 wins from 220 rides in 2015. He has been riding for Ian Williams Ed McMahon, and even Sir Michael Stoute recently and perhaps a big race win at Ascot or a large track might be coming.

FARNHAM (FREDDY) MAXWELL, BIRR AND FIGHTING CHARLIE

Wiliam Marshall, Ballincard, Derryard, died on 28th February 28th 1927(age 76) and he was the father of Farnham (Freddie) Maxwell. In earlier days was a good all round sportsman, judge and lover of horses. On the 1911 Census he was down as a 58 y/old Church of Ireland farmer married to Jennie (42). Two of his children were William Farnham Maxwell (Freddie) future jockey & trainer (aged 6) and John E. (age 5) a future jockey. In the 1870's he owned 447 acres, which was quite substantial.

Freddy (1905-1991 he retired in 1977) lived close to where Aubrey Hastings future trainer of four English Grand National winners lived. He joined the stable of Aubrey Hastings at Wroughton in 1923 and rode winners on the flat and then over the jumps (He also spent time with local trainer Wallace). He turned professional in 1927 and rode his first winner in December 1927 at Plumpton and then Windsor. He was riding in the Isle of Wight in 1928 and had 24 winners out of 89 mounts. In 1929, even though he was riding in England, he had some mounts at The Maze and Punchestown plus a ride in the Scottish Grand National. In the summer of that year he got a job riding in Sweden. When he returned to Britain he was riding for Robert Gore of Findon, who was a famous amateur rider before training horses. One of his first wins for him was on Prince Cherry. In 1931 he was the regular rider for Georginatown and he rode her in the Aintree Grand National (she had won 12 out of 13 races), where she ran well (eminent sports writer Geoffrey Gilbert praised him as a jockey). J.H.Wallace owned Georginatown and he flew over to see her at Derby races in January 1931 where she won twice in two days, carrying 12st 7lbs the second day. In the Grand National she got a bump from Easter Hero and ended up falling over Ballasport.

Maxwell came over to Mullingar in 1938 and rode Mr Mangan's Caperpeak to win. He had been riding successfully as an amateur and then a professional for some years for important stables in England. He was a famous amateur jockey in his day and then conducted one of the finest establishments in the kingdom. He eventually trained at Lamstown and before the war had a stable at The Curragh before joining the R.A.F. at the start of the war. He hoped to train again in Ireland after the war and even in November 1945 he trained the winners of two chases.

'NEVER GALLOP A HORSE WHEN THE WIND IS IN THE NORTH EAST'

I read somewhere that Freddy Maxwell once said *'Never gallop a horse when the wind is in the north east'*, as apparently it stressed out the horse. It was as a trainer on the flat that Freddie Maxwell established his name in racing with particular success with staying horses, which he trained at Lambourne, Berkshire. He won the Ascot Gold Cup three times between 1961 and 1966 with Pandofell (L. Piggott) in 1961 and Fighting Charlie who won two in a row from 1965 (L. Piggott) to 1966 (G.Starkey). After a few years as an Assistant Trainer, he set up in the mid-50's and had his first major win with Pandofell who won the Queen's Prize, Yorkshire Cup, Ascot Gold Cup and Doncaster Cup for him. He had a good touch with stayers. Fighting Charlie who won 2 Ascot Gold Cup's's, Alto Volante won a Yorkshire Cup and Horse Radish won a Northumberland Plate. Lady M. Bury of Mount Stewart, who started the first thoroughbred stud farm in Northern Ireland died (aged 88) in 2009, was the owner of Fighting Charlie who won the Ascot Gold Cup twice. Her filly, Northern Gleam, had previously won the 1953 Irish 1,000 Guineas.

The aptly-named Fighting Charlie ended the streak of one-time winners by capturing consecutive Gold Cups in 1965-66. Piggott guided him to a sharp 2 1/2 length victory in 1965, but deserted him in favor of Aegean Blue in 1966. For once, the master rider chose the wrong horse, as Aegean Blue trudged home fourth. Piggott's misjudgment would only become apparent after one of the most dramatic finishes in Gold Cup history. When Fighting Charlie went for the double in 1966 he was the first horse since 1932 to succeed. The Sunday before it had been discovered, that he had swollen legs but the vet Frank Mahon saved the day. He had the horse strapped up in a harness and gave him electrical treatment and an application of clay and camphor. Farnham Maxwell said that the odds against his making it to Royal Ascot were 100-1. Inflammation racked both forelegs, and one was as swollen as a *"telegraph pole."* Greville Starkey was riding him in place of Piggott and the reigning Gold Cup winner drifted far to his left turning for home. Winding up near the stands' side rail, he had lost the lead and was now about six lengths back. Then, just as abruptly, Fighting Charlie regrouped and unleashed a dazzling late rally to regain the lead, and he stormed home by eight lengths. He was then retired to stud.

The stallion Tenerani (1944) won 17 out of his 22 races, including the Italian Derby and the Queen Elizabeth Stakes, and he bred Ribot, but he also sired dual Gold Cup winner Fighting Charlie.

CAWSTON'S PRIDE A REAL STAR

At the other end of the scale he trained fast horses, Cawston's Pride (1968) who was Champion 2-Y-O Filly in 1970 (unbeaten in 7 races) and Merry Madcap who won a July Cup. The former won races like the Queen Mary Stakes, Molcomb Stakes, Lowther Stakes and Cornwallis Stakes. As a three year old she won the Ascot 1,000 guineas trial on her debut but became temperamental and was beaten when favourite for the 1,000 guineas and then refused to race in her next run. She was retired to stud where she produced star sprinter Solinus, Cawstons Clown etc. Cawston's Pride was a good broodmare before her untimely death getting Cawston's Clown and Solinus who both won the Coventry Stakes (she is considered one of the best 2 y/o fillies in the last 50 years). Maxwell also trained Young Christopher in 1965.

Lester Piggott, Brian Taylor and a few other jockey's rode for him and he had some international owners. One of his owners was Mrs Marion Frelinghuysen of New Jersey, who would wait for a telephone call from “Maxie” from Lambourn to tell her that her horse has a chance of winning, then she would jump on a plane to England. His brother J.E. Maxwell was also a jockey in the 1930's as an amateur with Mr Willett's stable at Pyecombe and both of them rode winners in Ireland.

Interestingly, a direct descendant of the Maxwell family going back to the 18th century is Roberta Maxwell who starred in the film *“Brokeback Mountain”* with Heath Leger. She has acted with Anthony Hopkins, Susan Sarandon, Julie Harris etc and also starred in the Tom Kilroy play *“The Shape of Metal”* in New York in 2007 plus other Movie and TV appearances. Her father Robert Maxwell went to Canada from Ballincard House in 1927 even though they hadn't suffered much from IRA threats in that era, when many large houses were burned down or were threatened. She has been back to the ancestral home many times since.

TOM MALONE, ARDEN VIEW, TULLAMORE

Tom Malone's career started as a 14 y/o in Ireland where he was taught to ride ponies. He took up a job with Tom Lacy and learned the value of hard work. He moved to J.A. Quinn on the Curragh where he spent a year and then to P.J. Rothwell. He became a conditional jockey and he rode over 100 horses winning his first race on Little Ora at Downpatrick. He then went to England to join Philip Hobbs where he won on his first 3 rides, but was injured with a dislocated shoulder and then later he broke his ankle, so nearly 6 months was lost. The future was looking bleak at Sandhill Stables, so he was moving back to Ireland feeling a failure, when he made a call to Martin Pipe, Pond House, looking for a job and surprisingly he got it.

He started there in 2001 and never looked back, riding as a conditional jockey for Martin Pipe at a very good time when A.P. McCoy had just left. He rode at the Cheltenham festival, (2nd in the County Hurdle was the closest) and he rode in two Grand Nationals (13th on Polar Red to Hedgehunter in 2005, and Milan Deux Mille 15th in 2008 to Cloudy Lane). One of his best rides was on Quick for Martin Pipe in December 2004 in a Pertemps Handicap Hurdle Qualifier. He had 7 runners but 22 y/o Malone slipped the field on Quick and won by 17 lengths. Pipe joked *"I told him to go quick- but not that quick."* It was his second Cheltenham winner.

In 2007, he was paying flying visits to Ireland to commentate on point to points.He also co-presented the Lester Awards Ceremony (called after Mr Piggott!) and he was on At the Races. He had 26 winners such as Dunbrody Miller, Bright Approach (bred in Dysart), Locksmith, Imperial de Thaix, and Milton Des Bieffes. In July 2008 the Tullamore jockey left the David Pipe stable at Pond House in the UK to return to Ireland after his career had stalled in recent seasons. Malone had won 73 races in Britain for David Pipe and his father Martin, as part of what was UK National Hunt's most successful stable for most of the decade, but the addition of Tom Scudamore to the stable in 2007 further pushed Malone down the pecking order. He had spent over six years in England. The 26 year old from Arden View decided to return home in order to concentrate on other career opportunities. He has been working for At The Races, as a TV commentator on Irish racing, including some point to point meetings, and he hoped to get more of this work in the coming years, while also becoming more involved in bloodstock trading.

He planned to develop the buying and selling of horses from Tullamore and then fly to England to sell them. He had a good list of clients in Britain who had winning horses from him. He also planned on resuming riding and was hoping to get going again. Malone's most successful season came in 2004/05 when he recorded 30 winners, and he will also treasure his two Cheltenham successes where he earned the most plaudits.

TOM MALONE BLOODSTOCK AGENCY

The Bloodstock Agency was set up to purchase and sell thoroughbreds both privately and at public auction, give advice on stallion selection, valuations etc. Tom race rode for 11 years, amassing a total of 70 winners, including five at Cheltenham. He also completed in the Grand National twice, before hanging up his boots and going in search of a new venture. The time he spent working for trainers and racc riding taught him an awful lot about judging quality in a thoroughbred, and this proved to stand him in good stead for a career as a bloodstock agent, as he was soon purchasing winners. In the first year of trading as a bloodstock agent his purchases accumulated 37 winners and now, in the six years since the inception of Tom Malone Bloodstock, there have been over 800 winners and counting.

Milton Des Bieffes was the first horse that Tom ever purchased, who was sourced from the Irish point to point field for an owner called Nick Shutts. This horse went into training with David Evans and went on to win seven races, three of which he won on the bounce with Tom himself in the saddle. Tom came across his most successful National Hunt purchase to date, Brindisi Breeze, winner of the Grade 1 Albert Bartlett Novices' Hurdle at the 2012 Cheltenham Festival. He also enjoys the challenge of buying three year old flat horses and watching them switch codes to a career over hurdle.

He had 56 winners so far in 2015 and from 2009-2014 he had 850 winners including 23 Graded/Group winners and 3 Cheltenham Festival winners. At Cheltenham 2015, Dodging Bullets bred by Frankie Dettori became the champion chaser 2 mile chaser and was sold privately through Tom Malone. Qualando bought privately through his agency won the Fred Winter Juvenile Handicap Hurdle for Paul Nichols. Qualando 28/1 and ridden by Nick Schofield was a French import who won a maiden at Exeter. Other winners included Milborough (Eider Chase Newcastle 2015), Mr Mole (G2 Game Spirit Chase), Irving (Fighting Fifth Hurdle Gr1 Newcastle), Casper Netscher (G2 Neartic Sts , Woodbine , Canada, Gimcrack Sts, Mill Reef Sts etc), Present View (G2 winner), Third Intention (G2 winner) etc.

THE ALLEGED PEADAR MATTHEWS, MULLINGAR

His father was Peter Matthews, Knockdrin, Mullingar. He rode mainly for P.J.Prendergast & Vincent O'Brien. He won the Irish St Leger with Arctic Vale in 1962; Linacre 40/1 won the Irish 2,000gns in 1963; he won the Athasi Sts and Gallinule Sts with After the Show in 1957 trained by Michael Hurley; the Royal Whip in 1977 with dual Prix de L'Arc winner Alleged 1/7, and Portail Rouge won the November Handicap in 1963 for Aubrey Brabazon. In 1957 he was second on After the Show in the 1,000gns. Alleged the dual Prix de L'Arc winner was surely the best horse he ever rode. He also rode for the Michael Hurley stable and owner Terence White. In April 1957 he had another good win at The Curragh when he beat Edenderry ridden Derby winner Chevastrid on Vie Rose.

The fact that he worked with both Vincent O'Brien and Paddy Prendergast was a great compliment to a quite jockey, who got on about his business and was well respected TP Burns said about Peadar Matthews that he was a *"far better jockey than he ever got the chance to show"*.

In June 2015 at Roscommon a young jockey called Robbie Dolan rode his first winner on Lady Ranger. His father Bobby worked for Dermot Weld for 25 years and his uncle Anthony rode an Irish Grand National winner. His grandfather is Peadar Matthews, so horse riding is in the blood. He often rides out on The Curragh with Rory Cleary, Athhlone and champion jockey Pat Smullen from Rhode. He is starting out and hopefully will do as well as his grandfather from Mullingar.

ADRIAN JOYCE, CURRAGHBOY, ATHLONE, CO WESTMEATH

He enrolled at 15y/o with RACE and it was hard to get rides and he moved to Tom Taaffe in 2006. His first ride as a 16y/o was with Phillip Rothwell on Erinella in a handicap at Leopardstown on 10th November 2002. He only had 3 rides in 2003 and his first winner was Shivermetimbers in a handicap hurdle at Punchestown by 11 lengths and six weeks later he had his second win at Punchestown on the same horse. A few weeks later he partnered the Francis Flood-trained Be My Leader to win a bumper at Punchestown. At this stage, the future looked bright for the 18-year-old 7lb claimer, but remarkably, he went almost two years without a winner after that success at Punchestown.

When he joined Tom Taaffe's stable in 2006 he won on Dead Sound in a novice chase in Clonmel. In 2006 he had his biggest win at 20 y/o when he rode a Westmeath horse 7 y/o Cane Break to success in the Paddy Power Chase at 14/1 with top weight & 7lbs taken off by Joyce. Cane Break went on to be 5th in Cheltenham Gold Cup in March 2007. He was owned by the Mount Temple Syndicate, Moate (Joe Ganley). The horse suffered a bad blood clot in his leg and ran well enough since his return & in his last race on 5th December 2009 he was fifth to Operation Houdini. Adrian Joyce (2002) produced a remarkably cool display aboard Cane Brake 14/1 to land the €110,000 Paddy Power Handicap Chase at Leopardstown by a 1/2 length. The 7lb claimer repaid the faith of trainer Tom Taaffe in style with just the eighth winner of his fledgling career and the first high-profile success. *"I was happier with the horse carrying 11.3 rather than 11.10 and I knew I had the right man in Adrian"*, the trainer said afterwards. Adrian said *"This is a dream come true. I knew from three out he'd keep galloping and he's a wonderful horse. I've been with Tom for six months and he has brought me on so much. I've learned so much from him"*, beamed Joyce, who has also ridden five winners for the Co Wicklow trainer Francis Flood. Trainer Taaffe was already targeting a possible tilt at the most famous handicap of all, the Aintree Grand National.

Joyce enjoyed another successful campaign in 2007/08 and on 17th June, he reached a notable milestone as having ridden Emotional Article to victory in a beginners chase at Fairyhouse, his claim was reduced from 7lbs to 5lbs. His progress continued throughout the campaign, with him riding plenty of winners for Tom Taaffe on the likes of In the High Grass, Emotional Article and Schindler's Gold. Pat Flynn also provided him with wins on Eritrea (2) and Cannery Row. However, having ridden nine winners to that point, the season ended on a low note for Joyce, with him breaking his arm in a fall from on In The High Grass in the Topham Chase at the Aintree Grand National meeting. He was plagued with injuries and this led to his early retirement. He broke his arm 3 times at critical periods when he was a conditional rider with Francis Flood in 2004. He was advised by doctors to retire but he carried on. In case it was necessary he had been adding to his stables over years as a back- up plan and was able to apply for a trainers licence. In 2009/10 he left Tom Taaffe's and went to Britain to ride for Evan Williams for a short time before returning to Ireland. He got a bad fall off a hunter and fractured his spine and this ended career Joyce.

As a trainer he had a flagbearer in the filly Majestic Timeline over the past 12 months. First time out she finished last at Dundalk. She had a wind operation and was then 2nd at Wolverhampton. A month later she won her first race at Dunstall Park and followed up with 4 more wins. He also had her half sister Times in Anatefka. They finished 1st & 2nd at Dundalk in November 2013. He hoped to attract some bigger owners into the future and build on the 7 horses he had at that time. Majestic Timeline won again at Dundalk on Fri 23rd Jan 2015. Other horses recently Coach Bombay and Times in Anatefka. His last winner as of 15th June was Coach Bombay at Dundalk ridden by Shane Foley.

SHANE SHORTALL, ATHLONE - ROAD TO RICHES, AFTER WALKING AWAY FROM RACING

It should be mentioned that the Derwin's in Athlone have played a significant part in the development of young jockey's in the area like Shane Shortall and Kielan Woods. Jim & Francis Derwin have carried on a family tradition in horse dealing in Ireland & abroad. They often have 200/300 horses for sale from hunters to show jumpers. They have been associated with horses like Mr Medicott ridden by Karen O'Connor USA in the Olympic Games (the horse won gold for Germany at Bejiing in 2008) and Joseph Murphy's Electric Cruiser, who represented Ireland.

Shane Shortall from Athlone, who went to school at Moate Community School, started out at Jim Derwin's in Athlone at the age of six *"It's not a racing yard but a dealer's yard, they have a riding school and that's where he started"* (his mother's name is Derwin). They got him doing a bit of pony racing and show jumping. He showed a lot of talent in pony racing and he also rode in point-to-points to gain experience. At 15 years of age, he started with trainer Tom Hogan, Nenagh as an apprentice. Unfortunately, he injured his ligaments and was out for over six months. He was then too heavy for the flat. Shane worked for Ian Williams in England in 2011. His first professional ride was in Stratford, riding an odds-on favourite and he was tailed off, beaten by 50 lengths. He was given five rides in three weeks of which he won two. His first winner, as a professional, was in Ffos Las for Williams on a horse called Manadam, but he wasn't happy there and came home in 2012 and as he said *"I walked away from racing really"*.

When he got interested again, Longford trainer Paul Flynn gave him a chance and later introduced him to Tony Martin, who gave him the opportunity to ride out. Shane started working full time at Tony's. *"Tony has been very good to me, he told me if I was good enough I would get rides and have been riding for him since"*. He then got a mount on a horse called Edeymi for Gigginstown House at the Cheltenham Festival, 2013 and was very unlucky being brought down when in contention in the Fred Winter Juvenile Handicap Hurdle. He was second on another Gigginstown horse called Marinero to the impressive future Cheltenham winner Dermot Weld's Windsor Park. His first winner back home was the brilliant mare Busted Tycoon, who is the first ever horse to win three times at the Galway Festival.

DREAMS CAN BE DOUBLED- GALWAY PLATE WIN IN 2014

In July 2014 at Galway, 22 y/o Shane Shortall had the biggest success of his career. His friend Ger Fox was due to ride Road to Riches 14/1 for Noel Meade in the Galway Plate but he was injured the week before and Shane was recommended to Gigginstown House by Tony Martin, as a good claiming jockey. He didn't know it but he was about to have the biggest win of his career. The horse took up the running very early and jumped from fence to fence, Basically, the field never got to him at any stage and it was clear that after the last fence he would not be caught, as he galloped away to win by 11 lengths from Burn And Turn and Balnaslow. He looked at the big screen and then looked back but couldn't believe how far he was in front. He said he could hear them in the distance behind him, and when he was jumping the last he mistook the sound for them jumping the last, even though they hadn't reached it yet.

It was Noel Meade's first ever success in the Galway Plate after a great and successful career and it was Shane's first ride for him. It was also a first win in the race for Michael O'Leary's Gigginstown House Stud and the winning trainer credited O'Leary's brother and racing manager Eddie with the foresight to tackle the Plate. Meade explained: *"After he ran second in Punchestown, Eddie suggested that he might be the right horse for the Plate and when the entries came out I was a bit surprised, as I thought he would have top weight. I think fast ground is the key to him and he jumped brilliant"*. When Shane won earlier in the day on Tony Martin's Greatness beating Tony McCoy on Golden Ticket, it is likely that he would have considered it a good day but dreams can be doubled. As he said afterwards, *"I was happy just to have a ride in Galway and the winner earlier made my day but this is a dream come through."* It was only his second win over fences. Success in a big race gives a young jockey a higher profile, but doesn't guarantee a better career and more winners. Shane still had to work hard as a jockey and hopefully many big days lie ahead. Road to Riches went on to be 3rd to Coneygree in the Cheltenham Gold Cup 2015. His last winner was in April 2015 on Phil the Flyer for Ray Hackett at Tramore (per 15th June 2015).

JAMES P. SULLIVAN - A STREETE JOCKEY

He learned his trade at RACE, Kildare and graduated in 2004. He joined trainer James Burns and his first ride was on Our Bluebottom in a maiden on 27th March 2005. He went through 2 years & 45 rides without a winner. In 2007 he rode for outside stables and had his first winner on 3rd June 2007 on the Pat Morris trained Royal Becky to win a 5 furlong apprentice handicap at Navan. A few months later he won on Thornfield Clo in a handicap at Ballinrobe in September. His yearly total was 82 rides & 2 winners. In 2008 he had a better strike & work rate. He had 7 winners for 5 different trainers from 138 rides. In November 2008, Sullivan nearly added a notable string to his bow by almost riding a winner over hurdles on just his second attempt, finishing placed on the Burns-trained Brosna Val in a juvenile maiden hurdle at Thurles. Sullivan began 2009 in fair style, but in mid-May he took the tough decision to leave Ireland and take up a new position with Mick Easterby in the North of England.

He rode for different trainers and he finished the year strongly with 4 wins from 14 rides in December & total of 11 wins from 202 rides. From May to August he was the hottest apprentice in the country riding 30 winners from 346 rides. Unfortunately, he only had another 5 winners just as it looked as if he might be Champion Apprentice. He lost by 4 to Martin Lane. Again in 2011 he got going when the turf season started and soon lost his 3lb claim. In 2014 he had 3 wins in 4 days-Klynch (Ruth Carr trainer) 11/2 at Epsom, Bickermet at Doncaster 15/2, and Nifty Fox (T.Easterby) at Ayr 5/2. His Season tally was 27. He had been side lined over the Christmas but the jockey from Streete came back. He had a double with Foxtrot Tango and Meshardal for Ruth Carr at Catterick on 8th April 2015. In his last 104 rides up to 15th June he had 8 wins. His principal trainers are Ruth Carr and Mick Easterby, but it is tough to get good quality rides. A major win at a featured meeting always helps to get good rides on better horses.On 19/20th June he had 4 winners in two days for Mrs Carr (21% strike rate in the week).

KIELAN WOODS, ATHLONE - FIRST THREE RIDES WIN IN BRITAIN

Kielan Woods, Athlone started riding with neighbours and he attended the riding school in Athlone at Derwins. He joined the pony circuit like many others and rode 46 winners. He found it a great learning experience and he went on to get a place at RACE apprentice school where he got a placement with Caroline

Hutchinson. She was very good to him and he got a 100 rides and three winners. He went from there to former jockey Paul Flynn and it was him that got a job with the Charlie Longsdon stable and he went there. It was a great place to work and Noel Fehilly was there and he was second jockey to him. Noel from Cork gave him help and Charlie Longsdon was very supportive and he learned a lot from him, as he was a trainer going places fast. His career highlight at that time was riding a winner for the boss at Aintree on board Ely Brown in 2012. He had a good season overall but not as good as the previous season. He was all set for the season ahead and hoped to boot home a few more winners and stay safe.

Kielan Wood seemed to be on an upward curve and if all went to plan in a few years, some thought Athlone could be boasting a champion jump jockey. Woods made a remarkable first impression when bursting onto the British scene in early 2011, winning his first three races, including trumping Tony McCoy in one. The 21 year-old had a notable win at Sedgefield in early March on Sacco D'Oro. He has a never say die and determined attitude and a great judgement of pace and natural horsemanship. All the attributes did not bring the major success. It was a tough world in winter and wins did not come easy. Out of his first 653 rides he had 86 wins. His success rate evened off with 23 wins in 2013/14 and in 2014/15 he had 21 wins. He rides for Ben Case, Alex Hales, Mrs P.Sly, Mark Wall and P.Middleton. Up to 15th June 2015 he had 5 wins out of his last 43 rides.

OFFALY

PAT GILSON - IRISH CHAMPION APPRENTICE IN 1979

He was born in Edenderry and became the Irish champion apprentice in 1979, when his 46 winners included the Naas November Handicap on Twinburn for Tony Redmond and the Leopardstown November Handicap on Singing Amah for Mick O'Toole. Other major wins included the 1981 Goffs Fillies' Challenge on Dedicated Lady for Con Collins; and that season's Irish Cesarewitch on The Neurologist for Edward O'Grady; in 1983 he won the Meld Stakes for R.Burns Sn on Bay Empress; the 1992 Naas Autumn Handicap on Yukon Gold for M.V. O'Brien; Killavullan Sts 1994 for Con Collins Kill the Crab; and the 1995 Moyglare Stud Stakes on Priory Belle for Jim Bolger. His sister married Manx-born Stephen Craine, who was also an Irish champion apprentice in 1977 and their son - also Stephen - rode successfully under both codes in Britain. His last winner was Rossmore Girl 5/1CF at Naas on Sunday 18th May 1997.

MAJOR W. TROCKE

In 1868 he won the Drogheda Plate at Punchestown with Lysander & the Conyngham Cup with Olympia; the United Service Plate with Gamekeeper 1871; & the Kildare Hunt Chase with Countess. The son of Rev William Trocke of Mount Ormons, Co Tipperary, he was a noted hard rider to hounds. He first rode for John Hubert Moore, father of Garrett who lived near them. In 1855 he won on his own mare Jenny Lind, and had a number of wins with Prince Ernest.

In 1858 he joined the 35th Royal Sussex Regiment & went to India. He rode at meetings there and had a small stud. He came to Ireland in 1866. In 1867 he was 2nd in the Conyngham Cup on Jolly Marine but rode mainly at small meetings. In 1870 he left the service and lived at Hillbrook, Parsonstown and rode until 1894. He rode winners at all the principal meetings and won all the major races. He had good horses like Gamecock who was said to have jumped 33 feet over the last fence in the Military Plate, Newbridge 1876. He had Brown Betty winner of the Irish Grand National and 7 races. His last winner was The Countess who won the Drogheda Stakes at Punchestown 1901, Kildare Hunt Plate 1902 and Prince of Wales 1904. He won 9 consecutive races in 1881/82 on Lady Wolseley and in the last beat Cyrus (H. Beasley). He remembered a well-known jockey Chiffney in a two horse race grabbing his opponent, out of view behind a hill, and throwing him out of the saddle. Those were the days!

OTHER JOCKEY'S with Westmeath and Offaly connections include **Aiden Howard,** Crowenstown- runs a successful horse racing yard at Trimblestown Stud near Kildalkey outside Athboy. He was flat race jockey and then amateur, but is now training. He had both flat and jump wins and one of his best horses was Enter the Indian, which won 3 handicap hurdles. He trained winners in point to points and his first Galway win was with Valamareha. He has a mare foaling service. **John Feehan,** Tullamore died in 1911 in Manchester from a cold. He was becoming a famous jockey. He had travelled to Belgium and was only 23 y/o. He rode in Classics and achieved many wins. **Brendan Mooney,** Mullingar was a successful jockey in the 1950's. He was with Atty Persse & Cecil Boyd Rochfort and had his first winner in 1956 on the Queen's horse Opera Score, at the age of 18. He rode for Jack Ormston in England for a number of years and after riding a double at Redcar one day, he changed out of his silks and said *"I must get back now, sir, to give them a hand with the hay making".*

James Kelly, Grange South, Mullingar, who rode Mavis of Meath to win Irish Grand National 1900 and his brother Thomas Kelly was also a jockey. **Frank 'Mull' McCormack,** Ballynacaragy, died in 2014 (82 y/o). He rode for Cecil Brabazon, Michael Dawson and Charles Mallon in England. He later became Head Lad for Eddie Harty. **Marcus Halligan,** Stonehall, Multyfarnham via Kildare was on the 1911 census, as a 26 y/o jockey working for P.W.McLoughlin at the above address. **Patrick Mullen,** Patrick Street, Mullingar was a jockey in England in the 1930's and he was retained by the Countess of Lindsay. **Peter Sullivan,** Mullingar was born in 1879. He rode for Lord Greville between 1890-98 on Admiral, Buckshot, and Flying Shot, winner of the Enniskillen Cup and the Belgium Grand National. In 1921, at the age of 42, he applied for a licence again and he was confident of a successful comeback. **Jack McCarthy,** Streamstown rode for the O'Roarkes and rode Jerpoint to win Irish Grand National in 1927. **Turlough Donnelly** rode for Pat Casserley at Slanemore for 3 years and was a good point to point rider. **John Donlon,** William Street, Birr, was a son of James and he was an apprentice jockey with J.J.Parkinson, Maddenstown Lodge. It was said that *"He had a great fondness for horses."* **Paddy Merrigan** from Athlone (born 1986) was probably one of the most controversial jockey's to come out of Westmeath. He was graduate of the pony scene like many other Irish jockey's, where he had 86 winners and at 15 he rode work for Willie Mullins and did the final schooling for Hedgehunter.He moved to Heather Dalton, Shropshire in 2004, then to Patrick Haslam and later Paul Nicholls, before coming to Peter Bowen for whom he rode Souffleur and other good horses. He won on Sir Monty and Souffleur at Aintree before being taken off for temperamental issues, which were to dog him over the next few years and he relinquished his licence.

Michael Murphy St Ruth's Park, Athlone joined Ian Williams stable in 2008 and on 24th October 2009, he rode a 13/1 double at Aintree in the Toteswingers Veteran's Handicap Chase on Lysander and later he won on Bob N You in a novice hurdle for Williams. Trainer Ian Williams praised the young Athlone rider's ability, after the Aintree win on board Lysander. He was a distant cousin of Pat Murphy from Limerick, who trained Supreme Glory to win the Welsh Grand National in 2001. **Derek Anthony McCormack,** Athlone rode for a number of years in Ireland & France (with Francois Cottin & Macaire for over 2 years). He rode Corker Hill 25/1 to win for N. Lawlor on 27th July 2015 at the Derby meeting. **Pat O'Connor,** Mullingar/Kilbeggan. In October 1983 the former dual Two Mile Champion Chaser Hilly Way (78/79) was sent to win in the North of England. The horse was trained by Pat O'Connor, who was brought up in Westmeath. His stables were in Derbyshire. He learned his trade with Peter McCreery in Kildare and Turlough O'Connor, Slanemore, Mullingar was his jockey. He was also associated with Grand National horses like Senator Maclacury, who was 2nd to Aldaniti the previous year. More recently there was the tragedy of **Jamie Kyne,** Moate, who died with his friend Jan Foster in a fire that ripped through a three storey block in Norton near Malton, North Yorkshire. He was an apprentice jockey at the start of his career with 29 winners. He loved boxing and was a member of the Monivea Boxing Club. He won the All Ireland boy 4 33kg title beating a fellow Moate boxer Gary Molloy in the semi-final in 2005.

Thomas O'Roarke's horse Aubeg running in the Galway Plate in 1917, where he finished 3rd

E.W. Hope Johnstone was Master of the Westmeath Foxhounds from 1913-1924 and the owner of Irish Grand National winner Ballyboggan

P.W. Shaw TD, who was associated with many successful horses in Ireland and Great Britain

George Webb, Corolanty, who bred the famous Brown Jack the most popular horse in Britain prior to Arkle

F.B.O'Toole (1894-1972), who was the Owner & Manager of Rathmoyle Stud, Edenderry from 1924-1965

The remarkable Brown Jack won the Champion Hurdle. He won 7 years in a row at Royal Ascot - the Ascot Stakes in 1928 and the Queen Alexandra Stakes from 1929-34

Insurance won the Champion Hurdle in 1932/33 and he was bred by Edward J. Hope, Gartlandstown, Westmeath

Races Day in Newbrook in May 1938

A scene from Captain Boycott filmed on Newbrook track in 1947

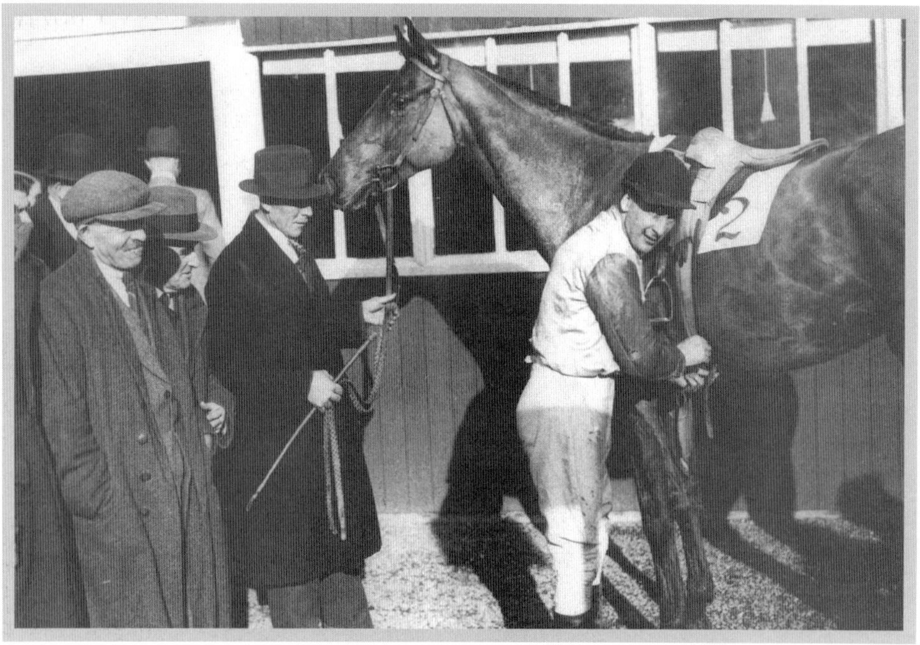

From Left to Right- "Quinny", Joe O'Roarke, Brian Fetherstonhaugh, and Tom O'Roarke with Forbidden Battle ridden by J.McNeill

Tom O'Roarke's remarkable horse Lady Barney was the dam of Battling Lady. Both of them continued racing and twice won on the same day at Longford and Kilbeggan (1937)

Marion Wallace, Belfield, Shinrone won the famous Barbour Cup outright in 1938, after three consecutive wins with her good horse Baykora ridden by J.J.Marshall

Larry Egan with Jack Chaucer ridden by Jimmy Brogan, who won the richest race in Ireland, the Red Cross Chase in January 1940

Aubrey Brabazon on one of his favourite horses St Martin, winner of the Galway Plate and Red Cross Chase in 1941 (Racing Through My Mind)

Eddie Newman, father of Gerry, was number one jockey to Tom Dreaper before Pat Taaffe. Here he is riding Glengormley, who won at Naas in 1943

J.J. Ham bred Revelry to win the Irish Grand National in 1947

Willie Ross won the Farmer's Plate at Slanemore in 1950 on "Fascination"

In February 1952, Cecil Ronaldson rode Cuskilay to win the Sportsman's Plate at Mullingar beating Lt Colonel Newell's The Beak and Toss Taaffe on Unconqueres

Christmas Card 1946 - Cecil Boyd- Rochfort with his son Arthur at Christmas 1946

The beautiful Gene Tierney attended Kilbeggan Races in 1953, when Prince Aly Khan won on Ynys

chapter 7
BREEDERS - ANOTHER FLASH TO SIZING EUROPE

R.G. ADAMSON

R. G. Adamson bred horses like Privit & Babes in the Wood. Privit won 30 races including on the flat, over hurdles, & chases between 1912 -1919. Privit made her debut at Mullingar on 10th June 1912 as 4 y/o and was unplaced in his colours, but was then bought by R.H. Walker but didn't win that year. In 1913 he won a maiden at Kells and 3 more races that year at Dundalk and a chase on St Stephen's day in Leopardstown. In 1914 she won 7 out of her 13 starts and was now owned by Capt D. McCalmont. She was 4th in the Galway Plate. Her best year was in 1916 when she won 9 out of 16 races. McCalmont had his biggest win in 1917 in the Galway Plate (she had 5 other wins that year). In her career she beat two subsequent Grand National winners on 17th July 1916, beating Sergeant Murphy by 15 length's in the Westmeath Chase at Mullingar, and in the Galway Plate she beat Shaun Spadah who won the 1921 Aintree Grand National.

TREVOR & ELIZABETH BADGER, BRIDGE HOUSE STUD

Trevor and Elizabeth Badger, Bridge House Stud, Ballynacaragy, Mullingar have had some stallions, while concentrating mainly on sport horses and other services. The stallions included Let the Lion Roar (Saddlers Wells) who was closely related to Saddlers Hall & Millenary and was 2nd in the Great Voltigeur to Rule of Law and 3rd to North Light in the Epsom Derby, in addition to winning two races from a mile to 1 1/2 miles. Superior Premium was a sprinter and prolific winner and Prince Arch was a Grade 1 winning 1/2 brother to juvenile Group 1 winner Kingsfort. Prince Arch (Arch-Princess Kris) won 6 races in the USA and retired in 2007. He wasrepresentative of the Roberto line. In 2008 Trevor & Elizabeth Badger, acquired Equiano the first Spanish trained horse to win at Royal Ascot in the King Stand Stakes. It is mainly a stud for event horses including Sirillio in recent years, a stallion who raced in Germany with Bruno Schultz & won as a 2 y/o but was then injured.

JOHN BELLINGHAM, GLENCARA, RATHCONRATH

John Bellingham, Glencara, Rathconrath carried on his family's long tradition of breeding and racing winners such as Rathconrath and Glencara. They were retained for the stud to perpetuate a longstanding bloodline. Glencara bred several winners, notably Admiral James. His father Colonel A Stuart Bellingham bred Kelling, winner of the Esher Cup, Britannia Stakes and Cesarewitch in 1950. In 1952, from the same dam, Monk's Fancy, Colonel Bellingham bred Cerise, winner of the valuable Acorn Stakes at Epsom in 1954. Kesrullah bred by him won the Coronation Stakes at Kempton. Hard Love (Hard Sauce-My Lady Love) was bred by JS Bellingham in the 1960's and came via Panama Cana to win a 6 furlong Spring Cup at Penang and had a brilliant win in the Kings Cup over 6 furlongs at Kuala Lumpur. In 1964, Col A.S.Bellingham had 7 horses with 13 wins and won £4,745; and J.S.Bellingham had 2 horses with 4 wins (£2,022). The family had a reasonable amount of success in the 1950/60's with their horses.

Sir Percy Nugent managed the lands of Colonel Bellingham at Glencara and at the same time developed his skill as an auctioneer in Goff's and became manager of Mullingar racecourse introducing evening meetings. Some of the mares over the years included Jungle Dreams, Welsh Poppy, Kessaway, Some Money, Bookies Money, Kessella, and Lovely Duck. In Oct 1949 the Princess Claire de Croy cousin of King of Belgium paid a visit to them and rode with hunt. Her father bred Nankin and Dark Legend in Belgium and was a friend of the family. During her stay she attended events including Irish methods of making silage and a Missa Contata in Mullingar Cathedral.

JOHN BOURKES, HYDE PARK STUD, KILLUCAN

John Bourkes, Hyde Park Stud, Killucan was a purpose built facility in Westmeath purchased in 2002 by him and ideally used for pinhooking, boarding, and sales preparation for yearlings (80 purpose built stables). The stud has had a number of successes on the track and through the sales. Modigliani (Danzig-Hot Princess) an Aidan O'Brien horse, three parts brother to Rodrigo de Triano and Hawkeye (winner of the G3 Desmond Stakes), Governor Brown by Kingmambo (winner of G3 Somerville Tattersall Stakes in 2002), and Tendulkar were amongst the early stallions associated with the stud, producing many horses for sale on the European market. As Bourke said, Modigliani was an outstanding individual who, during his racing career, defeated some high-class performers and shared the sames sire with Danehill.

TIM & FINOLA CAREY, TULLAGHANSLEEK STUD

The Carey's have been in Tullaghansleek Stud since 1867 and it covers over 200 acres. The cave at the entrance was built in 2400 BC and is the oldest & biggest in Ireland. There is one entrance into the cave and it has 4 rooms and 2 different passages; at the end of each passage there are two rooms (one with a rare cavity about 2 feet square. It is known locally as *"Carey's Cave"*.

Horses have always been a significant part of the life of the Carey's. In the late 19th century they kept shire stallions for local farmers, Irish Draught Stallions and as a rule supplied stallions to mare owners. One of most famous thoroughbreds was Blue Cliff who died a day short of 29th birthday, and he was an institution in the 1/2 bred industry. He holds the record in the RDS for the number of prizes won in the various show classes. One of his progeny Bueche Giorod was trained by Jenny Pitman to win the Massey Ferguson Gold Cup at Cheltenham. Other successful stallions were Merrion (Draught), Vivadari (Thoroughbred) and Tunbridge (Thoroughbred). Vividari has produced many successful point to pointers. Stallions standing in 1990 were Euphemism, Golden Cliff, Ireland's Pride and Silver Cloud.

One of the most interesting stallions was Tawriffic (Tawfiq-Joyarty) who won the Melbourne Cup in 1989. He was retired from racing in 1991 and eventually was sold in late 1998 to stand as a National Hunt Stallion in Ireland. He covered his first & only book of mares in 1999 at Tim Carey's stud before he died from a twisted bowel on 14 July 1999. The sole crop only had 8 wins from 85 starters of which Tawrific Laois won four. He beat Super Impose in the Melbourne Cup and he was the first of five cup winners for his Hall of Fame trainer Lee Freedman. He was ridden by Shane Dye in the Cup. He was 11 years dead when Tawrific Laois won as a 10 y/o won the Munster Handicap Hurdle at Thurles. Tim started running the farm with his father Ted and was involved with the Westmeath Foxhounds. Tim went to Warrenstown & the National Stud, before attending Allevmento Di Mirabello, Monza, in Italy working with Dr Malatti. He researched how stud farms worked and travelled to Canada, USA, Australia, Britain, and New Zealand. His most successful sire was New Frontier who bred Irish Grand National winner Lion na Bearnai. He was a Saddler's Wells horse out of a Mr Prospector mare but his career was cut short.

In 2008, his sires included King's Ride, Sayarshan, and Golden Lariat. Sayarshan was bred by leading French breeder Jean Luc Lagardere, from an Aga Khan mare who later purchased all the stock of Lagardere in a massive €200 million euro deal. He purchased Golden Lariat whose potential was pointed out by Sir Michael Stoute. He was by Mr Prospector out of a Sadlers Wells mare the opposite of New Frontier. He was a 1/2 sister to Ardross and his 1/2 brother won almost a million in prize money and from the same family as Scorpion. He was trained by Andre Fabre and bred by Maktoum Al Maktoum Crown Prince of Dubai. His first runner was Fayette County who when trained by for Muredach Kelly won a bumper at Downroyal by 5L's from subsequent Punchestown bumper winner Lots of Memories and won in Taunton in February 2014. The success of Fayette County over 2 years has assisted the stud, even as a 3 y/o he had the ability to jump fences. He was purchased by Tom Malone agent at Brightwell Sales for €55,000 and went to Tim Vaughan. J.P McManus bought him privately after his British debut and he won 2 more hurdles. Tim hoped he would be a good chaser as he had a great cruising speed and very scopey. Later J.P. McManus purchased him privately and left him with Tim Vaughan. The intention is to develop him as a chaser. Golden Lariat is increasing in popularity in 2013 and the aim is to produce quality & not quantity in keeping with a long tradition.

JOHN CONNAUGHTON BARRETTSTOWN STUD, MULLINGAR

John Connaughton Barrettstown Stud, Mullingar and Dunboyne Express, has always been a keen rider and huntsman but a number of years ago he began compiling a high quality broodmare band at his Barrettstown Stud in Mullingar, County Westmeath. Dunboyne Express's dam, Love Excelling, was an early acquisition, purchased out of the Lordship Stud for 220,000gns by his close friend Ted Naughton at the 2003 Tattersalls December Sale. The daughter of Polish Precedent hailed from one of Lordship's most active families, as a half-sister to Oaks winner Love Divine, and within two years she recouped that outlay when the Galileo filly she was carrying sold for 230,000gns. He liked Love Exceling, as a mare and this led to his association with Dunboyne Express. He saw Love Excelling as a big mare with a lovely conformation, a good pedigree. She only raced once for Henry Cecil as a 4y/o when breaking her pelvis.

Connaughton admitted to surprise that the bidding stopped at 48,000gns for Dunboyne Express (Shamardal-Excelling) and this led to him owning the horse when he first raced with Kevin Prendergast. He beat a horse of Aidan O'Brien's called Master of Hounds on his debut. He then ran in a select field in the Anglesey Stakes at the Curragh and won. *"Not selling him has turned out to be a great stroke of luck,"* said Connaughton. *"We're now going to enjoy him and hope he provides us with more thrills. And further down the line, he has the pedigree to be a stallion"*. In 2014 Dan Excel (Shamardal-Love Excelling) formerly Dunboyne Express beat stablemate Military Attack into third place to land the Singapore Airlines International Cup at Kranji over 10 furlongs in a record time. The 6 y/o no longer raced for his breeder John Connaughton and boosted his career earnings to £ 2.75 million. He has won 6 races (he had won Anglesey Stakes and Leopardstown 2,000gns trial in Ireland) and was rarely out of the money in 30 races. In Hong Kong his principal success was in The Champions Mile at Sha Tin. She produces wonderful looking stock and two recent yearlings by Teofilio & Shamardal grossed a million guineas at the sales. She was also in foal to Invincible Spirit and other top stallions. John Connaughton & Ted Naughton who helps to select mares have been very successful through Barretstown Stud in Westmeath in buying and selling high quality horses in association with John O'Shea, Farm Manager. He has been nominated as Breeder of the Year and has stated that prize money is a big factor that needs to be improved in order for people to cover their costs. He continues to occasionally own horses like Michael Halfords Sea the Lion, which won a maiden on Irish Oaks day a few years ago.

NOEL COLLINS - ALDERWOOD, TOTAL ENJOYMENT AND LUCKY WILLIAM

Noel Collins of Kilpatrick House, Mullingar is an owner/breeder from Tralee, Co Kerry who has settled near the Cleaboy Stud in Mullingar, where he is associated with the successful Garden Kingdom Syndicate as a founder member. He had bred high class horses in a short period like Alderwood, Lucky William, Total Enjoyment and The Sheperd King. In April 2012, he bred three winners at Fairyhouse. Two of them won black type races and both Alderwood (novice hurdle) and Lucky William (novice chase) went to Punchestown and won Grade 1's again (the other winner at Fairyhouse was Heavenly Brook). Both were foaled in 2004 like Total Enjoyment. The latter made his name winning the Cheltenham Festival bumper for the syndicate and Alderwood was also a festival winner in the County Hurdle for J.P. McManus and trained by Tom Mullins. Noel said *"I bought the dam of Alderwood carrying a colt foal by Anshan and I sent her to Alderbrook four times. Alderwood is the second of those and we still have two of the others. One of those is the seven year old Austerity Measures who has had a couple of point to point outings and the other is a full sister to Alderwood who is been kept for breeding"*. The Sheperd King was seriously injured and there was no guarantee that he would race again, even though he could have been the best.

Alderwood was consigned to the Goffs Land Rover Sale, as a 4 y/o and was bought by Tom Mullins for 19,000 euro. He is by Alderbrook who won the 1995 Champion Hurdle and stood at Alastair Pim's Anngrove Stud, Mountmellick, until he died aged 19 in 2008. His other star jumpers include For Non Stop, Glenfinn Captain and Ollie Magern. Noel is a beef farmer & his son Alan looks after family's 10 mares & other young stock. They had 40 horses there including lots of relations to the public stars. The Collin's sell their horses through Sean Gorman's Cleaboy & Coppice Stud.

PETER & ANN DOWNES, RUSSELSTOWN STUD, MULLINGAR

Peter had a number of unmarried uncles and the only one married was Robert. The family home was in Bellview and it was inherited by his uncle Toby Downes, before eventually being sold to the Bishop. Peter's father got Russellstown. The family had a bakery in town and going back in time there was a Downes Brewery in Enniskillen. Robert his grandfather invested in the Great Westrern Railway and Toby was more interested in racing then his father. He started by riding out with the hunt and in point to point's, due to encouragement by Toby and Reggie Bermingham. He had some rides on the track over the years and he rode in the last ever race at Mullingar in July 1967, which was won by the Finn family with Moigh Star. He was an amateur rider turned breeder. In 1981 he rode Swuzzlebubble bred by Jim Tormey of Bunbrosna and won at Downroyal, as part of a gamble on a horse trained by Cecil Ross.

He started in 1965 with 200 acres and 30 boxes. He has stood stallions like Bahrain, Dual, Our Mirage, Reformed Character, King's Ride, Celio Rufo and Persian Mews. Some of the winners bred by Russelstown Stud are Winter Squall,

King Lucifer, Carobee, Celestial Gold, and Fiveforthree.

He bred Celestial Gold (Persian Mews-What A Queen), which won the Paddy Power Gold Cup €90,596 in 2004 and the Hennessey Cognac Gold Cup €98,832 at Newbury for David Johnson and Martin Pipe (ridden by Timmy Murphy) and both G2's. The last horse to win these two races was Bright Highway in 1980. What a Honey the dam of What A Queen was a half-sister to L'Escargot. Fiveforthree won the Ballymore Properties Novice Hurdle at Cheltenham 2008 and he was a half brother to Celestial Gold. It was the same family as Mr What & L'Escargot through What a Queen (King's Ride- What A Honey), who was bred by Barbara & Arthur O'Neill (Barbara was given the family by Major Holliday, Cleaboy Stud according to some reports). Other good horses were Father Matt (4 wins, 2 over fences and 2nd in Gr1 Drinmore Chase & P.J.Moriarity Chase); Tipping Tim (14 wins over fences including the Mackeson Gold Cup Gr3 Cheltenham, Charlie Hall Chase & Ritz Club Chase, Cheltenham); King Lucifer (6 wins over hurdles& fences including the Kim Muir Chase, Cheltenham); and Carobee (5 wins including the Seagram Novice Hurdle, Liverpool), etc.

A horse called Celio Lucy (Celio Rufo-Cahore) was bred by him at Russelstown Stud. Celio Rufo was by Warpath-Counter Coup by Busted and was at the stud since 1986 and had been getting a fair share of winners. Prior to going to stud he won 11 races mostly in Italy including the Italian St Leger (Gr2). He also won the G1 named Gran Primo d'Italia in Milan. His most notable progeny at stud was Winter Squall and he is listed winner. Other nice horses by him are Counterbid, Trimmer Wonder, and Five From Home. Bahrain was also retired to Peter Downes Stud. He was a son of Irish Derby winner Tulyar who cost £250,000. He won the Amateur Handicap at Galway in 1962 when ridden by Sir William Pigot Brown and he later won the County Hurdle at Cheltenham beating the Queen Mothers Antiar. In 1978 he had been in existence for 13 years and the main stallion was Reformed Character, which went to England in 1982. He came in January 1976 from Major Holliday's Cleaboy stud. A 6 y/o by Reliance and he won at 3,4, and 5 and won £14,095.The fee for Reformed Character was £125 and the first crop in 1977 saw a price of 1,800 guineas and the previous year it was more. In 1982 Tower Shot arrived (Tower Walk-Sinful) and in 1982 King's Ride joined the stud (he won 6 times including the Lincoln). Unfortunately, Celio Rufo and Persian Mews (bred Persian Bold) were not very successful stallions.

More recently he bred the Gigginstown Stud owned No More Heroes, which was 3rd at Cheltenham and won races like a graded hurdle where he beat Willie Mullins's Shaneshill. The horse won a point to point, bumper, and over hurdles. He was unlucky at Cheltenham and its as a chaser he is expected to make a big impact. He is related to Fiveforthree and Celestial Gold. Peter has been very much involved with the Irish Thoroughbred Breeder's Association. Something very important to him has been the safety of horse riding helmets, ever since his 16 y/o son Stephen was tragically killed in a fall in 1995. He began a lengthy campaign and over ten years petitioned the European Parliament in Brussels to have new safety levels. Arising from this a new European safety standard on high performance helmets was developed in October 2005.

The family contributed a lot to Mullingar Racecourse and local racing. Robert Downes, (1861-1930) of Knocknagreena, Russellstown was a member of many committees in Westmeath & Mullingar including the County Council. He was the youngest son of Joseph Downes and educated at Clongowes Wood. He was a noted breeder of pure strain sheep and won many prizes at Ballsbridge. He owned race horses and had success locally & around the country and was Chairman of the Mullingar Race Committee. He brought about many improvements to the facility and Chairman of the committee for the Mullingar Agricultural Show. He was very much involved in the Irish Provincial Executive, which fought for provincial race courses in the 1920's.

T.P. Downes was a horse owner and on the Mullingar Race Committee. He won races like the Joseph O'Reilly Cup £100 at Fairyhouse in 1934 with Carraroe (Irish Battle-d by Fly Fisher). He rode it himself and beat Bachelors Heart (winner of Barbour Cup in 1933). He won on him at a Meath point to point in March 1935 & went for the Conyngham Cup. He bred Golden View II (Johney Roebuck-Rathview) and hunted with him before his sale to Margaret Lillingston & P.A.E.Reilly. He won the 1946 Irish Grand National but was later killed in a 3 horserace at Aintree. He also bred In View a half-brother to Golden View II that was favourite for the 1953 Irish National but was unplaced. Into View was the first Irish horse to win a jumping race in the USA in 1954. Other horses included Soir, Battlefort Graceful Anne, and Mariner's Dancer.

ANOTHER FLASH AND REVELRY IN THE LOCAL PUB

Anthony Duncan, Clonmoyle, Mullingar bred Another Flash (Roi d'Egypte-Cissie Gay) who was a half- brother to Sword Flash, Flash Bulb, and won 5 races in Ireland when trained by Cecil Ronaldson, and later scored 7 wins in England. Another Flash won in Mullingar in 1958 and won the Irish Cesarewitch in 1959 for trainer Paddy Sleator (he also won the two previous years with Sword Flash and Havasnack). Another Flash won all four races in 1958/59 aside from Cesarewitch. At that time he was owned by Mr N. Galway-Greer and it was rugby international J.T.Doyle, who advised J.J.Byrne to purchase him for £3,500. He was by Roi D'Egypte a full brother to Gold Cup winner Medoc II and just stood for £7. The dam Cissie Gay had changed hands on numerous occasions (once for nothing).

In a local history book '*Children of the Mound*', Mick Leavy mentioned that his father who owned Revelry winner of the Irish Grand National at one stage said that the horse was bought for £27 and Lord Harrington was due to send him to Tom Dreaper. It fell through and his father sold him for £400. The horse was later sold to J.T.Doyle for £10,000 and won the Irish Grand National in 1947. Various people used to ride the horse around in the area to exercise him. His father thought they were taking a long time each day and brought him out himself to see why it was taking so long, but the horse would not pass Tormey's pub in Bunbrosna without stopping. The secret was out and Revelry had a whole new meaning! When Revelry became well known, Andy Duncan an auctioneer in Mullingar found the dam's sister in Rooney's knacker's yard. He gave her to his nephew Anthony Duncan. He went on to breed Flashaway and Another Flash who won the Champion Hurdle.

FLASH OF GENIUS FROM SLEATOR

When Another Flash went for the Champion Hurdle in 1960 he was trained by the great Paddy Sleator who proved his ability to win top class races in both Ireland & Britain in the 1950's and 1960's. Another Flash ridden by Bobby Beasley ended up as 11/4 F and cruised around behind the leader and he came right away from Albergo and Saffran Tartan to win by two lengths in a new record time. Another Flash was out of the race in 1961 with an injury and in 1962 was 11/10F but he only finished 3rd to Anzio. This was the era when Sleator stabled his horses with Arthur Thomas in England and he was confident of victory, but it didn't happen on this occasion. He was out of the race again in 1963 because of a bout of enteritis over the year but he was 6/1F in 1964 in a field of 24 runners. He was only beaten by an outsider Magic Court, who veered across the track but held the race with Another Flash 4 lengths behind. He could have been the first horse to regain the title and after missing two years and probably was unlucky not to win the race twice. When he retired he carried on point to pointing.

CATHAL ENNIS, BALLABRIGGS AND ANNIE POWER

Cathal Ennis is based at Quill Farm, Castletown-Geo. His father Stephen was a mixed farmer who raised pigs and 7 cattle, but he retired from farming and the 80 acres at Quill house is now used for horses. One day he brought home a filly foal by Sheer Grit in the back of a trailer and her legacy lives on through her daughter Lemon Cello whose first offspring recently won a bumper. He was never involved with horses before that. Cathal was 11 y/o at the time and loved National Hunt racing, studying pedigrees and he became a big fan of Old Vic. A friend David Scally had a half-sister to Hi Cloy (won five Grade 1 races) who won the Power Gold Cup and the mare was in foal to Old Vic. He bought the mare named Papoose. Her last foal before the purchase was Ballabriggs who won the 2011 Grand National. She has provided 5 foals, one a full sister of

Ballabriggs and another was a half-sister. Cathal who is a newspaper advertising executive bought the horse on the advice of his uncle Seamus Ennis, who told him he liked a horse that was 2nd in an Oldcastle point to point called Letterman. His stud has grown to 15 National Hunt mares and Ballabriggs win increased interest in his horses, especially those that share the bloodline. He received help from Michael Ennis, Patsy Ennis, Gary Gleeson whose father Tony Gleeson, Rochfortbridge was a mentor and gave advice on stallions. His mother said he went white when Ballabriggs won the Grand National. She carried on producing mares after the big race.

ANNIE POWER

Annie Power (Sirocco-Anno Luce) was bred by Eamon Cleary who was the recipient of a ITBA Annual Awards for her. She came from top class flat family but who also had success over jumps. Her dam Anno Luce was a Group 3 winner and placed in the German Oaks. Her 6 winners included Atlaal a black type winner over hurdles and fences and was 2nd in the Tolworth Hurdle. Annie Power is the winner of 12 out of 13 races earning almost €300,000. Her only defeat was to More of That in the Grade 1 Irish Stallion Farms EBF Mares Novice Hurdle at Fairyhouse, until her fall in the mares hurdle at Cheltenham in 2015. Cathal was outbid by Eamonn Cleary for her but he spoke with him and agreed a deal for the mare Anno Luce, with the provision that Cathal reared the filly on his farm. It turned out that the filly was Annie Power and he reared her at Quill Farm before she went into training. Annie Powers went on to win a string of races in Ireland and Britain & was runner up in World Hurdle. On one occasion she had a narrow escape from a serious injury in the field, which could have changed her whole history. Cathal had 15 Mares in foal -5 to Oscar, 2 to Robin Des Champs. They are his favourite sires along with Beneficial, Presenting, Milan & Flemensfirth. His fillies are normally leased out, as he cannot afford to train them. He had one Kings Theatre in training with Peter Fahey. A promising 4 y/o full sister to Royal Alphabet called Queen Alphabet, who won in Kilbeggan. He has two dreams to breed a Gold Cup winner and see Westmeath win an All Ireland. The Gold Cup is his best chance!

He has had some promising horses but he has leased fillies including Queen of Mantua, a sister to Ballabriggs, to trainers like Fergal O'Brien and Tim Vaughan with the idea that they would return for breeding purposes after racing. At that time he had two horses in training with Irish trainer Peter Fahey. One was a King's Theatre four-year-old brother to Feathered Lady called King Rolfe, His job is to produce the foals in the best possible shape and it is critical they sell well. He bred the useful chaser Home Farm (Presenting-Tynelucy), who fell at the first in the Lexus Chase and he ran in the Hennessey in 2015 when unplaced. He has won three races but he has to have good ground. The Gigginstown Houses owned Identity Thief 7/4 won at Leopardstown on 28 December 2014 in a maiden hurdle, trained by Henry de Bromhead. He made a mistake but edged clear of favourite Snow Falcon 6/4 before the last to win comfortably. He has won 2 races and is a promising horse for the future.

Cathal is a regular correspondent to the Irish Field with particular reference to mares. He is passionate about the need for more incentives for breeders of National Hunt mares. He thinks there should be an additional mare's champion bumper at Cheltenham, and more chases confined to mares. He argues that there are not even half as many chases as against hurdles races for mares at present. It would be an incentive to owners to run better mares over fences. It looks like he might have some success with this aim.

FAGAN AND HOPE FAMILY - GOLD CUP AND CLASSIC WINNER'S

Edward J. Hope CC (1862-1940), Gartlandstown Stud, Crookedwood was educated in Clongowes Wood and was always noted for his hospitality. He bred classic winners like Lovely Rosa winner of the Irish Oaks in 1936 and he owned Santaria the Irish Oaks winner 1932. He also bred Dorothy Paget's Insurance (by Achtoi), which won the 1932 and 1933 Champion Hurdle and Prud'homme winner of the National Hunt Chase. He was engaged in the cattle trade; sales master at Dublin Cattle Market; and a Director of the Nelson Shipping Co. He supported the Westmeath Hunt and his horses ran nationwide. He died in 1940 and the funeral was attended by Sir James Nelson, Charles Flanagan TD, many local families including nieces and nephews from South America.

Insurance bred by Hope, was out of his home mare Prudent Girl, who was one of his best horses. He was owned by the eccentric Dorothy Paget when winning the Champion Hurdle in 1932 and 1933. When she died in 1959 at 54 y/o, she had won 1,532 races including seven Gold Cups, a Grand National and a Derby, making her the most successful owner in British history. Basil Briscoe her trainer got her Insurance, as well as Golden Miller the winner of five Gold Cups and one Aintree National. Philip Carr the original owner was ill and sold both for £12,000. One of his main opponents in this era was Weatmeath man Sir Hugh Nugents Song of Essex. Only three ran in the race in 1932 and Insurance (T.Leader) 4/5F won easily by 12 lengths and Golden Miller went on to complete the double in the Gold Cup. The following year Insurance now a 6 y/o was 11/10F and Song of Essex 3/1. The latter attacked Bill Stott, who was Insurance's jockey, at the start and his arm had to be bandaged. He was injured and had to retire after winning 8 of his 12 hurdle races. He was retired to Miss Paget's stud with Golden Miller and died at the age of 30 in 1957 just three months after Golden Miller.

His stallion Grand Inquisitor (His Reverance-High Prestige) won 12 races including the Liverpool Spring Cup as a 7 y/o in a lengthy career. He was 2nd in the Irish Derby in 1942 to Windsor Slipper. He was mated at stud with 21 y/o Duchess of Pedulas and sired Mr What the Aintree Grand National winner. He got few opportunities at stud and died 3 years before Mr What's win in 1955. Another son Take Time was 2nd in the Irish Grand National and won the Conyngham Cup in 1959, and his daughter Inquisitive Rose became the dam of Wrekin Rambler. Paddy Dunne Cullinanes Rupununi was also by Grand Inquisitor. He had other winners like Diamonds and Prudent Rose.

Charles Fagan TD carried on the tradition at Gartlandstown where he advertised Herodias (Ch 1920 Roi Herode - Oread) for the 1925-30 seasons on behalf of the horse's owner Margaret, Lady Nelson. He bred Poolgowran (Tangiers-Vin da Grave) who won the Irish National in 1934 for Sir James Nelson. Other good horses included Kitty's Pet, Snake Lightning (won 6 races) and Totaig (won the Royal Hunt Cup) and they stood here in 1947. In 1957 Mighty Apollo (Hyacinthus-Mighty Prudent) was bred by him and won the Kim Muir Chase at Cheltenham and was a half brother to Mighty Inquisitive (Grand Inquisitor-Mighty Prudent), who won the Baldoyle Handicap Hurdle in 1957 and the Leopardstown November Handicap in 1956.

Frank Fagan stood Royal Buck (bay 1957 Buckhound-Royal Charger) in 1970 for £100. Royal Buck (Buckahound-Royal Charge) won 13 races (Hennessy Handicap at the Phoenix Park etc). He bred Wrekin Rambler and Cheltenham Gold Cup winner Royal Frolic (1976). Royal Frolic the winner of the 1976 Cheltenham Gold Cup had connections with Gartlandstown Stud, as the 7 y/o gelding was owned by Frank Fagan. He sold the mare at the age of 20 and at the time she was in foal to Royal Buck and it was Royal Frolic. Royal Buck was the top National Hunt sire in Ireland with progeny earnings of £45,000. The O'Neills and What A Daisy bred 2 full brothers and a half brother to L'Escargot. The Pilgarlic What A Buck and Woverhampton were sired by Fagan's stallion Royal Buck.

In 1978 he had a new 5 y/o stallion Caribo (Sassafras-Petite). Sassafras had won the Prix De L'Arc (beating the great Nijinsky), and carried a good horse in France. He also had Major Point as a stallion. Caribo won the Prix D'Argenteuil at Longchamp and was 4th of 22 in the Grand Prix de Paris. In July 1983 a filly Rose Best won at Dundalk ridden by Christy Roche and was the first winner for Caribo. In 1976 Frank still had a half sister to Wrekin Rambler called Rose of the West and his two stallions were Meadsville and Major Point. Meadsville was trained by Stuart Murless and won some good races and also ran in the Irish Derby won by Ribero from Sir Ivor.

Frank Fagan's Rose of the West (Royal Buck-Inquisitive Rose) won the Lumville Stakes (J Roe) by and was a half sister to Wrekin Rambler. She had 2 wins at 2 and 3 years and was 2nd in the Pretty Polly Stakes. She traces to Western Rose (14 wins 4 hurdles including Tolworth & Kingwell Pattern Hurdles, 2nd in the Waterford Crystal Supreme Hurdle at Cheltenham and 10 wins over fences), Riva Rose had 7 wins with over £17,000 in prize money (placed in Spa Hurdle) and half sister to Western Rose. Inquisitive Rose (Darazari- Derravaragh Rose) never raced but the family included King Wah Glory who had 11 wins worth £81,000 (IAWS Novice chase Punchestown in 1996). Other horses included Roses Best 3/1 (Caribo-Rose of the West), who won the 3y/o Ashbourne at Fairyhouse, Orpheus Valley whose dam was Belle of the West and won the Grade A Guinness Chase. The horse was related to Minella Lad who won bumpers, the Drinmore Chase and 7 hurdle races including the Boyne, Slaney & Brown Lad Hurdle and was also placed in World Hurdle.

Wrekin Rambler was 3rd in the Irish St Leger and won the Goodwood Gold Cup. He retired to stud in 1968.

IRISH IVY SOLD FOR 35 GUINEAS "BECAUSE I COULDN'T GET 36 GUINEAS"

Sport visited Cornelius Hannon, Riverstown, Killucan, on March 1892. His best stallion was Marmiton and the brood mares were doing well at sales. The reporter had been there in January 1891 after Marmiton came from Britain and he advised people to send mares to him & many took the advice. Lord Roseberry bred him in 1885 and he ran well as a race horse without major success (£10 fee). Marmiton bred HRH who won the first 2 y/o race in 1900 and later won the Leopardstown Chase in 1903. He also had brood mares Deodar, All Right, Baby Girl, Cherry Blossom and Poor Clare. In March 1900 Hannon purchased St Gris (1896 Galopin -Isabel) from Mr Rothschild at 30 sovs. It was one of best & most organised studs he visited (his progeny won £1,348-19s in a year).

Hannon sired Mavis of Meath winner of Irish Grand National, trained by Larry Hope and ridden by T.Dowdall. Hope trained and rode the good horse Westmeath (Deodar out of Ascetic), which was originally owned by Hannan. As an unbeaten 4y/o, he was sold to Fred Leyland, London for £2,000 for whom he finished 5th in the 1897 Aintree Grand National. He won the 1895 Irish Oaks with Sapling (Marmiton-Deodar) and also bred Irish Ivy (Marmiton -Wild Ivy) to win Irish Oaks on 22nd July 1899. He owned both the sire & dam. In August the horse won the Leopardstown Prize of 1,000 sovereigns for owner Captain Peel. Hannon had disposed of Irish Ivy for 35 guineas and when he was once asked why he let her go for such a paltry figure, he answered *"Because I couldn't get 36 guineas"*.

However since then he had obtained very big figures for horses of the same breeding, which has added to the reputation of the stud. It was rumoured that the horse was sold to Captain Machell for £4,500. On 25th October 1899, Irish Ivy won the English Cambridgeshire at 20/1 by 3 lengths carrying 7st 11lbs. There was a great pride in Westmeath, as the horse had been bred in the county and it endorsed the breeding ability of the Hannon family. Another rumour spread that horse was sold to a patron of Richard Marsh's stable for 6,000 guineas. She was trained by W.Behan Herbert Lodge, The Curragh and owned by Captain Peel. Like many horses of that era she ran over all distances, as the records show. In April 1898, she was 2nd on her debut at The Curragh, then won at Leopardstown in the Londonderry Plate, which was run twice due to a mishap with the starting machine, but she won both times. She was unplaced in the Lincoln Handicap but then won four in a row - the Queen's Plate at The Curragh, over 2 miles on 27th June; the next day she won over 3 miles; then by 5 lengths at Curragh July meeting beating Sidewing; and then the Leopardstown Prize in August. She won the Park Hill Stakes at Doncaster and was then unplaced in Irish Cesarewich (didn't stay), before winning the English Cambridgeshire at 20/1. She was a very adaptable filly.

Another good filly to arrive was J. O'Reilly's Satin (Umpire-Silk). In 1897 at the Mullingar Horse Show, Poor Clare (Ascetic) and Baby Girl (Deodar) won 1st & 2nd Prize. In September 1900, Hannon sold a full brother to Irish Ivy for £1,500 at the Dublin Horse Show and he also bred Marpessa who won in 1903. On the 1911 Census, he was described as a 57 y/o magistrate for Westmeath, his wife Mary was 48 y/o from New Jersey, daughter Mary 25 y/o, and son Cornelius Hannan 19 y/o.

CAPTAIN H.B. GAMBLE, WESTMEATH

Captain H.B. Gamble, while serving with his regiment in Yorkshire, purchased Miss Pratt (1825) by Blacklock out of Gadabout, with whom he won some regimental races. The mare was low in stature under 15 hands, but very thick with good bone & length. The Captain's best horse was Volcano (Vulcan-Mansfield Liss), who won the Madrid Handicap at The Curragh in 1849. When he retired back to Westmeath, he brought Miss Pratt back with him to his Irish Stud, where she bred some indifferent foals. Gamble died suddenly in 1837 and an auction of his horses took place, with Miss Pratt purchased for 120 guineas by George Watts, a Devon born vet, who had moved to Ireland to breed thoroughbreds. He was in partnership with Bob Gore and later on his own. He attended an auction of Captain Gamble's effects and got Miss Pratt for 120gns. He was based at Jockey Hall, The Curragh and the leading owner of winners 5 times - 1833, 1844, 1846, 1848, and 1855. He put Miss Pratt to the good sire Economist (who sired the Irish Champion Harkaway) and bred the filly Echidna the dam of The Baron. She was never raced and was put to Birdcatcher to produce The Baron and is most famous for producing the great horse Stockwell.

ROBERT HOLMES MOYCASHEL, WESTMEATH

He was famous for his shorthorn cattle herd all over Ireland & Britain but he also bred horses. Verulam was bred by him at Moycashel near Kilbeggan. He also bred Vulcan winner of the Liverpool Cup in 1847 and the Cambridgeshire. He raced in Ireland & England and may have bred Aintree Grand National winner Wanderer 1855. Verulam stood at Killynon Stud, where the stallion Blackfoot was also located. The Vulgan mare produced a filly to the cover of Blackfoot (1833). The latter also got the dam of Gamecock the Aintree Grand National winner in 1887. His dam was Wire (1811) a full sister to Whisker & Whalebone. Humphry Clinker was one of the first horses to suffer from the malady of *"roaring"* with the Earl Fitzwilliam, Co Wicklow. Holmes sent a mare to him and bred a good horse Famine or Rush. He was described in *The Post & Paddock* by H.Dixon, as one of the best breeder's of young hunters who were often sent to Irish fairs between 6 and 8 year's old, but the best were usually bought before reaching the fair.

DAN KIERNAN'S, BALRATH STUD

Dan Kiernan advertised Gay Reveller (Muncaster - Revaillon) for the 1901 season, likewise Bealderg (Enthusiast - Enchantress) between 1901 and 1913 (who bred horses like James Pigg, Mawgoory, Cooldrea etc) and Monilea (Lesterlin - Marcella II) between 1910 and 1912. He owned Gay Reveller and he was injured in July 1905 and had to be put down. He had produced many champions and it was a great loss to Mr Kiernan. Other good horses included Cissy Gay by Gay Reveller who won over 50 races, Jolly Joy, Reveller (killed in Trim in 1902), Dysart (Bealderg), and Rathcore (Avidity). His horse Gay & Sweet won at Tullamore in May 1901, as did Cissy Gay in May 1899. J. Kiernan, Greenpark owned All Sorts, winner of 1916 Irish Grand National and runner-up in 1917/1918. He also owned Mask On, winner of the Conyngham Cup in 1921 when trained by Cecil Brabazon. James Kiernan Rathnamodagh, Dysart, Mullingar won with Piper's Hill at Mullingar in September 1913, as did Rathrua, both ridden by Willie Lynn. He owned useful horses like Royal Dennis, Lanigan's Ball and Irish Pride. Michael Kiernan, Rathcore, Dysart, started in 1982 and won the Dunmore Handicap Hurdle at Tramore with Grannies Pet and at one stage Paddy Mullin's great mare Grabel was retired there as a broodmare.

CYRIL MAGUIRE, COOLGAVNEY, BALLYNACARAGY AND THE STONE MAD HORSE

Cyril Maguire, Coolgavney, Ballynacaragy is best known as a breeder of poultry, but he bred a few promising horses. His horse Divine Rhapsody (City Honours-Cyrils Girl) won the Land Rover Bumper at Punchestown worth €50,000 ridden by M.Fogarty at 50/1 in 2010. He was sired by City Honours, who came second in the English & Irish Derbies in 1997. His mother was Cyril's Girl and she died of colic just an hour after he was born. He had to bring the foster mother, sourced from Fionnuals Cash's stud at Borris on Ossory, Tipperary. Divine Rhapsody was owned by Richard Walsh, Wicklow & the trainer was Phillip Rothwell. The foal sold for €5,700 at Tattersall's and was kept for 3 years & sold at the Land Rover Sale. It was a great day for Cyril at Punchestown. Divine Rhapsody has not been as successful as hoped with two wins in 11 runs and the last success was in February 2014 at Down Royal.

He also bred King Vuvuzuela who won the bumper at Punchestown & was a useful. The 6y/o bred by Maguire is out of Coolgavney Girl a daughter of Madam Madcap who was the dam of Comply or Die the Aintree Grand National winner. A year after giving birth to the foal that would become Comply or Die, Madam Madcap then owned by a neighbour (Martin Dibbs) of Maguire's gave birth to a Good Thyne filly foal that was blind. Instead of being put down Cyril agreed to take the foal & the mare. They named her Coolgavney Girl after a local townland. He said *"Madam Madcap was stone mad, daft. We put a bell on the foal or she was lead by the head collar".* He looked promising for the Red Menece Syndicate with a bumper and maiden hurdle win for Paul Nolan but then lost form.

A 'VAGUELY NOBLE' CHRISTY MAYE, MULLINGAR

The story of the great horse Vaguely Noble is told elsewhere, under the Cleaboy Stud, but when you speak to Christy Maye he is adamant about one thing, and that is Vaguely Noble is the greatest horse to come out of Westmeath and one of the greatest horses in the last half century in world racing. Not too many would disagree with him, but if you do be prepared for a vivid discussion.

In March 2009 the then former owner of the Bridge House, Chrisy Maye was honoured with '*This is Your Life*' compared by RTE journalist Colm Murray, Moate. He was joined by his wife Ellen, and family. He grew up on farm near Ballymahon one of 8 children and was a salesman, psychiatric nurse and launched the first mobile disco *(Disc A Go Go)* in Ireland or Britain. He started in 1965 in the Parochial Hall behind the Greville Arms and then moved to the Lake County Hotel. He played all over the midlands and after his marriage in 1973 he bought the old P & H. Egan premises, which became the Bridge House - the price was £27,000. The Bridge House became almost iconic over the years due to his work ethic and presentation. It won many prizes and almost every Irish musical star or band player there over the years. He was a founder member of the Tullamore Chamber of Commerce, which he served as President, and developed the Shopping Centre over 15 years and it was opened by Gay Byrne in 1995. He was part of every major event or organisation in Tullamore and Mullingar, whether it was Agriculture Shows or the Lions Club. He is still very much associated with the Greville Arms in Mullingar. He was also very interested in horse racing, as an owner, breeder and sponsor over the years.

He has owned many good horses over the years like Cloughtaney, Noble Thyne, and Stringfellows. The latter ran him ran at Fairyhouse in April 1986 and was unplaced to a horse called Cloughtaney. Christy was impressed with the winner and decided to meet the owner/trainer Eddie Hayden in Tipperary. Eventually, after some *"discussion"* they sorted out a price and that night Christy rang back confirming the sale (Eddie gave back a £5). The horse won three bumpers at Clonmel in December 1985; Limerick in March 1986, and Fairyhouse in April 1986. The horse ran in Sean Grahams Hurdle at Leopardstown on a bad day and surprised him with a good win. He always had great praise for Paddy Mullins and the horse won 8 races, including the inaugural running of the Bishop Cleeve Hurdle, in 1988 beating Mrs Muck & Beech Road by 20 lengths and the Red Mills Hurdle at Gowran in 1987. He was second favourite at 5/1 for the Champion Hurdle in 1988, but disappointed behind Celtic Shot. He was laid to lose about £250,000 by Hills & Ladbrokes. He was 8th of 15 runners to Beech Road in the Champion Hurdle in 1989, then 2nd beaten 7 lengths at Aintree and ran again at Punchestown in April 1989 to be 3rd to the good mare Grabel. He also won the Lismullen Hurdle three years in a row from 1988/90. At the end of his career he was trained for a while by Jim Tormey before he retired to Mullingar as a 14 y/o where he learned show jumping.

NOBLE TYNE THE FIRST HORSE TO BEAT CHAMPION HURDLER ISTABRAQ

Noble Tyne (Good Tyne -Tina O'Flynn) was also trained by Paddy Mullins and won 6 of his 16 races under rules. He had the distinction of beating Istabraq on his racing debut at Punchestown in November 1998 (Istabraq was not beaten again for 15 months). A fortnight later Istabraq comprehensively reversed the form in the Grade 1 Royal Bond Novice Hurdle at Fairyhouse. Another high class bumper horse and hurdler was French Holly, and in 1996 he was unbeaten when he travelled to Punchestown in April 1996 for the Jack White Memorial Bumper race. He was 2/1F but he was beaten by Noble Thyne. In the enclosure there was a very mixed group to greet the horse including 007 Sean Connery, Rolling Stone Ron Wood, and RTE's Ted Walshe. It was a great day out for all the staff from the two hotels. The celebrations continued at Finan's Naas where there was dinner for all staff and then back to the Greville Arms, where a video of the race was shown as they drank champagne. Another Good Tyne horse called Lady Thyne was trained by John Oxx and on 5th July 200 at Cork she gave Christy his first flat winner when beating the favourite Golden Hind.

In May 2007 Christy Maye, enjoyed his first success at his home track in Kilbeggan, when the Tom Cooper-trained Creme D'Arblay took the 3mile handicap hurdle. Niall Madden rode Creme D'Arblay to a length-and-a-quarter win. Tom Cooper said: *"I suppose you could say having a winner here, would be liking having a winner at Cheltenham for Christy. It means a lot to him, and the race being sponsored by a rival hotel (Mullingar Park) makes it all the sweeter!"*

He started up the Bridge Syndicate involving a group of local people. In 2009, Noble Galileo, bred by Christy, won a fillie's maiden at Galway and 14 members of the staff were in attendance. Bahrain Storm (Bahare -Dance Up a Storm) was bred at his Dunbroden Estate, Mullingar and won the Galway Hurdle at 20/1 and the next day he turned out again to win the Guinness Flat Race. In his lifetime he won over €360,000. Christy kept around 20 mares at his Mullingar Farm and said he did not know what to expect at Galway. He also bred Eagles Pass who finished 2nd in the Galway Hurdle in 2008 and Glenstal Abbey which was 2nd in the race preceeding the Galway hurdle beaten by Dual Gales (W. Mullins). He said *"We were associated with first in Galway Hurdle this year, second in it last year and third the previous year, so we're all delighted with that".* It was a remarkable achievement in many ways. Eagles Pass was 2nd to Indian Pace in 2008 beaten a length and was 3rd to Farmer Browne in 2007, before Bahrain Storm's win in 2009.

In 2013 Prince Chaparral (High Chaparral-Eilanden) won twice at the Tramore festival and Christy was the owner/ breeder and he was trained by Pat Flynn.

JIM McCARTAN, GAYBROOK LODGE

When he was young he started riding with Eamonn Finn in Ballymahon before he got into show jumping. He rode on the circuit for around 6 years including a good mare Easy Girl, owned by Ned Cash. When his brother Philip was assistant trainer to Noel Meade, Jim worked there for 6 months riding out horses and working in the stables. He then started working with Eddie O'Leary helping to break horses for the breeze up sales and he stayed there for three years. Tony O'Callaghan at Tally Ho Stud was also great to work for and encouraged him to buy breezers of his own. The first one he bought was a colt by Shack at Tattersalls Ireland and Michael O'Rourke, who was Managing Director at Tattersall's said he could pay for the second one as soon as he had money. The two horses cost Ir£4,200 and he resold them the following year for 9,500.

This was the start of been involved in pinhooking, except for a period when he concentrated on Adsell Productions which relates to stallion promotional DVD's for studs, Irish Thorougbred Marketing etc. He launched the company in 1987 to provide an audio visual communication service to the public & private sector as he had always been interested in photography and video production. In time he specialised in bloodstock promotion. He has used the best professionals in the business and people like Sir Peter O'Sullivan, Claire Balding, and Alastair Down have been voice over artists. It has been very successful and he has worked with the top studs in recent years. The bloodstock side of Adsell is called Bloodstock Vision, which aside from the studs and stallions provides a web-based design, health & safety training DVD's, TV commercial etc.

HORSES THAT "RUN LIKE ROCKETS"

He combines it with pinhooking at Gaybrook Lodge Stud which was set up in 2005. He has established itself as one of the largest and most successful consignors in Europe, with strong links to the USA market, purchasing most recently the progeny of Exchange Rate. Thorougbred's have always been a major part of his family and his brother Paul manages Croom House Stud in Limerick and other members of his family are also involved with horses. He concentrates to a certain extent on the American market, as he says you can get better value at Keeneland with 4-5,000 horses at a sale as against 7,000 at Goffs and other places. In May 2014 one of his most notable successes was the sale of a daughter of War Front, which was sold to David Redvers for 270,000 guineas. The horse had been led out unsold in 2013 for €85,000. As David Redvers said at the time *"Our experience of Jim's horses is that they breeze up like rockets, and run like rockets in races too"*. The horse called War Alert won on her second run for Qatar Racing and David Brown. Redvers had also bought Lighting Thunder from Gaybrook Stud for 115,000 guineas the previous year. She went on to be second in both the 1,000 guineas and the Irish 1,000 guineas for Olly Stevens.

One of Jim's most successful sales was at the Craven Breeze up sale when selling subsequent winner Moheet for 800,000 guineas to Al Shaqab Racing having bought the son of High Chaparral for 41,000 guineas as a yearling. He got her cheap, because the dam hadn't been successful with four previous horses and the horse had a scar from a flesh cut. The horse did an exceptional breeze up - the fastest time for 10 years at Newmarket! Moheet (he ran in the English 2,000 guineas and Epsom Derby in 2015 - tipped by Pricewise!) won first time out for Richard Hannon by 7 lengths. He is supported by a great team and the stud is consistently among the leading European breeze up consignors. In 2014 they were the leading consignors at the Craven Sale (by average) and at the Tattersalls Guineas Breeze-Up Sale (by total sales and average). He breeds a few horses himself and his brother Paul looks after them in the winter and he has one in training.

JOHN OXX, PARK STUD, KINNEGAD AND ARCTIC STORM

Arctic Storm is a horse that is remembered because he almost became the first Irish horse to win the Irish Sweeps Derby in 1962, when he was beaten a head by Tambourine who won in a record time with the Epsom Derby winner Larkspur behind in 4th place. He was unlucky because he was hampered at one stage. He was unfashionably bred being by the unraced Arctic Star out of Rabina, who failed to win on the flat but did win a £100 hurdle (It begs the question- how did he end up in a stable like John Oxx on pedigree?). He may not have had the breeding but he had the ability, as he won four races worth over £16,000 from 6 furlongs to 1 1/2 miles including the Irish 2,000 guineas in a record time, the Champion Stakes at Newmarket by 3 lengths and the Finglas Stakes. Arctic Storm owned by Mrs E. M.Carroll died due to a twisted bowel, which was a sad day for the owner and for John Oxx.

In a telephone conversation on 7th March 2014, John Oxx Jn explained that after he retired, the horse ended up in the The Park Stud, Kinnegad, which was purchased by Mrs John Oxx on the advice of the owner Peter Ennis, Ballyboggan, He said it was just a plain farm with a stone building & around 130 acres. Eventually, it was not economic and it was sold in 1976. Arctic Storm was the main stallion, but unfortunately he died young in 1968 without getting the chance to prove himself at stud. Peter Ennis who advised him about the stud, owned a horse trained by John Oxx called Our Shadow, who was 2nd to Mick Hurley's horse Gra Mo Chroi in the last ever flat race in Kilbeggan. Liam Browne had retired from the saddle and was a groom at the stud for a year and lived there. He decided to go back riding for a while before becoming a successful trainer. He was followed by Paddy Carroll as groom. In 1970 the Park Stud was standing Aglojo (Skymaster-Ballymaginathy) for 1970 and the well-bred Bally Joy (Ballymoss-Gladness).

Patrick Murphy and his wife Ann own Park Stud near Kinnegad, County Westmeath, bought the stud in 1989 and bred some useful jumps performers such as Lord Jay Jay and According To Dick, Morana winner of the Autumn Stakes was his first Group winner on the Flat.

OFFALY

LUMVILLE FARM AND DERRINSTOWN STUD

Lumville House, Edenderry, Co Offaly was bought in 1885 for the sum of £625 and it was on 365 acres of land. The original house fell into disrepair and was replaced in 1945 with a two storey residence of 4,000 square feet. It was purchased by Derrinstown Stud to develop the existing farm into a stud. Derrinstown Stud is Managed by Stephen Collins, part of Sheikh Hamdan's global Shadwell Stud. It has 10 farms set in 2,000acres, with most of it near Maynooth. The latest addition is the beef fattening farm near Edenderry. The Sheikh has about 220 mares between Europe & the USA, in addition to the 70/80 foaled at Derrinstown (Around 90 staff). Bobby Bryan the Farm Business Advisor ensures good quality hay, straw, and oats locally at the Lumville Farm in Offaly, which was purchased so that they could rest the paddocks when required. It was hard to find a large tract of grass, but it is fantastic free draining limestone land and and important addition to the stud, as they hope to expand the stallion operation.

The Stud Manager is Jimmy Lenehan on the day to day running. He was Assistant Trainer to Kevin Prendergast for 5 years and Manager at Gilltown & Kildangan and a great horseman. All European foals of Sheikh Hamdan's in Europe are weaned at Derrinstown. When yearlings are prepared to go into training the owners takes an interest in consultation with Collins, Lenehan, and Shadwell Racing Manager Angus Gold. The Sheikh visits Ireland more often than Britain or France, even though most of his horses are in Britain etc.

RICHARD BULL, ELMFIELD, TULLAMORE, DEPUTY SHERIFF OF KING'S COUNTY

He raced in partnership with Eyrefield Lodge trainer, Henry Eyre Linde. The talented but unsound Red Prince II (Ch 1889 Kendal - Empress) won the National Stakes as a juvenile, the Royal Whip, and the very valuable Lancashire 'Chase at Manchester as a four-year-old. Red Prince II was good looking and went on to become the leading National Hunt sire in 1904/09, and was subsequently sold on to Germany. He was out of the 1880 Grand National winner Empress. He won the Royal Whip (over 4 miles) as a 3 y/o. At 4 y/o he was a precocious jumper, winning 4 races over fences, including the Cork Park's Grand Stand Handicap Chase over 2 1/2 miles and Manchester's Lancashire Chase over 3 3/4 miles by 8 lengths. He was owned by Henry E.Linde of Eyrefield Lodge, The Curragh, who had a private steeplechase course at Eyrefield. Linde trained Empress to win the Grand National named in honour of Empress Elizabeth of Austria, who visited Ireland to hunt. He also trained Kirkwood's Woodbrook, and Too Good winner of the Grand Steeplechase de Paris and was 2nd in the Grand National. Red Prince II bred winners, that included Red Lad, who was 2nd to Ascetic Silver in the Grand National in 1906 and winner of the Irish Grand National; Conyngham Cup winners Fanius (1906); and Ruddygore (1914); and Galway Hurdle winner Red Damsel by Gay Lass (1913).

Other successful partnership horses were the full-brothers Mercury (11 wins) and Mercurius (6 wins) by Hominy - Princess. Richard Bull later saw his 'Daffodil, black hoop and cap' colours carried by Donnybrook (10 wins 1914/18, trained by Leslie Brabazon) and Kroo-boy (6 wins including the Irish Cesarewitch 1917/18 trained by S.C. Jeffrey). Richard Bull was also one of the original members of the Tullamore Golf Club Committee.

LORD DECIES, 5th & 6th BARON - KINNITTY CASTLE STUD

He advertised the stallions Reynard Volant (1942 Foxhunter - Flying Shell) at £148, Hunsingore (1941 Nearco - Springtime) at £75 and Appian Bridge (1941 Gold Bridge - Appian Way) at £48 to stand at his Kinnitty Castle Stud for the 1950 season. In Malaya in 1956, Irish horses dominated racing with Jolly Sailor a horse by Reynard Volant being champion of the year.

His predecessor, the 5th Baron Decies (1866-1944) owned Ballaghtobin (Morganatic-Fiorenza) bred by Colonel Chaloner Knox, unbeaten in six starts as a 2-y-o in 1914, and winner of both the Baldoyle Derby and the Irish Derby in 1915. Lord Decie's win with Ballaghtobin 7/2 (Morganatic-Fiorenza) in 1915 was very popular because he was followed home by UK challengers. He paid £4,000 for a 1/2 share in the horses, after his successful debut and he was the joint owner with Colonel Knox and G.W.Lushington. His colours were carried, *"scarlet, & green quartered cap".* Ballaghtobin reappeared in the Kings Plate at the Oaks meeting with General Symons a 6 y/o his only challenger and won by 20 lengths. He won 3 races as a 4 y/o and was unplaced at Newmarket in his only race in 1917. He went to India for 3 years and was sold in 1920 for 105 guineas. After his retirement he wasn't a success at stud. Decies was made a member of the Turf Club around 3 months before the race. He was a noted sportsman who represented Great Britain in show jumping on tours in North & South America & then was a polo player & yachtsman. He was appointed Military Press Censor in 1916 for three 3 years. He died in 1944 aged 87 years.

DR J.M. PRIOR KENNEDY JP, ELMFIELD, TULLAMORE - BALLINASRAGH STUD

He was a doctor, Justice of the Peace and former rugby international and a breeder for around 50 years. He was described on one local paper as *"Offaly's premier sportsman"* He purchased Killyleagh (Kendal - Abanico) a winner of the Sandown Grand Prize to stand him at Ballinasragh, which was managed by T.S. Elcoate. From his first crop (of only 2 to race) Killyleagh got Killeagh, winner of the 1906 Irish Derby and he also sired Punch winner of Irish Grand National. Dr Kennedy subsequently purchased Killeagh, at the end of his racing career to stand at Elmfield. He was not a success, his only decent winner being The County, winner of the 1915 Madrid Handicap. He sold Killanna (Killeagh-Annacross) to Mr Arnold at Ballsbridge sales September 1912 and also Joyful Morem (Killeagh-mare by Amphidamus) to P.Brophy.

In May 1940, Dr J.M.Kennedy's owned & bred Glendine trained by Jimmy Cleary, Bishopstown and he won a chase at Tramore. In May 1891, a cattle show was held at the Tullamore Show Grounds in 1906, and it attracted almost 300 entries with the gold medal for the best brood mare being won by Dr Kennedy, Tullamore. The committee of that year included many who directly or through their families were to maintain an interest in the Tullamore Show until its demise in 1938.

F.J. 'FRANK' LACY, BALLYCRYSTAL HOUSE, GEASHILL

Ned Lacy, Ballycrystal, Geashill initially had horses with Dan Kirwan, and he began training in the early 1950s, winning the 1956 Irish Cesarewitch with Limeona, ridden by his apprentice son, T.F. 'Tom' Lacy. He took over Height

O'Fashion, training her to win the 1964 Guinness Chase at Punchestown, in addition to finishing second to both Arkle and Flyingbolt in Irish Grand Nationals. Fashion's Fancy, Air Commodore and Balinagar were also good winners ridden by his sons Tom (professional) and Frank (amateur). He trained Ballyhassan Countess to win the Naas November Handicap in 1964. Frank was the younger son of Ned Lacy and he was a competent amateur rider, who eventually adapted Ballycrystal Stud to a stallion station, enjoying notable success with the unraced Sadler's Wells sire Accordion. Having said that it was Limona, who was also bred at the Co Offaly stud, and won the Cesarewitch, who originally helped to raise the profile of the Lacy's.

ACCORDION IN TUNE

Accordion was out of the Successor mare Sound of Success and a brother to Sonus, who was second in both the St Leger and Great Voltigeur, before winning the Goodwood Cup at four. He was also a half-brother to Hawaiian Sound, winner of the Benson and Hedges Gold Cup and runner-up in the Derby. Unfortunately, he never made the race track, so his subsequent success as a stallion has been amazing. It was at the Cheltenham Festival that Lacy's name came to the attention of people in racing, when he had his biggest success as a breeder when his homebred Katabatic won the 1991 Queen Mother Champion Chase. In his first crop was Dato Star, who was the first British trained horse to win the Champion Bumper at Cheltenham and went on to enjoy a very successful career over hurdles, scoring in the Christmas Hurdle as an eight-year-old and twice won the Champion Hurdle Trial at Haydock and the Fighting Fifth Hurdle. Accordion was quick to build on his early promise as a stallion, siring Yavana's Pace in his second crop. The Mark Johnston-trained gelding proved an exceptionally tough and consistent performer during his globetrotting career, making history as a ten-year-old when he became the oldest horse to win a Group 1 in Europe, when landing the Credit Suisse Pokal at Cologne in August 2002. He said: *"Accordion's had a good horse every year since Dato Star, and they seem to have just kept getting better."*

Other high-profile progeny of the 20-year-old stallion include high-class jumper Accordion Etoile, outstanding two-mile chaser Flagship Uberalles, Ladbroke Handicap Hurdle winner Graphic Equaliser, and Newlands Chase winner His Song. Amazingly, he only covered a small book of mares, so the percentage success was very high. In his first year he covered only ten mares, which included Dato Star. In his second year, he covered 15 mares which eventually rose to 70 mares a year. He died at the age of 21. Most of his progeny have been jumpers but Yavanas Pace was a *"great horse"* said Lacy. Accordion has spent his entire stud career at the family-run Ballycrystal Stud. He bought him at Ballydoyle when he was with Vincent O'Brien.

Dato Star won 10 of his 29 races and around £133,000 in prize money and he died in 2001 at Malton on the gallops, (trained by Malcolm Jefferson). Katabatic (Stong Gale) had 17 wins from 43 races and won over £362,000. In 2014, he was 31 y/o and living at Charlie Morgan's livery. In April 1994, he won the Melling Chase at Aintree by 15 length's beating Travado, Deep Sensation, and Remittance Man. His last race was in 1996 at 13 y/o. Yavanas Pace had 74 starts with 16 wins and he won £740,000, including the Credit Suisse Private Banking Pokal (G1), Prix Gladiateur (G3), Irish St Leger (G1), Canadian International (G1) etc. He died in 2010. Flagship Uberalles won the Arkle Challenge Cup (1999), Tingle Creek Chase (1999/2001), Queen Mother Champion Chase (2002), and the Punchestown Champion Chase (2003). He won around £1.38 million with 14 wins in 40 races (5 trainers/3 owners). Killegar, Limeona and Get Out of My Way were other horses associated with the stud. Lacy had other stallions at Ballycrystal - Gold Mark, Courtship and Where or When. Goldmark who was the third top rated 2 y/o in France in 1994 and won the Group1 Grand Criterium, bred Golden Cross and other winners include Missing You Too, Great as Gold and Red Knight. The other stallion is Courtship born in 1996 by Groom Dancer (trained by Henry Cecil) and a full brother to Pursuit of Love.

Tom Lacy, Rhode, was a successful apprentice and National Hunt jockey in the 1960's. He won the Gunness Handicap Chase with Height O'Fashion and the Troystown Chase at Navan. Height O'Fashion had 4 wins on the flat including the Irish Cesarewich and was placed 8 times and won 14 over jumps-including the Guinness Chase twice. She was placed 17 times, including 2nd in the Irish National to Arkle & Flyingbolt, 2nd in the Galway Plate, 2nd in the Thyestes Chase, and 2nd in the Leopardstown Chase. He set up his own public stable near Rhode, enjoying significant success with such as Scroll (ran in the Galway Plate), Welsh Bard, Bodelle and Ingabelle. Pat Smullen served his time to Tom Lacy, winning the apprentice championship in 1995 and 1996 en route to becoming multiple Irish champion as stable jockey to D.K. Weld. In 1976 he had Coramona in the Galway Plate and Barton in the Guinness Hurdle. The latter was a useful 4 y/o by Prominer who scored his third win just before Galway at Gowran.

DR GEORGE MOOREHEAD, ALIAS "R.M. DELEMERE", TULLAMORE

He was a doctor of Scottish descent, who raced under the name "R.M. Delamere". He bred & owned Roy Neil winner of the Irish Derby in 1892 and the National Stakes with Prodigal (1871) and Tyrconnell (1876), in addition to the Beresford Stakes with Prospector. Dr Moorehead also stood Lord Edward (1896 Enthusiast-Noble Duchess) winner of the National Breeders Produce Stakes and Monkchester Stakes. In 1873 his horse Knight of Erin (Behan) was 5th and last in Irish Derby. Turco was last in 1875, but proved to be the best horse for he won all sorts of races over the next 7 years. He won the Liverpool Hurdle (1879), the

Sefton Chase (1880), Beecher Hurdle and the Craven Chase on the same day in 1880. He was not so successful in the Aintree Grand National. He was ridden by Harry Beasley in these races and he also won in France in an Open Military Chase- the prize was a brown horse called Bibletto. He was retired to Richard Stacpooles stud, in Ennis, Co Clare. In 1877 he was 3rd in Irish Derby with Tyrconnell (J.Connolly) to Redskin.

At last in 1892, Moorehead won the Irish Derby with Roy Neil 5/1 (Kendal-Sylva by Sylvanus). He was trained by R.Meredith and ridden by M.Dawson. He won the Cork Derby before the Irish Derby and years later his grandson bred The Dikler winner of the Gold Cup in 1973. After the Irish Derby he won the Great Northern St Leger at Stockton, and was down the field in the Ebor Handicap, won at Manchester, and was 9th in the Cesarewitch. He came from the first crop of Kendal bred by the Duke of Westminister & won 5 out of 7 as a 2 y/o Two foals he kept were Blairfinde, who won the Irish Derby & Galtee More who won the Triple Crown in 1897. He bred Sylva who had had 8 winners and then Rusiaka who went on to breed Shaun Spadah.

In 1870 the King's County Chronicle referred to Dr Moorehead in an article and mentioned he Turf name "R.M.Delamere". They said he was *"the oldest supporter of the pastime in Ireland. It was nearly a half century since then, when worshipping at the shrine of Aesculapius not many miles from The Curragh his colours were first sported".*

JOHN NALLEN, BANAGHER AND A HORSE CALLED MINELLA

Jack Nallen was a native of Banagher, County Offaly and he died in December 2006. He owned horses like Hotel Minella who won four hurdle races and two bumpers when trained by Aidan O'Brien. He landed a hat-trick of major novice hurdles in 1995 - the Deloitte & Touche Novice Hurdle at Leopardstown, the Jameson Gold Cup Hurdle at Fairyhouse and the Country Pride Champion Novice Hurdle at the Punchestown festival. In 1996, Hotel Minella was beaten a head by Collier Bay in the AIG Europe Champion Hurdle. He also owned ten-time winner Minella Lad, who won two bumpers, seven hurdle races and one chase. O'Brien trained him to win the Brown Lad Hurdle, the Slaney Hurdle at Naas, and the Boyne Hurdle at Navan. Minella Man was another multiple winner and was trained by Anne-Marie O'Brien, with whose father, Joe Crowley, Nallen was involved for many years. He had horses with several trainers, including Michael Cunningham and Michael Hourigan.

John Nallen Junior carries on the family tradition and buys them as foals, because he prefers point to points, as did his father Jack. He moved up his team to one of Joe Crowley's old yard on "The Hill" in July 2010 and is assisted by Paddy Doody, who worked for Crowley for 16 years. He is now owner of the

Hotel Minella and buys them as foals. At Cheltenham's Brightwell sale in 2011, he sold Durrow winner Minella for Streak to Aiden Murphy for £230,000 and he went to John Jo O'Neill. The Templemore winner Minella Forfitness was sold to High Flyer Bloodstock for £130,000 and went to Nicky Henderson, while Minella for Party was sold for £75,000 and is with Tim Vaughan. He keeps foals on Lavly Farm and they are broken at 2 and 3, schooled before moving up to The Hill to go training. Jamie Codd and James Doody decide where they run. He had success with Minella Class who was runner up in a point to point to Cheltenian at Athlacca in 2009. In 2010 three sold well out of all his horses and he knows you need luck, a decent pedigree and some form before they sell. He sells mainly to wealthy British owners and 50/60 horses a year make good prices.

He has produced top class horses like Minella For Fitness, Minella Four Star, Minella Class and Minella Boys. He has been quoted as saying *"An ounce of breeding is worth a pound of feeding"*. He continues to buy the best quality young horses and stores, and employs the best people to work with him. He got €28,000 for a full brother of Minella Treasure, who was then sold to Tom Malone at Brightwells for €112,000. On 15th March 2014, J.P.McManus paid €260,000 for Minella Rocco at the post Cheltenham sale and the horse later won twice for Jonjo O'Neill. In March 2015, at the Brightwells Sale at Cheltenham during the race week, he had Minella Experience and Minella Awards.

PATRICK O'CALLAGHAN, BALEEK HOUSE, DURROW

He bred Tony Bin, Le Vita E Bella, and Light the Rocket. Tony Bin (1983-2000) was an Irish bred, who competed in Europe for his Italian owner from a base in Milan and became a leading sire in Japan. He was bred by Pat O'Callaghan. Tony Bin was foaled on 7 April 1983. He was a son of Rathbarry Stud's Kampala and out of the mare Severn Bridge by Hornbeam. The colt was a descendant of the great Nearco, through both his sire and his dam. O'Callaghan sold him for 3,000 guineas the Allevamento White Star breeding and racing operation of Italian businessman Luciano Gucci. Tony Bin was trained by Luigi Camici. As a three-year-old in 1986, he finished second in the GI Gran Premio de Jockey Club and as a 4 y/o won Group 1's Gran Premio de Jockey Club and Grand Premio de Milan. He was 3rd to Mtoto in the King George & Queen Elizabeth Stakes and then beat Mtoto to win the Prix de L'Arc in 1988. He ended up rated equal to Mtoto.

RAYMOND O'ROURKE, OFFALY

He sold For Non Stop (Alderbrook-Lost Link) the horse for €8,000 at Tattersall's Ireland in February 2006 to Gatterstown Stud. He had won a point to point, as a 4 y/o and then won a handicap hurdle at Chepstow. His best runs included a 2nd to Cue Card beaten 4 l's at Newbury on 31/12/11; and he was 2nd to Al Ferof beaten a neck on 3/12/11. In 2012 he won the Grade 1 Scilly Isle Novice

Chase and the Old Roan Chase, beating Wishful Thinking 23l's at Aintree on 27/10/12. He was 3rd beaten to Cue Card at Cheltenham on 14/3/13. He was trained by Nick Williams and ran against Sprinter Sacre, Cue Card, Al Ferof, Menorah, Captain Chris, Sir Des Champs etc. The horse won 4 races and earned €166,000. He had a good pedigree, as his sire won on the flat & also the Champion Hurdle. Lost Link never ran but she was a half 2 sister to Fiddling the Facts (Grade 1 Feltham Chase winner), and Facts Not Fiction. In August 2013, it was reported that he was sold for £175,000, as an 8y/o for Sean Clancy, and was going for the American National at Far Hills.

F B O'TOOLE, (FRANCIS-BRENDAN), RATHMOYLE STUD

The Rathmoyle Stud advertised resident stallions Catch the Wind 1902-1910, Mirador 1911-1919, Mountain Ash 1910-1911 and Cylden in 1919. T.F. O'Toole who was associated with the racing industry died in 1944. The Rathmoyle Stud at Edenderry was formed by the late Mr S.Rait Kerr who died a tragic death in the 1920's. It was bought from the representatives by F.B. O'Toole who at the first attempt bred Knight of the Grail a winner at Ascot in 1926 and he won the Irish Derby in 1927 (also the Coventry Stakes). He went on to win other classic races with Magnetic North in the Irish St Leger in 1956 (won £10,000 in career) and Jack Ketch won the 2,000 guineas in 1957 (won £40,000 in career), Sacarole Queen (Queen's Prize), and Royal Maid (Chesterfield Cup). In 1946, O'Toole was 5th in the breeders list to Harold Boyd Rochfort. In 1970 it was said that the stud had won 200 races to a value of around £100,000. Knight of the Grail was ridden by Michael Beary in the Irish Derby in 1927 and trained by Taylor in Britain. He was bred by O'Toole and was sold three times, initially to P.Day a Dublin horse dealer for 85 guineas, then to Andrew Young, Naas and on to the Newmarket Sales. He was unsold at 400gns, but was then bought for 350 guineas by Mr Broughton (which led to a court case a few years later). The stallion was Prince Galahad unbeaten as a 2 y/o in 1919 winning the Chesham Stakes and Dewhurst Plate. He became leading sire that year due to Knight of the Grail's win.

Jack Ketch (Abadan-Law) was foaled in 1954 and won £6,048 in Europe and $56,000 in the USA. The owner in Ireland was M.P Annesley & the trainer Stephen Quirke. He won 9 races from 30 runs. His major wins included the Maher Nursery (1956), Tetrarch Stakes, the International Stakes and the Irish 2,000gns (1957) and the Canadian Championship Stakes (1958). He was sold in 1958 to Allie R.Reuben, who raced under name of Hasty House Farm. He was trained by the future U.S. Hall of Fame trainer Harry Trosek. He made his American debut on 14 July 1958 at Chicago's Arlington Park and won the Morton Grove Purse. His biggest win was in the Canadian Championship Stakes on 25th October 1958 beating stable companion Mahan. He didn't have much success, as a 5 y/o in 1959 and retired to stud in Australia. Stephen Quirke died in 2001 at 68 y/o. He had been working part-time for the Turf Club for 3 years after his retirement. He was a son of the great Martin Quirke, who rode 9 classic winners and was champion in 1923. His biggest wins were Atherstone Wood (1967) and Mistigo (1968) in the Irish 2,000 guineas and Parnell in the Irish St Leger (1971).

B.B.TRENCH, LOUGHTON STUD, MONEYGALL

His father was W.T. Trench was a barrister and High Sheriff in 1885. He died in December 1911 and was Master of the Ormonde Hunt. Loughton was given to a private in his army by Cromwell and passed on to a Captain Pepper in exchange for a white horse. The house in 1896 was built in 1777. In 1828 Thomas Ryder Pepper was killed while out hunting, and his brother-in-law, Lord Bloomfield bought Loughton from his widow for a specific sum. Bloomfield enlarged and improved the house and estate. He sold Loughton to his brother-in-law, Mr Trench, father of the 1896 incumbent, B.B. Trench. The Stud was then run by W.H. Atkinson, Trench's cousin and agent. The resident stallions were Buckingham (Br 1890 Galopin - Lady Yardley), Sarawak (Borneo - Bathilde) and Arklow, an unraced full-brother to Ormonde. Castlereagh (deceased) previously stood at Loughton, where Richard Cooney was stud groom. Other stallions advertised at Loughton were Narellan (1893), St Hilaire (1896), Senanus (1905-07), Speed (1898-1901) and Spook (1902).

In April 1892, *Sport* visited the stud, which was operating for around 6/7 years under B.B. Trench. He had good stock and they were winning races. The previous August, five yearlings averaged 161 guineas at the Horse Show Sale 1891. Two by Castlereagh from Farina II and May Queen made 300gns and 200gns respectively. A brood mare, Allerton was sold (1/2 sister to Castlereagh) for 1,150gns to James Daly, Hartstown Stud. St Liz and Narella are two other stallions for hunters. Castlereagh was a successful racehorse and bred horses like Cliftonian, Givendale, Cornhill, Why Not, and Golden Crescent. Narellan was bred in Australia by James White and was brought to England to try to win the Derby but it didn't happen. When Arklow was a stallion, he had to have a paddock to himself or he would not produce. He still only covered 5 mares in 1895 but two were successful. He was firstly leased by Mr Trench from the Duke of Westminister, but his grace later gave him as a gift. He never raced because of an accident.

In the 1906 Scottish Grand National, of 440 sovereigns, two Offaly bred horses were 1st and 2nd. Colonel M.Lindsay's Creolin 100/6 by Arklow carrying 9st 13lbs was bred by B.B.Trench, Loughton, who also owned the sires and bred their dams of the winner and second. Mr C.R.Hodgins Do Be Quick 7/1 by Speed aged 6 y/o carrying 11st 8lbs was bred by his brother W.T.Trench, Redwood, Birr. They had two different owners & trainers. Creolin came through to win by 3 lengths Arklow was an obscure brother of Ormonde.

DAVID & CHRISTY MOONEY, TREASON STUD, PORTARLINGTON

It was run by David Mooney and his father Christy in 1970. The first stallion Even Say sired many winners and then in 1974 Charles Haughey's horse Aristocracy arrived (foaled in 1974). He won the G3 Whitehall Stakes and 5 races on the flat & 3 over hurdles (with Eddie O'Grady). He became one of the first sons of Lord Gayle to be used for jumps duty. In 1988 his first runners made their mark including Master Aristocrat. His other notable performers include prolific winner Imperial Vintage, Windy Bee, Marching Marquis and Mister Drum. He remained active for many years at Treascon Stud numbering 40-60 mares. In 2000 he was the leading sire of chasers in Ireland & Britain for the second time including horses like Limestone Lad. He lived past 27 years. Some of the stallions were Houmyan (won Italian Derby), TAOS (unbeaten 2 y/o), All My Dreams (German Derby winner), and Tocamadeira (won 2 Group races).

Treascon Stud had a small connection with Red Rum. Neron and Mared produced two fillies in 1963 and 1964 called Neared (sold for 110 guineas) and Quintula (190 guineas). Neared who had never raced owing to injury as her owner Christy Mooney reported to Donald McCain and Mr Mooney offered her to Donald McCain in 1974. She had been covered by Even Say. Christy died in 2011 and David Mooney carried on.

DONAl BRAZIL, GURTEEN STUD

In 2010, Berties Dream won the Grade 1 Albert Bartlett Novice Hurdle with Najaf 6 lengths behind. It was a great triumph for Galway trainer Patrick J.Gilligan, who had 30 previous winners in Ireland and Britain. It was his first runner in Cheltenham. He was owned by the Half A Keg Syndicate and ridden by Andrew Lynch with his second win at the Festival following Sizing Europe (also bred in Offaly). He was bred by Edward McEvoy and was by Golden Tornado (Sadlers Wells- Broadway Joan), who stands at Donal Brazil's, Gurteen Stud for a fee of £500 and was the first foal out of unraced mare Orla's Pride. The horse won for Conor Broderick and 7 other members of the syndicate. He was 33/1 and they had great celebrations at home. Gilligan said *"I'm speechless and can't believe it"* he said *"We really did think he would run well, but Cheltenham is Cheltenham and you don't come here thinking you are going to win".* The rain came at the right time.

Golden Tornado is the first stallion stood by Donal Brazil, Gurteen Stud. He was bought unraced in 2000, and covered mares owned by Brazil's neighbours. Now breeders were covering from further afield at €500. Dancing Tornado arrived from his first crop and won the Grade 2 Novice Chase at Gowran Park, then Ninety Two Team also trained by Gilligan. His progeny made sums from €20,000-26,000. He purchased 14 y/o Golden Tornado, who failed to sell as a 3 y/o at Goffs for 15,500 in 1999. He bought him from Michael J.O'Brien. People said he was mad and it was hard to get good mares at the start (he was a close relative of Fourstars Allstars). Golden Tornado wouldn't have covered more than 200-300 in 10 years. His fees rose to €800 after Berties Dream won at Cheltenham. He keeps his horses until 4 y/o and sells them from home. He is assisted by his son Clive and Oliver. It was his Uncles farm and his mother inherited it and passed it on. The mare was owned by Clonaslee man Edward McEvoy. He said *"Never buy a stallion when your 50, as you'll never see him made"* and so at 49 he bought Golden Tornado. In January 2011, Ninety Two Team won 3 handicap hurdles, one at Galway festival and M.Hourigan's Dancing Tornado won 2 bumpers and a maiden hurdle. He bred Ninetytwo Team out of his own mare Administer, who won over 12 furlongs, and she was also the dam of Broadstone Road.

He has sired point to point winners like Cloneen Storm, Golden Gem, and Spirit Tornado won Tallanstown.Other winners are Fortitsa, One Cool Tornado, Carsonstown Boy, (He was 2nd to Tammy's Hill in the Foxhunter), Waltzing Tornado. He got another stallion, Urban Poet in 2010 as a 4 y/o.

J.J. BEHAN, PORTARLINGTON

In February 1953, Johnny Behan's father purchased a mare Full House for £75. The mare was bred to the excellent stallion Buck Hound. This resulted in the foal Buckaroo, who is always associated with Portarlington. His won 18 times including the Tom Dreaper Cup at Tramore. Jack also bred high quality horses like The Illiad (Ladbroke Hurdle etc), Bertone (won 14 races), Ryker (Cambridgeshire), Hard Tarquin (Galway Hurdle winner) and Bolands Cross (3rd in the King George), Laurabelle, Red Datus, and Datus in 1960's. Tom Lacey is married to Jack's sister Peg.

EDMUND F DEASE , TURBOTSTOWN

He was born in 1856 and was a JP for Cavan & started hunting with the Westmeath Hunt. He won the Hunt Cup twice and played polo. One of best horses was Sparkling Hock. Devlin the sire stood at Turbotstown (1893), and like Dust Devil winner of Chester Cup in May 1893, was bred by Robert the Devil. Sir Gerald Dease set out to improve the pack in the Westmeath Hunt in the mid -19th century. In 1864, he erected kennels at Clonlost and a few year's later Culleen kennels. The stallion Monsigneur stood there in 1887. On 14th April 1868, at Culleen, Mullingar he sold valuable hunters like Mabel, Brunette, Hermit, Lancelot, Treasure, Commodore, Brilliant, Gypsy, Reform, Mechanic and Pat.

OTHER BREEDERS - Tom Lawlor bred Jackson's Lady. She raced on every type of event & track including polytrack and in the Irish Grand National. She won her point to point at Castletown Geoghegan over 3 miles, and she won 9 of her

41 races and over 200,000. Her lat run was at April 2015 when she won at Punchestown beating Upazo and Ned Buntline. She could be heading for the Galway Plate. **Mel Davies** and **Liam Wilson** set up a stud in Mullingar in 2006 and their first winner was John Charles at Wolverhampton, but their best day's were with **Barnbrook Again,** when he won two Champion Chases in 1989/90 and was second to Desert Orchid in the 1989 King George and 3rd to See You Then in the Champion Hurdle in 1987. He won 17 of 31 races and around £270,000. **T.B. Conroy,** Clonaslee, Laois bred and owned Irish Grand National winner Glebe Lad in 1999. **Thomas McCutheon,** Streete, who brought a stallion -with some success -called Sternchaser from New Zealand 1895 (he had also run in Australia); **James Gaynor,** Taughmon, had a stallion Young Magician, a brother of Foxhound in 1877, who was imported from England by William Price, Castlepollard. **Louis O'Neill,** Bryanstown House, Mullingar bred Assynt by Praxiyheles out of Miss Loch and Glasslough Monica. **John Robinson,** Streamstown House, Castlepollard stood Radical at his stud in 1970/80's. He was by Epsom Derby winner Relko. The dam Won't Linger traced back to Netherton Maid at Cleaboy Stud. The horse was 8th to Snow Knight in the Derby and Lester Piggott rode him to win at Ascot. Robinson had the successful stallion Roi D-Egypte at his stud in 1948.

Bernard Scally, Streete House, Rathowen had the stallion Explorer around 1900. **M.J.Saurin,** Harristown Stud, Kinnegad in 1890 had as his main stallion St Michael (Springfield-Land's End). Springfield was a very speedy horse and St Michael bred winners like Sour Saint and Auchovy (Leopardstown 1896). At this time he had some nice mares like Mrs Gamp, Laughing Girl, and James Coles Agnes. In more recent times **Dermot McIlveen,** originally from Northern Ireland but based at Monkstown House, Monilea. Mullingar bred some useful horses. In 1981, horses bred by him won 6 races and over £20,000 including sires like Solinus and Orchestra. In 2000 he sold Un Desperado for 16,500 guineas with a great female line that related to horses like Tiananmen Square, Arkle winner Oregon Trail, and Pat Hartigan.

chapter 8
THE JOYS OF BEING AN OWNER OR TRAINER

FRANK BARBOUR MASTER OF THE HUNT

Between 1913/16 Punch was second three times in the Irish Grand National recording his only success in 1915 at 7/2F when ridden by Reggie Walker for his father G.L.Walker. Ironically, two of the horses who won, Little Hack II 1913 and Civil War 1914, finished behind him in different years. The most interesting aspect of Punch's success was the owner Frank Barbour, who had been MFH of the Westmeath Hunt (1908-1912), and maintained strong connections with the midlands over the years (including acting as a Steward at Kilbeggan), with particular reference to the famous Barbour Cup worth £100, one of the most coveted prizes in the point to point field. He was a son John D.Barbour JP, Hilden & brother of J.Milne Barbour, Minister of Commerce, N.Ireland and described as a textile magnate. He was very popular and free of snobbishness. He played polo on English & Irish teams. When he retired as MFH in 1912 he was given a silver trophy representing a hound and fox breaking covert by Colonel James Smyth, and well-known local breeder and owner J.H.Taylor said he was *"kind, considerate, and indulgent"*. He was a keen hunter and point to pointer and eventually he set up a model racecourse for schooling at Trimblestown, Co Meath.

EASTER HERO AND "THE CHARGE OF THE COSSACKS"

Easter Hero was the best horse he owned. He was bred by Larry King, Ashbourne and Barbour purchased him for £500 in 1926 and when Cecil Brabazon was taking care of his horses he won with him at Ballinrobe that September. Barbour later sold him for £7,000 with a contingency of £3,000 if he won Aintree Grand National. In his career for Barbour, Easter Hero won 8 races for him including the Molyneux Chase and Beecher Chase, both at Aintree. He was unbeaten in 1927/28. He was sold to a Belgian financier Captain Loewenstein for 7,000gns & won the Prix De Drages in France. He was later sold to Jock Whitney, USA and won the 1929 Cheltenham Gold Cup for him by 20 length's. In March 1929 there was speculation in the media about Easter Hero in the Grand National as he was considered unbeatable. Frank Barbour said in an interview *"Easter Hero is a lovely horse now. I have no fear about the result. He will be just over the first jump and the others will never catch him"*. Jimmy Hogan the jocular Irish jockey on K.C.B had his own view of the race *"Wait until you see me leading the charge of the Cossacks"*. He carried 12st 7lbs in the Grand National and was a hot favourite and he finished 2nd to Gregalach. He had spread a plate three fences out and should have won. He won the Gold Cup again in 1930 by 20 length's after Gib fell. He was lame for the Grand National in 1930 and was brought down in the 1931 race, but turned out to win the next day in a dead heat with Coup De Chapeau. He was taken home to Kentucky by Whitney and died at 28 in 1948.

GALWAY DOUBLE FOR BRABAZON & BARBOUR

At Galway in 1925, Clonsheever carried 13 stone the in Galway Plate and finished 3rd to Miss M.D.Barbour's Blancona ridden by Charlie Donnolly (receiving 35 lbs) trained by Cecil Brabazon and an easy 8 length winner. He was good enough to go on and win the Irish Cesarewitch in October 1925 by 12 length. The following year Blancona became one of a small select number to win the Galway Hurdle after winning the Galway Plate when cantering home by 3 lengths at 4/7F. He was then trained by G.P. Braceridge and later by Alfred Brickley for whom he won the Beecher Chase at Aintree. Like many of the other horses he was sold off by Barbour and never reached the same heights in England. Barbour completed the big double at Galway in 1925 when Miss E.L.M.Barbour's won the Galway Hurdle with Alroi (both were nieces of Frank). She rode in point to points including the Conyngham Cup and was described on one paper as *"a pretty girl of sixteen"* and the youngest owner in the world, when her horse won in Galway. The Galway double was credited to G.P. Braceridge, but in reality Cecil Brabazon was in charge but didn't receive the licence until the end of the year.

Barbour moved his operations to Bishop's Canning, Wiltshire in England in 1926 where T.Pardy and then J.Bickley were his trainers. One of his leading horses Jerpoint owned by his nephew J.M.Barbour won the Irish Grand National in 1927, when trained by A. Bickley, Tarporly, Cheshire. His career was cut short by an accident in the Grand Steeplechase de Paris at Auteil in 1928, a race in which he had finished second the previous year.

KOKO - GOLD CUP WINNER AND" CABBIE"!

Another high quality horse in the stable was Koko (the only Gold Cup winner to run at Kilbeggan), who was only third of six in a handicap hurdle in 1923 at Kilbeggan, which was won by local hope P.W.Shaw's Broken Vow with J.Groarkes Dr Barney second. In his book *'Racing Through My Mind'* Aubrey Brabazon describes the unique way that Barbour dealt with Koko's leg trouble. He sent the horse secretly to a jarvey who ran cabs from Kingsbridge Station. The horse learned to draw cabs but it was on condition that Koko worked on the sets of the streets. The sets were wooden blocks laid down like cobblestones, which were found near the railway station and around Guinness's Brewery. He had done this with other horses and it had the effect of strengthening the horse's legs and clearing up the injury. The horse came back sound and won at Limerick and Mullingar in 1925, before being sent to trainer Bickley for Cheltenham. The Gold Cup only commenced in 1924, when it was won by Irish horse Ballinode and in 1926 Koko (Tim Haney) was a fine looking 8 y/o. He went off in front and led all the way to win by 3 lengths at 10/1 from Old Tay Bridge and Gerald L. He ran in the race again 1928 when he was the favourite, as he was in good form and finished third to Patron Saint, after bursting a blood vessel when travelling well and looking a certain winner. Before he ran in the 1928 Grand National there was a sensation, as he was sold to a Captain Guest MP and a Belgian Alfred Grisar for £4,000 with a contingency if he won the Grand National (which was usual for Barbour). He carried 12st 2lbs and was receiving 3lbs from his old stable companion Easter Hero but unfortunately he landed on Beecher's Brook and had to be hauled off by ropes. Frank said before the race *"I have good odds to my money, about £8,000 to £100 and the breeder's bet as well"*. He won 18 chases in a successful career including winning the Hurst National Trial in 1928 carrying 12 stone 7 lbs. He had other good horses and prolific winners like Cool Common, Gate Brook, Two Royals & Newsboy and Punch winner of 1915 IGN 2nd three times in 4 years.

He was an eccentric man and one story about him was that after riding at a meeting in Mullingar his horse bolted and threw him off near the road. He got up and hitched a lift into the town, where he caught a train to Dublin. He then boarded a ship sailing to New York and did all this while still wearing his riding clothes! Early in 1930 he retired due to ill health and went on a cruise around the world. All his horses were sold at Tattersall's on 20th January 1930. In November 1936, a paper stated that he died on the P & O Liner Rampura on the way home from Japan and was buried at sea.

ROBERT BAGNALL AND PANDORAMA

Robert Bagnall's horse Pandorama was an unusual horse in that he won his maiden hurdle, novice hurdle, beginners chase, and novice chase at the first time of asking. He also won four Grade 1's - Deloitte Novice Hurdle, Drinmore Novice Chase, Knight Frank Novice and the Lexus Chase. Robert Bagnall, Hillamar Hotel, Kinnegad, Co Westmeath owned or shared ownership in a number of horses with several trainers but this was the star. Pandorama was out of an unraced half-sister to useful hurdler/chaser Obie's Train and descended from the family of classy jumpers Mrs Muck and High Ken. He won a total of 9 out of 16 races and prize money of around €360,000. He was a horse with different problems he pulled a muscle before the RSA Chase at Cheltenham and when he went for the Hennessey Gold Cup his nose bled. His best day was in the G1 Lexus Chase when the horse who only cost €5,000, returned to the form that had seen him beat Weapon's Amnesty in the Fort Leney Chase. He was backed into 7/2 joint favourite with the disappointing Cooldine. He travelled well for Paul Carberry and won easily from Money Trix & Joncol and the intention then was to aim for the Gold Cup in 2011. As Robert Bagnall said *"this makes up for all the hardship. There'll be a drop of Guinnes had in the Kinnegad Hotel".*

Unfortunately, he could only finish 7th at Cheltenham in 2011 to the winner Long Run and afterwards he was in trouble with heat in his leg again, which meant a further rest. The ground was too quick for him on the day. The horse never fully recovered after that and in 2013 he was sold for £20,000 at Brightwell's December sale to dissolve a partnership. His last good run was the previous April when beaten 3 lengths by Roi De Mee.

The other horse that brought a significant victory was the admirable Native Jack who was owned with Gerry Burke, Niall O'Farrell, and Kevin Sexton. He was purchased privately for €6,000 on the advice of Philip Rothwell after winning two Open point-to- points. He won first time out in the PP Hogan Memorial Chase over the Punchestown fences, ridden by John Cullen. The latter was injured for Cheltenham and Davy Russell was brought in and he gave Native Jack a great ride over the Cross Country fences at Cheltenham at 12 y/o, beating the specialist Spot the Difference. Robert Bagnall compared it to *"winning the All Ireland final at Croke Park"*, as Cheltenham winners are rare. He had a number of other horses with Noel Meade and Philip Rothwell, like Parson's Pistol, Hotel Hilamar, Rochfordbridge etc., with different levels of success.

PAUL DALY, KILBEGGAN IS LUCKY AT LAST

Paul Daly grew up in a farming family but it was more likely to be pigs than horses, as equines did not run in the family. His father Sean and his uncle Jimmy became involved on the committee as young men, when the racecourse was under threat in 1956. They had a van that was used to draw birch back to the track to make the fences. Paul was only 16 when he became involved on the cross over on the opposite side of the track from his father. He later became involved in the office duties and when Jimmy as Chairman was ill, he became Acting Chairman. He was elected Chairman by the Committee on Jimmy's death. It was a labour of love which increased his interest in horse racing and partly led to him becoming involved as an owner.

He joined a local syndicate involving Jack Connolly, Patsy Ennis, Willie Smith, Alan McCormack etc and later it was through work and social occasions that he became involved in the Steel and Porter Syndicate with Peru Girl who won in 2003. The next horse he owned in a syndicate cost €20,000, but broke his pelvis. It was a while before they became involved again with the Liam Burke trained Give Chase (In the Wings-Silver Pursuit) bred by Juddmonte Farms, who won a bumper at Sligo on the 10/1 in July 2005, owned by the T.F.P. Syndicate.

Paul decided that he would like a horse in his own colours and Pat Martin recommended Lucky At Last (City Honours-Leixlip Belle), which he bought for €9,000. He finished an average third that day but received a bad ride, and the next day at Bellewstown he won a handicap hurdle. He backed him each way and was shocked, when he won. It was to get better at Ballinrobe in September 2008 when he was an easy winner of a grief filled finale in a handicap hurdle of €12,500 - he won by 12 lengths. He completed the treble when he won the Fairyhouse Handicap Hurdle in November 2008, carrying 11st 10lbs (A.P. Thornton 7lbs claim). He won by 2 1/2 lengths beating Get the Urge & Tryptonic. Martin said afterwards *"I'd imagine now that he will get a rest as he is on the go all summer".*

He won a few more races in 2009 and when running on the flat he was 2nd to Dermot Weld's Rite of Passage who won the Ascot Gold Cup. He ran at Galway in October 2009 and won a Qualified Riders race over 1ml 6 furlongs beating Torphicken & Natural High and in November he won the Paddy Power Handicap Hurdle of €28,500 at Cork carrying 11st 3 lbs. He won a Beginners Chase at Tipperary by 11 lengths. After the race which was the same day as Rite of Passage's win at Ascot, Martin said *"We got a boost from Rite of Passage's Gold Cup win at Ascot today, because he only collared us in the last 100 yards of 1 mile 6 furlong race at Ballinrobe last year (2009)".* He was 6th in the Amateur Handicap at Galway, but in October 2010 he won a novice chase there beating Chicago Grey by a head.The following year he was injured on the gallops when preparing for the Galway Plate. The horse won 9 of his 39 races and over €110,000 in prize money. He was a consistent and honest horse with a bit of class. Paul's biggest disappointment with him was when he slipped up at his native Kilbeggan track on the flat, when looking a certain winner.

One of his best and proudest days was when his horse Irish Poli won the Ballymore Handicap Hurdle at Kilbeggan on 16th July 2010. Pat Martin said afterwards *"That's great for us. Paul is the chairman here so we are delighted. It's a double edged sword as he loves to have a horse run well here, but hates to have a horse run badly. So we're always selective about what we run".* The horse also won at Sligo & Downroyal. She lost her form and some other horses since then were disappointing up to Rebel Laker. In reality Paul says the success of Lucky At Last paid for all the other horses, as it is an expensive game. He has a full sister and a 1/2 brother to Rebel Laker at the moment. Paul was also involved in the Wier Syndicate who owned Toomdeely who won two races at Listowel. Paul explained that sometimes winning is an anti-climax and that the best one is always the next one. As Chairman of Kilbeggan Races, he thinks a lot has been achieved and the foundations laid for the future, but they also have more plans over the next five years. Much has been done with the track and other areas, but he would like to see something more being provided for the punters.

J.J. DOLAN, AND FAIR ASTRONOMER

His stud was at Farnagh, Moate where Michael Scott is now based. He owned Fair Astronomer (Star Gazer-Fair Temair) who had the unique record of being the first two year to win in Ireland, England, and France. In the 1960's Fair Astronomer became the leading 2 y/o filly in the country. Fair Astronomer was raised by them in conjunction with local vet Jock Lyons and Don Beddy, Athlone. The horse won 10 of her 20 starts including the Cornwallis Stakes in England in 1962 and four other wins in Ireland, plus one race in France. In 1963 she won the Rous Memorial Stakes and Pretty Polly Stakes in England and was 2nd in the Kempton 1,000 guineas trial and Falmouth Stakes. She was trained in England by Harvey Leader and he managed to win with her over a mile even though she looked like a sprinter. He stretched her to a 1 1/4 miles and she was favourite for the English Cambridgeshire with a big weight where she finished an unlucky fifth. She was champion 2 y/o filly in Ireland and the second highest rated filly in England. She was fifth dam of the Champion Japanese horse Gentildonna, who won the Japanese Triple Crown in 2012, and also went on to win the Japan Cup and become Horse of the Year. When she went for the Cup again in 2013 she had not won any of her races but was still favourite and duly obliged by a nose (ridden by Ryan Moore). She had won 8 of her 123 starts by then and £7.9 million (she had lost to St Nicholas Abbey at Meydan). Her dam Donna Blini traced back to Fair Astronomer.

Phideas a half brother to triple crown winner Museum (1931) won the Irish 2,000 guineas and Derby and bred a filly called Ate who produced stakes winners in Prairie Oyster and Munch and Cow Girl II-all imported to the USA plus Mexborough (all by Mustang) and Princess Temair (by Democracy II). Munch won the Cherry Hinton Stakes (1957), Princess Stakes and three other races. (Mustavon won the Lincoln in a gamble). At 3y/o Munch won the Atlantic City Handicap and Cleopatra Handicap and was 2nd in the Arlington Matron. She was the only horse to beat Rich & Rare the English 2 y/o champion filly. She won €96,000 and in 22 races won 13 times. Prairie Oyster won the Haverhill Stakes and had 6 wins in 14 starts. He also had a horse called Right Drop who won a few races for him including at Mullingar.

Her late husband John was a former Director of Moate Livestock Sale's, who died in 1974. Mrs Elizabeth Dolan, Kilbeggan owned Gasoline who won the Lanesbrorough Novice Chase at Roscommon in May 1981 and was trained by Tony Redmond. On 11th May 1997 Elizabeth Mary (Noreen) Dolan, Brosna Lodge, Kilbeggan died aged 86. She was a poker & Bridge player, a Past Lady President of Bridge Club and Lady Captain of the Mullingar Golf Club.

MICK FOSTER & TONY ALLEN - NANCY MYLES

Francis Flood had great success for Foster & Allen with Nancy Myles who won 19 races (3 bumper, 3 flat, 3 chases and 10 hurdles) and more when she went to stud. He was given £12,000 to buy a horse and got her for reserve of £4,500. She was bought at the Derby Sales in Ballsbridge in 1988 and was called after song by a friend Kevin Sheeran. Her first race was in 1989 and she won on her 2nd race. She recorded three listed hurdle wins and retired in 1993. They went to a pub in Tralee and the owner explained it was called after a horse but he didn't know them (Foster & Allen). They bought other horses that won and the only one not to win was called Foster and Allen. Another popular horse was Westmeath Bachelor who won three races with Cecil Ross, with the last win in September 2011.

CAPT E.A. GARGAN, CULLION, MULLINGAR

He died in Feb 1960 (aged 71) and was Chairman of the Mullingar Race Company. He served as a Senior Steward of the INHSC in 1947. He was a Member of the Westmeath Hunt. As an owner/trainer he enjoyed his greatest triumph with the mare Southernmore in the 1935 Galway Plate. The fine chaser Southernmore (Drinmore-Southern Girl) bred and owned by him won at Leopardstown in March 1935, then won Galway Plate in 1935, and was unplaced in the Aintree Grand National. The prophets were mostly adrift over the Galway Plate in 1935 giving Southernmore a hopeful word but she won well by 4 l's from Lucky Fool. She was a consistent sort and won 4 races and was placed in 4 others that year. It was the greatest triumph for the well-known owner Capt E.A.Gargan. He subsequently bred Southern Coup (Coup de Lyon-Southernmore) who was 3rd in the Irish Grand National in 1953. Southerntown and Culleen's Actress was also successful. At Cullion his father-in-law T.M.Reddy bred Rhodine who produced Rose of Cullion, Cullion, and Oscuro. He rode many winners as an amateur including at Mullingar. Other successful horses included Mr Georgic, Southern Lass, Knightswood's, Culleen's Lass (Waivis Bay-Culleen's Actress) who won a maiden hurdle in 1958 at Mullingar, Culleenroi (won at Kilbeggan, Dundalk, & Naas), Southern Dago (won the Tostal Hurdle at Navan), and Furthermore. In 1954, Southern Coup was one of the finishers in the Aintree Grand National, behind Royal Tan.

H.KEANE, RATHCONRATH, WESTMEATH

His horses were with Dick Cleary and he owned two top class horses in half-brothers My Rath (Succoth- Bit-o'Thought) and My Royal (Avidity-Bit O'Thought). He sold them both in 1920 to England. He retained Sweet Home and kept Bit 'o Thought and had a half-sister to My Rath called Tiny Ways. On one occasion at Newbrook, My Royal lost over a furlong and a half in a race and came through to win amidst loud applause. My Rath won at Gatwick on 18th February 1921 in the National Trial Chase of £1,000 over $3^{1}/_{2}$ miles and carrying 11st 13lbs and in March he won at Leicester by 8L's beating Blazers and General Saxham.

TOM KILLIAN, GREENPARK

He bred Winter Break by Reformed Character and also Lady of the Lake a prolific winner. He had another good horse Koepenicker who in September 1910 won at Mullingar on 19th May; at Tuam on Wed 21st May ridden by T.Dowdall; and on Thursday 22nd May won again at Dunmore in Dunmore Plate for a total of 106 sovs. He owned other winners like Curry (Marmiton-Skoal), Coola II, and Royal Tange (Tangiers- Roi Allie).Tom Killian was a Westmeath owner of jumpers mainly and won the 1913 Conyngham Cup with Shaun na Scaub trained by Dick Cleary & ridden by J.Manley. He also owned Mawgoory (Bealderg) who won races for him in Ireland including at Mullingar before going to England where he won three races in a week in December 1921. He also finished 3rd in the Irish Grand National in 1912. He was bred by Dan Kiernan, Balrath. His father was James Killian, Dysart who died in November 1893 and is buried at Walshestown Cemetery. He was a farmer & worked on the Mullingar Poor Law Union Board. He owned the useful horse Lady of the Lake. Irene Neale and Helen Murtagh the sisters who owned Liberty Counsel who won the Irish Grand National are direct descendants of Tom Killian.

Shaun na Scuab was good enough to win the Conyngham Cup in 1913, when he was trained by Dick Cleary and ridden by J.Manley. He was also 3rd in the Irish Frand National. He was bred locally by Dan Kiernan, Balrath.

PAT CASSERLEY, SLANEMORE

He was based in Abbeyleix where he was a successful amateur rider. He took out a licence in 1970 and his best horses were Shuil Donn, Fourth Son, Ballyfin Lake, Mr Woodville, Madam Milan won 4 times in 1980 and Captain Noel (Mon Capitaine the same stallion as Captain Christy) won 3 races in 1979 including a good novice chase at Roscommon in October 1979. The trainer's biggest success was in the Munster National. He was originally farming and training at Slanemore. The *"Friends of Lilliput Organisation"* organised fund raising events in the early 1990's and Mullingar Bank Manager Ned Timlin won with Lilliput Queen in 1990. The horse was syndicated by Mr Timlin to Tom Nally, Mullingar Peter Burke, Clonmore, Peter Keegan, Tyrrellspass, and Andy Quinn, Mullingar and in late August 1992 when trained by Pat Casserly he ran twice in a week with a third and was an 8/1 winner in a handicap hurdle when ridden by Frank Woods. In 1983, Yer Man finished 3rd in Aintree Grand National and he had been trained earlier in his career by Pat.

FRANK ENNIS AND PADDY SLEATOR

Frank Ennis, from Ballinagore, Kilbeggan, spent 18 years with the legendary Paddy Sleator in Grangecon and was there during Sleator's successful involvement with Arthur Thomas. He travelled horses to Britain and back on a regular basis for Sleator and looked after the two prolific winners Black Ice and Harwell. He got plenty of rides for him but never rode a winner, as none of them were fancied. He said that the horses were never tried at home and everything was done on the bridle, with a lot of secrecy. There was a lot less information available in that era and many of the horses had nicknames and many of the lads didn't even know the real names of the horses. He spent six years with Ted Curtin and he rode some winners there before going to PV (Paul) Doyle in Shankill and later to The Curragh. He rode some good winners for him including Patent Slipper who was 4th in the Gloucester Hurdle at Cheltenham.

A KILBEGGAN “STING” BY BEESTON

He almost got in trouble with Doyle after the trainer fancied a horse called Beeston in a hurdle race in Kilbeggan and thought he would get a good price. However, Frank was so well-known in the area that many of the locals decided to back him and the horse duly won at a shorter price than expected and he was treated like a *“local hero”*. The problem was that he had to convince his boss that it wasn't a case of him giving out information and that took some doing! Eventually, he went on to take up training himself and in March 1975 he saddled his first winner at Naas with Mayfield Grove 5/1 (owner Mick Kirby) and won by 3 lengths in Maudlin Flat race, ridden by Bob Townsend. Some tempting offers were made for Mayfield Grove including £15,000 and they were all turned down (he was only 4 y/o). He had success with horses like Vipdanius and Colonel Honner. In October 2000 he trained Beep Beep owned by a syndicate including Pat McCormack, Kilbeggan and he was ridden by Pat Smullen to win by 3 lengths from Shoeless Joe when only having his second run for the trainer, and afterwards Frank said the plan was to send her back over hurdles. Pat had some success with horses like Ringned, Lilywhitedancer, and more recently Dantes Firth. Michael Kirby, Castletown-Geoghegan was his first patron and he had successful horses over a number of years like Mayfield Grove (4 wins), Wonder Gleam (4 races), Boy Island (5 races), and Saints Island (4 races), who won a bumper by 15 lengths and a hurdle race by 10 lengths in field of 29.

TRAINER AND STALLS HANDLER - ALL AT THE SAME TIME?

In 2001, Frank admitted that he was 39 years in racing and had been a stable lad, jump jockey, head lad, driver, stalls handler and then a trainer. He knew only too well what it was to struggle at the bottom of the training ladder. He had moderate horses, he drove his own horsebox and even brought other trainer's horses to meetings and he worked on the stalls just to keep going. The times were tough, even though he was a hard worker, but he was about to get some decent horses at the age of 54 years. He had his first listed race win with Annieirwin in 2000 and he won the renowned Rockingham Handicap at The Curragh with Inyourhearts. In 2001 he had Mahsusie, a grey daughter of Mukaddamah, and was owned in partnership by Jones and Norah Kennedy from Naas, County Kildare. He only ever had two runners in Britain and one of them was in a seller was so bad that he gave him away and he said that *"he would throw in the bucket and sheet as well".* Ennis had about 15 horses at this time and he was based near Lumville on The Curragh.

In 2002 he had a decent horses like Askthejudge who was bought as a hurdler but won three in a row on the flat, Miss Childrey who won the listed Swordlestown Stud Sprint Stakes at Naas ridden by Shamie Heffernan. As a 3 y/o she was 3rd in the Derrinstown 1,000 guineas classic trial to Alexander Goldrun, who later finished 2nd in the Irish 1,000 guineas (where Ennis's horse was unplaced). In 2006 he had 20 horses including a useful filly in Gee Kel. He had a string of winners in mid-season like Platonic Affair, Oxford City, Inyourthoughts (daughter of Inyourhearts), Ferneley, Dal Cais and Oxford City. He described the Dermot O'Rourke Ferneley as his best ever after wins at Galway & The Curragh and entered him in the best races. The highlight of the year was his first ever group success with Confuchias in the Group 3 Killavullen Stakes at The Curragh and he won two of his five starts (placed in two group races) including a third to Teofilo in the Futurity Stakes. Ferneley and Confuchias were both unplaced in the Irish 2,000gns and they went on to run at Royal Ascot without success. He had other winners in 2009 like Intapeace, Sebastian Flyte, Todds Forge, and Daisy Buchanan.

The better quality horses in this era were down to the Dermot O'Rourke owned Plantation Stud of around 187 acres in Newmarket, which was run on commercial lines and administered by a board of directors before being sold to him. The O'Rourke horses in training were spread among several trainers in Britain and Ireland, including William Jarvis and Richard Hannon, as well as Henry Cecil and Frank Ennis. Like many other things it was not to last and his career gradually wound down in the subsequent years.

MARK FAGAN, DERRAVARA GALLOPS, CROOKEDWOOD, MULLINGAR

Mark Fagan is a vet who set up in Derravarra Gallops in Castlepollard and Married Dubliner Deryn Mackey, Boutique owner in Blackrock called Khan and after moving to Mullingar set up another boutique. They met in 1997 and her in-laws owned Temple Spa. Award winning architect Neil Burke Kennedy designed their home. Mark Fagan still has veterinary practice. He has had some success with horses like bumper winner Mr Sykes and in October 2009 he had his first 2 y/o scorer Duchess of Foxland. One of his most satisfactory wins was with Derravarra Eagle in 2007 when he beat favourite Sweet Kiln in a conditions hurdle, as it was owned by his mother Margaret, bred by his father Edward, and it gave 19 y/o Conor Maxwell a 7lb claimer his first ever win. It was also a good advertisement for the public gallop operation that Mark runs at the stud in Crookedwood.

A.J. PILKINGTON AND HONEYMOON II

His family owned 1,683 acres at Tyrrellspass (1875 returns). He was educated in England and a graduate of Oxford Military College with training in horsemanship. He participated in the Westmeath Hunt and Polo Club. In 1898 he trained 13 horses for mainly Westmeath owners and he had 6 winners (£642-10s) and in 1899 had 10 winners (£1,172). William T. Brabazon, Johnstown House, Mullingar had horses with him and won a few races. Thomas Dibbs, Mullingar and James Brabazon, Mount Dalton, Rathconrath also had horses with him (he was owner and breeder of winners of good races in Ireland - died 1893). In 1899 he met with a nasty accident and it took some time to recover and P. Mulkearns ran his training establishment at Woodlands. His father Henry Mulock Pilkington died at Tore, Tyrrellspass in May 1899.

Some of his best horses included Mr A.B. Walkers Honeymoon II (Monsieur-Moonrise) ridden by himself, who won the Prince of Wales Stakes of 400 sovereign at Punchestown in 1902 and he also won the Punchestown Plate with Alderwood. At Galway Races in 1900, E.A.Shaw's horse Clear Case (Wiseman-Florida) won the Mervue Plate of 30 sovs over 7 furlongs and was trained by him. He trained Aristocrat, Oscuro, Min, Bonny Raith (Lord Grevilles), Convertor, Moonbeam & Annies Delight, for mainly local owners. In April 1900 he was injured at Punchestown in the Kildare Hunt Cup with muscle strain and couldn't ride Gay or Sweet in the Drogheda Stakes. In 1902 in a comparison with other local jockey's he was well clear - A.J.Pilkington 9 wins; E.A.Shaw 1, W.P. McLoughlin 1, J.Cheshire 3; T.Costello 4, M.Lowe 3, and James Kelly 2.

ROSS FAMILY AND THE POOKA

Willie Ross died on 20 April 1990 aged 80. In a full life he loved sports down the years including hockey, rugby, soccer, football, boxing, swimming and pitch & putt. He rode with the Westmeath Hunt and Harriers for years. He was on the point to point committee and acted as an official at meetings and also worked with the Agricultural Show. It was even recalled that 55 years before he took on the Wall of Death at the carnival in the Pound Field beside the old national school in Mullingar. Willie Ross bred and raced many successful point-to-pointers and bumper horses, ridden by his sons Cecil and Alan. Willie was a good rider and always had hunters and at least one pointer. There is a reference to Willie Ross in 1950 as a candidate for election as a Qualified Rider and he was proposed by Captain Gargan and seconded by Duke De Stacpoole. He had a licence until about 1976. Cecil's earliest point to point memory was in 1944 when his mother Imelda brought him & his brother Alan to Slanemore to see his father Willie riding. We went up to a fence & he remembers shouting *"Good man Daddy".*

Point-to-pointing, hunter chases, bumpers, hurdle races and steeplechases have been part of Cecil Ross's life, as an amateur rider and trainer. He said *"I've been on horses all my life, my father Willie always had a point to pointer at home and was always in the middle of them".* The home place is nearby as he was brought up in Johnstown in the same parish. Cecil said *"I mostly rode for local owners and trainers &and most of his best moments were with Bunny Cox, who was extremely well known in racing circles."* In point to points his best day was at Culleen, Mullingar when he had three winners.

He was raised on the family farm close to where he now lives, and he owns 140 acres. Training horses is still his business - and he had around 14 in recent years, some flat horses plus some cattle and sheep. He went to England and worked on the railway and in the Vauxhall factory in Luton. He met Norman Richards at the Dublin Horse Show, who specialised in hunters and went to work with him. He later worked with Peter Cazalet who was the Royal Trainer & had good horses like Lochroe, The Rip, and Blue Dolphin. He took care of the Queen Mother's horse Out of Town. Bill Rees and David Mould (described as a gentleman) were there at that time and eventually he came back to Ireland. Cecil said he rode about 90 winners in his career and had his first winner on a racecourse when he was 26. Over the years he had success with decent horses like Man of The West winner of the Hennessy Gold Cup in 1968 for Fulke Walwyn, The Inventor, Western View a locally owned horse bred by Michael & Rosie (Downes) Ross, the Oliver & Salome Brennan bred Benny the Bishop who won 6 races, Omas Glen owned by Gerry Carroll, Mullingar, and also flat horses like Princess Grand and his most successful horse Six of Hearts.

He also trained Foster & Allen's horse Westmeath Bachelor to win at Ballinrobe. Mick's nephew Danny Foster worked in the summer with Cecil. Our Eric described by him as *"a lovely durable little horse"* also won some races. The Inventor a graduate from the hunter chasing ranks under the Ross's guidance, won the Ladies' Cup at Punchestown in 1966 and both the Joseph O'Reilly at Fairyhouse and the Elveden Hunters' at Punchestown in 1967. He went on to pay his way for years in England, where he ran in consecutive Grand Nationals. The Inventor was formerly owned by vet Milo Cox, Pettiswood, Mullingar, but later raced in Britain for Robert Sangster. Cecil Ross is a remarkable man who contributed a lot to Irish racing and his 4 y/o The Inventor went on to run in 3 Aintree National's (fell in 1969 and refused in 1971/72) when owned by Robert Sangster and he was 4th to Garoupe in the Irish National. In February 1979, The Vintner another decent horse won the National Trial Chase at Punchestown at

25/1 beating Cheltenham & Aintree candidates. In 1981 Castlehaven (beat Deep Run) was 5th in Waterford Stayers Hurdle at Cheltenham and at Christmas 1982 he was 2nd over fences at Limerick, carrying 12st 5lbs. In 1983 he won the famous Barbour Cup at Castletown-Geo when he trained Lucky Marble to win with Ted Walsh as jockey.

In 1996 Benny the Bishop won a bumper at Kilbeggan ridden by Alan's son Anthony. Anthony 18 y/o rode the horse in a point-to-point at Castletown Geoghegan and also in 2 hurdle races. Benny the Bishop got his name from Benny Deegan a son of P.J. Clonminch, Tullamore, and the Deegan's stood his sire Bulldozer for his entire stud career. He was by Busted and won as a 2 y/o in England for Robert Sangster, but later met with an accident and was sold to Deegan's viz Stan Cosgrove, Moyclare Stud. Bulldozers best progeny were Dozing Bull, Clonminch, and Finnegan's Hollow. On 1st April 1990 Bulldozer met with freak accident and was put down. Benny the Bishop's dam was All Means, and her grand-dam was Serpentine Belle, who won at 5 y/o and bred 9 good horses. One of the best was Belle Artiste who won 14 races, and The Langholm Dyer, Serpentine Charge, Serpentine Lad, and Charlie Mouse. Benny was bred by Salome Brennan, Hollygrove, Belvedere.

THE POOKA OR THE "ILL-INTENTIONED LUBBERLY FAIRY"

The Pooka (who won Tetratema Cup at Gowran Park) ran in the 1972 Grand National ridden, owned & trained by Cecil. In an interview with the *Sports Illustrated Newspaper* before the race Cecil explained that the word meant *"an ill -intentioned lubberly fairy"* He was described as *"tall raw boned man of 32 who is riding overweight at 144 pounds"*. Cecil explained that the horse was a good jumper, very clever, sensible and only fell once in his life. When he walked the course a few years before he thought it was all right but added when *"I walked it again this morning and changed my mind. I'm not brave. I wish it was over."* I don't think anyone would doubt the bravery of Cecil Ross or any National Hunt jockey, but it was a revealing sentiment. He was with his friend Jim Tormey and the Newman family were also there with General Symons. The Pooka was a 10 y/o bred in England, purchased by him for £900. He had won two of his three races that year. He got as far as the Canal Turn on the second circuit and he was annoyed at what happened because the horse had struggled on the first circuit, but on the second circuit he was going well until the Canal Turn when he turned too sharp and sent Cecil out of the saddle. To this day he still thinks they would have been involved in the finish. The only thing that made him happy was that his friend Jim Tormey saddled General Symons to be third to Well To Do.

SIX OF HEARTS MAKES A "LOTTO" MONEY AND COMES UP TRUMPS

The best horse to come out of Cecil Ross's stable was nicknamed "Pat" and he was to make all his money on the flat (around €236,000 with 9 wins). In June 2011 Six of Hearts (S.H.James) brought Cecil to The Curragh on Irish Derby Day for the first time in 51 years (Chamour won in 1960), as just an hour before Treasure Beach won the Irish Derby for Aidan O'Brien his horse won €51,000 in the Paddy Power Sprint. In 2010, Six of Hearts who was owned by the Round Towers Syndicate, Kells won the G3 Ballychorus Stakes, which was a great occasion but he described his win on Derby Day as *"like winning the Lotto"* and *"this is as good as it gets".* Although only 73 y/o he attended with his wife Carol and said *"I feel about 100 but look about 110!"* For a National Hunt trainer all his life to succeed at this level was a dream. It was a field of 30 runners in a 6 furlong sprint and he won from Cheviot and Collingwood. In 2010 he had received a Special Award because of the horse's success in the G3 Ballychorus stakes.

He had the nice filly Princess Grand who won four races but it was nothing like the success of 7 y/o Six of Hearts (Pivotal-Additive). The horse made €100,000 as a yearling and was placed with Jamie Osborne and he joined Cecil's yard for 11,000 guineas after being bought at the Doncaster Sales by his nephew Alan in October 2007. John Butler & the Round Tower Syndicate bought him. He was gelded, started jumping in point to points, and then ran badly over hurdles, so they went back to the flat. The win at The Curragh was his 7th success, as he showed a new lease of life. It was the peak of Six of Hearts success and her last success on the track.

It is hard for smaller stables and you have to work hard. They start at 6am with his nephew Willie described by Cecil as *"The main man"* with stable work, tidying beds, giving hay and water. The lads finish up after riding out and Willie, his wife Carol and himself do the rest. He has a 3 1/2 furlong sand facility and in the recent past the other parts of the team were Dan Foster, Stan Finnemore and Johnny Geraghty. When he looks back on his career he regards his friend David Mould as *"probably the best jockey".* He is a great fan of Scobie Breasley and has a precious autographed picture of him in his living room. Looking back he remembers great point to point horses like P.P.Hogan's, Underway, Fearless Fred, Philliptown Hero and Corryvrekan. The best jockeys in the field then were Bill McLernon, John Fowler, and Ted Walshe. More recently he rates Derek O'Connor and Jamie Codd very highly. His best advice in the past for young people was to go to work with Jim Bolger and Dessie Hughes RIP.

Godsmejudge was bred by Cecil & Martin McCracken. His two greatest days were on 20th April 2013 when winning the Scottish Grand National at 12/1 beating Big Occasion & Mister Marker by 4 lengths and ridden by Wayne Hutchinson (24 runners/7 finishers). In April 2014 he was second to Alco (29 runners), when ridden by Aidan Coleman. The horse has won 5 races and €245,000 in prize money. He was pulled up on the Aintree Grand National in 2015 and is having a wind operation over the summer and aiming for Aintree again next year. The horse was with Cecil Ross as a point to pointer in Ireland before going to Britain.

ANTHONY ROSS AND FUNCTION DREAM

Anthony Ross Alan's son/Cecil's nephew, rode successfully in the north of England for a time in 2000/2001, principally for Saltburn trainer Mary Reveley. He had a great partnership with Function Dream and the 23 y/o was looking forward to the Champion Chase. She was rated 123 when coming over from Ireland to Mary Reveley. The 9 y/o was raised 38lbs. She only cost 7,000 gns at the sale as a foal. She was going for her 7th win in the Champion Chase. Anthony said *"It's the sort of thing you dream about but never really think will happen".* Ross came over to England 18 months before from Ballinacaragy, Westmeath after being recommended to Reveley by Ted Walsh (who was a cousin of the breeder). Ross had 19 point to point winners and 22 under rules. His grandfather Willie and his father Alan were riders (the latter with Paddy Mullins & Paddy Woods) and Cecil launched his career. It was 13 months before he had his first winner. The previous season he had 27 winners. He won the Castleford Chase at Wetherby, the Victor Chandler at Ascot, and the Game Spirit Chase at Newbury beating Flagship Uberalles the reigning champion by 17 lengths and was only 4/1 in the race. She was quick and accurate over fences with the odd mistake (she had won in Galway). Mary Reveley had 35 runners at the festival and no winners.

A few years can make a difference for every jockey and in January 2008 Anthony Ross (30) retired from the saddle and was still remembered for his association with Function Dream. He was having difficulties getting rides and decided to set up a livery yard outside Norton, while also riding out for Richard Fahey, who was very good to him. It was the dilemma for many young jockeys, as the rides become less and the horses get worse. When he was attached to the Mary Reveley stable for 3-4 years he rode Function Dream to win five in a row in 2000-2001. He said *"she was a great mare and lifted me to a bigger stage".* He hoped to maybe buy and sell a few horses.

SCOTT CLAN AT FARNAGH STUD

Richard Adamson owned the land at Farnagh up to around 1850, when it was sold to a Mr Fairbrother, who sold it to Edward Wakefield in 1895. He sold it to John Dolan around 1924 and the Scott family came around 1970 from the West of Ireland. Michael Scott was a horse dealer in Ballina, mainly hunters and point to pointers.

Barney Scott had his biggest success in 31 years as a trainer at Limerick when his best horse African Moon (owned by wife Katherine) won the Munster Grand National (ridden by Jayo Kane). He rode as an amateur for 27 years and he took out a trainers licence in 1949 at 29 y/o. His horse African Moon won at 6/1. John Fallon originally from Athlone but now living in Galway hunted with the South Westmeath Harriers. He bought a 2 y/o filly in 1975 called African Moon and leased her to Michael Scott. She won 11 races including the Munster National & Webster Cup. Fallon went on to have horses like Princess Leya (broken by Dot Love and Ciaran Murphy).

Barney when he started, he only trained his own horses and his stable was always small by racing standards-usually between 10 and 12 horses in training at any time. One of his best was Secret Vulgan around 1970/71. He won the Governor's Cup in the North, and was entered in the Aintree Grand National but ran in the Irish National and finished 5th, though he broke down three fences from home. In 1968 he beat Kinloch Brae and the next day Cappowillow won the Dunshoughlin Hurdle (2 winners in 2 days). The mare Capowillow won 8 hurdle races. Around the mid-1970's he had Petters and Barouche. The former won the Sandymount Handicap Chase at Leopardstown in February 1976 and Barouche won many point-to-points. None of his horses liked hard ground therefore he had few running at the time. He had no stable jockey, but the horses were ridden by John Harty, Sammy Shiels and young Gerry Newman. Other good horses included Carnroe, Lucifer's Dream, Speck of Leinster, Maud Milllar, and Hanley. His son Michael rode as an amateur and also a trainer and another son Phillip rode as an eventer and showjumper, who travelled the world. Susan Scott another member of the family has spent over 30 years working in Florida with horses.

Michael Scott, Farnagh Stud had some good horses like Dee Pee Cee (Tidaro) who won 13 out of 63 races including at York. Our Eric (Tidaro) who was sold to a syndicate & won 5/6 races. He bred Our Eric who was trained & owned by Cecil Ross. He won 5 of his 27 races. Speck of Leinster won 2 hurdle races and at Navan defeated Ruby Walsh's Undecided the horse who was drowned in Kilbeggan. He brought an entire Kadastrof to the stud in 2000. He had been unplaced in the Champion Chase the year before for Robin Dickin. They decided to go to Michael Scott as they liked his operation. The horse won 15 of his 67 races fron two to nine-4 on the flat, 4 over hurdles, and 6 over fences. He won over a mile at two and as a hurdler was 5th to Mysilv in the Triumph Hurdle and 2nd in the Glenlivet Hurdle. He switched to fences in 1997/98 and won 6 of 11 races and was a top novice chaser. He was 2nd to Ask Tom in the Game Spirit Chase with Viking Flagship & Celibate behind. He was eventually 10th of 11 in the Champion Chase. He was by Mill Reef Stallion Port Etienne and the dam was Kadastra. He had a few other good horses like Low Profile, when Barry Brogan

& Archie Watson came down and decided to purchase him after he won a bumper at Leopardstown and a maiden hurdle. He won 19 races and they brought off some gambles with him. Western Rambler won a few bumpers in the 1970's and another horse Quayside Charm. He sells colt foals and holds on to fillies for point to points, but pointed out that syndicates are gone and his would usully be winter horses.

JIMMY TORMEY, LENEY PRINCESS, AND "NOBBY", "TUSKY", & " TARKY"
He died on 24th October 2014 in the Midlands Regional Hospital, Tullamore Hospital but was from Mullingar. He was survived by his wife Pauline, sons Brian and Paul, daughters Carol and Una. He was reposed in Shaw's in Mullingar and removed to St Nicholas's Church, Multyfarnham, and buried in The Rock Cemetery.

It began in Leney, Bunbrosna where Edward (Ned), Tormey & his wife Nan bred & trained horses. He will forever be associated with horses like El Kekni, Grand Visier and Evilo but he was also linked to "Nobby", "Tusky" and "Tarky". The last three might not be familiar names but read on. Biddy Hawk produced Leney Princess (sire Roi D'Egypt) and Ned trained her as a 4 y/o to win a point to point at Slanemore ridden by his son Jimmy. She was then sold to Colonel John Thomson. He purchased her for £200 in 1956 because he had won the 1942 Cathcart Chase at Cheltenham with her sire Roi D"Egypt. John Oakey in his book *'Mince Pie for Starters'* explained his connection with some of the above. Apparently Thompson had nicknamed Roi d'Egypte "Nobby". He was a stallion based in Westmeath who sired around a dozen winners (like Regal Wine & Ernest) including Another Flash. As a 4 y/o she won a point to point at Slanemore and was second to the Duncan bred Flashaway in another point to point. She was placed four times over fences before being retired to the stud of Cecil Ronaldson, Clairmount Stud, Milltownpass.

Leney Princess was the dam of the winners of 83 races including Fort Leney (Fortina) winner of Cheltenham Gold Cup 1968 with a heart condition (13 wins-Power Gold Cup, Thyestes Chase, John Jameson Chase, and Leopardstown Chase etc), Proud Tarquin (9 wins including the Tote Champion Novice Chase & Guinness Chase at Punchestown and 2nd Irish Grand National), Lean Forward (by Bowsprit, 13 wins including the Leopardstown Handicap Chase), Prince Tino (21 wins), Tuscan Prince (15 wins-2 hurdles and 13 chases), all broken and trained by Cecil Ronaldson before going to Tom Dreaper. It was a remarkable result from an unsuccessful mare. John Oaksey was connected with several of the above horses when they went to England to Roddy Armytage. His favourite was Tuscan Prince ("Tusky"), who was a great jumper and was ridden by 20 men in his career. In 72 races he won 15 times and was placed 41 times. At the age of 27 he was cast in his box and was going to be put down, but he got up and lived three more years. He also rode Proud Tarquin ("Tarky") who won the Totalisator Novice Chase at Cheltenham in 1970 and was 2nd in the Irish Grand National in 1971. He was second to Red Rum in the Scottish Grand National and then won the Whitbread Gold Cup beating The Dikler, only to be disqualified. Lord Oaksey said about Proud Tarquin that *"I have never ridden a tougher or braver horse and never expect to".*

Jim Tormey held a licence for 47 years and was assisted by his brother Tommy. He trained General Symons (Paddy Kiely) to finish third in the Aintree National and he also won the National Trial at Punchestown. He recorded 21 wins with El Kekni and 18 with Grand Visier. He was an amateur rider who combined to run a quietly effective training stable. Jimmy was unfortunate when he fell on Lough Sheever and injured his shoulde at one stage. He was also Master of the Westmeath Harriers in Bunbrosna. El Kekni, was trained for Rex Beaumont of Belvedere, who paid numerous compliments to his handlers' skill, seemingly able to win whenever they wanted.

EVILO OR OLIVE ?

They also won the 1967 'Amateurs' Derby' at Galway with their own 6 y/o Evilo (100/7), as trainer & rider and was then second in the Galway Hurdle a few days later. He won by 6 lengths from Pappas Boy & Razors Edge. He shed 7lbs in 3 days after hours in the baths in Dublin. He gave the horse a great ride hugging the inside rail most of the way and came with a storming run in the dip. Jim said *"He attacked the hill to the straight like a tiger".* This was his first ride in Galway and he bought the horse from his neighbour M.F.Murphy and the horse got his name from Murphy's wife's name Olive, which spelled backways is Evilo. Tormey wasted to lose 7lbs and do the weight of 10st 5lbs. He motored from his home to a health spa on the Monday night to shed the last few pounds. After he won, it was no surprise to hear that that the thing he wanted most was a good meal. He hugged the inside rail behind the leader Strong Drop, then Extra Stout took the lead with Razor's Edge challenging into the dip, when Evilo made his move. The winner was owned & trained by Tormey and was treated very much as a pet. This was his 5th win with Tormey. It was no mean feat for Evilo to beat all but Muir in the Galway Hurdle two days after winning the Players Amateur Handicap. In 1982 he ran a total of 41 horses with 7 wins, including 5 by El Kekni (Ballinrobe, Killarney, Sligo etc). TP Burns was his favourite jockey and he always rode Grand Visier, when they backed it. Burns also rode for local owners who had horses with Kevin Bell like Mrs C.A. Ryans Irish Mist, Colonel Howard Bury's Everest Twenty One and Rex Beaumont's Merill Jane and Miss Mustang.

He also won with other horses like Brusna Boy, Right Rambler, Mektoub for Rex Beaumont, who won in Downroyal in 1981 and Rare Talk. His son Brian is carrying on the family tradition working with Darley Stud in Kentucky.

COUNT JOHN McCORMACK AND HIS BEAUDELAIRE

Count John McCormack (1884-1945) won acclaim in concert halls and theatres all around the world, as an opera singer and singer of old Irish songs and even appeared in a few movies. Racing was one of his favourite hobbies and in spite of a lot of bad luck he had some success.

In 1929 his horse Cragadour trained by R.More O'Farrell was 3rd in the Irish Derby won by Kop1. It was a strange race in that Fred Myerscough's Star Eagle was runner up and this was a horse "The Count" owned as a 2 y/o. When he went wrong they sold him to Fred Myerscough and then the horse recovered his form to win the Madrid Plate and Baldoyle Derby before being 3rd in Irish 2,000gns. He tried to purchase him back but failed, so he replaced him with Cragadour bought for £13,000, who had been 2nd in the English 2,000gns and 7th in the Epsom Derby. Neither of them did much afterwards though Star Eagle won his next race. In 1931 Beaudelaire (who cost 800 guineas) was 2nd to Sea Serpent in the Irish Derby (T.P.Burns), but then went on to win the St Leger in 1931. In a small field Beaudelaire won cleverly by a 1/2 length from the pacemaker Pahokee. It was his first classic success after having a lot of bad luck in the past and he was trained by R. More O'Farrell whom he bankrolled. In 1933 his horse Franz Hals was 4th in the Irish Derby to Harinero.

Tommy *"the Scot"* Burns rode for him and was his favourite jockey. He still rode for him as a free-lance on horses like Migronne to win the Turf Club Cup, but afterwards lost his licence when Philips Fancy ran down the field - many considered it unjust. Roderick More O'Farrell the trainer also came to the Stewards attention as a gambling trainer with fancied ones losing and outsider's winning. Burns won on the Count's horse Song of My Heart; in 1932 Smart Aleck won 3 races for the Scot and the Count as did Double Bell. It was said of Burns if the Count didn't get rid of him *"McCormack will be singing on the streets of Monastrevan and you'll be passing around the hat".* Thankfully, for all lovers of music the Count John McCormack managed to deal with the foibles of racing and continue his great career as a singer around the world.

BEENIE McDONNELL AND PETER SCUDAMORE

Beenie McDonnel (married Eileen Farry), Dunboden Park had red and white colours. In September 1978, the 5 y/o mare Pigeon's Nest had his biggest success in the J.T. Rogers Gold Cup. In 1979 she turned out for the 12th time to contest the Players Navy Cut Handicap ridden by Peter Scudamore (claiming 7lbs) since winning a maiden hurdle at Fairyhouse in January. He won by 3 lengths to Bracae Boy and Don Mobile. Scudamore said afterwards *"It was at Galway that I won the most prestigious race of my stay ... my first & only winner on the flat.... After the race we discovered that I had claimed a 7lbs allowance, whereas I was only entitled to five pounds...it was thought better that I slipped away to England and got myself out of sight and mind until it was too late for the authorities to disqualify me".* This was Peter Scudamore's only flat winner and he had 1,676 winners in his career and 8 National Hunt jockey championships.

In November 1979, Beenie was awarded the Irish Field Sporting Personality of the Month because of Pigeon's Nest, who ran 27 times and won 10 races (John T Rogers Memorial Cup in 1978, Player's Navy Cut in Galway in 1979 etc). She was retired to stud after refusing many offers and in September 1981 she had a colt by Persian Bold. In December 1983 she had her first 2 y/o foal which was sold at Ballsbridge the next year. In January 1987 she had Tried & True plus Sweet Downs and another successful horse was Gleaming Treasure (trained by Willie Treacy). Beenie's horse Gleaming Treasure won the Racing Post EBF Hand at Phoenix Park at 14/1, trained by Willie Treacy and ridden by Martin Lynch in 1987.

Francie '*Beenie*' McDonnell died on at Lynn aged 92. He was noted farmer, horse breeder, livestock judge. His family was originally from Blacklion, Co Cavan. He grew up at Dunboden farming the estate for many years until he retired in the 1980's and sold it to Christy Maye. He raised purebred Hereford cattle showing many prize winning bulls at shows and bulls from his farm called "Dunboden Prince". His motto was *"breed them big and strong, and they'll sell themselves".* He had great success in racing with Pigeon's Nest who won 13 races. He also won medals cycling in his youth. He was very generous and helped out people in trouble.

FRED MYERSCOUGH, MANAGER, AND AUCTIONEER

In 1943, Fred Myerscough achieved a new distinction that season winning two 2 Derbies when Scots Guard won the Baldoyle Derby after The Phoenix 2/5F won the Irish Derby by a length. He bought him as a yearling for 290 guineas and he won on his debut at Phoenix Park and won several other races including the Park 1500 in 1942. He won the Irish 2,000gns and then the Derby and was 1/8 to get the Triple Crown but faltered in final stages and was beaten 5 lengths by Solferino. He was retired to Ballykisteen Stud and was successful at stud (in 1949 he was syndicated for 160,000gns).

After business success he turned to racing and had sprinting mare Tut Tut, Diomedes, Prince Meteor and Star Eagle. His Tut Tut (H.H. Beasley) a 6 y/o daughter of Bachelor's Double beat the Irish Guineas winner Soldennis in 1921 in the 5 furlong Drogheda Memorial Stakes. It was his 10th win in 5 years and in 1919 he won the same race beating Loch Lomond, He was only just beaten in the Portland Handicap in England. In 1925 Myerscough & A.B. Coyle in partnership, won the Irish 2,000gns with St Donagh (RoiHerode) and also won the Baldoyle Derby. In 1941 he won the Irish 1,000gns with Milady Rose trained by Colonel Blake. He sold the Brownstown Stud & started training his own horses at Clonard, Dundrum and he was leading owner in 1941. He had six 2y/o winners and four were exported to the USA in spite of the war. He died 26 September 1954 at Clonard, Dublin at 73.

At 16 he worked with Coyle & Co., Brokers & Coyle Insurance with. In 1921 he got a controlling interest in bloodstock auctioneering firm R.J.Goff & built it up for Irish Breeders. A board of directors consisting of Frederick S. Myerscough, Patrick J. Brophy, Senator J. J. Parkinson and Col. A. J. Blake completed the new management team. In 1925, on the death of Edward Kennedy, Frederick Myerscough became chairman and managing director. Under him a branch office was maintained in Newbridge, but the company established its main offices in Dublin at Sewell & Son and Simpson's Yard in Mount Street, where sales were held in addition to those at the R.D.S. This was forging a connection with the company, which was destined to continue for three generations through his son, Cyril, and two grandsons, Robert and Philip Myerscough. In 1953 Frederick Myerscough retired and the chairmanship was taken over by Col. A. J. Blake, who continued in this position until 1963 when Cyril Myerscough took over the reins. He was succeeded by his son Cyril at who helped to develop Goffs.

SIR WALTER NUGENT MP, DONORE, MULTYFARNHAM (1865 -1955) 4TH BARONET

Generations of the family lived in Donore House until the 1950's. He was born in 1865 and died in 1955. He was a director of the Midlands Great Western Railway. From 1922-23 he was High Sheriff of Westmeath, Peace Commissioner, and Deputy Lieutenant Westmeath. He was a Senator from 1928-31. In November 1955 Sir Walter died at Donore, Multyfarnham (aged 90) and his wife died in 1957. In 1907 he entered parliament as a Nationalist MP for South Westmeath holding it until 1918. In 1917 he spent time in USA as journalist. In 1923 he was a Steward of Turf Club & National Hunt. Lady Nugent was an O'Malley and good horsewoman. An anecdote states that she saved a young girl at Dublin Horse Show 1934, as it was a runaway horse and that she made *"a dive from her own horse at the head of runaway horse, and hanging on desperately until she brought the runaway horse to a standstill".* She got a round of spontaneous applause.

He became a patron of the turf and his horses were trained by Michael Dennehy French House, The Curragh from 1898. He bred winners including hunters and race horses and followed the Hunt. He was the owner of King Frusquin (St

Frusquin) who won the Royal Whip in 1918. He won with horses like Sincerity (Hilaire-purity) at Dundalk in May 1904 and the same horse won at Baldoyle in March 1905 and Cork in May 1905. His father was Sir Walter owner of Clonave and other good horses trained by Dennehy. Clonave was a specialist hurdler in the 1890's. The biggest hurdle win was in the Croydon's Grand International Hurdle before the track closed in 1890 and Clonave also won the Great Metropolitan Chase on the same day in 1874. He was succeeded by Sir Percy Nugent.

MRS ROCHFORT-HYDE, LYNN HOUSE, MULLINGAR

She was a native of Canada and bred horses for racing, for horse shows and won many prizes in the dogs section at the Royal Dublin Show. In 1959 she won the Laidlaw Cup at the RDS with Brig o'Gold. She died and was buried on 21st March 1963 at Ballyglass Cemetery, Mullingar. She won with horses like Mint Sauce, Canibou Star, Flying Stella, Gay Nineties and Moonlight Bay. Cecil Ronaldson often rode for her.

SHAWS OF MULLINGAR

E.A.SHAW, MULLINGAR - BOUGHT A HORSE FOR 1 SHILLING AND SOLD ONE TO KING EDWARD VII

E. A. Shaw, Mullingar was born in 1872 and was a Solicitor and Owner. On the 1901 Census he was down as a 28y/o Solicitor of Carl Street, Mullingar North and his family were his wife Rosalie (28), daughter Mary Elizabeth (1) and Joseph (0). He was a Director of various companies and Governor of the Infirmary. One if his better horse's was Florida who won the Mervue Plate at Galway in 1894 and ran well in good races at The Curragh & Leopardstown. In 1897 Florida returned home to his owners place and was sent to local based stallion Enthusiast. In 1896 Shaw won on Larkfield at Mullingar races; in 1899 he won the Light Weight Hunt Cup on Diversion; he won the Whitworth Challenge worth 100 guineas on Little Boy, which he supposedly bought for one shilling. He sold another of his horses to King Edward VII. He won the Westmeath Hunt Cup 5 times. Other successful horses included Lord Rosmead (Gay Reveller-Delight) who won in Sligo; and Clear Case (Wiseman-Florida) won the Mervue Plate of 30 sovs over 7 furlongs with 6 starters and was 5/2 fav. Clear Case was trained by A.J.Pilkington, Woodlands, Multyfarnham.

Joseph A. Shaw, Solicitor, Lynn, Mullingar was Legal Advisor to the County Board of Health and Town Commissioners. He helped establish Penny Dinners. He had a good horse Little Clifter (by Cliftonhall) who won the maiden plate at Punchestown (£600) in April 1926 over 4 miles. He purchased the horse four months before on Bob Fethersonhaugh's advice. He won a flat race at Galway and later ran well in the Irish Grand National when second 2nd to Amberwave.

P. W. "STILLETTO" SHAW AND BELSIZE

P.W. Shaw was the member of the Shaw family, who was mostly involved with horse racing in both Britain and Ireland. The family's mercantile business was well- known across the country. He was a businessman, JP & also involved as Chairman on many committees in Mullingar. In sending telegrams related to horse racing he signed them "Stilletto", which had a significance readily appreciated & understood by their recipients. He divided his patronage between Carrick & Maddenstown. Belsize (Captivation-Chancery) was the best 2 year old in 1920 (winning at the Phoenix Park, Leopardstown & Baldoyle) & he was favourite for the Irish Derby in 1921. The name Belsize was the name of Shaw's home residence. He was a half- brother to Dunadry, Lissalinchey (Irish Derby winner), Dark Eyes & others. He made his debut at the Phoenix Park and won by 1 1/4 lengths for trainer Parkinson. His next race was at The Curragh in the Juvenile Plate of 6 furlongs for 300 sovereigns with E.Quirke up and he won by 6 length's. In May 1920, P.W. Shaw was offered £10,000 for Belsize, described as the best 2 y/o of the season, after winning the Irish Breeders Produce Stakes. In July he was offered £20,000 but he would not sell him. It was hoped that this great horse would bring acclaim internationally to Mullingar & Westmeath. The offer came from P.White a Cross Channel blood stock owner.

Captivation in 1920 was having a good year with Belsize, Oxendon won three 3 races, and Grandcourt who won the Newbury Spring Cup. Belsize was a 1/2 sister to the St Leger winner in 1905. In 1921 Belsize (Captivation-Chancery) was 3/1F for the Irish Derby. He was unbeaten in four races as a 2 y/o and Parkinson thought he was his best chance since Orby. He had no run before the race and was well- backed. He became upset at the start. He could only finish 7th to Ballyheron. He was brought back to sprinting and won a further 10 races and went to stud in Cork in 1927.

Shaw was also the owner of prolific winner Lomond Lake (Loch Lomond-Happy Moments) who won the Royal Whip 1927. Other older horses that won that year and were bred by Captivation were Grandcourt (won Newbury Spring Cup), Dunadry (formerly with Dick Cleary) won on Easter Monday in the Great Lancashire Chase, and Capstan who also won in England. He had a number of prolific winners like Loch Lomond, Llangorren (Bachelor's Double-Llangarren Lass), Huonora (Sir Huon-Kenora) and Tinode (Orby-French). In 1920 he was offered 2,300 guineas for Llangorren but did not sell him. He sent Huonora to Plumpton for a selling hurdle of 100 sovereigns and she won and was described by *"The Sporting Chronicle"* as *"a game mare"*. Llangorren won twice at The Curragh & once at the Phoenix Park before going to England. In March 1922 he won twice in 10 days at Leicester & Lingfield. The *'Sporting Chronicle'* this time wrote that it was *"a dapper little horse"*. Shaw had a number of horses trained in England and Neil Day was bought for 800gns at Doncaster by Shaw and won at

The Curragh. He was injured in April 1922 after a fall at The Curragh leading to a serious injury to his jockey Quirke. He did not run for 2 years and was then sent to G.N.Bennett in England to train and in a big field at Lewes he was gambled on near the off and duly won.

One of his favourites was Lomond Lake (Loch Lomond-Happy Hours) who in 5 weeks in 1926 had won five races at Curragh, Leopardstown, Baldoyle (Ballyscadden Hurdle), Mullingar and Powerstown Park (carrying 12st 10lbs). When he won at Baldoyle his young jockey Redmond also rode a flat winner for the stable and then a 3 mile chase winner. When only a 4 y/o, he carried 12st 2lbs to victory in Mullingar. In November 1927 Lomond Lake had a fatal collapse in a race at Liverpool & his jockey "Jimmy" Doyle got a severe fall but recovered. He had paid £800 for the dam, and he bred it himself. In 1919 the dam Happy Hours had won the Railway Plate at Limerick for him. Other winners included Chantress, Rushyford, Broken Vows and good filly Princess Salome (Roi Herode-Symington's Pride).

AIDAN SHEIL, KILLUCAN AND NEW YORK

Aidan Sheils has to fly in from New York to see his horses. He has lived there since 1985 and he runs The Irish Rover Bar in Queen's. He is a native of Killucan, County Westmeath and was part of a four man syndicate ("The Irish Rover Syndicate") with Niall Reilly, from Julianstown, Co. Meath who was in the building business and two other syndicate members in the US. He has been back home for all the big races featuring his horses in spite of all the travel. He likes to be there for winning days but has to accept the losing days. He sometimes thinks *"are we mad in the head"*, but it's all about the craic.

In August 2001 Aidan "Red Shiels" and wife Carmel of Killucan, Co Westmeath were at Tattersalls August sale when they bought a Mister Lord gelding. The horse called Oh My Lord won at point to points and on the track winning a maiden at Longford and a hunter chase at Down Royal. They travelled around to see the horse at Perth, Aintree and Cheltenham where he was 3rd to Spot the Difference in the Sporting Index Chase in Nov 2005. He fell in his next race and later died from colic. In 2009 they had another significant win with Northern Alliance 4/1F, trained by Tony Martin winning the Guinness Kerry Nation under Ruby Walsh from Royal County Star. This was a prelude to the big day at Cheltenham in March 2013. The horse, called Beneficient, was trained by Tony Martin (their trainer since 2001) and he was bought by Debbie Hartnett for 3,000 in 2004 and two years later was sold for 52,000. He looked him up on the internet after Tony bought him and found out he could have been bought for 11,000 the previous November and wasn't best pleased. He has won 2 Grade 1's in 4 successes. Aidan Sheils was celebrating his 50th birthday when the horse won the G1Deloitte Novice Hurdle and later won the 3 runner Arkle Novice

Chase in a race where Arvjka Legionnaire fell. He ran at Cheltenham under the name of the Irish Rover Syndicate. Aidan loves Cheltenham and doesn't like the flat. The horse won the Jewson Novice Chase at Cheltenham in March 2013. They had a big celebration in the Newgrance Hotel in Naas with 200 guests, including many from Delvin. They all watched the race on the big screen and remembered those missing, who played a part in the story.

HARRY WHITWORTH MFH

In June 1920 he won Irish Derby of £4,000 with He Goes (3/1) and in the Irish Field in December 1920 it was announced that Captain H.Whitworth was the leading owner of the year mainly due to He Goes his only runner in Ireland. He Goes (Prince Palatine-Feronia) was trained in Newmarket by J.Butter's. He won at Royal Ascot & Newmarket as a 2 y/o and was 10th in Epsom Derby on his only run at three. He won by 1 length from Wily Attorney but there was an objection by Canty on the runner up for bumping and boring but it was turned down. The horse had very little success after this race. Whitworth was the Joint Master of Galway Blazers in 1902/03 and hunted in Westmeath for 5 years, then he went to Yorkshire and he was also a keen polo player. He kept some horses in Ireland after the war and was the leading owner in 1920. His last good horse was Golden Oracle a sprinter in the mid-1920's.

He rode with the hunt, point to points in Westmeath and elsewhere. The horses were trained in England by Butters at Newmarket and his colours were cardinal & black hoops. J.J.Maher had trained chasers and he won the Metropolitan Chase a few years before with Break Out. His horse Genuine (Gay Reveller-St Evelyn) won Grand Stand Plate of 75 sovs at Bellewstown; Prince Henry won the Kildare Hunt Cup (8/1) at Punchestown in 1908; his chaser Moorside (St Aidan-Rudora) won in Baldoyle March 1908. Other winners were Shylock II Bonnie Joan (Peter of Skipaway), Excelite, Princess (won Galway Open Hunt Cup) and his horse L.B. was a strong fancy for the Galway Plate but ran out.

OFFALY OWNERS

H.DAVIS KENNY, BALLINGARRY

He died in August 1950. Even at an advanced age he rode his favourite hunter “Codex” at point to points. It was fitting that when he passed in a casket in accordance with his wishes it was drawn by Codex. He was a member of the Ormonde Hunt and Secretary for 17 years (retiring in 1939), a member of East Galway Hunt, Ormonde Club, King's County Knot of the Friendly Brothers of St Patrick, and was a Synodsman & Parochial Nominator of Ballinagarry & Lockeen Parish. On retirement as Secretary of the Ormonde Hunt he was presented with miniature of a fox mounted on a plinth. His greatest achievement was with his horses at Royal Dublin Society for three years in a row from 1923-25, when he won the cup for the best hunter in the show, and the Laidlaw & Babes in the Wood Challenge Cup outright. In February 1924 Harry Davis Kenny fractured a bone in his leg when on a morning school with his horse, who stepped in a hole but better news was on the way.

At the Dublin Horse Show in August 1924 he created a sensation by winning 3 cups for hunters. Bright Prospect (Green Emerald-Speed) an 8 y/o was bred by Mrs B.O'Meara, Eglish and sold by auction to Mr Read of High Park. He was passed on to Harry Kenny of Prospect and Mr Davis Kenny. He won first prize 14/15 stone class for hunters. The horse was top notch in his field and champion point to pointer and champion hunter in Ireland. He had refused tempting offers but was loath to part with him. Another prize winner was Harry Kenny's Virol (Vilko-Mithra Belle) and he was purchased by Capt H.A Gairdner. The three trophies won by Mr Kenny were the Coote Perpetual Cup presented by Sir Algernon Coote for best weight carrying hunter; the Laidlaw Champion Cup presented by T.K.Laidlaw for best hunter in show; and Babes in the Wood Challenge Cup presented by E.Hope Johnston.

Following these great wins he presented the "Bright Prospect Trophy" to the RDS, which was won out by Mr Galway Greer in 1949. In 1939 he showed the 5y/o "Wavering Bee", which he purchased at Goff's Sale and won the Samuel Ussher Roberts Championship cup as well as Bright Prospect Trophy, and Laidlaw Cup for best hunter. When the show commenced after WWII he won reserved championship and Samuel Ussher Cup with "Pampas Grass". He also had success with Ormonde Hunt teams in the Inter Hunt Championship. He was interested in point to pointing and racing under rules and his Comic Cuts won the Open Cup at the Ormonde Hunt in March 1925 and he was a full brother to Master Macree, who won a number of chases in England. A week later Comic Cuts won at Tuam and he also had two seconds with Lady Blighty & Tons of Money.

In October 1925 he sold Bright Prospect, who was a noted hurdler, to a Belgian businessman and he was considered the finest hunter bred in Tipperary, winning point to points and prizes at shows (£400). Comic Cuts had won a few points beating Mrs Jiggs who won several times under regular rules. He bred Agruide (Argosy) who was 2nd at Kempton in the Stewards Plate of £1,000 in May 1929 The previous week he had been well backed at Newmarket but was left at the start. At that time he still had the dam's sire and a couple of horses by Allenby. In November he had a deserved win in the Freckenham Stakes at Newmarket. He also bred a good horse a 4 y/o in 1931 in Battle of Killiecrankie trained by Maxwell Arnott at Clonsilla. He was a 1/2 brother to Irish Battle and the good English chaser General Advance. Kenny also bred Drinwood who was in the same race. He won at Ballinrobe in September 1931 and as 3 y/o won a prize at Ballsbridge. Interestingly, he bred Achtoi Lass who broke the mile record at Kings Park, Montreal on 19th September 1931. She was by Lass o'Killicrankie and a 1/2 sister to "Battle". He was very much a seller of horses and after Battle of Killiecrankie cantered home in the Stewards Chase in Baldoyle, over 2 miles 1 furlong he sold him to BBA in March 1932 for a Canadian customer. The horse had won a flat race and two chases. Maxwell Arnott, Clonsilla his trainer had a strong connection with Birr as he served with the military there.

H. SEFTON KENNY, CLYDUFF

Henry Sefton Kenny died in February 1940 after an accident getting off a train as a coat got caught in a carriage and he fell on the rails and fractured his ribs. Pneumonia occurred and he died in hospital. He was the eldest son of Harry D.Kenny late of Glebe House, Eglish, Borrisokane. He owned and bred hunters that followed the Ormonde Hunts. H Sefton Kenny followed in his father's footsteps footsteps and managed the stud of T.Kenny, Kilcarron, He then went to Rosemount, Co Westmeath. He trained the highest priced chaser Silvo belonging to his cousin H.V.Kenny. He won many good races and was placed in the National and won the big Paris Chase. Another good horse he trained was Greenogue. He was a magnificent horseman and rode winners under Turf and National Hunt rules. He was described as a *"Wonderful man and pleasant company"*. At his death he was Manager to Archie Willis well-known N.Ireland sportsman. Early in his career he had good horses like Ballybrack, Mithra Belle, Princel (who won at Punchestown) and Kilcormac. He had purchased Frank Barbour's good horse Dunadry for £22 and passed him on to Dick Cleary at Streamstown, who sold him for £900. In April 1925 he was training at Friarstown Lodge, The Curragh and he turned out his first winner from his new quarters when Prudent Lad won. He was owned by Captain Teague a stepson of Mr Kenny and he went on to win many races.

GUY ATKINSON CANGORT, SHINRONE

Guy H.Atkinson died at Cangort, Shinrone in April 1922 at an early age.He was an enthusiastic follower of the Ormonde Hunt and the family had a stud farm at Cangort, which turned out many successful thoroughbred yearlings. He owned and rode many point-to-point winners. He had his agriculture activities very much up to date and had the famous Yew Walk up to his residence. Mrs Guy Atkinson, Cangort who always rode side saddle was the mother of Major Anthony Atkinson, who lived at Cloughmoyle for many years before selling it.

CAPTAIN BERNARD DALY, TULLAMORE

Captain Bernard Daly owned the Tullamore Distillery when Alfred Barnard visited in 1886 (great nephew of original owner) and was a prominent figure in sports as Master of the Hounds, polo player etc. He also loved horse racing and in 1922 he won the Irish Oaks with Miss Hazelwood (it was said that Williams had his shirt on it!). In 1888 Bernard Daly and a cousin B.S.Mara went into a partnership to carry on under the name of "B.Daly & Co". After a number of difficulties the Distillery was saved by Captain Daly, B.S. Mara and E.J.Williams in 1903, when they came up with £20,000 to purchase it.

He lived near Dublin and Daniel E. Williams acted as Manager of the Distillery. He was also on the first board of the BBA (Bloodstock Breeders Association). He married Anna Maud Gray on 24th July 1897. He died in Lysadulas, North Wales aged 77 in 1940. He formerly lived at Templeogue House, Dublin at one time the residence of Charles Lever,who wrote some of his books there, which had numerous references to Offaly & Westmeath, as he spent time with his brother there. He had lived at Old Hall, Tullamore and was a J.P. He spent much of his time in India where he had great skill as a polo player, and in Ireland he was strong supporter of All Ireland polo club (James H.Locke owner of Kilbeggan Distillery was a friend involved with him in polo and Tullamore races). He had a stud farm at Kimmage and bred and raced many winners. His horses were trained by F.Grundy & Bob Fetherstonhaugh. Grundy won the Irish Oaks for him in 1922 with Miss Hazelewood and he also bred Tutbury who won races for King George V. In the early days he was interested in trotting horses and supported old £4-19s races. He was considered the chief organiser of Tullamore Races from 1885-1903 and he was renowned for his hospitality.

LORD ROSSMORE

The first owner to win over £5,000 was Lord Rossmore, who won £6,440 in 1813. He was part of the Westenra family from Sharavogue House, Shinrone, Birr and it was not until 1915 that this record was broken. Col. J.C.Westenra, Sharavogue House, was one of the leading owners in Ireland and won the most prize money from 1834-36 and in 1838 (£3,270 in 1836). His daughter married the Earl of Huntington and he inherited the property in Sharavogue (the house was burned down during the Civil War). In 1881 Passaic after winning the Cambridgeshire Trial Plate at Sandown Park was purchased by Lord Rossmore for 500gns. Freney was one of the finest and best bred horses in Ireland & United Kingdom. He won all before him at The Curragh. He was inclined to inbreeding of his horses but produced great horses. Warren William Westenra was 36 when his aunt's husband Baron Rossmore died and it brought him the title & estate and he was made a member of the Turf Club Stewards in 1811. Rossmore Lodge was his at one stage and although he was in racing since around 1811, it was not until the 1830's that it was built. He had Sir Hercules at his stud in 1832. Lord Rossmore won Irish Derby in 1905 with Flax Park (P.Hughes) with P.J.Dunne trainer.

WALLACES, BELFIELD, SHINRONE

Richard Wallace's father John Wallace died at Ballincor on 15th June 1911 aged. Richard himself died on 22nd September 1941 and is buried in Shinrone

Cemetery. His brothers Jim and Joe were famous rugby players and Tom played with the famous Sharavogue Polo team. His sisters were Mrs G.S.Webb, Mrs G Ryall, Mrs H.B. Kenny and they were well-known with the Ormonde Hunt. Richard was a good athlete and especially liked horses. One of his successes from the stud farm at Belfield was Glencorrig. It was said that he got £2,500 for him when he was sold to Mr Mackay after winning the Phoenix Park race, but he won previously at Downroyal. He had many good horses and didn't mind giving tips. No money would tempt him to sell if he liked a horse. His sires Cornkale and Baydrop were had for £4-4s and he also had Baydrop's full brother Gainsborough. He was a County Councillor for many years. He left one son John H Wallace in Australia and daughter Marion Wallace.

In August 1921 Dick Wallace provided a bit of a sensation with a double at Clonmel in the first and third race with his well-known horse Monocle. He purchased him as a youngster for a *"harmless price"*. The big horse was allowed to mature. After winning the Kilsheelan Plate he was very pleased and decided to go for the Kilcash Plate over the same distance in spite of a 10 lb penalty. He was 16ft 2ins in height and looked like a chaser. He started the year with 4 horses in training and scored 4 wins in his first year as a trainer. In July 1924 his horse Fast Asleep added to her success by winning over 9 furlongs at the Junction. Mr Wallace Belfield had good offers for her before she won anything, but he knew that he had a useful animal and refused to sell her. Wallaces horse Solus (he won 5 races in one year) ran very well for a long way in Galway Plate and he also ran very well the previous year. On this occasion he had the misfortune to hurt himself at the 2nd last fence and this undoubtedly kept him out of the first three. In April 1936 he had an advertisement for Baydrop & Corn Kale in the papers. In November 1938 Richard Wallace's horse Idrop (by Baydrop bred from a St Leger winner out of an Oaks winner) won the welter race at Naas. T.H.Wallace, Ballincor owned Vliko who sired chasers and hunters (1911 Santry Leucadia) £9-19s for 1927 season. J.H.Wallace rode his own horse Golden Ashe (Saxham - Auntie Ashe), he also won 4 flat races with Fast Asleep (Vliko - Sleepless), and rode Solus to win 5 (including the Galway Blazers 'Chase) and Mrs Jiggs twice in 1925.

COLONEL JOHN WESTENRA, SHARAVOGUE HOUSE

He was MP for King's County from 1832-52 & served as a Steward for 6 consecutive years from 1830. He was only 30 when he became a Senior Steward in 1832 and on his way to being a great trainer and breeder. He was Champion owner 1834-1836, & 1838. He won races like the Royal Whip in 1834 with Thump (trainer W.Cleary), Angelsey Sts 1838 with Wirrestrew and in 1834 with Whim. Thump was also second to Birdcatcher in the Kildare Stakes in 1837. Colonel J.C.Westenra lived in Sharavogue House. His daughter married Robin Hastings who later became the Earl of Huntington. The Hastings were an English family from near Sherwood Forest and were reputed to be descended from Robin Hood. Huntington inherited the Westenra property through his marriage to Westenra's daughter and they lived at Sharavogue House where they kept hounds. Sharavogue House was burned during the War of Independence and the land was later divided.

The Peel Cup was inaugurated in 1819 and he won it with Freney in 1833 (it was over 4 miles). Freney (Roller-Promise) was the winner of 27 races and he stood at Sharavogue in 1853 and also Redwing (Skylark-Perdita), who won 5 races and sired the chaser The General the winner of 16 races, and Hazard won the Corinthian Stakes at The Curragh. He bred Welfare by Priam and raced other horses like Leprechaun, Hannibal, and Trouncer.

SMALL WINNERS AND SYNDICATES

A few small owners as representative of the many others to have a few winners in the area over the years were **Brendan Arthur,** Rochfortbridge who won with Rahanine Melody (Orchestra -Jim's Cousin) at Kilbeggan in July 1999. The horse won 5 of her 25 starts and bred some horses like City Saint John, Frankfort, City Music etc. Rahanine Native was another horse who won a few races when trained by John Bowles. **J.J. Barry,** Delvin, Co Westmeath in September 2006 at Galway gave a great quote after his filly Perfect Memory won under Kieran Fallon when he said *"I'm from the Main Street in Delvin, Co Westmeath. In fact it's the only street in Delvin".* **Major Reggie Bermingham** was very involved in racing and the local courses and his horse Sorrel was 2nd in the Irish Cesarewitch in 1957 and he had some wins with Diamond Page. **Fr Barney Maxwell's** family in Empor had some success with Empor Star who won at Leopardstown and Empor Cross who was trained by Noel Meade. **John & Nora Donnelly,** Moneygall had success with a chaser Jamalade in the 1990's trained by Victor Bowens and this year they won with Long Journey Home at Leopardstown. **Tom Geoghegan,** Ballymore, has a decent horse running in Mallards in Flight trained by Gavin Cromwell. She won a mare's handicap chase at the Punchestown Festival and was being aimed for the Midland's National at Kilbeggan.

Joe Sheridan Independent TD had success with his horse Adeste Celeste in the 1970's when trained by Peter McCreery. Another great vote catcher in Westmeath was TD and former Minister **Willie Penrose** who had some success from Ballintue Road to Mr Dickens, more recently successful at The Pigeons. **Captain H.A Gairdiner** who was associated with the Wallaces & Kenny's in the 1920's with horses like Fizz and prolific winner Georginstown, who ran in the Aintree Grand National. In that same era **Hugh Horan,** Secretary of the Birr Show won races with his horse Dairy Man. **James A. Barry,** Banagher won the Naas October Handicap with Astrom in 1938.

Hundreds of Syndicates were set up down the years even with the top trainers and some are mentioned in various article's in the book. I will briefly mention a few more at random as representative of something that changed racing and allowed many people who loved the sport to have a chance to own some part of a horse, even if it was only a few hairs on his back. The **Ballyboggan Syndicate** was set up by Tom Scanlon Hotel Owner, Kinnegad, Tom Fox, auctioneer, Pauric Conlon former jockey etc who owned the great Galway specialist My Valley, who won there on both Tuesday and Saturday in 2007. They only bought her 3 months before and she had already won at Ballinrobe. The **Bradawn Breezer Syndicate** came to the attention of racing in August 1991 when the Kevin Prendergast trained horse won the Heinz 57 Phoenix Stakes valued at €150,000. He was bought by Michael Murray, Walderstown, Drumraney, Athlone and Michael Kearney, Clonave, Ballymore for 10,000 guineas as a yearling. He had two wins and was placed in five other races. He was third at Royal Ascot and won in Leopardstown at 14/1. Around 20 people were in the syndicate. The winner's enclosure was invaded by well- wishers after the race among them RTE's Colm Murray. He used Ted Walsh's quote *"racing needs more ordinary folk involved"*.

Quare Times owned by Mrs Cecily Wellmann won the Aintree Grand National in 1955, ridden by Pat Taaffe and trained by Vincent O'Brien

The Kilbeggan Challenge Cup is won after 117 years in 1957. The presentation was made by Chairman Paul Dunican to Mr R.Ussher, who won it with Icelough

Mrs Elizabeth Dolan leading in the filly Fair Astronomer, owned by John Dolan, Farnagh Stud. She was the first 2 y/o to win in three countries in 1962 - France, Ireland & Britain

Kilmore was bred by Gilbert Webb and traced back to Brown Jack in the 1920's, also bred by the family. He won the Aintree Grand National in 1962

Paddy Murray, Head Lad with Tom Dreaper, seems to be chatting Arkle. He was from Moate, where he started out at the Farnagh Stud

Fort Leney was the winner of the 1968 Cheltenham Gold Cup. He was out of Jim Tormey's great mare Leney Princess

Michael Scott's Secret Vulgan beating Kinloch Brae in the Easter Chase at Fairyhouse in 1970

Cecil Ross the owner, trainer, and jockey of The Pooka, who ran in the Aintree Grand National in 1972

In September 1974, Ted Walsh was a leading amateur jockey when he rode the horse Undecided who drowned in Kilbeggan

Barney Curley

In 1976, Royal Frolic won the Cheltenham Gold Cup and he was bred by Frank Fagan at Gartlandstown Stud

Night Nurse being led after winning his second Champion Hurdle in 1977, defeating Monksfield. He was ridden by Mullingar Jockey Paddy Broderick

From L-R: Lady Nugent owner of Blue Doc who just gave Wally Swinburn the jockey his 100th winner on the flat in 1977, and Sir Hugh Nugent the trainer

Local Jockey Mary Davey, had his first winner at Kilbeggan in 1983 on Timona

The Middleton Park draw in 1984 on the stairway.
Front Row L-F: Tony Robinson, Michael O'Hehir, Finian O'Brien, Kevin Deegan,
Centre Row: J.J.Gannon, Joe Leonard, Gilbert Carey, Tony Linnane, Sean McManus,
Sean McGee, Back Row: Martin Linnane and Ger Gannon

In June 1995, a young 21 y/o jockey called Anthony McCoy did his chances of getting the No 1 job at Martin Pipe's Pond House Stable no harm, when winning his first Irish chase aboard Crogeen Lass (4/1) by 7 lengths, for local Midland's trainer P.J.Casserley.

The great Vaguely Noble conqueror of Sir Ivor

Martin Brennan and Owen Brennan (his father) on the right, with 12 time winner Vulrory's Clown

The winner L'Escargot (T.Carberry) and French Tan (Pat Taaffe), jump the last fence in the 1970 Cheltenham Gold Cup

Kilbeggan Stand in the early 1950's

At Galway races in 1925 From Left to Right: jockey C.Donnelly, trainer Cecil Brabazon, Frank Barbour, Misses M & E.Barbour nieces of Frank, and Mrs Barbour

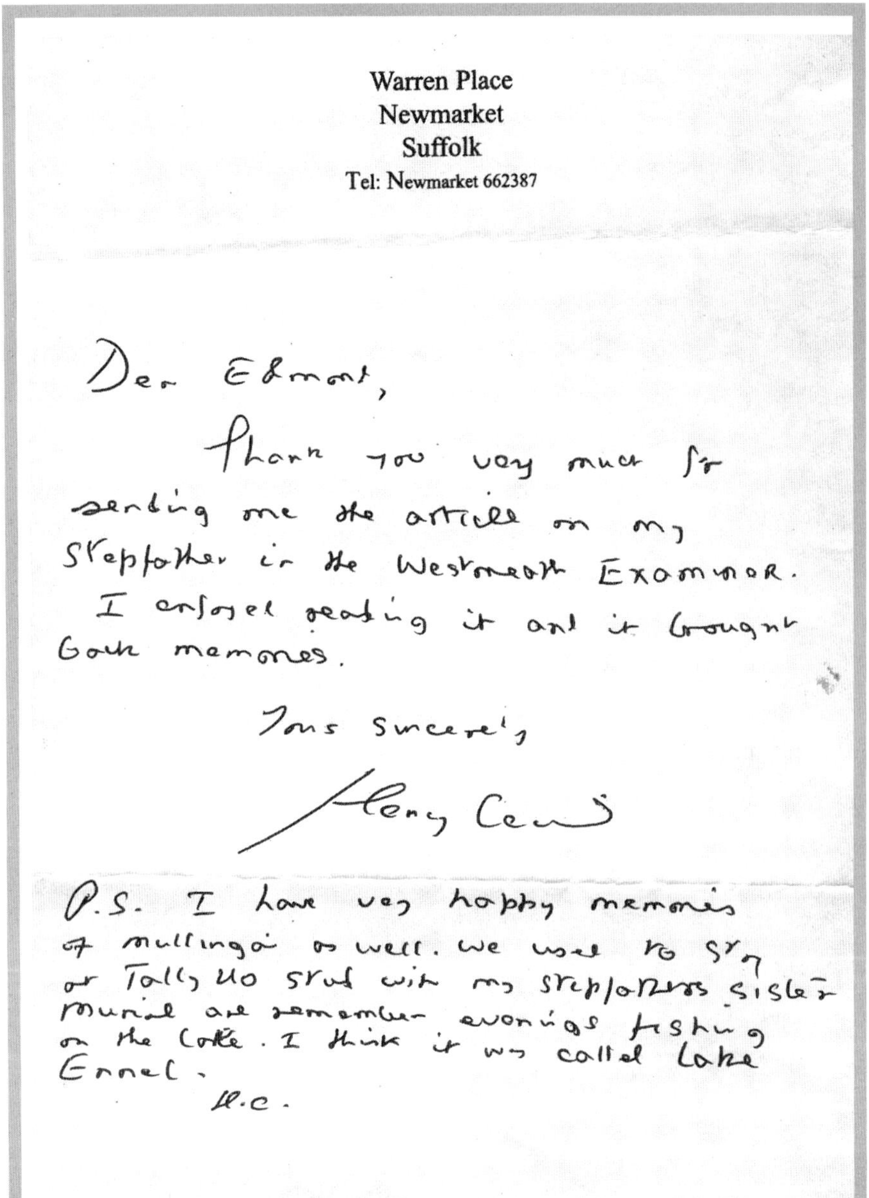

Warren Place
Newmarket
Suffolk
Tel: Newmarket 662387

Dear Edmond,

Thank you very much for sending me the article on my stepfather in the Westmeath Examiner. I enjoyed reading it and it brought back memories.

Yours sincerely,

Henry Cecil

P.S. I have very happy memories of Mullingar as well. We used to stay at Tally Ho stud with my stepfather's sister Muriel and remember evenings fishing on the lake. I think it was called Lake Ennel.

H.C.

A letter from Henry Cecil to Ted Bourke about his time in Mullingar, where he was very fond of Mrs Bourke's cooking

chapter 9
IRISH GRAND NATIONAL TALES

The jockey John Boylan won the Irish Grand National for its first two years in 1870/71, but tragically, he was killed at Killarney and never got the opportunity to do the treble. He was posthumously crowned champion jockey in 1871, a unique but sad event. In the second year there was a success for the midlands with Tom Kirkwood's, Woodbrook, Carrick-on-Shannon, horse The Doe 10/1, who was saved from the knacker's yard and paid back the price of 5 shillings in full with her win! Kirkwood raced his horses in Roscommon and Westmeath in this era. The Doe went on to breed his 1881 Aintree Grand National winner Woodbrook, trained by Henry Eyre Linde and another good chaser Usna, who was killed during Aintree Grand National after a great career, including a double success in the Prince of Wales Stakes at Punchestown. He also bred good horses like Paddy Maher winner of the Conyngham Cup 1908, Sugar Plum in 1882 and Apollo Belvedere in 1907, both won the Galway Plate. The White Knight, who won 10 races for Kirkwood and W. Wyndham the co-owner, including the Ascot Gold Cup twice, the Goodwood Cup, the Coronation Cup twice etc. He was not well-bred and was described as an ugly foal. His success saved the estate at a time when creditors were pursuing the family. Westmeath horses like Brabazon's Little Annie and Sir Walter Nugent's Clonave ran in the Irish National in this era without making much impact and the horse who dominated the race was J.H.Moore's Scots Grey who won in 1872 and 1875. In 1878, the Sir Walter Nugent's Westmeath owned Kiltoom (Haymaker-Rivulet) came with a late run in the race but failed to catch the 3/1 favourite Juggler by 3 lengths. Michael Dennehy, French Furze, The Curragh trained many of his good horses. Sir Walter Nugent was married to Maria, only daughter of a Richard More O'Farrell, another racing figure.

The closest Westmeath came to victory in the big race was Peter Nugent Fitzgerald's New Meadow (Haymaker-Souvenir) in 1884 where he attempted to slip the field before being caught on the line by The Gift. Fitzgerald was connected with the Mullingar racecourse and he kept a pack at Soho and the family bred Why Not winner of the Aintree Grand National in 1894. He was ridden by Westmeath amateur Robert Brabazon (1858-91), who was a brother of William Thomas (father of Cecil & Leslie Brabazon) and he shared the jockey's title in 1884. He lived at New Meadow House, Mullingar and presumably that is how the horse got his name. New Meadow 4/1 went on to lead all the way in the Galway Plate in 1884 and win by ten lengths. The horse was sent to England to compete in the Grand National, but broke a fetlock before the race and was put down. Brabazon won twice at Galway in 1887 on J.F.Brabazon's Gentle Annie (who won 23 races) and she was by Little Annie who won 18 chases between 1871 and 1874. The same year Brabazon rode G.F. Gradwell's Eglantine 4/1 to win the Irish Grand National and she was the dam of Drogheda winner of the Grand National and Galway Plate.

In 1890, the very popular favourite Greek Girl ridden by Harry Beasley beat Westmeath man W. Coghlan's Lochinvar (Lothario-Eileen Ogue) by six lengths. In 1891, Jimmy Cleary's Perfection (Pride of Prussia-White Rose) ridden by J.Hogan was only beaten 3/4 length in the race by Firewater. In 1892, Larry Hope rode S.A.Leonard's Springfield Maid to win the Irish Grand National and later in the year the horse won the Galway Plate. Hope was part of a family of which two branches of the family from around the Delvin area in Westmeath were associated with Grand National winners Drumcree 1903 and Ally Sloper 1915. Hope went on train Princess Hilda and Mavis of Meath to win the Irish Grand National. In 1893 Jimmy Cleary's horse Gondolier (Rhidorroch-Vivandierre) was second to Thurles the favourite in the big race. On the same day the Offaly bred Red Prince II (Richard Bull), won the Lancashire Chase and later was the sire of Red Lad winner of Irish Grand National).

THE ADMIRAL, THE KING, THE PRIEST AND THE WESTMEATH CONNECTION

National Hunt Racing in Ireland has produced many great equine stars like Arkle and Dawn Run, who aside from being great horses were loved by the people. Towards the end of the 19th century, Westmeath produced such a star in the form of a horse called The Admiral who became so famous that the future King of England Edward VII asked for a photograph of him, after the horse retired in 1899. The reason The Admiral was so famous was that he won 54 races under National Hunt rules and recorded another 25 wins in smaller races. No horse since then has beaten that record.

Fr Hegarty, Delvin, Co Westmeath bred the horse in 1884. He was by Young Toxophilite with a dam by Kildonan. The then unnamed horse was brought by him to Mullingar Fair on 6th April 1888 to be sold, but nobody was interested. Mr R.S.Fethersonhaugh from a great Westmeath racing family was friendly with the priest and he sent a message to Frank Mitchell, Tubberclair, Mullingar, the great trainer and jockey to come and look at the horse. Fr. Hegarty asked for £20 for the horse and Frank offered £15. The priest being a sport said, *"I'll divide five"*. Frank said *"I'll take him but what about the luck penny"*. The priest gave him 5 shillings but Frank replied, *"Shure your reverence would not soil my hand with that"*. *"Right"* said the priest *"we'll toss ten shillings or nothing"*. Up went the coin and Frank won. The horse was sold for exactly £17. The horse was originally called *The Curate* but Fr Hegarty had some objections, so Frank asked him to name the horse. The priest suggested calling him *The Admiral* and that became his name. When called *The Curate,* he won at the Rathowen Races in February 1889 as a five year old.

In 1888 he commenced his career running in races, which were recognised by the National Hunt Steeplechase Committee and were generally known as *"£4 19 shilling races"* and they were for young horses to get experience. Once they ran in races under the proper National Hunt rules they could no longer run in these small races. He won races at Dalystown, Culleen, Multyfarnham, etc eventually winning a total of 25 races at this level.

In his first race under proper rules, he won the Meath's Sportsmen's Farmers Light Weight Race worth 20/= ridden by Mr J.Seery. Frank Mitchell's father did not approve of racing as he was a farmer and considered it a luxury. However Frank Mitchell rode him to victory at Athboy and after he got a cheque for £70 his father became more interested in Frank's career as a trainer and jockey, and even invested 2/= on the horse, when he won in Mullingar. Between 1889 and 1897, when he recorded the last of his 54 wins, the horse had won from Westport across to Baldoyle & Dundalk and from Listowel to Enniskillen, and from Athenry to Inchicore. In June 1891, he won the last race at Dundalk and the next day won the second race at Birr. The horse was raced on a regular basis but he remained very sound even though he is said to have run 158 times.

A VERY CLEVER ADMIRAL

At that time the only means of travel was by train, as he did not have the luxury of a horsebox. One newspaper account stated that the horse was so used to trains that it was normal procedure to put him in the guards van on the train and tell the guard to let him off at the station nearest the racecourse, where he would find his own way to the racecourse. It's a good story but not true. Michael Geraghty, Killucan informed me that what really happened was that Frank removed the bridle after the race and The Admiral would find his way to the railway station and would be in his box when Frank was ready to leave. When Mickey Rock the lad brought him to the station and took off his bridle in the stable yard, he would wait until the horse boxes came, then he would make straight for the entrance to the platform himself and walk into the first empty box. When coming off the train in Mullingar he walked down the six steps outside along with all the other passengers. One night after coming home from another success in Loughrea young Rock left him with another lad, but he whipped round and jumped away and made his own way home to Tubberquill, which was 6 miles away. When he got to the gate he whinneyed and Mrs Mitchell had to come out to let him into his stable. He was very fond of apples and eggs and he often took apples out of Frank Mitchell's pocket. The horse travelled so much (sometimes running 3 or 4 times per week) that the great breeder and trainer J.J.Maher once said to Mitchell that *"You have a very easy way of training The Admiral". "What do you mean"* said Frank *"Well"* said Maher *"in horseboxes". "Is that so"* said Frank *"Well, I may tell you sir that there are plenty of horses trained on The Curragh and they don't win as many races".*

IRISH GRAND NATIONAL 1894 - "MR MITCHELL'S SLAVE"

Many of the races won by The Admiral were small races and in 1892 he ran 20 times between February and November, but he won the sum of £275-5s, which was a considerable sum and most of the time he was ridden by Frank Mitchell. However, he showed in 1894 that he also had the ability to win at the highest level when he won the Irish Grand National at Fairyhouse. Greek Girl the winner of the Irish Grand National in 1890 was 6/4 favourite and The Admiral was 8/1. He took up the running about halfway and was never caught to win from J. Cleary's Ravenwood and another well-known Westmeath horse Mr L.Yourell's Bass ridden by Ballynacarrigy's James Yourell. Bass was obviously as healthy as The Admiral, as he ran in an incredible 30 races in 1894 and won 10 times. When asked to describe his ride in the Grand National, Frank Mitchell said he intended to ride a waiting race *"but bang went the spring of the saddle and I got a hold of my leather and iron and he got a hold of me. He pulled me to the front and we were never caught".*

The Admiral raced from 5 years to 15 years and was commonly called *"Mr Mitchell's slave".* He only fell once in his career, when he slipped on a wet day in Mullingar when ridden by Bob Brabazon. He ran in the Galway Plate in 1895 and in one of his races at Dundalk he was beaten by The Soarer, who won the Aintree Grand National in 1896. His last win was at Enniskillen in 1897 and he ran his last race in Athlone in 1899 before being retired to the farm at Robinstown near Mullingar. He lived until he was 30 years old and was buried in a corner at the old training quarters at Tubberquill.

KING EDWARD VII

Albert Edward, Prince of Wales and the future King Edward VII was heir apparent to the throne for longer than anyone else in history due to the reign of Queen Victoria. He was known throughout his life as a playboy and sportsman before he ascended on to the throne in January 1901. He was also the most successful member of the Royal Family in terms of winning major horse races, as he won the Epsom Derby with Persimmon in 1896 (even as The Admiral was racing in Ireland) and in 1900 he won the Aintree Grand National with Ambush II a horse he ran in Ireland a number of times. When he was Prince of Wales he asked Major Fethersonhaugh, the Kings stud future racing manager, for a photograph of The Admiral. The Prince knew a lot about the career of The

Admiral, as Frank Mitchell had been over in England visiting the Royal Stud and he had spoken to the Prince about the horse. Frank sent a photograph of the horse to the Prince and received back a personal letter thanking him for it. The Prince attended Leopardstown & Baldoyle races when he was in Ireland. When coming to Leopardstown races he sent word to the stewards that he wanted to meet with Frank Mitchell. He had a long chat with Frank owing to the deeds of the great horse.

Frank Mitchell died in 1938 at the age of 77 and it's said his only regret was that he did not hold out for the Fairyhouse Grand National meeting, which he attended for over 50 years. He trained other good horses like Attractor, which won 34 races including 18 in England (4 for Frank Mitchell and 14 for Captain W.H.Lambton who bought him for £1,000). Oddly, a number of his horses that he ran in the 1890's had names starting with the letter "A"- Alfred, Ambrose, Amy etc. The Admiral may not have been the greatest chaser ever, but he won the hearts of many because of his courage, bravery and ability to win. He started with a priest and he finished winning the heart of a king. Not many horses or trainers achieved as much as The Admiral and Frank Mitchell in their long careers.

MAVIS OF MEATH AND F.J. KELLY

In 1896, the race was won by Gustavus Briscoe, Ballinter,with Royston- Crow 6/1 beating Captain Bob Dewhurst's favourite Breemount Oak. The Briscoe's and Brabazon association was to deliver many years of success. In 1899, Larry Hope owned & trained Princess Hilda (Brown Prince-Brunhilda) to win the race beating the unfortunate Captain Dewhurst's Morning Dawn. He was based at Clongiffen, Enfield and was a jockey, trainer, breeder, and farmer, with owners from a wide area around the midlands. In 1900, he repeated the success with F.J.Kelly's Mavis of Meath (Marmiton-Miss Rattle), ridden very well by Mullingar jockey James Kelly (23y/o). The horse carried 12st 12lbs & was 5/2 JF, which was a weight carrying record, which will never be beaten. He had other good horses like Silver Dart, Mistigris, Johnstown Lass (won at Punchestown in 1901), Tempo Bello (Punchestown 1908) and Cadamstown Lad. F.J.Kelly also owned Cathal, which was 2nd in the Grand National at Aintree in 1898. He was married twice and died in 1915 and is buried in Johnstown Cemetery. He also trained and rode Westmeath (Deodar out of Ascetic), which was originally owned by C.Hannan, Killucan. As an unbeaten 4y/o he was sold to Fred Leyland, London for £2,000 for whom he finished 5th in the 1897 Aintree National. When Mavis of Meath won the maiden plate at Punchestown in 1899 he was ridden by another jockey with Westmeath connections in Tom Dowdall.

PAT LANDER AND BOREENCHREOGUE

In 1901, W.T. Brabazon made a valiant attempt to win the National with Honeymoon II who was second to the great Tipperary Boy in 1901 and third to M.J.Cleary's Patlander (Sir Patrick-Theodora II) in 1902. He was a 39 y/o vet and a brother of Dick Cleary. He owned a horse called Hayden the year that Orby won the Epsom Derby in 1907 for Richard "Boss" Croker. Cleary from Kilpatrick, Streamstown, sold him for 2,500gns to Croker. He was bred in Westmeath by M.C.Ballesty by his sire Avidity out of Cleary's Langour. The horse won a Baldoyle and was 2nd in the Norbury Plate at Epsom. Hayden was bought as a pacemaker for Croker's Orby in a number of races, rather than racing on his merits. He had other horses like Annie Joy, Errigal and Ballywirra. The sire Sir Patrick was by Ascetic, who had many good horses like Aubrey Hastings Grand National winner Ascetic Silver and Drumcree plus the highly rated Leinster and Royal Meath. He had two attempts to win the Grand National and also challenged for the Grand Steeplechase de Paris, without success before breaking down. His jockey and trainer was James Cheshire who was originally from Monaghan, but he had his stables in Mullingar town up to 1900 stretching from St Mary's College to where the Post Office is now. He trained for Eddie Shaw and other locals. Anthony Cleary leased the stables to James Kelly and he had an Agriculture store there (apparently he had about 10 stalls with three horses in each stall). According to the Westmeath Examine, Cheshire was in Mount Druid, Castletown-Geoghegan before in January 1901.

His other major success as a trainer /jockey was with Boreenchreogue (Marmiton-Barberstown) in the Galway Plate in 1898, where he defeated Chevy Chase by a length. The horse was sold to England in 1899 by his owner Tom Cleary, Hightown, Killucan, even though he had been trained to compete in the Aintree Grand National. He had won six of his seven races that year and had great potential. After winning the Galway Plate he won at Baldoyle in September and a handicap at Leopardstown on St Stephen's Day. After negotiations, he was sold for 1,100gns.The horse finished 3rd in Cheltenham and his only significant win was in the Spring Handicap Chase and after injury he was never the same. His name was reduced to Boreen during his English career. Rapier writing in *"Illustrated Sporting & Dramatic News"* in 1905 wrote about him running for the last time in January 1905 in a race where the winner was sold for 50 pounds. The sad end of a horse destined for greatness. Tom Cleary died in January 1900 after a long illness. James Cheshire suffered many injuries which contributed to his retirement. In October 1899 there was a presentation to him in Cleary's Auction Room after his racing accident by all the racing people.

In 1904, Ascetic Silver won the Irish National ridden by Thomas Dowdall and beating Mr E.Taaffes Le Petit Pere, ridden by Longford jockey Johnny Lynn. Later he was bought for 850 guineas by Aubrey Hastings to win one of the four Aintree

Grand Nationals he captured.

LORD RIVERS 1908

The hot favourite for the Irish Grand National in 1908 was Lord Rivers (Riverstown), who was bred and owned by P.McLoughlin, Stonehall Farm. The hot favourite in the race was Moorside II 1/1, but he fell and Lord Rivers 10/1, who had won previously ran on to beat an old rival Harry Whitworth's Excelite (Red Prince II-Exe) by two lengths. Whitworth was Master of the Westmeath Hunt and he won the Irish Derby in 1920 with He Goes. Lord Rivers continued to win races in Ireland and later won the Champion Chase at Aintree. In 1912, four years after his victory at Fairyhouse he beat Excelite again at Kempton Park. Pat McLoughlin also had Rosy Symons (General Symons-Rosy May II), which went on to be second in two consecutive Galway Plates in 1908 to Shady Girl and in 1909 to Schwarmer. The McLoughlin's had other good winners like Lord D, Cooldrea, Stonehall and Pleasant Surprise, who was unplaced in the 1909 Grand National to Little Hack II, but won seven races subsequently before being unplaced to Schwarmer. Another horse bred by the McLoughlin's was Dysart (Bealderg-dam by Gay Reveller), which was even money favourite for the 1911 Irish Grand National. The horse had won in Mullingar and won the King's Cup the previous year therefore he liked the course and distance. The McLoughlin's had sold the horse to Captain H.Chippindall Higgin, Rathoath, and in a very competitive race, Dysart was beaten by the J.A.Trench ridden Repeater II. Trench was long associated with East Galway, but he had a close link to racing in Offaly. Tom Killian's Koepnicker ridden by Leslie Brabazon and Lady Symon's II were both unplaced in the race. Patrick McLoughlin died in April 1927 aged 60 y/o and was remembered as a notable breeder and sportsman. Dermot McLoughlin was later a point to point rider and the family continued to be involved with horses. A Joseph McLoughlin, Glascorn, Westmeath went to Argentina in the 19th century and became one of the founding members of the Mercedes Racing Club in San Jose.

Aside from the success of Lord Rivers, Riverstown's daughter Lady Rivers won ten steeplechases between the ages of four and six, and was later the dam of several winners of steeplechases and hurdles, including Lord Marcus, who won the Grand International and Grand Allies steeplechase. Riverstown's daughter Riversaint was a very good chaser, winning the Irish Grand Military in 1907. Riverstown also got many hunters and horses presented at various shows, including Easter Egg a winner of many championships and gold and silver medals between 1907 and 1910.

In 1911 Marcus Halligan, who was jockey to Pat McLoughlin that year was not as lucky, as his horse Simple Paddy bolted in the race won by Oniche. A Westmeath victory was foiled in 1912 by Reggie Walker's Small Polly, as she held off James Yourell's Lady Symon's by 1/2 length with Tom Killian's Shaun na Scaub back in third.

ALL SORTS WALKS HOME AFTER THE EASTER RISING 1916

As we approach the 100th anniversary of the Easter Rising, a small event that occurred in the background of history in Dublin on that faithful day in Irish history is generally forgotten. The Irish Grand National proceeded as normal at Fairyhouse (Civil War was a runner). One horse in the race had a full Westmeath background as James Kiernan, Dysart, owned All Sorts (Avidity-Piersfield mare), who was trained by one of the leading trainers Dick Cleary, Bishopstown Stud. The jockey was John Lynn from just across the border in Longford, who had been associated with Larry Hopes, Enfield stable, which also had strong Westmeath connections. Avidity (won 11 races) was bred by Sir John B.Maple by his sire Minting and owned by Michael Ballesty, Rathconrath Stud, who stood two successful sires in Avidity & Bergomask in this era. The dam of All Sorts had bred other winners like Lannigan's Ball & Pipers Hill and it was said *"she was out of a plain little pony,who had scored in a few £4-19s races".*

All Sorts had won his previous four races and was only 5/1 behind favourite Ballyneety. Punch & All Sorts pulled away from the rest and the latter galloped on to win by 12 lengths with Conyngham Cup winner Ruddygore third. We are used to major celebrations on TV and all through the night after a horse wins the Irish Grand National, but All Sorts reward for his victory was that he had to walk home from Fairyhouse over 60 miles taking several days to get to Streamstown, as all trains had been stopped due to the Easter Rising. As we shall see elsewhere the Cleary family contributed very much to Irish Racing and to sport in Westmeath, but it is worth recalling how they celebrated when another of his good horses Dunadry (a full brother to Lisnalinchey) won a £500 race at Leopardstown in 1918, when he beat Antipater and the remarkable Golden Fleece. Because they were held in high esteem friends and neighbours gathered at Skehana Hill and lit a huge bonfire to celebrate the victory dancing, recitations, and songs were the order of the evening and the family did not expect it, but they later entertained all at their home. All Sorts went on to be second in the race to Pay Only in 1917 and Ballyboggan in 1918 and was ridden by three different jockey's (Lynn, Mr T. O'Roarke and T.Carberry). James Kiernan also owned Mask On who won the Conyngham Cup in 1921,when trained by Cecil Brabazon.

All Sorts looked like winning at the last fence in 1918 but was caught by another Westmeath horse in Ballyboggan (Frustrum-Gentle Annie) 1/1F. He was trained by Bob Fetherstonhaugh one of the most successful Westmeath trainers, both on the flat and over jumps. E.W.Hope Johnstone was the owner and nephew of the renowned rider with the same name. He became Master of the Westmeath Hunt in 1913 and was married three times and once to Gussie Briscoes daughter (he won the Grand National in 1896 with Royston Crow). He owned other good horses like Ischevaha, Rising Moon, Callaly who was 2nd in the Irish National in 1938, and Mr Georgie. When the Land Commission acquired Fetherstonhaugh's lands in Carrick, Mullingar he moved to The Curragh and won two more Irish Grand Nationals with Dog Fox & Copper Court. Ballyboggan was a high class chaser who went on to win the Leopardstown Chase and was second in the Grand National in 1919 to Poethlyn. In 1925 Bob Fetherstonhaugh had his second success with Dog Fox who had been off the course for a few years with injury was still backed at 8/1. He was ridden by Joe Doyle, whose father and four brothers were all jockeys in this era. Other horses with Westmeath connections in the race were Easter Hero, Halston, Rathdrin, J.Kiernan's Mask On (Conyngham Cup winner 1921), Barretstown and E. Hope Johnston's Rising Moon. After the race Malcolm Arnott trainer of the latter, complained about his weight of 11stone 4lbs and amazingly the Steward'a agreed that the handicapper was *"too hard".* The horse went on to win five handicap's in a row before being fatally injured (It would be interesting to know the thoughts of the handicapper?).

In 1932, Fetherstonhaugh had his third win with Copper Court, who was by Goldcourt the sire of the great Golden Miller. The previous year, Charlie Rogers trained Impudent Barney to win the Grand National for Mrs B.M. Webster, but when that horse was injured they bought Copper Court, who was trained by Fetherstonhaugh. It was decided to leave the horse with him until after the race and then move him to Roger's stable. He ended up 2/1F carrying a nice weight of 10st 9lbs and in a close race beat Southern Hero and Red Park by 2 lengths and 1 length. The following year, Mrs Webster was foiled of a three timer by Red Park with her two horses Copper Court and Coolinolagh second & third. Copper Court went on to win at Mullingar. Ironically, it was Red Park the horse who was third to Copper Court the previous year that won the race. Copper Court competed again in 1934 before going to England where he was killed in a fall. Fetherstonhaugh also had the second J.A.Shaw's favourite Little Clifter in 1926, when the race was won by Amberwave.

HALSTON NATIONAL HERO

J.J. Ham, Halston, Moyvore (died 1945) purchased imported American mare Chimura and from her bred Halston (b 1912 by Bealderg). She was standing at Dan Kiernan's, Balrath Stud in Westmeath. Gay Reveller was injured in July 1905 and had to be put down. He had produced many champions and it was a great loss to Mr Kiernan. Cissy Gay by Gay Reveller won over 50 races. Dysart, P.McLoughlins Cooldreen' Rathcore, plus Gay & Sweet were other regular winners in this era bred by him.

Halston made his debut in the 1917 Ward Union Hunt Cup at Fairyhouse for owner-trainer T.P. Tyrrell, finished second in the 1918, and then won the National Hunt Cup at Punchestown. He was entered to be sold for £150 or more and was purchased for £440 by Major Herbert Dixon, who sent him to his private trainer Jack Ruttle. In 1920, he won the Irish Grand National and at Leopardstown at Christmas. In the Grand National he was 4/1 but raced clear in the straight to win by 12 lengths for trainer Jack Ruttle. In 1922, he won the Leopardstown 'Chase, a second Irish National (under 12st 11lb including a 5 lb claim) and Punchestown's Conyngham Cup (under 13st 5lb), his only starts. He was 100/8 to win in 1922, as two other horses with Westmeath connections were favourites Bob Fetherstonhaugh's Frances Brown and Dick Cleary's Doon Rossa. Giving nearly a stone to Frances Brown didn't stop Halston racing away after jumping the last fence to win by 6 lengths. As a veteran in 1924, he still managed to finish 4th to Kilbarry carrying 12stone 7 lbs, and as a 13y/o Halston finished third in the 1925 Irish National, conceding 33lb to the winner, Dog Fox.

Cecil Brabazon one of the most successful trainers in this era won the Irish National in 1921 with Archie Willis's Bohernore, with Dick Cleary having yet another second with Greenogue. The favourite was Frank Barbour's Fly Rose at 7/4. In his book Racing Through My Mind Aubrey Brabazon explained that his father had not booked a jockey but managed to get Danny Colbert to ride the winner. In addition they forgot about a babysitter for baby Aubrey, so they had to bring him to the races for his first Grand National. John McNeill jockey on Greeneogue objected to the winner, but it was overruled.

PIGG AND HAM

J.J.Ham also bred a horse called James Pigg (Bealderg-Gweebara), who was to be runner up in the 1923 Grand National. Tom Tyrrell who had lost out on Halston some years before bought him from Ham and trained the horse for the big race. He won the Ward Union Cup race before Fairyhouse and apparently, Tyrrell backed the horse to win £40,000 (his starting price was 6/1). It ended up as a two horse race with Jack Maloney getting up in a desperate finish to win by a head on outsider Be Careful and foil the great gamble. It would have been remarkable if J.J.Ham had three Grand National winners in such a brief period, but as we shall see he was not finished with the race, as he was to breed his third winner of the race in 1947 leading to great *"revelry"* at Halston. However, tragedy was to strike the family before that joyous occasion.

Mervyn Ham, son of J.J. Ham of Halston was tragically killed at Punchestown in April1930 (Age 27), when he fell in the La Touche Plate. He was a well know jockey from Mullingar to Punchestown & on the point to point scene. He was riding Mr Downes Carrigeenroe in a 4 mile chase. J.J.Bergin at the inquest said that the horse fell on his head and H.N. Nugent helped to lift the animal off him.

He died within a half hour. Dr Roantree said the deceased died from compression of the brain. Howard Clarke, Secretary of the Turf Club expressed his sympathy to the family and also Sir Bryan Malone, of the Punchestown Executive. Mervyn Ham had been associated with a racing stud kept by an uncle in France. He was buried in Milltown Cemetery and immense crowds attended because of the tragedy with many of the great racing families from Westmeath and nationally, in attendance.

J.J. Ham bred Revelry (Rejoice-Amy Gay), who was owned by the former rugby international Jack Doyle and supposedly trained by Dick O'Connell to win the 1947 Irish Grand National. The problem was that Dan Moore was still riding as a professional jockey and he had to be either a jockey or a trainer. Dick O'Connell was his Head Lad and the training licence was in his name. Rejoice the sire of Revelry stood in Westmeath & was by April the Fifth the Derby winner. He was purchased for only 26gns as 2 y/o by T.Leavy, who sold him at Ballsbridge in 1944 for 260gns to Lord Harrington. He was broken and schooled by Mr Leavy. Harrington sent him to Vincent Hartigan to train. He got plenty of experience in point to points and was unbeaten. He won the National Hunt chase at Navan and the maiden plate at Punchestown, where he was ridden by Dan Moore for the first time. Lord Harrington rode him in his last 2 races & hoped to go to Aintree, but was offered a substantial sum, said to be £10,000 and he sold him. He was unplaced in the Leopardstown Chase and then ran in the Aintree Grand National in 1947 but became unsighted and fell with Dan Moore on board. His next race was the Irish Grand National when Dan Moore, who had injured his neck in the fall, rode the horse with his neck in plaster and made all the running to win. He was the second favourite at 6/1 and beat Leopardstown Chase winner Cloncarrig. Doyle sold him to J.A. Clarke and he was sent to Fulke Walwyn, Lambourn, where he finished 12th of 43 in the 1948 Aintree Grand National. J.J.Ham had made a significant impact in the history of the Irish Grand National with Halston, Revelry and James Pigg, but he also had horses like Springfield, Kingfisher, etc who won races for him over the years.

DON SANCHO AND TOM O'ROARKE 1928

Don Sancho (Succoth-Woodbine) was bred by Tom O'Roarke who was breeder, owner and jockey (he rode All Sorts to be second to Pay Only in the 1917 Irish Grand National) and as a promising young horse he was sold for a four figure sum to Vivian H.Smith, who was later to become Lord Bicester owner of high class horses like Silver Fame, Royal Approach and Roimond. He was sent over from England by his trainer Fred Withington and carried top weight of 12st 1lb, but under a good ride from T.B.Cullinan he got up to win by a length. Cullinan is still the only jockey to win the Grand National, Gold Cup, and Champion Hurdle the same year with Shaun Goilin, Easter Hero and Brown Tony. In 1930, Don Sancho won the National Hunt Chase at Cheltenham his only other major success. He once ran at Haydock two days in a row but fell both times. Tom O'Roarke rode Awbeg to win the Conyngham Cup in 1917 and the same year he finished third in the Galway Plate on Awbeg to two good horses like Privit & Golden Fleece. He was in a four way tie with Cecil Brabazon, Hugh Delmege and. H.C.Alexander for the Irish Amateur title in 1922. He also had the notable distinction of running a mother and daughter at the same time and in 1937 Lady Barney and her daughter Battling Lady won eight races between them. Lady Barney (Martin Lightfoot-Lady May) ran in three Irish Nationals and twice finishing eight. She was a full sister to Double Cross and Jack McNeill was her regular rider. She had her first race as an 8 y/o in Longford and won her maiden at Leopardstown as a 9 y/o. At the Galway Festival in 1938, Battling Lady was 2nd in the Corrib Plate and 3rd in Stewards Plate. Tom & Joe O'Roarke worked in the Clonaboy Stud. The O'Roarkes had great success with Irish Battle bred horses in the 1930's, Forbidden Battle, Cool Battle, Irish Eve etc. Paddy M. O'Roarke was also an amateur rider and point to pointer, who had some success and was very much involved in developing racing in Westmeath. On one occasion he won at Ballinrobe with Southern Gale and his uncle T.Tynan also won with Collogen. At Leopardstown in December 1924 H.J.Kenny's good horse Hy Many was not able to run, as apparently there was foul play at O'Roarke's stable near Mullingar, when the horse was slashed around the legs with a sharp instrument and it was investigated. Paddy had a fall in Mullingar when his girths broke and he fell over a horse and got injured. He went back to collect his whip and couldn't remember and ended up going to hospital in a car. He had a mark for years where he was he was injured. There was plenty of rough riding in that era.

In 1934, Sir James Nelson won the Irish Grand National with Poolgowran (Tangiers-Vin de Grave). The full story of the family is told elsewhere but this home bred 5 year old with a light weight proved too quick on the run in and won at 8/1. He was ridden by Australian Bob Everett whose family had a connection with the Nelson's through aviation in the 1930's. Due to leg problems, like many previous Irish Grand National winners, Poolgowran never reproduced the same form again (4th in 1935 to Rathfriland whose only subsequent win was at Mullingar). His horse Owen Mor a winner at Mullingar was third in the 1938 race to Clare County. In 1937 Cecil Brabazon trained G.V. Malcolmson's Pontet to win at 3/1F beating Lough Cottage and future Aintree winner Workman (1939). He was also third to Shaun Peel in 1939.

In 1942, one of the great Irish Nationals took place with Tom Dreaper's greatest horse before Arkle and appropriately called Prince Regent (T.Hyde) 5/2F carrying 12st 7lbs, as a 7 y/o, against Dorothy Paget's 7 y/o Golden Jack (D.L.Moore) 11st 9lbs trained by Charlie Rogers, and Miss M.Mathison's 9 y/o St Martin (A.Brabazon) 12 stone. St Martin won the Galway Plate and Red Cross

Chase in 1941 and Golden Jack won the Plate in 1942, in addition to winning the Irish National in 1943. Prince Regent was only able to compete in the Gold Cup for the first time in 1946 due to the war and duly won it. In the Grand National as a veteran he was 3rd in 1946 to Lovely Cottage carrying 12st 5lbs and in 1947 was 4th to Caughoo at Aintree carrying 12st 7lbs, when well past his best. Most of this information was not available when these three horses met at Fairyhouse. Three great horses with three great jockeys jumped the last almost together and in a thrilling battle Prince Regent got home from Golden Jack by 1 length with St Martin 1 1/2 lengths behind. Aubrey Brabazon often said that St Martin was the best horse he rode although eventually admitting that three-time Gold Cup winner Cottage Rake was the best, in his autobiography. The Brabazon's may not have won this Irish Grand National but it will not be forgotten. The only other success for Westmeath was T.P.Downes breeding success with his Golden View II in 1948.

JACK CHAUCER AND THE BUS THAT DEPARTED WITHOUT LARRY EGAN

When World War II started in 1939 it was not clear that racing would continue in Ireland. It was provisionally agreed to proceed after discussions between the Government and the racing authorities. Given what was happening around the world it was extraordinary that the most valuable chase ever run in Ireland took place in January 1940. It was the Red Cross Handicap Chase over four miles at Leopardstown. It was sponsored jointly by the Irish Red Cross and the Hospital's Trust and the race was worth £2,610 to the winner. It was won easily by the favourite Jack Chaucer (Jackdaw of Rheims- Miss Chaucer who was by Tanglewood out of Clovilly) in the pouring rain. He won by 2 lengths from Sir Alexander Maguires Sterling Duke and Knockadroleen. Jimmy Brogan was due to ride West Point who met with an accident, which put him out of the race and Parkinson was due to ride Jack Chaucer, but he became ill and Brogan by default got the mount. He won at 4/1F with an attendance said to be around 20,000. He was trained by Westmeath man Cecil Brabazon. Jackdaw of Rheims was 13th of 15 in the Irish Derby in 1923 but went on to breed Jack Chaucer, in addition to Alice Maythorn winner of the Irish Grand National 1936 and Silent Prayer, who won the Galway Plate. Larry Egan bought the horse for £300 in 1937 from C.Malone and apparently he did not even canter until he was 6 y/o and he refused £2,000 for the horse in 1939. His first win was at Mallow in November 1938, then Mullingar, and he won a chase at Fairyhouse beating Dorothy Paget's Le Cynge.

The owner was H.L. (Larry) Egan of Egan's Bottling, Wholesale, and Retail Merchants, Tullamore and his colours were royal blue and yellow'. He controlled the family firm and had some success in horse racing for a few years. There was a huge crowd at the races. The book *"Racing Through My Mind"* about the life of Aubrey Brabazon recalls that Larry Egan picked up the tab for a huge round of drinks and by the time he headed back to the city centre he was penniless. With travel restrictions during the war he had to travel by bus. When the conductor asked for the fare he explained that *"I'm Larry Egan owner of Jack Chaucer the winner of the big race". "Oh yeah"* said the conductor as he flung poor Larry out the door *"and I'm Jaysus Christ"*. Because of the huge prize money in the chase, Larry Egan was just beaten for leading owner by the Aga Khan in 1940. The news that he won eventually reached the town, when Larry Egan sent a message to staff at P & H.Egan Ltd. (he was the eldest son of P.J.Egan). The news came by wires & radio and that he would be coming down on the Sunday evening. At about 4pm, two local bands (The Tullamore Brass & Reed and the British Legion Fife & Drum), were accompanied by townspeople, as they marched to the outskirts playing appropriate music. He arrived at about 8PM and the crowds assembled around a bonfire in O'Connor Square. Larry Egan was grateful but did not want to talk about himself. *"Praise the horse all you can"* he said *"He won a great race and he won it easily".* He said young Jimmy Brogan the jockey was a great factor in his win. At P.J.Egan's, Annaghmore House, Tullamore they had bonfires around the house and great cheers erupted for the family and all the staff congregated to enjoy the occasion. Michael J. Kelly a Director met Larry Egan on his return. Before the horse started training, he was stricken with illness at the owner's stable in Tullamore. He was attended by J. S. McCann VS and he was minded at night by Pat Geoghegan, who nurtured the horse and he returned to health.

JACK TRUMPS OPPOSITION IN IRISH GRAND NATIONAL

The Irish Grand National at Fairyhouse in the following March was only worth £740. Cecil Brabazon one of the most successful trainers in this era was going for his third Irish Grand National and Jack Chaucer was 5/2F. Cecil's son Aubrey decided to ride a different horse Baykora, who coincidentally had a strong association with the Wallace family near Birr in Offaly, but unfortunately the horse fell. Jimmy Lehehan was substituting for the injured Jimmy Brogan (whose previous luck ran out!). He dashed the horse into the lead about a mile from home and he came home, eased down, to win by 2 lengths. People all over Tullamore listened in to wireless sets and then hats were thrown in the air, with cheers from every quarter, as many backed him again. Lenehan said *"I had a most comfortable ride, for I felt that at any stage when challenged, he could come away again".*

He was by the very successful sire Jack of Rheims who traced back to Brown Jack, who was bred in Offaly by the Webb family. Jack Chaucer was the leading stakes winner in Ireland in 1950; Jackdaw of Rheims was the leading sire; and Cecil Brabazon the leading trainer. It was the only time that earnings under National Hunt rules determined the winners because of the huge prize money in the Red Cross Chase. Larry Egan was just beaten by the Aga Khan. Strangely,

Jack Chaucer never won another race and when he died he was buried in the tanyard in Tullamore.

Larry Egan had other horses like Ballyhooly, who won the Conyngham Cup and his horse Two Irish Eyes (Irish Battle-White Eyes) won a number of races, including at Mullingar where Jimmy Cleary was training.

A GOLDEN VIEW OF T.P. DOWNES

T.P. Downes was an owner, breeder and one of the most important figures in the development of Mullingar racecourse and horse racing in the midlands. He won the Joseph O'Reilly Cup at Fairyhouse with Carraroe (Irish Battle-dam by Flyfisher) in 1934 and he owned horses like Soir, Battlefort, and Mariner's Dance. The two most important horses bred by him were Golden View II winner of 1946 Irish Grand National and In View a half-brother, was the first horse to win a race in the USA in 1953. Golden View II (Johnny Roebuck- Rathview) was bred and hunted by him out was out of the half-bred local stallion Johnny Roebuck and was jointly owned. He was trained by Dan Moore but the records show that the trainer was his Head Lad Dick O'Connell because, as a professional jockey Moore couldn't hold a licence. Golden View II was carrying 12st 7lbs giving almost a stone to the favourite St Martin. He was ridden by Martin Maloney. He came through easily at the end of the race to win by 8 lengths at 7/1. He ran in a three runner Champion Chase at Aintree in November but fell breaking his neck. In View competed in the International Chase at Belmont Park in 1954, where Westmeath was well represented with Mrs Varney, Rathowen owning Nice Work ridden by Pat Taaffe and Eddie Newman riding Prince of Devon, winner of 6 of his 11 races. One of the leading National Hunt trainers in the USA at this time was James E.Ryan son of Owen Ryan who managed Cleaboy Stud, Mullingar and he had his great chaser The Mast in the race.

The International Race was won by Extra Points beating Mrs J.R.H. Thouron's The Mast by 18L's with Prince of Denmark 5th. Gerard Varney's Nice Work II fell. George Garrett (who visited Kilbeggan races) former Ambassador to Ireland presented the trophy. In View was well up but tired at the end. 1953 In View was favourite for the Irish Grand National at 5/2 after being second in the National Hunt Chase at Cheltenham but was unplaced behind the veteran Overshadow with Captain E. Gargan's Westmeath home bred Southern Coup (Coup de Lyon-Southernmore) in third place beaten 7 lengths.

EDDIE NEWMAN - THE MAN WHO KEPT HIS A KNEECAP IN A JAR!

The J.V.Rank owned Shagreen trained by Tom Dreaper was the mount of Eddie Newman, originally from Ballygarvey, Rathowen, Co Westmeath in the 1949 Grand National. Rank had won it with Prince Regent but Shagreen was not at that level. Shagreen had hunted with Fingall Harriers. In June 1947 at Mullingar, he ran his first race over hurdles and was unplaced. The other Westmeath jockey in the race Aubrey Brabazon looked like winning with Vincent O'Briens favourite Castledermot, until Eddie arrived on the scene with Shagreen to win by 4 lengths. The horse ran twice at Aintree and did win the Grand Sefton Chase. He was born in 1923 and got his initial training on the home farm. It started for Eddie Newman in 1938 at the age of 15 when he read an advertisement in the paper that Cecil Brabazon had put in which read, *"why are jockey's so scarce?"* He decided to answer the advertisement and got the job. He was paid 2/6 in 1933; he rode his first winner in 1939, and in 1942 was Champion Apprentice with 36 winners. While still an apprentice, he rode in the last race meeting at Longford in 1939. He joined Tom Dreaper's stable in 1944. He was competing against M.Moloney, T.P.Burns, Aubrey Brabazon, Morny Wing, M.Quirke, Joe Canty, Jack Moylan & by 1945 was one of the leading jockeys in Ireland. In 1947, he had a treble at Mullingar on Greenogue, Clover Mor, and Ardnacassa (who fell in the Aintree Grand National earlier in the year) for Tom Dreaper and he retired in 1954.

He was the first person to ride the winner of the Galway Hurdle in two successive years, when he rode Pride of Devon in 1953 and Cloudless Days in 1954, (the first to win two in a row). The latter beat Tantivy Cottage & In View. He joined the leaders coming down hill and drew away to win by 10 length's. He won an Irish Grand National on Shagreen, the Thyestes Chase, and rode 7 times at Aintree (his best result was 4th with Overshadow. His 6 other mount's from 1946-53 all fell. He said *"The course was much harder then. The fence between Beecher's Brook and the Canal Turn was the most dangerous. After the big Beecher's jump, the fence was wider than it is now, and the horses were inclined to plough through the next fence, so down they came".* He said *"It was a great life and very exciting. The phone would ring, and you didn't know where you'd be bound for, it could be anywhere in Great Britain"* Ironically, In 1953 Overshadow at 13 y/o won the Irish Grand National for Clem Magnier as Eddie was unplaced on Arctic Silver.

He also won the Gloucester Hurdle 1953 with Assynt for D.J.Morgan and won a few times on Cottage Rake. He rode for Ted Long, F.Walwyn, T.F.Rimell and G.Beaby and for many of the leading trainers. He received many injuries during his career - he broke his jaw, dislocated his shoulder thirteen times, broke 3 ribs, hurt his back, and split his kneecap into eight pieces (He kept the kneecap in a jar as a momento). On 2nd December 1949, he crossed over to England to ride Gallant Scot at Kempton Park, but they crashed through a fence and the horse had to be destroyed. He broke his kneecap in 8 places. Doctors said he would never ride again but he returned in 1950. In September 1954, he received a serious injury at Kilbeggan when his mount Sgiathan Dearg was brought down.

He was brought to the Mullingar Hospital. His injuries led to Tom Dreaper getting in another jockey, which was the great Pat Taaffe. Eddie said *"He was an absolute gentleman always out to help anyone".*

In 1947, he married veterinary surgeon Dolly Yourell, who came from a background of horses and he also bought Carrick. She bred and owned General Symons, which was third in the 1972 Aintree Grand National, ridden by his son Gerry and dead heated with Black Secret behind winner Gay Trip & Well To Do. Cecil Ross's The Pooka ran in the same race and fell at the Canal Turn second time around. General Symons was a half-brother to L'Escargot (sire Escart III-Flappy). He won the National Trial Chase at Punchestown, and the Webster Cup at Navan. His son Gerry Newman was third on Drumroan in 1978 and was associated with great horses like Captain Christy, before he went to the USA in the 1980's.

He was interviewed at his farm in Bunbrosna in 1974, where he kept a few hunters and 3 or 4 racehorses trained by Jimmy Tormey. At that time, he thought the best jockey was Fred Winter and of the present day (1970's) jockeys, Tommy Carberry and Frank Berry. One of his most enjoyable wins was in the Beecher Chase in 1948. In 1954, he was picked to ride at Laurel Park USA, which was one of the high points of his career.

Throughout the 1950's, Westmeath didn't have much success in the Irish Grand National although many of the contenders ran in Mullingar & Kilbeggan at different time, including Carey's Cottage, Sentina, Mr What, Kilmore, Killballyown, Knight Errant and Icelough. The latter was third in the race for R.H.Ussher in 1954 and 1956, but went on to win the Kilbeggan Challenge Cup in 1957 (after 117 years of competition going back to 1840) after winning in three consecutive years. When Umm won in 1955, his only run the previous year was a second over hurdles at Mullingar and shortly after his win, he had a crashing fall in the Mullingar Gold Cup. He was ridden by Pat Taaffe who became the first jockey to win the Irish and English Grand Nationals, the same year as he won the Aintree National on the Westmeath owned Quare Times. Umm, went on to become one of the few horses to also win the Galway Plate the same year as the Irish National.

1950 - 60's WINNERS SCARCE

The world may have been rocking and rolling to Elvis and later The Beatles, but success was scarce in this era in the Irish Grand National. T.P.Downe's Doctor Dandy was 5th in 1951, the Cecil Brabazon trained Barney's Link was 2nd to Alberoni in 1952, and Captain Gargan's Southern Coup was 3rd in 1954 to Overshadow. In 1959, Peggy St John Nolan won the Irish Grand National with Zonda and the story of that success is told under Women in Racing In 1960,

J.F.K. Farrell's Take Time (Grand Inquisitor-McKeogh's Girl) trained by Jim A. Wilson won the 1959 Conyngham Cup as an 8 y/o ridden by Mr Eddie Harty. He was the third favourite at 8/1 to win the 1960 Grand National, behind Blue Moth & Tom Dreaper's Olympia. Paddy Shortt his jockey tried to make all the running but made a mistake three out and Olympia took advantage to win by 6 lengths. It was to be the start of Tom Dreaper's seven in a row from 1960 to 1966. In 1961, F.D.Farmer's Owen's Sedge was second to Fortria in the Grand National.

The useful chaser Flying Wild (owned by American Ambassador Raymond Guest), who had the distinction of beating Arkle, was bred in Westmeath and was 4th to Last Link in 1963 and 5th to Arkle in 1964. Two years later, Height O'Fashion took on Flyingbolt with another close finish. Interestingly, Flyingbolt's sire Airborne was bred in Westmeath many years before, as outlined elsewhere. Cecil Ross's horse and good point to pointer The Inventor was 4th to Francis Flood's duo Garoupe and Glencarrig Lady in 1970. In 1971, three Westmeath connected horses were involved in the final stages of the Grand National. The favourite was the English horse Spanish Steps, with dual Gold Cup winner L'Escargot (Escart III-What A Daisy) carrying 12st 7lbs, and Colonel John Thompson's horse Proud Tarquin (Black Tarquin-Leney Princess) ridden by Peter McLoughlin and trained by Tom Dreaper was 11/1. The useful Secret Vulgan bred by Michael Scott, Moate and ridden by J.P.Bourke was also in the race. Proud Tarquin made the running, but was headed by King's Sprite (Arthur Moore), who faltered on the run in allowing Proud Tarquin and L'Escargot to come back. He held on by 1 $^{1}/_{2}$ lengths and $^{3}/_{4}$ length with Secret Vulgan back in 5th place. Proud Tarquin's dam was Leney Princess bred by Jim Tormey in Bunbrosna, Westmeath and she was the dam of the winners of 83 races mainly associated with Colonel John Thompson and Tom Dreaper including Fort Leney (Gold Cup), Prince Tino, and Lean Forward. Proud Tarquin won races like the Totalisator Novice Chase and the Guinness Chase at Punchestown, where he reversed form with King's Sprite. Mrs Barbara & Arthur O'Neill had the unique distinction of breeding two Aintree Grand National winners who were related, in Mr What (Grand Inquisitor-Duke of Pedulas) 1958 and Dual Gold Cup winner L'Escargot 1975.

DALETTA - "THE HORSE THAT PUT TULLAMORE ON THE MAP"

Guy St John Williams, son of Desmond J.Williams, came from a well-known Tullamore Irish distilling family that produced Tullamore Dew and Irish Mist. He was an executive of the company, specialising in brand creation and development for 14 years. He was very interested in horse racing, as an amateur jockey, trainer and owner, mainly under point to point rules. He married Ann Harty daughter of Cyril, therefore steeplechasing was a major part of the family life. He took out a licence to train in March 1979. Around the same time his interest in writing developed, when he wrote a history of the Irish Derby published in 1980. He later went on to be a freelance author, columnist, racing historian, and publisher. In 1979 all this was in the future and he was focused on being a successful public trainer.

The early days were not very successful, with a small stable and only a few winners. He even considered giving it up as a viable proposition. Mrs Frederick William Watson, Cloughjordan, then asked him to purchase a possible Gold Cup horse. He looked around at the novice chasers and decided that Daletta had enough class to be a contender. This horse was about to change his luck and he said at the time *"I owe him a great deal. I had a great stroke of luck in being able to buy him".* The horse arrived in the stable in February 1980 and his brother-in-law and jockey John Harty was impressed with the horse. The following Saturday he ran in the Amberwave Chase and beat Romany Count by six lengths. Just a few weeks later he went to England to win the Embassy Chase Final. The next step was the Irish Grand National.

I DO LIKE MONDAYS?

Daletta was an unusual horse, as he was flat bred from a sprinter Majetta and started with Tom Nicholson, who bought her for 620 guineas. He won a two year old race on his debut over 6 furlongs at Leopardstown at 25/1. He went on to be second in races from the Irish Lincoln on the flat to the Galway Hurdle and Arkle Chase (2nd to Chinrullah). He had 34 races on the flat and won four and a further 40 races under National Hunt rules winning 4 hurdles and 4 chases.

Twenty five runners lined up for the 1980 Irish Grand National with Jer the 7/1 favourite, who had won the Great Yorkshire Chase and Guy Williams's horse Daletta (Majetta-Dale Way) had top weight of 11st 4lbs, because he was going for a hat trick of wins after his two recent wins. Daletta ridden by John Harty was out the back until he steadily made up ground on the second circuit. He moved into third behind Tarquestral and Eggnog, with the former falling with Ted Walsh on board. Daletta hit the front, driven on by John P.Harty, and then had to fight off a challenge from a loose horse, who veered in front of him, with Eggnog renewing his challenge, as they crossed the line together. Guy Williams thought Eggnog won and it looked like a cruel defeat until the announcement came declaring Daletta the winner giving nearly 2 stone to the runner-up. At the time, he said Monday was his lucky day as he was asked to buy the horse by Mrs Watson on that day; he bought the horse on that day; and finally he won the Irish Grand National on Monday.

Following his success, he was the second highest rated chaser after Tied Cottage and ended up as favourite for the Gold Cup in 1981. Guy Williams had a stable of 21 horses within a few months and he received the Young Trainer of the Year

Award. Even at that time he said the two greatest attributes of a racehorse trainer were the ability to work at small details and a sense of humour. He needed the latter when Daletta suffered from a virus and was never the same again. He had some success with other horses like Poyntz Pass, who won Free Handicap Chase and at Fairyhouse in 1983. He eventually gave up on the training and went on to be a Stipendiary Steward for the Jockey Club in Yorkshire, which was not an entirely good experience. He went to work in the Macau Jockey Club and various areas of administration in racing, but his main call was as a racing journalist (including the pseudonym "Daletta") and author. He has contributed much to the history of Irish horse racing including a history of the Irish Derby with Francis Hyland, the Irish Grand National, Winner All Right 100 years of Irish Racing & Breeding, The Racing Lodges of the Curragh, books on Martin Maloney, T.P.Burns, Cheltenham Festival Centenary 1911-2011 etc including non-racing books like A Year in Connemara. Oliver St John Fogarty was his maternal grandfather and he has carried on the tradition. He is also been working on the development of an Irish Racing Archive.

GERRY NEWMAN AND KING SPRUCE 1982

Gerry Newman, the son of Eddie Newman who rode Shagreen in 1949 for Tom Dreaper, became only the second son of a previous winning jockey to win the Irish Grand National with King Spruce 20/1 in 1982 (the first was Dan & Arthur Moore). King Spruce whose sire Harwell was bred in Westmeath was trained by M.J.O'Brien, who had gone to the USA to learn his trade as a jockey but was seriously injured there after a Fall. A custom built wheel chair gave him the mobility to become one of Ireland's leading trainers, with horses like Bright Highway winner of the Hennessy & Mackeson Gold Cup's. O'Brien had worked in Virginia & Maryland where he met the horse's owner Rusty Carrier and the winner proved too strong for Francis Flood's, well backed Fethard Friend.

Gerry Newman with both parents having a racing background learned to ride with the Westmeath Pony Club before going to Kevin Prendergast at 16 and was then with Francis Flood for 3 years. His first win as an amateur was on T.Taaffe's Vulgan's Thistle at Thurles in 1973. He had his first win as a professional jockey with Romanogan at Listowel, as a 21 y/o on 25th September 1975. He rode out for Pat Taaffe, who was friends with his father Eddie and when Bobby Coonan was injured he gave Gerry the chance to win the King George VI chase in December 1975, with the great Captain Christy. It was amazing for a 21 y/o, with only 6 months as a professional, to win a major race on his first ride in Britain. The irony was that Pat Taaffe got his chance with Tom Dreaper, when Eddie Newman was injured. He replaced Tommy Carmody in the Peter McCreery stable in 1978. His major wins included the Sweeps Hurdle on Chinrullah in 1978 and the Mackeson Gold Cup on Bright Highway for M. J O'Brien and he rode King Spruce to win the Irish Grand National in 1982. He hoped to win the

Cheltenham Gold Cup in 1982 with Bright Highway, before the horse was injured. He had 8 rides in the Aintree Grand National. In 1976 he rode Roman Bar for Taaffe and fell at 19th fence. In 1978, he got round on Drumroan and was 3rd beaten half a length and neck. He then signed up for Michael Hourigan and also rode The Mighty Mac to win the Power Gold Cup. In October 1983, at 28 y/o with over 200 winners, he joined trainer Hugh O'Neill in the South of England. He said *"I always wanted to go to England if I was given an opportunity. Hugh O'Neill has now given me that and I think the experience will be tremendous".* It did not work out as planned and he went to the USA in 1980's and with his American born wife became involved in show jumping in Upperville, Virginia.

INSURE VICTORY 1986

In 1986, Right Hand Man was 3/1 favourite for the Irish Grand National after his 5th to Dawn Run in the Gold Cup. Insure was trained by Pat Hughes but was bred by T.B. Conroy from Laois. Mickey Flynn the jockey was from JKL Street, Edenderry, Co Offaly and he lived just a few doors from P.V. (Pat) Gilson a flat jockey. Insure was backed into 16/1 by the stable with Mickey Flynn under strict instructions to make the bottom weight of 9st 7lbs. He went off in front and it was up to the others to catch him. Nobody got near him and he won by ten lengths from Bold Agent & The Ellier. He went on to have further success as a jockey, in the Thyestes Chase on Olan Lad in 1989; and on Firion's Law in the Galway Plate where he beat Never Be Great and Ace of Spies; and the Ericcson Chase in 1991 for Victor Bowens. The downside of racing was illustrated at Kilbeggan in June 1997, when Micky Flynn recorded a double at Kilbeggan with Conagher Boy and Audacious Dancer. It would normally have been a scene of joy but not this time. It was an emotional evening for Flynn, who saddled his first and last double, because before the meeting he announced that these were his last runners as a trainer, because he was relinquishing his trainer's licence, which he received 3 1/2 years before. He said that the dwindling numbers left it *"no longer viable to train".* As a trainer he had saddled 24 winners with The Carrig Rua considered the best he trained. His family including his mother Dympna were in the parade ring for this strangely sad occasion. He was hoping that he would find employment within the racing industry.

Pat Hughes went to become a trainer, who pulled off gambles over jumps or on the flat, like Time Machine in the Wokingham Handicap sprint at Royal Ascot.

HEAR THE ECHO OF VICTORY AND TRAGEDY

One of the newspapers got it right in the 2008 Irish Grand National, when it mentioned that Hear the Echo at 33/1 silenced the crowd. Mouse Morris said *"He jumped well and it's great to win the race after being second a couple of times".* Paddy Flood jockey, Mouse, and Michael O'Leary's Gigginstown House team were only hopeful going into the race. Morris had tasted victory back in 1977 with Adrian Maxwell's Billycan but this was a welcome success as a trainer, because a number of horses were ill that year and missed Cheltenham. He jumped the 23 fences very well and took up the running coming into the straight and held off the challenge of 6/1 favourite Royal County Star and Jim Dreaper's Notre Pere. He was bred by Nuala Delaney the sister of the famous Tom Costello. The top weight Beef or Salmon made no show and it was decided to retire him after a great career and giving years of pleasure to many patrons of the turf. Hear the Echo brought Gigginstown their first Irish Grand National and the aim in 2009 was the big one at Aintree.

Just before the Aintree Grand National, Gold Cup winner War of Attrition was withdrawn, as Mouse Morris was not satisfied with the horse and Hear the Echo with Davy Russell on board was his replacement. Mouse said *"Hear the Echo is 100%"* and in another interview before the race, he very prophetically said about training horses *"It can break your bloody heart this business".* The eight-year-old, raced up with the leaders but then had dropped to the rear, when he collapsed and died near the finishing line. Davy Russell believed that Hear The Echo suffered a heart attack. It was a tragic end for a decent horse, who in 23 starts won four races and £164,006. In spite of his great success in many other races, Michael O'Leary would have appreciated his Irish Grand National success. Mouse Morris had many better horses from Buck House to War of Attrition, but as one of his owner's stated *"He is an artist as distinct from a commercial horse trainer".*

LION NA BEARNAI "FILLS THE GAP" IN THE IRISH GRAND NATIONAL

In 2011, Westmeath was to continue its contribution to delivering outsiders to win the Irish Grand National when Frank Daly, Tubberclair and Lorna Groarke, Athlone bred Lion na Bearnai (New Frontier-Polly Plum) to win. A big outsider, Lion Na Bearnai at 33/1 took the Ladbrokes Irish Grand National at Fairyhouse on Easter Monday 2011. Tom Gibney, who only had five horses, and jockey Andrew Thornton took centre stage for the greatest success of their careers. The horse had won at 50/1 in a valuable novice chase at Navan in February and this time battled on to beat Out Now (14/1) by four and a half lengths, with the Jonjo O'Neill-trained Alfie Sherrin (10/1), who came from some way off the pace, was best of the British raiders back in third. *"I only have the five horses. This is just brilliant,"* said Gibney. *"We were confident coming here but we were afraid to say it. Andrew is a brilliant rider, much underrated."*

Andrew Thornton had been struggling for the past four years and his total prize money for the season was less than he won in the Fairyhouse race. Tom Gibney's 12 y/o put in a great round of jumping. He said *"If he jumped he'd be thereabouts. That's how it turned out and he loves the place. He's in Aintree and hopefully we'll head there".* Frank Daly and his wife Lorna first bought Polly Plum, the dam of Lion na Bearnai, as a potential brood mare in 1994. New Frontier was a son of Sadler's Wells and the sire of Lion na Bearnai and at that time stood at Tullaghansleek Stud, Streamstown, with Tim Carey. Frank sold Lion na Bearnai at Tattersalls Ireland in 2006 for the sum of €8,800, as a four-year-old, to Tom Gibney, and has followed Lion na Bearnai's progress since. New Frontier won the Group 3 Prix de Conde over 1m1f at two and the Prix Berteux over 1m7f Prix Berteux at three for Andre Fabre. In 2000, he was retired to Tullaghansleek Stud, but died aged only ten. Lion na Bearnai had won a Grade 2 Ten Up Chase over 3 miles at Navan in February 2012. He is out of Polly Plum a Pollerton mare, who was placed in a bumper and over hurdles at Kilbeggan and only one of her 4 runners was ever placed. She was 1/2 sister to Merapi (won 6 races) & Powleyvale (won 7- 2 bumpers, 3 hurdles & 2 chases).

Frank Daly said *"It's great to have had some sort of contribution to Lion na Bearnai's success. When you sell at Tattersalls, you receive notification when the horse is named, so it's very easy to stay in touch with how it's doing. Lion na Bearnai had a few notable finishes, but it started to come together when it won the Conyngham Cup at Punchestown, which is the oldest steeplechase in Ireland".* He is originally from Mount Temple but is living in Tubberclair for many years, and is also the current chairman of the South Westmeath Hunt. His wife, Lorna, is secretary of the local Point to Point committee.

Sadler's Wells & his male line, like New Frontier have had big influence on National Hunt racing and another son of New Frontier was Welforth, who won the Imperial Call chase at Cork the same Easter weekend. Some of his other offspring include Sizing Australia, Frontier Dancer, Frontier Spirit, Glenfarclas, and Shanballa.

In 2014, three years after his big win in the Irish Grand National, Tom Gibney was hoping that Lion na Bearnai would give him another big win in the Aintree Grand National. Gibney only had 5 horses in his yard when he won the Irish Grand National. After that success he got some new owners and his string trebled. Just as things were looking up he had a bad year & the number of horses went down again. He had a bad bug in his yard and now he has 10 in training. He said *"Its tough work trying to make a living out of training at the moment. The dream is to win the Grand National, as that would be a great for the owners".* He admitted that he probably ran him too often, as the horse was running nearly every fortnight. In February 2014, he won a race at Fairyhouse before being pulled up in the Aintree Grand National behind Pineau de Re and was 11th to Shutthefrontdoor in the Irish National. Lion na Bearnai at that stage had won around £167,000 in prize money.

In 2012 Dot Love, Charlestown Stud, Mulllingar trained Liberty Counsel to win the Irish Grand National and in doing so became the first Irish based female trainer to train the winner. It should have been Peggy St John Nolan in 1959 but women were not allowed a licence to train at that time and her Head Lad Matt Geraghty is recorded as the trainer. The story of these two remarkable women is told in the chapter on Women in Racing.

GOLDEN WONDER AND THE MINISTER

Paddy Cooney, Athlone had a great political career and was Minister for Justice amongst many other position in Government. He also had an interest in horses and his father bred Ardnacassa who won the Conyngham Cup in 1948, when trained by Tom Dreaper and ridden by Mullingar jockey Eddie Newman. He was involved with the South Westmeath Hunt and as an Acting Steward at Roscommon races, plus an interest in a few unsuccessful horses until Golden Wonder. His neighbour Brian Dillon had a nice mare by Pollerton, which he gave to him for luck. She was bred by Tom & Brian Groarke, Drumraney, Co Westmeath. She was sent to Goldmark at Lacy's, Ballycrystal Stud, in Offaly and produced a colt foal which died. The Lacy's generously gave a free return even though it was a live foal. In May 2006 the foal arrived and was named Golden Wonder. As a 5y/o he ran in bumpers and maiden hurdles without success. He was then let home for summer, where Brian Dillon & Padraig Dunne rode and schooled him & he ran in a few point to points in 2012, where he jumped well. He eventually won his maiden hurdle at Bellewstown for Dessie Hughes. He was put over fences and ran in a novice chase and won at the Galway Festival in August 2013. He had two more races before Christmas and was then prepared for the Irish Grand National in 2014.

Jonjo O'Neill's horse Shutthefrontdoor justified being favourite at 8/1 by winning the Irish Grand National in 2014 (he won it previously with Butler's Cabin in 2007) and provided Barry Geraghty with his first success in the race. He travelled well in the race, but Dessie Hughes horse Golden Wonder16/1, showed his improvement by coming at him at the end of the 3 mile 5 furlongs finish, only to fail by 3/4 length. It was a brave performance. He also carried top weight in the Galway Plate, when over an inadequate trip he finished 6th to the easy winner Roads to Riches ridden by Athlone jockey Shane Shortall. Golden Wonder had his final run of the season in the Kilbeggan in Patrons Hurdle on 5th September, when second to Desertmore Stream.

LESS THUNDER AND MORE ROSES FOR GIGGINSTOWN IN NATIONAL

When Katie Walsh won the Boyle Sports Irish Grand National at Fairyhouse in April, she became only the third lady jockey to win the race. She rode Thunder and Roses (Ms K.Walsh) 20/1 to an emotional victory at Fairyhouse, because the horse was trained by Sandra Hughes. It was 31 years since Ann Ferris won aboard Bentom Boy, and then Nina Carberry also won on Organisedconfusion in 2011. On the positive side, two female jockey's and two female trainers won the race in the last five years. Sandra Hughes only took over her father Dessie's licence last year when he died. He had trained Timbera to win in 2003.

In a summary of the horse's chances before the race, he was described as a *"lazy jumper"* and *"unlikely to be involved".* He was neither, lazy or uninvolved, as he moved into the lead in the last half mile followed by his stable companion Rule the World (D.J. Mullins) and Band of Blood (A.P.Crowe), both trained by Mouse Morris, who had trained Hear the Echo to win for Gigginstown House in 2008. It looked like Gigginstown House would fill the first three places, as the three horses arrived at the last fence together with Jim Dreaper's Sizing Coal (Jonathan Moore). The latter managed to stop a clean sweep by taking 3rd place from Band of Blood with Rule the World 4 lengths second to Thunder and Roses. Five horses had come to grief at the first fence and by the end of the contest a number of others failed to complete. Eddie O'Leary said afterwards *"I thought our best chance of winning the race had gone, when Empire of Dirt came down in the melee at the first fence".* It was ironic, that Empire of Dirt and Jim Dreaper's Los Amigos were the two best backed horses in the race and neither featured as their stable companions dominated the race.

KATIE WALSH AND SANDRA HUGHES

Katie Walsh, sister of legendary jockey Ruby and daughter of trainer Ted (who both showed their joy with a hug and a kiss), who has the best Aintree finishing position for female riders in the Aintree Grand National with Seabass when he was third to Neptune Collonges and Sunnyhillboy in 2012, added to her great record by winning the Irish Grand National.

She said *"I've had some fantastic days, but this is an Irish National. They stopped in front and he kept going. It's great for women in racing."* Walsh added *"he loved the ground and he produced it all right on the day".* The horse had unseated Johnny King at Cheltenham but Katie spent her time looking at video's of the horse to help her on the day and it proved worthwhile.

The triumph was poignant and emotional for Hughes, who took over the training licence following the death of her father, Dessie, who trained Timbera to win the 2003 Irish Grand National, in November. Hughes said: *"Katie was absolutely fantastic, she just suited him to a tee".* She was brilliant and he (Thunder and Roses) was brilliant and added *"Someone above was helping us out. Dad always loved this race and to do it for him is wonderful. Dad was with us all the way today".*

It was not to be the perfect finish for Tony McCoy, as his well-backed horse Cantlow only finished 6th. On the day, Taoiseach Enda Kenny, presented McCoy with a specially commissioned frame print highlighting all his winners in Ireland since he started in 1992. There was no fairy tale ending for Tony McCoy but there is no doubt he was the *"Prince of Jockey's"* and his wife Chanelle was a suitable Princess. It was ladies day at its best and even though Michael O'Leary was not present it is certain that he enjoyed a very successful day.

They say there are no great statistical trends to follow in the Irish Grand National but in five years A Westmeath trainer (Dot Love), a Westmeath breeder (Frank Daly), and a Westmeath owner (Gigginstown House) won the race and another Westmeath owner Paddy Cooney finished second with Golden Wonder. Is that not a trend?

chapter 10
AINTREE GRAND NATIONAL VICTORIES

WESTMEATH AND THE AINTREE GRAND NATIONAL AINTREE

Sometimes people within racing think it is the greatest sport in the world and during the late 18th century and into the 19th century there is an argument for that view. It is certainly not true now, as BBC have dropped racing from their schedule in recent years and racing events make little impact on the news except for the Cheltenham Festival and the Aintree Grand National.

The Aintree Grand National has connotations for generations of Irish people and the world seemed to stop for a day when the big race was on with tips flying around. People who had never darkened a bookie's office, arrived in with a list of each way bets and if somehow you managed to get the winner, you were something of a hero in the locality. My first winner as a child was 6d on Mr What in 1958. I have no recollection as to how I got 6d, but I knew I was rich after the event. It was wonderful listening to it on Radio Eireann, as it allowed you to imagine the giant fence's like *"Beecher's Brook"*, *"Valentines Brook"*, and *"The Chair"*. The man behind it all was William Lynn of the Waterloo Hotel who leased land in 1829 and the history of racing at Aintree began initially as flat racing, until Lynn realised that steeplechasing was becoming very popular. The dispute about when it began relates to the two races in 1837/38, which some say took place at Maghull and others at Aintree. The race in 1838, was won by an Irish horse Sir William, ridden by owner/trainer Alan McDonagh from the well-known Galway family. I think the dispute about when the race commenced has been resolved and it is generally accepted that it was in 1839, when a syndicate of '1,000 proprietors of 25 sovereigns' was set up, as Lynn was in financial difficulty (sadly he was to die penniless). Reports at the time indicated that 30-40,000 attended the races travelling by horseback, coach, trap and cart and any vehicle that would get them there on time.

HARKAWAY THE FAMOUS IRISH FLAT CHAMPION TO RUN IN NATIONAL?
The Grand Liverpool Chase was a sweepstake of 20 sovereigns each with 100 added, 12 stone each rider and over 4 miles. Ireland was represented by Tom Ferguson, famous as owner of the great flat racing horse and champion Harkaway, who was reared in Westmeath. Harkaway was born in April 1834, but was leggy and ungainly, so they sent him to Thomas McEvoy's farm in Westmeath, who was a wealthy grazier, to run with his cattle on the rich midlands grass. He remained there for nearly two years at grass. When he was brought back he had his first run in the Angelsey Stakes at The Curragh. He won

18 out of his 23 races at The Curragh. One of the strangest reports in the sporting press took place in December 1838 when it was stated that Mr Ferguson was determined to *"have a dash at it with his famous horse Harkaway"*, who supposedly was practicing and turned out to be a *"prime jumper"*. It seems unlikely that Ferguson would allow the great champion to jump fences especially at Aintree. Ferguson had three runners in the race and Willie McDonagh brother of Alan had Rust in the race. The latter was hemmed in by a huge mob and kept there during the race to end his chances. It was very appropriate that the first ever winner of the Grand National was the well fancied Lottery 5/1 and he was owned by a Mr Elmore and ridden by Jem Mason.

In 1843, a horsed called Tinderbox ran in the Grand National in a race won by Lord Chesterfield's Vanguard. This horse was bred by Henry Murray, Mountmurray, Co Westmeath. He was sold at a hunt in Ballinasloe for £120. James Hunt owned him when he ran in the race and he was ridden by Garret Moore of Moore Hall. He fell at the wall and threw his rider who fractured his collar bone. He was going well at the time.

Even in the early years, there was severe criticism of the race for its cruelty to horses (in 1841 Lottery was carrying 13st 4lbs). Ireland had its first winner in 1847 when Matthew won, but the most famous Irish horse in the race was Brunette a 13 y/o mare, who had a remarkable record of wins in Ireland including Mullingar. She won the Kilrue Cup with 100 sovs. in 1843 and Mr Preston's Brunette won the Westmeath Urn of 100 guineas, four years in a row at Mullingar from 1842-45. She also won the Foxhunters Stakes at Ormond & King's County Races at Lismacrory in 1844. She had run at Worcester & Hereford, before the big race but was ill on the day. She was past her best and carrying 12st 6lbs, but still managed to be fourth in the 1847 Grand National. She became a broodmare and lived to the age of 22. She was probably the most beloved mare of the 19th century in Ireland, and it was ironic that in the Kilrue Cup in 1846 carrying 12st 7lbs she beat St Leger & Matthew (who were first & second in the 1847 Grand National). She was ridden by Alan McDonagh and it was rumoured he backed her to win £10,000. Little interest was shown in Matthew 10st 6lbs initially, but shrewd punters backed him and the gamble paid off for owner Mr Courtenay and jockey Dennie Wynne. At last Ireland recorded its first win in the race.

1855 - WANDERER FROM WESTMEATH

In 1855, John Dennis's Wanderer 25/1 by Verulam was carrying 9st 8lbs and ridden by John Hanlon. It is a race that was considered of low quality with the first three home bottom weights. Wanderer was described as a *"rough, undersized, common looking hunter"*. It seems that Hanlon and the owner backed the other Irish horse Boundaway to win, but when he faded he went on to win on Wanderer. Richard Coffey, Newcastle, Tyrrellspass bred many horses including Fertullagh, Theodora,Yaller Girl, Post Horn, Juryman and Will O'the Wisp. The family bred many good horses and the most famous horse he supposedly bred at Newcastle was Wanderer, who won the Aintree Grand National in 1855. Richard was involved in the Westmeath Hunt and in 1853 he kept harriers there and steeplechasers. The Coffey involvement with the hunt brought many distinguished visitors including Winston Churchill. It has also been stated that the horse was bred by Robert Holmes, Moycashel, who became famous in the mid-19th century for his Short Horn Pedigree Herd. H.Dixon in *The Post and Paddock* stated that *"he was known, as one of the best breeders of young hunters who were often sent to Irish fairs between 6/8, but the best were bought before they reached the fair".* He travelled a lot of the time to England and died living near London in 1870. In view of the above, it does appear as if the horse was bred in Westmeath either by Coffey or Holmes.

Martha was a horse who completed in Newbrook regularly in this era and she was unplaced in the 1864 Grand National. In 1862 three other horses that ran in Mullingar all ran in the Grand National but none of them completed the course - Anatis pulled up, Thomastown refused, and O'Connell fell. The fall of O'Connell led to the death of James Wynne when Playman rolled over him. It was a truly tragic day for the family, as he had been informed that his sister died in Ireland and Lord de Freyne tried to persuade him not to ride but he carried on bringing a double tragedy to the family. Four Grand National candidates appeared in the Westmeath Handicap Stakes in 1864, O'Connell 11st 11lbs (who won by a head from Orphan), Leonidas 9st, National Petition 10st 9lbs, and Martha 9st 11lbs.

THE GREAT THOMASTOWN

How Tom Naghten came into possession of Thomastown is not known for certain, but the best evidence is that he was won in a card game. Breeding records show that he was by Dean out of Fieldfare. The horse won a series of races including the Kilrue Cup of 150 sovereigns in 1859, when ridden by Ned Broderick. All the local tenants followed the horse through these wins. The story is that Mr Naghten then decided to send him for a race in England. He refused in 1862 he was 4th in 1864 to Emblematic, Unplaced 1866, and unplaced in 1867. A poem written about him indicates that Tom Naghten accepted a bribe to lose the race and it appears that when Broderick was taken off the horse he cancelled his bet. The replacement jockey J.Murphy (who rode the horse in both races), apparently, was involved and "supposedly" threw himself off, but even without the jockey Thomastown finished first. The story is that Tom Naghten had to sneak home in case he was caught by the losing tenants (he travelled home by a cattle boat from England). It seems that some tenants were evicted afterwards, as they could not pay their rent. Naghten's racing colours at this time were cherry & blue and he had other good horses like Sleeky Kitty, Ashplant, Nanny O'Leary, Joe North, and Youth. He died in 1876 and his widow Mrs Penelope Naghten carried on with the race meetings.

In 1866 Salamander won the race owned by Mr Studd's. He was a rich indigo planter from India, who settled in Rutland and trained his own horses and won a big bet on the horses at 40 and 50/1. Baily's Magazine was rather annoyed at his conduct in *"making the round of bookies and himself taking all the forties and fifties he could get"* and added *"it was not the sort of thing we are accustomed to expect from the landed gentry of England"*. There is a Westmeath connection in that Mr Studd met John Hartigan, Limerick at the Mullingar Fair and the outcome of that meeting was that he bought three horses - two hunters and the other was Salamandar a great Grand National winner. In a field of 30 runners, he cantered round and won by10 lengths. Unfortuntely, after a bad fall at Warwick he was put down. In 1875 Sir Walter Nugent, Donore (father of the future Sir Walter MP) ran his horse Clonave in the Grand National in 1875 carrying 12st 1lb and ridden by Gavin and also in 1876 without making any impact. The horse was related to Why Not, who was to win the race for the family in 1894.

THE MYSTERY OF CLOISTER AND GRACE II

At the first official race meeting in Kilbeggan at Ballard in 1879, Mr Talbot's Lady Newman beat a horse called Grace II in the Kilbeggan Plate of 30 sovereigns, who was said on the local paper to be owned by W.S.Kelly, Manager of the Hibernian Bank in Mullingar. He was a great supporter of hunting & racing in the county. She was the favourite for the race at even money, but could only finish second. She did manage to win a £30 plate at Loughegar that year. It cannot be confirmed that Mr Kelly was the definite owner and he died suddenly in October 1879. She was purchased for use as a hunter by Arthur Plunkett, Earl of Fingall, Co. Meath and used as a whip's horse in the hunt field. Grace II (Crown Prince-Marlyon) was bred to Ascetic when she was an 8y/o and dropped Cloister her first foal the following year. The earl was not impressed and sold both Cloister and Grace II to Percy Maynard for 31 guineas. Grace II had more foals until she died at 26 y/o.

Cloister ran three times in the Grand National winning and was second twice but also became famous for the two races she missed. Even as a 4 y/o Cloister won the Aintree Hunt Steeplechase over the Grand National fences and was sold to Lord Dudley and his first attempt to win the Grand National was in 1891. He came up against 4/1 favourite Come Away, over the last fence Captain Roddy Owen tried to get up on the inside but he was up against one of the best riders of the era in Harry Beasley, who boxed him in and took his space to win. Owen was furious and lodged an objection and in the weigh- room he wanted to settle the matter directly with Beasley, until Mr Marsh said the Captain might come in second again if he insisted on resorting to force. The Stewards over-ruled the objection and said Captain Owen should not have tried to go up the inside. Having ridden three seconds it was Harry Beasley's first win in the race.

Cloister was sold to Charles Duff and transferred to Arthur Yates stable, where Mr J. C. Dormer was given the ride. Captain Owen got the mount on C.G.Wilson's Father O'Flynn, a horse notorious for refusing in races. Owen took it so seriously that he jogged from Liverpool in a heavy sweater on the day of the race to shed weight. Dense fog obscured the far side of the track but when they appeared Cloister 12st 3lbs was challenged by Father O'Flynn 10st 5lbs and the weight made the difference as the latter won by 20 lengths. Owen achieved his ambition and returned to the War Offic, where he died in Egypt in 1896. Cloister only had one run before the big race, in the Grand Sefton chase, where he won easily, before his attempt to win it in 1893, where he started 9/2 F. He made most of the running before taking a breather and then racing away to win by 40 lengths. He was the first horse to carry 12st 7lbs and he won in the fastest time ever recorded. He was considered the Aintree King but the hero became a villain through no fault of his own, over the next two years through mystery and suspicion of skullduggery.

The public were backing Cloister at 6/4 F, even with top weight as the Grand National approached in 1894. In spite of the public support, the horse started to drift out in price and owner Mr Duff called in detectives suspecting that the horse might have been got at and eventually he was scratched. Yates the trainer thought the horse might have been injured in the race the previous year. This obviously did not satisfy the owner as he took the horse away and he was sent to Harry Escott at Lewes. The horse won the Grand Sefton Chase in November 1894 by 20 lengths and even though allocated 13st 3lbs he was still ante-post favourite. He seemed well and detectives were hired to watch the horse. After a gallop he rolled over after stumbling and even though the vet said he was lame, it was still believed that he was got at as he had drifted in the betting again. There are many who consider that Cloister was the greatest winner of the Grand National, in spite of the misfortune that affected him in his final two years. He won 18 of his 34 races over jumps.

COULD A WESTMEATH BRED HORSE WIN THE NATIONAL? - WHY NOT!

In the Aintree Grand National in 1889, Matthias Maher won the race with his horse Frigate on his seventh attempt having been second twice to Voluptuary in 1884 and Roquefort in 1885. The horse was sold on but didn't manage to win the race and amazingly Mr Maher bought her back for £500. It seemed like a foolhardy decision until at last in 1889 she got her head in front to beat Why Not by a length. The difference being that the great Tommy Beasley rode the winner and an amateur Mr C.J.Cunningham rode Why Not. In many ways Why Not's career was similar to Frigate, as he had seven attempts at the big race and won the race in 1894.

On the *Westmeath Guardian* newspaper dated 6th April 1894 a letter appeared from Percy Nugent Donore, Multyfarnham, Co Westmeath following Why Not's win, indicating that the Irish Times stated that the horse was bred by Colonel Thompson but this was incorrect. He stated that the horse was bred by his aunt Miss Nugent (afterwards Miss Nugent Fitzgerald) and sold by her to Mr Hilliard of Castleknock, when he was three years old. Twitter the dam of Why Not, was the property of Miss Nugent and Silverstream, grand dam of Why Not was also her property. Crystal the great grand dam of Why Not and dam of Clonave (who ran in the Aintree Grand National) was the property of Captain Nugent and bred by Sir P.Nugent. Twitter was sold sometime after Why Not was foaled to Colonel Thompson. Mrs P. Nugent Fitzgerald eldest daughter of Percy, who was a great lover of the turf, died in July 1905 and Percy Nugent died at Donore House in February 1896. He was the eldest son of the previous Sir Walter Nugent and grandson of Sir Richard More O'Farrell, Governor General of Malta.

Why Not (Castlereagh-Twitter) started his career as a four year old and he was a 13 y/o when he won the Grand National and made his final attempt as a 15 y/o in 1896. His record was 2nd 1889; 5th 1890 after remounting; fell at the 2nd last looking a winner in 1891; 3rd in 1893; winner in 1894; 5th in 1895; and 5th in 1896. Charlie Cunningham (1849-1896) was one of the most popular and successful amateurs in the north of England and Scotland. He rode from 1873 until his early death in 1906. He rode Why Not in his first three attempts and unfortunately came up against Tommy Beasley the first year, then he bravely remounted the horse in 1890, after falling at the fourth fence carrying 12st 5lbs. In 1891, he carried 12st 4lbs and was giving weight to the winner Come Away and the great Cloister was receiving 10lbs, yet he looked like winning at the second last fence, when he fell. He was over 6 feet in height and was a top class amateur but it was said that as Why Not was a small horse that Cunningham's long legs caught his feet in the fences when jumping them, and that this might have explained some of his jumping errors. He didn't run in 1892 and for his next three attempts he was ridden by Arthur Nightingall. When he won the Grand National in 1894 he was trained by Willie H.Moore younger brother of Garrett Moore, and then owned by Captain C.H.Fenwick who purchased him in 1892.

The 1894 Grand National was one of the most controversial in its great history because of rumours of cheating, when Cloister winner in 1893 and 6/4 favourite was withdrawn due to alleged lameness. Why Not ended up the 5/1 favourite.The race was won by the artistry of Arthur Nighingall and to some extent the over-eagerness of Joe Widger on Wild Man of Borneo (who learned from the experience by winning the race the following year). Under a strong drive Why Not who was giving over two stone to runner up Lady Ellen II and one stone to Wild Man from Borneo, pegged back his two rivals to win by 1 1/2 lengths and a head. The horse was past his best in his next two attempts but he showed that he was a great horse around Aintree and a great weight carrier in most of his attempts.

THE NUGENT FAMILY AND DRUMCREE

In the 1903 Grand National, the famous Irish stallion Ascetic bred 5 of the 23 runners and two others were grandsons. One of the horses Drumcree was by the half bred Witching Hour and was bred by C.Hope at Mabestown, Drumcree, Delvin. Witching Hour (1885) won over fences and she also traced back to Birdcatcher. What was historic was that Hope also bred Pride of Mabestown, who was a full sister to Drumcree. It was the first time that a brother and sister ran in the same Aintree Grand National. Drumcree was purchased as a hunter for Charles Newton by Owen J.Williams and he showed some talent as a jumper and was sent to Sir Charles Nugent to train at Cranbourne, Dorset. Pride of Mabestown was also bought by Owen Williams & won 6 races for him in England. In September 1899, Drumcree (Ascetic-Witching Hunt) won the Kilpatrick Plate at 8/1 in Mullingar and in 1900 his own sister Pride of Mabestown (Ascetic-Witching Hour) won the Farmer's Race.

Sir Charles Nugent was the son and heir to Ballinlough Castle in Westmeath and he rode in steeplechases, sometimes under an assumed name. He was wild in his youth through gambling and racing and was sent to England. He was bankrupt on a number of occasions, but he survived and inherited the lands in Ireland, as his older brother was killed tragically in a shooting incident. He was private trainer to Sir William Nelson for a while from early 1916. He won the Royal Hunt Cup and Chesterfield Cup with Illuminator in 1921 and the Stewards Cup 1924 and Wokingham Sts in 1925 with Compiler. It was regarded as a lucky yard as Bramble Twig, Cylgar, & Tetrachia won more races than all Sir William Nelson's at Stork House. He gave his own prescriptions such as *"Tonic Ball"* and *"Fever Ball"* to his horses. He had succeeded his brother in 1863 and died in May 1927 and handed over to his grandson Sir Hugh Nugent.

Drumcree was also a quirky horse and often refused to go into his stable, a relic of being scared by a squaking hen and banging his head going into a stable. Nugent trained a high class chaser Hidden Mystery, which was favourite for the 1900 Grand National carrying 12 stone, but the Prince of Wales won it with with Ambush II. He considered that Hidden Mystery was a much better horse than Drumcree, when he won the Grand Sefton Chase and also beating Manifesto at level weights at Hurst Park was an impressive result. He was a fractional favourite over the Prince of Wales horse Ambush II. During the race, Hidden Mystery was hampered by a loose horse and fell. Hidden Mystery subsequently ran at Sandown carrying 14 stone but broke his leg and had to be put down. His brother Leinster was also a good horse and won races around Liverpool on four occasions This allowed Ambush II to go on and beat Barsac and the great Manifesto, as the crowd acclaimed a royal victory. Ambush II didn't return to Aintree until 1903, when carrying 12st 7lbs he fell in the race won by Drumcree. In 1901, Drumcree ran in the Grand National for the first time and was 2nd beaten 4 lengths (having torn a plate) to Grudon. He was then sold to J.S.Morrison and was co-favourite for the 1902 Grand National, but was only 7th to another Irish bred Shannon Lass.

In 1903, Drumcree was the favourite at 13/2 with his sister Pride of Mabestown third favourite at 10/1. Charles Nugent's son Hugh was due to ride Drumcree in the big race, but he broke a collar bone shortly before the race and the replacement jockey was Percy Woodland. The famous Manifesto (winner in 1897 and 1899) was carrying 12st 3 lbs at the age of 15 and King Edward VII was in attendance to see his previous winner Ambush run and he went off into the lead. Drumree was also back to take on his old compatriot Drumcree. A number of horses were in with a chance and Drumree owned by the Duke of Westminister did a 'Devon Loch' by staggering and falling on the flat when looking like a winner and the King's horse Ambush fell at the last fence (the King loved racing and his first words after the misfortune were apparently *"I hope Anthony (the jockey) is not hurt. Is he up?")* Drumcree jumped the fence brilliantly and ran on to defeat Detail by 3 lengths, with the gallant Manifesto 3rd. Pride of Mabestown was unplaced and also fell in 1904. Hugh Nugent missed out riding the winner and sadly, tragedy was not far away. He was due to ride in Ostend, but his pregnant wife begged him not to go as she had a bad dream. He rode a horse called Red Dragon of Wales but the horse fell and he was killed. His son also Hugh was born just a few months later.

In 1906, Drumcree was 8th in the Aintree Grand National to Ascetic Silver, who amazingly was a 1/2 brother to Drumcree by Ascetic. He was trained by a good Offaly man Aubrey Hastings, who was to be connected to the Hope clan again a few years later with Ally Sloper. Drumcree fell in 1907 and his last race was in Sandown in 1909. He raced until the age of 15 and died in 1912. When Pride of Mabestown retired she bred Long Lough, who won 5 chases; Kilgar won 2 chases; Pride of Delvin won 7 chases; and Mabestown won 3 chases. The latter bred Pride of Drumrora who produced Drumrora, who was to be influential in future.

Pride of Mabestown's family carried on a great tradition, when direct descendants Tibretta was 2nd in 1958 (he won the Beecher & Sefton Chases at

Aintree plus 9 other races and 17 seconds) to Mr What bred in Westmeath, and Red Marauder won the race in 2001. Pride of Mabestown was the five great's maternal grandmother of Red Marauder. Edward Courage acquired the mare Drumrora after the war and three of Tibretta's daughter's Tiberetts, Tiberina, and French Colleen produced 22 winners including Spanish Steps (won 12 chases and 4 hurdle races), Royal Relief 2 mile Champion Chaser, Lictor (Topham Trophy winner) etc. Lira was another daughter and she bred Red Marauder, who won the Grand National in 2001 and was also the dam of his brother Red Striker. He was by Gunner B, who won the Eclipse Stakes in 1978. Red Marauder carried on the great family tradition of Drumcree & Pride of Mabestown by winning the Grand National.

NUGENTS AND RACING IN IRELAND

Sir Hugh Nugent lived firstly at Valley View, when his father was private trainer to Sir William Nelson and eventually he ended up in Windsor Cottages. He succeeded Sir Charles in 1927 and was the son of Hugh, who died in 1903. He has two sons John and David. He was an ardent Catholic and started the first chapel in the village (as a boy Paddy Prendergast attended). He left his home at Windsor House in 1940 and served as a Flying Officer in WW II & trained horses in Ireland at Clonsilla. He moved to Ballinlough Castle the family seat in 1938 and took over the stables of Mrs E.J.King (his mother), when she moved to Ireland in 1946. Some years before his death he lost his sight after a car accident. He died on 30th October 1983 (Age 79). Throughout his life he always used green writing paper. After the financial difficulties that Sir Charles Nugent had in Britain, it was Sir Hugh Nugent together with his own son John (died October 2009 at Ballinlough Castle), who restored the families finances through his business acumen. The family businesses included manufacturing the Lambourn tractor cab, Lambourn Horseboxes and running the UK's largest racehorse transport company, LRT. The Lambourn Horseboxes carried famous horses from Golden Miller to Grundy to their biggest successes.

Lady Nugent (Died 20th March 1963 aged 90 at Lohunda Park, Clonsilla) was the widow of Hugh who was killed in 1903. She later married E.J.King and her green & white colours were familiar for many years on the racecourse and they were trained by her son Sir Hugh. When she moved to Ireland, she became immersed in racing & breeding. She was a woman of decided views on bloodlines, and experimental inbreeding. She was also a great believer in astrology and sometimes insisted that her horse ran, as the stars dictated, rather on their trainers views.

Most of the horses had *"Slipper"* affixed to their name and they traced back to His Slipper. She owned Experiment winner of 3 races & a successful sire. She bred their first classic winner Diamond Slipper (His Slipper-Nanina), winner of

Irish St Leger in 1955 and was 5th in the Irish Derby to Panaslipper. Red Slipper won the Irish Cambridgeshire in 1963 and in 1964 also won £25,000 in prize money, with two raids on Longchamp and another at Maison Lafitte (Sir Hugh had another stable companion who won twice at St Cloud). The French were very upset by these results and brought in new regulations limiting the number of races open to foreigners. Red Slipper (Trouville-Ruby Slipper) won the Whitsun Cup with 9st 7lbs. He won 4 races in 1963 including the Irish Cambridgeshire with 8st 13 lbs and in 1964 won the Irish Lincoln. His Story won the National Produce Stakes in 1959; Wild Johnie won the Blandford Stakes in 1948; in 1957 Valentine Slipper (His Slipper-Sandra) was 3rd in the Irish Derby to Ballymoss beaten 5 lengths; and she won the Irish Lincoln 1952 with Rose Slipper. Sir Hugh trained many other good horses like Place Etoile who won the the Sun Chariot Sts in 1970; Miralife the Athasi Sts 1970 and Miralla who won Irish 1,000 gns in 1975 (owned jointly by his wife Lady Nugent & Lady Lister Kaye). Other good horses were Wolver Life (won 6 races and was placed in Group3 races) and Major Bee (won 10 sprint races). My Hollow won the Royal Whip & Desmond Stake's in 1980.

Nickolas Nugent, Ballinlough Castle, has taken over the family title, since his father John died, as 9th Baronet and they trace back to the O'Reilly's. He is an auctioneer and well known, as the Sales Director of Goffs Bloodstock Sales, after being Managing Director. He also likes to breed a few horses. He has one mare in foal to See the Stars, which will go to Richard Fahey. They bred Lily's Angel (Dark Angel-Noyelles), who won 10 of her 26 races and over €328,000. He also bred the Richard Hannon trained Zurigha, who won 4 races. He is known for his wit and ability at working people from his rostrum. He was born in London and lived at Lambourn, where his father Sir John ran the Lambourn Racehorse Transport. He was educated at Eton and spent summer holidays in Ireland. He has sold from the Magic Millions in Australia and Wrights Bloodstock Sale in New Zealand, Abu Dhala, Hong Kong Jockey Club, and breeze up at Sha Tin and in South Africa. He does a number of charity events on an on-going basis. He writes an interesting diary page in the Irish Field about his work, travels, and family. Tragically, they lost their young daughter Katie aged just six to leukemia in 2010 and they set up the Katie Nugent Fund to support families. Ballinlugh Castle is now a venue for weddings, concerts, exhibitions and much more since it was restored.

EREMON AND JAMES CLEARY 1907

Eremon (Thurles-Daisy) was bred in Ireland by James Cleary in Westmeath from the great racing family that included Dick Cleary, M.J. Cleary vet & horse breeder and P.J.Cleary from Coralstown. Eremon was a 1/2 brother to Christmas Daisy (Vitez-Daisy), who won the Cambridgeshire in 1909 and 1910. Thurles the stallion had also won the Irish Grand National. The horse appeared to be thick winded as a young horse, and was sold by dealer James Daly for a bargain price of £400 to Stanley Howard. He was trained by Tom Coulthwaite, who was not the usual type of trainer, as he trained athletes early on in his life and used the same principles for training horses. The horse made his debut as a 6 y/o and won at Newbury and added a few other wins, which meant that he ended up 8/1 second favourite in 1907 behind Red Lad and Ascetic Silver. Anthony Newey got a broken stirrup early in the race but ran near the front, even with just one iron, as he jumped like a stag. As many of the runners fell, Newey pushed on and got a big lead and he was still 6 lengths in front at the line. He beat Tom West and Sir William Nelson's Patlander. He was a good horse, as he received a 12lbs penalty for his win and still won the Lancashire Chase at Manchester for his fifth win of the year. Tragically, he escaped on the gallops at home after this, and after he was injured he had to be put down at 7 y/o.

GLENSIDE 1911

Glenside who won the Grand National in March 1911 was bred by W.G.Peareth but was foaled at A.T.F. Briscoe's place in Curristown, Killucan for a year and a half. The dam belonged to Mr Briscoe's cousin whose mares were with Briscoe for some years for Cornelius Hannon's stallion St Gris. A.T.F. Briscoe, Curristown, Killucan was a prominent political figure and member of County Council and was Hon. Secretary of the County Committee of Agriculture. He died in Feb 1944. The horse never raced in Ireland.

Glenside (St Gris-Kilwinnet) had been a cheap purchase. He had been bought for a partnership & only cost £150 (probably because he only had one eye) after winning a small race at Tenby. He was a good jumper and had a bit if class and speed in his pedigree. In 1909, he finished 2nd to Cackler in the Grand Sefton Chase in 1909 and was 2nd in the Valentine Chase to Leinster in 1910. In the race in 1911, he was 20/1 with Lutteur II 7/2F. Only four horses finished and three of them remounted, leaving Glenside (Mr J.R. Anthony) the only horse to jump the track. He won by 20 lengths from Rathnally & Shady Girl. He was trained by Captain R.H.Collins and the unluckiest person was Frank Mason, who was due to ride the horse but he broke his leg, giving the ride to Anthony who was familiar with the horse. The other piece of information that came to light was the horse had a temperature of 106 shortly before the big day. He fell in 1912, when ridden by Harry Ussher in the race won by Jerry M.

J.R. Anthony was a member of one of the most successful families in racing in this era. Jack steered Ally Sloper to victory in 1915 and Troytown in 1920, becoming the sixth jockey to win three Grand Nationals. He was also second on Old Tay Bridge in 1925 and 1926 and third the following year on Bright's Boy. His brother Ivor was a successful jockey and his other brother Owen a trainer. He became Britain's Champion Jockey on two occasions - in 1914 and again in

1928, after which he retired to become a trainer. His biggest success as a trainer was with Easter Hero, who won the Cheltenham Gold Cup in 1929 and 1930.

AUBREY HASTINGS - AINTREE LEGEND AND PROUD IRISHMAN

The Hon Aubrey Craven Theophilius Robin Hood Hastings was born on 9th January 1878 and died on 25th May 1929. When he died one paper recorded that *"he would never allow that he was anything else than an Irishman".* He grew up in Ireland in Sharavogue House, Co Offaly in the home of his brother Warner the 15th Earl of Huntington. The *"Robin Hood"* in his name relates to the legend that the original Robin of Sherwood was the heir to the Earldom of Huntington. George Hastings was created Earl of Huntington in 1529 by Henry VIII and since then the Hastings family have used *"Robin Hood"* in the name of the male heirs up to the present Earl of Huntington. Aubrey Hastings grew up in Sharavogue with a love of horses, hunting and polo. He was extremely popular and it was here he met with the accident that deprived him of sight in one eye. It seems that while taking part in a Sunday school excursion, he was cutting a stick, when the knife slipped striking him in the eye.

Hastings had inherited his great sporting abilities from his mother Lady Huntington, who was well known with the Kings County and Ormonde Hunt. In 1867, the Earl married Anne Wilmot daughter of Col H.J.C. Westenra and later inherited the property in Sharavogue, where he came to live. Col Westenra and his father Lord Rossmore had maintained hunting establishments there. Lord Rossmore was the first owner to win over £5,000 in Irish racing, when he won £6,440 in 1813 and it was not until 1915 that this record was broken. Col. J.C.Westenra was one of the leading owners in Ireland and won the most prize money from 1834-36 and also in 1838 (£3,270 in 1836). In view of the family history in racing, it was no surprise when Aubrey Hastings developed a career in the sport. He acted as whip with the hunt and at age 13 received a saddle and bridle from all the ladies, who rode with the harriers. In 1896, he rode his brother's horse Fairy Blast to win at Sharavogue Races.

As a young man Aubrey Hastings, without wealth of his own, had to earn a living. In 1905, he went to England and spent two years with W.Villiers at Cheltenham. He trained his first Grand National winner Ascetic Silver (1906) for Prince Hatzfeldt at Woodmancote, Gloucester and later he moved to Wroughton, Wiltshire purchased for him by the prince.

FOUR GRAND NATIONALS

Ascetic Silver won the Irish Grand National in 1904 for P.J.Dunne and was, later purchased by Hastings for £800 on the death of Dunne (for Prince Hatzfeldt), after he was impressed by Ascetic Silver's jumping. He was Irish bred and a half-brother to Drumcree (1903) and Cloister (1893), who both won the Grand

National. His dam Silver Lady died a few days after his birth and he had to be brought up by hand. As a two year old he was frightened by a thunderstorm and galloped into a ditch and dislocated his hip. A brother to Ardgreagh who was with him at the time was killed. He recovered but when still at Carrollstown being prepared for the Grand National, he dashed through a fence and hurt himself so badly that Mr Dunne decided to shoot him, but his son-in-law Mr Cullinan who owned Flax Park, persuaded him to give the horse a chance to recover.

In 1905, Ascetic Silver (Ascetic-Silver Lady) won the Grand National coming home in front of Kirkland, but unfortunately he left his jockey behind and Fred Bibby's Kirkland won the race. Hastings rode the horse himself and had to waste to make the weight. He won the race in 1906 by 10 lengths at 20/1 and the Prince gave all the credit to Hastings, who became the first man to ride and train a winner of the Grand National. The horse had proved his class by winning both the Irish & English Grand National. The Prince had three runners in the race, but it was Ascetic Silver that was expected to win. Sir Charles Nugent had the 7/2F favourite John MP, who was unbeaten in five races that year. He was travelling well up to the Canal Turn where he fell on the first circuit, and it was at the same place on the second circuit that Ascetic Silver made his move and took over to beat Red Lad by 10 lengths.

In 1915, war was raging across Europe and people, already, had an idea of the horrors that were unfolding and the cost in human life. Perhaps the Grand National was a distraction from the grind that was becoming part of their daily lives. Women's lives were never to be the same after World War 1, as all the work they did in factories, hospitals and at home meant that it was a different world after 1918, and women's right to vote, go out to work etc became national issues. In that context, it was appropriate that the first female owner was about to win the Grand National and she was from Delvin, Co Westmeath.

Ally Sloper (Travelling Lad - Sally in our Alley) was sold as a yearling at Doncaster September Sales in 1910 for 25 guineas to Captain Armitage, who sold the horse for 30 guineas to E Robson, the Wantage trainer. He was trained for the flat but was too slow, so he was given to H Randall, who found the horse a natural jumper and his day as a hack were over. Whilst taking part in a steeplechase, which was his maiden race and which he won, the horse caught the eye of Lady Nelson, who enquired if he was for sale. Not too keen to part with Ally Sloper, Randall asked 1000 guinesa. The offer was promptly accepted on condition of passing a "vet" and sent to Aubrey Hastings at Wroughton.

In 1915, Aubrey had Ally Sloper in the race and the 6 y/o had won the Beecher and Valentine Chases over the course as a 5 y/o, but was still not a great jumper.

Jack Anthony rode him and he was the brother of Ivor Anthony, who took over the stable after Hastings died in 1929. Ivor was riding in the race & lifted his brother back into the saddle at one point after a bad jump by Ally Sloper. When he took off too soon at the Canal Turn he lost both irons again but got back on an even keel. The horse battled on to victory and coincidentally set another record for the big race as the owner Lady Nelson (Margaret Hope from Delvin, Co Westmeath) was the first woman to win the Grand National (only three women had a runner in all the previous years). After the race, she praised the quality of Anthony's horsemanship. After the last race the course was closed and handed over to the War Department for four years. The National was transferred to Gatwick to be won by Vermouth (1916), Ballymacad (1917) and Poethlyn (1919). Ally Sloper ran each year with the best result being third place to Aubrey Hasting's horse Ballymacad (E.Driscoll) 100/9, when it was called the War National Steeplechase.

In 1924, a new race started for chasers at the Cheltenham Festival called the Gold Cup, which years later was to become the premier race on the calendar for the best chasers. Master Robert (Moorside II-Dodds) who was returned from The Curragh as a useless horse to his owner and breeder Robert McKinley, who then used him as a plough horse in Co Donegal. He was eventually purchased for £50, before ending up the property of Lord Airlie & Sydney Green who sent him to Aubrey Hastings. He had a diseased bone in his foot and poultices were used constantly to get him fit, right up to the start of the race. Hastings couldn't get a jockey to ride him, until Robert Trudgill accepted the offer even though he too had stitches on an injured leg after a fall in the Stanley Chase the day before. He won by 4 lengths from Fly Mask and Silvo and had to weigh in first and then go straight to a doctor as the stitches had split. It was a brave performance from a jockey who had not much success before this day. It was amazing that an Offaly man Aubrey Hastings trained the winner, a Westmeath man Michael Ballesty bred the runner up and another Offaly man H.Sefton Kenny trained the third horse.

BROWN JACK "A HELL OF A HORSE - WHO LIKED CHEDDAR CHEESE!"

Perhaps the most famous horse in Britain prior to Arkle and Red Rum was Brown Jack and Hasting's was strongly associated with this legend. He was born at Corolanty Stud in Ireland to George Webb, a local breeder not too far from where Aubrey Hastings grew up. He couldn't sell him at Goffs but afterwards Marcus Thompson from Cashel paid £110 for him. Aubrey Hastings saw him run in Ireland without success and purchased him for £750 for a client Sir Harold Wernher, as a jumper. He won 7 out of 10 hurdle races before winning the Champion Hurdle in 1928, but never ran over jumps again.

Aubrey asked Steve Donoghue to look at him and see if he had enough speed for the flat. He became associated with the great Steve Donoghue, as he won 7 years in a row at Royal Ascot - Ascot Stakes 1928 and the Queen Alexandra Stakes 1929/34. After Aubrey died in May 1929, the horse was trained by Ivor Anthony at Wroughton in the stables of Mrs Aubrey Hastings. He received presents & had parcels sent to him by the public of cheap American cheddar cheese (his favourite), apples, carrots etc. He received phone calls, had a sermon on goodness preached about him in church and at Steve Donoghue's retirement a receiving set was put in his stable so that the great jockey could talk to him. Before he died, Hastings said *"He was a hell of a horse"*. Ironically, the last horse saddled by him before his death was Brown Jack in the Manchester Cup. On 25th May 1929, he attended a match at Cirencester Polo Club and after playing a game he collapsed and died.

Aubrey Hastings left a legacy of success, which passed on to his family. Aubrey's son Peter Hastings (later Hastings-Bass) became one of the Queen's trainers in 1962 and in 1977 his son William Hastings-Bass also became the royal trainer. The Bass legacy led to the purchase of Kingsclere Estate near Newbury in 1953. Peter Hastings -Bass (age 42) died in 1964, and his young assistant Ian Balding took over the licence and later married his daughter Emma, thus carrying on the family tradition. Ian trained the great Mill Reef to win the Epsom Derby and Prix De L'Arc in 1971. Ian's brother Toby Balding trained two Grand National winners in Highland Wedding in 1969 and Little Polveir in 1989. His son Andrew took over at Kingsclere in 2003 and his sister Clare is even more famous, as one of the leading sports presenters on British television. Aubrey Hastings would have been proud of his legacy and his family's achievements. He was also very proud to be an Irishman.

SHAUN SPADAH - GRAND NATIONAL HERO IN 1921

The Aintree Grand National has a history of drama, excitement, equine heroes, brave jockey's and even braver punters sticking a pin in some dodgy horse and hoping he will win at 100/1. The 1921 race produced a winner who was Irish bred, Scottish owned, English trained and Welsh ridden and a horse Shaun Spadah, who was the only one to complete the course without falling but let's begin at the start of this equine adventure.

Patrick McKenna of Kilgarvan House, Streamstown, Co Westmeath was originally from Newtownforbes and spent most of his political life in Westmeath. He was elected for Longford-Westmeath in 1923 as a member of the Farmers Party, but lost the seat as an independent in 1927. He worked mainly for small farmers and wanted to break up the big estates to provide economic holdings. He joined the Fianna Fail party and presided over a meeting on the Hill of Uisneach, where Sean Lemass & Eamon De Valera addressed the people. He was campaigning in the 1909 General Election when he was invited to dine by

Michael J. Cleary, veterinary surgeon and well-known breeder and owner of good horses in Mullingar. Cleary persuaded him to buy a brood mare called Rusialka for £300, without even seeing the horse. At that time, Michael Cleary's brother Dick was a leading trainer of jumpers at Bishopstown, Streamstown and he had a horse called Easter Prize, formerly owned by John James a famous Irish bookmaker, in his stable. He said to McKenna that *"it was like a lottery breeding them"*, but that his was a good horse so the deal was done. When asked about Easter Prize after the Grand National, he is supposed to have said that the last he had seen of the triumphant sire Easter Prize was leaving Athlone *"tied behind a tinker's cart"*.

Dick Cleary, later trained All Sorts to win the Irish Grand National on Easter Monday 1916 Shaun Spadah ran that day at Fairyhouse but was unplaced. When Shaun Spadah won the Loughnagore Plate at Kilbeggan in May 1917, All Sorts was fourth in the same race.

JOHN THE BOGMAN

McKenna named the horse Shaun Spadah a character in a poem by a Meath priest Rev W. McCormack for years a professor at St Finian's College, Navan. (Spadah or spoddagh apparently means broken or wet turf clods, which usually remain after the turf has been drawn home). A report in the papers by writer E.E.Coussell after the big win read *"Shaun Spadah's Romance - Bred by Slap Dash Irishman under Queer Conditions"*. He wrote that McKenna had a houseful of children and frequently said as he left *"Well, I must be getting home to count the children"* and when Easter Prize was mated with his mare he asked *"for the blessing of the saints on the union"*.

As a foal the horse almost died after eating the seeds of a poisonous weed, but his strong constitution pulled him through. In 1915 he won at Downpatrick & Gowran Park before being sold to Frank Barbour ("Wee Frankie") linen magnate from Northern Ireland. In 1917, Shaun Spadah went to M.H.Benson the bookmaker who had a trade name of Douglas Stewart and the slogan *"Duggie never Owes"*, before being purchased by Scottish contractor Malcolm McAlpine who sent him to be trained by George Poole at Lewes. Poole brought off a unique double in 1921, with Soranus winning the Lincoln and Shaun Spadah the Grand National.

GRAND NATIONAL 1921

Another Westmeath horse Ballyboggan, a winner of the Irish Grand National, was dramatically scratched from the big race due to a set back and Shaun Spadah was left to represent Westmeath. A record field of thirty six horses started out but in the mayhem that ensued, on a very tough course, all of them except Shaun Spadah fell at least once or were knocked over by riderless horses.

Three jockeys broke their collarbones including Harry Browne an amateur jockey whose horse fell at the 2nd last fence and broke his reins and collarbone. In spite of this he remounted The Bore & finished second to Shaun Spadah (100/9). The irony of the result & all the fallers was that in 1922 Shaun Spadah fell at the first fence in the Grand National. What a difference a year makes! His jockey F.B.Rees a canny Welshman was one of the greats, winning the jockey's championship 5 times in the 1920's.

One of the amusing aspects of his victory was the guesses of the English papers at the translation of Shaun Spadah. Someone informed the Daily Mail that when translated it was *"James Good".* Another paper translated it as *"Jack of Spades".* One story is that he was a gentle horse, who even put up with the antics of children and because he could not be raised to a temper he was called a *"bogtrotter",* which apparently is supposed to be someone of extreme submissiveness. One other odd thing about the name was that in London cockney slang in the 1920's Shaun Spadah became slang for a car e.g. *"Blimey, I nearly got run over by that Shaun Spadah!"* In 1923 Shaun Spadah proved his ability, when finishing second carrying 12st 7lbs to another Irish bred horse,13 year old Sergeant Murphy. The Prince of Wales attended the races in 1923 and jockey Harry Brown) was his escort. The Prince fancied Sergeant Murphy, but Harry said *"Good God, don't do that. He's as old as I am. He's not a horse at all".* When Sergeant Murphy won at 100/6, Harry disappeared rapidly from the Royal Box with his head intact, but his pride dented. Shaun Spadah made his first appearance in the Grand National in 1919 and his final appearance at the age of thirteen in 1924 when he completed the course.

THE GHOST OF SHAUN SPADAH

Shaun Spadah is buried in Lewes (where he died) and there is a tombstone recording his memory. The ashes of his jockey Fred Rees, who died in 1951 are also in Lewes. A strange story was printed on the *Weekly World News* in May 1985 when a 21 year old female jockey Penny Ffitch Hayes, who was having lunch with her father at the site of the old Lewes racetrack, when she claimed she caught sight of a horse outside the window. When she went outside he was not there gone even though there was nowhere he could have gone. From photographs she identified the horse as Shaun Spadah and she was convinced it was the ghost of the Grand National hero of 1921. Could the spirit of the old champion be still haunting the old Lewes race track?

THE "SERGEANT", THE "CAPTAIN" AND THE PRESIDENT OF THE USA

In 1919, the Aintree Grand National was back home after being held at Gatwick during the war years from 1916-1918. The crowds flocked back to see the big race and the warm favourite was Mr Hugh Peel's Poethlyn at 11/4 carrying 12st 7lbs The field included Shaun Spadah winner in 1921, Sergeant Murphy winner in 1923, Lady Nelson's Ally Sloper, who won at Gatwick in 1917 and E.Hope Johnstone's Irish Grand National winner Ballyboggan who had been trained by Bob Fetherstonhaugh. All of these horses had strong Westmeath connections and had raced in Ireland. Bob Fetherstonhaugh at one stage had Shaun Spadah, Sergeant Murphy and Ballyboggan in his yard. Sergeant Murphy was placed when racing at Mullingar. The one that went closest was Ballyboggan who was beaten 8 lengths by the favourite Poethlyn, that had also won the previous year at Gatwick. Sergeant Murphy (General Symons-Rose Graft) ran seven times in the race from 1918-25. He was 4th to Troytown in 1920 and 4th to Music Hall in 1922 (after being re-mounted) before winning in 1924.

All of these horses have great stories to tell, as we will see, but Sergeant Murphy's win could match all of them. He ran seven times in the race, was a 13 y/o when he won, his jockey was killed the same year, the owner a student in Cambridge was the first American to win the race, in 1938 a future President of the USA starred in a film about him, 90 years later the winning trophy was stolen in America and much more. The horse went through many owners like James Nugent, Douglas Stuart, before Stephen Sanford. At one stage he became the property of S.Rait Kerr, Rathmoyle where he lived for a few years. In November 1921 an advertisement was put in the local paper that Kerr was giving up breeding and selling broodmares because of threats by the IRA. Tragically, he was found dead on the front lawn of the house in June 1922 having committed suicide. Rathmoyle Stud later produced another successful breeder in F.B.O'Toole who bred Knight of the Grail who won the 1927 Irish Derby, Magnetic North won 1956 St Leger, Jack Ketch won 1957 Irish 2,000 guineas etc.

Americans had been gradually getting more interested in winning the famous Liverpool Grand National (American bred Rubio won in 1908) and they owned four horses in the race. The first American to win the race was Stephen Sandford an undergraduate at Cambridge University, whose father was a carpet millionaire and gave him the horse as a hunter. The horse was still very frisky so he decided to put him back into training with George Blackwell and he went on to be 4th to Music Hall in 1922. The jockey in 1923 was Captain Geoffrey "Tuppy" Bennett a 28 y/o vet, who was a leading amateur jockey and rode Sergeant Murphy to win the Scottish Grand National in 1922. When the horse came to race in 1923 he was 100/6 to win, even though he was 13 y/o. He was not a great jumper but a dour stayer. Shaun Spadah was a 12y/o, carrying 12st 7lb, and priced at 20/1. Nobody told the two old horses that they could not win, as the unfortunately named Forewarned was 11/2 favourite. The course was covered in a mist and the horses could not be seen except at the first and last three fences even with binoculars. Sergeant Murphy took up the running at Beecher's on the second circuit and when they came out of the fog only three horses were in contention-Sergeant Murphy, Shaun Spadah, and Conjuror II.

Shaun Spadah faltered with his big weight and Sergeant Murphy stayed on to win by 3 lengths, with Conjuror II six lengths further back. Amazingly, the first five home, were aged in descending order from 13 y/o down to 9 y/o to show it was an *"old horses race"*.

One reporter recalled that at Sandown the previous December he was talking to jockey Charlie Hawkins, who said he was unlucky in 1922, but that *"he would win it the next time with Sergeant Murphy"*. A short time afterwards he was killed in a hurdle race in France. The irony of Captain Bennett riding the winner instead of Hawkins was that on 27th December 1923 he was also killed in a fall on a horse at Woverhampton, after being kicked on the head. He had ridden 62 winners that season and was only two behind the leading professional Fred Rees. Sergeant Murphy ran for another three years and died with his shoes on when he broke a leg at Bogside and had to be destroyed. General Symons was his sire, bred by R.A. Brice and he was a well bred horse being by Childwick. As a yearling he went wrong with his fore joints and by chance Westmeath breeder John Taylor, Mill House, Knockdrin, Mullingar, visited the stud, as they were considering putting him down, and pleaded for his life. Brice made a present of him and over time he became a very successful sire for Taylor.

The story of Sergeant Murphy was not quite finished yet as he had a special place in the USA as the first American owned winner. In 1938 a B movie called *"Sergeant Murphy"* starred a young Ronald Reagan in only his third film. It's the story of a farm boy who joins the army and follows his beloved horse Sergeant Murphy to Britain to win the Grand National (a bit similar to Elizabeth Taylor in '*National Velvet*'). Reagan went on to become an A list star and eventually, President of the United States. The director B (Breezy). Reeves Eason had directed the famous burning of Atlanta scene in "Gone with the Wind", 1939.

In September 2013, two steeplechase trophies were among five priceless trophies stolen from the National Museum of Racing and Hall of Fame in Saratoga Springs, N.Y. In a smash-and-grab robbery, which only took three minutes, the 1914 Brook Cup Handicap Steeplechase Trophy and the 1923 Grand National Steeplechase Trophy, won at Aintree in England by Sergeant Murphy. The 248-ounce Grand National Trophy was made of silver and was owned by Stephen Sandford. It was a professional job, with the intention to melt down the stolen trophies. In 2011, the Sergeant Murphy Cup was inaugurated for exceptional effort towards preserving land in Northern Baltimore and Harford County. The background was that the Sergeant Murphy point to point was held at Harford Hunt Races from 1925-34 and was sponsored by Stephen Sandford and named in honour of Sergeant Murphy. The name of Sergeant Murphy lives on through the Sandford family.

FLY MASK AND SILVO (1924/25)

The Laidlow Family, Castleknock were associated with two Grand National winners in Gragalach1929 and Grakle 1931, who were sold as five year olds and also Fly Mask,who ran in their ownership when 2nd in 1924 and 3rd in 1925. Fly Mask (Fly Fisher out of dam by Bergomask) was bred by Michael Ballety, Rathconrath Stud, Mullingar. Ballesty had the very successful stallion Bergomask (1891 Mask-Hermia) in 1899. Fly Mask's grand dam traced back to Ascetic and was originally trained in Dublin by James Daly, who bought him as an unbroken colt from Michael Ballesty. He was bought in 1929 by T.K. Laidlow for around £1,200 and was sent to Tom Coulthwaite at Hednesford, who later had charge of Gragalach and Grakle.

He was entered for the Grand National of 1923 and was 6/1 favourite, because he won at Haydock, Manchester, and Ludlow. However, after Cheltenham it was discovered that a nail was in his leg and he had to be withdrawn. In 1924 he was joint favourite at 100/7 with two other horses with midlands connections in Shaun Spadah & Silvo. H Sefton Kenny, Birr managed the stud of T.Kenny, Kilcarron, and then went to Rosemount, Co Westmeath to train horses with some success. He trained the highest priced chaser Silvo belonging to his cousin H.V.Kenny. The horse won many good races in Britain and was placed 3rd in the National in 1924 and won the Grand Steeplechase de Paris in 1925. He had been purchased by W.H.Medwood for 2,500gns. Silvo went for home after Valentines Brook, but was pursued by Fly Mask and Master Robert with the latter galloping on to win by 4 lengths from Fly Mask (ridden by Jack Moylan grandfather of Pat Eddery, champion jockey in 1926 and winner of seven classics) with Silvo (G.Goswell) six lengths behind. The following year Fly Mask (E.Doyle) was second favourite at 10/1 and looked like winning when taking over from Silvo (who finished 5th), but was collared by Double Chance & Old Tay Bridge on the run-in. It was a game performance with an extra stone on his back, carrying 11st 11bs, and his last attempt (now 11 y/o) at the big race.

GRAKLE AND THE OFFALY CONTINGENT

A total of 43 runners turned up for the race in 1931 and running in his fifth National Grakle again featured at 100/6. Gregalach led them out into the country with the favourite Easter Hero crashing out and Drin broke his hock. Ballasport was travelling well when falling and Georginatown only faded in the closing stages to fall at the last and Drintyre refused at the 2nd last. It turned out to be a titanic dual between Gregalach (winner in 1929 at 100/1) and Grakle with the latter winning by 1 1/2 lengths.

The Kenny family (or extended family) played a huge part in horse racing from breeding, training, to ownership in this era and were a major part of the Ormond Hunt. In March 1931, the local paper declared that H.Briscoe Kenny. Clyduff

House, Roscrea, bred Drintyre, Drin, Georginatown, and Ruddyman and that it would be a record when his four horses ran in the Aintree Grand National in 1931. It would have been but was it true? With the assistance of Guy Williams he supplied the following information and it was clear that Mr Kenny bred prolific winner Georginatown (1921 Kroonstad-Georgina Mac). The General Stud Book credits the breeding of Drintyre (1923 Drinmore - Lady Longwood) to Mr E. Foster, though the mare became Kenny's property by the time she had her foal in 1927. Drin (1924 Drinmore - dam by Balsamo) fell at Valentine's Brook 2nd time round, in the 1931 Grand National, breaking his hock and was put down. He was bred by Richard O'Keeffe, Corbetstown, Killucan Co Westmeath. Drin had won a Grand Sefton, Grand Military Gold Cup and the Prince of Wales' Handicap chase at Sandown Park (twice). [This was from F.M. Prior's Half-Bred Stud Book, Vol IV, 1934]. Prior gives Ruddyman (Ruddygore - dam May Lily by Hermit II), as a winner of 12 chases and twice second in the Welsh Grand National. He states that he was bred by H.B. Kenny, Clyduff House, Roscrea. On that basis, Kenny bred two of the runners Georginatown & Ruddyman, but he was also associated with Drintyre, which was no mean achievement in the greatest race in the world.

In October 1926, the welter race at Barronstown course was won by Capt Gairdiner's Georginatown bred by H.Briscoe-Kenny of Clyduff and purchased by her present owner as a 3 y/o unbroken filly. Georginatown was later owned by J.H.Wallace and in January 1931 she was described, as having won 12 of her last 13 races. The horse paid a flying visit to Derby in January to win a National Hunt Flat race the first day and a three mile chase carrying 12st 7lbs the next day. She was described as *"a little un with great courage"*. On the day of the race a contingent fron Offaly & Tipperary travelled to the Aintree Grand National including Messrs R. Kenny, R. Wallace, T.J. O'Mara, W.B. Hayes, and J.E. Maxwell a brother of the jockey Farnham (Freddie). A Mr Graham who drew the horse in the Hospital Sweep was also invited by J.H.Wallace, whose guests numbered 21. The horse got a bump, when Easter Hero fell and at the last Ballasport fell in front of her, and she fell over him.

H. Briscoe Kenny, Clyduff, bred other useful horses like Killadoon winner of the Victory Chase in 1931 at Manchester and later was sold to Colonel Tweedie. The dam Mithra Belle was also bred by him and won the Kildare Plate ridden by Harry Kenny Junior. He still had Mithra Belle at that time and Drintyre was related to her. In 1936, he purchased the sire Valois to stand at Clyduff. He had won over £3,000 in stakes including the Esher Cup & Chepstow Summer Cup of £1,000. He also won three hurdle races, carrying top weight in one of them.

QUARE TIMES -THE HORSE THAT WAS BURIED ON THE LAWN

When Vincent O'Brien won the Aintree Grand National in 1955 with Quare Times, he was completing a hat-trick of wins in the race, after the success of Early Mist in 1953 and Royal Tan in 1954. The owner of the horse was Mrs W.H.E Wellman (formerly Cecily Mildred O'Carroll Darby of Leap Castle, Co Offaly) of Gaybrook, Mullingar, Co Westmeath, who had an interesting life before this historic day. She married Anthony Minchin of Doorly Hall, Co Longford, which didn't last and then she married Major Robert Smyth of Gaybrook in 1935. He bought Quare Times for her in 1947 but he died in 1952. Her third marriage was to an American William Wellman who moved into Gaybrook. She was a familiar figure in the hunting fields of the midlands and a lucky owner with the only horse she had in training.

Quare Times was born in 1946 a son of Artists Son and was bred by Phil Sweeney, Orwell Stud, Thurles. He was bought at Ballsbridge in 1947 by Robert Smyth for 300 guineas, as a gift for his wife. The stayed in Gaybrook until he was five and when he was broken, he went to Vinvent O'Brien, who stated that the horse would take time to develop. He made his debut as a 6 y/o in 1952 but took until 1954, before he showed his form with a win at Gowran Park, and a win in the National Hunt Chase at Cheltenham as 5/2. It was an exhibition of horsemanship from Bunny Cox to win it two years in a row. It was also a great day for Mrs Wellman, as it was the only horse she owned. She said *"About ten months ago, Vincent O'Brien told us that we would make a bid for this race with Quare Times and he said he thought we would win it".* He jumped, stayed & quickened to victory by 5L's.

The next stop was Aintree, where O'Brien also had Royal Tan, Early Mist, and Oriental Way. The rain poured down giving heavy ground, which Quare Times did not normally like. Bryan Marshall going for three in a row picked Early Mist and young Pat Taaffe was given the ride on Quare Times. Sundew made a lot of the running in the race, as Pat Taaffe gradually brought Quare Times into the race and his brother Tom also travelled well on Carey's Cottage(trained by his father Tom) and briefly took the lead after Sundew fell. Coming to the last, Quare Times was full of running and galloped away to beat Tudor Line into second place for the second year in a row. Carey's Cottage got third place making it a great day for the Taaffe family. It was a brilliant piece of training and patience to get the horse at his best at the age of nine. The horse turned out a few weeks later at Leopardstown to win a 2 mile hurdle race by 6 lengths. He became one of the few horses to win a race again after success in the Grand National. Mrs Wellman was said to have put £50 EW on Quare Times at 100/8. She met the Queen Mother after the race and said she was sorry that her horse didn't do better and in turn she was asked all about Quare Times. She even suggested that the Queen Mother buy an Irish horse and got the reply *"Oh, yes,*

I know Ireland is where all the good horses come from".

On Tuesday 5th April, Quare Times was feted when he was paraded in style through the streets of Mullingar at 7pm. Thousands lined the street and the Chairman of the Town Commissioners D.Keelan and other members, plus County Manager M.G.McGeeney greeted Mrs Wellmann, Pat Taaffe & Vincent O'Brien. The Mullingar Brass & Reed Band and St Mary's Pipe band led the parade. Quare Times followed with the Master of the Hunt, Col Denis Purdon accompanying them. An open jeep was provided for the owner, trainer & breeder Mr & Mrs Sweeney. Newsreel film was taken of the event. Later at the Greville Arms, Rex Beaumont who owned a brother of Quare Times presented Mrs Wellmann with a bunch of flowers with a note *"to Quare Times from his brother".* He welcomed the trainer, jockey & breeder. Vincent O'Brien & Pat Taaffe also spoke. Major Wellmann spoke on behalf of both and thanked everyone. *"He was so confident of a win that he did not buy a return ticket for Saturday night".* There were free refreshments for everyone. A bonfire was lit at Gaybrook, where the horse stayed for the night after further celebrations.

Unfortunately for Cecily, re-marriage meant she didn't inherit Gaybrook, which was sold in the 1950's and in the1970's was acquired by the Land Commission. Mrs Wellman later moved to Ballymore Eustace, Co Kildare with her husband and Quare Times. The horse died at the age of 28 and was buried on the front lawn, close to home.

MR WHAT 1958 AND L'ESCARGOT 1975 - O'NEILLS

Barbara & Arthur O'Neill of Rathganny, Multyfarnham, Co Westmeath have a very unusual record in that they bred Mr What to win the Grand National in 1958 and 17 years later Ireland recorded its next win in a famous race, when the dual Cheltenham Gold Cup winner L'Escargot beat Red Rum. What was more remarkable was that they also bred L'Escargot and that he was directly related back to Mr What. When Barbara O'Neill (nee Malone of Shinglis, Westmeath, a well-known sporting family) married she had a mare called Duchess of Padula (she bred 5 winners including Inquisitive Pete, Colonial Jack, Battling Pedulas, Irish Duke and Carabawn-all $^1/_2$ brothers to Mr What) who was originally bought for £18 from Gerry O'Neill, Bellison Lodge, Castlepollard.

Even though she never raced, she turned out to be a remarkable mare because a filly she produced called What A Daisy who was the dam of L'Escargot, Havago (10 wins & won Gloucester Hurdle), What A Buck (won 9 chases); The Pilgarlic (7 chases and ran at Aintree); Flitgrove (8 wins); Rathganny (4 wins); and Master What(3 wins). The O'Neills and What A Daisy bred 2 full brothers and a $^1/_2$ brother to L'Escargot-The Pilgarlic and What A Buck both sired by Royal Buck, were owned by the Fagan's, Gartlandstown. In 1977, The Pilgarlic was 4th in the Aintree National & What A Buck 6th; 1978-The Pilgarlic was 5th, 1979- was 4th again, and 1980- was 3rd. Both were trained in England - the Pilgarlic by Fred Rimell & What A Buck by David Nicholson.

Arthur a native of Collinstown was commissioned in World War 1 and during World War II he served as a Group Leader in the L.D.F. He was a founder Director of the Mullingar Livestock Market, as well as an extensive farmer and keen on hunting and sporting activities. The horse was bought by Tom Taaffe (the father of Pat and Toss Taaffe) for £500. Apparently, he was called Mr What, because nobody could think of a name for him! Jim Tormey, Bunbrosna, (who died in 2014) had taken Mr What out hunting and he rode him in his first race in a Mullingar bumper in March 1954. The horse won a number of races over hurdles and fences (5 chases) including the Troystown Chase and was 2nd to Roddy Owen in the Leopardstown Chase. He was bought for £1,500 by businessman David Coughlan from Skibbereen but living in Bray, who left him with Taaffe to train for the big race.

In 1958 Wynburgh was the favourite at 6/1 and ESB with top weight was the only previous winner. Mr What was an 8 y/o, carrying 10st 6lbs, who beat Sentina in the Troystown Chase but as a novice was not a major fancy. Pat Taaffe was riding Sentina & Toss was riding Brookling, so the mount went to Arthur Freeman. He only saw the horse for first time in the parade ring and was a very late booking. There were 31 runners in the race and Freeman gradually took Mr What into the race and took up running on the second circuit and went clear at the Canal Turn. Well clear at the last fence he hit it hard and somehow Freeman stayed on board to go on and beat Tiberetta by 30 lengths, with Green Drill 15 lengths further back. Freeman said after the race *"At the last fence when I was looking around to see where the other horses were, Mr What nearly went down but it was all my fault".* Mr What was to make five more attempts to win the race from 1959 to 1963 but in 33 races he never won again (He was 3rd to Oxo beaten in 1959; fell at the 2nd fence in 1960; 11th in 1961; he was 3rd to the Offaly bred Kilmore in 1962; and finally in 1963 he was brought down at 13 y/o. Arthur O'Neill died in 1987 in Mullingar Hospital aged 93 and Barbara died in 1969. In December 1967, the 17 y/o horse died of old age at trainer Willie Stephenson's yard at Royston, Hertfordshire.

L'ESCARGOT - THE SNAIL WHO COULD RUN

After 17 years of failure, Ireland at last won the Aintree Grand National, with one of the most remarkable steeplechasers in our history, when Raymond Guest's L'Escargot (Escart III -What A Daisy) won the race in 1975. Mrs Barbara O'Neill bred L'Escargot, who won two Cheltenham Gold Cups in 1970/71; won the Grand National in 1975 (twice placed); and also won the Meadow Brook Chase in the USA for his owner former American Ambassador Raymond Guest.

The horse has been described has not having *"charisma"* and not really loved by the public like Golden Miller, Arkle, Red Rum, and Desert Orchid. He is probably best remembered because his name means *"The Snail"* or because he prevented Red Rum winning three in a row. All of the above maybe true, but when you look at the record of the horse he was more of a *"class grinder"* rather than a public star. He horse was originally purchased for 950 guineas by former jump jockey Jimmy Brogan, who tragically, died a few days later. His widow held on to the horse until 1966, when he was snapped up as a 3 y/o at the Ballsbridge Sales for 3,500 guineas by Irish trainer Dan Moore to race for one his regular owners Raymond Guest, former American Ambassador to Ireland.

Dan Moore was one of the most successful trainers of his era and trained a number of good horses with Westmeath connections. He trained Revelry bred by J.J.Ham, Halston to win the 1947 Irish Grand National although the licence had to be held in the name of Dick O'Connell his Head Lad. Westmeath bred Flying Wild was also owned by Raymond Guest, who had won the Epsom Derby with Larkspur in 1962 and Sir Ivor in 1967, but his main ambition then was to win the Aintree Grand National. L'Escargot won two bumpers at Navan & Naas and then won the Gloucester Hurdle at Cheltenham with 21 y/o Tommy Carberry riding. He won the Scalp Hurdle as a 6 y/o after a hobday operation and challenged for the Champion Hurdle, where he finished 6th to Persian War. He went over fences in 1969 and after winning a few novice chases, Guest went for the Meadowbrook Chase in the USA, which he duly won and he was voted Jumper of the Year in the USA in 1969. When he won the Wills Premier Chase early in 1970 it was decided to send the 7 y/o for the Cheltenham Gold Cup.

Kinloch Brae was hot favourite but fell at the hill leaving French Tan (P.Taaffe) and L'Escargot with young Tommy Carberry on board and he outstayed his opponent to win at 33/1. The horse challenged for the Colonial Cup at Camden, South Carolina but could only finish 4th, and it seemed to take a lot out of him as he lost his form. The following year he was joint favourite at 7/2 for the Gold Cup, after a good run under top weight in the Leopardstown Chase. When Glencarrig Lady fell, it was similar to the previous year as Tom Dreaper's Leap Frog and Fulke Walwyn's The Dikler challenged him, but he battled on to win his second Gold Cup. He was not greeted by the crowds like a true champion, even though he beat two future Gold Cup winners in the race. L'Escargot ran at Cheltenham an extraordinary eight times including two 4ths in the Gold Cup, and 2nd in the Cathcart Cup.

AINTREE GRAND NATIONAL 1972 - HIS HALF BROTHER AND THE POOKA

When L'Escargot went for his first Grand National in 1972 he was carrying 12stone and was 17/2 F but took a dislike to the place and he was knocked over at the third fence. Ironically, Mrs Eddie Newman (Dolly Yourell) ran her home bred horse General Symon's (Escart III-Flappy), who was a 1/2 brother to L'Escargot, in the race receiving a few stone but he ran a cracker dead heating with Jim Dreaper's Black Secret behind Well To Do and Gay Trip, only beaten five lengths. He took up the running, with Paddy Kiely on board, at the second last fence but though running on gamely couldn't hold on. General Symons was given an each way chance before the race after beating Beggar's Way in the Webster Cup Chase and also winning the National Trial Chase. He was trained by Jim Tormey, Bunbrosna, who travelled to the races with his neighbour Cecil Ross who was riding his own horse The Pooka. The latter fell at the Canal Turn on the second circuit when travelling well. He was bred in England and he was bought for £900. Cecil recalls the ride and struggling to lie up on the first circuit but he began to pick up on the second circuit. At the Canal Turn he said the horse went one way as he turned sharply and he went the other way and *"it was all over"*. He always said *"I thought then, and still do, that we were going that we were going to be concerned with the finish."* Having said that he recalls being very pleased that Jimmy Tormey RIP got joint third place.

In an article in Sports Illustrated in 1972, Cecil mentioned that The Pooka means *"a large ill-intentioned lubberly fairy"*. In an interesting comment on the famous course he said *"I walked the course a couple of years ago and that it wasn't too bad. I walked it again this morning and changed my mind. I'm not brave. I wish it was all over"*.

CRISPS'S CRACKLED BY RED RUM

One of the best remembered Grand Nationals was held in 1973 when Crisp galloped the field into the ground carrying 12stone, except for a horse who was to become a legend in Red Rum, who was receiving 23 lbs. It was a glorious performance by Crisp that deserved to win the great race but this time there was no happy ending as Red Rum and Brian Fletcher collared him on the run-in to win by 3/4 length. Dan Moore ran L'Escargot over the fences in November 1972, and this time he was better prepared for the big races in 1973, but he could only stay on to finish 25 lengths third, giving 23lbs to Red Rum. In 1974, Red Rum was carrying 12 stone and giving 1lb to L'Escargot now 11 years old, but he was in majestic form and gave Donald McCain his second win and Brian Fletcher's third win. He led from Beecher's Brook and L'Escargot beat Charles Dickens by a short head for second place. For his final attempt in 1975 the Moore family the horse had 11st 3lbs, he received a great preparation and a light season. All the signs were good, but Ginger McCain was not afraid of L'Escargot. Red Rum was backed into 7/2F to get the hat trick but a lot of money brought L'Escargot into 13/2. In the race itself, L'Escargot made one mistake at the 7th fence but that was his only worry, as he seemed to cruise around and it became clear that he was going much better than Brian Fletcher on Red Rum. He waited until they jumped the last and then raced away to win by 15 lengths. Even John Francombe said *"I have never ever seen a horse going so easily at that stage".*

L'Escargot became only the second horse to win both the Grand National and Cheltenham, which was first achieved by Dorothy Paget's Golden Miller. Red Rum went on to stamp his place in Grand National history and in the minds of racing followers around the world. Raymond Guest's aim of winning the Aintree Grand National succeeded, to add to his two Epsom Derby successes.He was inducted into the Hall of Fame in the USA in 1977 and he died at 21 at Raymond Guest's farm on his Powhatan Plantation.

MARTIN DIBB'S COMPLY OR DIE WAS JUST A "LUCKY PENNY"

On 5th April 2008, it was not a major surprise when David Pipe's useful horse Comply or Die won the Aintree Grand National, as he was 7/1JF but it suddenly brought into focus Martin Dibbs, Clinton House Stud farm the breeder of the horse, who slipped under the radar until this historic sporting moment. He certainly grabbed the media's attention because the other major racing news that weekend was the retirement of the popular veteran jockey Tony Dobbin. His last winner was on a horse called Ballyvoge and by a strange coincidence this horse was also bred by Martin Dibbs. To add to his fairy tale story on Sunday the day after the Grand National, Martin recorded a double with The Sliothar winning a novice hurdle at Southwell and Brotenstown a 6 y/o won a mare's hurdle at Limerick. Martin was at the races to see the latter's win as this was the first horse he had in training, in spite of being involved with horses all his life. Martin is related to the Cleary's, Kiernan's and Killian's, so there is a great tradition of racing blood in the family. His father inherited the place but had no no interest in horses. He paid £45 for a little filly by Duke of Mecklenberg, who was the dam of Bueche Giorad.

He watched Comply or Die (Old Vic-Madam Madcap) win the Grand National on television. He thought the horse had a great chance, as he had won the Eider Chase over 4 miles but he didn't back him. Northern Irish buyer Danny Doran had purchased the horse privately from Martin Dibbs and later Tom Costello got him and sold him to David Johnson. According to Martin the amazing thing was that Johnson bought five horses but when they were delivered to theyard, there was a 6th horse, which he didn't buy, included and when he queried it he was told he was thrown in as a *"lucky penny"* and cost nothing. Costello didn't believe the horse was any good. He went to Pipe's and was a great success.

He went to David Pipe as did The Sliothar later on. Martin had been breeding national hunt horses for over 25 years. He had around 10 broodmares in 2008.The dam Madam Madcap was a quirky mare that he had bought from a neighbour and he had three foals with her - one by Shardari (a dual handicap hurdle winner) called Paumafi, and another was a filly with one eye that he sold to a neighbour. Old Vic was a popular stallion around this time and he decided to try him. After Comply or Die's win he said *"I was on cloud nine. Everyone dreams of it, but they never think it could happen".*

He remembers that Madam Madcap was hard to catch in the field, as she would gallop off every time they went into a field. He decided to take her and got around the problem by catching another mare first and then she would follow her. He went for Old Vic as a dual Derby winner who he liked as a sire. His other successful dam was Annies Alkali, an unraced daughter of Strong Gayle, who was given to him by a friend and from the stallion Good Thyne produced winner's like Anniesthyne and Bar Gayne, a bumper and hurdle winner. When she visited Presenting in 2001/2002, he got The Sliothar and his full sister Brotenstown. The Sliothar was sold for 11,000guineas, as a foal but he kept Brotenstown who was trained by Paul Cashman a son of Liam Cashman, Rathbarry Stud, where Presenting stood. Annies Alkaki eventually had to be put down because of arthritis.

The other good horse he had was Bueche Giorod, who won the Massey Ferguson Gold Cup in 1980, and went on to be second in the Mildmay of Flete Chase at Cheltenham. Aside from Ballyvoge another horse that won for him was Even More at Wincanton. The family's involvement traces back to the 19th century and early 20th century when Thomas Dibbs, Rathconrath had successful horses in training with A.J.Pilkington like Rathgowan, Princess Hilda, Queen of the Valley, Hackler Huonora (who won a number of races in England) and Whinberry.

There is another notable Westmeath connection with Comply or Die and Martin Dibbs. The third dam of Comply or Die was Cecil Ronaldson's horse Lady Flame, who won the first race in which Arkle ever ran, the Lough Ennel Maiden Plate at Mullingar on December 9, 1961, a bumper for amateur riders. More recent runners include Ozark Queen, The Corby Glen, and Ceasan Desist. Martin was not known before Comply or Dies's win and some people who didn't know him just called him *"Comply or Die".*

TIMMY MURPHY HAS TO COMPLY OR DIE

Comply or Die won three of his four novice hurdle races in England ridden by Tony McCoy and was 4th in the Grade One Ballymore Properties Novices' Hurdle at the Cheltenham Festival in March 2004, and the following year won three of his four chases and was second in the Royal & Sun Alliance Chase at Cheltenham. After an injury he was off for a few years and only when he won the Eider Chase at Newcastle over 4 miles 1 furlong in February was he fancied for the Grand National. In the race itself Donald McCain's Cloudy Lane was early favourite to add to the family's previous successes. In 2002, Timmy Murphy's career was almost in ruins with alcohol addiction and spent three months in jail for an incident with an air hostess on a flight from Japan. It was a bad period, but with the support of trainers like Michael Hourigan he came back. Tony McCoy had got the job with J.P. McManus and J.J. O'Neill and David Johnson got him as a replacement. His quiet waiting tactics suited Comply or Die and now all he had to do was to live up to his name.

The horse jumped brilliantly and brought himself into the race and at the last he out-jumped Snowy Morning and then was challenged by King John's Castle, but he ran on to win by four lengths. Everyone was happy except the bookies that lost heavily on the winner. In the 2008/2009 season, he didn't show much form, but with the blinkers and the return to Aintree the horse put up a great performance to be second to Mon Mome beaten 12 lengths. He ran in the Grand National on two more occasions finishing 12th in 2010 and was pulled up before the 3rd fence in 2011. He was retired to Timmy Murphy's farm in Gloucester. He ran 26 times and won 8 races and Prize Money of £798,005. Timmy's first success on a track was also on Gay Loire, who finished third in a bumper at Kilbeggan and then three weeks later returned to win the bumper there in July 1993 at 5/2. When he went to England in 1995, his last winner in Ireland was also at Kilbeggan on African Dante.

OFFALY

KILMORE 1962 - "THE SHINRONE NATIONAL"

The National in 1962 was described on papers as *"The Old Nags National"* or *"The Pensioner's Race"*, but in Offaly it was called *"The Shinrone National"*. Three horses in the race were bred in the Shinrone area - the winner Kilmore, Cannobie Lee, and Solfen. The latter two bred by Mrs M.Willington, Belfield, who was a first cousin of Gilbert Webb who bred Kilmore.

Gilbert Webb, Corolanty House, Shinrone, was Secretary of Ormonde Hunt for 34 years. He bred Kilmore winner of the Aintree Grand National at 12 y/o in 1962. He was by Zalophus out of Brown Image, who was out of Brown Jill, which was a full sister to Brown Jack. Mr Webb had him broken as a 4 y/o by Jack Mooney, Cangort and he was hunted with the Ormond Hunt three or four times. On his return home after his honeymoon in June 1955, Mr Webb sold him to J. J. Ryan, Cashel for a sum just under £150. Mr Ryan raced him in Ireland where he won a number of hurdles & chases. He was trained by Willie Cullen, Dan Kinane, and Mick Browne at different times. Tommy Kinane rode Kilmore 7 times for his brother Dan, before Christy started riding him (he rode him 9 times and won the Munster Grand National 1960). His form did not indicate that he would be a Grand National horse but the shrewd Ryan Price saw something that others didn't see and purchased him for £3,000 guineas for owner Nat Cohen, then famous as the producer of the *"Carry On"* films. He also produced the controversial film *"Peeping Tom"* (1960) in this era.

Joe Cleare, a Farrier in Shinrone shod the first set of shoes worn by 1962 Grand National winner Kilmore, when still owned by Gilbert Webb. He still had one shoe after the horses win, which was nickel plated. It was given back to Joe Cleare and the Newbridge Cutlery Company agreed to plate the shoe, when they heard the story and mount it on a plaque of highly polished bog oak and added a silver plate inscribed with the words *"The first shoe worn by Kilmore winner of the Aintree Grand National 1962".* It was a unique and permanent momento, which will perpetuate the link between Shinrone and a lionhearted winner of the world's greatest steeplechase. In 1961 Kilmore went for the Grand National for the first time ridden by the great Fred Winter, who had just won the Champion Hurdle with Eborneezer and the Gold Cup on Saffran Tartan. He ran a sound race without ever looking like winning behind the grey Nicolaus Silver to finish fifth. In 1962 conditions were dreadful with very soft going. Two Irish horses Fredith's Son and Gay Navaree were spectacular front runners and made it an exciting race upfront, but as they tired, it was Kilmore, Wyndburgh, and old Mr What who fought it out with Fred Winter's horse winning by 10 lengths. Two other Offaly horses ran in the race and were bred by Mrs M.Willington (Marion Wallace), Belfield, by her sire Soldado (died in 1961) in 11 y/o Cannobie Lee (E.P.Harty) who was 8th and Solfen 10 y/o with 11st 2 lbs (T.Taaffe) who was 12th. Mr Webb only put a small bet on him as he didn't think he would win.

Unfortunately, the practice where the breeder of a national winner got £500 was discontinued but the sponsors said they would make a special presentation to him. In 1963 Kilmore was 6th in the race when only 100/8 and 13 y/o, before bowing out in 1964, as Fred Winter's last ride in the race before his retirement. The horse died at 31 in 1981and has a pub in Findon named after him.

FREDDIE - THE PEOPLE'S CHAMPION (1965-67)

H.B. Kenny of Clyduff House, Roscrea one of the many members of the family from the Birr-Roscre area had a theory in the 1920's that the ideal staying chaser might be produced by putting a three quarters bred mare to a thoroughbred stallion. It was only a theory but he tested it with the mare Nellie who was a bit of a savage, but produced Nell the dam of Freddie.

Bella Ringwood from Killballyskea, Shinrone, Co Offaly had the mare Nell (Soldado-Nellie), who apparently produced a foal every two years for Bella. In 1956, she was put to Steel Chip for a fee of around £5. Around 11 months later, a colt was produced and it was more than likely that if it looked good or showed any ability it would be sold. The foal got sick and she contacted her uncle

Frederick Ringwood a vet and diagnosed a bowel stoppage and gave a mild enema and waited over night to see if it would work. The next day the horse was much better and Miss Ringwood asked what she could do for him in return. He suggested *"You'd better name him after me"* and so a horse called Frederick came into being You won't find this name as a Scottish Grand National winner or a horse who was twice runner up in the Grand National. The locals in Shinrone from the start called him Freddie, which became his proper name. The horse is so associated with Scotland it maybe a shock to realize he was Irish, born in Offaly and named in Offaly. He remained on grass until 1961, when Stuart Wight came from Scotland to buy a few horses. He ended up on the farm in Shinrone on his travels and liked the horse. He offered a fair price for the horse and Miss Ringwood accepted. Back in Scotland he contacted his friend Reg Tweedie, Kelso, who hunted horses and ran them in point to points. He bought the horse after looking at him and a romantic racing tale began (Both Wight & Tweedie had races named after them at Kelso in later years).

Reg Tweedie was born on his father's farm at Coats, East Lothian, on July 6, 1911. He was taught to ride by family friend Stuart Wight (later a leading trainer) who brought Freddie to him It was not the first good horse that Tweedie owned or rode, because as an amateur he won the Foxhunters at Cheltenham by 15 lengths in 1934 & followed up by winning the Valentine Chase at Liverpool later in the year. In the Grand National in 1935, he fell on Ballybrack and finished fifth in 1940 on Venturesome Knight, who was going like a winner until breaking a blood vessel. He was also the regular rider of prolific winners like Belhector and Templebeg. He rode the winners of 128 races before retiring from the saddle in 1949. He owned horses like Berrymoss, Ashcrop, Ballybrack, Venturesome Knight, Belhector and Templebeg. He started training and his first winner was Winters Bark at Kelso in October 1954, but it was his association with Freddie for which he will always be remembered.

Freddie ran in 30 races, won 14 and was second 7 times. In his first two years year he became champion hunter chaser winning the Foxhunter's Chase at Cheltenham by 6 lengths in March 1964. It was when he went for the Scottish Grand National in April 1964 carrying 11st 8lbs against seasoned chasers, ridden by Bill Rees that he established his name when only beaten by Fulke Walwyn's horse Popham Down. Aside from his three Grand National races, he was second to Arkle in the Hennessy Gold Cup, he won the Great Yorkshire Chase, Mildmay Cazalet Chase and the Gallagher Cup Chase in 1966. He probably lacked a real turn of speed at the highest level and it was always likely that he would do best in a race like the Grand National.

"JAY" TRUMPS "FREDDIE"

In 1965, one of the few Grand Nationals that could be compared to the great race between Crisp and Red Rum took place when the Irish Scottish horse Freddie took on the American challenger Jay Trump ridden by the owner Tommy Smith a top amateur jockey. Both were 8 year old but Freddie was carrying 11st 10lbs against Jay Trump's 11st 5 lbs. The latter had twice won the famous Maryland Cup Chase and came to Britain to the stable of Fred Winter, who already had success in the big race as a jockey and had ridden the other Offaly bred horse Kilmore to win it in 1962 and also Sundew in 1957. Freddie (ridden by Pat McCarron) was the clear favourite at 7/2 to win the race with Jay Trump at 100/6. It was like a shoot-out in a western with on one side Reg Tweedie with Con Sheehan the stable lad, and Pat McCarron the jockey, all planning to win the race that Freddie was born for and all of Scotland wanted. On the other side stood a champion American chaser (Jay Trump), a champion English jockey (Fred Winter), and a Champion Amateur jockey (Tommy Smith). Tommy Smith went round on the inside, as Fred Winter used to do and gradually moved towards the leaders on the second circuit. Freddie was by then tracking the leader Rondetto and when he fell, Freddie took up the running with Jay Trump challenging. Neck & Neck they raced to the last where Jay Trump made a mistake but still got to the front. Pat McCarron got one more run out of Freddie and closed the whole way to the line only to fall short by ³/4 length. It was exhausting even for the supporters, who watched the race and heart-breaking for the Scottish connections. Freddie was now a hero in many people's eyes and tears were in Bella Ringwood's eyes too as she walked back with the horse, and in many ways his simple name made him part of the people. Tommy Smith was first amateur since 1946 to win the race and Fred Winter had struck gold in his first year as a trainer.

CARRY ON FREDDIE

In 1966, Freddie was 11/4 F and adjudged the best turned out-it seemed certain to be his year. Nat Cohen won the Grand National in 1963 with Kilmore ridden by Fred Winter. This time he was involved with Stewart Levy, who also produced the *"Carry On"* films. He had been purchased by Ryan Price but after his licence was withdrawn the horse went to Fred Winter. Fred Winter's Anglo was to be ridden by 22 y/o Tim Norman and was easy to back at 50/1. The jockey was in a car accident the day before and had to receive stitches in his face. He probably thought that least he wouldn't be interviewed on television! The going was heavy and Freddie was giving 21lbs to Anglo. At the last Anglo joined the leader Forest Prince and just galloped away from the opposition to win by 20 lengths from a staying on Freddie. It was disappointing for connections and his growing fans but they now had to wait until 1967. Would anything dramatic happen to prevent Freddie winning?

It was one of the few Grand Nationals I missed live on television, because we were brought into school on the Saturday afternoon by the nuns to study for the Inter Cert Exam. When I came home my mother explained that somehow every horse fell except one called Foinavon who was a 100/1. Freddie was not favourite to win the race carrying 11st 13lbs, but Josh Gifford's Honey End was 15/2 F and perhaps another unlucky loser. Foinavon had been once owned by Anne Duchess of Westminister and trained by Tom Dreaper but was no Arkle. Before the race it could have been stated that Arkle could give him a mile lead and still beat him! From Freddie's point of view it was strange that Popham Down, who was riderless was the horse that brought mayhem because he had beaten him in the Scottish Grand National a few years before. John Buckingham and Foinavon galloped into racing history but the brave favourite Honey End got within 15 lengths of him at the finish (Foinavon paid 444/1 on the tote). Freddie came home in 17th place.

Later in 1967 Freddie was retired with a strained heart, though he lived to the age of 28. While Freddie is remembered sometimes more for his defeats than his victories but in Grand National terms he is remembered fondly by many people. Tweedie became a member of the Jockey Club in 1969 and died in 1999 at 88y/o. He once said that Freddie was *"a character, more of a companion than a horse".*

THE MONEYGALL BUTTERFLY AND PRESIDENT OBAMA

Moneygall, Co. Offaly has become associated with President Barack Obama, arising out of research by Canon Stephen Neill, who discovered a connection with the President and his third great-grandfather Fulmouth Kearney, a shoemaker, who left the village and went to New York in the 1850's. Blood ties remained, as recorded by Henry Healy, who had traced his own family tree to the Kearney-Obama dynasty. He organised the village celebrations at Ollie Hayes' pub when it was discovered. He said *"The village itself hasn't seen attention like this ever and probably never will again".* The result of this research was that President Obama and his wife Michelle visited Moneygall on 23 May 2011 to retrace the steps of his ancestor and to visit a small house on the site where his relatives once visited. The President & Mrs Obama, famously, sipped Guinness in Ollie Hughes Pub. The village looked beautiful covered in flowers and peaceful again because of the by-pass. This is not the story of a great President tracing his links, which had full international coverage, but the story of a horse that made the village a little bit famous when winning the Grand National in 2000, ridden by Ruby Walsh & trained by his father. Papillon has been replaced as the most famous personality from Moneygall.

Eamonn McCormack who was a publican from Moneygall bred Papillon and the horses win was the greatest moment of his life. He owned an unraced fourth dam Rowley's Last and the third dam Glenawina was a point to point winner.

Her sire Soldado bred many winner's including Yer Man who was 3rd in the Grand National in 1983. The best of her four winners were Glen Owen trained by Neville Crump, who fell five out when L'Escargot won in 1975. Glenawina's unraced daughter Deep Glen bred Glen's Princess the dam of Papillon. His sire was Prince Hansel bred by Cecil Boyd-Rochfort and a winner of the Doncaster Cup. Glen's Princess had been placed in bumpers and won a maiden hurdle and two chases. She did well for the McCormack family before her death in 1997, but it didn't seem likely that she would produce a horse like Papillon. She also bred Le Meill, who won three chases including one at Cheltenham but she broke down. Even in 2010, Eamonn & Joseph McCormack bred point to point winners like Charming Lad, Glen's Boy etc. They had bred from half-sisters of Papillon in Melville and Comanche Glen. Lafontaine the stallion also bred Spot the Difference, who was so successful for J.P. McManus and Enda Bolger's the prolific winner Merry People; and Ever Blessed, winner of the Hennessy Gold Cup; hunter chaser Lakefield Rambler and on the flat Shambo who had 57 outings from two to nine.

Papillon was sold privately for 5,300 guineas to Ted Walsh after emerging from the ring at Doncaster Sales in 1995. He was a successful horse from the start for his new owner an American millionaires Betty Moran from Pennsylvania, who was much more interested in flat racing and not a great fan of the Grand National. In his career, he won the Paddy Power Dial-a-Bet Handicap Chase in 1998 and 2000, the Ladbroke Chase at Cheltenham, and was 2nd to Bobbyjo in 1998 (winner of the 1999 Aintree Grand National) in the Irish Grand National. Betty Moran had to be persuaded to run Papillon in the race. The horse was not in great form going into the race and Ruby Walsh was recovering from a fractured leg over the winter after riding in a chase in Czechoslovakia. On the day punters got 'stuck in' to Papillon backing him from 33/1 to 10/1, with McCoy riding the favourite Martin Pipe's Dark Stranger. Papillion crept into the race gradually, as there were many fallers and it ended in a battle between him and Mely Moss (N.Williamson). It looked like Mely Moss might get up but when challenged, Papillon produced a bit more to win by 1¼ lengths. The celebrations were about to be extensive in Moneygall also for all the locals that backed him. Ruby said afterwards that *"Mely Moss was a real thorn in my side".* Just a few weeks later the Walsh family added the Irish Grand National when Commanche Court won. In 2001, the race was run in horrific conditions, which didn't suit Papillon with every horse falling except the winner Red Marauder (Richard Guest) and second Smarty. The two jockey's who remounted were appropriately A.P. McCoy on Blowing Wind who finished 3rd and Ruby Walsh on Papillon (fell 20th fence), who was 4th. The winner was Red Marauder who traced back to Drumcree who won the 1903 Grand National and she was the five great's maternal grandmother of Red Marauder. Papillon missed the 2002 season and was retired in 2003 after being out of form.

Jimmy Tormey, RIP who was associated with horses like Evilo, Grand Visier, Leney Princess, and El Kekni

Peter Downes, Russelstown Marian Harkin MEP, Adrian McGoldrick, Chief Medical Officer of the Irish Turf Club and Mairead McGuinness MEP, at a meeting concerning safety helmets in horse racing

Angela Bracken, Tullamore breeder of the great and now retired Sizing Europe

The Kilbeggan Race Committee in the 1970's Front L-R; Tom Lynam, Pat Carton, Sean Daly, Paul Dunican, Sean Craig, Christy Carton, and Jimmy Daly. Seated: Tom McCormack, Frank Ryan, Frank Trodden, Artie O'Rourke, Kit Carton, Anthony Trodden, Joe McCormack, Paddy Carey, Tom Kelly, and Ger Cooney. Third Row: B.Corcoran, Ned McCormack, Mick Creevy, Ger Carton, Willie Fitzpatrick, Paddy Doyle, Joe McCormack, Joe Hanlon, Stephen Lynam, Mick Buckley, Martin Craig, Joe Keenan, Sean Keoghan, Jimmy Coffey, Frank Keoghan, Tony Daly, Brendan Fox, and Joe Ryan Back: Johnny Grehan, Ray Fox, PJ Lynam, Paddy Lynam, Fr Aidan Fox, Brendan Daly, Barney Ward, Sean Keegan, Mervyn Maxwell, Dr D.O'Sullivan, Sonny Carton, Hugh Murray, and T.J.Keenan

Peggy St John Nolan, who trained Zonda to win the Irish Grand National in 1959 but is not on the records, as women were not allowed to have a licence at that time.

Mary Kilduff, President of YITBA (Young Thoroughbred Breeder's Association)

Maria Cullen rode Pajanjo to success at Kilbeggan. She was the first female professional jockey to ride a winner over fence

Trainer Dot Love with jockey Ben Dalton, when Liberty Counsel won the Ladbrokes Irish Grand National Steeplechase

Tullaghansleek is managed by Tim Carey his wife Finola, together with their seven children, Left to Right: Muriel, Claire, Sinead, Fiona, Aislinn, Susan and Niall

The Scott family and guest's. Left to Right: Brian, Nina Carberry, Rachel (at Back), Susan (at front), Kathie Walsh, Heathe, and Michael

Aidan Shiels and Noel Hayes lead in Beneficient after his victory in the Arkle Cup

Donal Brazil, Gurteen Stud, Offaly, bred Berties Dream, who won the Albert Bartlett Grade 1 Novice Hurdle at Cheltenham

Oscar Time and Robbie Power

The jockey jumps into the lead at the last (Healy Photos)

Mouse Morris lifts the Totesport Cheltenham Gold Cup at Cheltenham in 2006, watched by Michael O'Leary on the Left and jockey Conor O'Dwyer on the right

Pandorama who was owned by Robert Bagnall, Kinnegad, and won the Lexus Chase in 2012

Edward Scally, who is originally from Athlone, and is now manager of Gowran Park Race Course

Cecil Ross with Six of Hearts

Gigginstown House Stud's horse Hear the Echo caused a surprise in winning the Irish Grand National in 2008

In August 2003, Kieran Kelly was tragically killed in Kilbeggan

Pat Smullen celebrating a successful Royal Ascot in 2014

Start of a Legend- Arkle defeats Mill House in the Gold Cup in 1964

Elaine Kelly, Penny Downes, Pat Gavin and Rosemary Ross from Mullingar at Castletown-Geoghegan point-to-point

The Offaly "butterfly" Papillion defeats Mely Moss in a thrilling Aintree Grand National

Cllr. Peter Burke, Mullingar and his uncle Ted Burke, who shared many memories with champion trainer Sir Henry Cecil at Lough Ennel

Sean Cleary who was tragically killed is seen here jumping off a horse in Frankie Dettori style.

From Left to Right - Tom Cleary, Rory Cleary and his mother Kathleen following Rory's emotional win at Galway in 2004 on Peter Casey's Palace Star in the McDonagh Handicap, the horse who won the race in which his brother Sean was tragically killed in 2003.

The inimitable Colm Murray, Moate, who loved racing and is sadly missed by all racing fans.

Kielan Woods, Athlone is still riding in England

L-R: Pippa Connor, Judge, Sarah Gene Loughnane, Birr, winner of the Best Dressed Lady Competition at Kilbeggan in 2012 and Roz Purcell, judge.

The mystery and tragedy of the Father Hayes coup in 1992

James P. Sullivan who rides for Ruth Carr in England

Stephen Donohoe, Athlone being presented with his apprentice's championship trophy by Pat Eddery in 2006 at Windsor. More recently he has been getting rides with Sir Michael Stoute.

Jim McCartan, Gaybrook Lodge, who sold Moheet, who ran in the English 2,000 guineas and Derby

Shane Shortall celebrates his Galway Plate win on Road to Riches in 2014

Kodiac the very successful stallion at Tally Ho Stud, who produced leading filly Tiggy Wiggy last year and she went on to be 3rd to Legatissimo in the English 1,000 guineas.

Let the Show begin with Dot Loves stable from Left to Right - Ciaran Murphy with Liberty Counsel; Jonathan Cuskelly with Shadow Eile; Liam Higgin's with Miss Bliss; and Dot Love with Let the Show Begin.

The opening of the New Complex in Kilbeggan in 1990. Back Row L-R: Anthony Scally, Ray Fox,Brendan Dly, Sean Daly, P.J.Lynam, Bernie Ward, and Paddy Dunican. Front Row L-R: Sean Keoghan, Tom McCormack, Hugh Murray, Mick Coffey, Paul Dunican, Mary O'Rourke, Minister for Education,Johnny Grehan, Jimmy Coffey, and Jimmy Daly.

Paul Daly, Westmeath CC and Chairman of Kilbeggan Race Committee with Bernie McCarthy, leads in his prolific winner Lucky At Last

Cilla Black's "Blind Date" at Kilbeggan in August 1996.
From left: Jimmy Daly, Chairman, Steve Tricker, Devon, Cathy Scott, Warrington and Paddy Dunican, Manager

Pat McCormack, Kilbeggan and Lucan has been associated with horses like Lilywhitedancer, Beep Beep, Ring Ned and more recently Dante's Firth, who made her debut in February 2012 at Gowran Park From Left to Right: Stan, Marian, Martin, David (all McCormack's), Tom Foley, Patrick Foley, Sarah Glynn, Pat and Alan McCormack, Kilbeggan

Racing People: Vincent Abbott, P.J. Carton, Frank Trodden, Art O'Rourke and Mrs Trodden

The gamble of the century by Tony Glesson, as Rotherfield Greys win's the William Hill Stewards Cup in 1988

If one more favourite wins I swear that...... (Healy Photos)

Paddy Dunican, Kilbeggan Manager, couldn't find a needle in a haystack, but he found Michael Hourigan, trainer of Beef or Salmon

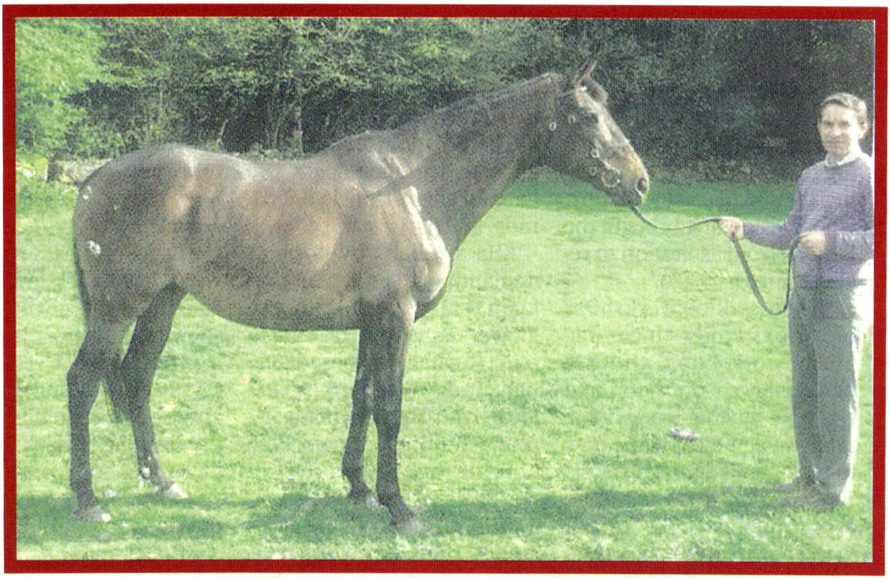

Cathal Ennis, Quill Farm, Castletown Geoghegan holding Papoose the dam of Ballabriggs winner of the Aintree Grand National

The Kilbeggan Knighthood Festival has an interesting connection with horse racing in Ireland and Rockhampton, Australia

Michael Dilger, Mullingar and his successful horse Wired Bryan in the US

Ciaran Fennessy holds the historic Barbour Cup, presented by Frank Barbour in 1909. Fennessy rode The Hard Hat to win the Greville Arms Barbour Cup race at Castletown-Geoghegan in April 2015. The Barbour Cup race was set up as a race open to all hunts in Ireland.

Paddy Nannery won €750 after the 100/1 shot. After the Ball won in Kilbeggan in 2003

chapter 11
KILBEGGAN RACES - 175th ANNIVERSARY (1840 - 2015)

KILBEGGAN RACES 1840 - 2015

It is probable that some form of racing took place in Kilbeggan, before the first recorded meeting on 9th March 1840, which according to tradition was held in the townland of Kilbeg. The main race was for a Challenge Cup, worth 40 guineas with £10 added by the Stewards and an entry fee of £3, which clearly indicated that it was for the gentry and not the common people. The race was held over 3 heats of 2 miles all held on the one day. The race started at 1PM and Rough Robin won the first heat.

The remaining four horses in the second heat that included Razor owned by Mr T. Crofton, who was too sharp for William Fetherston's Rough Robin. In the final heat it was a duel between Razor and Elson and as the local paper stated *"Neck and neck and touch and go, at and over everything to the last jump when Razor was still keeping up his edge"* won but *"not without very keen stroping".* The reporter said *"On every side was to be seen happy hearts, smiling countenances and sparkling eyes"*, with around 30,000 present at the meeting. The crowd may have been exaggerated, but it was a good day and an historic occasion for Kilbeggan Races. The races continued through the famine years and the mass emigration, which reduced the population of Ireland by around 2 million people. The following year, Mr Crofton won again with Mavourneen, but only after an enquiry. If he won the Kilbeggan Challenge Cup again in 1842 he could keep it and to lose it after just three years was going to be difficult for the locals to accept.

A BLACK BOTTLE OF GENUINE STINGO OR THE FIRST DOPING INCIDENT?

Mr Crofton's entry was Mickey Free, but as the local reporter stated *"it was evident from the start that Mickey from his first view of the course did not admire it"*. One fence had a steep fall into it, a stream and then a sharp breast. Amazingly, the winner Reformer outdistanced all the horses and all he had to do was jump over the first fence to get a walk over in the second heat and win the cup. However, when he came out he could not jump the fence and had to be rested before he came out and jumped it that evening. This led to an objection and a Steward's Enquiry was held the next day. It was discovered that the owner's friends had administered in one dose the contents of *"a black bottle"* of genuine *"stingo"*, which was to be used over the three heats, which completely unnerved the horse. The Stewards decided that this and the populace crowding the fence, put off the horse and allowed him to keep the race. The Challenge Cup was never threatened again until it was won by the Ussher family in 1957.

Racing up to 1855 was held in different places from Newtown, Dublin Road, Meldrum, Moate Road, Kilbeg, and for the first time ever at Loughnagore (the present site of Kilbeggan Races) in 1846. In 1850, it was a case of crushed bonnets and cracked skulls, as the heavy rain did great damage to ladies finery and a few of the traditional faction fights took place leaving a few people *"considerably softened in Donnybrook fashion"*. The local people involved in the races included John Locke, who in the 1840's had taken over the oldest pot still distillery in the world, when it was established in 1757; William Codd whose family also had a distillery in 1782; Dr William Gannon; Bernard Delaney of the Coola Mill, which may have dated back to the Middle Ages; James Palmer, Collector of Tax and Poor Rates; and James Clarke, extensive landowner. The successful owners in this era included the Fetherston's, Codd's, Clarkes, Odlums, Coffey's, Nugents, and De Blaquieres. The last recorded meeting was held in 1855, when Mr Davis's Fox won the Challenge Cup, but with secret societies, poverty, shortage of finance, faction fighting the races ended in 1855 for some years.

BALLARD 1879 - 85

This was the era of Parnell, Davitt, and the Land League, which was formed only six months after the first official Kilbeggan Races in April 1879. The town had a serious problem with smallpox in 1879 when a number of people died. The Locke family, who had an extensive interest in horse racing provided the course at Ballard in 1879. The track was laid out by whitewashed stones with coloured flags at various points. The fences were made of hazel or gorse bushes stuck into the ground and winged at each end. A stand was provided but there was a good view from the high ground. The races included a race open to all farmer's horses in Westmeath, which had been in their ownership for three months. The Midland Counties Plate of 20 sovereigns was open to Westmeath, Longford and Kings County. The Consolation Handicap was for all losers and a Pony Race for a saddle, bridle, and whip (they had to be under 14 1/2 hands high). The Stewards included John & James Locke; Richard Coffey, Newcastle; Michael Gorry landowner; and Matthias McManus who was a descendant of the Matthias McManus who set up the distillery in 1757, and also a descendant of John McManus, who was leader of the United Irishmen in Kilbeggan in 1798, before he was executed.

THE ILLEGAL HANKERCHIEF AND OVERHEIGHT PONY

The most important horse to race at the meeting was Grace II owned by William S. Kelly, Manager of the Hibernian Bank in Mullingar. She was the dam of the great Cloister, who won the Aintree Grand National in 1893 by 40 lengths carrying 12stone 7 lbs, the first horse ever to win with that kind of weight. At the meeting in 1880 there was four objections in different races including an objection for weighing in with a hankerchief that was not put on the scales weighing out; an objection to a horse that ran at an illegal meeting in the Strawberry Bed's; the others were for going the wrong side of a post and finally the inappropriately named Little Boy was objected to, for being over height in the pony race! Some very interesting personalities competed in that era including Willie Beasley who with his brothers Tommy and Harry, dominated Irish racing in this era. He rode The Glen 4/6 to win the Challenge Cup in 1883, when trained by Garrett Moore of Jockey Hall. The latter won two Irish Grand Nationals and rode The Liberator to win the Aintree Grand National in 1879. Rice Meredith trained Kentish Fire (1890), Roy Neil (1891), and Bowline (1893) to win the Irish Derby in 1883 and was a leading jockey and trainer in this era. He rode his own horse Elizabeth Cheff 4/6 to win the Farmer's Plate in 1883. He won races all over Ireland & Britain until he was warned off in 1893 and tragically was killed while out hunting in 1897. W.P.Cullen rode Huntsman to success in two races, and he was a famous gentleman rider from Galway like his brother Fred. He won three Galway Plates between 1885 and 1896, a Conyngham Cup with Royal Meath and his most famous success was with Wales in the Irish Derby in 1897, when the horse carried 7stone 13 lbs. Local jockeys like R.Brabazon had a treble in 1885 with Ringlet, Safe Home and Dynamite and J.Purcell won the two other races with Harristown and Laughing Girl.

It is not clear why racing ended in Ballard in 1885, but the political situation regarding land and faction fighting, which dated back to feats of strength and sport at fairs, gradually deteriorated into opportunities for a fight using cudgels and shillelaghs. Economically, it may not have been viable, as it depended on the support of the gentry and business people. In addition there was a surplus of meetings across the midlands.

REVIVAL AT LOUGHNAGORE 1901 - 1940

The present site of Kilbeggan Racecourse at Loughnagore on the Mullingar Road was to become the permanent home of racing in the town when it was revived in 1901. It was the generosity of Thomas Phelan that allowed the new Race Committee to start racing again. A meeting was held in the historic Volunteer Inn, where Thomas and Mary Cuffe were knighted in the 18th century by the Lord Lieutenant of Ireland and now the subject of the Kilbeggan Knighthood Festival for the past three years. The new committee was set up to organise the races for Monday 2nd September 1901. The Hon Secs were T & T Kelly and Joint

Treasurers Thomas Duffy and James Kelly. They travelled by foot, on bicycles, by ass and cart, dray and sidecar to arrive in Kilbeggan covered in dust. Kilbeggan had no railway station but stations at Tullamore, Clara, and Streamstown ensured large crowds in this period.

The track at Loughnagore (the lake of goat's) had been used in some form since at least 1846 and was rented by the race committee. With only one race meeting per year on rented land in a period of continuing land agitation, transport strikes, World War 1, 1916 Easter Rising, and the Civil War, it was always going to be difficult for the committee. The outbreak of World War 1 initially did not affect Ireland and it led to some of the top jockeys and trainers moving over. In August 1917, it looked as if Kilbeggan races would be lost, but continuous pressure by people like Sir William Nelson ensured that racing carried on. It was only a last minute telegraph by P. Dunne Cullinane MP that confirmed that the meeting would proceed. At one point, a photograph of a large number of people in the stand at Kilbeggan Races came to the attention of the military authorities giving them the idea that there was an unlimited man force in Ireland. It led to newspaper editors in Ireland not publishing photographs of attendance at meetings and Kilbeggan gained some fame as having put an end to rare picture making in Ireland during this period.

When Dick Cleary from Streamstown near Kilbeggan won the Irish Grand National on Easter Monday 1916, during the rising, he had to walk home the horse, as no trains were running. In 1922, around 40 race meetings were abandoned but Kilbeggan survived. The 1920's, saw the gradual collapse of Irish Racing, as prize money and attendances fell plus the international depression in the late 1920's.The introduction of the Entertainment and Betting Tax at a time of depression, only guaranteed disaster, as many race meetings disappeared and others could barely make a profit. This also led to a division between the Provincial race courses and those deemed to be favoured by the Racing Authorities within the pale around Dublin and the east coast. In 1932, the Government attempted to re-introduce it, but protests at many meetings from Ballinrobe to Kilbeggan, meant common sense prevailed and it was abandoned. The Totalisator was introduced in 1930 and it went some way to putting money back into racing, but prize money stayed low. In 1901, the prize money for the Challenge Cup was 30 sovereigns and in 1940 it was still the same. In 1939, a Government grant of £10,000 was given to the Turf Club and the Irish National Hunt Committee for allocation to racecourses.

GREAT HORSES IN KILBEGGAN FROM CLONSHEEVER TO BLAZING TEMPO

In the early days huge crowds turned up for the races, and J.H.Locke supervised the course on his polo pony and as one report stated he was *"worth more than a score of policemen"*. Local jockeys and trainers like A.J.Pilkington, T. Dowdall, Johnny Lynn, Cecil Brabazon, Leslie Brabazon, and Dick Cleary had plenty of success in the early days with some decent horses like Le Petit Pere (2nd in Irish Grand National), Rosy Symons, Annie Symons etc. Horses often ran twice at the meeting like Favonius ridden by P.J. Higgins in 1903 who won both races. An even more unusual event in 1937 was the success of the O'Roarke family's Battling Lady and Lady Barney at the same meeting, as they were mother and daughter. In the period from 1916 to 1923 the following great horses ran at Kilbeggan-Shaun Spadah who had his first race at Kilbeggan on 11th May 1914 when fifth in a flat race and in 1917 he won the Loughnagore Plate (he won the Aintree Grand National in 1921 and was 3rd in 1923), All Sorts finished 4th to Shaun Spadah in the above mentioned race carrying 12st 7lbs (winner of Irish Grand National in 1916), Koko (Cheltenham Gold Cup winner 1926), Punch (Irish Grand National winner 1915), Clonsheever (dual Galway Plate winner in 1923/24 and 3rd in 1925 carrying 13 stone), Privit won the Stand Plate in 1916 carrying 12st 10lbs (Galway Plate winner 1917), Red Damsel (winner of the first ever Galway Hurdle in 1913 when it was over 1 1/2 miles hurdle) and Dunadry, who went on to win big races in Britain. The full story of some of the above is told elsewhere.

The only other horse to run in Kilbeggan and win at Aintree was Rhyme N'Reason, who was trained by Jeremy Maxwell when unplaced at Kilbeggan in 1983, but when he was sold to England he won the Irish Grand National in 1985 and the Aintree Grand National in 1988. Apparently, Rhyme N'Reason missed fame for a different reason in 1983 during the time the police were searching for the kidnapped Shergar. A number of journalists and photographers came to Maxwell's yard and even looked in at Rhyme N'Reason with great disinterest not realising they were looking at a future dual Grand National winner. Jeremy had his own memories of the horse and said *"he hadn't shown much ability before running but the air must have agreed with him and he started to get much better after the race. As far as I can remember I was fined by the Stewards at Dundalk next time he ran (12/7/83) for not trying"* One of them asked him afterwards *"How do you know when trainers are lying?"* The answer was *"Easy-their lips move!"*. The horse improved after that and was sold to Michael Dickinson and the rest is history. Jeremy remembered thinking *"I must have been mad running him on the hard ground at Kilbeggan, as a four year old"*.

The Cheltenham Gold Cup was run for the first time in 1924 and in 1926 Frank Barbour's horse Koko trained at Trimblestown Co Meath by Bickley was sent for the race. Only three years before, as a five year old he finished third of six in a 1 1/2 mile handicap hurdle at Kilbeggan to P.W Shaw's locally owned Broken Vow (5/4) ridden by Tommy Burns. He won the Gold Cup in a canter from Old Tay Bridge and Gerald L ridden by Tim Haney. In 1928, he looked like winning the race again until he burst a blood vessel. He ran in the Aintree Grand National carrying 12st 3lbs and receiving 3lbs from the great Easter Hero. He landed on Beecher's Brook and had to be hauled off by ropes. In a successful career he won 18 chases. He is the only Gold Cup winner to run at Kilbeggan.

In 1956, Zonda won at Kilbeggan for owner Mrs Peggy St John Nolan and in 1959 Zonda won the Irish Grand National and the Leopardstown Chase before being third to Pas Seul in the 1960 Gold Cup. In 1971, Tartan Ace was unplaced in Kilbeggan but just two years later he won the Irish Grand National as a 6 y/o for Tom Costello. Jerry O'Neills Super Furrow owned by Mrs Margaret Marshall won a bumper at Kilbeggan in June 1985, before going on to win 12 races over 10 courses and over £100,000 in prize money from Punchestown to Galway. Michael Cunningham trained Greasepaint to win a novice chase in 1981, before being second to Corbiere in the Aintree Grand National in 1983 and to Hello Dandy in 1984. In more recent times, horses like Blazing Tempo Willie Mullin's first Galway Plate winner to Double Seven third in the Aintree Grand National in 2014, won in Kilbeggan before these succeses.

SENATOR J.J.PARKINSON CHAMPION TRAINER - KILBEGGAN CONNECTION

The leading trainers between 1901/1940 were R.Cleary 29, J.J.Parkinson 25, L.Hope 14, R. Fetherstonhaugh 8, M.Arnott 7, G.L.Walker 6, and C.Brabazon 6. Racing in this era at Kilbeggan was dominated by Dick Cleary, Bishopstown and J.J.Parkinson. The latter was born in Waterford in 1870 and was a qualified veterinary surgeon. He got into trouble with the authorities as an amateur and went to the USA, where he learned about new training and riding methods. He set up at Maddenstown Lodge and turned out winners from classics to 21 sovereign races at Kilbeggan. Between 1904/1939 he was the leading trainer for races won 23 times and leading trainer moneywise eight times. His record of 137 winners in a year under both codes set in 1923, stood until Jim Bolger beat it in 1990 and Dermot Weld beat his record of 2,577 wins in 2000 at Naas. He won two Irish Derbies with First Flier (1917) and Loch Lomond (1919) and won four Irish Oaks. His son W.J. (Billy) Parkinson was Irish Champion jockey in 1915 even as an amateur. He also trained for the notorious Richard 'Boss' Croker, who owned Orby the first Irish horse to win the Epsom Derby in 1907. He had his first success at Kilbeggan in 1907 with Premium and his final success in 1937 with Mrs E.McGrath's Ardanew, who carried 12st 9lbs in the Challenge. Cleary & Parkinson with their total of 54 wins in 228 races, had a 23% strike rate.

DICK CLEARY, SAVIOUR OF PUNTERS AND "CURER" OF SORE TOES

A winner for Dick Cleary was always popular and brought a great roar from the Kilbeggan crowd. He rode one winner himself at Kilbeggan on Pat's Girl in 1903. When Frank Barbour won the Challenge Cup in 1913 with Bachelor's Gift and

1914 with Roy's Daughter 1915, Cleary entered three horses to stop him taking the cup permanently in 1915 with Yours II (W.Lynn) winning and the other two placed Happy Go Lucky Girl II (T.O'Roarke) and Dernagarra. Barbour's horse Sore Toes had to be pulled and his name might be appropriate, as it would have been interesting to have had a camera patrol film for that race!

Cleary purchased Toin-na-Mona House & land in 1893 and after repairing it he started to develop his horse breeding and training career. He was formerly at the famed Cleaboy Sstud. He renovated Bishopstown House and built stables using railway sleepers. Amongst his great jockeys were his son James, Billy Lynn, Tom Madden, who spent many of his 80 years there. Cleary's stable was the only centre s of employment in the area. So many people were employed at the stables that the 'bread car' had to call regularly with deliveries. When it was too overcrowded the horses were then kept at Mosstown and Kilgarvan, and they were fed on oats & hay bought locally. To attend races they were walked the 'short cut' from Kilgarvan to the railway station in Streamstown.

His main stallions were Silvio II, Lustcrue and Irish Battle and each of them had plenty of success, both in Ireland & Britain. Irish Battle had great success with Clares Battle, Battleforth, Embattle etc. Even the year that he died in 1937, two of his produce won in England - Irish Vein and Irish dream. He trained many great chasers the most famous being Shaun Spadah winner of the Aintree Grand National in 1921 and also placed to Sergeant Murphy in 1923 (another horse which spent some time with him). All Sorts owned locally by James Kiernan won the Irish Grand National in 1916 and then took almost five days to walk home because no trains were running due to the Dublin Rising on Easter Monday. The dam of All Sorts had bred other winners like Lannigans Ball and Piper's Hill and it was said *"she was out of a plain pony that had scored in a few £4-19shillings races."* He also trained Dunadry (Captivation-Glenavy), a full brother to the famous Lissalinchy and also related to P.W. Shaw's high class horse Belsize, and he won the Leopardstown Chase of £500 in 1918. He carried 9st 9lbs and won easily from Antipater 11st 6lbs and Golden Fleece. When he returned home, there was great rejoicing at Skehana Hill beside his house. A Bonfire was lit with dancing, recitations, and songs being the order of the day. Dick didn't know it was on but invited people to his house afterwards for more celebrations. Dunadry also won the Weybridge Chase at Hurst Park and the Lancashire Chase. He was purchased at The Curragh a few years before by H.Sefton Kenny for £22. He passed him to Dick Cleary, and he sold him for £ 900. He trained winner's for local people like J.J.Ham (Kingfisher), J. Kiernan, Dysart, (All Sorts and Rathcore), Hugh Keane, Rathconrath, (My Rath) and many more.

He died in 1937, when he was described as genial, a pleasant companion, and a true friend. He supported the old Parliamentary Party and the agriculture community which included the Land League, United Irish League and the the Home Rule campaign. He was a member of the Westmeath County Council. He was removed from Boher Church and buried in Walshestown Cemetery.

MICHAEL JACKSON AND BISHOPSTOWN

Bishopstown was left in a dilapidated state and was purchased by Paddy & Claire Dunning, owners of Grouse Lodge recording Studios & Coolatore House. Michael Jackson arrived in Westmeath with his family in 2006 and stayed there for most of that year using the recording studio at Grouse Lodge, which has been used by other artists like REM, Paolo Nutini, Muse, Snow Patrol, Simple Minds, Dove and Will.I.Am. He worked on his music with Rodney Jenkins and Will.I.Am, while staying there and was able to drive around the area on occasions. He was interested in the local history and Irish Music. Apparently, owner Paddy Dunning even got to opportunity to play *"Billie Jean"* with him. When he stayed with them he visited Bishopstown House It was purchased for a client like Michael Jackson who hand- picked it when staying in Westmeath during 2006. With local labour, work was carried out on the house in line with some suggestions Michael Jackson made. Features included a state of the art wooden extension with 4 new bathrooms, a spectacular roof garden with a 360 degrees panoramic view. Bishopstown House was a three-storey fully-restored and renovated Georgian country manor with an incredible equine history combines. The courtyard where horses like Aintree Grand National winner Shaun Spadah and Irish Grand National winner All Sorts walked has been restored. In a small way, Michael Jackson almost connects with the 1916 Easter Rising, as he probably walked over the same ground as All Sorts did in the yard of Bishopstown House before the latter had to walk home over a few days because of the rising, as outlined above. Perhaps Dick Cleary and Michael Jackson are out there somewhere smiling at the irony of their strange connection with Bishopstown House.

DEVELOPMENT OF KILBEGGAN FROM 1946 - 1994

In 1945, the Racing Board was set up and given control of all aspects of racing and that each racecourse executive committee had to keep financial accounts. Prize money, entry fees, admissions, catering, and transport were all the responsibility of the Racing Board and grants for amenities and improvements. In 1946, prize money in Ireland was just over £184,000, but by the mid 1960's it was almost £750,000. Kilbeggan races re-commenced in May 1946, with prize money in each race of £100 and the first race was won by the appropriately named Wrong Note (Concerto-Thoughtless). In 1949, the American Ambassador to Ireland, George A. Garrett attended the races with his wife and won with Comic Dancer, a 4 y/o horse he bred himself in Virginia.

By 1950, many tracks around the country had received grants for improvements and gradually the introduction of course commentaries, photo finish cameras, better catering etc helped to increase attendances. Country meetings began to thrive after the war and when Kilbeggan improved the course in the early 1950's, one reporter said *"Kilbeggan has gone all pansy"* since his younger days, when attending a meeting was an ordeal. In 1948, two meetings were held for the first time but progress was slow and in 1963 the Committee could not raise the money to purchase the track, which was bought by Thomas Fox, who granted the Executive a long term lease and at least guaranteed the future of racing at Loughnagore.

The three main events of the 1950's were the visit of Prince Aly Khan to ride his horse in 1953, the tragic death of young jockey P.F.Conlon in 1952 and the crisis of 1956 when the races were almost lost. On 11th May 1953, Prince Aly Khan came to Kilbeggan to ride the unpronounceable Ynys in a bumper and with him was Gene Tierney one of the most beautiful actresses of the great Hollywood era. The horse won the last race at 5/4 from the P.P.Hogan ridden Organist. The last horse home was Leney Princess, who went on to be the dam of Fort Leney & other great horses. Just a year earlier, "Mutt" Conlon the jockey was killed when he rode Timber Topper in a flat race after 8 horses crashed to the ground. He was brought to Mullingar Hospital, but died from a fractured skull. The Race Committee were sued arising from his death and fell into debt of around £13,000.

In 1952, the Committee ran into financial difficulties, due to the compensation that had to be paid. Indeed, in 1956 there was almost a second tragedy on the course, when Pat Taaffe was seriously injured riding a horse called Ireland for George Rogers. He lay unconscious for a week with a fractured skull before recovering. The Race committee couldn't carry on and a new committee was formed with Michael Casey, Secretary and Paul Dunican, Chairman. The Committee had to organise a number of functions and events to raise money. A number of meetings were held with the Racing Board, but the main problem was payment of a debt of £312. The Racing Board provided an interest free grant of £300 to be paid back over three years. On the same day the Committee obtained a licence from the Turf Club to continue racing. In 1957 the famous Kilbeggan Challenge Cup was won after 117 years, when Icelough who was a very good chaser and favourite for the Irish Grand National in 1955, won the race for the third year in a row for trainer Tom Taaffe and owner R.H. Usher. The year 1958 was unique, as two new cups were presented when the Usher family gave a cup worth 50 sovereigns and the family of Joe Cooney recently deceased, presented a cup in his name In the late 1930's, the racecourse had been purchased by Joe Cooney, Manager of Locke's Distillery, who had a long association with the races. In 1959 the tote figure reached a five figure sum for the first time.

CHALLENGE CUP 1840/1957 - ICELOUGH SEES THE TROPHY AWAITING

The Challenge Cup as stated above was almost lost after three years, when Mr T.Crofton went for the treble in 1842, but through the three phases of racing it lasted. In 1880/1881 the well- known character Christy Coffey, Fertullagh won twice with Will O'the Wisp (Fertullagh-Lucky Star), who carried 12st 7lbs as a 6 y/o to win the race, but couldn't get the third win. Mr J .Yourell'd Lady Symons II won the race in 1911 and 1912 at odds of 4/5 and 1/7 for Frank Barbour, but his attempt to win the trophy with Bachelor's Gift in 1913 was foiled by Dick Cleary's Yours II. The only person to go close in the following few years was Thomas Killian, Chairman of the Westmeath Coursing Club and a great sports enthusiast. He won it twice with Mawgoory (3/1) in 1920 and Avickeen in 1924. Paddy Dunne-Cullinan's good horse Stage Management won in 1928 and then he won with Wild Cast in 1929. The Kiernan family stopped his run of victories with the useful Royal Dennis in 1930/31. Tragically, this horse collapsed and died at Baldoyle, while preparing for a third victory.

In 1955, Tom Taaffe laid out his useful horse Icelough (Icelough II-Faunlough) to win the Challenge Cup. Pat Taaffe had ridden the winner from 1951/1953 with Happy River (12st 7 lbs), Greenore, and Fort Wayne (12st 7 lbs), followed by Tom Taaffe winning with Carey's Cottage (12st) in 1954 ridden by Toss Taaffe. Even as Icelough was preparing for the race he was being tipped to win the Queen Elizabeth Stakes at Hurst Park on the following Monday. He was 85/40 on to win the race but the opposition included Tom Dreaper's Sentina (who was receiving 30 lbs), who went on to win the National Hunt Chase at Cheltenham in two consecutive years. Icelough was the favourite for the Irish Grand National in 1955 at 2/1 but was unplaced. In 1956, he was the favourite again at 11/2 even though carrying 11st 4lbs and finished 3rd to Air Prince and Richardstown. In the race at Kilbeggan, Icelough won by a 1/2 length from Magic King ridden and trained by Cecil Ronaldson & Sentina was four lengths back in third place. Each year Icelough (4/5) carried 12st 7lbs, and in 1956 there was a gamble on Silk Cottage (2/1), but he still won by an easy five lengths. In 1957 only three horses turned up for the race including his old rival Magic King only receiving 4 lbs, but this time he cruised home by six lengths.

The Cup was presented to Mr R.H.Usher the owner by Chairman Paul Dunican amidst loud applause and congratulations. Tom Taaffe had ridden the winner for the fourth consecutive year and one reporter wrote *"Icelough took this as if he saw the trophy awaiting him and stretched away for an easy win"*.

"IT'S SAD TO SEE THE SMALL MEETINGS GO"

In August 1963, a headline article in the Irish Field indicated that *"It's sad to see the small meetings go"*. The news behind the headlines was that the Racing

Board had withdrawn financial assistance from five racecourses - Thurles, Wexford, Roscommon, Kilbeggan, and Laytown from 1st January 1964. They said racing at Kilbeggan was *"uneconomic"*. There is a certain irony looking back on this decision, when you consider how successful the majority of the above courses have been for the HRI in recent times. Aside from the local Racecourse Executives, many small trainers and owners were worried about the decision. Apparently, the intention of the Racing Board to cater for them was Kilbeggan-style meetings on some of the larger courses. As one reporter said *"sentiment doesn't pay and I know I'm not with it but all the same I can't help feeling a twinge of sadness, at the passing of the little racecourses"*. There was no compulsion to close and in fact fixtures were allocated in 1964. After a huge effort by the courses and committees the racing survived. Unfortunately, in 1966 and 1967, Kilbeggan lost a meeting each year due to faults with the track. This was not a help when threats were renewed in 1969. In November 1969 it was announced that Ballinrobe, Tuam, Kilbeggan, Wexford, and Laytown were to go after *"December 1972"*. Representations were made to the Racing Authorities by all concerned. The logic of the Racing Board was not clear nor did they consult with racecourses. Meetings were arranged with politicians, as apparently the whole issue involved a legal battle between the Racecourse Association and the Racing Board, with the former arguing it was unconstitutional to take racing from Kilbeggan. Eventually, after a long and sustained fight, the races survived. Hindsight has shown that it was the correct decision. Even during this period, improvements had been made on the track and stand, a new photo finish tower was built, extra telephones etc. at a cost of £4,000. Improvements increased through the 1970's with a new Press Stand, horse boxes, Stewards Room, and better catering facilities.

NO FLAT RACES AND WHO NEEDS FIRST SPONSORSHIP?

The last flat race to be held in Kilbeggan was in August 1970, when the Mick Hurley trained Gra Mo Chroi (9/2) won a maiden plate from John Oxx's last Kilbeggan runner Our Shadow. The move to all National Hunt racing in 1971 was the deciding factor in changing the fortunes of Kilbeggan, as the track was never suitable for flat racing. In 1972 there were nine races at the May meeting with three divisions of races and in July 1972 there were 7 races. It meant larger crowds and more turn over on the tote. Kilbeggan was able to prove it was economically viable and no threat was to recur. Another landmark was reached in 1973 with the first ever sponsored races by Fabri-Cast, Kilbeggan and D.E Williams,Tullamore who sponsored the Czar Vodka Handicap Chase of £500. It was the richest race ever run in Kilbeggan and it included a framed oil picture of the winner, value £175 (by Janice Latham) to the owner and a clothing voucher of £25 to the groom. Fabri-Cast sponsored a Handicap Hurdle of £500. Guy Williams racing journalist, author, and trainer of Daletta the Irish Grand National winner was a member of the William's family. He had a meeting with the Kilbeggan Race Committee in St James's Hall with Tom McCormack and strangely, they had to persuade the members to take the sponsorship. It was new to many of the people, who had worked hard and voluntarily to help Kilbeggan survive, and they were suspicious of the implications of taking sponsorship.

Ultimately, they accepted the sponsorship and it was the start of a process that developed over many years. In 1973 a third meeting was held for the first time. In 1979 the Committee celebrated the Centenary Year since the first official meeting at Ballard in 1879. Sean Graham and the bookies sponsored races and the members themselves. In the 1960's, the Tote Jackpot commenced and for 5/- you could win a large sum and this led to a jackpot carryover of £3,697 and a tote turnover of £25,373.

RACECOURSE OF THE YEAR

In 1983, local jockey Marty Davey had his first success at Kilbeggan with Timona trained by Tom Lacy. He was given a great reception when he brought home the favourite by 5 lengths. His first winner was on Rough Course. He later went to ride for Mouse Morris and he rode the very useful horses like Cahirvillahow to several victories, Cranlome won the Munster Grand National and Willyoustop won the Tattersalls Novice Chase at Limerick worth £10,000. His brother Pat had ridden 6 winners for Lacy and was later Head Lad for Jimmy Coogan. The second race was won by Willie Glynn, who was to die tragically in 1984 in an accident in the USA a short time before he was due to come home for Christmas. The Willie Glynn Handicap Hurdle in Kilbeggan commemorated his passing and reminded people of the dangers for jockeys, as reflected in the tragic death of jockey's like Kieran Kelly in Kilbeggan, and Sean Cleary from Athlone and the serious injuries to Shane Broderick & many more. The course improved gradually in the 1980's and on 20th May 1990, a New Complex costing £165,000 was officially opened by the Minister for Education Mary O'Rourke. The same year Paddy Dunican was voted Manager of the Year by the Racing Club of Ireland. It was a prelude in the 1990's to further awards and Paddy Dunican was named Manager of the Year on several occasions. In 1992, the number of meetings was increased to four, in 1993 to five, and by 2006 there were eight meetings between May and September. In 1993 veteran trainer Paddy Mullins said *"Kilbeggan was a real race meeting. There is a great buzz to it unlike some of the deadly meetings we have to attend during the year"*. Kilbeggan featured regularly on TV news programmes and documentaries including *"From the Horse's Mouth"* in 1993, and *"Nationwide"* in 1995 etc.

KILBEGGAN BRINGS THE "BUZZ" BACK 1995 - 2014

In June 1995, Peter O'Hehir reported in The Irish Field *"that after weeks of dead and depressing midweek action, Kilbeggan was like a different world last Monday, when a crowd of 5,500 thronged the enclosure to enjoy the track's first meeting of 1995. The buzz is back".* It gave Conor O'Dwyer the opportunity to have a double with Masai Warrior and Vital Trix for two small trainers J.C. Harley and Tom Matthews. In June 1995, a young 21 y/o jockey called Anthony McCoy did his chances of getting the No 1 job at Martin Pipe's Pond House Stable no harm, when winning his first Irish chase aboard Crogeen Lass (4/1) by 7 lengths for local Midland's trainer P.J.Casserley. The year before he had joined Toby Balding's stable and rode 74 winners under National Hunt rules. Coincidentally, another potentially great jockey was riding that day when Mr T.J. Murphy rode Michael Hourigan's horse African Dante to win the bumper at this meeting. He was Timmy Murphy, who within a short time was to ride for Balding and eventually take over the riding duties at Pipes stable. Kilbeggan because of its undulating tight track, seems to suit some horses and during the year horses like Masai Warrior, Vital Trix, Finnegan's Wake, African Dante, Antarctic Wind and Muscovy Duck all won more than once at the four fixtures.

At the August meeting Stan McCormack's history of Kilbeggan Races *"Against the Odds Kilbeggan Races 1840-1994"* was launched by well- known trainer Michael Cunningham (who had a family connection with Kilbeggan), with the assistance of Michael Osborne. Ivan Yates, Minister for Agriculture was also present at this meeting. In 1995, the aggregate attendance increased to over 25,000 and 19 races were sponsored. Over £100,000 was spent on improving facilities including drainage and widening part of the track. Tarmacadam was laid in the enclosure at a cost of £90,000. In May 1996, veteran trainer Paddy Mullins won the Keenan Brothers Handicap Hurdle with Parskint, carrying the colours of his wife Maureen and the horse was a half-sister to five winners including Scottish Champion Hurdle winner Sayparee and Pargan, who won the Galway Amateur Handicap carrying 12 stone. In July, Paul Carberry had travelled from Killarney to Worcester to ride a winner for Ferdie Murphy, and then made the return journey 24 hours later to get a double for trainer Noel Meade with The Bould Vic and Legitman. Mr Ruby Walsh won the Coola Mills Bumper for Willie Mullins, a pre-cursor of their future relationship. The August meeting was the 40th anniversary of the formation of a new committee in 1956 to save the races, when they had to meet the Racing Board before getting their licence. In August they had sponsors in five races for the first time.

BLESSED BENNY THE BISHOP BRINGS BACK BUMPER

The most popular success of the day in August 1996 was when the very spiritual *'Benny the Bishop'* won the Tom Bermingham Menswear sponsored bumper. Cecil Ross from Slanemore, Mullingar trained the winner for Oliver & Salome Brennan and it gave his 18y/o nephew Anthony his first racecourse success, after providing his first ever win in a point- to- point at Castletown Geoghegan. The "Bishop" went on to win his maiden hurdle at the September meeting and give Anthony Ross his second success on a racecourse. Very Little won the novice chase for trained Pat Lally after being third at Galway, when ridden by Shane Broderick, before his serious injury. The wonderful veteran chaser, John Queally's Merry People recorded the 10th win of his career in the Joe Cooney Memorial Handicap Chase beating Galway Blazers Chase winner Beet Statement. Richard Dunwoody made a flying visit to Kilbeggan in August and recorded a double with on Allatrim & Cuban Crisis. Aidan O'Brien also had a double with Loughloone and Sup A Whiskey (an appropriate winner in the town!).

During World War II when there was no racing in Ireland all the great jockeys of the time rode in the *"Kilbeggan Grand National"* for donkeys. When a local won the race one reporter wrote *" the laurels were torn from the brows of racing giants".* The expression came to mind when Kilbeggan decided to have the first running of the Midlands National sponsored by Elan, Athlone, in July 1997. During the summer months it has become the most important handicap chase outside of the Galway Festival.

Kilbeggan started off the season with an attendance of 7,000 at the May meeting, where Enda Bolger had a double with the top hunter chaser of the season Dixon Warner (Mr R.Walsh) and Legitman (D.Casey), who were both then aimed for Galway. A young jockey called Barry Geraghty lost his right to claim 7lbs (down to 5 lbs), when he won on Swift Pick for Noel Meade in a maiden hurdle. Tom Foley had a winner by Danoli's sire The Parson at this meeting when Tisrara Lady overcame a nine month absence to win the novice. A teenager, Jason Maguire took the riding honours with his first ever double on My Blue and Peter McCreery's Greek Magic, before going to better things. Richard Dunwoody was in Ireland because of his motor racing exploits, but came to Kilbeggan to win on Edward O'Grady's Dunferne Classic.

MIDLAND NATIONAL AND THREE CONSECUTIVE MANAGER OF THE YEAR AWARD'S 1996 - 1998

In July, the Elan Midlands National of €50,000 provided a very appropriate winner when the Ramojo Syndicate's Cristy's Picnic (D.Casey) 14/1, trained by Mouse Morris won easily from Graphic Image and Mubadir. The horse went on to win the Galway Plate Trial at Tipperary two days later. A touch of Hollywood and the movies came into play when it was discovered that Neil Jordan, Director and the actor Stephen Rea were part of the syndicate. Interestingly, Merry People who finished fifth in the race went on to beat Irish Grand National winner Feathered Gale at Tramore and also won the Grade 3 Denny Gold Medal Handicap Chase vale £20,000 at Tralee. The highlight for many was the appearance of the most popular horse in Ireland & Great Britain the grey Desert Orchid, who walked around the parade ring. He was top class over hurdle & fences winning the King George VI Chase at Kempton, the Gold Cup, and Irish

Grand National.

At the end of the season an estimated 40,000 people attended the races and over £2 million was wagered by punters (Sponsors had provided £55,000). To win the National Hunt Manager of the Year Award on one occasion could be described as fortunate, but to win it in three successive years was downright phenomenal. Paddy Dunican received the award in 1996 for the first time and in spite of Kilbeggan having its most successful year ever in 1997 it was difficult to believe that the award would fall to him again with competition from Punchestown, Fairyhouse etc. Many sportsmen and managers are never recognised for their achievements in their lifetime, but for the Irish Racing Industry, which is renowned worldwide, to effectively say that Kilbeggan is the best managed National Hunt course in the country for two consecutive years, was unprecedented. It was not just a compliment to the skills and organisation of Manager Paddy Dunican, but of the massive team effort by the voluntary committee under the Chairmanship of Jimmy Daly, to deliver an exceptional service to race goers in the midlands and Ireland. In 1996, major political figures like An Taoiseach John Bruton had visited Kilbeggan Races in August and also Ivan Yates, Minister for Agriculture, Food and Forestry. It was recognition of all the effort put in by members of the voluntary committee since 1956 that brought Kilbeggan from near extinction in the 1950's and 1960's to this level of success.

It seemed that it could not get better for Kilbeggan, but in the racing success story of the decade Paddy Dunican won the Racing Club of the Year Award for the third time in 1998. Winning awards whether it is an All- Ireland Final or an Olympic medal it is measured by the quality of the opposition, which was very high in Ireland. The various Kilbeggan Voluntary Committees down the years since then must have been reading Oscar Wilde when he stated *"nothing is worth doing except what the world says is impossible"*, because by leaps and bounds it had climbed up the ladder of racing success. It was a credit to the Manager, Jimmy Daly, Chairman, Tom Lynam, Treasurer and all the committee. Over £700,000 had been spent in eight years and the number of meetings increased from 3 to 6 and a New Plan was launched for £$^1/_2$ million. The developments were for the benefit of the public and the improvement of the track. Kilbeggan was also nominated in 1998 for the Racecourse of the Year by the Irish Racehorse Owners Association, together with Cork and Tramore.

RACING TOWARDS THE 21ST CENTURY WITH "THE PATRON SAINT OF KILBEGGAN PUNTERS"

In May 1998, Michael Hourigan the man, who was once described as *"the patron saint of Kilbeggan punters"* because of all his fancied winners, delivered another winner with Coolree Lord in the Usher Cup. Frank Lacy, Rhode had a welcome winner with Brisbuck Lady (20/1) after a virus stricken season, but it was tempered by his stallion Accordion's full book of mares for the season. Local trainer Michael Kiernan, ran his Roscommon winner Lough Suedy but the mare was unplaced. In June, Tony Redmond, Irish Racehorse Trainer's Association praised the re-development of the dip on the far side, which was also praised by Willie Mullins and champion jockey Charlie Swan. There was also a new road and car parking. In June, 29 y/o Mark Roper won the featured race the £12,000 Bank of Ireland Handicap Hurdle with Tidal Princess (12/1) ridden by David Evan's, who lost his 3lb claim. After the race he said *"she is a decent mare"* and she proved it by winning the Apprentice Derby at The Curragh during the Derby week-end.

Bertie Aherne, An Taoiseach flew down in a helicopter to attend the Elan Midland National in July with Noel Ryan, IHA, Chief Executive, who was unable to disguise his incredulity at the popularity of the fixture (even though he was from Mullingar). The Irish Independent headline was *"Bertie on a Winning Break"*, as he had a 14/1 winner ridden by Barry Geraghty, who was shortly afterwards heading to Australia as part of the competition between Irish and Australian jump jockeys. It was the kind of meeting where the phrase *"A horse is a friend of man so long as man doesn't bet on him"* seemed to be coming through, until the favourite Betseale won the last leg of the jackpot for 4 lucky punters. During the meeting the bookmakers handled £305,000 more than The Curragh the previous Friday. Cristy's Picnic was the favourite to win the Midlands National race again with Tony McCoy on board, but Hemisphere 12/1 trained by Dessie Hughes and ridden by Norman Williamson from the front proved too strong. Ruby Walsh received a great endorsement at the start of his professional career from Gerard Stack who trained Plettenburg Bay to win the first race, when he said *"I thought he gave him a brilliant ride".*

When Timmy Murphy came for a ride in Kilbeggan in August he had ridden 60 winners in Britain the previous season, with 46 for his retaining stable of Paul Nicholls. He won the first race on French By Chance 12/1 on a day when all favourites were beaten. The special *"Laois GAA Day At the Races"* took place in August with 1,500 tickets sold in advance and it led to a jackpot of £29,968. I recall the unusual incident of Michael Cunningham's horse The Tollah in the opening race, when I backed him at 7/1 and he jumped the last 20 lengths in front with a short run-in. I turned away briefly and when I looked back the jockey was falling off about 50 yards from the line. Shane McGovern said afterwards *"My leather opened on the run-in, I lost my balance and came off".* Many a punter quietly cursed that evening.

In 1999, a crowd of 8,000 poured through the gates as the new £1 million pavilion was opened, although there was a problem with the new Auto Tote system. The pavilion was for corporate entertainment, with a private balcony on the first floor for 300 guests and in May it was opened by Joe Walsh, Minister for Agriculture, Food, and Forestry. The tented village overlooking the track was also a success. Around 45,000 attended the races in 1999 (up 5,000 on the previous year). The tote take on Midlands National Day was £131,000 and only Galway festival could match that figure. Sponsorship for the year was around £85,000 and was expected to increase in 2000. This meeting was the last of the 1998/99 National Hunt season with Noel Meade leading trainer & Ruby Walsh was champion jockey. Antarctic Wind was with Jessica Harrington for the second time in her career, after a spell in England with Micky Hammond, when winning the Elan Midlands National in July. Kieran Kelly made the running on the horse that was having his first win over fences and he comfortably beat Triptodicks by 9 lengths.

At the first August meeting it was noted that the attendance of 7,000 patrons was almost 1,500 more than the Heinz 57 meeting at Leopardstown on the previous Sunday. The most popular winner was Michael Cunningham's The Tollah in the Joe Cooney Handicap Chase, as the horse had fallen on the run in at a previous meeting. He won after going well in a Galway chase when he also fell. Rathoath Gale gave young Philip Carberry a win a handicap chase giving him two winners and leading to the need to put "P.A.Carberry" on race cards, to distinguish him from his more famous brother Paul. Even in 1999, Charles Byrne knew how to get a horse to run up sequence of wins. In September Beacon Lane recorded his second win in less than 24 hours and his sixth since July, when winning the Foster & Allen Handicap Hurdle.

A NEW MILLENNIUM

The IHA honoured Kilbeggan in 2000 by presenting their Annual Report at the track for the first time, as they hosted a Press Conference at the popular Westmeath venue. Denis Brosnan announced the Capital Development Programme that ploughed so much money into improvements in places like Kilbeggan. The crowds were now bigger with an average of around 8,000 and turnover was £2.7 million. The exclusively National Hunt racing has made a big difference, Kilbeggan ranked fifth in the average attendance table well ahead of The Curragh and Fairyhouse and behind only Galway, Listowel, Leopardstown, and Punchestown and also fifth on Tote betting. Christy Roche produced a gamble on J.P.McManus's Aerleon Pete in the Belvedere House & Gardens Handicap, cruising home with bottom weight. Roche said afterwards *"He cost twice as much as Istabraq (82,000 guineas) out of Michael Stoutes stable, compared to 38,000 for the Champion Hurdler out of John Gosden's stable but he is such a villain".* He went on to repeat the dose with Aerleon Pete 13/8F in the Bank of Ireland Hurdle in June,with a win at Navan in between. Over £1/2 was bet with the bookies but the most unusual feature was when five jockeys rode out a finish with a circuit to go. The crowd loved it because the first three in the betting took the first three places.

Over 12,000 turned up for the Elan Midlands National in July. Michael Hourigan's horse Scallybuck (N.Williamson) 8/1 had won in Kilbeggan the previous June, loved the fast ground and beat River Cora (R.Walsh) by a length, before heading to Galway. Williamson went on to have a double with Brandy Galore. Hourigan was one of the owners in the Scallybuck Syndicate and this was his first winner of the season. A Grangecon permit holder Helen Markham had her first success as a trainer in September. Her father Johnny had played a major role in the Paddy Sleator stable, as a jockey and headman when the maestro had his great years. The winner was Master Bounce after 31 attempts on the racecourse. Michael Cunningham won the bumper with Glenbar, who provided Mr Gordon Elliott with his first winner in Kilbeggan, before going on to be one of the top trainers in Ireland and a challenger to Willie Mullins.

I'M ON THE LINE-FIRST WINNER FOR DOT LOVE

In 2001, a horse who was to make a big impression in Kilbeggan and go on to international success in the future was J.P.McManus's Spot the Difference 7/2. In May he won the hunter chase ridden by J.T. McNamara beating Gordon Elliott on Father Andy. Enda Bolger said afterwards that he would not make up into a top hunter chaser and go for handicap (his prediction was not exactly correct!). After Kieran Kelly won on Ojay for Dessie Hughes the latter stated *"You need an experienced jockey around here to keep horses balanced"*, which was very true. Spot the Difference went on to win at Roscommon before returning to Kilbeggan to win the £20,000 Eircell Handicap Chase by 15 lengths ridden by Ruby Walsh. The best finish of the night was in a handicap hurdle when Philip Carberry on Ask the Moon beat his brother Paul on Royal County Buck by a head giving Michael Halford a winner. The highlight for locals was when I'm On The Line won the Coola Flat Race, as it was Mullingar permit holder Dot Love's first winner and ridden by Ciaran Murphy, who was also having his first winner as a jockey. He had to switch the horse around a wall of horses to beat Dale Creek by a 1/2 length winning at 25/1 and he paid £160.50 on the tote. They received a huge reception in the winner's enclosure and they were mobbed by well-wishers. Dot Love only received her permit a month before.

It was the 100th anniversary of racing at Loughnagore (Lake of the Goats) on the Mullingar Road, Kilbeggan in 2001 and it was celebrated at the July meeting. On the first day at Galway Races RTE featured a piece commemorating the anniversary and showing the atmosphere at the races on Midland's National day. The prize money for the Elan Midlands National meeting rose from £55,000 to £100,000. The feature race had Spot the Difference (R.Walsh) as 11/4 favourite with Michael Hourigan's previous year's winner Scallybuck considered as the main danger. Hourigan succeeded all right but it was with his outsider Rockholm

Boy (Philip Carberry) 12/1 who won from Spot the Difference. He gave an exhibition of jumping from the front and the trainer said afterwards *"He's entered for the Plate but is more likely to go for the Blazers Chase".* He went on to win the Galway Plate, the first Midland's National winner to do it. Paul Gilligan had his first winner, since he took out a licence, when Broadstone Road won with Barry Geraghty on board. Paul Carberry was at his brilliant best with a treble at the August meeting on John Bowles Back to Bavaria, Butterscotch, and Ask the Moon and he followed up in September with a double on Noel Meade's Blue and Henry de Bromhead's Dale Creek.

PAUL CARBERRY SUSPENDED FOR DROPPING HIS HANDS

Paul Carberry has always been one of the jockey's that divides opinions about his abilities. He is one of the most naturally talented, but some think he has lost races due to exaggerated waiting tactics or overconfidence. In May 2002, he dropped his hands at Kilbeggan on the run in when riding the hot favourite Heart of Midlothian in the novice hurdle and didn't see Danny Howard coming on the inside to get up and win by a short head on High Tower. The Irish Field reported that *"in fairness to the crowd little very little if anything was said to Carberry".* He held his hands up and admitted the error and after a Steward's Enquiry he was suspended for a week. This meeting provided a little bit of history as Polaris Flame (Mr P.Buchanan) trained by Mrs D.Foster, became the first horse to win a handicap run for hunter chasers. At the following meeting, Carberry paid back the punters their losses with a 112/1 treble with Carlesimo, Borora King and Cappaduff (the first two for Noel Meade).

The Elan Midlands National was won by 10 y/o Keeponthesunnyside, who was recording his fourth course win. He jumped brilliantly, except for one fence and stayed on stoutly to win by twelve lengths from Dodger Nash, with Ferdy Murphy's English challenger Occold in third place. Doyle stated afterwards *"we said we would test them all with his light weight, even though he would ideally prefer better ground. This is my biggest success as a trainer".* Ruby Walsh was stood down at this meeting after being unconscious for a short time after a crashing fall on Horse Chestnut. The most interesting winner was Barrow Drive in the novice chase for Charles Byrne, because he went on to become one of the top novices in Ireland. Four runners at this meeting (Consalvo, Native Sparkle, Barrow Drive, and Lord of the Turf) went on to win at the Galway Festival. The tote aggregate was €150,000 (up €30,000 on previous year). In August, Bernard Brogan the star Dublin footballer was part of the Speculators Syndicate, who were all Dublin based and their horse Madonna Fan (B.M.Cash) 11/2 won a maiden hurdle for trainer Arthur Moore. The Lear Fan colt was bought out of the Luca Cumani stable for 6,000guineas and it was the syndicates first ever winner. The famous Ireland's Own Magazine was celebrating their 100th anniversary, by sponsoring a race at Kilbeggan. All fans of Miss Flanagan, Cassidy, and Dan

Conway's Corner were all at the big occasion. Very appropriately the race was won by veteran course specialist Benny the Bishop trained by Cecil Ross. The 12 y/o recorded his fourth win on the track when ridden by Shane McCann. Ross said *"He loves it around here. When he gets fast ground this place is probably worth a stone to him".*

TURF CLUB REVOKE KILBEGGAN'S LICENCE TO RACE

One meeting was lost in 2002 because of the inclement weather, but in 2003 two extra meetings were granted bringing it up to eight for the summer season. The committee carried out many developments including widening the track, improving the bends, a new plastic running rail, and a new medical facility was built. In view of all the praise and wonderful support of the racing community, it was a major shock in Kilbeggan and racing circles in May 2003 when the Turf Club revoked their licence, because the ambulance road did not meet the required health & safety standards. It was pointed out to them by Manager Paddy Dunican that two different standards seemed to be applied by the Turf Club, as Kilbeggan took Health & Safety very seriously. Kilbeggan had applied to the HRI for grant aid for a new race track service road and they were appealing the decision Work was done on the road pending the appeal and decision on the grant aid. It brought back the possibility of what happened in 1956, 1963, and 1969, when many racecourses were under threat. After an inspection on 12th May 2003, the Licensing Authority issued a license for the year. It was not good for racing that a racecourse that won awards, national praise, had great attendances etc had to go through this whole process to justify their health & safety policy. On a more positive note Horse Racing Ireland (HRI) announced in June a €60 million capital development project. The featured Midlands National Handicap of €32,500 in July, was won by Kirmar 14/1 trained by P.A.Fahy and brilliantly ridden by Barry Geraghty to win by a short head from Just in Debt (Derek O'Connor).

THE TRAGEDY OF KIERAN KELLY ON 8TH AUGUST 2003

It is sometimes forgotten that National Hunt jockey's live on a knife edge of danger as they ride around a variety of race courses on ground varying from soft to firm, on dodgy jumpers, poor quality horses and always wary of the element of chance. Kieran Kelly (25 y/o) had ridden winners around Kilbeggan on a number of occasions and just before the Joe Cooney Memorial Handicap Chase, he won the 6pm race on Martin Brassil's Barrack Buster 6/4F, making all the running and winning comfortably. He rode Dessie Hughes horse Balmy Native 8/1 in the race with Timmy Murphy on the favourite and eventual winner Central Billing. During the course of the race Balmy Native fell on him and Kieran Kelly appeared to be kicked by the remaining runners and he suffered head injuries. He was quickly removed to Tullamore Hospital, before being transferred to the Beaumont Hospital Intensive Care Unit, where he was on a life support system before he lost his life on the following Tuesday. The tragic loss of Kieran Kelly overshadowed the entire racing year, as he was a popular young National Hunt jockey. He had started out with Micky Flynn, Edenderry, Offaly before going to Dessie Hughes. He had already ridden good horses like Hardy Eustace, Timbera and Colonel Braxton. He had his greatest success the previous March at Cheltenham in the Sun Alliance Novice Hurdle for his greatest supporter Dessie Hughes (who died in 2014). Poignantly, he could have gone on to ride the great Hardy Eustace to win two Champion Hurdles.

At the meeting on 22nd August a large number of people gathered around the Parade Ring between the 3rd and 4th race to honour Kieran, by remembering him during a minutes silence. His father John and sister Bridget were present, and asked Colm Murray to thank people from all over the world, who sent messages of condolences. All lovers of National Hunt racing will remember him for his character & courage, which is representative of all jockeys in National Hunt racing. Daryl Jacob from Wexford, who rode for Paul Nichols said that if he won a Grade 1 race he would look to heaven and dedicate it to his great friend Kieran, as they had shared a house together in Kildare. I thought it was very moving when he said that he had a photo of Kieran at home and in his car *"so he is with me wherever I go"*. They did everything together and Daryl said *"You never get over a thing like that"*. Kieran thought him never to take things for granted and used to talk him through tapes every night after racing. When Daryl won the Aintree Grand National in 2012 on Neptune Collonges, he looked to the heavens, and dedicated his victory to his best friend and inspiration Kieran Kelly, in a wonderful moment. Ruby Walsh explained it very well in his autobiography. How they started out at the same time, his place was beside Kieran in the weigh-room in Kilbeggan and his good sense of humour. He has always said in interviews *"that was the worst day I ever had in racing"*, which even people who have never ridden a horse would understand.

A WONDERFUL YEAR IN 2004

It was a very successful year for the Kilbeggan management, as the high profile of the course and the ability to give people what they wanted led to 8 very successful meetings, which attracted over 50,000 people. The betting turnover was over 5.2 million and corporate sponsorship over €160,000. One of the many highlights was the presence of the Westmeath team and supporters at their big celebration on the course following their first ever success in the Leinster Football Final. A happy wedding together of the two great Irish sports of National Hunt racing and the GAA and hopefully, they will both live happily ever after! It was also the year of the first ever Saturday meeting, with a massive attendance, although it was in danger of not taking place because of a dispute with the valets, who insisted on receiving €130 for working on Saturday. It was resolved when a sponsor paid the amount. The People in Need Races in May raised over €50,000 with tremendous support from the community. The highlight was when Paddy Dunican auctioned an Offaly jersey and Condron Concrete paid €10,000 for it. Items varied from nominations to stallions at Tally Ho Stud and Ennel Lodge Stud to a signed Michael Schumaker signed cap.

Philip Myerscough family had a long association with Mullingar racecourse before it closed, and Jessica Harrington trained his horse Colca Canyon (R.Power) in a chase at the meeting. Fairytales don't always work out, but when Fable won the Irish Stallion Farms EBF Handicap Chase it was yet another win for Noel Meade and Paul Carberry. The horse won €35,000 for the Up To Six Syndicate in 12 months. The featured Midland's National was won in August by the famous Westmeath maroon colours of Michael O'Leary's, Gigginstown House. Night Busker 5/2F was an Accordion gelding that had won in May, and was only having her third run in a chase in the big race. Paddy Flood kept him towards the front and the lively Oh So Lively (D.Casey) was his main challenger, but he won by a length. Dessie Hughes said *"He jumps well enough to run in the Plate and if he gets into the handicap he'll run in it".* Michael O'Leary was interviewed afterwards by Colm Murray, and delighted the crowd by tipping Westmeath to beat Dublin in the Leinster Final. The Suffolk based Dedham Vale syndicate were well represented, when Persue A Head won the bumper to bring a new element to the track. In September, Barrack Buster (R/Walsh) 7/4F, who was the last winner that Kieran Kelly had as a jockey, won in September and course specialist Keeponthesunnyside added to his successes in the Kieran Kelly Memorial Handicap Chase- a fitting end to the season. Barrack Buster 4/6 also went on to win his novice chase at Kilbeggan in May 2005, when for the first time in many years a jockey rode three in a row at Kilbeggan. Ruby Walsh's other winners were Glacial Moss 4/5 and Dr Julian 4/1.

LADBROKES SPONSOR THE MIDLAND'S NATIONAL FOR THE FIRST TIME

The 2005 season, brought an interesting start involving connections with Haydock, Cheltenham, and Aintree. The opening May meeting proved to be a memorable one for two staunch supporters of the venue with two wins for Cecil Ross and Robert Bagnall. Cecil Ross pulled off a great win in the Bridge House Handicap Hurdle with 20/1 shot Never Say No, while Bagnall's Fairwood Present skated home in the novice chase. The latter had already sponsored the second race on the card and his horse had already run in Cheltenham and Aintree before winning in Kilbeggan. Paul Carberry rode Definite Spectacle in the 1.50PM at Haydock and arrived by helicopter in Kilbeggan around 5.15pm to ride favourite Ikitaf to victory in the 5.30pm.

In July the Midland's National had a new sponsor, when Ladbrokes stepped in to sponsor the race giving a significant promotional development to the track and making it a €50,000 race. Paddy Dunican, Manager stated *"The sponsorship by Ladbrokes is the most significant since Kilbeggan Races began in 1840 and will be a great stimulus to a quality field and competitive races. This made it the biggest summer meeting outside the Budweiser Irish Derby and Galway Festival".* It was a long way from Russia to Kilbeggan, but there was a shock in the race when Paddy Flood dashed the Dessie Hughes trained Trotsky 20/1 (paid €80.70 on Tote) into the lead and he held off the late challenge of Il En Reve by 3/4 length. He cost just 3,100 guineas at Goffs and was owned by the Horseplay Syndicate. In August 2005, the Galway Blazers winner Mon Oiseau grabbed defeat from the jaws of victory after cruising up to take the lead he drifted left, as Robbie Dunne the jockey lost his whip. Victory went to Michael Darcy on Il En Reve in the Kieran Kelly Memorial Handicap Chase. When Legal Express won the novice chase it was the first training success for permit holder James Halpin, Co Meath and the first winner as a professional for Andrew Lynch then claiming 5lbs. It should be noted that over the years sponsors with Kilbeggan connections like the Joe & Christy Keenan, Loughnagore, Padraig Thornton, Tom Lynam, Coola, Pat McCormack, and many others supported races at Kilbeggan in different ways.

In 2006, one of the highlights of the year was the Carroll Cuisine meeting in June, as they had a historic connection with the midlands through local man Mark Gavin, Dalystown, who was Commercial Director. They sponsored five races on 26th June a handicap hurdle worth €20,000 and a chase worth €25,000, with victories going to Air of Confusion owned and trained by I.Madden and Phillip Fenton's Kings Orchard 10/1 (D.Russell) won the handicap chase to repeat an earlier win on the track. Syndicates were proving very popular and five syndicates won at the June meeting, where there was a social element, a sense of fun, and a touch of Irishness in their titles. The *"Ceili House"* (won with Mellow Music) and *"Bodhran Makers"* danced to success in two races and the *"In the Rough"* syndicate drove straight and true to win the novice hurdle, with the very impressive Proud To Be. In July, the Up At Six syndicate (who had won previously at Kilbeggan with Fable) had another big success when Noel Meade's Patton 5/2F (N.P.Madden) ran away with the Ladbrokes Midland's National by 13 lengths from Lorry Boy & Trotsky.

In August, Martin Brassil's Cunningham's Folly (R.Walsh) 1/1 completed a hat trick of success at Kilbeggan in three months. Ruby's father Ted saddled Collingwood 4/5 to win the bumper, ridden by his sister Katie. At the last two meetings of the year Noel Meade and Paul Carberry delivered for punters with four winners -Restoration (6/4), Deep Return (11/8F), Yarra Maguire (7/2F) and Rock On Tom (9/4).

€2.3 MILLION DEVELOPMENT ADDS GLAMOUR TO KILBEGGAN RACES

Kilbeggan was able to announce a fabulous new development for 2007, which cost €2.3 million. The development included a new parade ring and elegant presentation area, weigh room, administrative offices, saddling stalls and fibre stand cross overs on the track itself. The familiar old parade ring, weigh room, and saddling stalls were all gone. It was only possible because their neighbours the Fox family, who had played a major positive part in the history of Kilbeggan races sold additional land at the back of the old parade ring to the Race Committee to allow the new development. The superb new facilities were officially opened at the July meeting by the Tanaiste and Minister for Finance, Brian Cowen and present were Brian Kavanagh, CEO Horse Racing Ireland, the Most Rev.Michael Smith, Bishop of Meath (who blessed the new facilities) and many other senior officials and dignitaries. The air conditioned Jockey's Room had seating for 62 jockey's, a valet's bench, and separate facilities for lady jockeys. It also included a new Press Room for 20 journalists, new toilets near the parade ring, 16 new saddling stalls, With the new pavilion, extended enclosure and an improved track and parade ring Kilbeggan was prepared for the future.

THE IRONY OF GORDON ELLIOTT, LIQUID LUNCHES AND CHRISTY MAYE

The word *"Irony"* comes to mind when you look at the results at the first Kilbeggan races on 5th May. Gordon Elliott is now one of the leading trainers in Great Britain and Ireland but back in 2007 he started out in spectacular style when winning the Aintree Grand National with Silver Buck (who had won a point-to-point in Westmeath before the big race) in April 2007. The irony was he did not have his first winner in Ireland until Barstool Prophets Syndicate horse Toran Road (5/1) won the M.A. Stephens & Co Handicap Chase at Kilbeggan on 5th May 2007 ridden by his brother Joey. Elliot said afterwards *"That's great and it's for local lads in Summerhill, which includes my father and my uncle. One of the owner's sons had a wedding last night and it looks like we're going to have another night of it tonight".* (Barstool Prophet's indeed!). Anyone, who is familiar with Irish politics, would also see the irony of Liquid Lunch (R Walsh) 8/13F winning the Fianna Fail Maiden Hurdle for trainer Brian Hamilton. Local hotelier Christy Maye, long associated with the Bridge House Hotel, Tullamore and Greville Arms, Mullingar, won with his outsider Crème D'Arblay 14/1 and the irony in this case was that it was the Sean Hughes, Mullingar Park Hotel Hurdle sponsored by Josephine Hughes! Who said fate doesn't have a sense of humour?

At the June meeting, Robert Bagnall's good local horse Hilamar Hotel (Denis O'Regan), trained by Noel Meade got a well-deserved win in the Carroll Cuisine Novice Chase, strongly supported by all of Wesmeath. A very interesting bumper winner was Colm Murphy's Zaarito, who went on to better things. The Ladbroke Midland National was won by Dessie Hughes First Row (R.Loughran) on just his fourth start over fences. He got up on the run-in to beat Mullica Lad and Il En Reve by a short head and 1 1/2 lengths. The novice chase brought a 1-2 for Gigginstown House Stud when Mouse Morris's War of the World beat Warrior Drive. The unlucky horse was Piano Star who fell when clear, but Michael Cunningham's horse was to go on and win two Midlands Nationals. Hector O hEochagain presented his *"Big Bash"*, a cabaret style celebration of racing, and it was the new Racing Ambassador's first visit to Kilbeggan.

"ALL MY CHILDHOOD FRIENDS WERE THERE AND I WAS PERFECTLY HAPPY"

Looking back on the horses that ran in Kilbeggan in 2007, and it was interesting that winners like J.J.Mangan's Conna Castle ended up favourite for the Galway Plate; Colm Murphy's Zaarito, who won his bumper in Kilbeggan was favourite for the Champion Bumper at Cheltenham and finished third; and champion trainer Willie Mullins had won with useful horses like Taipan's Way and Uncle Junior. The track had been widened and extensive drainage carried out to create a better surface for trainers and jockeys.

John Kiely's King Rama (P.Carberry) won the Belvedere House Gardens & Park Handicap Hurdle very easily in May and quickly followed up with another win at the first ever Sunday meeting in June. The trainer said the aim was the Galway Hurdle at the festival. Thomas O'Leary came from Clonakilty in West Cork to get his win at Kilbeggan with Hamelsmead Lady 1/1F, as the bookies had a bad day. The first ever Sunday meeting was a great family occasion, which has continued on as a Family Fun Day at a time when other racecourses were struggling with Sunday meetings. It was an opportunity for adults to bring out the child in them, as one writer at Kilbeggan races stated in 1906 *"all my childhood friends were there and I was perfectly happy"*. The world had changed from Punch & Judy to Bouncing Castles, but the child inside was still the same?

Michael Cunningham had a wonderful record at Kilbeggan, but his Piano Star 12/1 ridden by Paddy Flood did not seem an obvious choice to win the Midland's National, until it was highlighted on the race card that he had been unlucky at Kilbeggan previously and was tipped to win. He didn't just win in 2008 but went on in 2009 to win the race again and prove it was no fluke. Strangely, these were the last two wins of his career. Michael Cunningham said afterwards that the ground suited him better than 2008 and he would be aimed for Galway. The Midland Breeders had been sponsoring a race at Kilbeggan for years and in 2008 they had a great year with three winners at Cheltenham and an Aintree Grand National winner. The winners at Cheltenham were Alberta's Run in the Royal Sun Alliance Chase Grade 1 over 3 miles; High Chimes winner of Kim Muir Chase 3m 1furlong; and Fiveforthree winner of the Ballymore Properties Novice Hurdle Grade 1 over 2 miles 4 furlong and Comply or Die won the Aintree Grand National. It was a great boost for midlands breeding and a presentation was made to them at the races.

It was with great sadness that many people heard that Jimmy Daly, Chairman of the Race Committee died on 23rd August 2008 after being ill for some time. He had given great time and energy over the years to many local organisations, but it was perhaps for his work with the Race Committee that he will be remembered most. When he took over he committed himself to it with intelligence, vision, leadership, and hard work to ensure his legacy.

In 2009, the meeting on 16th May had to be abandoned due to the weather and the effect on the track was a big consideration. When Borrowoody won the Sean Hughes Handicap Hurdle in April it was Patrick Mullin's 49th winner of the season to break Ted Walsh's post-war record in 1976, for the number of winners ridden by an amateur in a season. Mullins said: *"I'm delighted but if Ted had been riding the horses I've been on he'd have had sixty or seventy winners!"* In May, there was a popular local win for Robert Bagnall, who was a great supporter of Kilbeggan as a sponsor and owner, when Rochford Bridge won the Coola Handicap Hurdle (sponsored by Tom Lynam, Coola who was Treasurer of the Race Committee). It was his second win at Kilbeggan, as he stayed on really well to get up and beat favourite Sadler's Native. He said afterwards that he liked smaller tracks and could come back again. The Last Derby won the Kieran Kelly Novice Chase before going on to better things and in 2009 he won the United House Gold Cup Chase in England for Eoin Griffin.

2010 - D FOUR DAVE GAMBLE AT KILBEGGAN BY NEWLY WED

On Monday 21st June 2010, Kilbeggan was holding a relatively quiet meeting with no major race on the card. By the end of the evening Kilbeggan had hit the sporting headlines on newspapers and on-line after one of the biggest gambles on an Irish course in recent times. The race selected was the Hurley Family Kilbeggan Handicap Hurdle (80-96 rated horses) of 5,175 over 3 miles. My cousin Pat McCormack sponsored the race on behalf of our family and it looked an open race. Amongst the runners were a horse called D Four Dave trained by Conor O'Dwyer and owned by Douglas Taylor, Co Kildare and John McSharry, Leitrim. Douglas Taylor was the Managing Director of the MCR Group who sponsored races in Dundalk and Leopardstown. He was the mastermind behind the gamble, which involved an estimated 150 people being driven around by 50 drivers to betting shops in Kildare & Dublin to put on bets. Apparently, the plan involved Taylor's recruitment company giving each employee 200 in cash, with a completed betting slip and a set of instructions. They were given an alarm set to go off at 6.55PM (five minutes before the race at 7pm) and to take the price, which was expected to be around 14/1. Some of the employee's did not do it correctly (which caused the price to be only 7/1 on the track) but the vast majority of bets were put on successfully.

In the race itself, Conor O'Dwyer saddled his second winner of the season when D For Dave landed the gamble from 14/1 in the morning and finished up 5/1. He received a vey cool ride from Mark Walsh, who did not know about the gamble but cruised home by five lengths. O'Dwyer stated later that *"three miles suits him well and he jumped great. He handled the ground well enough but I've no plans from here. His part-owner Douglas Taylor was married on Saturday, so today will help pay for that party!"* If you had looked at his previous race which was also at Kilbeggan it would have been hard to back him, as he was 40 lengths 9th of 13 runners. The group did not win the full €200,000 expected, but it was a considerable sum and amazingly, Mr Taylor pulled it off just two days after he was married to his wife Stella. In terms of the gamble the bookies like Paddy Power and Ladbrokes admitted to five figure losses, but the general attitude was that it was just an old fashioned gamble in the Barney Curley style and they all paid up.The Stewards had an issue because of the improvement in form of the horse. Conor O'Dwyer explained that they had employed different and more positive tactics plus the horse was running over a longer distance. The explanation was noted and accepted by the Stewards.

The story was broken by The Irish Field and picked up by all the Irish & English papers. In an interview with the racing paper Douglas Taylor explained the background. His interest had started when he bought a horse for €1,200 and she won three times. He continued to own horses and sponsor races. He planned the coup at his office in Capel Street, but it was not inspired by Barney Curley or Dick Francis but by *"six pints of Guinness"*. He was at the races with his wife Stella and co-owner John McSharry when the gamble was on. It wasn't a total success, as not all the staff followed instruction, but they won a considerable sum and went back to Murphy's Pub in Kilcock to celebrate. He did state that the Kilbeggan gamble *"was only a dry run"* for something bigger? When Barney Curley was asked for a comment he referred to those who didn't do their jobs and said *"If they were working for me I'd sack them"*. Another aside was that the coup resembled a plot in the novel Extra Money written by Felix & Dick Francis, where juveniles are given instructions to put on bets of €200 in different bookie shops on an outsider that wins.

The big question was why was the horse called D Four Dave? The answer per Douglas Taylor was that *"He was called after an iconic figure from Dunlavin, who thinks he's from Dublin 4"*. Interestingly, a while after the race Conor O'Dwyer sent a nice letter to my cousin Pat thanking him for sponsoring the race and adding *"racing needs sponsors, so well done"*. It was a nice gesture to end a fascinating tale. Below is a Copy of the Instructions issued to the Employees:

"Dear Employee,

Enclosed you will find:

1. *A completed betting slip for the betting shop that you have been sent to.*
2. *€200 in cash for which you need to place the bet.*
3. *You should also have a watch with an alarm set to go off at 6.55pm.*

Your job is to place the bet exactly when the alarm goes off at 6.55pm. You need to be at the counter before the alarm goes off to be in position to hand over the betting slip and say to the person at the counter "I WILL TAKE THE PRICE". When the person hands you back the betting slip you will pay over the €200. You then have to place the betting slip back into your envelope and return the slip immediately to your supervisor/driver along with the watch when he comes to pick you up. You can then return with your driver/supervisor to MCR office to get paid.

Thank you"

Nothing could match the above in 2010, but Adrian Maguire's good horse Golden Kite won the Midland's National, Hairy Molly who won the bumper at Cheltenham in 2006 won a handicap chase at Kilbeggan; and Chairman of the Race Committee Paul Daly won on the track with the Pat Martin trained Irish Polie.

KILBEGGAN 2011 - 15

One of the most unusual races at Kilbeggan in recent years was the opening maiden hurdle at the Sunday meeting on 5th June 2011. Dermot Weld had a rare runner at Kilbeggan in Daffern Seal, ridden by Robbie McNamara and owned by Dr R. Lambe one of his top owners. The horse was a promising 4th in a bumper when 13/8. What was extraordinary was that he was freely available at 10/1 and started at 9/1. He raced away to win by 13 lengths with hardly a cheer from the crowd!

The Gigginstown House Midland's National on 15th July 2011 was a sad day for Michael O'Leary and the family with news of the death of his father Ted. The jockey's on Gigginstown Horses sported black arm bands for their respective races, while the traditional parade of horses at the start of the evening was cancelled. The featured Midland's National was won by Col Murphy's Future All Star (J.L.Cullen) with the Gigginstown horse Campbonnais in third place. Murphy said afterwards *"They went a better gallop today than the last day and the extra two furlongs suited him"* The Beginner's Chase ended in a driving finish with a dead heat for the first time in many years at Kilbeggan between Willie Mullin's horse Otay Kawn (D.Casey) and Gordon Elliott's *Trendelenburg* (P.Carberry). The latter was owned by the Barstool Prophet's Syndicate (including his father and uncle), who had given him his first victory in Ireland at Kilbeggan the year Silver Birch won at Aintree.

The first meeting of the year in May 2012 had a number of interesting winners and runners like Gordon Elliot's *Cause of Causes,* who won the opening maiden hurdle in the first race race; Mallowney (Grade 2 Chaser now) ran in a maiden; Liberty Counsel (Irish Grand National winner), and Zuzka in the bumper. Others like Mister Benedictine won the Michael Moore Handicap Hurdle and Fay Bookmakers Hurdle in June and he was favourite for the Galway Hurdle at one stage; Tastiocht won a bumper in June 12; Seefood, Passage Vendome won a T&V Novice Hurdle in June and had a previous win at Punchestown; and Cheltenham winner Carlito Brigante was only third in a novice chase to Dazzling Susie.

Local successes in 2012, included Let the Show Begin in September trained by Mrs Dot Love, who won the Angus Beef Hurdle and Liberty Counsel also won for her in the Dunbia Chase. Excellent as Usual won in July and was bred by Christy Maye, Mullingar and won The Ladies Day Handicap Hurdle over 3 miles for owner Padraig Barron & trainer Garrett J.Power, Kilkenny. Philip Byrne, the Offaly trainer won a bumper with Roisin Dubh, and also in August 2012 Adrian Murray, Westmeath trainer won a Novice Chase with Loughnagall (B.Geraghty). Blazing Tempo won a mares hurdle in September before going to success in Galway and Special Tiara won a maiden hurdle on 20 July 2012, before going on to win the Grade 1 Maghull Novice Chase at Aintree and most notably in the Desert Orchid Chase at Kempton when Barry Geraghty made all the running and ran the field ragged.

Over the years Kilbeggan featured many events at the races from GAA events involving n Westmeath and Laois; companies like Elan, Athlone; People in Need; Ireland's Own etc. On 17th May 2013, the Tullamore Rugby Club celebrated their 75th anniversary. They won the Midland's League, Provincial Town's Cup etc. They also won the Leinster Rugby Club of the Year Award and the captain Aaron Deverell got Leinster Player of the Year. It was the ideal place to celebrate their success and there was a great atmosphere.

In 2013 Mark McNiff from Sligo, could be deemed a small trainer, but he recorded his first ever double in May with Seskinane and Balboni. Ruby Walsh recorded his first win of the new season on Willie Mullin's Alelchi Inois 1/1in a maiden hurdle, who was winning on his Irish debut after being bought in France. Dessie Hughes continued his good Kilbeggan form with a double with Datokepe (33/1) in the novice chase and Wise Oscar (7/2) in the handicap chase. J.P.McManus's Double Seven came into form with a win in May in a handicap chase for trainer Martin Brassil that was to be the start of an upward curve that lead to victory in the Gigginstown Midlands National in July, when he reversed form with Wise Oscar & Tom Horn. He went on to be in 3rd place in the Aintree Grand National in 2014.

Oliver Brady who had brought so much to every racecourse in Ireland recorded his last Kilbeggan win with Maccas Lad (14/1). Noel Meade had a nice double at both June meetings with Six Stone Ned (3/1) in the novice chase and Nina Carberry won the bumper on Devil's Paintbrush (9/4F) a very nice horse by Shantou. He followed up with Honourable Emperor (5/2) and Tom Horn (6/4F) at the next meeting. Barry Geraghty's only ride was on Coolnagorna Giggs (3/1F) for Tom Hogan who stated afterwards it was a happy occasion, as *"I had my first winner in the owner Patrick McLoughney's colours. He is a long-standing owner of mine and I'm delighted to train a winner for him".*

DOUBLE CELEBRATION ON THE HORSE THAT DOESN'T LIKE FENCES

The year 2014 will not be remembered by Philip Fenton for the right seasons, but one of the highlights was Caim Hill's win in the Midlands National at Kilbeggan in July. The horse repeated his win of 2012. He had won 14 races in 6 years and at the age of eleven still had a bit of class. The winning jockey was Brian O'Connell, who had previous success in the race, and he had a double celebration, as his wife Donna had a baby the day before. He was backed from 14/1 to 7/1 and beat Rivage D'Or (future Cheltenham winner) by 3½ lengths with Fever Pitch 3 lengths further back. The owner Mick Dempsey from West Cork said *"He's not in love with fences, as it's a big effort for him to get over them, although he found the smaller fences easier".* Fenton had another win with Desertmore Stream 7/2, who beat Paddy Cooney's Irish Grand National runner up Golden Wonderin a hurdle race.Seefood shocked the crowd that day in another race when unseating Barry Geraghty giving John Berry's Croghill Tuppence 20/1 a lucky win in the race. It was a successful year for some locals as Athlone jockey Shane Shortall won in April on the well fancied Seaboru 7/2 for Stephen Ryan, Tipperary before receiving great public attention when winning the Galway Plate on Road to Riches for Gigginstown House Stud. Dot Love pulled off a nice win at Galway with Lucky Pat in a bumper after finishing 6th earlier in the week. The horse turned out a week later to win his maiden hurdle at Kilbeggan. In August, Offaly trainer Philip M.Byrne pulled off a surprise win with Whispering Hope (Mr P.J.Cawley) bred by Paul Guinan in the

Tom Bermingham Menswear bumper.

Other highlights varied from John Bowes course specialist Akatara recording his third course win by beating another course specialist in Kalico Kim in June and an interesting novice chase at this meeting was won by Henry De Bromhead's Bally Longford (Ann & Alan Potts owners), with Willie Mullin's beaten favourite Indevan (Mrs Ricci owner) disappointing. Aidan O'Brien had a novice hurdle winner in King Leon, and Cailin Annamh recorded her 8th career win at Kilbeggan in a novice chase before going on to further success.

In Apri 2015, the opening race of the year was won by Paul Nolan's appropriately named Illtakeitfromhere ridden by Luke Dempsey and he should go on to win a chase. Francis Slevin who only has two horses near Enfield had his first winner with Luckynumberslevin, who liked the ground. Jessica Harrington has a good strike rate in Kilbeggan and Fresh By Nature well ridden by Mark Bolger won the novice chase at 9/4F. Mark later suffered facial injuries at the June meeting, when he fell on Annie Oakley.The Gigginstown House Stud horse Ravished trained by Mouse Morris was quite impressive in the handicap chase beating Mallards in Flight.

Jessica Harrington's Duckweed put in a smooth performance in May with Robbie Power riding to win the At The Races Novice Hurdle at Kilbeggan. The horse had a local connection, as she was owned and bred by Kieran Guinness, Halston and she was a daughter of Wolfe Tone. She won cosily by 2 1/2 lengths over Captain Von Trappe and Nickname Exit (4th) both owned by Gigginstown House Stud, who were out of luck all day. She said *"I decided to come here, as it was three miles and she got all the allowances. She jumped really well and was a good point-to-point winner"*. She could be worth following over the summer. Guinness also bred / owned Nautical Nitwit (Let the Lion Roar-Mrs Pugwash) who was 3rd at Punchestown on 16th May 2015 at 100/1 and other horses like George Catt, Teucrium, Chester Charlie, Skeffington, Perfect Percy and Chatty Ted. Brian Hayes rode a double with Aunt Alice and Abolitionist to claim the rising spoils. Dot Love's Lucky Pat returned to record his second win on the track as a 4/1F with Davy Russell. This was his first run since a wind operation, which was obviously successful.

Michael O'Leary's horse Akorakor was part of a double for Gordon Elliott at the bank holiday meeting in May, which started with Mustadrik 9/10F,who was gambled on to follow up a win at Down Royal just two days earlier. Akorakor was the horse who won the bumper at Fairyhouse on Easter Monday on the same day that Dot Love won the Irish Grand National with Liberty Counsel. Michael O'Leary pledged €200,000 to the winner of the bumper but he won the race with Akorakor. He rang from Portugal to say that the money was to be donated to the Injured Jockey's Fund. This was shortly after the serious injury to John Thomas McNamara and it was a very generous gesture. Tom McNulty was a different type of owner in that it was the first time he led in a winner when the appropriately named Stay With It won. Willie Mullin's horse Daisy Gift (R.Walsh) was an uneasy 2/1F favourite in the mares hurdle but won comfortably in the end.

DESSIE HUGHES RIP

Dessie Hughes recorded 8 single wins at 8 meetings during 2014 with horses like Sugar Bullet, J.P.McManus's Nearly Nama'd, Rivage D'Or, Indian Icon, Roger Roo, Seefood, Sheamus, and Swiftmarc. Seefood and Sheamus went on to further success over fences and hurdles. His final winner was Swiftmarc (Ian McCarthy) 14/1, carrying bottom weight in the J.P. McManus sponsored Martinstown Handicap Hurdle Hurdle. It was appropriate that he was yet again Leading Trainer at Kilbeggan. He was the most successful trainer in recent years at the course and was very popular as a trainer and just as a man with all the patrons. He will be badly missed by everyone in racing and in Kilbeggan, which he always supported.

DEDICATION TO SEAN DALY AND TOM LYNAM

Sean Daly has been part of the Kilbeggan Race Committee since 1956, when the new committee was formed. The Kilbeggan Race Committee was sued arising out of the death of P.F.Conlon the jockey in 1952, and they owed £13,000 to the banks and £312 to the Racing Authorities, leading to their licence being revoked. After a series of meetings a new committee was formed, which led to young Sean Daly and his brother Jimmy being brought on to the committee. The financial issues were ultimately resolved and the licenced to race granted. The two brother's job initially was to use their van to get birch for the fences, which they duly did. A large number of fund raising events were run by the Social Committee such as draws, dances, and carnivals in which Sean helped out willingly. He was also there when Kilbeggan was threatened again in 1963 and 1969. He is the last of that great voluntary committee that took Kilbeggan back from the brink of closure to be the only racecourse in Westmeath & Offaly to survive.

As a young man he thoroughly enjoyed the dances, carnival etc., and the sense of achievement in saving the races. He was asked to go on the gate at the cross over into the stand at that time and he has been doing it for almost 60 years. He has seen all the changes from two meetings to eight; the improvements in the course and facilities and the great position Kilbeggan is in now. He remembers when most people were on the outside with entertainment and two bars (Dufficy's and Fagan's). If you happen to be going into the races at the cross over, you will have the pleasure of meeting a wonderful man, who is representative of that generation and all the families, who contributed to Kilbeggan over the years.

The Lynam Family in Coola are an institution in Kilbeggan through farming, the ploughing, the races and they have constantly given their time to the community. Tom Lynam's father "Locky" was part of the Kilbeggan Race Committee and naturally Tom became part of it in the 1960's to be followed by his brother P.J. (their sisters Mary and Eileen were also on the Ladies Committee). As young people might say, Tom Lynam is a *"legend"* in Kilbeggan, before his time. He has been part of most of the good things that have happened down the years from the race committee, involvement in the church, the hall, and many other organisations in the town. He is a farmer and uses all that knowledge to take care of the race track, as an essential part of his life.With eight race meetings each year it is a major job to have it ready in different weather conditions and with limited space on the track. He knows every blade of grass and every corner of the track. He has been Treasurer for many years with responsibility for the expenditure of million's of euro, during a period of rapid change. Tom has also sponsored a race at Kilbeggan for a number of years and has even tried owning a racehorse. He can only be described as the heart and soul of Kilbeggan races. In a world of change, he is the equivalent of the old committees that voluntarily saved Kilbeggan Races. It is for this reason that with Jim Tormey & Cecil Ronaldson, I decided to dedicate the book to Sean and Tom, as representative of that generation and the good things in life.

PADDY DUNICAN, MANAGER AND KILBEGGAN'S FUTURE

It started with his grandfather Paddy and then his father Paul was involved in the race committee from 1956. He became Chairman and was there during the difficuly years in 1963 and 1969. Because Paddy grew up with the races at home, he became involved at an early stage doing all kinds of jobs from working on the hurdles, turnstiles, on the phones or assisting in the office. In this way, he learned all the basic jobs involved. He loved farming and rural life, so the races fitted into this category.

When Tom McCormack retired in 1988 he was asked to be Secretary by the committee in a part-time capacity, under the supervision of Tom McCormack. At that time there were three race meetings per year and an attendance of about 12,000 per year. He didn't look for the post but his attitude was *"always to do your best"*. It was a big challenge but he didn't know the job and had to learn everything. This involved the ability to listen, watch, and learn quickly. He was very young at the time but the committee wanted to develop and improve the racecourse.

He said *"We started to develop the racecourse and the big objective was to purchase additional land from the Fox family".* The committee had no security, only a lease. The purchase of the racecourse lands (90 acres) took place in 1992, and it then allowed the committee to develop more meetings. The first development was the building of new complex in 1990 incorporating bars, self service restaurant etc. The bank and the Racing Authorities gave full support, as more grants became available in the 1990's. It should be remembered in this era that the committee signed personal guarantees for the money, which was an amazing commitment and belief in the races.

Paddy said *"Once we bought the land, we could increase the number of meetings".* They started looking at the race track, as could only take 3 or 4 meetings. They removed timber railings and put in a plastic rail's. He said *"We improved structures by putting in underground facilities for water etc".* The racetrack was widened, extended and drained to improve the surface and help deal with the fact that it is a tight track. In line with developments Paddy said *"We started a sponsorship drive, which increased the quality of racing and received corporate sponsorship from companies like Elan to sports groups like the Buccaneers".* Gradually, over the years, the number of meetings increased from 3 to 8 with attendances averaging around 5,000. As Manager, Paddy could promote it and develop it more.

Paddy sees his job as an administrator rather than a racing person, *"as you can never afford to take your eye off the ball".* The real issue in recent years is the emphasis on Health & Safety, the track, and watering. In the past you paid insurance once a year, but now it's a major part of the industry. In *"what other industry would you have two doctors and ambulance's following people, as they do their job riding around a race track".*

Like any organisation you need to keep improving. Sponsorship began with a few thousand pounds and grew to a six figure sum, with support from Mullingar, Tullamore, Athlone and surrounding areas and now it's a big part of Kilbeggan's success. Paddy works closely with the HRI and Turf Club to provide good racing and he would know all the other racing managers in the industry, as part of the Association of Irish Racecourses. He has received the National Racecourse Manager of the Year Award on three occasions in recognition of his commitment. It is not a 9-5 job, as he has to keep a permanent eye on the track plus attend many meetings regarding racing, sponsorship, and any other aspects of the industry.

With any organisation, it is the future that matters and plans for the future take into account the central location, all National Hunt Racing in the summer and it is now well established with strong local support, as the only course in the midland region. The advantages are it is situated on the M6 motorway, with around a $^1/_2$ million people within an hour's drive from Dublin to Galway. It is competitive, both within racing and against other sports and leisure activities. Kilbeggan describes itself as *"The Heart of Ireland, the Soul of Racing"* and both literally and metaphorically, it is close to the truth. The obvious danger to any summer meeting is the weather, which has been very poor in recent years, but Kilbeggan continues to provide Family Fun Days, Best Dressed Ladies competitions, music, for those who want a day out, with better quality racing including the featured Midlands National in July each year. Paddy say's *"Over the next 5 years the track will continue to be developed to attract more and better horses, which together with improved facilities to attract patrons and new people, should add to the attraction of racing".*

The major change in recent years is the development of a website, social media, texting etc, which has altered the landscape and increased the number of people who purchase tickets on-line, and brought new interaction with a new generation. With the economy now on an upward curve, it is hoped that Kilbeggan will continue to thrive with more sponsorship, better racing and make a great day out for everyone, who loves National Hunt racing.

KILBEGGAN TALES AND TITBITS

THE PRINCE, THE ACTRESS, THE DAM OF A GOLD CUP WINNER AND 150 SOVEREIGNS

On Monday May 11th, 1953 Prince Aly Khan came to Kilbeggan Races together with a beautiful actress, a horse with an unusual name, one of the greatest trainers and breeders in Irish racing, the mother of a Cheltenham Gold Cup winner and all for a race worth 150 sovereigns! Aly Khan was one of the biggest punters in racing and invariably thousands of pounds changed hands with big bookmakers like William Hill. His greates horse was Petite Etoile winner of the English 1,000 guineas and Oaks in 1959, when trained by Noel Murless. He was also an amateur jockey and rode over 100 winners. Aside from his racing interests he was often described, as a playboy and in 1949 he married Rita Hayworth, the actress and one of the leading pin-up's of World War II. The stormy marriage lasted around two years and in that time they had an extended honeymoon in Europe, where she attended race meeting's but not Kilbeggan. However, in 1953 one of the most beautiful actresses in Hollywood history was in Kilbeggan. Gene Tierney who came from a wealthy New York family, started on Broadway and eventually ended up at 20th Century Fox starring in a western *"Belle Starr"* in 1941. Her most important role was in the film noir thriller *"Laura"* in 1944, which is unusual in that her beauty is spoken about for around $^1/_2$ hour (based on a painting), as it is assumed that she has been murdered.

When she eventually appears she was one of the few actresses that could live up to the expectations. She starred in films like *"Leave Her To Heaven"*, *"Razor's Edge"* (with Tyrone Power), as a villain and also in the comedy *"The Ghost and Mrs Muir"*. She had a nervous breakdown in 1955 and in 1961 married W.Howard Lee, Houston. She died aged 70 from emphysema.

At the races, the autographs of Aly Khan and Gene Tierney were very popular with the locals. Everyone was waiting for the last race (the bumper), where Aly Khan was riding the unpronounceable Ynys, a four year old by Owen Tudor trained by H.M. Hartigan. He was 5/4 favourite and went straight into the lead before being pursued by P. P. Hogan, the great trainer and breeder of high class National Hunt horses, riding Organist (5/1), but he held on to win by 2 1/2 lengths - a perfect finish to a perfect day! Following the race, the road was cleared into town to allow him to rush back to his stud. Tragically, he was killed in a car crash in a Paris suburb in May 1960 at the age of 48. He was one of the most important influences in horse racing and the bloodstock world. There is a story that Gene Tierney was presented with a case of Locke's Whiskey, which she threw out of the car somewhere on the Mullingar Road. Is there anyone who would believe that whiskey from the oldest Pot Still Distillery in world (1757), would be thrown away?

One final note is that no one noticed the last horse in the race who was Mrs E.Tormey's Leney Princess, an unconsidered outsider. She went on to become one of the most successful dams of her era with horses like Fort Leney, Cheltenham Gold Cup winner in 1968, Lean Forward, Prince Tino, King Frost and many more. All in all, May 11th, 1953 was an unusual and historic day in the history of Kilbeggan Races.

A KNIGHTHOOD FOR A DINNER AND THE RACING CONNECTION

In 2012, a festival was started in Kilbeggan based on the knighting of a local innkeeper Thomas Cuffe in the late 18th century. The Coach belonging to the Lord Lieutenant of Ireland broke down near Kilbeggan, and Lord Townend and his party had to stay in the local Volunteer Inn (visited by John Wayne in 1950). They did not expect much from the local innkeeper, but he provided the best of food and topped it up with the famous Kilbeggan Whiskey from the oldest pot still distillery in the world (1757). The Lord Lieutenant decided to knight the innkeeper and despite the best efforts of his companions he dubbed him Sir Thomas Cuffe. The following morning he explained that it was only a *"joke"* due to excess alcohol. Sir Thomas was perfectly willing to give up the title for *"compensation"*, but he declared that his good wife Lady Mary would not even consider it. They kept their title for their lifetime and a painting of the knighthood was above the door up to 1994. The racing connection arises from a direct descendant Ada Cuffe Quinn marrying Hugh Morgan Byrne and their daughter Peggy married Gerald St John Nolan. The story of Peggy St John Nolan is recounted elsewhere but she trained Zonda to win the 1959 Irish Grand National, but as women were not allowed to have a licence it was in the name of Head Lad Matt Geraghty. Her daughter Anne married Michael Cunningham, who was champion trainer in Kilbeggan but more importantly trained champion filly Cairn Rouge and he won the Champion Hurdle with For Auction 40/1, in addition to training Greasepaint who was 2nd in the Aintree National to Corbiere.

The racing & international connection goes further, as Edward 'Paddy'Wilson the great grandson of the Lord & Lady, as a young man hunted and attended race meetings before going to Australia in 1837. His father was the Rev. Edward Wilson and his mother Elizabeth Cuffe. After many adventures across Australia and racing horses at different times he ended up in Rockhampton on the east coast, where he became Chairman of the Jockey Club and the Tattersalls Club.

Thomas Cuffes knighthood which is still celebrated in 2015 began with a coach pulled by horses breaking down in Kilbeggan. He might have smiled at the idea of his descendant's being so successful in horse racing, both in Ireland & Australia.

TED WALSH AND THE HORSE WHO FINALLY MADE UP HER MIND

The headline *"Undecided finally makes up her mind"* appeared in a newspaper in connection with one of the most extraordinary incident ever to occur at Kilbeggan on Thursday, 19th September, 1974. It was an eight race card and the fifth race was the Fabri-Cast Amateur Handicap Hurdle for 4 year olds and up and it had a field of 14 runners. The favourite was Tullow Lass, ridden by Mr R.O'Neill and she looked like obliging, as she had a clear lead coming to the fifth lass where she fell. Undecided was not in touch with the leaders at that stage, so it must have been a surprise to her when she was brought down by the favourite. Ted Walsh was the rider of Undecided for his father Ruby and this is his version of what happened next:

> *"She fell at the hurdle past the stands and crashed through the running rail on the inside. When she got to her feet she proceeded to follow the horses that had gone on quite a bit in front of her. When they turned at the bottom bend, she also turned to take a short cut. I ran after her to see if I could catch her, as she ran towards the pond, which was covered with a green coat of slime and grass. As she was running downhill towards it, she jumped the water at the edge. I am presuming she thought the green coat was solid and she landed about 15 feet into the middle of the pond. As I got to her, all I could see it was her rear end sticking up and her hind legs kicking. She appeared to suffocate*

> *quickly. I remember when we pulled her out with a tractor and rope tied to her tail, the suction was so great it pulled the bridle off her head. A sad memory, but nonetheless one which will be part of Kilbeggan folklore for time to come. It has also been used in many tracing quizzes around the country. The daily paper next day carried a picture of my father standing at the edge of the pond looking in with a grim face. The caption on the paper read "Undecided finally makes up his mind". It was a 'sad memory' for the Walsh family, but for Kilbeggan Races it has been something that racegoers always remember and associate with the course more as a "joke" than anything else".*

Dermot Weld who had a number of rides on the course recalls that particular incident also and as he says *"I will always remember a horse that Ted Walshe rode getting loose and drowning in the quarry in the middle of the race track. It is one thing to explain to an owner why his horse didn't win, but to tell him that his horses has drowned is another."*

Even now it is difficult to understand how the horse actually drowned, but some of the local committee considered that when she jumped into the pond, one of her legs got caught in the reins thus preventing her getting out and that she panicked and drowned before anyone could get to her. It was an unusual, sad, and I suppose funny incident. The winner of the race was Donegal Road ridden by Michael Furlong and trained by D.O'Keeffe, Shanballymore, Co Cork.

An addendum to this incident gave another dimension to the story. It was written by W.P.Carter in the *"Cork Holly Bough 1990"* It stated:

> *"Undoubtedly, the unluckiest animal I ever followed was a horse named Undecided, owned and trained by Kildorrery-born Ruby Walsh and ridden by his champion amateur son Ted. The misfortunate Undecided was the perpetual bridesmaid-nearly always finding one just a little bit too good for her on the run in. However, I felt confident of recovering previous losses when I plunged on her in an amateur hurdle at Kilbeggan. I believed Undecided's day had finally come and despite my erratic tipping experiences, I was just flabbergasted when his name wasn't mentioned in the racing results broadcast on the 5.55pm radio sports news. On opening the following morning's Examiner racing page, I was startled by the headline "Kilbeggan Runner Drowns". I thought -surely not mine but yes, you've guessed, the unlucky Undecided, finally had its fate decided- and in most distressing circumstances."*

THE DRAMA OF 1991

The first meeting of the year on Monday, 2th May, 1991 was destined to be one of the most notorious in Kilbeggan's long history going back to 1840. Two chases on the day were to become international news items in the following days. The Usher Cup had Tommy Kinane's mount, Sharp Comment a hot 5/4 favourite to defy a 4lb penalty for winning at Roscommon the previous week. He won cleverly, defeating Forgestown by a comfortable 2½ lengths. Eddie O'Grady's good horse Caddy, who won the race the previous year was well fancied but after jumping off well he faded out of contention and was pulled up. In the following race, Francis Flood's Dominick's Cross was an obvious favourite for the Hunter Chase. The horse appeared lifeless in the parade ring and on the way to the start. Eventually, he was withdrawn by order of the Stewards on veterinary advice. Lagan Valley Rose was made the new favourite at 2/1 and won by 8 Lengths. When punter's went home that evening they did not realize the controversy that was about to ensue!

The front page headlines on national newspapers varied from *"Fears of Big Race Scam"* (30th May The Star) to *"Stables On Dope Alert"* (8th June, Irish Press). Basically, the story was that Eddie O'Grady's Assistant Trainer Tim Finn noticed that Caddy was lifeless in the parade ring prior to the Usher Cup and told one of the Stewards. The vet checked the horse at the start, but neither he nor jockey Tommy Carmody were sure if there was anything wrong with him. Carmody knew very quickly during the race that something was wrong and pulled him up on the first circuit. In the Hunter' Chase, Dominick's Cross the obvious favourite was a drifter in the betting and Francis Flood noticed he stumbled in the Parade Ring a few times and seemed very sleepy. He was brought down to the start, but after a vets inspection he was withdrawn by the Stewards. In an interview on the Irish Independent, Francis Flood said *"I have always been wary of scare stories, but this time there was something suspicious. His head was down and it took us quite a while before we could load him on Monday night"*. He had three stable lads with the four horses, but it was not possible to watch the horses all the time. The case of Caddy was not as bad and he was much better after a few hours.

Samples from both horses were taken for analysis by the Equine Forensic Unit in Trinity College and the Horse Racing Forensic Laboratory Ltd in Newmarket. The original results were not positive but by Saturday, 8th June tests confirmed that the horses were "nobbled". The question was how did it happen? Speculation varied from the use of aerosol sprays to direct injection. The general conclusion was it was injection, as they were affected so quickly. The next issue was the lack of security. The conclusions of the investigation into security were that the general security for the stabling of runners at Kilbeggan was not sufficient e.g. 20 boxes inside the main entrance were only fenced off by "twine".

The Turf Club also came in for criticism for not dealing with the issue. Paddy Dunican, Manager of Kilbeggan Racecourse pointed out the amount of money spent by the Kilbeggan Committee to improve the track in recent years and that it was never possible to cover all aspects in a totally satisfactory manner. He admitted that the stabling area was not properly fenced off. Hindsight is 20/20 vision and it was easy for members of the press to be judgemental, afterwards about what should have been done. Unfortunately, history had shown that sophisticated security at high level courses had not stopped the problem, if the culprits really wished to achieve their aims. There was also an onus put on trainers to provide their own security.

The Irish Independent headline of 18th June was *"Bookies Investigated in Kilbeggan Affair".* There was speculation that Kilbeggan was only a testing ground for a big sting, because there was no real evidence of a major coup. It was confirmed by the Racing Authorities that a few bookies were under investigation and all bookmakers working at Kilbeggan had to submit their sheets, and most of them did. The Gardai interviewed several people named by the Turf Club, because it was felt that a small group of punters had formed an organised ring to beat the system. In spite of all the furore, there was little enough evidence of any great gamble, and the attempt to drug the horses was somewhat clumsy and obviously miscalculated. Perhaps Kilbeggan was only a testing ground, but any failed attempt which alerts every racecourse in Ireland and increases security, cannot be deemed all that successful.

On 25th June the Irish Independent headlined that *"Kilbeggan Goes High Security".* Between the Turf Club and the Kilbeggan Executive, seven people were on duty supervising the stable area. The stables were still not fenced in, as it would take time and money. The Irish Turf Club's own security officer directed operations and each stable ensured that they had enough staff to police all the horses in the stable area. Someone commented (unsurprisingly) *"it was like closing the stable door, after the horse had bolted"*, which was true in so far as it went, but if everyone had the power of foresight, racecourses (or even punter's) would never have any problems.

KILBEGGAN PRODUCES REPUBLICS LONGEST PRICED WINNER SINCE 1935

When Museum won the Irish 2,000 guineas in 1935 at 100/1, little did anyone know that it would be almost 70 years later before this would happen again. The strange thing about Museum's victory is that he went on to take the Irish Triple Crown by winning the Irish Derby (100/8) and the St Leger (1/2). It must have been the only time in racing that a horse was 100/1 and 1/2 on The Curragh the same year! The Horseleap Maiden Hurdle at 6 PM on 6th June 2003 in Kilbeggan was as insignificant race, with an 8 y/o horse called After the Ball having his fourth race in a month. He had been 9th beaten 33 lengths on 9th May in Wexford (25/1); fell at the first in Navan on 18th May (25/1); and was 8th in Kilbeggan beaten 31 lengths on 26th May (50/1). It was therefore no surprise that he was generally unbacked and ended up 100/1 on the tote. Paddy Nannery was a local fence builder, and related to Willie & Paddy O'Toole, who were long associated with racing & the building of fences at Kilbeggan. Paddy Nannery placed a bet on After the Ball on the tote and won over €750 when the horse galloped home in front of a silent stand. It was a case of celebrating *"after the ball was over"* for Paddy! Experts like Tony Sweeney and Tony O'Hehir confirmed at the time that they could not recall a 100/1 winner in Ireland between 1935 and 2003. Maybe someone out there knows of one?

KILBEGGAN AND LIGHT TITBITS

FAVONIUS ON THE DOUBLE

In April 1903, Favonius (4/1) walked away with a handicap hurdle ridden by P.J.Higgins and immediately turned out for a $1^1/_4$ mile flat race to win by 5 lengths at 1/1, ridden again by Higgins.

DAM THE WINNER

In May 1937, there was a very unusual double at Kilbeggan by Tom O'Roarke. He won the Midland Plate with Battling Lady, who was by Irish Battle out of Lady Barney. In the next race the same Lady Barney turned out to win the Loughnagore Chase by 10 lengths (her second run of the day after being 4th in a $1^1/_2$ mile hurdle race). Battling Lady was the only foal bred by Lady Barney, who was barren after this and was returned to racing with profitable results. The two horses had also won at Longford and repeated the feat at Kilbeggan. A remarkable family!

EITHER WIN OR DIE?

At the May meeting in 1949, locals were delighted when Cealthra won the Midland Flat race at 4/1, as he was owned near the course by Joe Kelly, Streamstown and most of them backed the horse. What they didn't know was the owner's last words to the jockey when the horse was being saddled up. He said *"either win or die"* to the jockey. Clearly Mr Tyrrell was a jockey who could ride under pressure!

YOU GO OR ON YOU GO, THAT IS THE QUESTION

An unusual incident occurred in September 1977, when the riderless You Go jumped the wire fence separating the course from the enclosure and came straight for the stand, scattering the crowd and was caught at the front steps of the stand. By an extraordinary coincidence the next race was won by the Clem

Magnier trained On You Go!

CHARLES J. HAUGHEY AND JOE McGRATH

At the May meeting in 1980, two of the best known figures to bestride life in Ireland won consecutive races at Kilbeggan, with horses they both bred. In the Midland Novice Chase, Mr Haughey's home bred Blasket Sound (5/2) won by 4 lengths, with Gerry Dowd riding. In the following Usher Cup, Chevalid (8/13) brought a change of luck for local jockey Gerry Newman and trainer Tom Shaw. This horse was bred & owned by Joe McGrath one of the great figures in business & racing in Ireland un the 20th century.

A POULTICE OF COW DUNG!

At the August meeting in 1991, held on Nations Cup day at the RDS, the hitherto disappointing Midsummer Fun trained by Joe Byrne and ridden by Conor O'Dwyer won. The winner had originally been purchased from Jim Bolger and was an intended runner in the Guinness Chase at Galway but suffered an injury. Joe Byrne used the old remedy of a poultice made from hot (should that be fresh?) cow dung to cure the bruising! The same day Orient Melody won the handicap chase and his stammering form figures of PPPP did little to explain why he was backed from 12/1, and even less to explain how he won the race?

KILBEGGAN BEATS ROYAL ASCOT

On the second day of Royal Ascot in June 1991 they had a jackpot carryover of £53,000, but Kilbeggan had a carryover for their meeting and the jackpot grew to £66,000.

TOM DREAPER AND PUGILISM

In May 1929, the great Tom Dreaper rode his first winner at Kilbeggan when Orange Grove won the Loughnagore Plate by 4 lengths. It was on a day when trick of the loops flocked into town and one report said *"the exhibition of their pugilistic abilities was enjoyed by those in the vicinity".*

A DEAR HORSE AT 6d

In August 1955, Martin Quirke champion jockey in 1923 and winner of 8 classics, one day visited a friend George Mullen, Naas and he was offered a yearling. A price was made and Quirke parted with his 6d - in cash. The horse was appropriately called Dear One and on 29th August 1955 he won the Tullamore Handicap at Kilbeggan.

PRIEST GIVES NEW HOPE FOR CONDEMNED HORSE

In 1960 New Hope won the Usher Cup ridden by R.Hanly for trainer D.Kinane. He had previously finished second in two Galway Plates and was fourth in the Irish Grand National. He was once condemned to the kennels, but got an eleventh hour reprieve when the owner's brother-in-law, Fr John Sweeney "nursed" the ailing horseback to health, when it was feared his racing days were over.

A HONEYMOON HIT

In September 1976, Ted Walsh rode Dream House to win the Fabri-Cast Hurdle at Kilbeggan. It was perhaps an appropriate winner for Ted, because he had only come back from his honeymoon the previous day. There was an enquiry into the result (not I hasten to add because Ted rode a winner after his honeymoon), because Dream House had been last of four at Limerick in his previous run. Thankfully, he got a wedding present when the horse kept the race.

HOURIGAN SWOOPS TO CONQUER

Michael Hourigan has a great record over the years at Kilbeggan and at the meeting in September 1994 he was in second place in the race for Leading Trainer at Kilbeggan. Aidan O'Brien was in the lead with six winners and Hourigan had three winners, so it seemed like no contest. However he produced four winners on the day in Muscovy Duck, Butler John, Lantern Luck, and Dancingcinderella (three ridden by Kevin O'Brien) to take the title against the future champion trainer. On the same day, Shawiya who had won at Cheltenham the previous year failed to win at Kilbeggan, when falling at the last fence in a novice chase.

LORRA LORRA LAUGHS WHEN "BLIND DATE" VISITS KILBEGGAN

In August 1996 Steve Tricker, Devon and Cathy Scott, Warrington, won on Cilla Black's show "Blind Date" and visited Kilbeggan Races and Kilbeggan Distillery, as part of their prize. Colm Murray, Commentator marked their cards and Sean Graham, Bookmaker gave them a free bet in each race, leading to a profit for the lovely couple. They were given a royal time when wined and dined on the track for the day. The show was shown in February 1997 to an audience of around 12 million people. Did Sean Graham quote odds on whether Cilla would need a new hat?

€8,292 ADDED TO €115 EUROMILLION'S WIN

In 2005, Dolores O'Riordan won €115 million in the Euro Lottery. In August 2007 at Kilbeggan Races, her husband Adrian won €8,292 with his mare Carraig na Capaill (a daughter of Prix De L'Arc de Triomphe winner Carroll House) Dolores had bought the horse the previous October, after it won a point to point at Templemore. Adrian was described as *"cock-a-hoop"* after the win.

chapter 12
THE INTERNATIONAL CONNECTION

We are living in a world that is getting smaller and smaller, as access through travel or communications is making everything possible, but in the past you emigrated to make your fortune and returned home or else stayed in your new land. In racing terms, many breeders are selling most of their horses abroad, as there is now a huge market over five continents. In the past, some of the breeders in the midlands made their fortunes in Argentina or Australia,then returned home to own horses or set up their own studs.

In Argentina in the 19th century, there was huge emigration from Westmeath. The Irish Sheperds and the gauchos of the Pampas were united in their love of horses. Horses and horse racing was part of their lives. When the English & Irish came they wanted more organised racing with heats and breeding, part of the game. In 1826, the Buenos Aires Race Club was founded by a group of British & Irish merchants and gradually they developed with more betting and runners. In the 1850's, local mares were bred with imported stallions. The racing became more like home in style and presentation. Owning race horses and having private races was a mark of social prestige in Ireland & Argentina. Races became the most important social event of the year. Wexford people had contempt for the Midland immigrants from Westmeath, Offaly, and Longford, as they perceived themselves as better educated with a higher culture and moral standing. Murphy even wrote about one meeting where Wexford people won all the races, and those from Ballinacarrigy, Westmeath caused trouble and the races had to be abandoned.

In the 1880's, the Stud Book was inaugurated and names like Duggan, Maguire, Murphy, or Gay now appeared. Almost 20 of the 100 founders of the Jockey Club of Buenos Aires in 1882 were Irish immigrants. Joseph McLoughlin, Glascorn, Mullingar (1831) and estancia "San Jose" Mercedes 1896 was one of the founders of the Mercedes Racing Club.

SIR WILLIAM NELSON

William Nelson was the son of Hames Nelson, from Battstown, Co. Westmeath. He was prominently connected with the South America meat trade, and Chairman of the well- known packing firm of Nelson & Son and also principal of the Nelson line and steamers, which went between Liverpool and Argentina. He emigrated to Argentina, where he built up an extensive business and made a fortune killing, marketing, and exporting meat. His early interest in horse racing began in Argentina, where he had a string of horses. He came back to

England around 1900 and Steve Donoghue rode for him. In the New Year honours, he was conferred with a baronetcy in 1912. He was a gambling owner & Robin Goodfellow in the Daily Mail described him as a '*dead meat merchant*', which may have referred to his business, but also referred to his numerous non-triers in a race. Nelson thought it was unfair and resented it. He did send a small string of fillies to Argentina to be raced and eventually bred with the best sire's there. He married Margaret Hope, Gartlandstown, Westmeath, who became Lady Nelson. Her brother E.J.Hope was a great breeder of good horses in Gartlandstown. Christopher Hope her other brother had been manager of Las Palmos Frigorifico and as legal representative of the late Sir William Nelson, he had administered his wide commercial & shipping (Nelson Line) interests in Argentina. He also had his own extensive properties, the estacias "Los Leones" in Suipacha and "San Bernardo" in the Partido de San Antonio de Areco. He was a keen sportsman and well known golfer, as in 1910 he won the Argentine Centenary Cup presented by the Government. He was good at polo, tennis, pigeon shooting, and fishing (Charles Fagan TD was their nephew). In September 1948 he died in Buenos Aires at the age of 81 having lived there since 1887 and was buried in Chacarita Cemetery. His wife was Isobel M Duggan, daughter of Thomas Duggan, Calle Bartolome, Buenos Aires. He visited Ireland many times before WWII and had 4 daughters and 2 sons. The Nelson's are still breeding horses in Argentina, mostly devoted to polo playing and Jack Nelson was an outstanding polo player and President of the Argentine Polo Association. As you can see both the Hope and the Nelson families were related to the Duggans, the most famous Irish landowners in the pampas.

Having established his wealth, Sir William Nelson went on to win the Irish Derby with Bachelor's Wedding in 1913 and the National Stakes with Skymon's Pride in 1908. He owned Patlander (Sir Patrick-Theodora II) Irish Grand National winner in 1907 (bred by M.J.Cleary). He had good horses like Grammont, Duke of Padua, Vencedor etc, but not too many high class horses and he set up at Clonbarron in Meath. He made a great contribution into saving racing in Ireland during WW1 with Lord Decies. He was later very much involved in having the Totalisator (Pari-Mutuel) accepted in England and Ireland. He died in July 1922.

A LITTLE HELP FROM HEAVEN

In more modern times Tommy Nelson, Buenos Aires whose family was originally from Moyvore, Westmeath, before they emigrated to Argentina during the Famine, had racing success in Argentina in April 2008. His father Raul Nelson was fond of horses and when he was home, his Irish relatives in Moyvore called a foal *"Lady of Moyvore"*. In April 2008, on the date of his mother's 93rd birthday the horse won its first ever race. A friend from Mullingar believed *"that the horse received a little help from heaven"*. One of her brothers, "De Pizarra" retired early due to injury, but had won a Group 1.

REDDY FOR RACING

T. M.Reddy, Culleen, Westmeath (1839-1915) was born in 1839 and emigrated to Buenos Aires, Argentina as a 17 y/o in 1856 and became a major sheep, cattle, and goat farmer. The Southern Cross recorded in March 1893 the following. *"One of the greatest bargains of the Estancia Land is the purchase by Thomas M.Reddy of the well- known Estancia El Sermon of Laro in the partido of Vacine, the land measures about 4 1/2 leagues, all wired in, and contains some well-built estancia houses and fine mounts of old trees, the price paid 250,000 or 22.3 per hectare. We are happy to congratulate Mr Reddy".* Even after he returned to Culleen, Mullingar, he maintained his interest in the Argentinian properties and in 1905 he was the owner of 45,000 acres of land near Buenos Aires. In 1910 he owned 30,000 sheep, 8,000 horned cattle and 500 horses and mares. The horses were bred from 8 Irish mares he imported in 1874, and he also purchased well-bred sires from Ireland.

He was a JP and a Colonel of the National Volunteers Corps, aside from his involvement in racing, hunting and sport in the area. He was a member of Westmeath Hunt and a racecourse was set up on his Culleen lands for the Westmeath Hunt and point to points. His horses were successful locally, but also at The Curragh, Leopardstown and Phoenix Park. His horses included Garcon winner of Westmeath Hunt Cup & other races, Whisper, Oscuro, Rose of Culleen (General Symons-Rhodine), Pride of Culleen and Culleen. A.J. Pilkington was his trainer. Even after he returned to Culleen he continued to visit his property on occasions in Argentina. In September 1913, one of his favourite flat horses Culleen, met some mishap at a meeting in the Phoenix Park and it did not show for a while and when the vet Mr Patrick called, it was decided to put him down (he apparently had 2 fractures and gangrene set in). He was a front runner usually over 7 furlongs or a mile.

His wife Alicia died in March 1939 and was a niece of Cardinal Cullen, Archbishop of Dublin and her daughter was Mrs Edward Gargan, who was Farm Manager at the time. His own daughter Mina (19 y/o) appeared, as a racehorse owner in Mullingar in 1904-5. In 1911 he was popular and generous in the community and in April 1894, "Celtic" GAA Football Club presented him with an address. They welcomed him and his family home from abroad and thanked him for the use of his grounds for the GAA, and declared they had won *"almost every match"* since he left.

JAMES YOURELL, PIERSFIELD, BALLYNACARRIGY

He emigrated to Argentina in 1870, and returned 20 years later with finance. It is not clear as to how he made his money, but he owned 95 acres at Ballynacaragy & Sonna. He used income from his farm to race horses. He rode his own horse at many races in Mullingar in the late 19th century. He reputedly had no interest in gambling. His best-known horse was Bass who was 3rd in Irish Grand National in 1894 to Frank Mitchell's horse The Admiral, an even more prolific winner. In that year, Bass won 10 races out of 31 runs from Cork to Kilkenny back to Mullingar. In 1894, Yourell had 12 wins and won prize money of £298. In the 1901 census,Yourell was described as a 40 y/o bachelor living with his mother at Piersfield on 118 acres. He owned useful horses like Lady Symons II (General Symons), who finished 2nd to Reggie Walker's Small Polly in the 1912 Irish Grand National, Lady Blane, Lady Angelos, and he rode his own horse Workman to win the Tally Ho plate at Tullamore in May 1897. In 1934, a member of the family Jimmy Yourell was killed at the Westmeath Hunt point to point ar Ardivahan when riding E.Tormey's Never Say Die, when his foot was caught in a flag post and he was thrown from the saddle. He had a fractured skull and died at Mullingar Hospital.

AUSTRALIA

FREDERICK HENRY HANDCOCK

He was born in 1815 in Athlone a member of the Baron Castlemaine family, Moydrum Castle but he emigrated to Australia in 1837, to seek his fortune. In Adelaide, he was quickly a respected member of the community and in January 1838 his brown mare Taglioni raced in one of the earliest events held in South Australia. As an adventurer, he played a big part in discovering the Barossa Range and with James Fisher established one of the earliest sheep runs outside Adelaide called *"Fisher & Handcock Station"* in 1838. With a group of young colonists, he was amongst the founding members of the South Australian Club formed before the Adelaide Club. In 1838, he rode a gelding Charley to win the first steeplechase held in South Australia.

J.H. TAYLOR, (1858-1919), MILL HOUSE STUD, KNOCKDRIN, MULLINGAR

He experienced sport all around the world. He went to Australia in the late 19th century where he had an excellent sheep farm and he managed a stud for a number of years, where he became wealthy. When he came back to Ireland he set up the Mill House Stud at Knockdrin, Mullingar. He advertised stallions like General Symons (1897 Childwick - Hamiltrude) from 1900 to 1909 and subsequently the sires Atlas (Isinglass - The Gorgon), Glenesky (Lesterlin - Stella) along with "General Symons' best son" Drinmore between 1910 and 1917. He had horses at different times with Matthew Dawson, The Curragh, R.Fethersonhaugh, Mullingar, and in England with P.F.Hartigan & F.Hunt.

He imported a few stallions from Britain like General Symons, who was in Knockdrin for many years. He was bred by R.A. Brice and was described by E.B.Hutchins, as the best looking yearling he had ever seen, but he met with an accident and was ordered to be shot. Before it was done, Mr Taylor's brother asked Brice to give the horse a chance at stud where he bred many winners including Drinmore, Monilea, Royal Arch, and Atlas. In 1905, Taylor's progeny by General Symons did well when General Killian (General Symons-Killian) won the National Produce Stakes at The Curragh (6frsl 60 yds). In Gartlandstown & Skymons Pride he had bred & owned winners of the valuable Breeders Produce Stakes at the Phoenix Park and the latter won the National Produce Stakes at The Curragh when she was bought by Sir William Nelson. He had other winners like Worthy Earl, Cresley, General's Pride, Sensitive Simon, and Knocknacarriga. Other horses bred by General Symons included Witching Hour, Rathowen, Lady Symon's II, Oscuro, Rose of Culeen, Jack Symons etc and many of them were owned or trained in Westmeath.

Drinmore, who did not win as a 2 y/o but won three three races in Ireland as a 3 y/o, and was leased to George Edwards in England, who won the City & Suburban Handicap with him. In 1911, Taylor took a case against the Yorkshire Insurance Co for £1,000 for the life insurance policy of General Symons, who died on 27th October 1910. He lost the case and applied again against Judge Dodd's ruling, but in the appeal in January 1912 the Lord Chief Baron confirmed the decision on the grounds, that information was withheld from insurers on the health of the horse.

Taylor was Chairman of the Westmeath Farmer's County Association and a member of the Westmeath County Council. He died on 22 January 1919 at his residence. His horses were sold a few months before because of ill health. In August 1918, he sold Drinmore for 600 guineas to J.Doyne, at a sale at Mill House. Others sold were Gartlandstown (General Symons) 150 guineas and Nellie Symons (General Symons). Other horses were sold to local breeder's & owners like E.J.Hope, R.Downes, H.Garahan, P.Killian, Mr McCall, J.Nugent (a colt by Drinmore -Simonsworth for 300gns), and T.Killian. He also sold horses in training at the Phoenix Park on 28 August 1918 including Cresley (Atlas-Rossleagh) 650 guineas to L.Brabazon, and Lediston (Atlas-Simonsworth) for 450 guineas.

STALWARTS OF THE AUSTRALIAN JOCKEY CLUB

Cuthbert Fetherstonhaugh (1837-1925), Dardistown, Co Westmeath was born in Dardistown and in May 1853, he moved to Victoria, Australia to join his father & siblings. He worked as a clerk, carrying contractor, and other jobs. He was always interested in horses & became a dare devil rider in the Western District. He laid out the Coleraine steeplechase course with Tom Clibborn Fetherstonhaugh also from Westmeath. He went to Queensland in 1862 and bought a lease of Burton Downs, 300 miles north of Rockhampton, but sold it in 1863 after a drought. He was a great adventurer and a sporting man. He had a religious experience in 1865 & became an Anglican Minister. **Thomas Strettel Clibborn,** Holmsby, Elizabeth Bay, Sydney (1837-1910) was born in Moate Castle, son of Cuthbert. He qualified as an engineer and went to Australia in 1859, as a qualified engineer from TCD. He was a great administrator and became identified with racing as Secretary of the Ballarat Turf Club in 1872 & he became Secretary of the Australian Jockey Club in March 1873, at a salary of £350, when it was in a poor state in Sydney. The added prize money in his first year was £3,740 and when he retired in 1910 it was £44,950. He had principles, but he was fearless and tireless.

He started the Hunt Club races at Randwick and promoted yearling sales. He was a friend of Governor Sir Hercules Robinson a fellow Irishman with an interest in the turf. The AJC Derby became Australia's premier classic under him with £4,000 added and the same with other races like the Sydney Cup. All the country clubs in New South Wales were registered under the rules of racing and they built new headquarters in Bligh Street in 1901. He had a uniform system of registration brought in, a revised weight for age scale etc. Ill health led to his retirement in 1910 & he died that year. The Clibborn Stakes (Handicap) at Randwick honours his memory.

Sir Hercules Robinson (first Baron Rosmead) 1824-1897 was born at Rosmead, Co Westmeath in 1824 and was educated at Sandhurst and joined the 87th Royal Irish Fusiliers in 1843, but the enforced sale of family lands led to his resignation & he supervised the Famine Relief Works up to 1849. He was also the Chief Commissioner, investigating Irish Fairs & Markets. He had various jobs from Montserrat, Hong Kong, and was Governor of Ceylon, until he came to Australia as Governor of New South Wales in 1872-1879, New Zealand and the Cape of Good Hope. He made a major impact politically over many years but one of his great hobbies was horse racing.

He attended Sydney and Melbourne and had many good horses like Kingsborough, winner of the Australian Jockey Club Derby in 1874 and St Leger in 1875. He became a patron of the Australian Jockey Club and did much to improve the tone and administration of racing. When his daughter got married in 1878 her travelling dress featured her father's colours. It was said that his interest in horse racing made him very popular with the people. His younger brother Sir William Robinson followed the same diplomatic route and was Governor of Western Australia three times between 1875 and 1895.

Sir Charles Gairdner (1898-1983) was born in Batavia, Netherlands East Indies & was the son of an Anglo Irish merchant. He was brought up in Galway and he was in WW1 but received a serious injury to his leg. After the war he was in the cavalry & also a versatile sportsman at polo, hockey, golf etc. He married Evely Handcock, daughter of 5th Baron Castlemaine in Westmeath in May 1925. He won rapid promotion in WW2 and in March 1945 he was sent to the HQ of General McArthur, as Sir Winston Churchill's personal representative. He purchased New

Forest, Tyrrellspass in 1950 and subsequently was appointed Governor of Western Australia in 1951-63 & sold New Forest in 1954 to Scandanavian shipping magnate H.Hannevig. He was on the Kilbeggan Racing Committee in 1953. In 1963, he became Governor of Tasmania for 5 years. He hunted 2 days per week while in New Forest and was interested in horse racing and sport (He also apparently enjoyed knitting!). Joe Broderick, New Forest, Tyrrellspass, worked for Sir Charles Gardiner in New Forest and went with him to Western Australia. He trained horses and won the WATC Australia Derby for him in 1971 with Ride Easy (he was a brother in law of Phyllis Maxwell, Kilbeggan).

BANAGHER AND AUSTRALIAN RACING

Flour miller Marc Foy came to Ireland from France at the time of the French Revolution and started his own mill at Banagher in County Offaly, where he married an Irish girl and raised an Irish family. His son Mark Foy married Mary Macken in 1848 and they had six children. In 1859 they decided to go to Victoria, Australia. He started a shop in Bendigo and soon had other branches, and then he sold up and opened a store in Melbourne. His son Francis was a great help, but after a quarrel he returned to Ireland, but after three years he returned to Australia, and within a short time was running his father's business (age 21). He went into partnership with a James Gibson, but eventually sold the family shares for €16,000. He named the new shop he set up in Oxford Street, Melbourne, as *"Mark Foy's"* Plazza and it was a great success. He set up the first escalator in the store in Sydney and the first motor delivery vans.

THE IRONIC RACING WIT OF FOY AND HIS LAST BET

Outside business, his real interest was horse racing and he set up a Stud Farm called "Monastery" near Parkes. He imported many racehorses from Ireland & England and sent mares to stud in France. He clearly had a sense of humour, as he called his first sire His Reverence. He tried to be very original in naming his horses. He called a son of His Reverence, Skin the Goat (meaning having an axe to grind), but this was rejected, so he called him No Shenanagan. He imported an unnamed English colt and when he was due to be entered the trainer John Allsop remembered that they never registered a name. He raced around to Foy's office to get a name but he was too busy to be bothered and said *"Call him anything you like but let it be something Irish".* The trainer took him at his word and called the horse *Something Irish.* He was registered as that and went on to be good on the track and as a sire. One of his sons he named The Christian Brother. He raced for pleasure and it was said that he gave away his prize money and winnings.

Francis Foy loved Melbourne Cup day and always invited friends to a picnic lunch on tables under the trees at Flemington and champagne flowed freely. His horse Voyou was second in 1899. In1918 on Cup Day, he was 64 y/o and his health was failing. During the normal party at the races a bookmaker asked him if he wanted to have a bet on the Melbourne Cup. He said he wouldn't have a bet on the Cup but said "I'll bet you 3/1 that I don't get back to Sydney alive". Two days later this very interesting business magnate suffered a heart attack travelling home. He died on the train as it pulled into Goulburn, New South Wales on 12th November 1918.

UNITED STATES

JAMES E.RYAN, UNIONVILLE, CHESTER COUNTY, PENNSYLVANIA, USA (1900-1976)

James E. Ryan was the son of Owen J.Ryan, who originally was breeding horses at Cleaboy Stud, Mullingar before it was sold to Major Lionel Holliday. Owen continued as manager for many years and James's sister Sheila also managed the stud for 13 years. He married Oonagh, Aunt of Betty Galway Greer. Her family had a stud farm, but unfortunately turned down Easter Hero (won 2 Gold Cups) because the vet said he did not like his legs. After that, Nat Galway Greer examined the legs himself. Golden Miller also passed through his hands (Gold Court-Millers Pass). He was sold at Goff's but he didn't buy him until he was a 3 y/o. He won 5 Gold Cups (1932-36) and one Grand National in 1934. Other famous horses were Amber Point (won 14 races) & Knight Errant (won 9 races), both successful at Galway and Another Flash, Poor Flame, and Workboy were also successful.

While working in a dye works factory in England (Major Holliday's factory), he began riding steeplechasers in his teens at the weekend. He moved to the USA in the 1930's and became a trainer & breeder. It was said that Ryan's was fired from the dye factory, after he beat his boss Major Holliday in a race (as told by his daughter Patricia in Sports Illustrated). She said that he married her mother in Dublin at 6am in order to get to England on time to ride a horse. His owners included very important figures in USA racing in Paul Mellon, Richard King Mellon, Mrs F.Ambrose Clarke, James Cox Brady Jn, and Esther du Pont Thuron for whom he trained Royal Governor, the American co-sprint champion in 1949.

He was a trainer but rode Drinmore Lad in the USA for Paul Mellon before the horse went to Britain. *Country Life Magazine* (1941) said he had a stranglehold on hunt racing in USA, as he won 4 out of 5 races at one of the meetings. In 1944, the chaser Boojun II, bred by Harry Beasley was trained by Ryan for F.Ambrose Clarke and won the Governor Ogle Stakes at Laurel Park and seven races in total. Burma Road owned by Mrs Esther de Pont Weir won seven of his 20 races and was 2nd in the Brook Chase and won a total of $37,125. His biggest win was in his last race in the Temple Gwathmey Memorial Steeplechase.

He was widely respected for his knowledge of horse anatomy. He later became a trainer and was an esteemed buyer and seller of racehorses. Tattersall's said he was the second best judge of horseflesh in their 200 year history. Patricia said her grandfather (the Old Man) would have been annoyed, as he was only judged 4th best. She recalled that even though attired in a tuxedo, after a night at the casino's, waking her sister, her brother and herself at 3am and positioning them with flashlights at the 1/2 mile pole, 3/8 pole and 1/4 pole. The Ryan children were instructed to put on the flashlights, when her father's horse passed. Although the clockers seemed to be outwitted, someone in the stable ratted and his horse was only 2/1 when he won. Patricia worked for the Jockey Club for 4 years, and owned Anxious Moment, who once finished second to Round Table and was trained by her father.

His best horses also included Country Delight, Royal Vale, and The Mast (who won the North American Steeplechase in 1953). In June 1952 he had three stakes winners in a week in New York and at one stage he was planning to run Country Delight in the Ascot Gold Cup but she lost her form. He won the New York Turf Writers Cup with Clive of India, the Temple Gwathney Chase with his great chaser The Mast and the Queens County Handicap with Country Delight (at this stage the horse had won $201,860). Royal Vale an English bred horse arrived in 1952 and won none of his seven races but in 1953 he won 5 out of 8. He was as much at home on the dirt, as the grass, and he equalled the North American record for 1 1/2 miles on the turf in Miami Beach Handicap, then won the Bowie Handicap on the dirt, the Gallant Fox Handicap, New York, and the Dixie Handicap for owner Mrs Esther du Pont Weir. Amazingly, Jim Ryan schooled him as a jumper before converting him to the flat, a reversal of the usual order.

PAUL MELLON AND THE MILL REEF CONNECTION

Paul Mellon (most famous for owning Mill Reef) bought his first horse in 1933. It was an Irish Thorougbred, Drinmore Lad whom Jim Ryan brought to the USA, as a 3 y/o in 1932. He ran in a timber race at Far Hills N.J. and won it. His fellow Virginian, Ambrose Clarke had won the Aintree Grand National with Kellsboro Jack. When Mellon tried to win his own Aintree Grand National with Drinmore Lad, Clark took him to Mrs Aubrey Hastings training yard and to trainer Ivor Anthony. It was a connection that spanned his entire career. Drinmore Lad won a number of good races and twice was an early co-favourite for the Aintree National, with the great Golden Miller, with whom he dead heated in the Crawly Chase at Gatwick in 1937. Drinmore Lad was never sound and healthy enough on National Day to contest the big race and was returned to Virginia, where it was discovered that he had a heart condition.

Mellon had a problem of duelling trainers between Jack Skinner and Jim Ryan, as there was a good deal of animosity between them, so he gave up Jim Ryan because he lived too far away. Ryan trained his first important flat race winner

County Delight, a son of Triple Crown winner Count Fleet, purchased at the 1948 Keeneland sales. He won the Dixie Handicap at Pimlico, and the Gallant Fox Handicap at Jamaica 1951 and 1952. Ryan also bought Tap Day, as a yearling, and more importantly the mare Red Ray who became respectively dam of Belmont Stakes winner Quadrangle and third dam of the great European Champion Mill Reef. Red Ray by Hyperion cost 50,400 dollars, when purchased in England was Ryan's contribution to the career of the great Mill Reef.

INTERNATIONAL STEEPLECHASE AT BELMONT 1954

In 1954, Westmeath had a great interest in the big International Chase at Belmont Park covering 9 fences, over a 1¼ mile track, with a stand that could hold 20,000 seats and space for 100,000 elsewhere. Westmeath had an interest in three of the European challengers with Eddie Newman riding Mrs Vernon G.Cardy's Pride of Devon, who had won 6 out of 11 races and had finishing speed; Mrs Verney, Rathowen, Mullingar owned Nice Work II, who had won three races: and T.P. Downes bred Leslie Brand's In View (P.J.Doyle jockey), who had won at the Ward Union point to point. The other European runners were Dorothy Paget's Prince of Denmark, who had run at Cheltenham; Dick Francis on Rose Park; Mrs Griffin's Louis Seize ridden by amateur Bunny Cox; and Campari. The International Race was won by Extra Points by 18 lengths beating Ryan's horse The Mast with Prince of Denmark best of the visitors in 5th place. The Cup was presented by the former American Ambassador to Ireland George Garrett, who had attended Kilbeggan races just a few years before to see one of his horses win in Ireland. Jim Ryan ran many of his best chasers at Belmont Park since 1938 and The Mast was one of his best, winning top chases including the Brook Chase and Broad Hollow chase. He was bred by Mrs Jim Ryan and foaled at Fairy House the Ryan home in Unionville, Pennsylvania in 1947. He was by the noted steeplechase sire Annapolis a son of Man O'War-Claddagh. The Mast was voted *"Steeplechaser of the Year"* in 1953 and ran a great race on his seasonal debut behind Extra Points, but couldn't overturn the result in the International Chase. Jet Action owned by Elizabeth Graham Arden was a runner. She first raced under the name of "Mr Nightingaile". When the horse was injured in a race with cuts and bruises Ms Arden became "Florence Nightingaile" and treated him with her own medications.

James E. Ryan always kept contact with home and purchased many horses in Ireland & Britain over the years and was a very successful trainer.

MICHAEL DILGER, MULLINGAR - USA

Michael Dilger grew up in Mullingar with an interest in outdoor activities and the family had a strong connection with horses. He was a graduate of the Darley Flying Programme and he decided to make his career in the USA and was lucky enough to be become Assistant Trainer to Todd Pletcher for seven years. As one report said he earned an unofficial master's degree as a long-time assistant to

Pletcher. He spent summers at Arlington and Delaware and some winters in South Florida during those years. He said that he came to America not for a job but for experience. He hadn't expected to spend seven years with him but in that time he had learned a lot. Before striking out on his own Dilger worked overseeing Pletcher's string of runners at Delaware Park, and also travelled to major races with his Triple Crown contenders.

In January 2013, at the age of 35 he decided to take out a licence and go it alone. He used Saratoga as his northern home base, as it was a good place to train horses and everyone has equal access to the best vets and farriers, which is a great help to new trainer's. Stuart Subotick, New York sent him 15 horses plus a few others from friends and supporters. He only had two winners before his big day in the Grade 2 Sanford Stakes. Wired Bryan (by Stormy Atlantic), a grey was the only New York-bred in the field, gave trainer Michael Dilger the first graded stakes winner and the first stakes victory of any kind in his brief career when winning over the 22-1 shot Southern Blessing in the $200,000 Sanford Stakes at Saratoga in 2013. Wired Bryan broke quickly to lead taking the early advantage while racing along the inside under jockey Shaun Bridgmohan. He was briefly headed by Hollywood Talent but fought back to win by 1 1/2 lengths.

Michael was quoted as saying *"He was my first winner, my first stakes runner, my first stakes winner, and my first graded stakes winner. We decided to run him in this race because there was really no place to run him"*. He was nervous when he lost the lead but his horse responded very well. The Sanford has been won in the past by champions such as Secretariat, Affirmed, and Forty Niner.

In August 2013, Wired Bryan was beaten a nose in a desperate finish to the €200,000 Saratoga Special (G2) by Todd Pletcher's front running horse horse Corfu, owned by the Coolmore connected Michael Tabor, John Magnier, and Derrick Smith. After being 5th in the Hopeful Stakes (gr. II) on September 2 to Strong Mandate, Wired Bryan went to Finger Lakes, where he easily beat five other New York-breds in the New York Breeders' Futurity, winning by 7 lengths in that six-furlong race.

"It was a fairly emphatic victory," said Michael Dilger, who trains Wired Bryan. *"I don't think we ever lost faith in him. In the Hopeful, I think he came up against a drying-out track he didn't like. Of those who showed early speed, he was the only one who hung around at the end. He's doing great and we're excited to run him on Saturday".* In his final run of the season in October, he won the Bertram.F.Bongard Stakes of €150,000 at Belmont Park over 7 furlongs to show his versatility. At the start of the season the people involved were hopeful. Mike Dilger was hopeful, but said *"til you get up here and start to train them a little bit you just don't know"*. At the end of the season he won over €530,000. Unfortunately, he was retired and

did not compete as a 3 y/o.

In 2015, Michael Dilger won two more stakes races with EH Cumpari winning the €150,000 Palm Beach Stakes (G3) and Steet Babe winning the Mineshaft Handicap (G3). In February 2015 in her third race Street Babe won the Mineshaft Handicap (G3) of €125,000 at Fair Grounds Racecourse at 21/1 ridden by Kerwin Clark and she won by 3/4 length. *"He is a late starter and we still don't know how good he is"* winning trainer Michael Dilger said. *"It's fun having him around. You're going to see a lot of this horse".* In June 2015 he had 38 wins from 211 runs. More success still beckons for Michael Dilger.

FROM CAPTAIN CHRISTY TO VIRGINIA - LIFE IN THE USA

Gerry Newman lives in Upperville, Virginia and he has a career there as a jockey, trainer, and breeder for many years but it all started back in Ireland (outlined under the Irish Grand National). In 1985, Gerry went on a working holiday and for a few rides to the USA and decided to stay when he was offered a job. He was a jockey in Middleburg, Virginia for Douglas Fout a champion racer and trainer based near Middleburg. He went on to be second leading rider two years in a row. His first winner was Sports Writer at the Rolling Rock Hunt Club, Ligonier, Pennsylvania. He had won five times on the horse in Ireland. The biggest race he won in the USA was the Temple Gwathney Chase at Middleburg in 1990. At that time there was a number of Irish people working with horses in some form in the area that he knew very well, which was a help. He had a job as starter with the National Steeplechase Association, but when he quit in 2001, he no longer attended many meetings, as he was concentrating on training show jumpers and hunters.

He met his wife Kathy in Middleburg in 1986 and at that time she had a business going called Allwyn Court. He purchased land near the show grounds and sold his land in Virginia. They had a 32-acre farm and 16 boxes. He did a lot of hunting and was an honorary whip to the Piedmont Foxhounds and an accredited steward with the National Steeplechase Association.

His daughter Katherine was born in 1990 and is a very good rider. They got her a pony when she was six and within a short time she was a champion with pony Dot Comm and later she went to win the North America Young Riders in Virginia, when she won individual gold over 3 days on her horse Costa Sur (4 clear rounds and one fault in the fifth). Tragically, the horse had to be put down 6 months later, which was very difficult for the young rider. At Allwyn Court they have hunters, jumpers, equitation classes and it is now located in Wellington, Florida. Over the years, he always travelled home especially around Christmas but his mother died in March 2012.

RHODEMAN SEAN SMULLEN AND FRANK STRONACH AT ADENA SPRINGS

Pat Smullen is Irish Champon jockey and arguably in the top ten jockey's in the world, but it all began when his 46 y/o brother Sean started by bringing him to Joanna Morgan's stable many years ago. He went a different route and aside from being a multi-tasker he has a small string at Woodbine, while mainly overseeing a larger contingent at the Ontario branch at Adena Springs Farm. More importantly he works for Austrian & Canadian businessman Frank Stronach (Born 1932), founder of Magna International in Ontario and worth over a billion dollors. His son Andrew Stronach is involved in the Adena Springs Farm Thorougbred Enterprise. Frank Stronach owns and operates some of the most prominent racetracks in the United States. Among his early successes was his partnership with Nelson Bunker Hunt in the filly Glorious Song who was voted the 1980 Canadian Horse of the Year. He has won races like the Queen's Plate in 1994 and 1997; the Belmont Stakes in 1997 with Touch Gold, and the Preakness Stakes in 2000 with Red Bullet. His horse Ghostzapper won several major races including the 2004 Breeder's Cup classic, and he got the Eclipse award for Horse of the Year, and named the World's top ranked horse for 2004 (he won almost €3.5 million in prize money). In Canada, he was selected as the outstanding owner 9 times. He was outstanding owner in the USA from 1998/2000 and in the latter year outstanding breeder.

Sean Smullen does most of his training at Frank Stronach's nearby Adena Springs Farm, where he oversees a constant stream of horses coming in from the racetrack, and then shipping them back to their various trainers at Woodbine. He also maintains an ontrack operation, which is overseen on a daily basis by his assistant Patrick Dixon, and while his charges often are not at the top of the stable's hierarchy, he also has been known to have a runner in his stable. Sean Smullen trained Daddy Cool who won the Singspiel Stakes in 2005 and the Valedictory Stakres at Woodbine in 2004. In 2014 he had Pink Trillium, who ran in the $500,000 Woodbine Oaks, a 9 furlong for Canadian-3 y/o fillies in June 2013, but only finished 7th. He trained different quality horses from Gazuma in 2010 to City Wolf, who was under Spollen's care from 2011/2013 and won four in a row in 2011 including the Durham Cup(G3). In 2012 he was 2nd in the Seagram Cup (G3) and 4th in Singspiels Stakes (G3). He was bred in Kentucky at the Adena Spring Farm. That four-race win streak comprised the highlight of City Wolf's career. He retired to stud with a record of four wins and four placings (including a runner-up finish in the Durham in 2012) from 18 starts, with total earnings of $293,686 and was one of Smullen's most successful horses.

ADENA SPRINGS AND BILBY RANCH

In January 2015, Frank Stronach's Adena Springs South has reopened the stallion operation at its 3,800 acre facility in Williston, Florida, for the 2015 breeding season. Stallions include Breeders' Cup Classic winner Fort Larned, Capo Bastone, Hunter's Bay, and City Wolf. Except for newcomer Capo Bastone, the other three are second-year sires relocating from farms in Kentucky, Maryland, and Florida, and City Wolf which is by the great Giant's Causeway at $4,000 live foal. His pedigree is better than some of the others, who were better on the track. Giant's Causeway is the sire of many young sires at stud, including successful stallions Shamardal, one of the best in Europe; First Samurai; Footstepsinthesand; and Intense Focus etc. Sean Smullen plays a huge part in the Stronach operation in Adena. Another aspect of the job is taking care in the recovery from injury of good horses. Rock Again was shifted to the Bilby Ranch in Ontario, owned by Sean Smullen, before going back into a training program again. The main function on the Bilby Ranch, Ontario, run by Diane and Sean Smullen is to teach some Western lessons for families on horses from riding to jumping in a holiday atmosphere. Both of them have worked with horses all their lives. Diane runs Bilby Ranch 7 days a week, 24 hours a day providing training, lessons, boarding and horse breaking services. David Moran when he came over to ride for Carolyn Costigan, also spent some time with Spollen. The Irish ex-pats had a small share in the Queen's stallion Motivator and bred Mobilizer. As shareholders they were invited to the Windsor Palace for dinner. Sean Smullen said that Mobilizer was a good looking 2 y/o. Success with horses is obviously in the Smullen family. It's also a long way from Rhode to Windsor Palace (via USA & Canada).

JAMES "PLUNGER" McMANUS, DRUM, ATHLONE

He was born in 1868 and was probably educated at Drum National School, which was opened in 1861. He then went to Deerpark, Athlone, and on to St Jarlath's, Tuam. He entered the Civil Service in London and he developed journalist skills & contributed articles to the "Evening Mail". Eventually, he went to New York in 1890 and later settled in Seattle. From an early age, he liked horse racing and it became his main interest. He became a successful punter & then an owner. A list of horses in the American Racing Calendar 1914 shows he had 15 horses in different stables. He named one *"Curraghleen"* and some of the others were called *"O'Sullivan"*, *"Chesterton"*, *"Chief Lally"*, *"Rocky O'Brien"*, *"Star O'Brien"* *"Medallion"* (sold to Captain E.Cassatt for €10,000- he also won for the new owners), *"Adriuche"*, *"Roselare"* and *"Adeline Patricia"*. His biggest success was in the Hopeful Stakes in 1909 with Rocky O'Brien, who won at 40/1 ridden by Vincent Powers. The horse was sent from Arcadia to Emeryville to win this top juvenile race. He didn't have a penny on the horse (the first time he never backed it). It was said that he paid Powers €2,500 for winning. It was a year that Irish horses did well, as they used to gather at the Worden Hotel in the cool of the evening, while discussing plans to rid "Erin of Sassenachs". Kimball Patterson arranged to have a number of his 2 y/o's broken. He became well known and was a survivor of the 1906 earthquake. It was said that at one point he drove a cable car in San Francisco He moved to Chicago and travelled extensively, including visits to Ireland. He lost financially in the Wall Street Crash in 1929. He moved to London and died there in London at 94 y/o in 1962 and he is buried in Drum Cemetery.

EUROPE

Rex B. Beaumont (1914-88), born in Yorkshire in 1914 to a French mother Beaujolie from whom he got a love of language, literature and culture, and his father was a botanist and veteran of WWI. He served in the RAF during World War 11. He met Col Howard-Bury, while he was travelling as Assistant Commissioner of the British Red Cross during the 1940's. For over thirty years he was friend and companion to Howard-Bury and inherited Belvedere on his death. He was a talented actor praised by John Gielgoud and Sir Laurence Olivier. His great friend was Michael Wilding, husband of Liz Taylor. He acted for the Royal Shakespeare Co & knew Noel Coward, Marlene Dietrich and stood in for Rex Harrison. He joined the RAF in WW2 and knew Colonel Howard Bury at this time & stayed at Belvedere House. He came back to Belvedere & developed the gardens. People like Elizabeth Arden (who had horses with the McCall's at Tally Ho Stud in Westmeath not far from Belvedere) and Constance Spry visited there.

"TO QUARE TIMES FROM HIS BROTHER"

He was a member of the Horse Breeders Assocation, and Jimmy Tormey trained his horses and usually there was a big celebration in Greville Arms, when his horses won. In 1950's and 60's Rex had horses like El Kekni, Khemis, Mabrouk, Merill Jane and Miss Mustang and Bury had a horse appropriately called Everest Twenty One. He won the Irish Cambridgeshire in 1967 with Khemis ridden by Johnny Hunter, who described how a furlong out he tried to barge his way through and *"I knew it was absolutely hopeless, so I spotted a gap and shot my mount for it. I started to weave my way across the course towards the stand side, hoping to find a gap before having to go too far over".*

Beaumont who had just been beaten the previous year with Mabrouk, held a celebration for up to 200 guests in the Greville Arms. The horse won £2,000 in a field of 19 runners. His main challenger Sweet Jewel was ridden by Mullingar jockey Peadar Matthews. The horse was trained by Kevin Bell (who also trained Mabrouk for Beaumont). He was returned at 100/6 and he paid 65 shillings on the tote. Amazingly, the horsebox had been involved in a collision with a motor car on route to the race but the horse was not affected by it. On the same occasion, he presented a cup for a race he sponsored in Tralee to Mrs Helbush an American who won it. In April 1955, Pat Taaffe won the Knockdrin Novice Chase at Mullingar on Modernist owned by Beaumont, and a full brother to Aintree Grand National winner Quare Times. Rex Beaumont was part of the celebration in Mullingar when Mrs Wellmann won the Grand National with Quare Times. He presented flowers to her in the Greville Arms with a note *"To Quare Times from his brother".*

WALKER AND JORISTOWN STUD, KILLUCAN

John Reid Walker (1855-1934) was the older brother of four and he was a J.P. and High Sheriff of Shropshire. He was one of 4 brothers with Lord Wavertree (R.Hall Walker), associated with the history of the Irish National Stud, Sir Peter Walker and Barclay Walker. He was very much a British Sportsman but he did set up the Joristown Stud in Killucan, Co Westmeath. He was educated at Rugby. He was an accomplished sportsman especially in polo and as a breeder of horses. At the Barton Polo Club in Lichfield he rode 6 winners in succession. He established the Ruckley Stud Farm in Staffordshire. His most famous horses were Invershin who won the Ascot Gold Cup in 1928 and 1929 and a number of other good races and the brilliant Inkerman, who won the Jockey Club Stakes in 1923, Chester Stakes, Jockey Club Stakes etc and won over £12,000. In 1904 he stood Dinna Forget (1892 Loved One- Barometer) won 8 of 31 starts including the Leopardstown Grand Prize, Kempton Park Jubilee, and Liverpool Cup. Diamond Jubilee was the younger brother of Epsom Derby winner Persimmon and was bred by the Prince of Wales (later King Edward VII) to win the treble crown. In his union with Red Virgin he produced the colt Queen's Advocate foaled by Reid Walker in Killucan, as was his younger sister Elizabeta who won the Northumberland Plate (both of them were trained for Reid by Alec Taylor).

Dinna Forget (earned over £8,000 in his racing career) as a stallion bred Dinneford, and Invershin. Walker was a well known member of Jockey Club & of a famous racing family and he died at Albrighton, Salop after being ill for some time. He was a staunch supporter of racing and breeding for a half century. In 1929 owing to poor health he disposed of some of his horses, but he was always interested in the Turf. He won many great races but not the classics (Invincible was 4th in the Derby and 2,000gns). He died in March 1934. He had several trainers from P.P. Gilpin, H. Cole, W. Robinson, Alec Taylor, Digby etc.

A *Badminton Magazine* reporter arranged a visit to the Joristown Stable in early 1900's. It was arranged through Captain Bernard Daly and the reporter spent a day on site. He left Broadstone by train with Captain Daly for Killucan. He was met by a Jaunting car and introduced to E.H. Elliott the manager and stud groom. The first horse they saw was Dinna Forget. The horse was bred in 1892 by Captain Peel. Reid Walker's ambition was to revive the Herod blood and Dinna Forget was a direct descendant. Other horses included the mare Trance (Royal Hampton-Sublime), Virgin (Gallinule-The Sabine) and another mare Goosander (Gallinule-Rose D'Amour), who had a Dinna Forget foal and it cost Reid Walker 1,000gns). Reid Walker had spoken to Captain Daly about getting a farm in Ireland. He came over to inspect Joristown and sent an agent Frank Sugden to make a valuation. He went into negotiation with owner Cornelius Hannan the breeder of Irish Ivy and he did not want to part with it. He eventually got his way and purchased the 300 acres. He designed new buildings and altered the old ones but he only made a few flying visits. The house was described as charming, and the neighbours benefit from the stud farm. He came down another day for more photos and cycled the 3 miles from Killucan meeting Elliott, Mrs Woods (the housekeeper) and Prudence the retriever. In 1924 the Land Commission purchased 229 acres at Joristown from Reid Walker for division and the Joristown Stud was offered for sale at Mullingar in August 1925 but was withdrawn at £4,600.

John Keegan, originally from Mullingar, Westmeath trained Smokey Cinders (Incinderator-Minett) who won the 1997 edition of the Canadian Derby. The owners were Ed and Jim Pawluk and the rider was Tom Adkins. The horse also won the Wheat City Handicap (twice over a mile), the Speers Stakes (twice), Westerner Handicap, Free Press Handicap, and the Sydnry Halters. He was Sprinter of the Year in 1999, 2000 and 2001, but he also won the Speers twice. He won 18 races and earned over 389.000 between 1997/2002.

DAVID MORAN

Davy Moran has been a great success as a jockey in Canada and he is from Tipperary. However he has strong Westmeath connection, as his uncle Jimmy Moran was a well- known garage man in Mullingar and he also worked with trainer Frank Ennis from Castletown Geoghegan plus riding for Westmeath trainer Cecil Ross. Moran began his career in 1999 with Frank Ennis, having his first ride in public for that yard on Forest Princess at Fairyhouse in August 1999. His workload increased significantly in 2000 and he got into the frame on no less than seven occasions, without winning that term. However, after the conclusion of that season Moran made the significant decision to become an apprentice rider to Jim Bolger in 2001. He grew up in Templemore, Tipperary and his father Eddie bred David's Lad winner of the Irish Grand National. Like many Irish jockey's he started with ponies. He enrolled with RACE at The Curragh and became an apprentice with Jim Bolger. His first winner was Margarula in a 2y.o nursery, as he was second jockey to Kevin Manning. Early on he broke his leg when thrown from a horse but didn't get much sympathy from Jim Bolger. He had 38 wins from 321 starts. Moran continued in that role until the spring of 2009, when he won out his three-pound allowance and became a full-fledged jockey.

His association with Bolger led to his acquaintance with Costigan, who had worked as an assistant trainer there before striking out on her own in Canada. He had ridden in Canada because of his connection with Carolyn Costigan and he won on Roan Irish in the €250,000 Princess Elizabeth Stakes and €500,000 Woodbine Oaks in 2010 and was third in the Queen's Plate. Roan Irish had been with Jim Bolger and Carolyn asked Davy to ride her and then commit to travel over for the 2010 season. The horse was second in the Fury Stakes and won the Woodbine Oaks (Costigan was the first lady to train the winner).

Roan Inish spent her early days in Ireland with Bolger, and the Costigans brought her back to Canada for the Princess Elizabeth Stakes at Woodbine in October 2009, after a roundabout trip. Roan Inish was the first horse trained by Carolyn and then became her first winner. It just happened to be in a major stakes race in Canada. It was a tremendous race with Todd Pilcher's horse Emburs Song favourite and looking a winner until Roan Irish and Moment of Majesty came late to nab her with Davy Moran, the meat in the sandwich winning by a head. Moran said *"She gives you a proper fight".* The Oaks win, was the largest purse ever won by Moran, who also rode the filly the previous October at Woodbine.

He decided to go to Canada in April 2011, after considering a move there with his family. He was married with five children aged 7 months to 7 years. The visa had only come through a few weeks before and he linked up with veteran agent John Bell. The first two years were hard but he gradually he settled in and he received good support from Brian Lynch and Mike Doyle. In 2012 he won the Woodbine Canadian Stakes for Richard Fahey on Barefoot Lady. Back home he had won the King Edward Stakes at Ascot and the G2 Ballychorus Stakes on Cecil Ross's Six of Hearts.

In 2014, he had 38 wins in 321 starts with purses over $2million-he won the King Edward Stakes on Grand Arch; the Algoma Stakes with I'm a Kittyhawk and the $300,000 Turf Monster Handicap in Pennsylvania on Sharp Sensation. He is enjoying it and maybe there is more to come.

chapter 13
WOMEN IN RACING

In Britain, Norah Wilmot was the first British female racehorse trainer to officially train a winning horse. Her historic win came with a filly called Pat at Brighton in August 1966. The day before, she became one of the first two women to be granted a training licence by the Jockey Club in Britain. Just like Ireland, before 1966 women could only train in an unofficial capacity, and were forced to put the licence in a man's name, such as a family member or as in the case of Norah Wilmot in the name of her Head Lad(s). She had applied for the licence but was always turned down. It was ironic that Wilmot trained for Queen Elizabeth II and when her horse No Fiddling won at Kempton the Queen's Racing Manager Captain Charles Moore took her into the winning enclosure. Eventually, Wilmot & Florence Nagle took a case against the Jockey Club, which reached a Court of Appeal in 1966, when the three judges ruled in their favour. Jenny Pitman was the most successful trainer in Britain but Henrietta Knight, Vanessa Williams, Rebecca Curtis, Emma Lavelle and Lucinda Russell are currently competing at a high level.

In Ireland, when the rules were changed, Anne Bullitt Biddle made Irish racing history at Naas on 31st August 1966 by becoming the first official woman trainer to have a runner and she started off with a winner, when Flying Tiger won the Cork Stakes. Peggy St John Nolan should be on the records, as the first woman to train the winner of the Irish Grand National, when Zonda won in 1959 in the name of her Head Lad Matt Geraghty. Joanna Morgan was the first lady jockey to make a significant impact riding over 200 winners and becoming the first woman to ride in a classic, when she rode Riot Helmet in the 1976 Irish Derby; and she was the first to be placed in a classic on El Cito in the Irish St Leger in 1980. She took out a training licence in 1985 until her recent retirement in 2014. Since then many ladies like Ann Marie Crowley, Frances Crowley, Jessica Harrington up to Nina Carberry (Irish Grand National on Organised Confusion), Kathie Walsh (Irish Grand National on Thunder & Roses and 3rd at Aintree on Seabass), Jane Mangan etc have highlighted the abilities of ladies at the highest level. When Nina Carberry won the Foxhunt Hunter's Chase at the Cheltenham Festival in 2015, it again re-iterated the progress made by women in racing. Nina, Katie Walsh, Hayley Turner & Lizzie Kelly are the most publicised female jockey's in the media. The most progress has been made in the training sphere, with many more women competing on equal terms with their male compatriots. From Mrs Anne Biddle to Jessica Harrington, a number of female trainers have competed successfully over jumps and on the flat.

In Westmeath & Offaly, a number of women have made notable contributions to racing. The first woman to own an Aintree Grand National winner was Lady Nelson (Margaret Hope, Gartlandstown, Co Westmeath) the wife of Sir William Nelson with Ally Sloper in 1915. The first Irish based female trainer to train a winner of the Irish Grand National was Dot Love, Mullingar with Liberty Counsel in 2012. Mrs Barbara O'Neill, Rathganny, Mullingar with her husband Arthur, bred Mr What to win the 1958 Aintree Grand National. Amazingly, the next Irish horse to win the race in 1975 was the dual Cheltenham Gold Cup winner L'Escargot, who was also bred by Barbara and her husband Arthur (The two horses were directly related). Mary Dowler, Lacken, Co Westmeath in 1974 at Phoenix Park she made history, when she became the first women jockey to compete with men as a professional jockey. She was attached to Seamus McGrath's stable and was on Dream House and finished 5th in a field of 11. She also had the distinction of riding in the first ever race for ladies at the Phoenix Park in 1972. In addition, Maria Cullen at Kilbeggan races in June 1987 was the first female professional jockey to win a steeplechase (she was also the first to win over hurdles in Ireland).

A MULLINGAR LOVE STORY IN 2012

I remember on the morning of the Irish Grand National being in a bookies office in Kilbeggan looking at the form, when a local woman asked me if Liberty Counsel (a daughter of Leading Counsel) would win. The horse had twice won in Kilbeggan and was around 50/1. I said that it was a great race for outsiders, therefore every horse had a chance, but I wasn't backing it myself. If you believed in fate it was a missed opportunity, as the local horse from Mullingar galloped into the record books.

Liberty Counsel had made no show in the Kim Muir Chase at Cheltenham and being from a small stable like Dot Love's, Charlestown Stud in Mullingar was not expected to succeed against the big stables. The irony was that she denied champion trainer Willie Mullin's his first success in the race, as his horse Away We Go finished second at 25/1 with Home Farm & Sweeney Tunes behind. Ben Dalton the jockey was a 5lb claimer and he settled the horse in the middle of the field before coming through the field to challenge and hold off Paul Townsend on Away We Go, and become the fourth mare to win the race. He had won on the horse the previous May at Kilbeggan and the 10 year old showed an incredibly game attitude to grind out a memorable success, prompting wild scenes of celebration. It made Dot Love the first female to train the Irish Grand National winner, since Jenny Pitman, who struck with Mudahim in 1997. It was Liberty Counsel's 4th win over fences and the first since Kilbeggan the previous September.

The owners were sisters Irene Neale and Helen Murtagh. Irene said: *"I'm on top of the world. It's the best day of my life apart from my daughter being born in 1986. She's a gutsy little mare and nearly died three times with ailments."* The owners of Liberty Counsel always knew she was destined for success despite three brushes with death. Mullingar native Irene said: *"I always knew that she had ability, but there were lots of mishaps over the last few years. We'd get her right and the next thing she'd be at the vet. Last year was the first time she did well for a period of time uninterrupted."* The sister's explained that their great grandfather James Killian also owned a useful horses like Lady of the Lake and Winter Break, before he died in 1893, and their grandfather Tom Killian of Greenpark owned jumpers like Shaun na Scuab who won the then famous Conyngham Cup in 1913 when trained by Dick Cleary. The plan was to parade the mare at the foxhunt point-to-point where their father and grandfather were very involved.

Helen's late husband Bernard ("Ber") Murtagh first discovered Liberty Counsel at a stud farm near their home. He made a deal with Winston Honner of Clongiffen Stud Farm, near Enfield. Winston said that he could become a partner in the horse and if it was no good at racing then it could be a horse for Vivienne for eventing. The horse fell at her first outing, at a Horse and Jockey point-to-point race in Tipperary behind Seabass. It was the only time Ber saw her running, as he died of a heart attack in 2007 at 56 y/o. When Winston decided to sell his share in the horse, Irene & Helen became partners and the horse went to Dot Love. She showed promise but illness would get in the way of her success. She won her first point-to-point in 2009, but then nearly died of colic, and it was only for Ned Gowing, a vet that she was saved.

She ran a few times again and then had a tendon injury. She had to be taken care of and Vivienne would bandage her and put her on the walker, but it was unlikely that she would run again. The treatment went on for 1 1/2 years before she got better and won a race on their local rack in Kilbeggan. Another infection followed and she was nearly put down before she recovered. Dot Love & Ciaran Murphy realized she was good enough, when she won another race at Kilbeggan. Ciaran revealed: *"She spent her holidays with her owners to get a break from the yard and then came back to us three months before competing."* A lot of work was done with her and when the ground was dry on Irish National day she had a chance. They couldn't believe that they won €141,000.

SUNSHINE AND A CHAMPAGNE BREAKFAST

After the race, Denmark born Dot Love, who had just become the first Irish based female trainer of the Irish Grand National said *"this was a team effort and Ciaran Murphy, who works for me and rides her out and schools her, deserves a lot of credit"*. She said *"She's a super mare and a very good jumper"*. After all the excitement of the day Dot said: *"We arrived in the doors of the local pub and there must have been 100 people out to welcome us home. It was fantastic to see all the support for us and for Liberty of course. She was paraded up and down the place and went trotting off, enjoying the attention I'm sure. We celebrated into the night and it was fantastic."* The celebrations were in Clarkes Bar, Mullingar with hunting enthusiasts and other racing people including the joint owner's mother Rose Kiernan, aged 90. The occasion was like Westmeath winning an All- Ireland final with singing and dancing, as they looked at the race 100 times. She admitted that she did not back the horse leaving it to her grandchildren. The super mare had colic, bad legs, an operation but still came out on top. As Dot Love said *"We woke up to a champagne breakfast and sat in the sunshine".*

The horse was paraded at the point-to-point meeting in Castletown Geoghegan on the Sunday. Dot added: *"I'm sure she'll have all the attention she could handle there."* Dot Love was in racing for 40 years and worked closely with Gigginstown House in the preparation of their horses for racing. In the day of Liberty Counsel's success Michael O'Leary started a fund for J.T. McNamara paralysed at 38, when he donated the €200,000 prize won by his horse Akorakor in the point to point bumper.

Dot Love was born in Denmark but has been 40 years in Ireland. She mainly break's in and pre-train horses for Gigginstown, but has about 10 others in training. She has always acknowledged the role of her assistant Ciaran Murphy and stated that he deserved huge credit, as he has done great work with the horses. She came to Ireland in the mid 1950's from Denmark. She spotted an advertisement by a Danish woman Mrs Kjaer living in Rathmolyon, Co Meath. Her employer took her hunting which gave her a love of riding cross country. She met & married Jim Love in a few years and had two children Mickie & Melanie. Mickie farms in Rathmoylan and Melanie runs a livery yard beside Dot. In 1976 when her marriage was over she moved to Charlestown. She rode her horse The Professional at the three day event at Punchestown and got round safely and she went to Burghley and Badminton in the 1980's. She qualified for the Danish team with Macrello for the 1988 Seoul Olympics but they forgot to enter her. Dot bought Charlestown from Joe Moorehead in 1989 when he retired and he still lived there, until his death. He got her interested in racing and taught everyone about the whole business.

She was joined by Ciaran and they began training point to pointers with success and Dot rode for about 5 years on Innisfallen, whom she bought off Ted Walsh. She won two opens and was placed about 12 times and then hunted. They began breaking, pre training and schooling horses for Gigginstown House and now virtually all pass through her hands. Five days after getting a licence in 2001 she had her first winner I'm On the Line in Kilbeggan in June 2001. Unfortunately, she didn't get her second winner until the 2006/7 season, with What A Lad winning a hunter chase at Down Royal in May 2006. After that she had a few winners each year but it was tough as horses broke down, were put down, and were killed. In 2012, Liberty Counsel won twice at Kilbeggan including the Dunbia Cup.

STABLE STAR SHADOW EILE

It was in 2010 that Love's first stable star emerged in the shape of Shadow Eile owned by local breeder Sean O'Reilly, Glascorn. Shadow Eile was a daughter of Beneficial and made steady progress starting with a win in bumper at Down Royal on St Patrick's Day in 2011, then a maiden hurdle at Galway and a novice hurdle at the Listowel Festival later that year. In 2012, she gave Dot Love her biggest win as a trainer up to then when winning the Grade 2 Irish Stallion Farms European Breeders Fund Mares Novice Hurdle Championship Final at the Fairyhouse Easter Festival. She continued her sequence with a maiden win on the Flat at Ballinrobe prior to winning twice at the Galway Festival, namely in a conditions race on the Flat and in a handicap hurdle two days later with Joseph O'Brien on board. She went on to win a conditions hurdle at Bellewstown later in August and finished off a remarkable 2012/13 campaign with an excellent fourth to Quevega in the Grade 2 David Nicholson Mares' Hurdle at the Cheltenham Festival.

The most recent star to emerge in the stable is Lucky Pat who was 6th in a bumper at the Galway Festival in 2014 on the Monday and on the following Saturday won a bumper beating two horses Call Vinnie & Old Storm that were in front of him on Monday. Martin Carey owned and bred the front runner and he won by 3/4 length ridden by Mr D.Lavery. After the success Dot Love said *"Chasing will be his game and he's a magnificent jumper and so may go straight over fences"*. Lucky Pat went on to win his maiden hurdle at Kilbeggan and a handicap hurdle. It can be difficult for smaller stables, but she is hoping that another star like Liberty Counsel will appear on the horizon?

PEGGY ST JOHN NOLAN AND ZONDA

Peggy St John was related to a number of families in Kilbeggan through marriage, as her mother was Mrs Ada Cuff-Quinn, Ivy House, Kilbeggan. Bessborough House,near Dublin was her original home. She was a pioneer of equal opportunity for women not just in Irish Racing but other sports. As Peggy Morgan Byrne she was a champion swimmer and she helped pave the way for ladies in show jumping with her horse Swaztika Rose and she won the Grand Prix at the RDS in 1949 with Outdoor Girl. Zonda was given to her as a 3 y/o by Captain G.Maguire and became her star chaser. In 1956 an amateur jockey Mr Willie Robinson rode Zonda to success at Kilbeggan and he also rode him to success in the Leopardstown Chase, but on the day of the Irish Grand National in 1959 he was booked to ride Quinta Que the 2 mile Champion Chaser. It was ironic that it was Pat Taaffe who took the mount on Zonda as a prelude to their great rivalry in the 1960's on Arkle and Mill House. The field also included Roddy Owen (Cheltenham Gold Cup winner), Gold Legend ('58 National winner), and Knight Errant.

The problem for Peggy was that women were not allowed to have a trainer's licence in 1959 and her Head Lad Matt Geraghty was on record as the trainer. In the race itself, Zonda took the lead at the second last, but then was challenged by Toss Taaffe (Pat's brother) but he readily held him off. She was leading owner that year with £2,776 in prize money. The horse had a touch of class and was 2nd in the Hennessy Gold Cup, third in the Irish Grand National in 1960 and also third in the Cheltenham Gold Cup to Pas Seul. The horse was unfortunate in that in December 1960 after an Enquiry by the Irish National Hunt Committee, Matt Geraghty as trainer was notified that his licence had been withdrawn for 12 months following a test of saliva and urine, which showed a stimulant had given a positive test. When she attempted to clear her name the Stewards of the National Hunt Committee in Britain declared they were *"incompetent to evaluate the scientific evidence she introduced in her defence"*. She stated that she had been informed that several grains of a drug or stimulant had been found in the test, which was positive. Even at this distance at time there is not much doubt that an injustice was done. He was disqualified from the Rathfarnham Chase. On top of that poor Zonda, after racing in Britain, could not return because of the Foot & Mouth outbreak in the country.

In 1973 when women were allowed to ride under rules she was already a grandmother but won a bumper at Fairyhouse on Another Paddy. In 1978 one of her big moments was when she trained Drumroan who was third in the Aintree Grand National (ridden by Westmeath jockey Gerry Newman) to Lucius & Sebastian V. In 1983 she was in hospital following a fall when riding one of her own horses, which was said to be a novice chaser called King Jaguar. Her last runner in Kilbeggan before she died was the same King Jaguar in the Old Distillery Novice Chase, which he won at 5/2 ridden by Martin Lynch (associated with Oscar Time). On the same day the Jeremy Maxwell trained Rhyme N'Reason could only finish 6th of 12 to Kerr Pink Shoes in a hurdle race before becoming the first horse to win the English & Irish Grand National double. Her first runner at Kilbeggan as an owner was Nanny Bank's ridden by Dan Moore in May 1939-she finished last!

Her daughter Anne married trainer Michael Cunningham, who carried on her great tradition and trained 17 winners at Kilbeggan between 1972 and 1994. He trained the brilliant Cairn Rouge to win the Irish 1,000guineas, Coronation Stakes and Champion Stakes. Over jumps he won the Champion Hurdle with For Auction 40/1 in 1982 and in Cheltenham he almost brought off a unique treble when Greasepaint won the Kim Muir Memorial Challenge Cup, Churchtown Boy won the Grand Annual Chase and For Auction was 3rd in the Champion Hurdle. His biggest regret was the narrow defeat of Greasepaint in the 1983 Sun Grand National at Aintree ridden by Mr Colm Magnier. He was beaten 3/4 length by Corbiere, thus making Jenny Pitman the first woman to train the winner.

Greasepaint 2/1 won the novice chase at Kilbeggan in 1981 before going on to be twice second in the Grand National. He also won at Kilbeggan with useful horses like Derrymoyle & Bavard Dieu.

MARIA CULLEN - FIRST PROFESSIONAL FEMALE JOCKEY TO WIN A CHASE AND A HURDLE

On Monday 22nd June 1987 a small but unique event occurred at the Kilbeggan meeting. The Old Distillery Novice Chase of £1,175 had a field of 12 runners. Liam Burke's Take Beating 6/4F was a course specialist (winning three races out of five on the track) and favourite for the race with Jim Kavanagh's 8y/o Pajanjo a steady 5/2 second favourite. Kavanagh who was a night telephonist at one stage had no great racing background, but he served time with Martin & Stephen Quirke, plus Brud Fetherstonhaugh when he had horses like Busted. He saved up enough to start a riding school and later got horses like Brookville and Reflex Action who won a number of races. One person with him from his riding days was Maria Cullen from Maddenstown, who was to become the first female professional jockey to win a steeplechase under National Hunt rules (she had already won the first hurdle race). He gave Maria & her younger sister Caroline some rides and they were a major part of the stable set up. In 1984 she took out a professional licence and even with 22 wins (1991) it was a tough life as she couldn't ride in ladies races. She was 11th of 24 runners at a race in Cheltenham.

When Pajanjo lined up for the novice chase, his record was not notable and it was more in hope than confidence that he set off in pursuit of leader Gentle Flight, who was 40 lengths in front at one stage but then started to make mistakes. Pajanjo closed in over the last few fences and ran on to win easily by 15 lengths from Refute and Barnham VI, with Take Beating a disappointing fourth. Maria Cullen was not the first woman to ride a winner over fences, but she became the first female professional jockey to ride a winner over fences. It was Maria's 20th winner and she remembers the occasion.

"I must say I have great memories of my success in Kilbeggan. It was my second ride over fences and it's true I was the first professional jockey to win a steeplechase and also the first to win a hurdle race in Ireland. My memories of Kilbeggan that evening are still clear to me, it was a beautiful evening and the ground was perfect. In the race, I remember one horse went into a long lead and at one stage was about a fence in front. However, I didn't panic and with about six furlongs to run he started to slow down. I passed him three out and won very easily".

OBVIOUSLY - MISS DEIRDRE COGAN BREEDS A WINNER

A Westmeath bred horse was one of the fancied runners in the Breeders Mile at Santa Anita in 2014. Obviously was a 6 y/o bred at Woodleigh Stables, Castlepollard by Deirdre Cogan (24). She is a graduate from NUIG with a Masters in Science and was named Breeder of the Month for June 2014 after his 1$^{1}/_{2}$ length win in the €400,000 Gr1 Shoemaker Mile on the same track when 2/1F. That was his 11th win in 21 races and he made all the running in the race. *"We were rolling right along. He's all class,"* said winning jockey Joe Talamo. *"He was going fast, but he was doing it fairly easily. With him, you didn't have a choice though. His thing is going to the front. If I would have taken him back, we wouldn't have won. You give him his head and let him do it. He is one of the best I've ever sat on",* Obviously then boasted seven graded stakes wins, all in Southern California, in his career. He has won 11 of 20 career starts and has earned $1,337,361.

Obviously was born in the yard to Laela (a daughter of Montjeu) was bought by Deirdre's father Noel and was sired by Coolmore's Choisir. He won twice in Ireland at Dundalk and Cork in 2011 with Joseph O'Brien riding and was trained by Peter Fahey. The Cogan's had sold him at Goffs as a yearling in 2009 to the WE Syndicate. In 2011, after a number of good runs in Gr3 and Gr2 races, he was sold for 130,000 guineas to his present owners Anthony Fanticola and Joseph Scardino (trainer Phil d'Amato and jockey Joe Talamo). His win in the Shoemaker Mile was his second of the year and he was amongst the first horses to qualify for the race. The race was won by Wise Dan for the previous two years.

Noel Cogan started the stud in Castlepollard some years ago and he has three children. Prior to Deirdre's success with Obviously, the stud had other winners. Noel bred African Chimes who won 18 races in Britain (1990-95) and Lady Bear who won 8 times including the Atalanta Stakes (listed) in 2003. African Chimes was trained by Bill O'Gorman notable for his prolific winning two year olds like Provideo & Timeless Times (16 wins each as 2 y/o).

Noel Cogan owns five mares and likes to pinhook (buy foals and sell them as yearlings) and he had great success with Desert Bloom by Shamardal who was sold for three times the original cost. Noel was a doctor in the USA for a number of years and is now in Castlepollard, specialising in intellectual disabilities. He is also a Medical Doctor with the Turf Club and the doctor for Navan Racecourse. Obviously was 3rd in the Breeder's Mile in 2012 and 5th in 2013. The 2014 the race was won by Karakatonic from Anodin and Trade Storm. Obviously finished a respectable 5th one place ahead of Pat Smullen on Mustajeeb and Toronado with Richard Hughes riding was 8th.

SALOME & OLIVER BRENNAN, MULLINGAR

Oliver & Salome Brennan (died in May 2012), Hollygrove Stud, Belvedere, Mullingar were very much part of the racing community in Mullingar.

They bred Royal & Sun Alliance Chase winner the Trevor Hemmings owned

Albertas Run (Accordion-Holly Grove) 6/1 to win at Cheltenham for trainer John Joe O'Neill. He was one of Tony McCoy's favourite horses. He said *"You need a horse that wants to win".* He said *"He loves the ground, loves the track, and is always a better horse at this time of year"*. He won 15 from 36 runs and netted just over £900,000. Alberta's Run (Accordion-Holly Grove Lass) main wins were the Reynoldstown Chase (2008) RSA Chase in 2008, Amlin Chase (2009), Ryanair Chase (2010, 2011), and the Melling Chase (2010). He won the Grade1 Ryan Chase in 2010 (beating J'y Vole and Poquelin) and in 2011 (beating Kalahari King and Rubi Light). Trevor Hemming's decided to retire him at the age of 12 after he ran poorly in the Ryanair Chase in 2013 and was pulled up. As Jonjo said *"he was a flagbearer for many years and ran his heart out for you every time".*

They were introduced to thoroughbred breeding by Peter & Ann Downes. In 2008 they were nominated for Breeder of the Year and the victory of Albertas Run in in the GR 1 Royal & Sun Alliance Chase in 2008 was sweet, as their foundation mare Girseach was still hale and hearty at the age of 28, before passing away at the age of 30 in 2010. Girseach bred 7 winners including the top class Mister Morose 10 wins (won Grade 1 Aintree Hurdle), Southolt (3 wins), The Proms (8 wins), King Girseach, Fine By Me, and Miss Orchestra. They were also nominated in 2010 as Albertas Run won the Melling Chase at Aintree. Holly Grove Lass ran in 2 bumpers and 3 hurdle races and was the dam of 2 winners from 6 runners.

He was by the very successful sire Accordion, who bred Flagship Uberalles, Dato Star who was bred in Offaly, Accordion Etoile etc, out of the mare Holly Grove Lass, who also bred High Gears who won a few races. He was notable for having two white feet and the Brennan's sold him for €11,000 to John O'Byrne and he was returned to the 2004 Derby Sale by Landscape Stud to be purchased by Highflyer Bloodstock for €20,000. He was sent to Jonjo O'Neill's at Jackdaw's Castle Stables. As an owner Salome Brennan's most successful horse was Six of Hearts on the flat, who won 9 races including the Group 3 Ballychorus Stakes trained by Cecil Ross (total Prize Money won was over €236,000). She also owned Benny the Bishop who won 6 races and over €33,000 and Lughnasa (trained by Robert Tyner) who won 3 out of 9 races. She also bred Whatwillwecallher a very promising horse, now owned by J.P. McManus and trained by Robert Tyner, who has been so successful in point to points and now on the racecourse with horses like Footy Facts, Byerley Babe,etc. Whatwillwecallher was ridden to success by the Tyner's son Jack before his tragic death at Dungarvan point to point in February 2011. The horse won a point to point, and under rules 3 bumpers including the Punchestown Festival and 2 hurdles races (5 wins from 8 races). Whatwillwecallher was sold at the 2005 November National Hunt Sale by Hollygrove Stud for €20,000 to Moy Stud and returned to the 2009 Derby Sale to be sold by Hillview Stud for €10,000 to Mr. P O'Connor. He was later owned by J.P. McManus.

Salome Brennan bred other horses more recently, like Big Farmer (won a point to point), Scarlet Feather, Benjanim Button, Saddleeruppat, and Haddington Road (Old Grove -Hollygrove Cezanne) trained by Dot Love and a recent winner for Kieran Guinness. She died on the 17th May 2012 having contributed a lot to racing in the Westmeath area over many years.

THE FIRST WOMAN TO OWN THE WINNER OF THE AINTREE GRAND NATIONAL

Margaret Hope, Gartlandstown, Co Wesmeath was the daughter of Michael Hope and sister of E.J.Hope, the very successful breeder of Dorothy Paget's horse Insurance a dual winner of the Champion Hurdle and also several classic winners. She was married to Sir William Nelson, who was Chairman of the Nelson Line, Liverpool and the Nelson Steam Navigation. Lady Nelson bought Ally Sloper for 700 guineas after he almost was sold to Frank Bibby, but his agent dropped out because the horse had one of his toes out. She had already become the first lady owner to win a race at Aintree, when winning the Stanley Chase and also the Valentine Chase in 1914 with 5 y/o Ally Slope. When Ally Sloper won the Grand National in 1915, she became the first registered female owner in the history of the race to succeed. The jockey was Mr Jack Anthony, champion amateur in 1914 with 60 winners. He rode Glenside to victory in 1911 and the great Irish champion Troytown in 1920, when there was a rumour that a lot of the Sinn Fein war fund was bet on him. The trainer was Aubrey Hastings from Sharavogue House, Co Offaly, who trained 4 Aintree Grand National winners including Ascetic Silver in 1906 (when he became the first man to both ride and train a Grand National winner), Ballymacad in 1919 and Master Robert in 1929. It was to be the last race at Aintree until 1919, due to WW1 when the race took place at Gatwick.

In the race itself, Ally Sloper made a hash of the second fence and nearly threw Anthony out of the saddle until the hand of another jockey reached out and pulled him back. The hand belonged to his brother Ivor riding beside him on Ilston. His jumping improved and by the 2nd last fence he went into the lead and in a rousing finish held off Jacobus and Father Confessor. He ran three times at Gatwick from 1916/19 and was third in 1917. He failed to finish when racing at Aintree again in 1919. Ally Sloper was the first 6 y/o since the King's horse Ambush II in 1900 to win the Aintree National (His pedigree traces back to the Chester Cup winner of 1870, Our Mary Anne). Lady Nelson generously, gave 1/4 of the prize money to soldiers and sailors in need after the race.

In 1918, she had 6 wins with £8,900 in prize money (top winner Bramble Twig). In 1919 her horse Tetrarchia ran in the Irish Oaks won by Snow Maiden. In 1923 Juggernaut was a good stallion with 1,000gns winner Silver Ern, Silver Image who won the Jubilee Stakes and also Silver Jug. Lady Nelson bought Juggernaut, which was in Ireland & brought him to England. When Sir William died in 1932 she assumed the responsibilities of his racing interests and ownership of the Clonbarron Stud, Athboy plus the well-known stallions Tangiers and Vencedor. Tangiers had won the Ascot Gold Cup, Newbury Summer Cup and Jubilee Handicap, while Vencedor was a fast horse winning the Fern Hill Stakes at Ascot and other races. In 1929, she decided to restrict her activities and sell the thoroughbred mares, foals, and yearlings. She kept a few horses with Ivor Anthony, Wroughton and J.Ruttle, Clonbarron. The week before she died, her horse Glen Warrior won at Lingfield ridden by Steve Donoghue and another horse Graphic won several races. Margaret Hope died in London in April 1932 and ironically, she was outlived by Ally Sloper the horse that put her name on the Aintree records forever. Much of the bloodstock was sold after her death. Hugh Hope Nelson, Chavey Lane, Ascot had managed her stable and he was involved in the International Horse Show, when it was revived in 1934. He was well-known in the polo field before he died in 1937. Her son Sir James Nelson was in 1942 on the Advisory Board and also an INHS Steward and he came to resent the Central Racing Advisory Committee (CRAC) and their role in allocating fixtures.

ANN FALLON HELPED BY PRINCESS ANNE

Ann was was born in Dublin, her father Tony was from Tullamore and her mother Mary from Westmeath. Tony was a well known in greyhound circles with dogs with prefix "Shureen"- Shureen Dove won the Oaks Trial Stakes, while the Irish Cup winner Ballyduff Bobby was by Best Man out of Shureen Pride. Tony was involved in a horse syndicate that included Paul Daly, Jack Connolly, Alan McCormack, Patsy Ennis etc in a horse Nora Ann that won three races. Ann rode her first pony at 8 that belonged to a friend and then Tony bought her a pony called Tootsie. At nine she was hunting with the Westmeath Hounds, a member of Westmeath Pony Club, and taking part in eventing, hunter trials, and showjumping. She won rosettes and qualified for the RDS through the Pony Club. All her sporting interests related to outdoor field sports and her father bought a horse Lean Times, which broke a leg when in the lead in a bumper at Clonmel. She got a job with trainer Andrew McNamara, Croom, Carlow, where she rode many good horses like Boreen Prince. She spent 1983/84, as an exercise jockey in America, where Lester Piggott was also riding at the time on the track, before returning to work in the stables of Kevin Prendergast. Charlie Swan & Kieron Fallon, were working there at the time. Her father gave Kieron his first ever greyhound. She once had an amateur riders licence. She says *"I finished down the field in a couple of races in which I rode, but I enjoyed it nevertheless".* She initially applied for a judge's licence to the Irish Coursing Club, which was of great interest to her even though she was working in racing in 1985, but her racing days still carried on. She was helped by bookmaker Michael O'Mara, who got her an interview with Epsom trainer Phillip Mitchell, but she didn't like the place and instead managed to get a job with David Nicholson, after a chat on the phone. She rode out top class horses like Waterloo Prince & Charter Party.

PRINCESS ANNE TALKS HER DOWN THE HILL

At this time, the work riding staff included a very important personage *"Princess Anne saw it as her way out of getting away from it all".* At this time the Princess sent her horse Cnoc na Cuile to Nicholson's yard. The horse won at Worcester to register her first win over fences for the Princess. Ann said *"She would ride out a couple of times a week. We started at 6.AM every morning and she was never late".* The horses were tacked up for her but she always gave a helping hand. Ann felt she could always ask the Princess for advice. She was very much into helping people and she's a caring lady. Ann said *"I will always be indebted to Princess Anne. At one time I had a bad fall off a horse going down a hill and going down hills always held a fear for me, but one day when we met a drop, the Princess helped me get over the fear. It took about three minutes but she talked me down the hill".* When she returned home she worked with Frank Dunne, Hamwood Stud, Dunboyne for about 5 years on his stud farm, looking after mares and foals.

She was the first ever lady coursing judge in Ireland. She was part of the team for the major meeting in Clonmel and was a judge at Clounanna in Limerick. She travelled all over Ireland to meetings. In 1988 at Westport, she judged Merry Colina as a short head winner in the Derby Trial over her father's Shureen Smokey. Her father's dog was in front all the way but was just passed, as they reached the hare. She was also a judge at her local Castletown Geoghegan meeting. It was very physical and so she took up another career. She works for the Irish Greyhound Board since 2007 in Thurles, dealing with the public etc and likes the job.

ANGELA BRACKEN - SIZING EUROPE

In 2009, Angela Bracken, Tullamore, was up for the Breeding Awards with her husband Padraig Bracken and all because of one horse Sizing Europe (Pistolet Bleu-Jennie Dun). The two sons Rory & Michael are continuing the family tradition breeding horses. He was bred by Angela and was bought, as a foal by Hugh Bleahan at Tattersalls November Sales in 2002 for €9,000. He did not have a great pedigree, as there wasn't a winner in the first two generations of the family, but based on physique and demeanour it made up for the lineage. He was the 3rd foal of an unraced mare Jennie Dun (Mandalus), whose first was The Spoonplayer, a useful horse who won four races and was placed in a Gr 3 race. He is by Accordion and a half brother to Sizing Europe. The third dam Charlie Girl was unraced but is the dam of Lady Aylmer who is the dam of Zelda's Fancy. Jennie Dun was plagued by laminitis during 2009 and lost a foal by Scorpion. She had at that stage a 6 y/o son of Flemensfirth that M.V.Magnier gave €230,000 for at the Derby Sale and a 4 y/o filly by the same sire in 2009.

Pistolet Bleu won the Criterium de Saint Cloud and Grand Prix de St Cloud and after covering his only Irish crop he died from colic at 13 y/o. The horses he sired in France included Triumph Hurdle winner Katarino and Christmas Hurdle winner Geos, and others like Cappa Bleu, Merigo, and Vodka Bleu. The only other sibling of Jennie Dun to win was The Spoonplayer. Sizing Europe was purchased by Ann & Alan Potts and became the best horse they ever owned.

The horse recorded the first of his eight Grade 1 wins when beating Hardy Eustace by 8 lengths to win the AIG Hurdle at Leopardstown in 2008. He had come to the attention of the public, when he won the Greatwood Handica Hurdle in 2007. The most disappointing performance was in the Champion Hurdle in 2008 when he looked like a winner, but was suddenly pulled up with a back injury and he also missed Cheltenham in 2009 with an injury. The performance of his career took place in 2011 at the Cheltenham Festival, when he won the 2 mile Champion Chase beating two great horses in Big Zeb and Captain Cee Bee. He almost made all the running under Andrew Lynch with brilliant accurate jumping. Potts and the stable had also won the previous day with Sizing Australia, in the Cross Country Race. After his brilliant win in the Champion Chase in 2011, there was the controversial race at Cheltenham in 2012 when beaten by Finian's Rainbow. He went on to win the Gowran Park Handicap Chase four years in a row up to 2014. When he won the Gowran Race in October 2014 he showed he was as good as ever beating Galway Plate winner Road to Riches, who went on to be 3rd in the Gold Cup, when getting up by a head. He was now heading for 13 y/o after a stellar career, so a watching brief was held on his continuing ability. It was decided to let him take his chance at the festival in the Champion Chase where his stable companion was better fancied. He continued competing in the Champion Chase for the past three years including finishing second to Sprinter Sacre but in a not very vintage 2015 chase won by Dodging Bullets he was no longer ompetitive.(Finishing 7th of 9 runners). The decision was made to retire a great and classy horse.

Harry Bromhead later said the 13 y/o horse was to be re-trained to take part in the racehorse to riding shows at the RDS and would be sent to Rosemary Connors to do that. Let's hope that this great champion has a wonderful and deserved retirement.

His greatest wins since then include the following Greatwood Handicap Hurdle (2007), Irish Champion Hurdle (2008), Craddockstown Novice Chase (2009), Bord Na Mona Novice Chase (2009), Arkle Challenge Trophy (2010), Queen Mother Champion Chase (2011, Gowran Park Champion Chase (2011, 2012, 2013, 2014), Tingle Creek Chase (2011), Tied Cottage Chase (2012, 2013), Punchestown Champion Chase (2012, 2014),Clonmel Oil Chase (2012), and Paddy Power Dial-A-Bet Chase (2012). He has won 22 races from 45 starts and around €1.6 million in prize money.

MARY KILDUFF, OFFALY - PRESIDENT OF YITBA

Mary Kilduff grew up on a dairy farm in Belmont, Co. Offaly. Her family are breeders and producers of flat, national hunt and half-bred horses. Both her parents Noel & Eithne grew up on farms and her grandfather Patrick was a horse dealer, so it ran in the family. Her father Noel, continued the family tradition of breeding and horse dealing. Many of the horses were sold to Dessie Devlin, Jonesborough, Co. Armagh and the farm was a hive of activity, when she was young. She started riding at the local riding school with Anna & Tadg Camon and eventually took part in show jumping and showring competitions including the Tullamore Agricultural Show. She was a member of the Offaly Pony Club and later the East Galway Pony Club. In winter, she hunted with the Glasson Farmers and East Galway Hunt.

Racing was always a big part of her life and she has fond memories of going to Ballybrit each August and evenings at Kilbeggan racecourse. Her Uncle Tony bred many horses and has horses in training over the years. Mary's passion for horses led to her career in the racing industry. She completed a degree in Equine Business from Gurteen Agricultural College and Athlone IT and was subsequently selected, as part of the YITBA apprenticeship scheme. This year-long scheme was a great experience during which time she learned a lot about the business of thoroughbred breeding and met some great people from the industry along the way. During college holidays, Mary worked at Ballylinch Stud in Kilkenny. After completing college and receiving a bachelor degree in Equine Business, Mary went on to work in Newtown Stud in Kildare.

YITBA (Young Irish Thoroughbred Breeder's Association)

Mary was fortunate enough to be chosen for the YITBA apprenticeship, where she worked in some of Ireland's top farms. She is currently office manager in Forenaghts Stud in Naas, owned by the Smurfit family, and she has also worked alongside Dermot Cantillon, who owns Tinnakill House, particularly during the sales season, when they could sell up to fifty horses in one sales season.

In August of 2014, she was appointed Chairperson of the Young Irish Thoroughbred Breeders Association, an arm of the Irish Thoroughbred Breeders Association to meet the needs of younger people in the thoroughbred industry. She was delighted with the opportunity to stand at the helm of this organisation and bring her passion for horses and skills to the table. She think's it is important for young people in the industry to have a strong support network. She says *"Through our work, we also aim to encourage people into the thoroughbred industry and also to promote the Irish industry and establish ties with those in the industry further afield".* Mary knows the value of YITBA and said in 2014 *"The standard is rising all the time and we're delighted with the apprentices and looking forward to having them on board, as reps of ITBA.The first placement will be a great start for them and provide a great footing".* As she says *"my own door is always open for advice and help. We are the future and it's important for young people to get opportunities".*

In September 2014, they hosted the first European Young Breeders Weekend, held during the inaugural Irish Champions weekend. Representatives from similar organisations in Germany and England joined them for the weekend, which was a great success, and highlighted the importance and benefits of strong relationships with others. They are currently planning and looking forward to the European Young Breeders weekend 2015.

MARGARET MARSHALL AND HER SUPER FURROW ("JOE") - "LIKE A CAT FIRED OUT UPSIDE DOWN"

Margaret & Seamus Marshall, Drumcullen, Co Offaly have been horse owners since the early 1980's & cattle farmers. Undoubtedly, the best horse Margaret Marshall owned was Super Furrow(who was nicknamed "Joe"). The story began with Jerry O'Neill a vet from Borris, Co Carlow, who started training with a small string in the 1980's after being a successful owner. He owned Dim Wit the winner of the 1972 Irish Grand National and other good races like the Thyestes Chase and Jameson Gold Cup.

Margaret Marshall sent Super Furrow to run in the Cools Mills Flat race in Kilbeggan, as a 5 y/o on Monday 24th June 1985. He was backed in from 6/1 to 3/1 and duly obliged by 4 lengths. The £835 collected that day was only a deposit for the future. Amazingly, he only finished 5th in a novice chase the following year at Kilbeggan. Super Furrow won 12 races over 10 different courses and over £100,000 in prize money. Some of the main races he won were the Champion Novice Chase (Gowran), PZ Mower (Galway), Kerry National(Listowel), Northern Telecom and Guinness Chase (Galway) and at Punchestown in April 1989, he won twice within 48 hours. Firstly, he gave weight all-round in the two-mile Motor Import Chase on the Tuesday and under a 3lb penalty, he won the Festival Handicap Chase over an extended 3 miles on the Thursday. It was a remarkable feat of endurance and versatility (the horse ran 60 times and was in the money 29 times). In spite of all that success it was perhaps in defeat that he ran his best races including seconds in the Power Gold Cup and Galway Plate (under top weight) and his best race in February 1990 in the Vincent O'Brien Gold Cup, when he had a titanic struggle with Maid of Money & Waterloo Boy on the run in, only giving way in the last 150 yards. Jerry O'Neill summed him up when he said *"He was like a cat fired out upside down, he'd always land on his feet".* The Marshall's were related to the great jockey Bryan Marshall ,who won the Grand National in 1953 with Early Mist and with Royal Tan in 1954. They have won 61 races with their horses and on every racecourse except Sligo, Ballinrobe, Fairyhouse, and Tramore. Seamus buys all the horses and more recently they have had horses like

Brian's Express, Lisa's Lionheart and Devil's End, plus some point to pointers to be trained by Leslie Young that they bred themselves.

MARION WALLACE (MRS M.WILLINGTON) SUCCESSFUL BREEDER AND BARBOUR CUP WINNER

Marion Wallace was the daughter of Richard Wallace, Ballingarry House, Shinrone and when John Wallace went to Australia in the 1930's, she inherited the stud farm of her father. She had the very successful stallion Baydrop at her Belfield stable in this era and his most famous produce was Baykora, who won the famous Barbour Cup three times in a row from 1937-1939, thus enabling her to keep the cup and the horse was also very unlucky in the La Touche Cup at Puncherstown, when swerving at the last fence, looking a winner. In this era, she bred some useful horses like Drop-a-Wink (Baydrop-Never-a-Wink); Golden Patriot; Battle Eve (Irish Battle-Never-a Wink) usually ridden by local jockey W.Murray, son of a popular Roscrea doctor and this horse gave him his first winner; Vliomonde bred by local stallion Vilko (the dam Lisduane was owned by T.H.Wallace, Ballincor); and Baygina (Baydrop-Georginatown), a winner in Mullingar. Miss Wallace's Drop-a-Wink was 3rd in the Naas November Handicap to Stormy Current, which ran well in Irish Derby and was beaten a head by Owenstown in the Ulster Derby.

Marion Wallace married R.M.Malcolm Willington, who took over the training licence, which had been held by other employee's. He and his wife enjoyed continuous success with many home-bred National Hunt winners, selling on the proven geldings and retaining the fillies for their stud. The latter category included Troubled Sole (Turmoil II - Royal Sol), successful in the 1965 'Amateurs' Derby' at Galway and a great-granddaughter of Mrs Jiggs. Among the stallions they stood at Belfield was Soldado (1938, Umidwar - Athasi), who was a half-brother to the 1929 Derby and St Leger winner Trigo and Irish Derby, and St Leger winner Harinero and Primero who dead heated in the Irish St Leger with Patriot King. Primero went to Japan in 1936, where he was amongst the top five leading sires thirteen times, second twice, and third twice and was leading broodmare there in 1958. On his death in 1961, Soldado had sired the winners of 89 National Hunt races, notably Solfen, twice successful at the 1960 Cheltenham Festival (Sun Alliance Chase in 1960 & Stayers Hurdle), the multiple winner Solbina and Soltown who won the Troystown Chase in 1958. Other horses include Soldrop, Solbaygina, Solflame who won at 4/1 in Mullingar in 1956 causing a *"Shinrone Invasion"* to the bookies. In the 1962 Aintree Grand Nation won by the Gilbert Webb bred Kilmore, two more local horses bred by Soldado ran in the race - Cannobie Lee an 11 y/o ridden by Eddie Harty was 8th and Solfen 10 y/o ridden by Toss Taaffe was 12th. Mr W.J.Kennedy, Borrisokane, Auctioneer had a mare at that time out of Kilmore's dam Brown Image and sired by Soldado, who sired the above two unplaced horses. Marion Wallace (Willington) died in 1961.

The above is just a sample of some of the women who have contributed so much to racing in the midlands either directly or as partners, which cannot be quantified. Many others have also contributed through point to points like Ita Kiernan, Linda Groarke, Jessica Cahalan etc. Sheila Ryan as outlined under Cleaboy Stud worked and managed the stud for many years before setting up Littlewell Stud. Bela Ringwood bred the great Aintree Grand National runner, point to pointer and all round chaser Freddie, as outlined under the Grand National. Anna May Mullins (nee O'Connor), Rosemount produced a DVD *"Horse Racing Syndicates-It Could Be You"* some years ago. She was a member of a syndicate called River Syndicate who owned *"Presenting Lucy"* and also Goat Racing who owned the popular and successful *"Forpadydeplasterer".* Jean Fetherstonhaugh originally from Bracklyn who died in 2012 aged 93, told her story in a book called *"The Last Laugh".* She also loved horse racing and was a member of the syndicate who owned Mysilv who won plenty of races.

chapter 14
POINT TO POINTS

WESTMEATH HUNT HISTORY

It could be argued that official Westmeath Hunt history started around 1697, when Bishop Dopping had a pack of hounds kennelled near Killucan and in 1738 Thomas Pakenham MP had a private pack at Pakenham Hall. In 1800 John Fetherstonhaugh hunted near Killucan and Grangemore and around 1802 the Sonna Harriers were started by Hugh Tuite with the kennels at Coolnahay. Hugh Morgan Tuite MP succeeded his father and kept the hounds. Richard Reynell of Killynon hunted around Clondalever and in 1835 his son Sam Reynell, who was to become famous as Master of the Meath Hunt, started a scientifically bred pack of hounds.

In 1854, Sir Richard Levinge, Knockdrin, who was the first Master of the Westmeath Hunt, started a pack with hounds from Britain. In 1856, George Boyd-Rochfort took over after a meeting in Middleton and he was followed by John Fetherstonhaugh Briscoe of Grangemore and he increased hunting to 5 days a fortnight. Captain Gerald Dease 1861-68 got all classes to join the hunt (his father John was the first Catholic Magistrate in 1793) and took over in 1861 at Turbotstown House. On one occasion he broke a leg, but got a trap specially made to go through the fields and gaps, so he could hunt. The Midlands Great Western Railway (MGWR) was used for distant meetings. In 1866, a new kennel was opened at Culleen with Gerald Dease and Sir William Trockmorton running it. Mr Dease resigned in 1868 and was presented with a Plate valued at £300.

Dease was succeeded by C.McDonald Moreton, who had good hunters like Marchioness, Plum, and The Colonel and then in 1871 Captain R Coote took over for a year and held a champagne breakfast at Culleen. In 1872 Captain R. Greville-Nugent took over. He was one of the best known amateur riders in Britain & Ireland (riding 4 winners at Punchestown on one occasion) under the name of "Mr St James" until his tragic death in 1878 at Sandown. A committee (including Captain J.R.Malone, Ambrose More O'Ferral, Sir Walter Nugent and Lord Kilmaine were involved) took control under Sir Montagu Chapman in 1876, followed by Sir William McNaughton (1882/83) and Captain James T. Clarke (1883/86). Other riders and racing breeders who were involved in this era included Henry Murray of Mount Murray, and Christy & Richard Coffey, Newcastle. Lord Greville MFH 1886/93 always started with a breakfast, and he made it very popular with other hunts around the country. He was very much involved with the development of Mullingar Racecourse. His horse Bonnie Rath was very successful, winning at local meetings and as far as Ballyhaunis and Loughrea. In September 1898, he sold a lot of his horses including yearlings by Strathblane, Marmiton, Lourdes to locals like E.J.Hope, James Cole and P.P.O'Reillly. In 1903, he announced his intention of giving a beautiful cup to be run at Newbrook value 100 sovs, to which the Race Company were adding 100 sovereigns. He was fond of racing in a quiet sort of way but bet very little. He died in 1909 at 68 y/o. He was Deputy Lieutenant in Westmeath and succeeded to the title in 1883. He owned Mullingar and generally always tried to do his best for the town and county.

In 1894 Lord Longford & E.M.Pakenham became Joint Masters. Lord Longford was somewhat eccentric and apparently on one occasion was the only one to cross a flooded river with his horse, but when he got to the other side he realized he forgot his hat and swam back again to collect it! J.B.Charters was MFH 1900/03 and was followed by two people who made a big impact in horse racing in Ireland and Britain as outlined, with Harry Whitworth 1903/08 and Frank Barbour who was MFH from 1908/1912. He also inaugurated the famous Barbour Cup.

In 1912, the hunts first American MFH was Harry Worcester Smith, who was well known in the USA's Master of Foxhounds Association. An expert breeder he came to study conditions in Ireland, but had many problems during his stay and he wrote an interesting account of his time in Ireland and Europe. In 1913, E.Hope Johnston had 4 days of hunting a week and he was followed by Norman Field in 1924 (His brother Marshall Field was a very influential figure in horse racing in this era with strong connections to Tally Ho Stud). Captain C.E Winter was Master/Joint Master from 1927 to 1935. Mrs Winter's had to cover for him during World War II and she travelled on a motor cycle. Other Masters to follow were Patrick Pickersgill 1945, Sir Dermot Cusack-Smith and in May 1950 Miss Joyce Hansel from a New York/Virginian family, became involved and was Joint Master with Lieut-Colonel Denis Purdon. Some of the other MFH's in this era included Major M.P.O'C Tandy, well known breeder J.S.Bellingham, Glencara, Hon. Kieran Guinness, G.M.and J.Delamere, Colonel & H.D.Harvey Kelly etc.

Many famous people have been part of the Westmeath Hunt from the 19th century, including the Duke of Marlborough, Lord Lieutenant of Ireland, Lord & Lady Randolph Churchill, famous trainers & jockeys like Atty Persse, Harry Ussher, Greville Starkey, the British Ambassador to Singapore, the Governor of Australia, Liam Cosgrove, Taoiseach and even Mandy Rice -Davies, who was famous in the 1960's when she and Christine Keeler were involved in the Profumo Affair. Many racing families in Westmeath go back to the 19th century with their involvement in the hunt and point to points including Downes, Ross, Kiernan, Nugent, Ronaldson, Tormey, Cleary, Boyd Rochforts, O'Roarke,Gavin families etc. The most famous equine animal running with the Westmeath Hunt in modern times has to be Gigginstown House's War of Attrition winner of the Cheltenham Gold

Cup in 2006.

The Hon Kieran Guinness is Chairman with his nephew Sebastian joint master. Other Joint Masters were Wendy O'Leary and Dr Mark Mortell.Field masters included Paddy Gavin & Helen Moorehead and hunts man James Lowry. A notable charity raiser is €10 raised by every faller in the Hunt through year. Former point to point rider Sonya Kiernan acts as Secretary, while her parents Frankie & Ita are the driving force behind Castletown Geoghegan point to point, with 2 meetings per year on the left handed circuit, with a steep uphill finish to the last fence. In recent times Jacksonslady, Backstage, and Carrigeen Lechuga have all run at the venue. Many improvements have been made on the track, with a permanent railing around the parade ring and an all white railing for both sides of the course.

WESTMEATH POINT-TO-POINT RACING

In the 1970's, some of the great hunters included Pat Hogan's Under Way, Rusty Tears, Gus O'Brien's Corryvreckan, Philiptown Hero, Any Crack and in the 1980's/90's horses like Eliogarty, Attitude Adjuster, Elegant Lord, Risk of Thunder, Spot the Difference, up to the present with Tammy's Hill, Salsify, On the Fringe, and many more. The other type of horses are those who went on to major success on the racecourse and for this you have d a long list like The Thinker, Midnight Court, Cool Dawn, Florida Pearl, Best Mate, War of Attrition, Beef or Salmon, Amberleigh House, Denman, Imperial Commander and many more. Tied Cottage ran and won at Castletown-Geoghegan point to point in January 1983. He won the Cheltenham Gold Cup in 1980 only to lose on a technicality. Even at Cheltenham in 2015, there was a list of horses that came through point to points like Faugheen, Martello Towers, Milsean, No More Heroes, Road to Riches, The Druid's Nephew etc.

WESTMEATH HUNT POINT-TO-POINTS 1873 - 2015

The first recorded point to point meeting of the Westmeath Hunt was considered to be at Loughagar in 1873, when the Hunt Committee joined in with the 8th Hussars and Royal Fusiliers to put on the event. It was held on land provided by George Cuming and subscriptions were submitted to J.H.Vize, National Bank, and W.Kelly, Hibernian Bank in Mullingar. A young Captain Reginald Greville -Nugent was the originator of the meeting due to his love of horse racing. He set aside an apartment to provide a lavish luncheon by invitation. The other Stewards included Lord Greville, Lord Kilmaine, Sir Percy Nugent, W.Pollard Urquhart, High Sheriff, John Malone, Ralph Smyth, R. Rochfort Boyd, J.F.Montgomery, C.McDonald, and T.Maher. Others who became involved were Sir Charles Nugent, R.Coffey, A.More O'Ferrall and W.S.Kelly, who were very much racing people. Races included the Greville Handicap Plate of 150 sovereigns won by Mickey Free from Little Annie and The Torrent. All of these competed in the Irish Grand National at some stage. The Westmeath Hunt Cup was won by T.Jackson's Lightfoot 5/4F ridden by Mr

Exshaw. The meeting was held over two days and crowds were good even with other meetings being held in the area.

In 1875 *"Mr St James"* rode Ildrem to win the Westmeath Handicap by a 1/2 length. In this era a number of horses that ran in the Aintree Grand National or Irish Grand National participated, like A.Croftons Sultana, Major Browne's Scots Grey, Mr G.Gubbins Thiggin Thue, J.Purcell's Harristown, Sir William Nugent's Kiltoom, M.Ballesty's and T.Cleary's Boreenchreogue (Irish Grand National winner) etc. The point to point's were held at Catherinstown in 1879, the first at Slanemore in 1880 and in Rathconrath in 1881, Culleen in 1886 (occupied by T.M. Reddy) and at Clondalever in 1892/93. In 1887, it switched to Mr T.M. Reddy's place again at Culleen (2 miles from Mullingar). From 1890, it was held at Newbrook a number of times with P.J.Carroll, Secretary in the 1890's. In 1900, at Newbrook, the most interesting winner was C.Hopes, Pride of Mabestown in the Farmers Race. She was unplaced in the Aintree Grand National in 1903 but her full brother Drumcree, also bred in Westmeath, won the big race.

Harry Whitworth MFH won the Welter Hunt Cup at Clondalever in 1904 on Penelope. P. McLoughlins Irish Grand National winner Lord Rivers was only second in 1908 at the point to point and in some accounts it was said to be held at Johnstown Fort, where there was a great view from the hill. In 1909, Frank Barbour presented the Barbour Cup and it became one of the most important cups with hunts from around the country competing for it. The cup was purchased from James Tuite, jeweller, gold, and silversmith and it was a beautiful piece of work being a replica of the Punchestown Grand National Cup. It was open to all hunts in Ireland and regiments quartered in Ireland. Twenty one entries were received from around the country the first year. It was won then by William Uprichard (Co. Down Staghounds). T.M. Reddy acted as starter and James H. Locke from the famous Kilbeggan Distillery acted as the Judge.

Westmeath's only winner in the early years was G.A.Boyd-Rochfort' s good horse Kilhugh ridden by Cecil Brabazon in 1909. It had to be won three times in succession to become anyone's property and Miss Dorothy Reynolds was the first person to win it twice with Roxborough in 1910 and I.X.L in 1912. It was held in Slanemore up to 1923 except for Multyfarnham in 1914 and Ardivahan in 1924/25. In 1913 at Slanemore, the Conyngham Cup winner Merri Merri won the Barbour Cup and in a tremendous finish J.P.Hogan's horse from Limerick Hunt beat the Meath Hunt representative Too Clever by a neck. It was over 4 miles in natural country with the weight to be carried 13st and to be ridden in colours by gentlemen riders. Tents were on the hill and the Highland Light Infantry gave hospitality. Atty Persse the famous trainer had Hubert Martin running. Lady Levinge dropped the flag to start the race. He was impressed with Merri Merri and later saw him win the Conyngham Cup, on a day when former Aintree Grand

National winner Covertcoat was killed in the race and on the same course as he had his first win.

THE BARBOUR CUP AND BAYKORA

When Paddy Dunne Cullinan won the race in 1922 with Burgama it was a popular success, because of his strong Westmeath connections and again in 1924 Mrs L.Garahan's Jack ridden by P.J.Casey won the race for Westmeath. From 1928 to 1939 it was almost a case of Ladies only as Miss P.Ryan's Connie won in 1928, Mrs P.Dunne Cullinan's Heza in 1930 ridden by the great Tom Dreaper; and then a dead heat between Miss P.Irvine's Shiela and Miss Ruth Murphy's No More in !931. Miss Irvine's Shiela rode her own horse to win in 1932, having broken a collar bone just a month before, she was just resuming riding; Lady Dumfries Bachelor's Heart (1933); and Miss E. Lysaght's May Star II winner of seven races (1934). Miss Dorothy Reynolds horse St Bruno II of the North Mayo Harriers was expected to continue the sequence in 1935 and win the cup for the third time, but W.P.Hanley (Tipperary Hunt) well known in racing circles won the race with Hurdy Gurdy Man to spoil the sequence, as St Bruno came down at a drain. Jimmy Cleary gave local supporters a fillip with a treble on the day. The dominance of the ladies was to continue with Dorothy Reynolds winning with St Bruno in 1936, before Miss Marion Wallace with her high class chaser Baydrop won three in a row between 1937 and 1939 to win the cup. The horse was unplaced in the Irish Grand National in 1940.

MARION WALLACE

Marion Wallace (later Mrs M.Willington) was a very successful breeder in Shinrone, as accounted elsewhere, with successful stallions like Baydrop and Soldado. Baykora was one of her most prolific winners in the 1930's. The Barbour Cup was described as the best trophy within point to point racing, and as the rain poured down on Ardivahan it seemed that the trophy would be lost to the Westmeath point to point committee. Only five horses ran in the race with J.Marshall (related to Bryan Marshall) up. She won the race easily from Toby Downes on Caviare. Toby Downes had been second in the race five times (including twice behind Baykora). It was a sad occasion in many ways when the cup was presented to Marion Wallace, but it was not to be the end of the story for the Westmeath Hunt.

TRAGEDY AT ARDIVAHAN IN 1934

The meeting in 1934 brought tragedy to Ardivahan when popular young amateur Jimmy Yourell was tragically killed on E.Tormey's Never Say Die in the Farmer's Lightweight Race. He jumped the last obstacle looking like a winner when his foot was accidently caught by a flag post and he was thrown. It seemed that the horse struck him on the ground and he was knocked unconscious. He was attended by Dr P.J.Keelan on the course and removed to Mullingar Hospital where he died. His family had made a great contribution to racing in the midlands for many years. The local Hunt Cup had runners from well- known breeders like Sheila Ryan (associated with Cleaboy Stud) with the winner Caramana, Betty McCall (Tally Ho Stud) with Bit of Luck, and T.P ("Toby") Downes with the hot favourite Another View who fell. In 1935, Jimmy Cleary performed an amazing feat on Tom O'Roarke's prolific winner Clares Battle,when riding the last mile with a broken rein and he jumped seven fences to win by $1^{1}/_{2}$ lengths.

Captain E.A.Gargan had been Secretary in the 1930's and he presented the Gargan Cup to replace the Barbour Cup, as the point to point continued through WW II. Gargan won a race at the meeting in 1944 with Valiant Son but it was most notable for the jockey Peggy St John Nolan, who was to become one of the most significant female figures in racing over many years. The most important race in the 1940's was the Westmeath Perpetual Challenge Cup (value £50) with £25 added, presented by Westmeath Polo Club. In the 1950's the highlight was the re-introduction of the Barbour Cup. In a rare act of gracious sportsmanship, Mrs Marion Willington (Wallace) re-presented the Barbour Cup to the Hunt Committee. The cup went to Brigadier A.D.R. Wingfield, when his horse Proud Kitty (Rejoice) won. In 1963 the prize money at Slanemore was £235 with races including the Barbour Cup (£75 added), Open Heavyweight Race (£40 added), Westmeath Perpetual Cup (£40 added), Westmeath Hunt Cup (£40 added) and Armytage Perpetual Challenge Cup (£40 added). Sponsorship was now a necessity to ensure that the point to point would continue. The Secretary at this time was Edmund R.Nugent, Jamestown Court, Castletown-Geoghegan. Peter Downes rode Nugent's horse Quo Vadis to win the Hunt Cup twice in 1962/63 and Helen Bryce Smyth did the same double in the Barbour Cup on Still William. In 1967 the Barbour Cup was won by P.C.Heron's Barberstown in the absence of Cecil Ross's The Inventor, who had won at Fairyhouse.

Surely, one of the best point to point meetings was held at Culleen in 1969 when Cecil Ross's two money spinners The Pooka (Westmeath Hunt Cup) and The Inventor (Barbour Cup) both won. Lord Fingal's Champion Hunter chaser No Other also won the Culleen Cup and Jim Dreaper trained & rode Black Secret (placed 2rd in the Aintree Grand National in 1971 to Specify)) to win the Westmeath Perpetual Challenge Cup. Tom Cruise's Artists Slave gave Cecil Ross a treble at the meeting. In 1969, Cecil Ross rode The Pooka in the Aintree Grand National (fell on the second lap) on the Saturday & came back in time to the point to point races at Newbrook on the Sunday to ride a double on Sunny Chief (Guy St John Williams racing author, rode the runner up The Jolly Doctor) and Tribal Chief. Moate vet Mick Cooney won the Barbour Cup with Vipsanius. A great reception was given to jockey Eddie Newman and trainer Jim Tormey after their horse General Symons dead heated the day before with Black Secret, when they were 3rd to Well To Do in the Grand National.

In 1974, Ted O'Leary's horse Knockmark ridden by Alan Ross was a popular winner of the Barbour Cup beating Ted Walsh on Dot Loves horse The Innisfallen. In 1976 the point to to point was held in Abbeyshrule, Co Longford outside the county, due to difficulty in getting a course. Miss Joan Vandeleur, Secretary was a good organiser. Ned Cash's Barouche won the opening Hunt Cup and then attempted to win the Barbour Cup, but was beaten by J.Jones's Summer Storm. The races at Castletown Geoghegan in 1978 brought two notable figures in Pat Taaffe and Tommy Carberry to the event. Taaffe's Super Dub VI won a maiden race and Carberry's horse Cottage Tudor was beaten a neck by Sicilian Princess in the Patton Cup qualifier. The brilliant hunter chaser Corryvrecan came to win the Barbour Cup in 1979 by an easy 10 lengths. In Castletown Geoghegan in 1983, Ted Walsh had a double, winning the Barbour Cup with the Cecil Ross's Lucky Marble by a distance at 5/2 and followed up with M.Butterly's Arctic Beau.

In 1987 Tony Martin had a treble with three favourites in Marked Impression, Knockshegowna, and in the Barbour Cup with Gallagher, who had been third to Observe in the Christies Hunter Chase at the Cheltenham Festival a short time before. The winner of the Paddy Connell Memorial Cup was by Lighter Than Air bred by Paddy Clarke, Cleaboy Stud with the sire Rarity, and coincidentally they sponsored the race. A very important introduction this year was the form & racing sheet, which was included with the card for the first time. Pat Hogan had a double in 1989 with the useful horse Howyanow and Moon Run, both ridden by Enda Bolger. In 1990, Colonel Lemon had his 17th win in point to point's in the Westmeath Cup and he was owned by Eamonn Finn (who had the last winner in Mullingar races in 1967 with Moigh Star). In 1998 Frank Kiernan won with Toarlite (his third win of the season) at Castletown Geoghegan.

WILLIE PENROSE TD GOES DOWN BALLINTUE ROAD

In 1997, Dixon Varner won the opener and went on to become Champion Hunter Chaser for Enda Bolger & Mrs J.Magnier. Ruby Walsh rode him to win the Champion Hunter Chase at Punchestown. The Barbour Cup was won by Kildare jockey John Robinson on Sally Willows 1998. Westmeath's most popular TD in 2008 was Willie Penrose the Labour Party's spokesperson on enterprise, trade, and employment and he had Ballintue Road running in the Barbour Cup. He was ridden by Ciaran Murphy and when the favourite fell at the last he went on to win. This was the second leg of a double for them as favourite Haze Blue won earlier for the Goosebump Syndicate (Micky Love, Joe & Noel Murphy). Tom Cleary, Athlone trained Jack Monday for his brother and he also won before aiming for Punchestown.

George Webb from Shinrone whose family bred Brown Jack & Kilmore had a winner with Little Inch, owned by Offaly breeder Patsy Kelly. Robert Brabazon upheld the great name of the family in racing by winning with favourite The

Snuffler. In 2010 local jockey Danny Foster had two winners with Glenark and Alright Benny trained by James Robinson. On the Net who was 5th in the Cheltenham Foxhunters Chase won at the meeting after a tough duel. In 2013, Martin Lynch trained Oscar Time to be 4th in the Aintree Grand National and he added a local win to his CV, when a son of Vinnie Roe called Royal Caviar was ridden by his son Mark to win at his local meeting. Mark went on to have a double with the 8 y/o Face the Music. The applause that greeted the winner was matched by the greeting for Dot Love's Irish Grand National winner Liberty Counsel at the meeting. Mark Fagan another local trainer added to the joy by winning with Kanesh (J.P.McKeown) in the Barbour Cup. He said *"We really wanted to win this race, as it is for the Barbour Cup, one of the oldest Cups around".* In April 2014, Bank on Time won the Tullaghansleek Stud winners confined hunt race and gave local handler James Kiernan his 6th win in the race, which he also won as a jockey. In October 2014, Dot Love's veteran 11 y/o Loughnagall with Ciaran Murphy riding brought off a surprise win (10/1). They had only purchased him three weeks before.

HISTORY OF THE SOUTH WESTMEATH HUNT CLUB

In 1888, a group of people in the Athlone area purchased a pack of hounds from Captain Fetherstonhaugh, they formed themselves into a hunt Club known as the South Westmeath Staghounds. Some of the early hunts chased a stag over open country, covering distances from ten to twenty miles, the stags being supplied by the Ward Union Hunt for a rent of approximately £16. By 1906 the stag disappeared, his place being taken by the fox. In 1926 the name of the Club was changed to the South Westmeath Harriers and in 1931 to South Westmeath Hunt Club, which it has been called ever since. The pack was kept in the early years by Broughton Adderley of Ballykeeran and was looked after by Billy Berry, Garrycastle, Athlone, and when he died his son Billy Berry Junior took over. His only means of transport was his bicycle and he was paid the princely sum of 30/- per month for his dedication. The hounds were then kept at Retreat Heights, Athlone and also the Army Barracks, but are now kennelled at Annagh gortha, Ballykeeran and ably looked after by Tom Barlow, Parnell Square in Athlone. Joint Meets were held with the Longford Harriers over the years, the venue being Tang & Ballymahon.

MASTERS

Lord Castlemaine 1888-99; Edward Wakefield, Farnagh 1899-1908; Colonel Carter, Athlone 1908-11; E.J.Bolton 1911-1930; Cecil Johnson 1930-33; Lionel Lyster 1933-1938; Captain W.M.T.Magan 1938-1939; Lionel Lyster 1940/41; Gerry Groarke 1941-43; M.Mahon 1943-1953; J.Berry (Joint) 1952-53; Lt Colonel M.J.Higgins 1953-56; Col J.Lewis (Joint) 1954-55; P.McCormack 1957-58; M.Kearney 1958-59; G.Collins 1960-80; Mrs D.English 1980-82; and Martin Dibbs 1982-88 (breeder of Comply or Die).

From its foundation the Club has held a point-to-point. For the first six years races (1889-95) they were held at Aughafin, Moate, on the farm of John Gaynor, then at Lissanode, Mount Temple and at Drumraney for one year only. In 1898 and the following year's at Kilkenny West until it eventually moved to Listisson,The Pigeons in 1978, in the heart of Goldsmith Country, from where it has been run ever since. In 1891, John Gaynor was also Joint Secretary with J.J.Hurley, Moate and the meeting was held under the auspices of Broughton Adderley's Staghounds of Ballykeeran at Aughafin near Moate. The Treasurer was Columb Kelly, Moate, and the committee were John Egan, Simon Boland, Pat Duff, P. Fallon, L.D. Byrne, George Woodburne, Dr Fitzmaurice, John Lynch, John Lowe, John Murtagh and James McCormack. The meeting consisted of a Farmers Plate of £25 for half-bred hunters from the district; Welter Cup of £21 (presented by R.Hodson) for hunters the property of members; Farmers Plate of £10 for hunters the property of Farmers; and Light Weight Cup of £21 (presented by H.B.Adderley son-in-law of Lord Castlemaine). In 1892, two of the Committee, John Gaynor with Sunset and John Lowe with My Queen won races and in 1893 repeated the feat with two different horses in Sunfield and Gunshot.

One of the better horses in this era was L.Yourell's prolific winner Bass, who won two races out of four in 1894 and was good enough to be third to The Admiral in the Irish Grand National. The cost of running the meeting in 1894 was £177-10s-10d covering stakes £85, stand & Course over £6, band over £14, timber, flags etc £4-8s, printing,post etc £13-5s-11, Rent £15, Charles Murray's wages £1-10s, etc. The Kilkenny West meeting of 1907 had plenty of entries but Colonel Hall's Needful was the only favourite to win on a cold wet day, when two horses won at 10/1. By the 1930's, Jimmy Cleary was the man to follow, as he had three winners and a third in the five races at Kilkenny West including his father's Irish Thorn (Irish Battle-Twinthorn), Ballybrickeogue, and Arkinsaw. He was beaten in the South Westmeath Hunt Club by the Marquis de Brissac a leading amateur rider in France, who owned the winner Blarney Castle.

In 1989, Miss Carmel Connaughton recorded a double with J.C.Fahy's Carhoon and Eamonn Finn's prolific winner Colonel Lemon. Kieran Guinness won the maiden with Lady Easton with Frank Kiernan on board. The Secretary at this time was Mrs N.Moore and Arthur Moore was Chairman of the Hunt. In more recent years at The Pigeons the locals have had some success with Ciaran Murphy riding Dot Love's Valentines Beauty to win in 2008 when Tom Cleary, Athlone won with Jack Monday. In 2009 Cecil Ross trained Another Whiparound ridden by Jamie Codd to win a division of the mare's maiden. In the other division, Adrian Murray trained Leney Lou to win with young Danny Foster riding him for the A.B.P. Syndicate from Bunbrosna.

In 2011, Gordon Elliot's Backstage (1/2) ridden by Jamie Codd (who had five winners at the meeting) won a 14 runner open lightweight race at The Pigeons and immediately was aimed for the Aintree Grand National, where his odds started to shorten for the Grand National. He had won at The Pigeons in 2009 before being 8th of 29 in Foxhunters Chase at Aintree, so he knew the fences. The reason why this happened was that as a rookie trainer in 2007, Gordon Elliott won the Grand National with Silver Birch, who had his first run for him at Castletown Geoghegan point to point just 6 weeks before the big race. The amazing thing was that this was his first win as a trainer and it happened outside Ireland in the biggest jumping race in the world. The horse won by 3/4 of a length at 33/1 ridden by Robbie Power. He finished 10th in the Grand National to Ballabriggs and was fancied for the Grand National in 2013, but was pulled up at Cheltenham (after 7 point to point wins) in the Christies Foxhunter chase.

In 2012, the star performer was 6 y/o Living Next Door, who raced clear with purpose and Tony Martin looked to have a nice staying chaser in time. Tom Cleary's Jack Monday (by Black Monday) won the opening confined winners' race ridden by Peter Flood. Katie Walsh rode Dermot Desmond's Hinesight to beat Jennifer Pugh on Schindlers Rock. In March 2013, Paddy Hughes was in attendance reminiscing about his Irish Grand National winner Insure running there and another good horse in Buck Rogers. Jack Monday had won in 2012 for Tom Cleary and at 14 y/o was bidding to win the Confined Hunt race for the 4th time but he slipped on the turn. It was won by Brian Scott's Jiggle Joules under Aaron Murphy and the inimitable Paddy O'Roarke presented the award and remembered that he had won his first race there many years before (Richard Pugh reporter on the Irish Field had ridden his first winner 20 years before at this meeting). Robert Brabazon won with Viewvic (5/2) ridden by Ben Brabazon and owned by Penny Downes. Willie Penrose TD recorded yet another win with Mr Dickens, who is trained by Adrian Murray and ridden by local jockey Danny Foster.

In March 2014 local based Brian Dunning who was owner, trainer, and jockey of Mr Michanda won the confined Hunt's Winner's race on his £200 purchase. Former Kilbeggan specialist The Last Derby was proving to be one of the best open horses in point to pointing and added a very comfortable win by 15 lengths, on a day in which his jockey Rob James had a treble. This was also the meeting where there was a 'Foinavon' type pile up of horses leaving just five to get around. In 2015 the meeting was postponed from 1st March to the 8th March due to weather conditions, and then only five races took place with J.J.King having a double on Champers on Ice & Western Marrior.

WESTMEATH HARRIERS

In 1953, Cecil Ronaldson won the Large Cup on J.Tierney's Luxury IV and completed a double with Attempt II. One of the luckiest winners was A.Duncan's

Flashaway in the Leavy Cup, who was well behind Major Bermingham's Diamond Page II, when the latter failed to pass between the posts at the finish. The winner came from the same family as future Champion Hurdle winner, Another Flash in the 1962 Champion Hurdle. Tom O'Roarke won on the local horse Dalystown and Paddy won on Southern Gale. In 1955 the Leavy Cup was won by Major Bermingham's Keoltown, after a great ride by Cecil Ronaldson to beat Paddy O'Roarke on No Sale. In 1957 J.V.Leavy's Atout Noir won the Leavy Cup ridden by V.Leavy Jn and the trophy was presented by Mrs Leavy to keep it all in the family.

The Harriers race in the 1987 was won by Pat Hogan's No Other Way, who improved on a recent run at Patrickswell, when third to Attitude Adjuster, to win the Open Lightweight Race and the useful Gallagher ridden by Tony Martin won the open heavyweight. Incidentally, Attitude Adjuster went on to be 8th in the Aintree Grand National to Maori Venture in 1987 and was 5th to Rhymn N'Reason in 1988 ridden by Niall Madden. The meeting in 1983 brought one of the best point to points held at Castletown Geoghegan, when the former Irish Grand National winner Tied Cottage owned by Mrs J.Moore and ridden by John Fowler won the Lightweight Race after star hunter chaser Eliogarty fell at the last and Mrs J.Magnier's Colonel Heather finished second. Ted Walsh recorded a double with his own horse Needless to Say and E Hope Johnstone's Lucky Marble. The officials for this meeting were Cecil Ross, Secretary, A.Casserley, H.Tynan, J.F.Tormey, T.Tormey, A.Ross, J.Dolan, J.F.Moorehead, C.Ronaldson, W.Ross, and T.Daly.

ORMONDE HUNT

Sir Charles Coote stated in 1801 that *"Near Shinrone they breed their own horses, particularly for the saddle, and have a very fine kind in this vicinity".* The Hunt has a long history going back to 1778. Colonel Giles Eyre, Galway hunted this area around 1809. It roughtly covered from the Birr area into North Tipperary. Colonel J.C.Westenra best remembered for his success in horse racing hunted here in the 1830's and he was related to Lord Rossmore who also participated. Captain John Hammersley kept hounds at Northlands near Cloughjordan. Families like the Wallaces, Kenny's, Ringwoods, and the Webbs were horse breeders and part of the Ormonde Hunt. Other families tracing back to the 19th century were the Drought's, Hackett's, Maxwells, Falkiners, Stoney, Jackson, and Smith. Thomas Stoney, Borrisokane, kept the hounds for a number of years followed by John Drought, Banagher,who was a great supporter of steeplechasing. Drought bred horses like The Cob, Smarger, Mountjoy, and was associated with Dan O'Connell, who supposedly made a jump of over 32 feet at the down fence in Lismacrory. In 1872, Lord Hastings (Earl of Huntington) re-united the Ormonde & King's County Hunt. William Trench was followed by the remarkable Assheton Biddulph, who had been with many hunts in Britain and Ireland.

The Ormond Hunt races were held many places from Grennanstown, Ballygiblin, Lismacrory, Norwood and Kylenagoona. The rise of the Land League in the 1880's brought local agitation in 1881/82 and also 1908. The Ormond was re-started in 1912 by Sir William Austin and G.S.Webb continued the Corolanty connection with the hunt, when he was made MFH in 1914 before he retired in 1919. He is best remembered as the breeder of the great Brown Jack the most famous horse in Britain in this era. In 1924 he returned as Joint Master with H.M.Reid, Roscrea. In 1940 he was succeeded by his nephew George Ryall and his son Gilbert was Secretary of the Hunt from 1940. A Miss M.O.Mathison from Scotland was in charge around 1940 and she owned the chaser St Martin winner of the Galway Plate, when trained by Aubrey Brabazon. In 1950 J.F.Cahalan, Ballingarry, was joint secretary and when Gilbert retired in 1965, Mr Cahalan continued as Secretary for 15 years. The Wallaces & Kenny's have a long association with the hunt going back to mid 19th century.

Donald Swan hunted with the Ormond Hunt (MFH 1974-84), as did his son Charlie who was Champion Jockey and associated with Champion Hurdler Istrabraq (He also went to School at Wilson's Hospital, Multyfarnham, in West-meath). In 2014 John Kenny was Chairman and the Secretary was Jessica Cahalan whose father is Morgan Cahalan owner of the remarkable sprinter cum miler Gordon Lord Byron. John Kenny's association goes back through his brother, father, and grand uncle over 60 years.

ORMOND & KINGS COUNTY POINT-TO-POINT

Lismacrory Races was renowned in North Tipperary & South Offaly over many years. In 1843 the meeting on Simpson Hackett's land was over 11 fences including a wall. Colonel H.C.Westenra presented a Gold Cup value 100gns. Mr Drought's The Cob won the race even though he was described as *"slow and a baulker"*. His rider John Kelly was one of the best jockey's around and he led all the way on the *"slow horse"*. A meeting was held in April 1845, which caused great excitement in the area, as it was picked for a faction fight between two neighbouring parishes. Captain Kelly RM, Shinrone, Birr ordered in the cavalry & infantry. The Parish Priests Fr Nolan, and Fr O'Meara, Lorrha strongly condemned the plan from the altar. The end result in this case was that the two groups pledged to keep the peace. At the meeting on 4th April 1848, which was organised by the Ormond & Kings County Hunt, was not quite as successful in that the stand came crashing down injuring around 20 people including Fr O'Malley PP, Shinrone, with many having serious spinal injuries and other broken limbs.

Horse Racing in Kylenagoona, Borrisokane, originated in 1863 on the farm of John Reddan and continued up to the early 1900's. The Stewards in 1872 included e Lord Hastings, G.Jackson, Captain Saunders, R.H.Falkiner, R.Reeves, David Clarke, Thomas Sadler,and J.J.Kennedy. It was a warm and dusty day and one reporter was upset at the peasantry forcing their way on to the stand without paying a half crown. The Hunt Plate was described as *"the Derby of the day"* and was won by J.N.Russell's The Knight (Mr Exshaw jockey). In 1876, Gerald Foley's Iniquity won the race by 6 lengths beating Harry Beasley one of the great family of jockeys on Tatters. In 1877, the Stand House was turned into a beer garden and P.H.Steven's, Secretary and the committee were criticised for not controlling the crowds. It was a very popular race meeting and it was said that some liked The Curragh and some liked Punchestown, but they all liked Kylenagoona. In 1888 the Committee were Patrick H. Stephens, Hugh Delaney, Matthew Dunne, John Reddan, Daniel Darcy and Secretary M.Costello, Kyle Park House.

In 1902 the Hunt Races were held in Ballingarry, where it was hard to see the race, as there was said to be 26 fences. H. Briscoe Kenny won the Ormond hunt Cup outright when his horse Countess Belgrave won it for him for the third consecutive year. In 1903 it was in Caherhoerigh, Moneygall with 5 foot walls and other big fences and it took place in the shadow of the Devil's Bit. In the 1930's the meeting was held in Knockarlow Mill's, Clareen, Birr with 6 races including an Open Challenge Cup. It was dominated by the Kenny family as owners, trainers, and jockeys, as they won with Sunkist, Another Prospect, and Little Brown Boy. Amazingly, in 1935 they hadn't a single runner as the ladies dominated proceedings. Marion Wallace won with The King, Miss McCutheon won with Kilmore and Mrs McMasters rode two winners.

Racing continued during the war and in 1944 J.F.Reid won with his brave horse The Nipper and A.J.Burris's horse Moneygall won the Farmer's Plate ridden by Mr "Bubbles" Burris. In 1947 Harry Kenny was Secretary and Clerk of the Course and he was ably assisted by regulars G.S.Webb, Gordon Ryall and R.H.Wallace. The most popular win in 1948 was G.C.Webb's Juryman in the Belfield Cup maiden race. In 1951, H.Davis Kenny died and it was a sad occasion at the meeting. In 1955 the Belfield Cup described as the "Ormond National" was won by Pat Hogan's Art Foot (D.Hogan). In 1962 a meeting was held in Ballincard, Kilcormac owned by Jack Maxwell with £250 and five cups. The Ormond and (sometimes) King's County races continued in various places over the years and more recently in Ballingarry. In 2000, fourteen races took place on a single day at Ballingarry, the equivalent of two meetings on a single day.

JAMIE CODD BECOMES CHAMPION AT BALLINGARRY RACES

Derek O'Connor had dominated the point to point scene and even reaching 1,000 wins in the process over the years, but when he came for the two day Ballingarry meeting on 6th and 7th June 2014 he knew the title was almost gone. He had no winners on the Sunday & Jamie Codd won with Port Rock for Robert Widger. At the end of the Monday meeting Jamie Codd was confirmed as champion by 6 winners. He rode his 95th and final winner on Exhibit Five. It was his first ever title and he received a tremendous reception in the Parade Ring, when presented with the Robert C.D. Kenny Memorial Trophy by Olive Kenny, as leading rider at the meeting. He said *"I'm over the moon to have won the riders title. I'v had a few disappointments over the last few years but today makes up for it all".* The Gatechecker received the biggest cheer when he won, as he was owned by local man Aiden Fogarty whose house was right at the end of the backstraight. He never had a runner at the meeting in previous years. He named the horse after his father who was a gate checker for the GAA over the years. He buys one horse every year and this was one of the better ones. There was also a local success for handler Brendan Madden from Moate when he won with Glebeparkhawk, which was his first ever success. He thanked his neighbour Tom Cleary who helped him train the horse. In a day of firsts, 22 year old Fintan O'Toole from Loughrea, had his first ever winner as a jockey on Where'd ya Hide it, in the older horses maiden, and described it as an *"unreal feeling".*

The Ballingarry two day point to point early in June 2015, clashed with Kilbeggan races, and unlike the previous year Derek O'Connor had already won the jockey's title. Colin Bowe and Donnchadh Doyle had already decided to share the handler's title. The Westmeath based vet Mark Fagan trained Super Scorpion to win the gelding's maiden ridden by Jamie Codd. He was bred and owned by Siobhan Kiernan daughter of Sean. Over the two days, both Jamie Codd and Derek O'Connor had two winners. Codd was the leading rider but had to dash to ride at Listowel. Aaron Synott a 19 y/o from Enniscorthy had his first win on Gem & I. A new meeting was held in 2015 in Longford by the Longford Harriers and Westmeath Foxhounds at Corbeagh House to add to the meetings.

BROSNA FOXHOUNDS

It was founded in 1995 and they hunt a country that hasn't been used since the demise of the Kings County Hunt in the early 1900's (from Birr, south to Ferbane and Kilbeggan in the north). Founders include Barney Glennon, Chairman John Moriarity & Colm O'Brennan. Since 2006 Ian Colton has served as second joint master and Aisling Carter was field master.

The Brosna Durrow Point to Point in March 2014 had three runners from Gigginstown, including a 1/2 brother to Champion Hurdler Punjabi, who cost €97,000 at the Derby sale called Attribution. The Gordon Elliot trained Attribution ridden by David O'Leary won for them, with Jamie Codd on the better fancied Guerilla Tactics unplaced. Derek O'Connor had a treble with Cailin Aileann, Change the Rules, and Zero Visibility. On the Sunday there was fresh ground but it was still heavy after the rain. Ciara Duffy a competitor in the first series of the TG4 reality programme *'Jockey Eile'* won on Likeable Rogue, whom she trains. The horse had twice been placed for Paul Nichols and was bought at Doncaster. Roger Quinlan had a treble with Annie Oscar, Heroes or Ghosts, and Shannon Smacker.

The featured Glenwood Tullamore open lightweight was restricted to women riders for the first time in the 12 years of racing at the Offaly venue. Rachel Blackmore brought 13 y/o Powerfulpaddy through to win for a third career win.

Jennifer Pugh (nee Mayne) was a Doctor in Tyrrellspass (29y/o) for a number of years and she married Richard Pugh in 2005. She had her first success in Tramore in a bumper on Carrig Cottage for trainer Michael Fitzgerald. She was joint leading point to point rider in 2008/9 with Liz Lalor (with 8 wins each). In 2003/4 she had her first win with Match Maker owned by her father-in law Derek, where she beat her her identical twin Jacqueline(Kidd) at Necarne Castle. Her second success didn't come until October 2008 on Captain Gucciat. During her winning year, she fractured her right collar bone twice. At this time she was in General Practice in Tyrrellspass. She is often down as honorary medical officer at point to points. Her 8th winner, to share title, was Butler's Storm owned and trained by her husband Richard. Jennifer & Liz decided jointly not to ride in the last two meetings of the year so they would stay level

JAMIE CODD AND DEREK O'CONNOR

With over 650 Point to Point winners to his name Wexford native Jamie Codd is the second winning-most rider in the history of the sport. He is the only modern day rider to ride all six winners on one card emulating, both John Berry who went through the card at Caim in 1988 and Brian McLernon back in 1959. He has been going head to head with Derek O'Connor in the title race for many years. In 2011, he went to the final weekend only to finish second to O'Connor at the very last meeting and had been second to O'Connor for seven successive seasons going into last term. In 2014 he got off the mark very quickly and opened up a clear lead before Christmas when collecting his first ever HRI award. He maintained an advantage right the way to the end of the season winning the title for the first time by a score of 95-89. Along the way he also managed to squeeze in riding his first ever Grade 1 winner, when steering ex pointer Shaneshill to success for Willie Mullins at the Punchestown festival. A dual Cheltenham festival winning jockey he is one of the strongest and most talented point-to-point riders of all time. He is one of only two riders ever to score 100 winners in one season and in a title battle, which was followed intensely by many within the sport, he managed to hold off the ten times champion Derek O'Connor and win his first ever title. He failed to retain the title in 2015 but he had success at Cheltenham with Cause of Causes for J.P.McManus and The Package for David Pipe.

Derek O'Connor has won more races than any other rider in history. Since being Champion Novice rider he went on to win ten successive Point to Point titles and was one half of a wonderful title battle in 2014. The Galway-man fought right to the final day only giving best to Jamie Codd at the final meeting in Ballingarry. Before Derek O'Connor was champion the record for the number of winners in a season was 56 held by both John Thomas McNamara and Davy Russell. Not only has O'Connor beaten these two great riders but he has doubled that record when he rode 113 winners in a season. He has three times ridden over 100 winners in a season. In the history of point to points, only seven six timers have been recorded and O'Connor is responsible for three of them. He enjoyed a Cheltenham festival double with Zemsky and Chicago Grey in 2011. He has now ridden well over 950 winners and rode his 1,000 winner this season in February. It may have been Jamie Codd in 2014 but in 2015 it was Derek's year with his 90th winner of the year in Ballingarry at the Ormonde Hunt in May. He had a double with Elusive Theatre and Chosen Dream. It was his 11th title and he was the first jockey to win 1,000 races, when Death Duty for Pat Doyle and Gigginstown House Stud won on 15th February in a 4 y/o geldings maiden. He rode his first winner in February 2000.

Liz Lawlor won her 4th title with 11 wins. Faugheen the Champion Hurdler & Road to Riches were the two most successful point to pointers on the track (also Thunder & Roses winner of the Irish National). Everything is relative in life and sport so in February 2015, the 22 y/o Simon Cavanagh from Mullingar rode his first track winner aboard Jack Aboo, owned and bred by his father Richard, in the concluding Woodrooff Maiden Hunters Chase at Clonmel. Winning trainer Dot Love said: *"I'm delighted for the Cavanagh family and he'll stay point to pointing and hunter chasing now. We might look for a hunters chase in England with him".* For his part Cavanagh disclosed: *"I've had four point to point winners and I ride out for John Joe Walsh and Dot Love".*

chapter 15
PERSONALITIES - FROM COLM MURRAY TO A GREAT BETTING COUP

COLM MURRAY - "A LOVABLE ROGUE"

Maybe it is appropriate that the final chapter should include a piece about Colm Murray, who is mentioned a number of times through the book, as he gave horse racing a personality of its own, when the red light went at RTE. I spoke to Robbie Irwin who was a great friend of Colm's at Kilbeggan races this year and he described him affectionately, as *"a lovable rogue".* Robbie lived near him in Dublin and they shared lifts into RTE over many years. They shared an interest in horse racing, golf, and went for walks together. He spoke about Colm's great generosity with time, which people did not know about and his work for charity. He would drive all over the country to help out but he always had a mischievous glint in his eye. He recalled one day out walking with Colm in the wheelchair, when he had Motor Neurone Disease. As they walked over the iconic wooden bridge near the Royal Dublin golf course a man came towards them and said *"What happened to you?"* and Colm said *"Did you ever hear of Motor Neurone Disease?".* The man replied *"When did that come out?"* Colm with a glint in his eye said *"I don't know when it came out, but I have it!"*

He was born in Moate, County Westmeath, and his parents had a shop in the town. Colm Murray took an interest in horse racing at an early age and he went to Kilbeggan races and places like Galway & The Curragh. He started school in the Convent of Mercy, Moate and did his Leaving Certificate in 1969 in the Carmelite College in Moate. He participated in local dramas in the school and later graduated from University College Galway with a degree in French, & History in 1972. He was a teacher for a while locally in both Athlone and the Vocational School Tullamore, where he met his wife Ann. He also spent three years in Ballymun before joining RTE. They married in Charleville and had two kids Patricia & Kate. They made their home in Clontarf, Dublin. Apparently, before they went on their honeymoon he stopped off at Galway Races to raise a few bob for the trip.

His life and career changed when he left teaching and became a continuity announcer in RTE in 1978 starting with *Hospital's Requests,* then as a newscaster in 1983 with Charles Mitchell, Maurice O'Doherty & Ann Doyle, before he reached his goal of first sports newscaster on the evening news. In his outside broadcasts he is especially remembered for his reports from Bejiing in 2008. He brought racing more into the reports and he covered Cheltenham each year for almost 20 years, when because of cut backs he was not sent. Even Foster & Allen offered to finance the trip deeming it a *"national disgrace"* that he wasn't there. He could show great initiative to his own benefit such as when he was in Sydney for the Special Olympic's the Melbourne Cup was on. He convinced RTE that John Oxx's horse Enzeli might win it and that he should be there for it. The horse finished near the back and his boss was not impressed, when he returned home.

THE TROUBLE WITH HORSES

It was a natural progression to want to become involved in horse ownership, His first horse was a mare called Gerise with some friends. He went on to be trained by Paddy Mullins. As the group were leaving the Parade Ring, Com asked Paddy Mullins what were the chances and the great and wise trainer said *"Have a pound each way"*. He informed his cohorts and based on the belief that this was the nearest thing to a tip from the trainer they all put on a score each way and the horse won, leading to a party on the way back to Dublin.

When Willie Mullin's started training he only had a small number of horses and record Group1's at Cheltenham & Punchestown were only a dream in his head. On Willie's suggestion they bought a horse called Magic Oats which won a three mile hurdle race in Galway at 33/1. Willie suggested that they back the horse and Colm backed him at 14/1 'without two'. He won and added to it shortly afterwards at Roscommon. Toureen Girl was another horse that carried Colm's colours to success in a bumper at Wexford and later won the Richard Power Handicap Hurdle at Tramore. In 1994 Colm had the choice of two horses either Sambara for £7,500 or Mystical City £5,000. He chose Sambara who proved her worth by winning 4 races over hurdles and three on the flat, and she later bred Equus Maximus. The only downside was that Mystical City went on to win the Galway Hurdle. The syndicate also bought a horse called Creux Noir to be trained by Dermot Weld. In June 2003 they backed him from 14/1 to 8/1 at The Curragh and he won with Pat Smullen on board.

The Demure Syndicate had other wins with Shadow of the Wind, Katie Stobling, and Madam Leader (3 wins). One of the more interesting ones was Sweet My Lord which Colm owned with Jonathan Mullin & Aiden Devaney. He won a number of races but his potentially biggest moment was when leading in the Leopardstown Chase worth around €50,000 he fell at the last looking a winner. This horse gave him his last win at Tramore the following April. In March 2011 he was honoured by his Alma Mater for his contribution to sport (at a time when he was battling Motor Neurones Disease) by UCG. Throughout his career he excelled in his presentation of sport with his knowledge and wit, whether it was an interview or a Cheltenham Preview night. He also received an award from Horse Racing Ireland.

MOTOR NEURONE DISEASE AND A CELEBRATION OF LIFE

Motor Neurone Disease is probably one of the most feared diseases because of the implication of helplessness, as it gathers momentum. Ironically, Colm Murray got the news after returning from Cheltenham, one his favourite places, and it was devastating. A visit to Willie Mullin's yard at Clonsutton, apparently, helped convince him to return to work. We can all recall watching him on television in the public limelight and being as professional and ironic, as ever each evening. When he was confined to his home in Clontarf he continued to back horses. He was one of the few people to get a definitive tip from Aidan O'Brien, when he told him about Camelot for the 2,000 guineas and Epsom Derby. He backed the double at 8/1 and celebrated his great success.

Perhaps the bravest thing he did was to do the excellent documentary about his fight with Motor Neuron Disease. He fought back with strength and energy and even put forward his name for trials and tests in the hope that someday a cure will be found. It was inspirational and moving not just to those with the debilitating disease, but anyone with a serious illness. When he died the mass leaflet described it as *"A celebration of the life of Colm Murray"*, which was very appropriate. It was attended by the President Michael D.Higgins and Enda Kenny, Taoiseach amongst many. He was 61 y/o when he died from the disease but he had helped raise awareness of Motor Neurones Disease. People remembered his enthusiasm, zest for life, flair of language and love of sport including his friend and colleague Robbie Irwin. His daughter Kate described him as *"warm, generous, kind, and loving"* and it was poignant that he died on the opening day of Galway, where his marriage had started many years before.

CYRIL HACKETT - AN INDEPENDENT BOOKMAKER WHO COULD HACK IT!

Cyril and Monica Hackett, started their bookmaking business in 1965, when they paid £3 to rent their first shop and took in £34, and by 2005 their turnover figure was €116 million and a listing at number 278 in the country's top 1,000 companies.

In the early 1960s, Cyril Hackett worked his summer holidays from UCD (where he studied science) in a Great Yarmouth, Norfolk pea factory. He collected bets from the staff and gave them to a lorry driver to put them on but after a while he took the bets himself. He was there for 5 summers, as he made good money. In 1965 he opened his first shop in Kilcormac, Co Offaly, his home town and put in a girl to look after things and went back for the summer to Great Yarmouth. He married Monica (nee McNabb) that year. It was simple then with bets written on a pad and hand stamped. On the Monday he opened he took in £34. Cheltenham opened on Tuesday and he took in £400. At that time you got the results from Extel, if you were in Dublin, but from the radio down the country.

He opened up their first three shops in Dublin, in 1971, to add to the additional bookie shop's in Mountmellick, Tullamore, Portarlington and Edenderry. The Dublin shops were bought from bookmaker Cecil Fine, who retired when the Hackett's bought the rest of his shops in 1976. In just 11 years it had become a huge business. English bookmakers first came to Ireland in the early 1980s and the Hackett's were offered €3.5 million by Coral's and Ladbrokes but refused, which was a brave decision. The family home at this time was 230 acres at Geashill and they had six children. In 2013 they had 48 shops, 19 of them in Dublin with 3 more going to be opened. In the 1990's the SIS moved in with live pictures of racing and computers changed everything making it better & easier to operate. At that time there was no evening or Sunday racing. Modern technology changed the face of bookmaking in Ireland. Nearly all of the small, old-time bookies were gone in the country towns. In the 1960's bookies offices were smoke filled discreetly placed offices, where no woman would enter but now they were acceptable business premises in a change of culture.

Horse racing had changed, with a huge volume of bets being placed and the biggest change was that 50 per cent of betting was now on other sports, and on the Lotto. All the children became part of the business in some form with Paul responsible for Dublin, John around the country and Mark ran the Geashill farm. Their other son Peter was tragically killed in a car crash in 1993. Cyril & Monica also became involved in breeding horses. Their yearling Eden Rock was sold for €700,000, a filly Shanghai Lily was also sold for €300,000 and a colt, Golden Arrow, for €180,000. Monica had enjoyed success as an owner with the Paul Nicholls-trained Natal.

In 2015, Cyril Hackett died at the age of 75 and at that stage nine of the shops had been sold to Paddy Power to streamline the business. He had remained the leading independent bookmaker through his lifetime, with almost 70 shops nationwide, two on-course offices and online & telebetting services to support those. Hackett's also sponsored races at a number of Irish racecourses including Kilbeggan (which he always liked to support as it was his local course) and the Irish Cesarewitch at the Curragh. Cyril & Monica Hackett contributed a lot to Offaly & to racing in general in a competitive business. They worked hard but in many ways their work also seemed to be their hobby.

John Hackett who has carried on the business was also interested in the breeding side and he kept 8 brood mares for breeding. He had Maradyke Bridge a two time winner, Ard Lane a winner first time out, Aughan Villa a 4 time winner trained by Peter McCreery. He also had Fruit Defenu bought in France for £90,000 and trained by Noel Meade. He won his first race at Fairyhouse. Cyril's son Mark & his wife Pippa, Geashill, have run the Moat House Farm since 2005 and it comprises 45 acres. Interestingly, it has an historic Norman Motte

(Moat of Down) & Bailey. They breed thoroughbreds mainly for the British & Irish market. The Hackett's do everything themselves from foaling to sales, with some success, as breeder's and pinhooker's. In 2006, they had their first winner on the track with a 2 y/o Patrick's Well at Down Royal, which they had sold as a yearling. Pippa took a career break to help out with the kids and the farm. In 2012, they had their biggest success when they turned 53,000 guineas to 500,000 guineas in 18 months, through Roger O'Callaghan, Tally Ho Stud with a 2 y/o son of Shamardal out of a Swain mare Balloura. John Ferguson signed the docket for the breeze up and it had been purchased by O'Callaghan as a foal.

It was a great boost for them at the time. It has been mixed over the past few years with their foals. In February 2015, Gladstone Street went to Zebedee and Balloura went to new sire Morpheus (both at Tally Ho Stud). The mares Amaniy went to Baltic King, Balloura to Morpheus, and Christmas Cracker to Sir Prancelot. A lot of luck is involved and there can be mixed fortune with mares in foal.

BREON CORCORAN, CHIEF EXECUTIVE OF BETFAIR (1971-)

When I went to the Primary School in Kilbeggan many years ago we had to pass the shop of Tom Walsh, where we would occasionally buy something, if we could afford it. Mrs Walsh was a teacher in the school for many years and lived all her life in the town. Her daughter Dolores, also a teacher became a very successful Principal of the Primary School in Kilbeggan. Her husband Liam Corcoran was also a teacher, and they lived in Mullingar, Co Westmeath. They had a son Breon who grew up in Mullingar, who has gone on to become one of the most important figures in horse racing as Chief Executive of Betfair, the on-line betting exchange. Betfair operates in a system where the customers bet against each other, with the company taking a small commission. They are guaranteed to make a profit regardless of the results. In 2014, around £150 million was wagered on Betfair and Betfair Sportsbook at Cheltenham. It is the world's biggest internet betting exchange with around $^3/_4$ million customers. However, all this success was not as clear cut as it seems. Before the arrival of Corcoran as Chief Executive they were struggling.

He left Mullingar and did a degree in Maths at Trinity College in Dublin. He wanted to be involved in business and he came to London in 1993 to work for Banker's Trust as a trader. He spent seven years there and then tried a few business ideas from a language school to a scooter taxi service, without success. He did an MBA at INSEAD and arising from that he joined Paddy Power Bookmakers in Dublin. He had no real interest in racing but understood risk management and electronic commerce. He stayed there for around 10 years up to November 2011 and ended up as Chief Operating Officer. It was at that point that he accepted the offer of Chief Executive Officer at Betfair (a post he could not take up for 10 months). He was married with three children and living in Barnes not far from the Betfair offices in Hammersmith. He is not unlike Michael O'Leary in that he is casual in dress.

Betfair was founded in 2000 by Andrew Black and Edward Wray and in 2010 it was valued at £1.4 billion. However share prices had collapsed on the stock market in 2010 with problems over new products, costs etc. It took around four years to recover. One of the main problems was the cost of overheads, so he cut the worldwide workforce from 2,300 to 1,800 thus reducing costs by £35 million. He built up the software development facilities and added to them from Romania to Dublin (where the fixed odds operation is setup). An interesting & successful development was to make the on-line facility seen more like the old style bookie office. As the situation was improving attempts were made to buy shares but they were turned down. It showed that the product was good and worth continuing the developments. The emphasis was on technology and speed for their customers.

Breon Corcoran brought additional success to a good product, even if it was a long journey from Mullingar to London. He was on the Irish Times Irish Rich List, as worth €33 million in 2015 and it can only get better.

SIR PETER NUGENT, (1920 - 2002) 5th BARONET

He was the son of Sir Walter Nugent, Donore 4th Baronet. He enlisted in the Irish Guards and served in World War II in the Jungle Warfare School in Bombay. After the war he returned to the family seat intending to run the estate but he had difficulties in his relationship with his mother. He married Anne Smyth, Gaybrook and they moved to Jamaica to run a banana plantation. He later tried to work Donore but again it did not work out and he bought land in nearby Reynella. It was difficult in the 1950's and he had to sell the farm. He took over the baronetcy in 1955 on his father's death and after his mother's death in 1960 he sold the Donore estate to the Land Commission. He managed the lands of Colonel Stuart Bellingham at Glencara and at the same time developed his skill as an auctioneer in Goff's, and he also became manager of Mullingar racecourse introducing evening meetings and other improvements.

He managed Mearscourt Estate for Lady Lister Kaye and started selling for Goff's and Tattersall's (he was with them from 1965-89). In 1983 he was made a Director of Tattersall's. He contributed to Tattersall's setting up a sales complex in Fairyhouse. In 1980 he took over management of the Blackhall Stud in Kildare owned by Lady Zia Wernher and moved there. He retired in 1990. He is succeeded by his son Richard who was born in 1947. He was noted for his flamboyant, jovial style and booming voice. Edward Mahony said he was *"one of finest auctioneers ever"* in the time he acted as his understudy from 1981. He got others started like Philip Myerscough & Robert Hall.

NOEL RYAN, MULLINGAR - FIRST CHIEF EXECUTIVE OF THE IHA

In March 1999 Noel Ryan (1942-1999), who was Chief Executive of the IHA (Irish Horseracing Authority), died at the age of 56, following a long battle against cancer. He was appointed as the IHA's first chief executive in late 1994, just after the authority was established in the Dail and he had many challenges in front of him to steer the new organisation through a series of crises. He had to fight some strenuous opposition from the industry's many competing groups.

He was born on Christmas Day 1942 and educated at St Mary's Christian Brothers, Mullingar and then University College Dublin. He lived most of his life in Palmerstown in Dublin. He obtained a law degree at UCD and was called to the bar in 1979. He joined the Public Service in 1960 and worked in many departments from Defence to Foreign Affairs. He had a good record in the Irish Civil Service and had been an Assistant Secretary in the law division of the Department of Justice and in the Department of Foreign Affairs. As Director General of the Law Society he was involved in the negotiations that led to the Anglo- Irish Agreement. He was married to Una and had six children. He was interested in racing as an annual member at The Curragh & Leopardstown, but it was still a shock when he was appointed by Denis Brosnan, as he did not have experience regarding the workings of the racing authorities.

The birth of the IHA clearly had implications for the Turf Club, which dated back to the 18th century, and naturally they feared a loss of their historic powers (echoes of the current position between the HRI and the Turf Club some twenty years later). Disputes varied from the financing of racings integrity service to disputes over fixture lists (again echoes of the Irish Provincial Executive in the 1920's/30's). The basis of Noel Ryan's work was the five year plan from 1997-2002. He had disputes with the on-course bookmakers, with the lowlight being the bookmaker's strike at Leopardstown in 1997, when no prices were returned. Ryan proved to be a strong negotiator and managed to achieve a compromise. He struggled right up to his illness in his attempts to re-organise the tote. He brought some drive into the industry, which had been lacking but this did lead to personality clashes. He helped to increase funding to racing through his contacts and also improved facilities in tracks around the country.

He contributed to making the IHA a strong force in racing and in summary, he brought about a significant increase in prize-money, in the Capital Development fund, the modernisation of the Tote and of the industry itself, which covered many aspects of the five year plan. He was diagnosed with cancer of the colon in 1997 and he was confined to the Mater Private Hospital for the last few months of his life. Dermot Weld said at the time of his death *"For a man to die at 56 is tragic. In a very short time as chief executive of the IHA he helped co-ordinate the different factions and aspects of the industry to move Irish racing forward".*

EDWARD SCALLY, ATHLONE - MANAGER GOWRAN PARK

On 30th July 2012, 32 year's old Edward Scally, originally from Kilmacoo Lane, Athlone, Co Westmeath, was appointed General Manager of Gowran Park Racecourse and Golf Club. He is the son of Edward who was a sales rep. and Margaret and he has four sisters. He graduated from the Marist College in 1997 and studied accountancy in Athlone Institute of Technology (AIT in 1998), where he met his wife Bríd from Connemara. He went to Germany for a few years and it was then he became involved with the hotel and hospitality sector. He became Manager of Treacy's Hotel in Enniscorthy and then moved to the Carlton Hotel Group. His last job, before Gowran Park, was in their hotel Bunclody in Wexford.

He had studied strategic management in the USA in 2008 at Cornell University Ithaca, New York and it gave him a broader view of the hospitality sector. His appointment as General Manager of Gowran Park Racecourse and Golf Club was a natural step for him, as he is interested in sports and horse racing. As Gowran Park is a Grade 1 racecourse with 16 meetings each year, including the famous Thyestes Chase, it is very much part of the hospitality sector to present it at its best. The objective is to develop the racing and golf club, but also to look at the wedding and conferencing facilities. It was a great challenge to the young man from Athlone, who lived in Wexford at the time. He maintains contact with Athlone, and visits as often as possible especially to support Garrycastle GAA team. In Wexford he managed the Duffry Rovers senior football team, which has tasted success. Gowran Park was opened on 16th June 1914 with prize money of £130. The present Race Company was formed in 1948. They had the first race course commentary, the first tote jackpot in 1966, and the first televised race. It is a great opportunity for the young man from Athlone where racing ended at Garrycastle in 1923 to make his mark, especially as the economy is beginning to improve.

MARK BOYLAN, BANAGHER

Mark Boylan from Banagher has been singing since the age of three, and no doubt he made a strong positive impression on people for the following ten years of his life, with no idea about how his life would change after a visit to Cheltenham racecourse with his father David in 2010. Inspired by the trip and his love of horse racing he wrote a song called *"The Festival"* for the Injured Jockey's Fund, which became a huge hit on You Tube. In 2011 he opened Channel 4's coverage of the Cheltenham Festival by playing the song leading to A.P.McCoy commenting on his Twitter account that *"I ain't no Simon Cowell but how good is 13 y/o Mark Boylan's Song about the Cheltenham Festival"*. The other biggest compliment was that normally racing songs are not very good, but even his favourite newspaper the Racing Post endorsed the catchiness of his song, which appealed to all ages and groups. The 13 y/o was now on the world stage, raising money for his favourite sport and that does *"beat Banagher"!*

At the end of 2012 and now aged 14 y/o he attended the Breeder's Cup. He wrote a song called *"Stateside"* as a tribute to the Breeder's Cup. The organisers brought him out for a week to sing to 65,000 people at the meeting. It was an unique experience, as the lyrics were printed on the card and all the crowd joined in to create an amazing experience. His whole trip was covered on local TV, radio, and all other media forms including the New York Times. He met many people from the great jockey Pat Day to Bo Derek. All funds from the song went to the Permanently Disabled Jockey's Fund. Already in his short life he had played Vicar Street and with the High Kings. He has also played from California to Holland. In 2013 he wrote a song about Campbell Gillies a 22 y/o, who died tragically in Corfu in an accident. It was at the request of his mother and for charity. The song was called *"A Song for Campbell"* and it ended up competing with Ed Sheeran and other major stars on the play list.

The major event in British and Irish Racing in 2015 was the retirement of A.P.McCoy, 20 times champion and arguably the greatest National Hunt jockey ever. The night before he competed in his final Aintree Grand National on Shutthefrontdoor, Mark Boylan got a call from BBC1 to play at a celebration in Liverpool. He is doing his Leaving Certificate this year at 17 y/o, but luckily was on his Easter holidays and he took the opportunity to sing the song *"Greatest"* in front of 1,000 people in an auditorium. He was hoping that McCoy would win his second Grand National but it was not to be.

DENIS EGAN, CEO, TURF CLUB - FERBANE, CO OFFALY

He is a Chartered Accountant but his passion for horse racing made him perfect for the job as financial controller. He became Chief Executive in 2001 when Brian Kavanagh moved to Horse Racing Ireland. He is only the 15th Keeper of the Match (the Matchbook was the original hand written record of racing results) since the Turf's Club foundation in 1790. Looking from the outside it does seem strange that in a world where everything is amalgamated that racing still has two bodies running the racing industry in the Turf Club & HRI. In the past few years Denis has had to deal with recent issues including the High Court challenge to its right to regulate, the anabolic steroid scandal and the possible loss or reduction of it's power due to government legislation, which is trying to streamline the running of Irish Horse Racing. As CEO he was very relieved to win a case in April 2014 by a jockey & trainer about the Turf Clubs right to regulate Flat racing. The judge decreed that under the 1994 Act, the Turf Club could make and enforce the rules of racing. It guaranteed that fair play & integrity could be maintained in racing. The other major issue was anabolic steroids after several well publicised cases, which led to the Turf Club expanding their drug testing regime in 2015, and the aim was also to increase the powers of veterinary office to search and seize. Denis Egan said *"The Turf Club will use every resource at its disposal to ensure that Irish racing is kept as clean as possible and free from drugs"*. Another recent issue that is less serious, but nonetheless an indicator of the on-going problems, that arise under the current structure. In February 2015, he stated that the Turf Club would challenge the HRI Amendment Bill due before the Dail in June in relation to a section about the Hunter Registration Certificates affecting point to points. The HRI provides €7,300 to point to points to help them survive and the Turf Club supports them, allocates meetings and sends some staff to the meetings. The problem was that the issue of Hunter Registration Certs was being transferred to the HRI, which meant the Turf Club would lose revenue.

The task for Denis Egan into the future will continue to be very difficult in a changing world within racing, but over a difficuly period he has shown that he has the qualities to deal with the serious issues.

TONY GLEESON'S GAMBLE OF THE CENTURY

Tony Gleeson is originally from Streamstown and he went to England at 18 years old. He started as a barman but had four pubs at one stage. He bought one of the most popular nightspots in Ealing called the Spinning Wheel in 1981. He was part of a syndicate that owned a horse Borara Lad who won a few races with David Elsworth. Rotherfield Greys won a few races as a 2 y/o and was valued at around £250,000, but later got a virus and he started dropping out in races. Mr Bingley the owner eventually sold him as a sprinter and he was bought for 7,500 guineas in 1985 in the name of his wife Dolores. He was trained by Chris Wall. Tony said he was *"highly strung, hard to control, and with a mind of his own".* In view of that they decided to geld him.

The first gamble on him was in an apprentice handicap at Warwick when he was ridden by Jonathan Leech. He covered the bets of the group, in Ireland and not on the course. He put £200 on another horse at the track, which led to Rotherfield Greys drifting to 20/1 SP. He won easily by 3 lengths and he made £100,000 (£5000 bet at SP). He had other successful bets on the horse, who gradually went up the handicap. They ran him in 7 furlong races in soft ground and he was dropped 14 lbs in the handicap, as his form became erratic. He also had a burst blood vessels problem, which was a worry in a gamble.

FAIRYTALE OF THE STEWARDS CUP 1988

He ran 4th at Salisbury before the plan to win the Stewards Cup at Goodwood. They set up 9 accounts with bookies and disguised bets with doubles and other bets. At *"City Index Bookmakers"* the horse was 33/1, but when he wanted to put on £1,000 at that price they would only give 25/1. He eventually got on £2,000 at 25/1. One of his biggest and trickiest bet was a double with Seve Ballesteros in the golf. He had £150 EW on Seve at 9/1 and 8/1 with Rotherfield Greys at 33/1 (he also doubled up with other golfers with the horse - just in case!) and won £53,000. Ballesteros had already won the British Open, so the pressure was on trainer Chris Wall to deliver and Nigel Day the jockey. They weren't worried about the size of the field or the draw, as long as he was no further back than 5th or 6th, as he had loads of speed. He put on £6,000 at 33/1 and his wife had £2,000 at 25/1. It took him four days to collect all his winnings from the various shops totalling around £1/4 million. The family and friends all backed the horse. It was also backed from London to Mullingar with huge celebrations that night at the Spinning Club. One man who saved up 6 weeks rent put it all on the horse. The horse was later injured, as they planned another coup on the Stewards Cup and was retired to Streamstown. At this time he had other horses with Chris Wall like I'm Electric, Little Chanter, and Back Spin. He also had Blazing Success with John Oxx. Tony said *"It's been like a fairytale. We were just lucky to get a horse like that".*

FATHER HAYES AND "DIVINE GUIDANCE"

He was bought in Keeneland for $35,000 through Dermot Browne with whom he had horses, but (in view of the subsequent stories) he took them away and brought them to Matt McCormack. He had problems with Keeneland over the sale that were eventually resolved. This led to Father Hayes being gelded and sent home to Westmeath. He was trained by William Pearce in Yorkshire and he started in a bumper at Hereford. They ran him on the flat at 7 furlongs or a mile which was too short until he got a handicap mark. He was a 1/2 brother to John Oxx's good horse Highland Bud. They entered him in seller's race, which influenced the handicapper to rate him at "57". They then went for the gamble in June 1992 at Sandown in a 1 1/2 mile race. The horse was backed in from 14/1 to 5/2 before going to 4/1. Dandy Nicholls famed sprinter trainer rode him and he stood on the saddle after he won. The Racing Post reported *"he punched the air so hard just before crossing the line that he seemed in danger of falling off".* He won anything from £100,000-£500,000 on this gamble, depending on sources. Tragically, the trainer William Pearce committed suicide just a few days after the race.

The story was not over as the Jockey Club launched an investigation as to whether the correct horse was running in the name of Father Hayes (who incidentally was named after a priest in England, who liked to do Yankees on a

Saturday). He was by Stage Door Johnny and the Turf Club Inspectors came and took blood samples. They confirmed that he was Father Hayes and not a *"ringer".* Part of the problem was that he was originally called Johnny Be Good before the name was changed. The same Father Hayes (the priest) helped put on and collect bets when the horse won at Southwell. Surely, this was a case of *"Divine Guidance",* as he said afterwards *"I never had such a thrill".*

Tony eventually sold up his places and came home to live in Rochfordbridge in 1998. He has a few mares but he missed out badly on the dam of Excelebration, as he had her for a few weeks. He paid 22,000 guineas for her but she was a "windsucker" and it was confirmed by the vet. She was eventually taken back and bred one of the top horses of her era. Tony Costello said he gambled on his horses to even the odds. The reality is that bookies have an 80% chance of winning and the punter has a 20% chance.

BIBLIOGRAPHY

Blew, W.C - *A History of Steeplechasing* Nimmo London 1907
Bird T.H.- *A Hundred Grand National's* Country Life 1967
Bland, Ernest- *Flat Racing since 1900* London 1950
Brabazon, Aubrey, - *Racing Through My Mind* Vota Books Waterford 1998
Browne, Noel P- *The Horse in Ireland* Pelham London 1962
Carberry, Paul & Gibson, Des Paul - *Paul Carberry the Autobiography* Paperweight 2011
Cox, M- *Notes on the History of the Irish Horse* Dublin 1897
Curling, Bill-*The Captain a biography of Captain Sir Cecil Boyd Rochfort* Barrie & Jenkins 1970
D'Arcy, Fergus- *Horses Lords and Racing Men* Turf Club, Kildare 1991
Dixon, H- *Silk and Scarlet* Rogerson & Tuxford London 1859
Fitzgeorge -Parker, T- *The Ditch on the Hill* Simon & Schuster London 1991
Fitzpatrick, B.M.-*Irish Sport and Sportsmen* Gill & Sons Dublin 1878
Green, Reg-*A Race Apart : The History of the Grand National* Hodder & Stoughton 1988
Green, Reg-*The Grand National* the official illustrated history 2000
Harman, Bob *Ultimate Dream 75 years of the Cheltenham Gold Cup* Mainstream Publishing
Herbert, Ivor -*Arkle* London 1974
Herbert, Ivor & Smyly, Patricia - *The Winter King* Pelham Books 1989
Holland, Anne - Kinane *A Remarkable Racing Family* O'Brien Press 2012
Holland, Anne -*The Grand National the Irish at Aintree* O'Brien Press 2008
Hyland, Francis - *History of the Galway Races* London 2008
Kelly, James -*Sport in Ireland 1600-1840* Dublin 2014
Kelly, Ger- *Irish Racing Memories 1900-1908* Leinster Leader 1998
Lantry, Margaret & O'Keeffe, Jack -*Racing Reflections The Life and Times of Irish Racing People* 2012
Lewis, C- *Horse Breeding in Ireland* - A.Allen London 1980
Magee, Sean - *The Life & Legacy of Himself* Highdown 2005
Mason, Finch & Richardson, J.M-*Gentlemen Riders Past and Present* Vinton London 1909
McCoy, A.P. -*My Autobiography* Orion 2011
Oakley, Robin- *Britain & Ireland's Top 100 Racehorses of All Time* -Corinthian Books 2012
Oaksey, John-*The Story of Mill Reef*- Aurum Press Ltd 2006
Oaksey, John- *Mince Pies for Starters* Magna 2004
Peters, Stewart- *The Irish Grand National* 2007
Peters, Stewart- *The Grand National since 1945* (NPI Media Group 2005)
Peters, Stewart-*Festival Gold -40 years of Cheltenham Racing* NPI Media

Group 2003)
Richardson, Charles-*Racing At Home & Abroad* London 1927
Sargent, Harry- *Thoughts Upon Sport* London 1895
Sharpe, Graham-*Turf Accounts* Guinness Publishing 1990
Smith, Brian-*The Horse in Ireland* Wolfhound Press Dublin 1991
Smith, Raymond and Costello C.-*Peerless Punchestown Sporting Book* Dublin 2000
Sweeney, Tony & Ann- *Sweeney Guide to the Turf* Dublin 2001
Taaffe, Pat -*My Life and Arkles* Stanley Paul London 1972
Tanner, Michael -*The Champion Hurdle* Pelham London 1972
Watson, S.J.-*Between the Flags* Allen Figgis Dublin1969
Welcome, John- *Irish Horse Racing An Illustrated History* Gill & McMillan Dublin 1982
Williams, Guy St John-*Cheltenham Festival Centenary 1911-2011 an Irish Tribute* Daletta Press 2011
Williams, Guy St John-T.P.Burns *A Racing Life* Hillgate 2006
Williams, Guy St John-*The Racing Lodges of the Curragh* Daletta 1997
Williams, Guy St John & Hyland, Francis- *The Irish Derby 1866-1979* J.A.Allen London 1980
Williams, Guy St John & Hyland, Francis-*Jameson Irish Grand National* the Organisation Dublin 1995
Williams, Guy St John - *Winner All Right 100 Years of Irish Breeding & Racing* Daletta Press 1999
Wilson, Julian-*The Great Horses* Little Brown 1998

LOCAL HISTORY BOOKS

Cox, Liam- *Moate* 1980
Dease, E.F-*A Complete History of the Westmeath Hunt* 1898
Egan, Oliver-*Tyrrellspass Past & Present* 1986
Hunt, Tom- *Sport & Society in Victoria Ireland* Cork University Press 2007
McCormack, Stan -*Against the Odds, Kilbeggan Races 1840-1994* (1995)
McMahon, Noel-*In the Shadow of the Fairy Hill Shinrone & Ballingarry* Kilcommon Press 1998
Moyvoughly Historical Committee - *Moyvoughly and its hinterland*
Nugent, Nicholas- *The Sir the memoirs of Sir Hugh Nugent*
O'Brien, Gearoid-*Athlone in Old Photographs* Gill & McMillan 2002
O'Brien, Gearoid- *Athlone Miscellany* History Press 2011
O'Brien Seamus- *A Town in Transition Post Famine Mullingar*
Sheehan, Jeremiah- *South Westmeath Farm and Folk* Blackwater Press 1978
Sheehan, Jeremiah- *Worthies of Westmeath 1982* Wellbrook Press 1987
SS Peter & Paul's Foroige-*Our Local History Streamstown, Horseleap & Boher*

1990
Smith, Harry Worcester - *A Sporting Tour Ireland through, England, Wales and France in the years 1912- 1913* Vol 1 & 2 Columbia S.C. The State Company 1925

NEWSPAPERS, ANNUALS, PERIODICALS AND MAGAZINES

Newspaper's- Faulkner's Dublin Journal, Dublin Evening Post, Freeman's Journal, Westmeath Examiner, Westmeath/Offaly Independent, Westmeath Guardian, Kings County Chronicle, Irish Times, Irish Independent, Irish Press, Irish Field, Racing Post, Sporting Life, Irish Sportsman and Farmer and New York Times. **Annuals** - Sean Graham Racing Annual, Irish Racing Annual, and the Irish Racing Yearbook. **Periodical's and Magazines** - Baily's Magazine, Badminton Magazine, Sporting Magazine, Ruff's Guide, the Irish Horse, Irish Racing Calendar, The Sportsman, Racing Calendar, Sports Illustrated, and Journal of the Old Athlone Society.

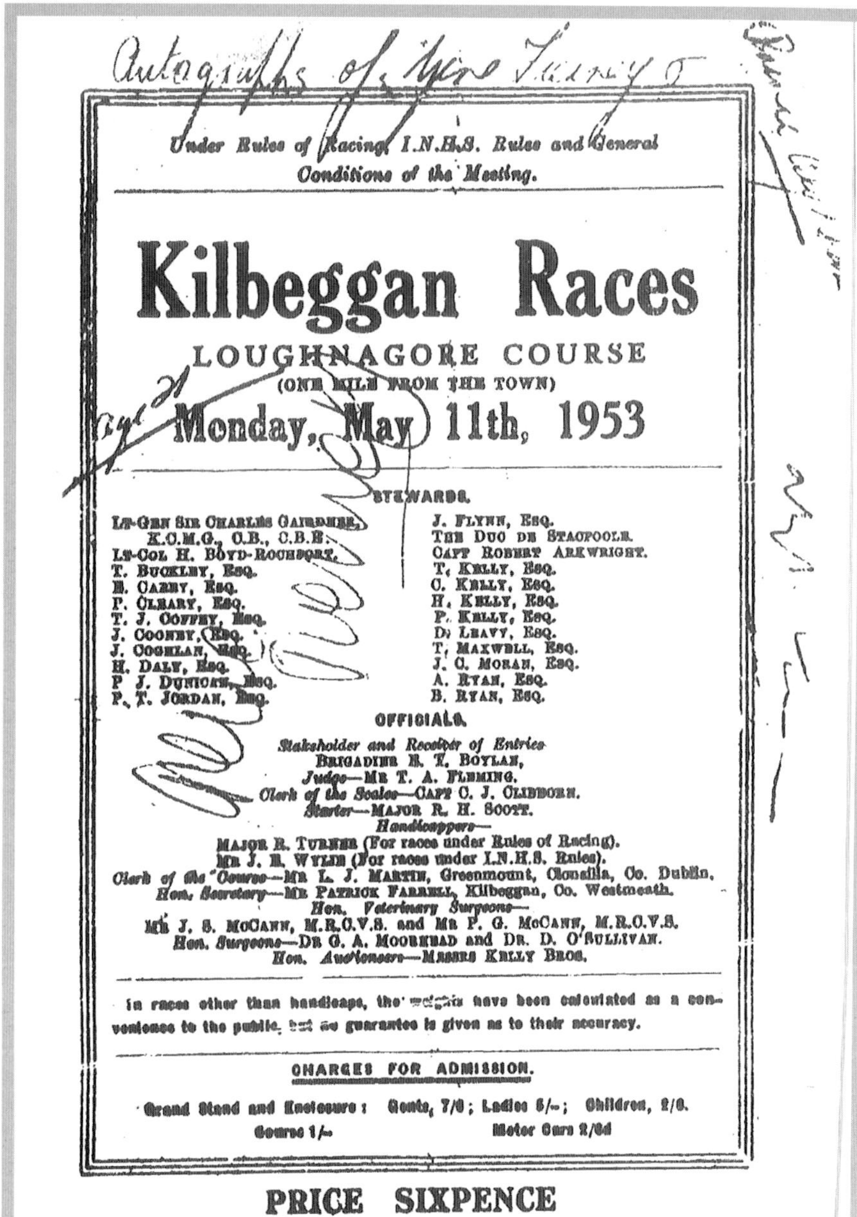

Under Rules of Racing, I.N.H.S. Rules and General Conditions of the Meeting.

Kilbeggan Races

LOUGHNAGORE COURSE

(ONE MILE FROM THE TOWN)

Monday, May 11th, 1953

STEWARDS.

LT-GEN SIR CHARLES GAIRDNER, K.C.M.G., C.B., C.B.E.
LT-COL H. BOYD-ROCHFORT.
T. BUCKLEY, ESQ.
E. CARRY, ESQ.
P. CLEARY, ESQ.
T. J. COFFEY, ESQ.
J. COONEY, ESQ.
J. COGHLAN, ESQ.
H. DALY, ESQ.
P. J. DUNICAN, ESQ.
P. T. JORDAN, ESQ.
J. FLYNN, ESQ.
THE DUC DE STACPOOLE.
CAPT ROBERT ARKWRIGHT.
T. KELLY, ESQ.
C. KELLY, ESQ.
H. KELLY, ESQ.
P. KELLY, ESQ.
D. LEAVY, ESQ.
T. MAXWELL, ESQ.
J. C. MORAN, ESQ.
A. RYAN, ESQ.
B. RYAN, ESQ.

OFFICIALS.

Stakeholder and Receiver of Entries
BRIGADIER E. T. BOYLAN,
Judge—MR T. A. FLEMING.
Clerk of the Scales—CAPT C. J. CLIBBORN.
Starter—MAJOR R. H. SCOTT.
Handicappers—
MAJOR E. TURNER (For races under Rules of Racing).
MR J. E. WYLIE (For races under I.N.H.S. Rules).
Clerk of the Course—MR L. J. MARTIN, Greenmount, Clonsilla, Co. Dublin.
Hon. Secretary—MR PATRICK FARRELL, Kilbeggan, Co. Westmeath.
Hon. Veterinary Surgeons—
MR J. S. McCANN, M.R.C.V.S. and MR P. G. McCANN, M.R.C.V.S.
Hon. Surgeons—DR G. A. MOORHEAD and DR. D. O'SULLIVAN.
Hon. Auctioneers—MESSRS KELLY BROS.

In races other than handicaps, the weights have been calculated as a convenience to the public, but no guarantee is given as to their accuracy.

CHARGES FOR ADMISSION.

Grand Stand and Enclosure: Gents, 7/6; Ladies 5/-; Children, 2/6.
Course 1/- Motor Cars 2/6d

PRICE SIXPENCE

Race Card with the autographs of Prince Aly khan and actress Gene Tierney

Advertisement for Kilbeggan Races in 1974

Michael Casey, secretary of Kilbeggan Races with Michael O'Hehir

BACKED THE WRONG HORSE.

PUTTING ON HIS LITTLE BIT.

A TYPICAL RACE-GOER.

A WELL-KNOWN BOOKIE.

Sketches showing Mullingar Races in the early 20th century